Lecture Notes in Computer Science 13049

More information about this series at https://link.springer.com/bookseries/558

Lejla Batina · Thomas Bäck · Ileana Buhan ·
Stjepan Picek (Eds.)

Security and Artificial Intelligence

A Crossdisciplinary Approach

Editors
Lejla Batina (iD)
Radboud University Nijmegen
Nijmegen, The Netherlands

Thomas Bäck (iD)
Leiden University
Leiden, The Netherlands

Ileana Buhan
Radboud University Nijmegen
Nijmegen, The Netherlands

Stjepan Picek (iD)
Radboud University Nijmegen
Nijmegen, The Netherlands

ISSN 0302-9743   ISSN 1611-3349 (electronic)
Lecture Notes in Computer Science
ISBN 978-3-030-98794-7   ISBN 978-3-030-98795-4 (eBook)
https://doi.org/10.1007/978-3-030-98795-4

This Springer imprint is published by the registered company Springer Nature Switzerland AG
The registered company address is: Gewerbestrasse 11, 6330 Cham, Switzerland

Preface

In recent years, artificial intelligence (AI) has become an emerging technology to assess security and privacy. There are many security challenges and potential solutions for AI systems at the algorithm, architecture, and implementation levels. So far, research on AI and security has looked at the various sub-problems in isolation, primarily relying on best practices in the domain. At the same time, future solutions will require fostering the sharing of experiences and best practices between those domains. To address some of those challenges, we organized a Lorentz workshop in 2019 called AI+Sec that considered several research topics on the intersection of AI and security. We covered topics like side-channel attacks and fault injection, cryptographic primitives, adversarial machine learning, and intrusion detection. The Lorentz workshop had around 50 participants, where 45% were junior scientists. During the group discussions, we realized that no texts provide a broad view of security and AI, and we decided to write a book covering such topics. After more discussion, 41 people showed interest in contributing to the book, and we selected 14 chapters to be included. We approached Springer, who agreed to publish the book, and helped in the procedure.

The book chapters were evaluated based on their significance, technical quality, and relevance to the topics of security and AI. Each book chapter submission was reviewed in a single-blind mode by at least three authors of other book chapters. After the first review round, the authors had the opportunity to improve the book chapters and update the manuscripts to keep them up-to-date.

Part I, "AI for Cryptography", contains five chapters. We discuss how AI can be used to construct cryptographic primitives. Next, we provide a detailed exposure on AI for implementation attacks, first side-channel analysis, and then fault injection. Finally, the last chapter of this part discusses physically unclonable functions and AI.

Part II, "AI for Authentication and Privacy", contains four chapters. We focus on AI techniques to improve privacy in the first two chapters, which are followed by two chapters on authentication approaches.

Part III, "AI for Intrusion Detection" contains two chapters. This part discusses how AI can be used for malware detection and network intrusion detection.

Finally, Part IV, "Security of AI", contains three chapters. In the previous book parts, we focused our attention on how AI can be used in security. Now, we discuss the security of AI. This part presents topics like adversarial examples, backdoor attacks, and implementation attacks on AI.

A long list of volunteers invested their time and energy to create this book. We are grateful to the PhD students who helped in coordinating the effort, the Lorentz workshops staff (Wendy van der Linden, Tara Seeger, Sietske Kroon) for their support in organizing the event that led to this book, Marina Krček, who helped with the editorial tasks, and the team at Springer.

Last but not least, we thank all the authors for putting much effort into producing the high-quality content we are proud to present here. With this book, we hope to provide the community with insights into recent and latest developments in artificial intelligence and security.

February 2022

Lejla Batina
Thomas Bäck
Ileana Buhan
Stjepan Picek

Organization

Editors

Lejla Batina   Radboud University, The Netherlands
Thomas Bäck   Leiden University, The Netherlands
Ileana Buhan   Radboud University, The Netherlands
Stjepan Picek   Radboud University and Delft University of
     Technology, The Netherlands

Reviewers

Lejla Batina	Radboud University, The Netherlands
Thomas Bäck	Leiden University, The Netherlands
Shivam Bhasin	Nanyang Technological University, Singapore
Jakub Breier	Silicon Austria Labs, Austria
Lukasz Chmielewski	Radboud University and Riscure, The Netherlands
Fatemeh Ganji	Worcester Polytechnic Institute, USA
Giuseppe Garofalo	KU Leuven, Belgium
Carlos Javier Hernandez-Castro	Complutense University, Spain
Julio Hernandez-Castro	University of Kent, UK
Annelie Heuser	French National Center for Scientific Research (CNRS), IRISA, France
Xiaolu Hou	Slovak University of Technology, Slovakia
Domagoj Jakobovic	University of Zagreb, Croatia
Dirmanto Jap	Nanyang Technological University, Singapore
Sander Joos	KU Leuven, Belgium
Wouter Joosen	KU Leuven, Belgium
Alan Jovic	University of Zagreb, Croatia
Marina Krcek	Delft University of Technology, The Netherlands
Martha Larson	Delft University of Technology and Radboud University, The Netherlands
Huimin Li	Delft University of Technology, The Netherlands
Shaofeng Li	Shanghai Jiao Tong University, China
Zhuoran Liu	Radboud University, The Netherlands
Shiqing Ma	Rutgers University, USA
Luca Mariot	Delft University of Technology, The Netherlands
Azqa Nadeem	Delft University of Technology, The Netherlands
Servio Paguada	Radboud University, The Netherlands, and Ikerlan Technological Research Centre, Spain

Contents

AI for Intrusion Detection

Security of AI

AI for Cryptography

Artificial Intelligence for the Design of Symmetric Cryptographic Primitives

Luca Mariot[1]($\boxtimes$), Domagoj Jakobovic[2], Thomas Bäck[3],
and Julio Hernandez-Castro[4]

[1] Cyber Security Research Group, Delft University of Technology,
Delft, The Netherlands
L.Mariot@tudelft.nl
[2] Faculty of Electrical Engineering and Computing, University of Zagreb,
Zagreb, Croatia
domagoj.jakobovic@fer.hr
[3] Leiden University, Leiden, The Netherlands
t.h.w.baeck@liacs.leidenuniv.nl
[4] School of Computing, University of Kent, Canterbury, UK
J.C.Hernandez-Castro@kent.ac.uk

Abstract. This chapter provides a general overview of AI methods used to support the design of cryptographic primitives and protocols. After giving a brief introduction to the basic concepts underlying the field of cryptography, we review the most researched use cases concerning the use of AI techniques and models to design cryptographic primitives, focusing mainly on Boolean functions, S-boxes and pseudorandom number generators. We then point out two interesting directions for further research on the design of cryptographic primitives where AI methods could be applied in the future.

1 Introduction

Cryptography can be broadly defined as a discipline that studies how to enable *secure communication* between two or more parties in the presence of *adversaries*. Historically, cryptography has been associated with *encryption*, which aims at protecting the *confidentiality* of messages transmitted over an insecure channel. On the opposite side, the goal of *cryptanalysis* is to analyze a particular encryption scheme to search for eventual vulnerabilities that can be exploited to attack the scheme and violate message confidentiality. Collectively, *cryptology* encompasses both the fields of cryptography and cryptanalysis.

Modern cryptography stands on the use of precise mathematical definitions and rigorous proofs to guarantee a certain security level under a particular model of the adversary's strategy. As such, designing a sound cryptographic primitive or protocol is usually a hard task, as well as it is cryptanalyzing it. In this respect, *Artificial Intelligence* (AI) provides a host of interesting approaches and tools to address problems in the design of cryptographic schemes. By looking at the existing literature, one can find many works that use various approaches from the field

© Springer Nature Switzerland AG 2022
L. Batina et al. (Eds.): Security and Artificial Intelligence, LNCS 13049, pp. 3–24, 2022.
https://doi.org/10.1007/978-3-030-98795-4_1

of AI to address several use cases relevant to cryptography. One may classify such works in two main areas, depending on the nature of the underlying problem:

Search and Optimization. Several questions in the design of cryptographic primitives can be cast as combinatorial optimization problems over a discrete search space, such as, among others, the search of *Boolean functions* and *S-boxes* with desirable cryptographic properties, which are fundamental building blocks in the design of symmetric encryption schemes. To this end, AI-based heuristic techniques such as *Evolutionary Algorithms* [51], *Simulated Annealing* [14] and *Swarm Intelligence* [37] have proved to be quite useful to tackle optimization problems related to cryptography.

Computational Models. The second area concerns the use of computational models belonging to the domain of AI as components in the design of crypto-graphic schemes. In this case, the underlying idea is to link the overall scheme's security to the complex dynamic behavior of such computational models, which in principle are difficult to cryptanalyze. Perhaps the best known examples in this research thread are *Cellular Automata*, which have been mainly studied to design symmetric encryption primitives such as Pseudorandom Number Generators (PRNG) for stream ciphers [66,67] and S-boxes for block ciphers [20,39].

This chapter aims to provide a broad overview of the state of the art concerning the use of AI methods and models for designing cryptographic primitives and protocols, focusing on the two areas mentioned above. In particular, we consider the most significant use cases of AI-based cryptography, namely the design of Boolean functions, S-boxes, and Pseudorandom Number Generators (PRNG). For each use case, we introduce the corresponding cryptographic design problem, and then we give an overview of the related literature. We conclude by considering two new directions along which this research field could evolve in the next years.

The rest of this chapter is organized as follows. Section 2 gives a concise introduction to the basic notions of cryptography, and covers the basic notions related to AI-based heuristic techniques and cellular automata. Sections from 3, 4 and 5 focus on AI techniques used to design cryptographic primitives, addressing, in particular, the use cases of Boolean functions, S-boxes and pseudorandom number generators. Finally, Sect. 6 concludes the chapter by discussing open problems and directions for future research in the field of AI-based cryptography.

2   Background

In this section, we first illustrate the basic terminology and concepts related to cryptography over which we ground the discussion of the next sections. Next, we introduce the basic AI techniques and models that have been used in the literature to design cryptographic primitives, namely heuristic optimization techniques and cellular automata. Clearly, given the broad scopes of these research fields, a complete treatment is well beyond the scope of this chapter. For more information on the topic, we refer the interested reader to standard textbooks such as [27,64] for cryptography and [17,23] respectively for heuristic optimization algorithms and cellular automata.

2.1   Cryptography

As we mentioned in the Introduction, one of the goals of secure communication is *confidentiality*, which ensures that only the intended recipient is able to read a particular message. The main tools studied in cryptography to achieve this goal are *encryption schemes*, which are applied to the following basic communication scenario. Suppose that a *sender*, Alice, wants to send a *plaintext message P* to a *receiver*, Bob, over a communication channel. In particular, the plaintext message P can be thought of as a finite string over an alphabet Σ. However, the communication channel is eavesdropped by an *adversary*, Eve, who can intercept and read everything transmitted over it. To solve this problem, Alice and Bob adopt the encryption scheme depicted in Fig. 1, which works as follows. Alice first feeds P in input to an *encryption function*, which also depends on an *encryption key K_E*. The encryption function output is a *ciphertext C* that Alice sends to Bob over the insecure channel tapped by Eve. On his end, Bob applies a *decryption function* to the received ciphertext, which similarly depends on a *decryption key K_D*, and whose output is the original plaintext message P. The encryption and decryption functions must be the inverses of one another so that Bob can decode the correct message from the ciphertext.

The confidentiality property of this scheme rests on the assumption that Eve cannot recover the plaintext message P by just observing the ciphertext C transmitted over the communication channel. In particular, *Kerchoff's principle* states that the security of an encryption scheme should not rely on the secrecy of the encryption and decryption functions used by Alice and Bob, but rather only on the secrecy of the decryption key K_D. Thus, one may assume that Eve knows the encryption and decryption functions, so they must be designed not to leak any useful information on the plaintext message or the decryption key if the latter is not known.

Depending on the nature of the keys employed by Alice and Bob, one can classify encryption schemes in *symmetric* and *asymmetric* ones. In a symmetric encryption scheme the same key is used both for encryption and decryption, i.e. one has that $K_E = K_D = K$. Since this key must be kept secret, Alice

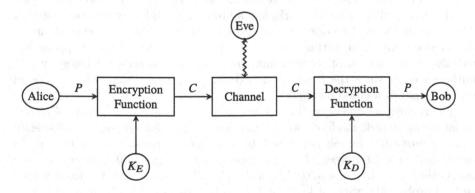

Fig. 1. Block diagram of a generic encryption scheme.

and Bob have to figure out a way to share it securely before the communication takes place. Symmetric encryption schemes can be further divided in *block ciphers* and *stream ciphers*. In a stream cipher, each symbol of the plaintext P is combined with a corresponding symbol of a *keystream* z, computed from the initial secret key k through a *keystream generator algorithm*. Perhaps the most widely studied model in this context is the *Vernam-like cipher*, where the plaintext, the keystream and the ciphertext are all bitstrings of the same length, and the encryption operation corresponds to the bitwise XOR between the plaintext and the keystream (see Fig. 2a). In a block cipher, on the contrary, the plaintext is processed in fixed-size *blocks*, that are iteratively combined with several round keys derived from the secret key through a scheduling algorithm. One of the most common paradigms for the design of block ciphers is the *Substitution-Permutation Network* (SPN, see Fig. 2b). In this case, the plaintext block undergoes first a *confusion phase*, followed by a *diffusion phase* and finally by the *key combination phase* with the current round key. This process is repeated for a certain number of *rounds*.

Confusion and *diffusion* are two general principles stated by Shannon [62] that every symmetric encryption scheme should satisfy, to frustrate statistical attacks. In particular, the aim of the confusion phase in an SPN cipher is to make the relationship between the plaintext and the secret key the most complicated as possible. This property is accomplished by processing the plaintext block through a set of smaller *Substitution boxes* (S-Boxes), which we will discuss more in detail in Sect. 4. On the other hand, the goal of the diffusion phase is to spread the statistical structure of the plaintext over the ciphertext, so that each symbol of the ciphertext depends on many symbols of the plaintext. In a SPN cipher this is done by using a *permutation box* (π-box, also called a *diffusion layer*) right after the confusion phase.

In an asymmetric (or *public-key*) encryption scheme the keys used for encryption and decryption are distinct. Typically, there are no key-sharing issues in this case since Bob can make its encryption key public while he keeps only the decryption key private. Alice will then use Bob's public key to encrypt the plaintext and send him the corresponding ciphertext.

Most of the applications of AI techniques to cryptography concern the symmetric setting, although a few works also address the public-key case (see e.g. [1]). Therefore, in the next sections, we will focus on the use cases related to symmetric cryptography. Also, in this chapter, we will not consider AI-based approaches to solve other aspects of secure communication such as message integrity and authentication, since the mass of the existing literature about AI methods in cryptography is focused on encryption and confidentiality.

The security of an encryption scheme is usually analyzed in terms of adversarial goals, attack models and security levels. The *adversarial goals* specify when a particular attack performed by Eve can be considered successful. In particular, in a *total break* of the encryption scheme the goal is to recover the decryption key, while in a *partial break* Eve is able to decrypt ciphertexts with a certain probability, without knowing the decryption key. Finally, Eve achieves a *distinguishing break* if is she can tell apart the encryption of two distinct ciphertexts (usually corresponding to a plaintext chosen by Alice and a random one) with a probability higher than $1/2$.

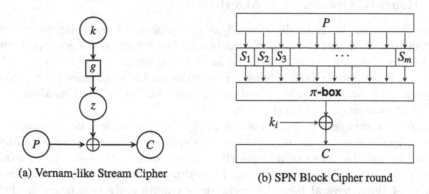

(a) Vernam-like Stream Cipher   (b) SPN Block Cipher round

Fig. 2. Encryption diagrams for Vernam-like stream ciphers and SPN block ciphers.

The attack models define the type of information available to Eve to perform an attack on an encryption scheme. These vary from very weak assumptions, as in the *ciphertext-only attacks* where Eve only knows some ciphertexts encrypted under the same unknown key, up to more sophisticated ones such as *chosen-ciphertext attacks*, in which Eve can choose some ciphertexts and obtain the corresponding plaintexts decrypted under the same unknown key.

The *security level* models the *computational resources* that Eve has at her disposal to carry out a particular attack. In particular, in the *unconditional security* level an encryption scheme cannot be broken under a particular attack model, even if the adversary has unlimited computational resources. While this is the most robust definition that a cryptographer can adopt, unconditional security usually yields encryption schemes that are hardly usable in practice, typically because the encryption key has the same length of the plaintext and the ciphertext. The *provable security* level is often employed in the design of public-key encryption schemes. Here, the goal is to reduce a particular computational problem assumed to be hard (such as factoring integer numbers or computing discrete logarithms) to the task of breaking the encryption scheme. Finally, in the *computational security* level the best known attack that Eve can perform on an encryption scheme requires at least N operations, where N is a very large number. In particular, a scheme can be shown to be computationally secure only for certain specific attacks, and there is no guarantee that it is not vulnerable to others. Despite this drawback, computational security is perhaps the most widespread security level considered in the design of *cryptographic primitives*, especially in the symmetric key setting. One of the reasons is that low-level cryptographic primitives are simpler to analyze, and few classes of attacks are known on them. Thus, it makes sense from a practical point of view to defend these primitives in light of such attacks. Further, this is the security level underlying most of the literature of AI-based cryptography and cryptanalysis, which is why we will mainly consider it in the rest of this chapter.

2.2   Heuristic Optimization Algorithms

Optimization can be generally defined as the process of searching for a best solution to a particular problem. Formally, one has a finite set S equipped with an *objective function* $f : S \to \mathbb{R}$ assigning to each *candidate solution* $x \in S$ a measure of how good x is in solving a particular problem instance. The goal of *combinatorial optimization* is to find an *optimal solution* x^* that maximizes f, that is, $x^* = argmax_{x \in S}\{f(x)\}$.

In most combinatorial optimization problems of practical importance, the solution space S is usually too huge to be explored in an exhaustive manner. One of the possible ways to address this shortcoming is to resort to *heuristic optimization algorithms*, in order to find a (sub)optimal solution in a reasonable amount of time. Several heuristic techniques traditionally belong to the field of AI. The general characteristic shared by these techniques is that they are *iterative algorithms*, i.e., they start from an initial solution and iteratively tweak it using the objective function to drive the search. After a certain number of evaluations, the best solution found so far is returned.

We now give a short overview of the main heuristic algorithms that have been used to design cryptographic primitives, which of course is far from being exhaustive. The reader is referred to [2, 10, 17] for more comprehensive treatments of this topic.

Single-State Optimization Methods. The idea underlying single-state optimization methods is to optimize a single solution at a time, and to search in its *neighborhood* to find a solution with a better objective function value. This approach assumes that a topology is defined on the solution space, usually induced by the Hamming distance in the case of binary strings. Two of the most widely used single-state optimization methods in cryptography are *Hill Climbing* (HC) and *Simulated Annealing* (SA). Hill Climbing replaces the current solution whenever another one having a better objective function value is sampled in the neighborhood. This strategy tends however to get stuck in *local optima*. To overcome this drawback of HC, simulated annealing accepts with a certain probability a *worse* solution in the neighborhood than the current one. The acceptance probability in SA is controlled by a *temperature* parameter, which is decreased throughout the optimization process. Hence, at the beginning SA favors *exploration* of the search space, making the escape from local optima more likely. In later iterations, the algorithm focuses on *exploitation* of the current region of the search space.

Population-Based Optimization Methods. In population-based optimization methods the main idea is to optimize a set of candidate solutions instead of a single one. This approach allows for a more global search on the solution space, decreasing the risk of getting stuck in local optima.

In this domain, the most popular methods are *Evolutionary Algorithms* (EA), which are loosely inspired by the principles of biological evolution. Each individual in the population is represented by a *genotype* which decodes to a candidate solution of the search space, also called a *phenotype* in this context. At each iteration, an EA manipulates the genotypes of the individuals in the population by following a three-step process. First, the objective function (also called a *fitness function* in this case) is evaluated on all individuals. Then, a *selection operator* is used to choose the individuals that will reproduce in the next generation, using their fitness values to drive the selection in a probabilistic way. Next, *variation operators* are used to create the new generation from the selected individuals. This step usually consists of a *crossover operator*, where the genotypes of two parent individuals is mixed to create an offspring, and then a *mutation operator* is applied on the offspring to introduce random variation in its genotype.

Several variants of EA have been considered in the literature depending on the encoding adopted for the genotypes and the variation operators used to modify them. For example, in *Genetic Algorithms* (GA), the genotypes are usually encoded by fixed-length bitstrings, but integer vectors and permutations have also been used. In *Genetic Programming* (GP), on the other hand, the aim is to evolve syntactically correct programs that are usually represented by trees.

Finally, another type of population-based heuristics used in cryptography are *Swarm Intelligence methods*, among which *Particle Swarm Optimization* (PSO) is the most common one. In PSO, the elements of the population are *particles* that move over the search space. Each particle is described by its current position and velocity. During a single PSO iteration, each particle updates its position by adding its velocity. Then, the velocity controlled by taking into account the *global best* solution found so far in the particle's neighborhood and the *local best* solution found so far by the particle itself.

2.3   Cellular Automata

A *cellular automaton* (CA) is a discrete computational model described by a regular lattice of *cells*, where each cell updates itself by considering its current state and those of the neighboring cells. In its simplest form, a CA is defined by a one-dimensional array of n binary cells and by a *local rule* $f : \{0,1\}^d \rightarrow \{0,1\}$ of *diameter* $d \leq n$. The update of the array's global state is performed by evaluating in parallel f on each cell and the neighborhood formed by the $d - 1$ cells on its right (although variations on the center of the neighborhood exist, e.g. by considering also the cells on the left). There are several approaches to update the cells at the boundaries that do not have enough neighbors to apply the local rule. One common solution is to consider the array as a ring, with the first cell following the last one. This induces a *global rule* $F : \{0,1\}^n \rightarrow \{0,1\}^n$ that defines the next state of the CA array as:

$$F(x_1, x_2, \cdots, x_n) = (f(x_1, \cdots, x_d), f(x_2, \cdots, x_{d+1}), \cdots, f(x_{n-d+1}, \cdots, x_n)) \ ,$$

for all $(x_1, x_2, \cdots, x_n) \in \{0,1\}^n$. Thus, a CA can be viewed as a vectorial function defined by a *shift-invariant coordinate function*, with periodic boundary conditions. Traditionally, CA have been studied in the domain of *natural computing*, and thus belong to the larger class of nature-inspired AI computational models. The reason underlying the interest of CA for implementing cryptographic applications is twofold. First, the shift-invariance property that characterizes CA allows for uniform and efficient hardware implementations. Second, depending on the underlying local rule, the dynamic evolution of a CA can be quite complex and unpredictable. We point the reader to [26] for a broader introduction to the basic concepts concerning CA.

3   Boolean Functions

Boolean functions are a fundamental class of cryptographic primitives used in the design of stream and block ciphers. This section gives a brief introduction to Boolean functions and the optimization problems related to their cryptographic properties. Next, we survey the main works in the literature addressing the design of cryptographically strong Boolean functions using AI techniques.

3.1   Background

One of the most common models for the keystream generator in the Vernam-like stream cipher defined in Sect. 2.1 is the *combiner model*, where the bits produced by several *Linear Feedback Shift Registers* (LFSR) are combined by a *Boolean function*, whose output is used as the next keystream bit. The computational security of this model can be reduced to the study of the combiner function's cryptographic properties, the reason being that some attacks become more efficient if the function does not meet certain criteria.

We now give a concise overview of the properties that Boolean functions used as cryptographic primitives in stream and block ciphers should satisfy, referring the reader to [6] for a thorough treatment of the subject. In what follows, we denote by $\mathbb{F}_2 = \{0, 1\}$ the finite field with two elements, and $\mathbb{F}_2^n$ the set of n-bit vectors endowed with a vector space structure, with bitwise XOR as the vector sum and logical AND as the multiplication by a scalar. A Boolean function of n variables is then defined as a mapping $f : \mathbb{F}_2^n \to \mathbb{F}_2$. There are mainly three unique representations of Boolean functions used in cryptography, the most natural one being the truth table. Assuming that the vectors of $\mathbb{F}_2^n$ are totally ordered, the *truth table* of a function is a 2^n-bit vector Ω_f that specifies the corresponding output value $f(x)$ for each vector $x \in \mathbb{F}_2^n$. The *Algebraic Normal Form* (ANF) represents a Boolean function as a multivariate polynomial over $\mathbb{F}_2$, i.e., as a sum (XOR) of monomials, where each monomial is the product (AND) of a subset of input variables. Finally, the *Walsh transform* represents a Boolean function f in terms of *correlations* with *linear functions*, which are defined as the XOR over a subset of the input variables. Hence, each monomial in their ANF is composed of a single variable.

These three representations can be used to define several cryptographic properties for Boolean functions used in stream ciphers. We briefly mention the four most important criteria below:

- *Balancedness*: the truth table of f should be composed of an equal number of zeros and ones. Unbalanced functions present a bias that can be exploited in statistical attacks.
- *Algebraic degree*: the degree of the polynomial represented by the ANF of f should be as high as possible, to avoid attacks that exploit the low linear complexity of the LFSRs used in the combiner model.
- *Nonlinearity*: the distance of the truth table of f from the set of all linear functions should be as high as possible. This property can be measured by considering the highest absolute value in the Walsh transform of f. Functions with low nonlinearity can be vulnerable to fast-correlation attacks in stream ciphers.
- *t-th order correlation immunity*: Each subset of t or fewer variables should be statistically independent from the output value of f. This condition is met if and only if the Walsh transform vanishes for all input vectors with at most t ones. Functions used in the combiner model should be correlation immune of a high order to avoid *correlation attacks*.

As we touched upon earlier, all the above properties are always considered in a computational security setting. Therefore, using a Boolean function that satisfies a subset of these properties protects from the specific attacks for which they are tailored, but does not grant security concerning other attacks. Moreover, as there exist several theoretical bounds among these properties, most of them cannot be satisfied simultaneously. The problem thus becomes to select a Boolean function with a suitable trade-off of the most important criteria. Finding such a function can be formulated as a *combinatorial optimization problem*: given the desired number of variables n, the designer's goal is to find an n-variable Boolean function which is balanced and has the highest possible degree, nonlinearity and order of correlation immunity. However, this problem cannot be solved by enumerating all Boolean functions of n variables. Indeed, the size of the resulting search space is 2^{2^n}, which hinders exhaustive search already for $n = 6$ variables. To give an intuition of the search space size, for $n = 8$ variables, there exist $2^{256} \approx 1.16 \cdot 10^{77}$ functions, which is approximately equal to the number of atoms in the observable universe. Since in practical stream ciphers a larger number of variables is required (at least $n = 13$ for the functions in the combiner model), the designer needs to resort either to *algebraic constructions* (for which the reader can refer to [6]) or to *heuristic optimization algorithms*, which include the AI-based methods introduced in Sect. 2.2. There are two main reasons for using heuristic algorithms to find proper Boolean functions in place of algebraic constructions. The first one is *diversity*: although algebraic constructions are easy to use and there is a formal proof that they satisfy specific cryptographic properties, the resulting functions usually belong to only a few known classes under affine equivalence relations.

On the other hand, heuristic algorithms from the AI domain are "blind", that is, they base their search solely upon the optimization of an objective function. Hence, heuristic algorithms can provide a wider variety of optimal Boolean functions, and in principle, they can discover new ones belonging to previously unknown classes. The second reason is that heuristic algorithms are more flexible than algebraic constructions. Indeed, the designer can take into account more properties of interest by merely combining the appropriate terms to optimize in the objective function. Notice also that these properties do not need to be all related to cryptographic criteria: one may also include, for instance, properties concerning the *implementation costs* of the resulting Boolean functions in hardware, such as gate count or circuit area.

3.2   Survey of Related Works

Most of the AI-based approaches that tackle the search of Boolean functions and S-boxes with good cryptographic properties revolve around the use of genetic algorithms (GA) and genetic programming (GP). Especially among earlier works, one can see that simulated annealing (SA) was also a quite popular technique employed on this problem. At the same time, a minor research thread considered the use of swarm intelligence optimization algorithms such as particle swarm optimization (PSO).

Historically, GA have been extensively investigated to evolve the truth tables of Boolean functions with good cryptographic properties. The first attempt in this area can be traced back to Millan et al. [44]. There, the authors used the classic bitstring representation of GA to encode the truth table of Boolean functions, to maximize their nonlinearity. The same authors refined their approach in [45] by forcing the GA to generate only balanced Boolean functions, through the use of a custom crossover operator. The authors further combined their GA with a hill climbing step, and the fitness function maximized the correlation immunity order, besides the nonlinearity of the candidate Boolean functions. The idea of designing ad-hoc crossover operators to reduce the space explored by GA when searching for cryptographic Boolean functions has been later adopted in other works [36,38]. However, its advantage over classic operators such as one-point crossover has been systematically confirmed only recently by Manzoni et al. [33].

The first work considering the use of SA to generate Boolean functions with high nonlinearity is that of Clark et al. [11], where the authors adopted a two-stage optimization approach. In the first stage, SA was used to drive the search into a region containing highly nonlinear Boolean functions, which were then located in the second stage using a hill climbing algorithm. Successively, SA has also been investigated by Clark et al. in [14], where correlation immunity was also considered in the optimization process, and by Clark et al. in [12], where the authors adopted a different representation for the candidate solutions. In particular, they proposed to use the *spectral inversion method*, where the candidate solutions are represented as Walsh spectra already satisfying specific properties (e.g., vanishing for all coefficients with at most t ones to meet t-th order correlation immunity). The optimization objective is to minimize the deviation of the *pseudo-Boolean function* resulting from the inverse Walsh transform applied on the spectra searched by SA; when this deviation is zero, the corresponding map is a Boolean function with the desired cryptographic criteria. The authors adopted this approach to design *plateaued* Boolean functions, which satisfy the best possible trade-off among algebraic degree, nonlinearity, balancedness, and correlation immunity. More recently, Mariot et al. [36] investigated the spectral inversion method with GA, remarking that it is more efficient than SA in finding plateaued Boolean functions.

The approach considering swarm intelligence algorithms also gave interesting results and insights in this optimization problem. However, this research line is not as developed as those based on GA and SA. Saber et al. [60] used a Particle Swarm Optimizer (PSO) to evolve Walsh spectra of plateaued functions, leveraging on the spectral inversion method of Clark et al. mentioned above. In particular, the position of a particle is updated by permuting the coefficients of the Walsh spectrum. Interestingly, this method allowed them to discover balanced Boolean functions of 9 variables with nonlinearity 240, algebraic degree 5, and correlation immunity order 3, whose existence question was open until then. Mariot et al. [37] designed a discrete PSO algorithm to search for Boolean functions with a good trade-off of nonlinearity and correlation-immunity, using the truth table encoding. The position update operation only swaps the bits in the truth table, to preserve balancedness.

To date, Genetic Programming turned out to be the most successful optimization technique for designing Boolean functions with good cryptographic properties. Although GP shares the same evolutionary algorithm structure of GA, the candidate solutions are *computer programs* instead of bitstrings, which are usually represented as trees. In this case, a Boolean function is encoded by a tree where the leaves represent the input variables, while the internal nodes are Boolean operators, and the root node gives the output of the function. The truth table is thus obtained by evaluating the GP tree over all possible assignments of the input variables on the leaf nodes and then taking the corresponding output value on the root. Castro et al. [7] were the first to address the design of Boolean functions for cryptographic applications. In particular, the authors considered the *average avalanche effect* as an optimization criterion, which is relevant for Boolean functions used in cryptographic hash functions. Picek et al. [50] applied GP to the evolution of Boolean functions with good cryptographic properties, comparing its performance with GA. Successively, Picek et al. [54] experimented with several EA algorithms, including GP, and combined them with algebraic constructions to investigate the maximum nonlinearity value achievable by balanced Boolean functions of 8 variables, which is today still an open question. More recently, Picek et al. [51] performed a systematic comparison of four evolutionary algorithms under three different fitness functions, that took into account several combinations of cryptographic properties of Boolean functions. The results showed that *Cartesian* GP (a GP variant where the solutions are represented as graphs, instead of trees) obtained the best results.

Pushing the hybrid approach of [54] further, Picek et al. [49] used GP to directly evolve secondary algebraic constructions of *bent* functions, which are those Boolean functions reaching the highest possible nonlinearity value. Although they exist only for even numbers of variables, and they are always unbalanced, bent functions can be used to construct highly nonlinear balanced functions (see [6] for an overview of related methods). The search for bent functions with heuristic optimization algorithms is nonetheless an interesting problem, even though bent functions cannot be directly used in the design of stream ciphers. Using this approach, the authors of [49] were able to construct bent Boolean functions of up to 24 variables, which are practically impossible to find using direct search methods based on more traditional representations such as the truth table encoding. Along this research direction, we also mention the work by Hrbacek et al. [22], who evolved bent functions up to 16 variables with Cartesian GP. Picek et al. [53], on the other hand, used GA ad GP to design *quaternary* bent functions, that can be turned into bent Boolean functions of a larger number of variables. Finally, Mariot et al. [34] applied GA and GP to search for *hyper-bent* functions. Hyper-bent functions are a subclass of bent Boolean functions at the highest possible distance from the set of linear functions represented by bijective monomials. This property is useful to thwart approximation attacks.

The merits of evolutionary algorithms concerning the property of correlation immunity have been investigated by Picek et al. in [46], where the authors compared the performances of GA, GP, and Cartesian GP in the design of correlation immune functions. Besides its utility in stream ciphers, correlation immunity is relevant in masking countermeasures for *side-channel attacks*. In this context, the goal is to find a t-th order correlation immune function with minimal *Hamming weight* (i.e., with the lowest possible number of ones in the truth table), in order to minimize the implementation cost of the countermeasure. To this end, Picek et al. [48] employed GP to design low-weight Boolean functions with various orders of correlation immunity. Correlation immune functions can also be defined in terms of different combinatorial objects, such as binary *Orthogonal Arrays* (OA). Indeed, the rows of an OA form the *support* (that is, the set of input vectors mapping to 1) of a correlation immune function. Therefore, a different approach to designing low-weight correlation immune functions of order t for side-channel countermeasures is to construct binary OA of strength t with the smallest number of rows N possible. Along this direction, Mariot et al. [38] investigated the use of GA and GP to evolve binary OA of various sizes, remarking that GP is much more effective at generating them.

4   S-Boxes

S-boxes, which we already introduced in Sect. 2.1 as cryptographic primitives for block ciphers based on the SPN paradigm, are the parallelization of several Boolean functions computed on the same input vector. In this section, we cover the background notions concerning S-boxes. Then, we overview the literature about using AI methods to construct S-boxes with good cryptographic properties.

4.1   Background

An S-box is a vectorial mapping $F : \mathbb{F}_2^n \to \mathbb{F}_2^m$, mapping n-bit to m-bit vectors, also denoted as an (n, m)-function. In SPN block ciphers, usually, one has $n = m$

since the S-boxes are required to be bijective for decryption purposes. An S-box is defined by m *coordinates functions* $f_i : \mathbb{F}_2^n \to \mathbb{F}_2$, which determine the i-th output bit of F for $1 \leq i \leq m$. The *component functions* of an S-box, additionally, are all the linear combinations of its coordinate functions (excluding the null combination). Similarly to Boolean functions in stream ciphers, the S-boxes composing the confusion layer in an SPN block cipher must also satisfy certain cryptographic properties to thwart attacks, among which we describe the most important ones below. The reader can refer to [6] for a deeper treatment of the cryptographic properties of vectorial Boolean functions.

- *Balancedness/Bijectivity*: Analogously to the single-output setting, an S-box $F : \mathbb{F}_2^n \to \mathbb{F}_2^m$ needs to be *balanced*, meaning that each output vector in $\mathbb{F}_2^m$ must appear the same number of times 2^{n-m}. When $n = m$ as in the case of S-box for SPN ciphers, balancedness corresponds to bijectivity.
- *Nonlinearity*: The nonlinearity of an S-box S is defined as the minimum nonlinearity among all its component functions, and it should be as high as possible to withstand *linear cryptanalysis* attacks.
- *Differential uniformity*: The differential uniformity corresponds to the minimum value that can be observed in the *difference distribution table* of the S-box, where each entry is indexed by a pair of vectors $a \in \mathbb{F}_2^n \backslash \{\underline{0}\}$, $b \in \mathbb{F}_2^m$ and it reports the number of times that the value of $F(x) \oplus F(x \oplus a)$ equals b. Ideally, the differential uniformity of an S-box should be as low as possible to avoid *differential cryptanalysis attacks*.

The unfeasibility of exhaustive search is even more prominent for S-boxes than in the case of Boolean functions. The number of (n, m)-functions is 2^{m2^n}, since each S-box is defined by the m truth tables of its coordinate functions. Considering only bijective (n, n)-functions, their number is approximately $2.6 \cdot 10^{35}$ already for $n = 5$ variables, which is not amenable to exhaustive enumeration. Hence, the use of heuristic optimization algorithms is even more motivated when searching for an S-box that is optimal with respect to the three properties above. Indeed, as in the Boolean functions' case, the designer can resort to algebraic constructions of good S-boxes, which, however, cover only a tiny fraction of all possible optimal S-boxes. Heuristic algorithms can provide a wider variety of S-boxes, that can also be optimal concerning additional properties such as those related to their implementation costs.

4.2   Survey of Related Works

The body of literature regarding the use of AI methods to construct cryptographically strong S-boxes can be roughly divided into two main approaches. The first one seeks to solve the optimization problem related to the cryptographic properties of S-boxes using nature-inspired optimization algorithms, which is the straightforward extension of the same approach applied to single-output Boolean functions discussed in Sect. 3.2. On the other hand, the second direction leverages on AI-based computational models to synthesize S-boxes with good properties.

Perhaps the best known example in this regard is the *cellular automata* (CA) model, which we introduced in Sect. 2.3.

We start with an overview of the first approach. The first work adopting evolutionary algorithms to optimize the cryptographic properties of S-boxes dates back to Millan et al. [43]. There, the authors designed a genetic algorithm to evolve S-boxes with high nonlinearity and low autocorrelation, a property that is closely related to differential uniformity. Burnett et al. [5] designed a heuristic method, mostly based on hill climbing, to generate S-boxes with the same structure of those used in the MARS block cipher, one of the AES finalists. Fuller et al. [19] proposed a multi-objective optimization approach for the heuristic construction of cryptographically strong S-boxes. In particular, they showed that power mappings (S-boxes whose polynomial representation is defined by a single monomial) could be evolved through iterated mutations to obtain solutions with the best possible trade-off of nonlinearity and autocorrelation. Clark et al. [13] employed a two-stage process inspired by that adopted for Boolean functions in [11] to search for highly nonlinear S-boxes, using simulated annealing and hill climbing to minimize a new objective function motivated by Parseval relation. Picek et al. [57] applied GP and Cartesian GP to the evolution of S-boxes, devising a method to adapt these two heuristics to the permutation encoding which limited the search space only to bijective (n, n)-functions.

Further, Picek et al. proposed a new fitness function in [47] to design S-boxes with evolutionary algorithms, experimentally assessing that it allows one to find highly nonlinear solutions more quickly than other objective functions already defined in the literature. Ivanov et al. [24] set forth an interesting *reverse* approach where one starts from an initial pool of optimal S-boxes in terms of nonlinearity and differential uniformity (obtained, for example, through algebraic constructions based on finite field inversion). Then, they apply a GA to tweak these S-boxes and generate new ones with slightly suboptimal properties. The motivation for this strategy is to generate a large set of S-boxes with similar cryptographic properties. The designer can then choose among them those that satisfy additional implementation requirements for a specific block cipher.

Let us now turn to the second approach based on cellular automata. Daemen et al. [15] were among the first to pioneer the use of CA for the design of S-boxes in block ciphers. There, the authors studied a simple local rule called χ, which flips a cell's state if and only if the two cells on its right present the pattern 10, and proved that the resulting S-box is bijective only when the size of the CA is odd. Moreover, they showed that rule χ induces CA-based S-boxes with good nonlinearity and diffusion properties. Interestingly, the only nonlinear component used in the design of KECCAK [4], the cryptographic primitive that has been adopted as the SHA-3 standard for hash functions, is a CA of 5 cells defined by rule χ. Seredynsky et al. [61] investigated S-boxes defined by *second-order* CA, whose invertibility is granted by the fact that the next state of each cell is computed as the XOR of the result of the local rule evaluated on its neighborhood and its previous state. In particular, the authors analyzed the *avalanche properties* of the S-boxes defined by such CA equipped with local rules of 5 and 7 variables. Szaban et al. [65] investigated the set of all 256 local rules of 3 variables. They selected those which resulted in the best nonlinearity and autocorrelation values by evolving a CA-based S-box of size 8×8 for a certain number of steps. Ghoshal et al. [20] considered 4×4 S-boxes with optimal nonlinearity and differential uniformity defined by multiple iterations of CA rules, and presented efficient *threshold implementations* for them that can be used for the design of lightweight SPN block ciphers.

We conclude this section by mentioning some works at the intersection of the two approaches discussed above, i.e., those based on the use of heuristic optimization algorithms to construct S-boxes defined by CA. Up to now, this last direction turned out to be the most successful one, since it can produce S-boxes on par with those yielded by algebraic constructions from the cryptographic point of view and also having good implementation properties. Picek et al. [55] used GP to evolve CA-based S-boxes with sizes ranging from 5×5 to 8×8, obtaining optimal solutions for nonlinearity and differential uniformity up to size 7×7. Picek et al. [56] further explored this optimization approach based on GP by considering the S-boxes defined by CA rules also from the implementation perspective. Under this experimental setting, they managed to evolve CA-based S-boxes with optimal nonlinearity and differential uniformity, and having hardware implementation costs to those of other state of the art S-boxes. Finally, Mariot et al. [39] performed a systematic theoretical investigation of the cryptographic properties of CA-based S-boxes and developed a reverse-engineering approach based on GP to find what is the shortest CA rule resulting in a specific S-box.

5 Pseudorandom Number Generators

Pseudorandom number generators (PRNG) are a crucial component for the security of basically any cryptographic scheme. In this section, we first cover the basic notions about PRNG and the statistical tests used to assess the quality of pseudorandom sequences. Next, we survey the main applications of AI methods to design PRNG.

5.1 Background

Random numbers and sequences are fundamental for several cryptographic tasks, such as the generation of keys, nonces, and masks for side-channel countermeasures. However, truly random numbers are difficult to come by since they can be generated only through physical phenomena such as radioactive decay, atmospheric noise, or reflection of photons in semi-transparent mirrors, which require specialized (and expensive) hardware generators. Consequently, the designers of cryptographic primitives mostly rely on *Pseudorandom Number Generators* (PRNG), which stretch a short initial random *seed* into an arbitrarily long pseudorandom sequence.

The term "pseudo" comes from the fact that a PRNG is a deterministic function; hence it always generates the same pseudorandom sequence if it starts from the same seed. In particular, achieving unconditional security under a distinguishing attack is not possible with a PRNG, since given enough time any pseudorandom sequence can be trivially distinguished from a true one. Thus, cryptographic PRNG are usually designed under the computational security setting. One of the possible approaches is to model the PRNG with Boolean functions, thus leveraging the cryptographic properties discussed in Sect. 3.1. Indeed, the keystream generator used in the Vernam-like stream cipher can be considered a PRNG and can thus be designed using the combiner model, for instance.

On the other hand, the most common way to assess the quality of a cryptographic PRNG is by applying a battery of *statistical tests* on a sample of its sequences. The rationale is that if the pseudorandom sequences do not pass one or more tests in the suite, then the PRNG that produced them should not be used in cryptographic applications. Examples of statistical tests for cryptographic PRNG include the DIEHARD suite [40] and the NIST suite [3].

5.2   Survey of Related Works

Like S-boxes, one can remark two common trends in the use of AI methods for the design of cryptographic PRNG. The first one is centered on the use of cellular automata (CA) to define the structure of a PRNG. The second direction employs evolutionary algorithms to directly optimize the structure of a PRNG, or to evolve a CA whose dynamics is then used to produce pseudorandom sequences.

Wolfram [67] was the first to propose a PRNG based on a cellular automaton for stream ciphers. Specifically, he suggested using a CA equipped with local rule 30, which is known to induce a chaotic behavior in the CA dynamics. The seed of the PRNG is represented by the initial configuration of the CA, while the *trace* of the central cell (i.e., the sequence of states assumed by the central cell through multiple iterations) is taken as the pseudorandom sequence produced by the CA. However, Meier et al. [42] proved that Wolfram's PRNG is very weak from a cryptographic standpoint since it is vulnerable to a known-plaintext attack that exploits the *quasi-linearity* of rule 30, which allows to rewrite it in an equivalent way where the initial seeds are not equiprobable. Martin [41] remarked that this weakness is linked to the fact that rule 30 is not first-order correlation immune when interpreted as a Boolean function. Thus, later works in this direction, such as Formenti et al. [18] and Leporati et al. [31], focused on the search of larger CA local rules with a good trade-off of nonlinearity and correlation immunity. In particular, they assessed the quality of the pseudorandom sequences produced by the selected CA rules, respectively, with the DIEHARD and NIST statistical test suites. More recently, Manzoni et al. [32] considered CA-based PRNG from the *asynchrony* perspective, where the cells do not update all at the same time. Interestingly, through the NIST suite, the authors remarked that the quality of the pseudorandom sequences produced by certain local rules improves by allowing a small degree of asynchrony.

Concerning the approach based on evolutionary algorithms, Koza [28] used genetic programming to evolve Boolean trees used as CA local rules in Wolfram's PRNG model. In particular, the fitness function measured the *entropy* of the sequence produced by a CA equipped with the local rule defined by a GP tree, and the optimization objective was to maximize it. Remarkably, the best local rule resulting from Koza's experiments turned out to be equivalent to rule 30 used by Wolfram. Sipper and Tomassini [63] proposed a *cellular programming approach* based on a *hybrid CA*, where each cell can update its state according to a different local rule. In particular, the rule map was evolved using a genetic algorithm variation, where the fitness function to maximize was again Koza's entropy. Castro et al. [8] applied GP to design PRNG not based on the cellular automata approach; instead, the trees evolved by GP directly represented computer programs to generate pseudorandom numbers. In order to drive the GP optimization process, the authors adopted a fitness function based on the *avalanche effect*, which measures how many bits change in the output of the generator when only a single bit is complemented in the seed. Martinez et al. [30] later refined this approach, by proposing the PRNG Lamar designed through GP, and assessed through the DIEHARD test suite. Picek et al. [58] investigated the construction of PRNG with cartesian GP, showing that the evolved generators passed all NIST randomness tests and were quite efficient and small to be implemented in hardware. Along a similar research line, Picek et al. [59] presented three different methods based on Cartesian GP to design PRNG for masking countermeasures in side-channel attacks, each one allowing for a different degree of reconfigurability in hardware implementations.

6   Conclusions and New Directions

As we have seen in the previous sections, the field of AI-based cryptography is characterized by an extensive literature. We remark that our overview is far from being exhaustive. As a matter of fact, in this chapter, we did not cover several other minor research threads, such as the construction of ciphers with co-evolutionary methods [52], the design of secret sharing schemes based on cellular automata [35], construction of quantum key distribution protocols with evolutionary algorithms [29], and AI-driven cryptanalysis [9, 21]. However, we believe that the use cases of Boolean functions, S-boxes, and pseudorandom generators are representative of the main research trends in this area, both for the variety of methods adopted to address their design and also for the research challenges underlying them.

We conclude by discussing two new directions of research regarding the design of cryptographic primitives, where AI methods could be applied in the future.

Concerning the area of Boolean functions and S-boxes, most of the related literature focuses on applying a particular heuristic and then experimentally assessing its performances by verifying the cryptographic properties of the solutions produced by it. However, different heuristic techniques can have a very different degree of success in generating good Boolean functions and S-boxes. The reasons underlying these performance gaps are still not very clear. It would thus be interesting to perform a meta-analysis of the main heuristic techniques used up to now (e.g., evolutionary algorithms and swarm intelligence methods), and investigate more closely why some approaches are more successful than others. Along the same direction, it would also be useful to study more in detail the difficulty of the combinatorial optimization problems related to Boolean functions and S-boxes, for example, by employing *fitness landscape analysis* techniques on the underlying search spaces. As far as the authors know, only Jakobovic et al. [25] performed an analysis of the fitness landscape associated with S-boxes, and there are still several avenues for further research that could be explored in this domain.

Joan Daemen suggested an alternative approach to the design of block ciphers where AI techniques could help, which does not focus on the cryptographic properties of S-boxes[1]. This approach starts from the observation that recent lightweight primitives inspired by the structure of KECCAK [4] employ very simple and small S-boxes, whose optimality can be easily achieved without having to resort to heuristic algorithms. Examples in this class of primitives include the cryptographic permutation XOODOO [16], which employs a 3×3 S-box defined by the same CA rule χ of KECCAK. The design of XOODOO depends on several real-valued parameters, such as *round constants*, used to break the symmetry produced by the shift-invariant structure of χ. An interesting direction of research in this setting would be to use heuristic techniques, such as evolutionary algorithms, to optimize the parameters of XOODOO for different dimensions, for example, by considering more constrained hardware implementations.

References

1. Applebaum, B., Ishai, Y., Kushilevitz, E.: Cryptography by cellular automata or how fast can complexity emerge in nature? In: Proceedings of ICS 2010, pp. 1–19 (2010)
2. Bäck, T.: Evolutionary Algorithms in Theory and Practice - Evolution Strategies, Evolutionary Programming, Genetic Algorithms. Oxford University Press, Oxford (1996)
3. Bassham III, L.E., et al.: Sp 800–22 rev. 1a. a statistical test suite for random and pseudorandom number generators for cryptographic applications. National Institute of Standards & Technology (2010)
4. Bertoni, G., Daemen, J., Peeters, M., Assche, G.V.: The Keccak reference, January 2011. http://keccak.noekeon.org/
5. Burnett, L., Carter, G., Dawson, E., Millan, W.: Efficient methods for generating MARS-like S-boxes. In: Goos, G., Hartmanis, J., van Leeuwen, J., Schneier, B. (eds.) FSE 2000. LNCS, vol. 1978, pp. 300–313. Springer, Heidelberg (2001). https://doi.org/10.1007/3-540-44706-7_21
6. Carlet, C.: Boolean Functions for Cryptography and Coding Theory. Cambridge University Press, Cambridge (2021)

---

[1] Personal communication.

7. Castro, J.C.H., Viñuela, P.I., del Arco-Calderón, C.L.: Finding efficient nonlinear functions by means of genetic programming. In: Palade, V., Howlett, R.J., Jain, L. (eds.) KES 2003. LNCS (LNAI), vol. 2773, pp. 1192–1198. Springer, Heidelberg (2003). https://doi.org/10.1007/978-3-540-45224-9_161

8. Castro, J.C.H., Seznec, A., Isasi, P.: On the design of state-of-the-art pseudorandom number generators by means of genetic programming. In: IEEE Congress on Evolutionary Computation, pp. 1510–1516. IEEE (2004)

9. Castro, J.C.H., Viñuela, P.I.: New results on the genetic cryptanalysis of TEA and reduced-round versions of XTEA. New Gener. Comput. **23**(3), 233–243 (2005)

10. Chopard, B., Tomassini, M.: An Introduction to Metaheuristics for Optimization. Natural Computing Series. Springer, Heidelberg (2018). https://doi.org/10.1007/978-3-319-93073-2

11. Clark, J.A., Jacob, J.L.: Two-stage optimisation in the design of boolean functions. In: Dawson, E.P., Clark, A., Boyd, C. (eds.) ACISP 2000. LNCS, vol. 1841, pp. 242–254. Springer, Heidelberg (2000). https://doi.org/10.1007/10718964_20

12. Clark, J.A., Jacob, J.L., Maitra, S., Stanica, P.: Almost boolean functions: the design of boolean functions by spectral inversion. Comput. Intell. **20**(3), 450–462 (2004)

13. Clark, J.A., Jacob, J.L., Stepney, S.: The design of s-boxes by simulated annealing. New Gener. Comput. **23**(3), 219–231 (2005)

14. Clark, J.A., Jacob, J.L., Stepney, S., Maitra, S., Millan, W.: Evolving boolean functions satisfying multiple criteria. In: Menezes, A., Sarkar, P. (eds.) INDOCRYPT 2002. LNCS, vol. 2551, pp. 246–259. Springer, Heidelberg (2002). https://doi.org/10.1007/3-540-36231-2_20

15. Daemen, J., Govaerts, R., Vandewalle, J.: Invertible shift-invariant transformations on binary arrays. Appl. Math. Comput. **62**(2), 259–277 (1994)

16. Daemen, J., Hoffert, S., Assche, G.V., Keer, R.V.: The design of Xoodoo and Xoofff. IACR Trans. Symmetric Cryptol. **2018**(4), 1–38 (2018)

17. Eiben, A.E., Smith, J.E.: Introduction to Evolutionary Computing. Natural Computing Series, 2nd edn. Springer, Heidelberg (2015). https://doi.org/10.1007/978-3-662-44874-8

18. Formenti, E., Imai, K., Martin, B., Yunès, J.-B.: Advances on random sequence generation by uniform cellular automata. In: Calude, C.S., Freivalds, R., Kazuo, I. (eds.) Computing with New Resources. LNCS, vol. 8808, pp. 56–70. Springer, Cham (2014). https://doi.org/10.1007/978-3-319-13350-8_5

19. Fuller, J., Millan, W., Dawson, E.: Multi-objective optimisation of bijective S-boxes. In: Proceedings of CEC 2004, pp. 1525–1532 (2004)

20. Ghoshal, A., Sadhukhan, R., Patranabis, S., Datta, N., Picek, S., Mukhopadhyay, D.: Lightweight and side-channel secure 4 × 4 S-boxes from cellular automata rules. IACR Trans. Symmetric Cryptol. **2018**(3), 311–334 (2018)

21. Gohr, A.: Improving attacks on round-reduced speck32/64 using deep learning. In: Boldyreva, A., Micciancio, D. (eds.) CRYPTO 2019. LNCS, vol. 11693, pp. 150–179. Springer, Cham (2019). https://doi.org/10.1007/978-3-030-26951-7_6

22. Hrbacek, R., Dvorak, V.: Bent function synthesis by means of cartesian genetic programming. In: Bartz-Beielstein, T., Branke, J., Filipič, B., Smith, J. (eds.) PPSN 2014. LNCS, vol. 8672, pp. 414–423. Springer, Cham (2014). https://doi.org/10.1007/978-3-319-10762-2_41

23. Ilachinski, A.: Cellular Automata: A Discrete Universe. World Scientific Publishing Co. Inc. (2001)

24. Ivanov, G., Nikolov, N., Nikova, S.: Reversed genetic algorithms for generation of bijective s-boxes with good cryptographic properties. Cryptogr. Commun. **8**(2), 247–276 (2016). https://doi.org/10.1007/s12095-015-0170-5
25. Jakobovic, D., Picek, S., Martins, M.S.R., Wagner, M.: A characterisation of S-box fitness landscapes in cryptography. In: Auger, A., Stützle, T. (eds.) Proceedings of GECCO 2019, pp. 285–293. ACM (2019)
26. Kari, J.: Basic concepts of cellular automata. In: Rozenberg, G., Bäck, T., Kok, J.N. (eds.) Handbook of Natural Computing, pp. 3–24. Springer, Heidelberg (2012). https://doi.org/10.1007/978-3-540-92910-9_1
27. Katz, J., Lindell, Y.: Introduction to Modern Cryptography, 2nd edn. CRC Press, Boca Raton (2014)
28. Koza, J.R.: Evolving a computer program to generate random numbers using the genetic programming paradigm. In: ICGA, pp. 37–44. Morgan Kaufmann (1991)
29. Krawec, W., Picek, S., Jakobovic, D.: Evolutionary algorithms for the design of quantum protocols. In: Kaufmann, P., Castillo, P.A. (eds.) EvoApplications 2019. LNCS, vol. 11454, pp. 220–236. Springer, Cham (2019). https://doi.org/10.1007/978-3-030-16692-2_15
30. Lamenca-Martinez, C., Hernandez-Castro, J.C., Estevez-Tapiador, J.M., Ribagorda, A.: Lamar: a new pseudorandom number generator evolved by means of genetic programming. In: Runarsson, T.P., Beyer, H.-G., Burke, E., Merelo-Guervós, J.J., Whitley, L.D., Yao, X. (eds.) PPSN 2006. LNCS, vol. 4193, pp. 850–859. Springer, Heidelberg (2006). https://doi.org/10.1007/11844297_86
31. Leporati, A., Mariot, L.: Cryptographic properties of bipermutive cellular automata rules. J. Cell. Autom. **9**(5–6), 437–475 (2014)
32. Manzoni, L., Mariot, L.: Cellular automata pseudo-random number generators and their resistance to asynchrony. In: Mauri, G., El Yacoubi, S., Dennunzio, A., Nishinari, K., Manzoni, L. (eds.) ACRI 2018. LNCS, vol. 11115, pp. 428–437. Springer, Cham (2018). https://doi.org/10.1007/978-3-319-99813-8_39
33. Manzoni, L., Mariot, L., Tuba, E.: Balanced crossover operators in genetic algorithms. Swarm Evol. Comput. **54**, 100646 (2020)
34. Mariot, L., Jakobovic, D., Leporati, A., Picek, S.: Hyper-bent boolean functions and evolutionary algorithms. In: Sekanina, L., Hu, T., Lourenço, N., Richter, H., García-Sánchez, P. (eds.) EuroGP 2019. LNCS, vol. 11451, pp. 262–277. Springer, Cham (2019). https://doi.org/10.1007/978-3-030-16670-0_17
35. Mariot, L., Leporati, A.: Sharing secrets by computing preimages of bipermutive cellular automata. In: Wąs, J., Sirakoulis, G.C., Bandini, S. (eds.) ACRI 2014. LNCS, vol. 8751, pp. 417–426. Springer, Cham (2014). https://doi.org/10.1007/978-3-319-11520-7_43
36. Mariot, L., Leporati, A.: A genetic algorithm for evolving plateaued cryptographic boolean functions. In: Dediu, A.-H., Magdalena, L., Martín-Vide, C. (eds.) TPNC 2015. LNCS, vol. 9477, pp. 33–45. Springer, Cham (2015). https://doi.org/10.1007/978-3-319-26841-5_3
37. Mariot, L., Leporati, A.: Heuristic search by particle swarm optimization of boolean functions for cryptographic applications. In: Silva, S., Esparcia-Alcázar, A.I. (eds.) Companion Proceedings of GECCO 2015, pp. 1425–1426. ACM (2015)
38. Mariot, L., Picek, S., Jakobovic, D., Leporati, A.: Evolutionary search of binary orthogonal arrays. In: Auger, A., Fonseca, C.M., Lourenço, N., Machado, P., Paquete, L., Whitley, D. (eds.) PPSN 2018. LNCS, vol. 11101, pp. 121–133. Springer, Cham (2018). https://doi.org/10.1007/978-3-319-99253-2_10
39. Mariot, L., Picek, S., Leporati, A., Jakobovic, D.: Cellular automata based s-boxes. Cryptogr. Commun. **11**(1), 41–62 (2019)

40. Marsaglia, G.: The marsaglia random number CDROM including the diehard battery of tests of randomness (2008). http://www.stat.fsu.edu/pub/diehard/
41. Martin, B.: A Walsh exploration of elementary CA rules. J. Cell. Autom. **3**(2), 145–156 (2008)
42. Meier, W., Staffelbach, O.: Analysis of pseudo random sequences generated by cellular automata. In: Davies, D.W. (ed.) EUROCRYPT 1991. LNCS, vol. 547, pp. 186–199. Springer, Heidelberg (1991). https://doi.org/10.1007/3-540-46416-6_17
43. Millan, W., Burnett, L., Carter, G., Clark, A., Dawson, E.: Evolutionary heuristics for finding cryptographically strong S-boxes. In: Varadharajan, V., Mu, Y. (eds.) ICICS 1999. LNCS, vol. 1726, pp. 263–274. Springer, Heidelberg (1999). https://doi.org/10.1007/978-3-540-47942-0_22
44. Millan, W., Clark, A., Dawson, E.: An effective genetic algorithm for finding highly nonlinear boolean functions. In: Han, Y., Okamoto, T., Qing, S. (eds.) ICICS 1997. LNCS, vol. 1334, pp. 149–158. Springer, Heidelberg (1997). https://doi.org/10.1007/BFb0028471
45. Millan, W., Clark, A., Dawson, E.: Heuristic design of cryptographically strong balanced Boolean functions. In: Nyberg, K. (ed.) EUROCRYPT 1998. LNCS, vol. 1403, pp. 489–499. Springer, Heidelberg (1998). https://doi.org/10.1007/BFb0054148
46. Picek, S., Carlet, C., Jakobovic, D., Miller, J.F., Batina, L.: Correlation immunity of boolean functions: an evolutionary algorithms perspective. In: Proceedings of GECCO 2015, pp. 1095–1102 (2015)
47. Picek, S., Cupic, M., Rotim, L.: A new cost function for evolution of S-boxes. Evol. Comput. **24**(4), 695–718 (2016)
48. Picek, S., Guilley, S., Carlet, C., Jakobovic, D., Miller, J.F.: Evolutionary approach for finding correlation immune boolean functions of order t with minimal hamming weight. In: Dediu, A.-H., Magdalena, L., Martín-Vide, C. (eds.) TPNC 2015. LNCS, vol. 9477, pp. 71–82. Springer, Cham (2015). https://doi.org/10.1007/978-3-319-26841-5_6
49. Picek, S., Jakobovic, D.: Evolving algebraic constructions for designing bent boolean functions. In: Friedrich, T., Neumann, F., Sutton, A.M. (eds.) Proceedings of GECCO 2016, pp. 781–788. ACM (2016)
50. Picek, S., Jakobovic, D., Golub, M.: Evolving cryptographically sound boolean functions. In: Blum, C., Alba, E. (eds.) Companion Proceedings of GECCO 2013, pp. 191–192. ACM (2013)
51. Picek, S., Jakobovic, D., Miller, J.F., Batina, L., Cupic, M.: Cryptographic boolean functions: one output, many design criteria. Appl. Soft Comput. **40**, 635–653 (2016)
52. Picek, S., Knezevic, K., Jakobovic, D., Derek, A.: C^3po: cipher construction with cartesian genetic programming. In: López-Ibáñez, M., Auger, A., Stützle, T. (eds.) Companion Proceedings of GECCO 2019, pp. 1625–1633. ACM (2019)
53. Picek, S., Knezevic, K., Mariot, L., Jakobovic, D., Leporati, A.: Evolving bent quaternary functions. In: 2018 IEEE Congress on Evolutionary Computation, CEC 2018, Rio de Janeiro, Brazil, 8–13 July 2018, pp. 1–8. IEEE (2018)
54. Picek, S., Marchiori, E., Batina, L., Jakobovic, D.: Combining evolutionary computation and algebraic constructions to find cryptography-relevant boolean functions. In: Bartz-Beielstein, T., Branke, J., Filipič, B., Smith, J. (eds.) PPSN 2014. LNCS, vol. 8672, pp. 822–831. Springer, Cham (2014). https://doi.org/10.1007/978-3-319-10762-2_81

55. Picek, S., Mariot, L., Leporati, A., Jakobovic, D.: Evolving S-boxes based on cellular automata with genetic programming. In: Bosman, P.A.N. (ed.) Companion Proceedings of GECCO 2017, pp. 251–252. ACM (2017)
56. Picek, S., Mariot, L., Yang, B., Jakobovic, D., Mentens, N.: Design of S-boxes defined with cellular automata rules. In: Proceedings of CF 2017, pp. 409–414. ACM (2017)
57. Picek, S., Miller, J.F., Jakobovic, D., Batina, L.: Cartesian genetic programming approach for generating substitution boxes of different sizes. In: Companion Proceedings of GECCO 2015, pp. 1457–1458 (2015)
58. Picek, S., Sisejkovic, D., Rozic, V., Yang, B., Jakobovic, D., Mentens, N.: Evolving cryptographic pseudorandom number generators. In: Handl, J., Hart, E., Lewis, P.R., López-Ibáñez, M., Ochoa, G., Paechter, B. (eds.) PPSN 2016. LNCS, vol. 9921, pp. 613–622. Springer, Cham (2016). https://doi.org/10.1007/978-3-319-45823-6_57
59. Picek, S., et al.: PRNGs for masking applications and their mapping to evolvable hardware. In: Lemke-Rust, K., Tunstall, M. (eds.) CARDIS 2016. LNCS, vol. 10146, pp. 209–227. Springer, Cham (2017). https://doi.org/10.1007/978-3-319-54669-8_13
60. Saber, Z., Uddin, M.F., Youssef, A.M.: On the existence of (9, 3, 5, 240) resilient functions. IEEE Trans. Inf. Theory $52(5)$, 2269–2270 (2006)
61. Seredynski, F., Bouvry, P., Zomaya, A.Y.: Cellular automata computations and secret key cryptography. Parallel Comput. $30(5–6)$, 753–766 (2004)
62. Shannon, C.E.: Communication theory of secrecy systems. Bell Syst. Tech. J. $28(4)$, 656–715 (1949)
63. Sipper, M., Tomassini, M.: Generating parallel random number generators by cellular programming. Int. J. Mod. Phys. C $7(02)$, 181–190 (1996)
64. Stinson, D.R., Paterson, M.: Cryptography: Theory and Practice. CRC Press, Boca Raton (2018)
65. Szaban, M., Seredynski, F.: Cryptographically strong S-boxes based on cellular automata. In: Umeo, H., Morishita, S., Nishinari, K., Komatsuzaki, T., Bandini, S. (eds.) ACRI 2008. LNCS, vol. 5191, pp. 478–485. Springer, Heidelberg (2008). https://doi.org/10.1007/978-3-540-79992-4_62
66. Tomassini, M., Perrenoud, M.: Cryptography with cellular automata. Appl. Soft Comput. $1(2)$, 151–160 (2001)
67. Wolfram, S.: Cryptography with cellular automata. In: Williams, H.C. (ed.) CRYPTO 1985. LNCS, vol. 218, pp. 429–432. Springer, Heidelberg (1986). https://doi.org/10.1007/3-540-39799-X_32

Traditional Machine Learning Methods for Side-Channel Analysis

Alan Jovic[1]([✉]), Dirmanto Jap[2], Louiza Papachristodoulou[3],
and Annelie Heuser[4]

[1] Faculty of Electrical Engineering and Computing, University of Zagreb,
Zagreb, Croatia
alan.jovic@fer.hr
[2] Temasek Laboratories, Nanyang Technological University, Singapore, Singapore
djap@ntu.edu.sg
[3] Fontys University of Applied Sciences, Eindhoven, Netherlands
[4] French National Center for Scientific Research (CNRS), IRISA, Rennes, France
annelie.heuser@irisa.fr

Abstract. Traditional machine learning techniques (excluding deep learning) include a range of approaches, such as supervised, semi-supervised, and unsupervised modeling methods, often coupled with data augmentation and dimensionality reduction. The aim of this chapter is to provide an overview of the application of traditional machine learning methods in the field of side-channel analysis. The chapter encompasses the common methods used in side-channel attacks, a historical overview of the use of machine learning methods in side-channel analysis, and a brief description of various machine learning approaches that have been used in related studies. Both machine learning methods and side-channel specific methods such as Principal Component Analysis, Linear Discriminant Analysis, Template Attacks, Random Forests, Multilayer Perceptron and many others are compared and the current status of their use in side-channel analysis is presented. Several research avenues are still incomplete and the chapter points out some of the open questions.

1 Introduction

Recently, there has been a lot of interest in applying artificial intelligence methods, especially from the field of machine learning (ML), to improve the practical attacks on electronic devices that use cryptographic algorithms for data protection [28,33,52]. All of these devices create an information leak (unintentional release of information) from the device. This leakage, known as *side-channel leakage*, can be exploited after taking measurements to extract secret cryptographic keys. Obtaining the secret key (or keys) is the main goal of *side-channel analysis*, also called *side-channel attacks* (SCA) approaches [58]. The main reason for using ML methods in this area is that some of the approaches belonging to SCA can be formulated in a way that allows efficient use of ML methods in the construction of cryptographic device leakage models, which facilitates the

L. Batina et al. (Eds.): Security and Artificial Intelligence, LNCS 13049, pp. 25–47, 2022.
https://doi.org/10.1007/978-3-030-98795-4_2

attacks [60]. On the other hand, there are some approaches to SCA that do not justify the use of ML methods, but rather focus on SCA's information-theoretic aspects [37].

The aim of this chapter is to present an overview of various ML methods that have been used and are still being explored in SCA. This chapter is limited only to the traditional ML methods, which excludes the newer deep learning approaches. It includes an introduction to SCA and its information-theoretic models, gives a historical overview of the approaches used, and then reviews various methods of data preprocessing [46], data modeling, and model evaluation in SCA, focusing on the use of ML methods in this area.

2   Side-Channel Analysis

SCA leakage can be simulated by information-theoretic models that show the attacker's ability to recover the secret key, which would allow him to decipher the protected messages. In practice, the leak can be exploited by an attacker who is able to measure it with specific tools, even if he does not know all the details of the cryptographic algorithm implementation. SCA attacks have been successfully used to break the hardware or software implementations of many cryptosystems, including: block ciphers, stream ciphers, public key ciphers, implementations of signature schemes, message authentication code schemes, implementations of cryptographic protocols, implementations of cryptosystems, and even network systems [67]. Leakage of information from devices and algorithms cannot be avoided, and the use of countermeasures, either hardware or software ones, such as data randomization [12] and masking [31][1] is necessary to ensure security. There are several types of SCA that threaten the security of cryptographic implementations, as explained below.

2.1   Types of Side-Channel Analysis

SCA was first presented by Kocher [26] in 1996. Kocher showed that timing differences in the execution time of a modular exponentiation operation can be used to break instances of the RSA algorithm [55]. Subsequently, Kocher *et al.* [25] investigated instantaneous power consumption and found that it can reveal information about internal (or intermediate) states of any cryptographic algorithm. It was also shown that electromagnetic emanations (EM) around a device can be exploited in the same way [18,53]. When measuring any type of leakage, one or more traces are usually measured with a probe, displayed on an oscilloscope, and recorded on a connected computer. A trace used for SCA typically consists of a time-series of M measurements, and N of such traces

---

[1] Data masking is the process of hiding original data by altering its content. It is based on the simple idea that the message and the key are masked with a randomly generated mask at the beginning of the computation, after which the rest is performed as if there were no mask. At the end, the mask must be known so that the original data can be recovered.

form a dataset. The sampling times are considered as features (variables) of the dataset. An example of a test-bed for taking power consumption measurements and analyzing them may be found in Martinasek *et al.* [39]. The types of SCA commonly encountered in the literature are shown in Table 1.

Table 1. Common types of SCA

Classification category	Examples
Signal type	power consumption, electromagnetic emanation, acoustic, visible light, timing, fault, caching
Profiling device	profiled, non-profiled
Statistics order	first-order, second-order, higher-order

The attacks on cryptographic devices based on power consumption and EM traces are commonly referred to as Simple Power Analysis (SPA), Differential Power Analysis (DPA), Simple Electromagnetic Analysis (SEMA), and Differential Electromagnetic Analysis (DEMA). Correlation Power Analysis (CPA) also uses power consumption traces, but unlike the other methods, it considers the information-theoretic model of Hamming-distance (see Sect. 2.2), from which the best estimate of the secret key is derived based on Pearson's correlation coefficient. Another distinction between types of SCA is that between profiled and non-profiled attacks, a concept similar to white-box and black-box approaches to testing or threat modeling. Namely, in profiled attacks, we assume that the attacker has in his possession a profiling device that is highly similar or identical to the attacked device (target), and he can train different models on his profiling device that emulate how the target device works [49]. In non-profiled attacks, the attacker is assumed to have less knowledge about the target and no way to train the models. In this case, a typical attacker can only collect a limited number of side-channel traces for a fixed unknown key value from the target device and then use some SCA technique (e.g., DPA) to infer information about the secret key [62].

There is also a distinction between first-order and higher-order SCA. The order level refers to the number of outputs from a SCA model used for mounting an attack on the secret key. The modeling based on first- and second-order statistics are usually sufficient to quantify the secret key. For example, DPA is mainly based on calculations related to the first-order statistic, the mean [56]. In standard SCA, the masking countermeasure typically requires combining several time samples involving a mask operation to "remove" the mask, which is referred to as higher-order SCA because it uses higher-order statistics.

2.2 Information-Theoretic Models

To perform SCA, special measurement equipment is required that allows power signals to be captured[2]. Power simulations describe the behavior of a device executing algorithms with certain values. From an attacker's perspective, behavior-level power simulations are interesting because they reveal data dependencies that can affect the security of the implementation.

The most widely adopted information-theoretic models used to map simulated transitions to power traces are the Hamming-weight (HW) and Hamming-distance (HD) models.

Definition 1. *The* Hamming weight *of a value v is defined as the number of ones in its binary representation. Therefore, the HW model is based on the number of ones in a certain value.*

Definition 2. *The* Hamming Distance *of two strings of the same length v_0, v_1 is the number of bits in which v_0 and v_1 differ. This means that $HD(v_0, v_1)$ can be defined as follows: $HD(v_0, v_1) = HW(v_0 \oplus v_1)$.*

The HD model is used to deduce the power consumption values from the transitions that occur in the dynamic power consumption of a circuit at the output of logic cells, such as registers. In principle, by counting the $0 \rightarrow 1$ and $1 \rightarrow 0$ transitions that occur in a digital circuit during a given time interval, exploitable information about the manipulated secret key can be derived. According to [38], the Hamming-distance model in power simulations assumes, for simplicity, that all cells contribute equally to power consumption, and that there is no difference between $0 \rightarrow 1$ and $1 \rightarrow 0$ transitions. In practice, however, the power consumption of a $0 \rightarrow 1$ transition is higher than that of $1 \rightarrow 0$ transition. The HD model is mostly used to describe the power consumption of buses and registers, and is therefore suitable for performing hardware SCA. Since all software runs on hardware, this leakage model is implicitly used for software attacks as well. The choice of the appropriate model depends on the measurement setup.

The HW model is simpler in the sense that it considers the power consumption of the processed data. The attacker assumes that the power consumption is proportional to the bits set to 1 in the value of interest. By observing the value of a bit before and after it is processed, we can detect differences in power consumption. If the cell processing the value v always stores the same value before processing v (for example, it is a register that is always initialized to 0), then the power consumption is directly or inversely proportional to the initial bits of that value. If the value stored in this initialization register is a random variable, then comparing the initial and processed values does not give the attacker any useful information; the results are independent. The HW model may be easier

---

[2] It is possible to perform SCA with power, electromagnetic, acoustic, or other signal types, see Table 1, but in this chapter, for simplicity and because they are common, we will consider only power signals. Similar models can be described for other signal types.

for a cryptographic device to simulate, but it provides less side-channel information to the attacker and is used when the HD model does not provide useful information.

3   Historical Overview of the Machine Learning Research for SCA

Some of the earlier applications of ML for acoustic SCA include neural networks used to learn information about what was typed on a keyboard [3,68], or the sound of a printer [4].

In the context of power or EM SCA, many works using ML have also been reported. There are some pre-2011 publications that have used ML-related techniques, but do not explicitly state or claim to have used an ML-based approach:

- Karlof and Wagner [24] reported an attack on Elliptic Curve Cryptography (ECC) protected with randomized side-channel countermeasure using Hidden Markov Model (HMM) to model the intermediate state values and mask values as probabilistic finite state machines.
- Lemke-Rust and Paar [27] reported a higher-order attack on a Boolean masking implementation using a Gaussian Mixture Model (GMM).
- Batina et al. [7] proposed to use cluster analysis in DPA to identify key candidates that lead to maximum cluster separation.
- Souissi et al. [56] proposed to use Principal Component Analysis (PCA) method as a basis for finding the secret key.

In 2011, some researchers started to state that they use ML for SCA. Hospodar et al. [22] used the Least Square Support Vector Machine (LS-SVM) to perform a binary classification that uses the values of the logic cells of the cryptographic algorithm output during an intermediate state of the algorithm as a class label (called the intermediate value model). This work highlights the ability of the ML-based approach over SCA data. Lerman et al. [28] compared several methods: random forests (RF), SVM, and self-organizing map (SOM) with a classical template attack (TA, see Sect. 5.6) for a profiling-based attack on an FPGA board protected by the 3DES algorithm. Heuser and Zohner [20] proposed the first work on ML in SCA information-theoretic framework. They used the multi-class SVM for attacking multi-bit values (HW model) and incorporated maximum likelihood principle for key recovery. This was later extended by Bartkewitz and Lemke-Rust [5] with a new multi-class classification strategy based on probabilistic SVM using ordered class predictions for attack evaluation. Other similar works, but based on neural networks, was also done by Martinasek et al. [40,41].

Several threat models have also been explored for possible ML applications in SCA. Lerman et al. [32] presented the model when the attacker may not have full profiling capability. They used semi-supervised learning, where the attacker was assumed to have access to a similar device with multiple known and fixed secret keys (partial knowledge), and attempted to attack the target device with unknown keys. Another consideration relates to the time-series nature of SCA data. This was investigated by Lerman *et al.* [30], who proposed a method for detecting a profiling attack based on the time-series behavior in the measured traces. The attack on an implementation protected by countermeasure was presented in [31]. They proposed an ML-based attack against the Rotating S-boxes Masking countermeasure on AES.

Some of the unsupervised learning methods have also been studied for public key cryptosystems. According to Heyszl *et al.* [21], clustering is generally useful for SCA when profiling information is unavailable and exhaustive partitioning is computationally infeasible. This study addressed an attack on an FPGA-based implementation of ECC scalar multiplication using the k-means method. In [45], Perin *et al.* used unsupervised learning to attack exponentiations with randomization.

Lerman *et al.* showed in [33] that ML techniques provide better classification results when the adversary's ability to perform device profiling is limited and in a high-dimensional context where many parameters affect device leakage. Therefore, the combination of multiple side-channel leaks and a clustering-based approach provided higher success rates for non-profiled attacks than traditional TA, as shown by Specht *et al.* [57]. The success rate of online TA was significantly improved in [69] by using the k-nearest neighbor, Naïve Bayes and SVM methods for template classification.

More recently, since 2016, research on the use of traditional ML techniques for SCA has focused on testing various feature selection and other methods for data preprocessing [46,49] (described in the next section), as well as to a more thorough consideration of many supervised and unsupervised ML methods [47] (see Sects. 5 and 6) and their evaluation criteria (see Sect. 7).

In Table 2, we summarize the traditional ML methods used in SCA, some of which are explained in detail in the following sections. For each method, a reference to its use in the SCA literature is included. Methods for data preprocessing are not shown here as there are many variations of these methods, see Sect. 4.

Table 2. Traditional ML methods commonly used in SCA

ML methods	
Type	Methods
Supervised	k-nearest neighbour [69], Naïve Bayes [47], Support Vector Machines [34], Random Forests [46], Multilayer perceptron [41]
Unsupervised, cluster	k-means [21], Expectation Maximization [27], Self-organizing Map [28]
Unsupervised, latent variable	Hidden Markov Model [24], Gaussian Mixture Models [27]
Semi-supervised	k-medoid [32], Tri-training [35], Self-training [50], Graph-based Learning [50]

4 Data Preprocessing for SCA

Raw measurement datasets for SCA can suffer from several problems. For example, the number of traces recorded may be too small in relation to the sample size (feature set), resulting in a sparse dataset, as there are too few samples to cover the extended feature set. This fact, in turn, leads to the Hughes effect, which is a reduced classifier prediction due to high dimensionality. Therefore, quality selection of points of interest (features) is an important issue for SCA datasets, which has often been neglected. Other common problems are:

- class imbalance, where, for example, in the HW model, there is a disproportion in the number of samples for each of the nine classes,
- misalignment of traces, often as a result of introduced countermeasures,
- low signal-to-noise ratio, which prevents accurate quantification of the underlying signal properties.

In order to improve the preprocessing of the raw data, several techniques have been introduced in SCA. They can be divided into two general groups:

- data augmentation techniques, which deal either with changing the values or the size of the samples, or with transforming the measured feature set, and
- feature selection techniques that attempt to solve the problems by selecting those points of interest that contain more relevant SCA leakage information.

In any case, the goal of the data preprocessing step is to prepare the dataset into a form that allows for more efficient SCA. Data preprocessing, when considered in the context of traditional ML techniques, is usually unavoidable, as traditional ML techniques are somewhat more dependent on the carefully performed preprocessing step than deep learning techniques. In the following subsections, we describe various techniques that have been used for data preprocessing in SCA.

4.1 Data Augmentation and Dimensionality Reduction Techniques

Dimensionality reduction based on Principal Component Analysis (PCA) transforms the original features into new features [57]. The new features yield a new base of time samples in which the inter-class variance is larger, taking into account the covariance of the samples. Typically, only a few principal components are selected to adequately represent the larger initial dataset [2]. Linear Discriminant Analysis is also a dimensionality reduction technique and a competitor of PCA in the context of supervised learning problems. LDA forms a linear combination of the data that attempts to separate classes by scattering the inter-class difference (centroids) and considering and minimizing intra-class variance. Both methods have been used successfully in the SCA context, although LDA requires that the number of traces measured is greater than the number of features, which may prevent its use on some datasets [14]. There are other existing dimensionality reduction approaches that may be related to PCA, such as in [11]. Here, the aim is to maximize the higher-order CPA coefficient, which has been shown to be equivalent to maximizing the data covariance. Dimensionality reduction techniques based on manifold learning [65] and similar approaches may offer additional improvement in SCA compared to PCA and LDA under certain assumptions and dataset properties. This remains to be investigated.

Countermeasures that use time-domain traces misalignment can cause problems for DPA. Traces realignment can be considered as a data augmentation technique that can contribute to successful SCA. There are some approaches in the literature that offer traces realignment. For example, Tian and Hus [61] proposed a new general method to handle misaligned traces by dynamically localizing the peak shift in the amplitude domain while partially aligning the traces in the time domain. Yang *et al.* [64] addressed the problem by proposing two alignment approaches: a local alignment based on shotgun distance and a global alignment based on weighted edit distance. They demonstrated their efficiency under three scenarios and different noise levels.

Adjusting the class imbalance is a common issue in ML. In SCA, attack scenarios that consider HW model in the profiling phase may suffer from this problem. To mitigate the effect, which is typically problematic in high-noise scenarios, various ML techniques, such as data resampling, are commonly used. Picek *et al.* [49] show that when the data is highly imbalanced, results using the SMOTE technique [16] are encouraging, as some scenarios are observed where the number of measurements required for a successful attack is reduced by more than eightfold.

4.2 Feature Selection Methods

Feature selection in SCA has mostly been performed using Pearson correlation (similar to CPA), where a subset of information-rich features is selected based on the correlation between the target output of the substitution box (S-box) of the cryptographic algorithm and the measured power consumption at a given time point [20,29].

A paper by Gierlichs *et al.* [19] introduced some feature selection metrics for SCA called Sum Of Squared Pairwise Differences (SOSD) and Sum Of Squared Pairwise T-Differences (SOST). It has been shown that SOST performs better than SOSD on noisy datasets and that the use of the metric improves the overall efficiency of the classification model. Zheng *et al.* [66] investigated several feature selection techniques, including mutual information analysis (MIA) and KS-test (Kolmogorov-Smirnov) based analysis, to achieve efficient SCA. They did not use any ML classifier to evaluate the feature selection techniques. Another approach to feature selection for SCA was given by Reparaz *et al.* [54]. They used a technique to identify $d + 1$ tuples of time samples, where d is the masking order, for multivariate[3] DPA attacks. The approach suggests the use of MIA

---

[3] Multivariate SCA considers multiple time points of the measured traces when building the model.

before attempting a key recovery attack. Moreover, an interesting feature selection metric called Normalized Inter-Class Variance (NICV) has been proposed by Bhasin *et al.* [8]. It is a metric that can be used to characterize the measurement differences between different devices and different keys. The purpose of NICV is to return the total variation of the traces at each time sample to test which leakage model causes variation between classes.

In review paper on ML-based SCA, Picek *et al.* [52] investigated the influence of the number of features in SCA by applying information gain feature selection in several scenarios. One of the conclusions is that the feature set can be reduced to only 20% of the original set in most scenarios without significant loss of accuracy. In a recent paper specifically addressing feature selection for SCA, Picek *et al.* [46] analyzed a number of feature selection methods for SCA, including those traditionally used only in the ML domain, i.e., the chi-square (χ^2) measure, L1 regularization with linear SVM for wrapper-based feature selection, and some hybrid feature selection techniques. Using the hybrid-based approach, which proved to be the most successful, χ^2 was first used to reduce the number of features in all datasets to 250 (out of more than a thousand) in order to reduce the running time of the other selection techniques and eliminate irrelevant features. Subsequently, it was shown that both the linear SVM wrapper selection and stability selection techniques were applicable for SCA. In addition, the work showed that using appropriate feature selection for SCA is more important on the highly noisy datasets, including those with countermeasures, than on the lowly noisy ones.

Additional research on feature selection methods is needed in order to establish the best approaches in SCA under a range of attack scenarios.

5 Supervised Learning Methods for SCA

In this section, we present the most common supervised learning methods used in SCA for profiling and template matching. ML techniques for classification are widely used in SCA, particularly on datasets with high-noise ratios.

5.1 Naive Bayes

The Naïve Bayes classification method is based on probability concepts, more precisely on the Bayes theorem for conditional probabilities of independent events [9]. The conditional probability model considers $\mathbf{x} = (x_1, \ldots, x_n)$ as the vector of values of independent variables that need to be classified. Each vector is assigned a probability $p(c_j | x_1, \ldots, x_n)$, for $1 \leq j \leq k$ and k possible classes. The set of classes $c_1, c_2, \ldots, c_k$ is mutually exclusive and exhaustive. Using Bayes theorem, the posterior conditional probability can be calculated as $p(c_j | \mathbf{x}) = \frac{p(c_j) \, p(\mathbf{x}|c_j)}{p(\mathbf{x})}$, for $1 < j < k$. Assuming that each event and posterior probability are independent of any previous event, the conditional distribution over the class variable c is $p(c_j | x_1, \ldots, x_n) = \frac{1}{Z} p(c_j) \prod_{i=1}^{n} p(x_i | c_j)$ for $1 \leq j \leq k$, where the evidence $Z = p(\mathbf{x})$ is a scaling factor depending only on $x_1, \ldots, x_n$, i.e., a constant when the values of the feature variables are known.

The Naïve Bayes classifier combines the Naïve Bayes probability model with a decision rule. A common rule is to choose the most likely hypothesis, i.e., the maximum value of the a posteriori probability. For each class c_i, a classifier is chosen as the class index that gives the maximum value for an event. The Naïve Bayes classifier has been widely used in SCA, due to its computational efficiency [47, 69].

5.2 Random Forests

RF are one of the best-known and most successful stochastic ensemble methods. The forest consists of a number of decision tree learners [10]. It accounts for randomness in its construction in two ways: it uses bootstrap data sampling and feature selection at each node splitting. Feature selection for splitting is done from a random subset of k features at each internal node of a decision tree. Only the best informational splitting is taken among the selected features. The forest is usually constructed with trees built without pruning. The model makes a voting-based decision on new samples and returns a class probability distribution. RF has been successfully used in many SCA works for profiling attacks [32, 34, 46] due to its ability to accurately assess the class probabilities, which is necessary for estimating the secret key. In fact, RF can be considered, along with SVM, as the complex traditional ML algorithm of choice for demanding classification tasks.

5.3 Support Vector Machines

SVM is a deterministic, nonparametric supervised learning model that builds a discriminative classifier defined in N dimensions by an optimal separating hyperplane, given a set of labeled training data. An optimal hyperplane, as defined in [1], is the one that has the largest minimum distance to the training points, because in this way noisy data is still correctly classified. Thus, the optimal hyperplane maximizes the margin between training data from different classes. New samples are mapped to the same N-dimensional space and class membership is predicted based on the side of the margin they fall on. SVMs are supervised learning models with associated learning algorithms that analyze data and recognize patterns, and are used for classification and regression analysis. Given a set of training examples, each labeled for belonging to one of two categories, an SVM training algorithm builds a model that assigns new examples to one category or the other, making it a non-probabilistic binary linear classifier that can be extended for multi-class cases. In addition to linear classification, SVMs can efficiently perform non-linear classification by using the so-called kernel trick, which implicitly maps their inputs to high-dimensional feature spaces. Its use in profiling SCA is well established [5, 22, 28, 34, 46] (Fig. 1).

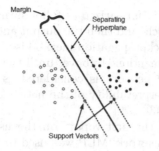

Fig. 1. SVM: distance to the hyperplane for two sets of training data

5.4 Multilayer Perceptron

The simplest type of neural network is called a perceptron, which is a linear binary classifier. It is a learning algorithm based on the idea of mimicking the action of neurons in the human brain, in the way they process a signal. A perceptron classifier only works for data that are linearly separable, i.e., if there is a hyperplane separating all positive points from all negative points [42].

To improve the classification for non-linear problems, more layers of perceptrons can be added to obtain a multilayer perceptron (MLP). MLP is a feed-forward neural network that maps sets of inputs to sets of corresponding outputs. It consists of multiple layers of nodes in a directed graph, where each layer is fully connected to the next layer. MLP typically consists of at least three layers: an input layer, an output layer and hidden layer(s). The input layer receives the input vector, then the hidden layer(s) processes the data, which is later passed to the output layer. The nodes of different layers are interconnected, and each layer contains an activation function. Each input to a node is multiplied by its weight and processed by the function to determine whether the node should be activated, depending on some threshold values (hence the name *activation function*). A simple example of a basic MLP is shown in Fig. 2. Note that if there is more than one hidden layer, then it can be considered as a deep learning architecture.

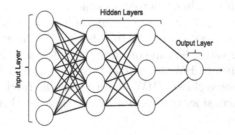

Fig. 2. Multilayer perceptron

The main concept can be summarized as follows: the input vector of training data is sent forward in a batch, and then the output and the corresponding error are computed. Then, the backpropagation method is used to reduce the error by readjusting the weights as mentioned above, until the training data is learned. Often the resulting trained network is considered as black box, and there is ongoing research on the interpretability of the network to fully understand and optimize the performance [43].

In the context of SCA, the first report on the use of MLP was given by Martinasek *et al.* [41]. In this work, MLP was used to perform classification for an AES key. During the training phase, the profile was built based on different candidate keys. Only a crisp classification was performed, which returned the predicted output class, and the model was evaluated using the accuracy metric. In later work, the MLP output was instead adapted as a probability (i.e., softmax output), which is more suitable for use with guessing entropy (see Sect. 7), a type of attack success metric, in the context of SCA evaluation.

MLP has recently gained traction after it was shown that it can be used to help break mask-protected implementations [36]. In this work, the authors argued that some of the built-in functions of MLP implicitly perform these combinations of feature data samples automatically, which behaves similarly to a higher-order SCA.

5.5 Hierarchical Classification

In an ordinary classification problem, each trace is associated with a flat label, i.e., each label stands by itself. However, for some problems this may not be appropriate due to the hierarchical nature of the data. For example, when classifying animals, dogs and cats are both considered mammals, while lizards are considered reptiles. In this case, if the classifier is to predict the class of each animal, the number of classes increases significantly.

In hierarchical classification, instead of working directly with the flat labels, some labels are grouped under a parent node based on similarity, forming parent-child clusters. In this case, the data can be first divided into M nodes (representing intermediate classes), and then into the leaves (the final classes). In some scenarios, it may be useful to include multiple layers of nodes, resulting in a higher hierarchy depth to achieve better accuracy.

In the context of SCA, the first successful application of hierarchical classification was reported by Picek *et al.* [51]. In this work, if the attacker is targeting the 8-bit intermediate value, he can consider the following case: first classifying into 9 classes accordance to HW and then classifying into all values for the corresponding HW. For some classes (HW 0 and 8), the hierarchical approach does not make any difference, since one cannot divide them further.

5.6 Template Attack vs Traditional Machine Learning

Template Attack (TA) [15] is considered the strongest SCA from an information-theoretic point of view. From ML perspective, the common Gaussian formulation is a supervised learning approach called Quadratic Discriminant Analysis [13]. TA is used as a profiling SCA method. Namely, the attacker is assumed to have full control over a profiling (clone) device that highly similar or identical to the target device. The attacker has full ability to collect as many traces as possible with different parameters to characterize and model the profiling device. The resulting model is then used to attack the target device. During the profiling phase, the attacker can build different profiles for different classes $M \in \{M_1, ..., M_{N_c}\}$, where each class corresponds to different intermediate values. For example, in AES, the number of profiles for an S-box output is equal to $2^8 \times 2^8$ for all possible 8-bit key candidates and 8-bit plaintext values. If a leakage model is introduced in later work, it could reduce the number of classes used to build the profile. For example, the classes HW or HD of the S-box output are commonly used, so the number of classes could be reduced to 9 classes (0 to 8). During the template matching phase, the attacker compares the traces from its model with real traces obtained from the attacked device for each corresponding bit. The traces with the highest correlation correspond to the correctly guessed bit value.

One of the main assumptions is that the side-channel leakages are drawn from a multivariate Gaussian distribution. Given the profiling measurements $\mathbf{T} = \{\vec{T_i} | 1 \leq i \leq N\}$ from clone device, where $\vec{T_i}$ defines each trace, the attacker groups the traces according to their classes to obtain the sets $\{\mathbf{T}_{M_1}, ..., \mathbf{T}_{M_{N_c}}\}$. Each $\mathbf{T}_{M_i} = \{\vec{T_{M_{i_1}}}, ..., \vec{T_{M_{i_{n_i}}}}\}$ contains all the traces corresponding to class M_i. For each class M_i, the attacker calculates the mean and covariance matrix:

$$\mu_{M_i} = \frac{1}{n_i} \sum_{j=1}^{n_i} T_{M_{i_j}} \tag{1}$$

$$\Sigma_{M_i} = \frac{1}{n_i - 1} \sum_{j=1}^{n_i} (T_{M_{i_j}} - \mu_{M_i})(T_{M_{i_j}} - \mu_{M_i})^T \tag{2}$$

The pair $(\mu_{M_i}, \Sigma_{M_i})$ is referred to as *template* for a class M_i. Hence, in total, N_c templates are required for N_c distinct classes.

During the attack phase, after measuring a new set of N_A traces $\mathbf{I} = \{\vec{I_i} | 1 \leq i \leq N_A\}$ from the target device, the attacker uses the maximum likelihood (or log-likelihood) as classifier.

$$k = argmax_{k^*} \log p(k^* | \mathbf{I})$$
$$= argmax_{k^*} \sum_{i=1}^{N_A} \log \frac{p(I_i | \mu_{M(k^*)}, \Sigma_{M(k^*)}) p(k^*)}{p(I_i)}. \tag{3}$$

Here, log-likelihood is often used to avoid numerical problem when taking exponentiation. Due to the monotonicity of the logarithm function, the key with the highest $p(k^*|\mathbf{I})$ will also have the highest $\log(p(k^*|\mathbf{I}))$. Then, some constant terms in the log-likelihood that are not key-dependent can be removed.

$$k = argmax_{k^*} \sum_{i=1}^{N_A} -\frac{1}{2} \left(\log \left((2\pi)^{N_P} |\Sigma_{M(k^*)}| \right) + \left(z_i^T \Sigma_{M(k^*)}^{-1} z_i \right) \right), \tag{4}$$

where $z_i = (\vec{I_i} - \mu_{M(k^*)})$. Here, $(\mu_{M(k^*)}, \Sigma_{M(k^*)})$ refers to the template for class $M(k^*)$, based on the intermediate value obtained from the key hypothesis k^*.

The advantage of TA is that the attack is easy to perform, since it is a simple calculation of the means and variances of the traces for different classes. In this case, the attacker can rank the candidate keys based on their likelihood instead of performing a direct classification. So, if the most likely key is incorrect, the attacker can search for the next most likely key and so on.

In [34], the authors conducted a study to compare the performance of TA versus ML techniques. TA was compared to the two most commonly used ML-based methods, SVM and RF. Several scenarios were considered. The first scenario was the one where the leakage samples contain non-informative (useless) points in the perfect profiling model (where the attacker model and the target chip are identical). In this case, if the useless leakage points are independent of the useful ones, a ML-based attack cannot be more efficient than TA, if the profiling performed is sufficient. In the next scenario, assuming imperfect profiling, the number of useless points is varied to compare TA and ML-based methods. The results showed that when the number of points can be kept reasonably small, TA outperforms ML-based methods. However, once the size becomes very large or the profiling set is limited, the ML-based methods begin to outperform the TA-based methods. It has also been shown that RF can perform well due to its built-in randomization-based feature selection.

For effective implementation, one of the proposed approaches is pooled TA [17], where only one pooled covariance matrix is used. The performance of pooled TA was also compared with various ML-based attacks. For example, in [48], it was shown that using Naïve Bayes as a wrapper for feature selection achieves better performance than pooled TA. In [47], the performance of TA and pooled TA was compared with different Bayes classifiers. The work showed that the Bayes classifier alternatives are better than even pooled TA, when the number of profiling traces is limited and therefore no correct estimation of the covariance matrix can be performed. Another variant of TA is Online Template Attacks (OTA) [6], which is typically used for attacks on public-key cryptosystems. With OTA, the attacker can only obtain a single target trace, which executes the targeted secret from the target device. The template is then generated by the target device or a clone device with limited attacker control. The target trace is then compared to the template to find a pattern of specific operations.

6   Other Learning Methods for SCA

Besides supervised learning, other learning paradigms have also been applied to SCA, such as unsupervised learning and semi-supervised learning. The difference is illustrated in Fig. 3.

6.1   Unsupervised Learning

In unsupervised learning, the goal is to determine the hidden structure or pattern in the data without using class labels. One of the major challenges in

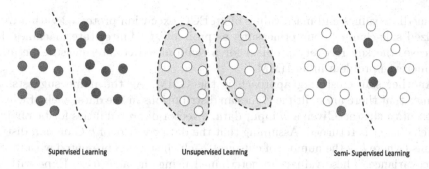

Supervised Learning   Unsupervised Learning   Semi- Supervised Learning

Fig. 3. Illustration of different learning paradigms

unsupervised learning is that it is more difficult to evaluate the performance of the learned model since the labels are not available.

Cluster analysis attempts to find a structure or pattern in the unlabeled data. Given a set of unlabeled data, the learning algorithms return different clusters of data based on a "similarity" or "closeness" metric. As a result, the data within one cluster can be considered "similar" and "dissimilar" to the data in the other clusters. This is typically referred to as hard clustering. In soft or fuzzy clustering, the data is not assigned to a label or cluster, but to a degree of membership or probability of belonging to a cluster (a value between 0 and 1).

An example of a basic unsupervised ML algorithm is the k-means clustering algorithm. It starts with k random clusters, and in each learning iteration, the data is then assigned to a cluster with the closest mean value. Once the cluster assignment converges, the algorithm terminates. Each data sample is assigned a label based on the final cluster assignment. In the field of SCA, some work has been reported using the k-means algorithm, mostly for public-key cryptography attacks. Some examples of single-trace clustering-based attacks on FPGA implementations have been reported by Heyszl et al. [21], Perin et al. [45], and Specht et al. [57]. Some attacks have also been reported on embedded devices, e.g., Järvinen and Balasch [23] on an 8-bit AVR, and Nascimento and Chmielewski [44] on a 32-bit ARM Cortex-M4F processor.

Another example of clustering method is SOM, which is a kind of neural network. In SOM, each data sample is mapped to a neuron and the network is organized so that similar data samples are clustered together (mapped to neighboring neurons). In the context of SCA, so far only Lerman et al. [28] used SOM, for a single-byte profiling-based attack, where it has been compared to other approaches.

HMM is one of the methods that has been used fairly early in the SCA literature [24]. HMM attempts to model finite-state stochastic (Markov) processes. In this case, there are some states that are not observable, instead the outputs of the states that are affected by these "hidden" states are observable. Thus, the goal of the HMM is to infer the hidden states based only on the output observations. Using the HMM approach, Karlof and Wagner [24] modeled the intermediate values and mask values of an ECC execution protected with a randomized side-channel countermeasure, as probabilistic finite state machines. In this case, the key recovery problem for a randomized countermeasure became the inference problem in an HMM.

Another soft clustering approach is the GMM. As the name suggests, it assumes that there are multiple Gaussian distributions in the data, each of which represents a cluster. Given any input data, a vector of probabilities for belonging to each cluster is returned. Assuming that the data consists of k Gaussian distributions (where k is the number of clusters), each cluster is represented with mean and covariance. These values are determined using the algorithm Expectation-Maximization (EM). In [27], GMM was used for a higher-order attack against a masking countermeasure. It was shown that if the attacker does not have access to the mask during profiling, GMM can be applied with EM algorithm to estimate the cluster distribution parameter. For second-order attack, the performance is shown to be comparable to profiling TA and better than second-order DPA.

6.2   Semi-supervised Learning

Semi-supervised learning represents the middle ground between supervised and unsupervised learning. Here, most of the available data are unlabeled, but there is a small subset of data that is labeled. This may be due to the limitation of resources in labeling the data, such as the lack of a human expert. Therefore, the learning algorithm can use these data to guide the prediction of the unlabeled data.

Unlike supervised learning in SCA, which assumes the strongest attacker model (where the attacker has full control over the target device), semi-supervised learning assumes a more realistic attacker scenario. The first reported attack using semi-supervised learning was reported by Lerman *et al.* [32]. They used the Partitioning Around Medoids (PAM) or k-medoid algorithm to cluster the traces from a similar device. The known fixed key of this device was used to determine the correct features (time points), as well as to help label the traces. During the attack phase, the attacker used the trained clusters to determine the class (or label) of the traces. The authors compared the semi-supervised attack to the supervised attack and showed that the latter was better, but the preliminary results with semi-supervised learning were promising.

Another study used collaborative learning, more specifically tri-training as a semi-supervised learning [35] method and applied it to the DPAv4 dataset. The authors have shown that even a small number of labeled traces is sufficient to achieve high accuracy, but that the results can be unstable. Moreover, the method has not been tested on an actual secret key discovery task, but rather evaluated only with respect to classification accuracy.

In [50], Picek *et al.* conducted a more thorough investigation on semi-supervised learning. In this case, two approaches were used: self-training and graph-based learning. In self-training or self-learning, any classification method can be used and the classifier is trained with the labeled data in the first iteration. After training, the classifier is tested on unlabeled data. Once the output probabilities are known, only the data with the highest output probabilities that exceed a pre-selected threshold are selected and added to the set of labeled data. This process is then repeated several times. In graph-based learning, each data sample is represented as a node. The nodes contain the set of labeled and unlabeled data and the edges represent the similarity between neighboring nodes. In this work, the label spreading algorithm was used, where the labels of a node spread to neighboring nodes. Therefore, nodes that are closer to each other are more likely to have the same label. The results of this work showed that the semi-supervised method, especially the self-learning method, can provide some improvements. This was established by comparing the results of semi-supervised and supervised-based attacks on the same labeled datasets.

7 Evaluation of ML Models in SCA

Machine learning classifiers use various evaluation measures that allow to assess the quality of the built models and to compare the models resulting from different hyperparameters or from different classifiers. Common examples of such measures are: accuracy (total classification accuracy), precision, recall, F1-score, area under the ROC curve (AUC), G-mean, κ, and others. The definitions of these measures for binary and multi-class classification can be found in the literature [49,63]. All these measures are based on the data confusion matrix, which relates the actual class of instances to the predicted class, where the results can be true positive (TP), false positive (FP), true negative (TN), and false negative (FN). In unsupervised learning, such as non-profiled SCA, the silhouette index can be used for result evaluation [57], while in semi-supervised learning, the classification metrics mentioned above are usually used.

SCA can use ML classifiers in the profiling phase to obtain classification models, including the output probabilities of the models that assign a prediction percentage to each instance for belonging to individual classes. However, the comparison of attack success should not be based on the aforementioned evaluation measures, but on SCA-specific measures, such as success rate and guessing entropy [59]. Indeed, a paper by Picek et al. [49] discusses the relation between the evaluation metrics of the ML model and SCA-specific measures and concludes that ML metrics should not be used to assess a priori whether SCA attacks will be successful. They show that there is at least no evidence that higher accuracy in the profiling phase leads to lower guessing entropy (i.e., a more successful attack). The problem with using SCA-specific measures instead of ML metrics for ML classifier evaluation is that the former are computationally intensive. An ML-based metric called data confusion factor was proposed by Picek et al. [52], which takes into account both the number of classes and the distance of a hit from the true positive for HW model. While initial results suggest a potentially successful application to a limited number of datasets, no comprehensive study has currently been conducted to determine whether this measure could be used for ML model comparison for SCAs prior to the use of SCA-specific measures.

A problem with some of the ML methods is the lack of robustness (or high variance) of the models, i.e., a small variation in the input dataset can lead to significant variations in the class predictions. This problem is particularly pronounced for SCA datasets, as they typically have high levels of noise. Therefore, to increase the robustness of ML models, only classification methods that do not suffer from high variance should be used, such as ensemble models (e.g., RF [34]). High robustness of models increases their value, especially in the case where the changes in the data distribution are made with the aim of confounding the models, which is the case for countermeasures. Note that high robustness can also be achieved by collecting larger datasets over time, which would account for various changes in the distribution in the target device.

As for the interpretability of models, there is very little work that considers interpretable models for SCA. Although decision trees and induction rules can be used to obtain comprehensive models, leakage measurements are usually voltages measured in time, which are strictly numerical features. Therefore, the use of explainable models is questionable, since usually the only goal in SCA is to find the secret key. When SCA involves the use of other, non-power related features (e.g., time-series driven cache attacks on AES [60]), the use of interpretable models to validate the features may be justified. Moreover, an elaborate ML-based feature selection can be used to analyze the importance of points of interest to obtain additional information about leakage. However, successful feature selection has been shown to be significantly hampered in datasets with countermeasures [46].

8   Conclusion

We have shown that significant efforts have been made to apply various traditional ML algorithms in SCA to increase the effectiveness of the attacks. The current research focuses on evaluating a range of scenarios (e.g., different cryptographic algorithm implementations, different countermeasures, different dataset noise levels, different dataset dimensions) in which SCA could be improved by the proper application of ML methods. Both different methods of data preprocessing and data modeling are carefully studied in order to achieve better results. Further work in this area should elucidate some application details to establish specific ML methods and their combinations as solid alternatives for traditional SCA methods such as TA. Since ML is inherently data and algorithm dependent and there is no silver bullet, determining the best practice under different scenarios is expected to be the likely outcome of future research.

References

1. Alpaydin, E.: Chapter 13, Kernel machines. In: Introduction to Machine Learning, 2nd edn. The MIT Press (2010)

2. Archambeau, C., Peeters, E., Standaert, F.-X., Quisquater, J.-J.: Template attacks in principal subspaces. In: Goubin, L., Matsui, M. (eds.) CHES 2006. LNCS, vol. 4249, pp. 1–14. Springer, Heidelberg (2006). https://doi.org/10.1007/11894063_1
3. Asonov, D., Agrawal, R.: Keyboard acoustic emanations. In: 2004 IEEE Symposium on Security and Privacy (S&P 2004), 9–12 May 2004, Berkeley, CA, USA, pp. 3–11. IEEE Computer Society (2004). https://doi.org/10.1109/SECPRI.2004.1301311
4. Backes, M., Dürmuth, M., Gerling, S., Pinkal, M., Sporleder, C.: Acoustic side-channel attacks on printers. In: Proceedings of 19th USENIX Security Symposium, Washington, DC, USA, 11–13 August 2010, pp. 307–322. USENIX Association (2010). http://www.usenix.org/events/sec10/tech/full_papers/Backes.pdf
5. Bartkewitz, T., Lemke-Rust, K.: Efficient template attacks based on probabilistic multi-class support vector machines. In: Mangard, S. (ed.) CARDIS 2012. LNCS, vol. 7771, pp. 263–276. Springer, Heidelberg (2013). https://doi.org/10.1007/978-3-642-37288-9_18
6. Batina, L., Chmielewski, Ł, Papachristodoulou, L., Schwabe, P., Tunstall, M.: Online template attacks. In: Meier, W., Mukhopadhyay, D. (eds.) INDOCRYPT 2014. LNCS, vol. 8885, pp. 21–36. Springer, Cham (2014). https://doi.org/10.1007/978-3-319-13039-2_2
7. Batina, L., Gierlichs, B., Lemke-Rust, K.: Differential cluster analysis. In: Clavier, C., Gaj, K. (eds.) CHES 2009. LNCS, vol. 5747, pp. 112–127. Springer, Heidelberg (2009). https://doi.org/10.1007/978-3-642-04138-9_9
8. Bhasin, S., Danger, J., Guilley, S., Najm, Z.: NICV: normalized inter-class variance for detection of side-channel leakage. In: 2014 International Symposium on Electromagnetic Compatibility, Tokyo, pp. 310–313 (2014)
9. Bramer, M.: Introduction to classification: naïve bayes and nearest neighbour. In: Bramer, M. (ed.) Principles of Data Mining. Undergraduate Topics in Computer Science, pp. 21–37. Springer, London (2013). https://doi.org/10.1007/978-1-4471-4884-5_3
10. Breiman, L.: Random forests. Mach. Learn. 45(1), 5–32 (2001). https://doi.org/10.1023/A:1010933404324
11. Bruneau, N., Danger, J.-L., Guilley, S., Heuser, A., Teglia, Y.: Boosting higher-order correlation attacks by dimensionality reduction. In: Chakraborty, R.S., Matyas, V., Schaumont, P. (eds.) SPACE 2014. LNCS, vol. 8804, pp. 183–200. Springer, Cham (2014). https://doi.org/10.1007/978-3-319-12060-7_13
12. Bucci, M., Guglielmo, M., Luzzi, R., Trifiletti, A.: A power consumption randomization countermeasure for DPA-resistant cryptographic processors. In: Macii, E., Paliouras, V., Koufopavlou, O. (eds.) PATMOS 2004. LNCS, vol. 3254, pp. 481–490. Springer, Heidelberg (2004). https://doi.org/10.1007/978-3-540-30205-6_50
13. Cagli, E.: Feature extraction for side-channel attacks. Ph.D. thesis, Sorbonne Université, December 2018
14. Cagli, E., Dumas, C., Prouff, E.: Enhancing dimensionality reduction methods for side-channel attacks. In: Homma, N., Medwed, M. (eds.) CARDIS 2015. LNCS, vol. 9514, pp. 15–33. Springer, Cham (2016). https://doi.org/10.1007/978-3-319-31271-2_2
15. Chari, S., Rao, J.R., Rohatgi, P.: Template attacks. In: Kaliski, B.S., Koç, K., Paar, C. (eds.) CHES 2002. LNCS, vol. 2523, pp. 13–28. Springer, Heidelberg (2003). https://doi.org/10.1007/3-540-36400-5_3
16. Chawla, N.V., Bowyer, K.W., Hall, L.O., Kegelmeyer, W.P.: SMOTE: synthetic minority over-sampling technique. J. Artif. Int. Res. 16(1), 321–357 (2002)

17. Choudary, O., Kuhn, M.G.: Efficient template attacks. In: Francillon, A., Rohatgi, P. (eds.) CARDIS 2013. LNCS, vol. 8419, pp. 253–270. Springer, Cham (2014). https://doi.org/10.1007/978-3-319-08302-5_17

18. Gandolfi, K., Mourtel, C., Olivier, F.: Electromagnetic analysis: concrete results. In: Koç, Ç.K., Naccache, D., Paar, C. (eds.) CHES 2001. LNCS, vol. 2162, pp. 251–261. Springer, Heidelberg (2001). https://doi.org/10.1007/3-540-44709-1_21

19. Gierlichs, B., Lemke-Rust, K., Paar, C.: Templates vs. stochastic methods. In: Goubin, L., Matsui, M. (eds.) CHES 2006. LNCS, vol. 4249, pp. 15–29. Springer, Heidelberg (2006). https://doi.org/10.1007/11894063_2

20. Heuser, A., Zohner, M.: Intelligent machine homicide - breaking cryptographic devices using support vector machines. In: Schindler, W., Huss, S.A. (eds.) COSADE 2012. LNCS, vol. 7275, pp. 249–264. Springer, Heidelberg (2012). https://doi.org/10.1007/978-3-642-29912-4_18

21. Heyszl, J., Ibing, A., Mangard, S., De Santis, F., Sigl, G.: Clustering algorithms for non-profiled single-execution attacks on exponentiations. In: Francillon, A., Rohatgi, P. (eds.) CARDIS 2013. LNCS, vol. 8419, pp. 79–93. Springer, Cham (2014). https://doi.org/10.1007/978-3-319-08302-5_6

22. Hospodar, G., de Mulder, E., Gierlichs, B., Verbauwhede, I., Vandewalle, J.: Least squares support vector machines for side-channel analysis. In: Second International Workshop on Constructive SideChannel Analysis and Secure Design, pp. 99–104. Center for Advanced Security Research Darmstadt (2011)

23. Järvinen, K., Balasch, J.: Single-trace side-channel attacks on scalar multiplications with precomputations. In: Lemke-Rust, K., Tunstall, M. (eds.) CARDIS 2016. LNCS, vol. 10146, pp. 137–155. Springer, Cham (2017). https://doi.org/10.1007/978-3-319-54669-8_9

24. Karlof, C., Wagner, D.: Hidden Markov model cryptanalysis. In: Walter, C.D., Koç, Ç.K., Paar, C. (eds.) CHES 2003. LNCS, vol. 2779, pp. 17–34. Springer, Heidelberg (2003). https://doi.org/10.1007/978-3-540-45238-6_3

25. Kocher, P., Jaffe, J., Jun, B.: Differential power analysis. In: Wiener, M. (ed.) CRYPTO 1999. LNCS, vol. 1666, pp. 388–397. Springer, Heidelberg (1999). https://doi.org/10.1007/3-540-48405-1_25

26. Kocher, P.C.: Timing attacks on implementations of Diffie-Hellman, RSA, DSS, and other systems. In: Koblitz, N. (ed.) CRYPTO 1996. LNCS, vol. 1109, pp. 104–113. Springer, Heidelberg (1996). https://doi.org/10.1007/3-540-68697-5_9

27. Lemke-Rust, K., Paar, C.: Gaussian mixture models for higher-order side channel analysis. In: Paillier, P., Verbauwhede, I. (eds.) CHES 2007. LNCS, vol. 4727, pp. 14–27. Springer, Heidelberg (2007). https://doi.org/10.1007/978-3-540-74735-2_2

28. Lerman, L., Bontempi, G., Markowitch, O.: Side channel attack: an approach based on machine learning. In: Second International Workshop on Constructive SideChannel Analysis and Secure Design, pp. 29–41. Center for Advanced Security Research Darmstadt (2011)

29. Lerman, L., Bontempi, G., Markowitch, O.: Power analysis attack: an approach based on machine learning. Int. J. Appl. Cryptol. 3(2), 97–115 (2014). https://doi.org/10.1504/IJACT.2014.062722

30. Lerman, L., Bontempi, G., Ben Taieb, S., Markowitch, O.: A time series approach for profiling attack. In: Gierlichs, B., Guilley, S., Mukhopadhyay, D. (eds.) SPACE 2013. LNCS, vol. 8204, pp. 75–94. Springer, Heidelberg (2013). https://doi.org/10.1007/978-3-642-41224-0_7

31. Lerman, L., Medeiros, S.F., Bontempi, G., Markowitch, O.: A machine learning approach against a masked AES. In: Francillon, A., Rohatgi, P. (eds.) CARDIS 2013. LNCS, vol. 8419, pp. 61–75. Springer, Cham (2014). https://doi.org/10.1007/978-3-319-08302-5_5

32. Lerman, L., Medeiros, S.F., Veshchikov, N., Meuter, C., Bontempi, G., Markowitch, O.: Semi-supervised template attack. In: Prouff, E. (ed.) COSADE 2013. LNCS, vol. 7864, pp. 184–199. Springer, Heidelberg (2013). https://doi.org/10.1007/978-3-642-40026-1_12

33. Lerman, L., Poussier, R., Bontempi, G., Markowitch, O., Standaert, F.-X.: Template attacks vs. machine learning revisited (and the curse of dimensionality in side-channel analysis). In: Mangard, S., Poschmann, A.Y. (eds.) COSADE 2014. LNCS, vol. 9064, pp. 20–33. Springer, Cham (2015). https://doi.org/10.1007/978-3-319-21476-4_2

34. Lerman, L., Poussier, R., Markowitch, O., Standaert, F.: Template attacks versus machine learning revisited and the curse of dimensionality in side-channel analysis: extended version. J. Cryptogr. Eng. **8**(4), 301–313 (2018). https://doi.org/10.1007/s13389-017-0162-9

35. Liu, B., Ding, Z., Pan, Y., Li, J., Feng, H.: Side-channel attacks based on collaborative learning. In: Zou, B., Li, M., Wang, H., Song, X., Xie, W., Lu, Z. (eds.) ICPCSEE 2017. CCIS, vol. 727, pp. 549–557. Springer, Singapore (2017). https://doi.org/10.1007/978-981-10-6385-5_46

36. Maghrebi, H., Portigliatti, T., Prouff, E.: Breaking cryptographic implementations using deep learning techniques. In: Carlet, C., Hasan, M.A., Saraswat, V. (eds.) SPACE 2016. LNCS, vol. 10076, pp. 3–26. Springer, Cham (2016). https://doi.org/10.1007/978-3-319-49445-6_1

37. Mangard, S., Elisabeth, O., Standaert, F.X.: One for all - all for one: unifying standard differential power analysis attacks. IET Inf. Secur. **5**, 100–110 (2011)

38. Mangard, S., Oswald, E., Popp, T.: Power Analysis Attacks: Revealing the Secrets of Smart Cards. Springer, Heidelberg (2007). https://doi.org/10.1007/978-0-387-38162-6

39. Martinasek, Z., Clupek, V., Krisztina, T.: General scheme of differential power analysis. In: 2013 36th International Conference on Telecommunications and Signal Processing (TSP), pp. 358–362 (2013). https://doi.org/10.1109/TSP.2013.6613952

40. Martinasek, Z., Dzurenda, P., Malina, L.: Profiling power analysis attack based on MLP in DPA contest V4.2. In: 39th International Conference on Telecommunications and Signal Processing, TSP 2016, Vienna, Austria, 27–29 June 2016, pp. 223–226. IEEE (2016). https://doi.org/10.1109/TSP.2016.7760865

41. Martinasek, Z., Hajny, J., Malina, L.: Optimization of power analysis using neural network. In: Francillon, A., Rohatgi, P. (eds.) CARDIS 2013. LNCS, vol. 8419, pp. 94–107. Springer, Cham (2014). https://doi.org/10.1007/978-3-319-08302-5_7

42. Mitchell, T.M.: Machine Learning. McGraw Hill Series in Computer Science. McGraw-Hill (1997)

43. Montavon, G., Samek, W., Müller, K.R.: Methods for interpreting and understanding deep neural networks. Digit. Signal Process. **73**, 1 – 15 (2018). https://doi.org/10.1016/j.dsp.2017.10.011, http://www.sciencedirect.com/science/article/pii/S1051200417302385

44. Nascimento, E., Chmielewski, Ł: Applying horizontal clustering side-channel attacks on embedded ECC implementations. In: Eisenbarth, T., Teglia, Y. (eds.) CARDIS 2017. LNCS, vol. 10728, pp. 213–231. Springer, Cham (2018). https://doi.org/10.1007/978-3-319-75208-2_13

45. Perin, G., Imbert, L., Torres, L., Maurine, P.: Attacking randomized exponentiations using unsupervised learning. In: Prouff, E. (ed.) COSADE 2014. LNCS, vol. 8622, pp. 144–160. Springer, Cham (2014). https://doi.org/10.1007/978-3-319-10175-0_11
46. Picek, S., Heuser, A., Jovic, A., Batina, L.: A systematic evaluation of profiling through focused feature selection. IEEE Trans. Very Large Scale Integrat. (VLSI) Syst. **27**(12), 2802–2815 (2019). https://doi.org/10.1109/TVLSI.2019.2937365
47. Picek, S., Heuser, A., Guilley, S.: Template attack versus bayes classifier. J. Cryptogr. Eng. **7**(4), 343–351 (2017). https://doi.org/10.1007/s13389-017-0172-7
48. Picek, S., Heuser, A., Jovic, A., Batina, L., Legay, A.: The secrets of profiling for side-channel analysis: feature selection matters. IACR Cryptol. ePrint Arch. **2017**, 1110 (2017). http://eprint.iacr.org/2017/1110
49. Picek, S., Heuser, A., Jovic, A., Bhasin, S., Regazzoni, F.: The curse of class imbalance and conflicting metrics with machine learning for side-channel evaluations. IACR Trans. Cryptogr. Hardw. Embed. Syst. **2019**(1), 209–237 (2018). https://doi.org/10.13154/tches.v2019.i1.209-237, https://tches.iacr.org/index.php/TCHES/article/view/7339
50. Picek, S., Heuser, A., Jovic, A., Knezevic, K., Richmond, T.: Improving side-channel analysis through semi-supervised learning. In: Bilgin, B., Fischer, J.-B. (eds.) CARDIS 2018. LNCS, vol. 11389, pp. 35–50. Springer, Cham (2019). https://doi.org/10.1007/978-3-030-15462-2_3
51. Picek, S., Heuser, A., Jovic, A., Legay, A.: Climbing down the hierarchy: hierarchical classification for machine learning side-channel attacks. In: Joye, M., Nitaj, A. (eds.) AFRICACRYPT 2017. LNCS, vol. 10239, pp. 61–78. Springer, Cham (2017). https://doi.org/10.1007/978-3-319-57339-7_4
52. Picek, S., et al.: Side-channel analysis and machine learning: a practical perspective. In: 2017 International Joint Conference on Neural Networks, IJCNN 2017, Anchorage, AK, USA, pp. 4095–4102 (2017). https://doi.org/10.1109/IJCNN.2017.7966373
53. Quisquater, J.-J., Samyde, D.: ElectroMagnetic analysis (EMA): measures and counter-measures for smart cards. In: Attali, I., Jensen, T. (eds.) E-smart 2001. LNCS, vol. 2140, pp. 200–210. Springer, Heidelberg (2001). https://doi.org/10.1007/3-540-45418-7_17, http://dl.acm.org/citation.cfm?id=646803.705980
54. Reparaz, O., Gierlichs, B., Verbauwhede, I.: Selecting time samples for multivariate DPA attacks. In: Prouff, E., Schaumont, P. (eds.) CHES 2012. LNCS, vol. 7428, pp. 155–174. Springer, Heidelberg (2012). https://doi.org/10.1007/978-3-642-33027-8_10
55. Rivest, R., Shamir, A., Adleman, L.M.: Method for obtaining digital signatures and public-key cryptosystems. Commun. ACM **21**(2), 120–126 (1978)
56. Souissi, Y., Nassar, M., Guilley, S., Danger, J.-L., Flament, F.: First principal components analysis: a new side channel distinguisher. In: Rhee, K.-H., Nyang, D.H. (eds.) ICISC 2010. LNCS, vol. 6829, pp. 407–419. Springer, Heidelberg (2011). https://doi.org/10.1007/978-3-642-24209-0_27
57. Specht, R., Heyszl, J., Kleinsteuber, M., Sigl, G.: Improving non-profiled attacks on exponentiations based on clustering and extracting leakage from multi-channel high-resolution EM measurements. In: Mangard, S., Poschmann, A.Y. (eds.) COSADE 2014. LNCS, vol. 9064, pp. 3–19. Springer, Cham (2015). https://doi.org/10.1007/978-3-319-21476-4_1
58. Standaert, F.X.: Introduction to side-channel attacks. In: Verbauwhede, I.M. (ed.) Secure Integrated Circuits and Systems, pp. 27–42. Springer, Boston (2010). https://doi.org/10.1007/978-0-387-71829-3_2

59. Standaert, F.-X., Malkin, T.G., Yung, M.: A unified framework for the analysis of side-channel key recovery attacks. In: Joux, A. (ed.) EUROCRYPT 2009. LNCS, vol. 5479, pp. 443–461. Springer, Heidelberg (2009). https://doi.org/10.1007/978-3-642-01001-9_26
60. Sönmez, B., Sarıkaya, A.A., Bahtiyar, S.: Machine learning based side channel selection for time-driven cache attacks on AES. In: 2019 4th International Conference on Computer Science and Engineering (UBMK), pp. 1–5 (2019). https://doi.org/10.1109/UBMK.2019.8907211
61. Tian, Q., Huss, S.A.: A general approach to power trace alignment for the assessment of side-channel resistance of hardened cryptosystems. In: 2012 Eighth International Conference on Intelligent Information Hiding and Multimedia Signal Processing, pp. 465–470 (2012). https://doi.org/10.1109/IIH-MSP.2012.119
62. Timon, B.: Non-profiled deep learning-based side-channel attacks with sensitivity analysis. IACR Trans. Cryptogr. Hardw. Embedd. Syst. 2019(2), 107–131 (2019). https://doi.org/10.13154/tches.v2019.i2.107-131, https://tches.iacr.org/index.php/TCHES/article/view/7387
63. Witten, I.H., Frank, E., Hall, M.A.: Data Mining: Practical Machine Learning Tools and Techniques. Morgan Kaufmann Series in Data Management Systems, 3 edn. Morgan Kaufmann, Amsterdam (2011). http://www.sciencedirect.com/science/book/9780123748560
64. Yang, W., Cao, Y., Zhou, Y., Zhang, H., Zhang, Q.: Distance based leakage alignment for side channel attacks. IEEE Signal Process. Lett. 23(4), 419–423 (2016). https://doi.org/10.1109/LSP.2016.2521441
65. Zheng, N., Xue, J.: Manifold Learning, pp. 87–119. Springer, London (2009). https://doi.org/10.1007/978-1-84882-312-9_4
66. Zheng, Y., Zhou, Y., Yu, Z., Hu, C., Zhang, H.: How to compare selections of points of interest for side-channel distinguishers in practice? In: Hui, L.C.K., Qing, S.H., Shi, E., Yiu, S.M. (eds.) ICICS 2014. LNCS, vol. 8958, pp. 200–214. Springer, Cham (2015). https://doi.org/10.1007/978-3-319-21966-0_15
67. Zhou, Y., Feng, D.: Side-channel attacks: ten years after its publication and the impacts on cryptographic module security testing. IACR Cryptol. ePrint Arch. 2005, 388 (2005). https://dblp.org/rec/journals/iacr/ZhouF05
68. Zhuang, L., Zhou, F., Tygar, J.D.: Keyboard acoustic emanations revisited. ACM Trans. Inf. Syst. Secur. 13(1), 3:1–3:26 (2009). https://doi.org/10.1145/1609956.1609959
69. Özgen, E., Papachristodoulou, L., Batina, L.: Template attacks using classification algorithms. In: 2016 IEEE International Symposium on Hardware Oriented Security and Trust (HOST), pp. 242–247 (2016). https://doi.org/10.1109/HST.2016.7495589

Deep Learning on Side-Channel Analysis

Marina Krček[1], Huimin Li[1], Servio Paguada[2,4], Unai Rioja[2,4], Lichao Wu[1], Guilherme Perin[1], and Łukasz Chmielewski[2,3(✉)]

[1] Delft University of Technology, Delft, The Netherlands
[2] Digital Security Group, Radboud University, Nijmegen, The Netherlands
L.Chmielewski@cs.ru.nl
[3] Riscure, Delft, The Netherlands
[4] Ikerlan Technological Research Centre, Arrasate, Spain

Abstract. This chapter provides an overview of recent applications of deep learning to profiled side-channel analysis (SCA). The advent of deep neural networks (mainly *multiple layer perceptrons* and *convolutional neural networks*) as a learning algorithm for profiled SCA opened several new directions and possibilities to explore the occurrence of side-channel leakages from different categories of systems. This is particularly important for designers to verify to what extent an adversary can extract sensitive information when possessing state-of-the-art attack methods. Deep learning is a fast-evolving technology that provides several advantages in profiled SCA and we summarize what are the main directions and results obtained by the research community.

1 Introduction

Side-channel attacks (SCA) are a well-known and powerful class of implementation attacks against different types of systems, such as cryptographic implementations, processors, communication systems, and, more recently, machine learning models. What makes these attacks powerful is the fact that they use unintended leakage of information conveyed from different sources: power consumption, electromagnetic emanations, time, temperature, acoustic, photonic emission, etc. An adversary uses specialized equipment to monitor some of those side-channel leakages to extract secret information. For example, the amount of time needed to process a specific secret byte in a computer might be different from the amount of time needed to process other possible values for this byte. The monitoring of a side-channel can lead an adversary to recover secret information from time measurements.

In this chapter, we focus on the predominantly used form of side-channel attacks that are based on power consumption and electromagnetic analysis to extract secret cryptographic keys. Embedded devices make use of cryptographic primitives to protect the processing and storing of sensitive information. However, the cryptographic algorithmic implementations (e.g., AES, 3DES, RSA, etc.) in software and hardware also need protection on their private keys. Side-channel attacks can extract those keys from unintended leakage of information if

© Springer Nature Switzerland AG 2022
L. Batina et al. (Eds.): Security and Artificial Intelligence, LNCS 13049, pp. 48–71, 2022.
https://doi.org/10.1007/978-3-030-98795-4_3

the device is not properly protected. Differential power analysis (DPA [22]) and correlation power analysis (CPA [6]) appeared in 1999 and 2004, respectively, as powerful statistical methods to recover private keys. These attacks, classified as non-profiled attacks, assume that an adversary can query multiple encryption (resp. decryption) executions from a target crypto operation by controlling, at least, the plaintext (resp. ciphertext). All the executions represent a set of side-channel measurements. Usually, an adversary split the target key in chunks (divide-and-conquer strategy) and for each possible value of a key chunk, he or she creates a list of predicted labels based on the crypto algorithm (e.g., when attacking an AES implementation, an adversary predicts what are the values of S-box output in the first round based on possible byte key guesses). As a final act, the adversary performs a differential or correlation analysis between side-channel measurements and all possible sets of predicted labels. The key guess associated with the highest difference-of-means or correlation value is assumed as the correct key chunk value.

In 2002, Chari et al. [10] proposed a different category of SCA known as Template or Profiled Attacks. Profiled SCA is a specific class of side-channel analysis that is conducted in two phases: profiling and attack phase. To profile a crypto implementation, the adversary collects a set of side-channel measurements where the key of the target cryptographic execution is known and may vary from measurement to measurement. Thus, the adversary creates statistical models (commonly called templates) that can describe the leakage and noise of the device under control. In a second phase, a separate set of side-channel measurements is collected from another and (usually) identical device running an unknown key. The attack (also known as the matching phase) applies the learned templates to this second device, which can indicate what are the most likely key values ordered according to their probabilities.

After the aforementioned publications, several countermeasures to protect crypto implementations were proposed and applied by the security industry. Randomization of sensitive information, boolean masking schemes, noise addition are among the most common forms of protection against side-channel attacks. However, the research on SCA is constantly discovering new capabilities of side-channel attacks when adopting more advanced statistical techniques. The main goal is to investigate how far an adversary can go when using the most advanced and realistic attack techniques. Results in this sense are important for developers to know what kind of protections their crypto designs need depending on their applications and risk. Recently, publications considering deep neural network approaches demonstrated the ability to break protected crypto implementations [7,19,56]. This is the main reason why deep learning is the predominant form of profiled side-channel attacks nowadays. Indeed, deep neural networks perform extremely well on a wide variety of learning tasks. Observe that in the profiled SCA setting, the profiling and attack phases are similar to learning and prediction steps of a deep neural network-based supervised classification task. The deep learning field is continuously evolving and impacting side-channel attacks in general even beyond profiled SCA. In this chapter, we summarize results from recent publications where non-profiled SCA attacks also leverage from powerful deep neural networks.

This chapter's focus is on deep learning-based SCA. We start by providing background knowledge on deep neural networks and profiled SCA. Section 3 provides an overview of the state-of-the-art in the application of deep neural networks to profiled SCA. In Sect. 4, we analyze the advantages of using deep learning in the context of profiled side-channel analysis. The main idea of Sect. 4 is to highlight why deep neural networks can be seen as powerful alternatives to classical profiled attacks such as template attacks and traditional machine learning, which have been considered as the most powerful class of SCA for many years. Section 5 brings an important discussion about the correct interpretation of metrics for deep learning-based profiled side-channel analysis. As reported in recent publications, the usage of well-known supervised classification metrics (e.g., accuracy, loss, recall, etc.) can be meaningless in the context of SCA when evaluating protected targets. In Sect. 5, we describe solutions for such an important problem.

Another important aspect of training deep neural networks is the hyper-parameters tuning. In Sect. 6, we describe this problem in the context of profiled SCA. As we will see, there are still no published efficient solutions for this problem for SCA, and we describe possible alternatives. Section 7 describes different applications of deep learning to SCA. Finally, Sect. 8 concludes the chapter while gives an overview of what we believe to be the most important perspectives and directions for future work.

2   Background

In this section, we explain the notation we use throughout the chapter and deep learning-based profiled SCA.

2.1   Notations

Throughout this chapter, we use $\mathcal{X} = \{X, Y\}$ to denote a dataset composed of feature array X and label vector Y. The feature array $X = \{x_{i,f}\}$ defines a set of N side-channel traces, where i indicates the trace index and f indicates the feature index (a sample) inside a trace. In the label vector $Y = \{y_i\}$, each element y_i indicates the label associated to a side-channel trace i. The terms $\mathcal{X}_{train}$, $\mathcal{X}_{val}$ and $\mathcal{X}_{test}$ denote the training, validation and test sets, respectively. The terms profiling traces and training traces are used interchangeably throughout the chapter.

The term k refers to a single key byte belonging to the full encryption or decryption key $\mathcal{K}$ with dimension $|\mathcal{K}|$. An input plaintext byte used as input to the encryption or decryption operation i (executed in order to obtain a side-channel trace) is referred as pk_i. The plaintext byte pk_i belongs to the full input plaintext PK_i. Let also $f(pk_i, k)$ denote the function that returns the label associated to one execution of a cryptographic operation.

Let also $p_{i,j} = P[y = j | X = x_i]$, where $p_{i,j} \in \mathcal{P}$, denote the probability that a side-channel trace x_i contains the label j. In this chapter, bold letters and bold acronyms, e.g., **a**, denote vectors of dimension 2^b, where b is the bit-length of the target intermediate value in a cryptographic execution.

2.2 Profiled SCA and Deep Learning

Deep learning-based profiled side-channel attack requires a training set of size N for the learning or profiling phase. Ideally, the training set should be composed of side-channel traces where each trace is measured with random input data (ciphertext or plaintext) pk and random key k. To create a labeled dataset for SCA, also referred to as the training set $\mathcal{X}_{train}$, it is important to firstly choose a leakage model that better describes the physical side-channel leakage present in the underlying measurements. Commonly selected leakage models against symmetric crypto implementations (e.g., AES, DES) are Hamming weight (HW), Hamming distance (HD), identity (ID), or bit-level models. In this case, the leakage is modeled for an intermediate value represented by a single byte or a bit. This intermediate value in an encryption or decryption operation depends on a key byte k and input (i.e., plaintext or ciphertext) pk.

The number of possible classes to label a dataset is directly derived from the selected leakage function $f(pk_i, k)$. As an example, the target intermediate value of an AES implementation is usually a byte in the S-box state in the first or last encryption/decryption round. In this case, HW or HD models define 9 classes for the datasets. In case the ID model is used, the dataset is defined for 256 classes. Attacks on a single intermediate bit define only two possible classes. The bit-level leakage model is also a common situation when attacking public-key implementations (e.g., RSA, ECC). In this last case, the attacker has specific knowledge about the target implementation such as scalar multiplication or modular exponentiation method.

For training a deep neural network, the labeled set is split into training, $\mathcal{X}_{train}$, and validation, $\mathcal{X}_{val}$, sets. As we will discuss in Sect. 5, classic validation metrics (e.g., accuracy, loss, recall, precision, etc.) obtained during training may not indicate the leakage detection performance of a neural network, especially for protected targets. Therefore, to have a meaningful validation metric for SCA, the best possible scenario is to compute guessing entropy or success rate during training. For that, it is crucial to have a validation set $\mathcal{X}_{val}$ where the key $\mathcal{K}$ is fixed for the full validation set. If $\mathcal{K}$ is random for each trace in $\mathcal{X}_{val}$, then a different efficient validation metric must be found.

The understanding of deep learning metrics in the context of SCA is an essential background knowledge to train efficient models. Conventional deep learning metrics usually are accuracy and loss (or error). *Accuracy* indicates the ratio between correctly predicted data and the total number of predictions. *Loss* is based on a *loss function* selection (the most common form of loss function for profiled SCA is *cross-entropy*) and it indicates the overall error for the evaluated set. These metrics are monitored during the training phase and can indicate different phases that can occur while the parameters (weights and biases) are being updated by stochastic (or adaptive) gradient descent methods.

Common metrics in SCA are success rate and guessing entropy [47]. In profiled SCA, these metrics are not aimed only at predicting correct labels as is the case with machine learning metrics, but also to reveal the secret key. In particular, let us assume that given Q amount of traces in the attacking phase, an attack outputs a key guessing vector $\mathbf{g} = [g_1, g_2, \ldots, g_{|\mathcal{K}|}]$ in decreasing order of probability with $|\mathcal{K}|$ being the size of the keyspace. So, g_1 is the most likely and $g_{|\mathcal{K}|}$ the least likely key candidate. The first-order success rate is defined as the average empirical probability that g_1 is equal to the secret key k^*. The guessing entropy is the average position of k^* in $\mathbf{g}$. When predicting an attack set $\mathcal{X}_{test}$ with a fixed key k^*, we obtain a prediction array $\mathcal{P} = \{p_{i,j}\}$. This array has the number of rows equivalent to Q, and the number of columns is equivalent to the number of possible classes. For all key candidates, we compute the probability that k is the correct key k^* in $\mathcal{X}_{test}$ as follows:

$$P[k = k^*] = \sum_{i=0}^{N-1} log(p_{i,j}) \tag{1}$$

where $p_{i,j}$ is the j-th class probability (or prediction) of the neural network for side-channel trace i. The class index j is determined according to a leakage model function $j = f(pk_i, k)$.

In profiled attacks, the main goal during the training phase is to reach a generalization performance so that the trained deep neural network can obtain a low guessing entropy (resp. a high success rate) after predicting Q attack traces. The generalization phase usually happens after the model starts fitting the side-channel leakages (after *underfitting*) and before this same model starts to degrade its performance, i.e. when it usually reaches an *overfitting* phase. Fitting refers to how well the model approximates the unknown underlying mapping function given the input and output variables. When overfitting occurs, the neural network can fit the training set with very high accuracy and small error, but it cannot fit the validation or test sets. Ideally, we should always train a neural network until it achieves the maximum quality in terms of generalization concerning the validation set. If this happens, we should be able to assess whether the model is in the generalization phase or not. This seems to be an easy task, but there are quite some difficulties in the interpretation of metrics to identify what phase the model belongs to while the training evolves. An interesting observation would be the detection of the boundaries between two of the phases above. These boundaries may be detected with the observation of conventional metrics (loss, accuracy, recall, or precision) using validation data. In Sect. 5 we discuss potential solutions to identify the generalization phase during training in the SCA context.

3 Recent Results in Deep Learning-Based Profiled Side-Channel Attacks

This section provides an overview of recently published results on deep learning-based SCA. Various types of deep neural networks have been used, and we summarize what is state-of-the-art regarding the selection of neural network topologies. The information contained in this section is a summary of recent results that mainly target cryptographic primitives based on AES [12], RSA [41], and ECC [21,31].

3.1 From Machine Learning to Deep Learning in SCA

Machine learning techniques are quite successful in a lot of different fields, such as image classification [23] or speech recognition [15]. Due to the shared similarity between profiling SCA and supervised machine learning, researchers started experimenting with machine learning techniques in profiled SCA. They utilized standard machine learning techniques, such as Support Vector Machines (SVMs) and Random Forests [25], neural networks [28], and, more recently, deep learning [7,26,40,58].

Deep learning is a class of machine learning where the learning algorithm (i.e., a deep neural network) extracts higher-level features from the raw input. Usually, in the case of deep neural networks, it is considered that the neural network has multiple layers. Therefore, multi-layer perceptrons (MLP), with more than one hidden layer, are deep neural networks. Some other examples of deep learning techniques include deep belief networks (DBN), recurrent neural networks (RNN), convolutional neural networks (CNN), and residual neural networks.

The first publication to explore deep learning-based profiling SCA results is from Maghrebi et al. [26]. In this case, the authors applied MLP with one hidden layer (which is not considered a deep neural network), Stacked Auto-Encoder with three hidden-layers, and also introduced the application of CNNs for SCA. The authors also applied a specific RNN architecture called a long short-term memory (LSTM) network with two layers of 26 LSTM units and a Random Forest algorithm. Except for the Random Forest algorithm and the MLP the authors used, other algorithms are considered deep learning techniques. The authors also suggested hyper-parameters tuning for SCA with a genetic algorithm, as stated in the appendix of their paper. Since then, there has been a variety of different architectures with different hyper-parameter settings. We provide an overview of the deep learning techniques that were applied to SCA and discuss state-of-the-art results.

3.2 Deep Learning Techniques in SCA

After the appearance of the first publication with deep learning results for SCA, researchers started to investigate the benefits of well-known learning techniques, such as regularization, visualization, hyper-parameters optimization, and model interpretation, to improve the attack performance.

Regularization techniques are used to avoid overfitting during the training phase. Examples of regularization techniques are data augmentation, noise addition, weight decay, dropout layers [46] and early stopping. In [7], the authors presented the first results with data augmentation techniques for CNNs to bypass desynchronization in side-channel measurements. The adopted techniques are based on random trace shifting and trace warping during the training phase. This way, the trained CNNs can generalize to side-channel measurements where the leaking samples appear in random time locations due to desynchronizations caused by measurement setup or countermeasures. Results achieved for protected AES implementations demonstrate the benefits of these well-known regularization techniques. Kim et al. [19] explored how additional noise can be used as a regularization for preventing overfitting, and they also present their CNN architecture. Here the authors compare the performance of their CNN architecture to the CNN architecture introduced in [40] paper. Also, the authors explore more datasets, and their neural network is larger in the number of layers, indicating the benefits of more convolution layers for leakage detection.

The selection of hyper-parameters for deep neural networks is also explored in some of the publications. In [40], the authors provide several results for different CNN and MLP configurations and also introduced the open ASCAD dataset to serve as a basis for further work on the SCA. The authors also tested Self-Normalizing Neural Networks (SNN), but the performance compared to the MLP did not show any significant improvement. Considering how to develop an adequate CNN architecture for SCA, the authors chose to test some state-of-the-art CNN architectures from the image recognition field, such as VGG-16 [45], ResNet-50 [16], and Inception-v3 [48]. From the initial architecture, the authors performed tuning of the hyper-parameters having guessing entropy as the metric to define the model. Another relevant paper to mention is the paper where authors present a methodology for creating neural network architectures for SCA application [58]. The paper introduces several CNN architectures, each fine-tuned for certain characteristics of utilized datasets, showing how the initial CNN architecture can be light-weighted by searching for appropriate hyper-parameters.

Visualization techniques are also explored for profiled SCA. These techniques indicate the main features in input data which the trained model considers as most important for its classification decisions. For instance, Masure et al. [30] provide results with gradient visualization. In [18], the authors compare the performance of different visualization techniques. These results are discussed in more detail in Sect. 4.5.

In the line of model interpretability, the work presented in [51] provides first results with Singular Vector Canonical Correlation Analysis (SVCCA) tool to interpret what neural networks learn while training on different side-channel datasets. All the aforementioned deep learning techniques provide different perspectives for profiled SCA.

In the next section, we explore what are the main advantages of deep learning in comparison to classical profiled attacks, such as template attacks or machine learning.

4 Advantages of Deep Learning for Profiled Side-Channel Analysis

In this section, we analyze the advantages of deep learning for profiled SCA in comparison to classic techniques such as template attacks and traditional machine learning. First, in Subsect. 4.1 we discuss the fact that deep learning does not require preprocessing or feature selection. Subsection 4.2 describes results indicating that convolutional neural networks are less sensitive to trace desynchronizations. Subsequently, Sect. 4.3 discusses results indicating that deep neural networks can learn high-order leakages. Then we explain how deep learning can take advantage of the domain knowledge in Subsect. 4.4. Finally, Subsect. 4.5 describes various attribution methods (or visualization techniques) for leakage detection.

4.1 Side-Channel Analysis Without Preprocessing

Template attacks (TA) [10] are commonly considered to be one of the most powerful side-channel attacks from an information-theoretic point of view. However, in practice for template attacks to be successful, one needs to choose some special samples as the interesting points in actual side-channel traces [11]. These points are usually referred to as *points-of-interest (POIs)*.

Up to now, much research has been performed on choosing POIs that lead to the most successful TAs (see [13]). This choosing process is often called *POIs selection* and many different approaches were introduced for it over the years. However, it is unknown that whether or not these approaches of choosing interesting points will lead to the best classification performance of TAs. For example, it is hard to quantify whether all useful points for TA have been chosen. In general, we do not know which approach is the best for all possible devices and implementations, as the proposed techniques are only validated experimentally and there has not been a universally optimal solution presented. Moreover, significant processing of the samples, including, most notably, alignment, is necessary before both POIs selection and TAs are being run.

Related to the POIs selection is the problem of feature extraction from the traces. The goal of the extraction is to find the most leaking components in the traces and filter out the noisy components. There has been performed a significant amount of effort in this research direction. For example, Principal Component Analysis was used to extract features and use them from TA [2]. Feature selection is also necessary for machine learning techniques, such as SVM, random forest, or decision trees.

The significant problem of both the POIs selection and feature extraction techniques is that they are not an integral part of TA and that they introduce additional complexity. I comparison, the techniques based on deep learning suffer to a much lesser extent from these problems. In particular, feature extraction is a part of the problem that deep learning aims to solve. The input layer of a deep neural network directly receives the side-channel trace interval corresponding to the interval of interest. It is expected that during training, the backpropagation algorithm (often using stochastic or adaptive gradient descent) will learn network parameters (e.g., weights and biases) in a way that only some of the input features will be relevant in the neural network classification decisions.

As a result, an adversary does not need to identify leaking samples (or features) beforehand, as this process is automatically done by the backpropagation algorithm. Of course, the neural network selects input features representing points-of-interest as long as it can fit the leakage contained in the side-channel measurements. During the training process, it is possible that the neural network overfits the training data and poor generalization is provided. In this case, the neural network will mostly make a decision based on different input features for each classified side-channel traces, meaning that automated POI selection was not successfully made. To address overfitting problems, the most recommended method is regularization.

4.2   Bypassing Desynchronization

Well-synchronized traces can significantly improve the correlation between the intermediate data and the trace values. The alignment of the traces is, therefore, an essential step to enhance the efficiency of the side-channel analysis. Static alignment is the most commonly-used approach to align the traces. Usually, an attacker should select a distinguishable trigger/pattern from the traces, so that the following part can be aligned using the selected part as a reference. There are two limitations to this approach. First, the selected trigger/pattern should be distinctive, so that it will not be obfuscated with other patterns and lead to misalignment. Second, when the countermeasures such as random delay interrupts are implemented, the selected trigger should be sufficiently close to POIs in minimizing the countermeasure effect. From a practical point of view, a good reference that meets both limitations is not always easy to find. Although the other optimized alignment methods, such as Elastic Alignment [55] and Rapid Alignment Method [33], could be candidates to reduce the effect of the countermeasures, the rising of the pre-processing cost makes the traces synchronization a challenging task.

Deep learning provides alternative approaches to bypass desynchronization, which can be realized by either traces pre-processing, or direct attack on the misaligned traces. For traces pre-processing, autoencoder (AE) [42], an unsupervised-learning model well-known for the ability for feature extraction [1,49], could be applied for denoising purpose and lead to an improvement of attack efficiency in both non-profiling [24] and profiling side-channel analysis [56]. Specifically, to train an AE for the denoising purpose, the input and output are represented by noisy-clean traces pairs. A well-trained denoising AE could keep the most representative information (i.e., traces leakage) in the latent space while neglecting the less important features such as random noise. Once the denoising AE is trained, much cleaner traces can be recovered by feeding noisy traces to the input of the AE. Back to desynchronization, it can also be considered as a type of noise that introduces variation in the time domain. As stated in the paper [56], by training the denoising AE with a limited amount of traces, the reconstructed traces can lead to a good performance that comparable to the original one.

In terms of deep learning-based side-channel analysis, several works have presented their effectiveness when compared with classical methods [29,39,40]. There are two reasons in general: 1) deep learning-based attacks do not require critical preprocessing (i.e. realignment), as it is covered in the learning phase; 2) deep learning-based attacks automatically reduce the dimension of the traces by combining the raw features non-linearly with the interconnection of neurons and transferring them to the low-dimensional representations. Thanks to these two characteristics, the effect of misalignment can be reduced during the training of the network. Among different deep learning models, convolutional neural networks (CNNs), thanks to their spatial invariance property, were demonstrated to be the most preferred architecture in coping with desynchronization and the random delay countermeasure [40]. To further enhance the capability of CNN in handling the desynchronization, two possible techniques could be applied: first, exploit the leakage in traces' frequency representation by transferring the traces with short-time Fourier transform [57]; second, applying data argumentation, such as artificially adding random delays, clock jitters [7] or Gaussian noise [20], as it could help increase the diversity of the training sets and balance the class distribution of the profiling data.

In summary, compared with conventional profiling attack methods, deep learning architectures are more resilient to the variation in the time domain. Together with their attacking performance compared with classical profiling attack methods, deep learning becomes a preferable method for profiled side-channel analysis.

4.3   Deep Neural Networks Can Learn Second-Order Leakages

Side-channel attacks exploit the dependency between the power consumption of a cryptographic device and the intermediate values of the implemented cryptographic algorithm. Side-channel countermeasures try to obfuscate the aforementioned data-dependency. In particular, masking countermeasures achieve it by randomizing the key-dependent intermediate values of the algorithm. The goal is to make the power consumption of the device independent of the intermediate values. This is achieved with the Boolean operations between random values (masks) and intermediate data. At the end of encryption/decryption execution, the mask are removed from the result [9,14,27].

Conversely, with the inclusion of deep learning techniques in the side-channel analysis field, masked cryptographic implementations have a new threat: neural networks have shown their capability to break masked cryptographic implementations. Up to now, publication results only demonstrated the capacity to break protected software implementations in the profiled setting. Benjamin Timon in [50] proposed a deep learning solution for non-profiled attacks against masked AES implementations. Even if the attack does not require the profiling on an identical device, it still requires the training of a deep neural network for each key candidate, drastically increasing the attack complexity. The results provided in [50] demonstrate the efficiency of their method against ASCAD dataset [40] and custom ChipWhisperer implementations, however, it is difficult to assume that this method will not be restricted by its high complexity limitations when applied to different devices. Nevertheless, it was demonstrated with input-based sensitivity that deep neural networks can fit high-order leakages. Figure 1 provides results from [50] demonstrating that deep neural networks fit high-order leakages when training set is labeled based on correct key candidate.

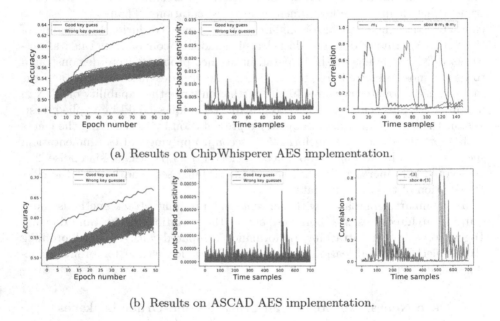

(a) Results on ChipWhisperer AES implementation.

(b) Results on ASCAD AES implementation.

Fig. 1. Results from [50] (Fig. 12) illustrating the ability of deep neural networks to fit high-order side-channel leakages.

Masure et al. in [30] used loss function-based input activation gradients to demonstrate that convolutional neural networks can learn second-order leakages, as indicated in Fig. 2. Input activation gradients based on loss function indicate what are the samples where the loss function is more sensitive. As Fig. 2 indicates, the input activation gradients are higher for the samples representing the processing of mask values.

Although there are no formal explanations for the fact that deep neural networks are able to fit second-order leakages, it actually combines multiple samples in order to make its decisions. As stated in Sect. 4.1, deep neural networks can

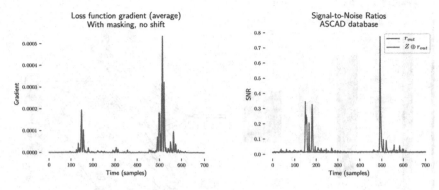

Fig. 2. Results from [30]. Input activation gradients are indicative that CNNs can fit second-order leakages.

learn high-order representations from data and it is expected that these complex learning systems would be able to learn high-order side-channel leakages.

4.4 Take Advantage of the Domain Knowledge

Domain knowledge (DK) [32] assumes that the information domain can be used as part of the dataset to improve the generality (to different datasets) and robustness (towards noises interference) of classifiers. The usage of DK neurons is first introduced to the side-channel domain by Hettwer et al. [17] in 2018. The authors provided the plaintexts as additional information into the neural network to learn the leakage regarding the secret key directly. Specifically, by concatenating the traces' latent representation (a dense layer of CNN) with the one-hot-encoded plaintexts at the byte level, better results can be obtained when performing attacks. Figure 3 illustrates this procedure: the features were extracted from the input by the convolution layers, which are then combined with DK neurons containing the plaintext information to enhance the classification performance. Following this, researchers found that combining the DK neurons (bit-encoded plaintexts) with the denoising autoencoder could reduce the effect of the masking countermeasure [24]. Indeed, merging domain-specific information with extracted features of the convolution layers enables the network to converge to different statistics at the decision level [52]. In other words, leakage traces are generated conditionally on the provided plaintext and the secret key. Although the correlation between plaintext and secret key may not exist, the extra information could be still helpful in extracting more meaningful features. By applying DK that may be not limited to plaintext (i.e. ciphertexts), we see the potential of DK in performing more powerful attacks.

4.5 Visualization Techniques to Identify Input Leakage

As we have already mentioned, profiling attacks are classification problems, and in this type of problem, it is always meaningful to have a method to visually

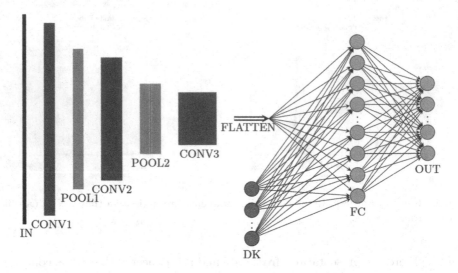

Fig. 3. Image from [17]. A convolutional neural network with domain knowledge in a fully-connected layer.

interpret how the learning model is using the features to conduct the classification. Visualization techniques are very useful for manufacturers to evaluate the side-channel security of their design. This is a useful fact to take advantage of. Recall that an important aspect of evaluating a supposedly secure device is to be able to point out where the leakage is being generated. This way, it is possible to propose modifications and recommendations to limit adversarial possibilities. Knowing where the leakage is generated becomes crucial to improve security and eliminate the main flaws in the crypto implementation.

In general terms, visualization is conducted by analyzing what input features (given by a neuron in the input deep neural network layer as a one-to-one mapping) have more influence in classification during training. After the activation of the neurons, the learning algorithm back-propagates the error to update the weights in those neurons until they reach the first layer. In [30] the authors proposed the visualization of input activation gradients as a technique to characterize the automated selection of points of interest by deep neural networks. The result is a vector of gradients that are computed by the backpropagation algorithm as the derivative of the loss function with respect to the input activation. Gradient visualization is the technique that computes the value of the derivatives in a neural network regarding the input trace, such a value is then used to point out what feature needs to be modified the least, to affect the loss function the most. In [50], the authors proposed the same solution, defined as sensitivity analysis, and they used it in the context of non-profiled side-channel analysis where input activation gradients are used as distinguishers. Input activation gradient method has already being used as a tool to show that neural networks can actually fit high-order leakages (see Sect. 4.3).

Another technique employed for this purpose is Layer-wise Relevance Propagation (LRP). LRP propagates the classification score through the network until the first layer and then conducts the one-to-one mapping [3]. The work in [53] applied a method gradient visualization to show how MLP could be used for the Leakage Assessment Methodology (see Sect. 7). In [18] authors used the LRP technique to identify which samples of the power trace have a greater influence on the learning process. They compared three attribution methods (Saliency Maps [44], LRP and Occlusion [59]) on three different datasets, showing how LRP is the most suitable for finding POIs. Finally, one of the most recent approaches is to use heatmaps (or feature maps) to interpret the impact of filters (also known as convolutional matrices or kernels in the context of CNNs) in order to adapt the neural network model according to how the features are selected [58].

5 Metrics for Deep Learning-Based Profiled SCA

Supervised classification tasks require correct metrics to determine the performance of the algorithm as well as to measure its learning capacity. Accuracy, precision, recall, AOC-ROC, and log-loss are commonly used metrics in supervised classification tasks for many application domains. Computer vision and natural language processing are among applications where the classification accuracy must be very high to solve the underlying problem. Each element in a test set is classified separately. Thus, we are only interested in the generalization capacity of the trained algorithm as long as it provides a high classification accuracy. In particular, deep neural networks have performed extremely well over a wide variety of supervised classification tasks.

When a profiled side-channel attack makes use of a deep neural network as the learning algorithm, we are interested in verifying how effective these highly complex learning systems are in order to learn side-channel leakages and retrieve the cryptographic secret by classifying side-channel traces according to a leakage model. If we strictly consider a side-channel attack on an AES implementation (where the attacker trains a profiling model to attack each separate key byte), a profiled attack is theoretically able to recover the correct target key byte with a single side-channel measurement. This scenario would be possible if the identity leakage model of S-box output in the first encryption round is defined as the leakage function. However, real side-channel measurements are noisy, and several (from hundreds to thousands of) traces are required to conclude attack capability. This is done by summing up the output class probabilities for each classified side-channel trace, in which the selected output probability value for each trace corresponds to the class associated with the guessed key. For each key guess candidate, we compute a probability that key guess k is correct, $P[k = k^*]$, according to Eq. (1). Therefore, in a situation when a deep neural network is trained in a way that it can fit the existing leakages, classifying multiple traces and combining their predicted class probabilities is necessary to estimate the success rate or guessing entropy for a certain amount of traces.

Sometimes, the number of classified side-channel traces in a test or attack phase needs to be very large to reach a consistent conclusion about the model generalization. In such a scenario, the output class probability for the true label (or class) is not always the highest value in the output layer. As a consequence, the overall test accuracy, precision, or recall will stay close to random guessing. In the same way, the cross-entropy loss function for the test set also does not inform enough about the model generalization. This brings us to an important question: what metric should a deep learning-based SCA consider? The authors of [38] demonstrated that conventional machine learning metrics are not very informative for the side-channel analysis domain, concluding that the best metrics are guessing entropy and success rate. In [35], the authors proposed a didactic analysis of output class probabilities obtained by attacking protected AES targets. They once more provided evidence that guessing entropy and success rate become the main metrics for deep learning-based profiled SCA. Based on that, the analysis can be improved in many different directions. Analyzing the guessing entropy during the processing of training epochs can lead to the identification of an efficient early stopping metric. As a result, the neural network will be regularized for side-channel analysis. This is similar to what has been recently proposed in [60].

Therefore, to improve side-channel leakage detection with deep learning, side-channel metrics at a validation level still offer the best alternatives. The selection of correct metrics in deep-learning profiled SCA is also important in hyper-parameter tuning algorithms. As we discuss in the next section, these optimization algorithms converge according to a metric direction (minimum or maximum value) and if the selected metric is not consistent with SCA, the optimization algorithm may have convergence problems.

6   Tuning Neural Network Hyper-Parameters for SCA

This section discusses the problem of selecting efficient hyper-parameters for deep learning-based profiled SCA. The performance of deep learning-based profiled side-channel attacks depends greatly on the selection of hyper-parameters for neural network topology. Different from other profiled attack methods, such as template attacks and machine learning-based attacks, deep neural networks have tenths of hyper-parameters to be defined.

The hyper-parameters definition can be strictly related to the attacked dataset. Several aspects in the dataset may directly affect the selection of specific hyper-parameters: countermeasures, noise levels, number of measurements, number of points in a side-channel measurement, or trace and appropriate leakage model. This already means that one of the main challenges in deep learning-based profiled SCA is the difficulty (if not impossible task) of finding a universal deep learning model that works well on a variety of datasets.

Hyper-parameter search is a common task in all kinds of deep learning applications. For profiled side-channel attacks, the situation is not different. Usually, several combinations of hyper-parameters are evaluated against a dataset and the best possible combination that solves the problem (i.e., recovers the target key byte(s)) is assumed as an optimal model for the underlying task. Depending on the dataset features and target implementation details, manually finding efficient hyper-parameters can be very hard or near impossible. Therefore, there are two main paths to solve this problem: by deeply understanding the role of specific hyper-parameters and their effect on specific datasets or, more recommended, to adopt an optimization algorithm to automatically find the best possible configuration given restricted computation time and resources.

Even if the second path is chosen, the analyst has to set hyper-parameters ranges and possible options to be searched by the optimization algorithm. If the search range for a specific hyper-parameter is completely wrong, it is very likely that the search or optimization algorithm will never identify an efficient combination of hyper-parameters that solves the underlying problem. This can be a serious problem when evaluating the target with profiled SCA, as the analyst can draw wrong conclusions about the security of the device. If deep learning-based attacks can't recover the sensitive information from side-channel leakages, one of the main reasons can be the wrong definition of a deep neural network architecture.

If a dataset is too large (with few million side-channel measurements) and strong countermeasures are present, we expect that a larger model is chosen. This can result in MLP or CNN with several hidden layers, similar to competitive architectures such as VGG-16. However, an appropriate definition of the size of the neural network (and consequently the number of trainable parameters), is not sufficient to ensure its efficiency. A very large deep neural network can overfit even large datasets. This means that alternative solutions to restrict the overfitting to the training set are necessary to improve the performance in terms of generalization. Widely adopted techniques to improve generalization are *regularization techniques* and some of them can directly affect the selection of hyper-parameters and their ranges in a search problem. Some of the hyper-parameters are directly related to the way weights and biases are updated during network training. In [36], the authors investigate the impact of different widely used optimizers in profiled SCA. Their results indicate different performances concerning different amounts of profiling traces and neural network sizes. Moreover, they demonstrate that some of the optimizers (Adam and RMSprop) tend to provide fast convergence, however more chances to overfit the network. For other cases, Adagrad and Adadelta optimizers are appropriate for large network models and large datasets and tend to work better when large amounts of training epochs are considered while offer smaller chances to overfit. Although not investigated in [36], learning rate, batch size, and the number of epochs are also training hyper-parameters that have a huge influence on the attack performance. The learning rate scheduler (by changing the learning rate during training) is an important artifact to reduce overfitting and to stabilize the generalization even if a large number of epochs is considered.

A viable approach when manually tuning hyper-parameters is their modification according to observed metrics. As discussed in Sect. 5, accuracy and loss function are inconsistent metrics to evaluate attack performance (key recovery). However, these two metrics can still be used to analyze how fast a neural network overfits the training data. If this happens very early in the training phase while the guessing entropy or success rate indicates no key recovery, the neural network model is probably too large for the evaluated dataset. Alternative solutions are to increase the number of training or profiling traces, reduce the size of the network or adopt regularization techniques (e.g., early stopping, data augmentation, noisy/batch normalization layers, regularization L1/L2, etc.). Other SCA options, such as leakage models, number of attack/validation traces, also directly influence the learning capacity of the model. For instance, to ease the computation cost, it is crucial to verify if what is more efficient is to search for optimal hyper-parameters or to change the amount of profiling traces. The same principle may apply for the number of attack traces, as a trained model could require a large amount of traces to be able to select the correct key as the most likely one. Therefore, this trade-off between the number of profiling traces, the number of attack traces, and hyper-parameters needs to be taken into account. In order to analyze the effect of each of the aforementioned aspects, the authors in [37] propose a new framework, where they explore the number of traces and hyper-parameter tuning experiments required in the profiling phase such that an attacker is still successful. One important benefit from [37] is the identification of what is the main attack component (hyper-parameters, number of attack traces, or number of profiling traces) that affect mostly the performance of the profiled attack. With such a framework, an analyst can explore the minimum amount of (profiling and attack) traces if the number of hyper-parameters combinations can be very large due to little limitations in time complexity.

Some hyper-parameter selection techniques in deep learning domain also apply to the specific SCA field, such as Grid and Random Search Optimization [4,5,39,40,58]. In terms of Grid Search Optimization, a step-wise search is defined by setting a range of values for specific hyper-parameters. Specifically, to get the optimal parameter combination, the network training is implemented sequentially for every value in the grid. Thanks to its simplicity, Grid Search Optimization is the most widely (although not efficient) used strategy for hyper-parameter tuning in SCA. For instance, in [40], the authors adopted Grid Search to experimentally show the process of choosing each hyper-parameter for MLP and CNN respectively and presented the impact of each hyper-parameter on the performance of SCA. Besides, Grid Search is proved to be reliable in low dimensional spaces [5].

For Random Search Optimization, similar to its counterpart, a fixed range of values is required to be defined for each hyper-parameter. Then, a set of hyper-parameters are chosen randomly from their range as a combination, which is applied to the neural network for evaluation. The authors in [39] used Random Search to find the most optimized CNN model for the datasets by tuning 13 hyper-parameters. Indeed, Random Search Optimization can be implemented automatically with high efficiency in selecting the optimal hyper-parameters. However, the impact of each hyper-parameter is not taken into consideration [4, 40].

Other optimization methods are also proved to be efficient in tuning the deep learning model. In [58], architecture hyper-parameters were chosen by using the visualization techniques to understand how each hyper-parameter impacts the efficiency of the CNN, and each optimizer hyper-parameter was selected by Grid Search from a finite set of values. Moreover, Evolutionary algorithms, such as genetic algorithms and simulated annealing, could also provide better solutions as they implemented metric-based optimizations. Note, Bayesian optimization and Gaussian processes could provide optimal solutions when the training effort is very expensive, which is the case of profiled side-channel analysis. For that, a proper metric needs to be defined in order to correctly judge the performance of a deep neural network for profiled attacks, as discussed in Sect. 5.

7   Different Applications of Deep Learning to Side Channel Analysis

The feasibility of the deep learning for side-channel analysis goes beyond the design and test of new threats. In this section, we summarize different applications of deep neural networks on side-channel attacks that differ from using deep neural networks as a supervised trained classifier.

Deep Learning in Leakage Assessment: To the best of our knowledge, the work [53] was the first to present a version of leakage assessment methodology, where the mathematical foundation involves a function inferred by a learning algorithm. The architecture of the neural network model used could be categorized as a multi-layer perceptron shallow network. Taking into account its relation with the neural network we include this work as a different application of deep learning for side-channel. The task of the learning algorithm is set for classification, where two types of classes are aimed to be distinguished, to do so, the acquisition procedure in the methodology remains the same, and the classes are defined regarding the combination of input data, i.e. random class and fixed class. Nevertheless, an extended version using more than two classes is also possible, the evaluator can compose different sets using different values of fixed data and group them by an identifier, creating more than two classes. Although experiments with more than two classes are not conducted in the original work, we could think that by doing so, a modification in the architecture might be required to deal with the overfitting that having more classes could originate.

The leakage detection also involves a way to analyze graphically where the leak is located. Having computed the statistical moments using even Welch's t-test or Pearson's χ^2-test, a plot pointing out where the spikes exceed a fixed threshold is depicted, showing up what operation of the crypto-algorithm is being compromised. This is a particularly easy task for the statistical-based approaches. In the case of the learning algorithm, deal with the detection of the time sample where the leak happens is trickier. Authors dealt with this by using sensitivity analysis [43]. By using this measure, it is possible to backtrack the activated neurons until the most relevant time samples for the classification task are showing up. Using this measure, it is still not possible to appreciate a

p-value that exceeds the threshold where the leakage happens like as is the case for non-neural network approaches. The only information that it brings is the time samples where the leakage is located.

A Deep Neural Network as a Side-Channel Distinguisher: Timon in [50] presented the first non-profiled deep learning solution to attack protected AES implementations. The way the analysis leads to the conclusion that a trained deep neural network is used as a key distinguisher in a non-profiled setting. For that, the authors train an identical deep neural network architecture for each key byte candidate. Separate training is then conducted based on training traces labeled according to the current key guess. In a divide-and-conquer strategy, which is usually applied to AES, this analysis would require at least 256 training phases to recover a single key byte. The authors demonstrated that the complexity is not too high for some specific targets. However, besides the great contribution offered by this paper, the complexity can easily escalate beyond control if training a single model for a single key byte candidate requires too much time.

Deep Learning Against Public-Key Implementations: state-of-the-art public-key implementations, such as RSA or ECC-based protocols, are nowadays protected with randomization techniques that make single trace attacks the only feasible side-channel solution. These attacks are commonly referred to *horizontal attacks*. In [8], the authors proposed a supervised single trace deep learning attack on a real RSA target. Weissbart et al. in [54] applied CNNs to single trace EdDSA implementations based on Curve25519. These two reported applications of deep learning to public-key designs are supervised techniques and require the knowledge of random blinding and secret variables to label the traces. As an example of a realistic scenario application, the adversary would need to have access to the random number generator in a chip to be able to label the single traces for training purposes. The main difference from the application on symmetric crypto, where class probabilities from multiple traces are combined in a summation probability for each key candidate, classifying single traces resort again to conventional supervised classification metrics to analyze the attack results. In [34], authors proposed a combination of horizontal attack to deep learning techniques. Their proposed framework is able to break protected public-key implementations with CNNs by assuming that an adversary is able to provide initial labels (with large amount of errors) to a trace set after applying an unsupervised horizontal attack. In the end, the attack from [34] is kept unsupervised as no knowledge about private key bits is assumed for the whole framework application.

8   Conclusions and Perspectives

This chapter described a general overview of state-of-the-art in deep learning-based profiled SCA. The main advantages of deep learning against tradicional methods were described. Important discussion about the correct usage of metrics in a deep learning-based attack were addressed as well as the main concepts involving hyper-paramaters tuning in SCA domain.

The research on deep learning techniques for side-channel analysis still leaves several open questions. The main challenge in profiled SCA is the ability of a trained model to generalize to different devices. In deep learning-based SCA, we suggest that this problem could be addressed with efficient regularization techniques able to understand the variations that need to be applied to training traces to improve generalization.

The selection of an efficient metric for deep learning-based profiled SCA still poses difficulties for security evaluators. As conventional deep learning metrics may be meaningless in scenarios with SCA countermeasures, SCA metrics remain a solution. However, the calculation of guessing entropy or success rate during the training phase can face complexity drawbacks, as these calculations can involve thousands of attack traces. Therefore, interesting research could focus on defining efficient loss functions that are based on SCA paradigms.

Finally, one of the main difficulties found by the SCA community in this domain is to propose a non-profiled attack solution based on training a single deep neural network. Auto-encoders are usually suggested as unsupervised methods, however, their efficiency for non-profiled SCA is still an open research question.

References

1. An, J., Cho, S.: Variational autoencoder based anomaly detection using reconstruction probability. Spec. Lect. IE **2**(1), 1–18 (2015)
2. Archambeau, C., Peeters, E., Standaert, F.-X., Quisquater, J.-J.: Template attacks in principal subspaces. In: Goubin, L., Matsui, M. (eds.) CHES 2006. LNCS, vol. 4249, pp. 1–14. Springer, Heidelberg (2006). https://doi.org/10.1007/11894063_1
3. Bach, S., Binder, A., Montavon, G., Klauschen, F., Müller, K.R., Samek, W.: On pixel-wise explanations for non-linear classifier decisions by layer-wise relevance propagation. PloS One **10**(7), e0130140 (2015)
4. Bergstra, J., Bardenet, R., Kégl, B., Bengio, Y.: Algorithms for hyper-parameter optimization, December 2011
5. Bergstra, J., Bengio, Y.: Random search for hyper-parameter optimization. J. Mach. Learn. Res. **13**, 281–305 (2012)
6. Brier, E., Clavier, C., Olivier, F.: Correlation power analysis with a leakage model. In: Joye, M., Quisquater, J.-J. (eds.) CHES 2004. LNCS, vol. 3156, pp. 16–29. Springer, Heidelberg (2004). https://doi.org/10.1007/978-3-540-28632-5_2
7. Cagli, E., Dumas, C., Prouff, E.: Convolutional neural networks with data augmentation against jitter-based countermeasures - Profiling Attacks Without Preprocessing. In: Fischer, W., Homma, N. (eds.) CHES 2017. LNCS, vol. 10529, pp. 45–68. Springer, Cham (2017). https://doi.org/10.1007/978-3-319-66787-4_3
8. Carbone, M., et al.: Deep learning to evaluate secure RSA implementations. IACR Trans. Cryptogr. Hardw. Embed. Syst. **2019**(2), 132–161 (2019). https://doi.org/10.13154/tches.v2019.i2.132-161, https://tches.iacr.org/index.php/TCHES/article/view/7388

9. Chari, S., Jutla, C.S., Rao, J.R., Rohatgi, P.: Towards sound approaches to counteract power-analysis attacks. In: Wiener, M. (ed.) CRYPTO 1999. LNCS, vol. 1666, pp. 398–412. Springer, Heidelberg (1999). https://doi.org/10.1007/3-540-48405-1_26
10. Chari, S., Rao, J.R., Rohatgi, P.: Template attacks. In: Kaliski, B.S., Koç, K., Paar, C. (eds.) CHES 2002. LNCS, vol. 2523, pp. 13–28. Springer, Heidelberg (2003). https://doi.org/10.1007/3-540-36400-5_3
11. Choudary, O., Kuhn, M.G.: Efficient template attacks. In: Francillon, A., Rohatgi, P. (eds.) CARDIS 2013. LNCS, vol. 8419, pp. 253–270. Springer, Cham (2014). https://doi.org/10.1007/978-3-319-08302-5_17
12. Daemen, J., Rijmen, V.: The Design of Rijndael: AES - The Advanced Encryption Standard. Information Security and Cryptography, 1st edn. Springer, Heidelberg (2002). https://doi.org/10.1007/978-3-662-04722-4
13. Fan, G., Zhou, Y., Zhang, H., Feng, D.: How to choose interesting points for template attacks more effectively? In: Yung, M., Zhu, L., Yang, Y. (eds.) INTRUST 2014. LNCS, vol. 9473, pp. 168–183. Springer, Cham (2015). https://doi.org/10.1007/978-3-319-27998-5_11
14. Goubin, L., Patarin, J.: DES and differential power analysis the "duplication" method. In: Koç, Ç.K., Paar, C. (eds.) CHES 1999. LNCS, vol. 1717, pp. 158–172. Springer, Heidelberg (1999). https://doi.org/10.1007/3-540-48059-5_15
15. Graves, A., Mohamed, A., Hinton, G.: Speech recognition with deep recurrent neural networks. In: 2013 IEEE International Conference on Acoustics, Speech and Signal Processing, pp. 6645–6649 (2013)
16. He, K., Zhang, X., Ren, S., Sun, J.: Deep residual learning for image recognition, pp. 770–778, June 2016. https://doi.org/10.1109/CVPR.2016.90
17. Hettwer, B., Gehrer, S., Güneysu, T.: Profiled power analysis attacks using convolutional neural networks with domain knowledge. In: Cid, C., Jacobson, M., Jr. (eds.) SAC 2018. LNCS, vol. 11349, pp. 479–498. Springer, Cham (2018). https://doi.org/10.1007/978-3-030-10970-7_22
18. Hettwer, B., Gehrer, S., Güneysu, T.: Deep neural network attribution methods for leakage analysis and symmetric key recovery. In: Paterson, K.G., Stebila, D. (eds.) SAC 2019. LNCS, vol. 11959, pp. 645–666. Springer, Cham (2020). https://doi.org/10.1007/978-3-030-38471-5_26
19. Kim, J., Picek, S., Heuser, A., Bhasin, S., Hanjalic, A.: Make some noise: unleashing the power of convolutional neural networks for profiled side-channel analysis. Cryptology ePrint Archive, Report 2018/1023 (2018). https://eprint.iacr.org/2018/1023
20. Kim, J., Picek, S., Heuser, A., Bhasin, S., Hanjalic, A.: Make some noise. unleashing the power of convolutional neural networks for profiled side-channel analysis. IACR Trans. Cryptogr. Hardw. Embed. Syst. 148–179 (2019)
21. Koblitz, N.: Elliptic curve cryptosystems. Math. Comput. **48**(177), 203–209 (1987)
22. Kocher, P., Jaffe, J., Jun, B.: Differential power analysis. In: Wiener, M. (ed.) CRYPTO 1999. LNCS, vol. 1666, pp. 388–397. Springer, Heidelberg (1999). https://doi.org/10.1007/3-540-48405-1_25
23. Krizhevsky, A., Sutskever, I., Hinton, G.: ImageNet classification with deep convolutional neural networks. Neural Inf. Process. Syst. **25** (2012). https://doi.org/10.1145/3065386
24. Kwon, D., Kim, H., Hong, S.: Improving non-profiled side-channel attacks using autoencoder based preprocessing (2020)

25. Lerman, L., Poussier, R., Bontempi, G., Markowitch, O., Standaert, F.-X.: Template attacks vs. machine learning revisited (and the curse of dimensionality in side-channel analysis). In: Mangard, S., Poschmann, A.Y. (eds.) COSADE 2014. LNCS, vol. 9064, pp. 20–33. Springer, Cham (2015). https://doi.org/10.1007/978-3-319-21476-4_2

26. Maghrebi, H., Portigliatti, T., Prouff, E.: Breaking cryptographic implementations using deep learning techniques. In: Carlet, C., Hasan, M.A., Saraswat, V. (eds.) SPACE 2016. LNCS, vol. 10076, pp. 3–26. Springer, Cham (2016). https://doi.org/10.1007/978-3-319-49445-6_1

27. Mangard, S., Oswald, E., Popp, T.: Power Analysis Attacks: Revealing the Secrets of Smart Cards. Advances in Information Security, Springer, Heidelberg (2007). https://doi.org/10.1007/978-0-387-38162-6

28. Martinasek, Z., Hajny, J., Malina, L.: Optimization of power analysis using neural network. In: Francillon, A., Rohatgi, P. (eds.) CARDIS 2013. LNCS, vol. 8419, pp. 94–107. Springer, Cham (2014). https://doi.org/10.1007/978-3-319-08302-5_7

29. Martinasek, Z., Malina, L., Trasy, K.: Profiling power analysis attack based on multi-layer perceptron network. In: Mastorakis, N., Bulucea, A., Tsekouras, G. (eds.) Computational Problems in Science and Engineering. LNEE, vol. 343, pp. 317–339. Springer, Cham (2015). https://doi.org/10.1007/978-3-319-15765-8_18

30. Masure, L., Dumas, C., Prouff, E.: Gradient visualization for general characterization in profiling attacks. In: Polian, I., Stöttinger, M. (eds.) COSADE 2019. LNCS, vol. 11421, pp. 145–167. Springer, Cham (2019). https://doi.org/10.1007/978-3-030-16350-1_9

31. Miller, V.S.: Use of elliptic curves in cryptography. In: Williams, H.C. (ed.) CRYPTO 1985. LNCS, vol. 218, pp. 417–426. Springer, Heidelberg (1986). https://doi.org/10.1007/3-540-39799-X_31, http://dl.acm.org/citation.cfm?id=18262.25413

32. Mirchevska, V., Luštrek, M., Gams, M.: Combining domain knowledge and machine learning for robust fall detection. Expert. Syst. 31(2), 163–175 (2014)

33. Muijrers, R.A., van Woudenberg, J.G.J., Batina, L.: RAM: rapid alignment method. In: Prouff, E. (ed.) CARDIS 2011. LNCS, vol. 7079, pp. 266–282. Springer, Heidelberg (2011). https://doi.org/10.1007/978-3-642-27257-8_17

34. Perin, G., Chmielewski, L., Batina, L., Picek, S.: Keep it unsupervised: horizontal attacks meet deep learning. IACR Trans. Cryptogr. Hardw. Embed. Syst. 2021(1), 343–372 (2021). https://doi.org/10.46586/tches.v2021.i1.343-372

35. Perin, G., Chmielewski, L., Picek, S.: Strength in numbers: improving generalization with ensembles in machine learning-based profiled side-channel analysis. IACR Trans. Cryptogr. Hardw. Embed. Syst. 2020(4), 337–364 (2020). https://doi.org/10.13154/tches.v2020.i4.337-364, https://tches.iacr.org/index.php/TCHES/article/view/8686

36. Perin, G., Picek, S.: On the influence of optimizers in deep learning-based side-channel analysis. IACR Cryptol. ePrint Arch. 2020, 977 (2020). https://eprint.iacr.org/2020/977

37. Picek, S., Heuser, A., Guilley, S.: Profiling side-channel analysis in the restricted attacker framework. IACR Cryptol. ePrint Arch. 2019, 168 (2019). https://eprint.iacr.org/2019/168

38. Picek, S., Heuser, A., Jovic, A., Bhasin, S., Regazzoni, F.: The curse of class imbalance and conflicting metrics with machine learning for side-channel evaluations. IACR Trans. Cryptogr. Hardw. Embed. Syst. 2019(1), 209–237 (2019). https://doi.org/10.13154/tches.v2019.i1.209-237

39. Picek, S., Samiotis, I.P., Kim, J., Heuser, A., Bhasin, S., Legay, A.: On the performance of convolutional neural networks for side-channel analysis. In: Chattopadhyay, A., Rebeiro, C., Yarom, Y. (eds.) SPACE 2018. LNCS, vol. 11348, pp. 157–176. Springer, Cham (2018). https://doi.org/10.1007/978-3-030-05072-6_10

40. Prouff, E., Strullu, R., Benadjila, R., Cagli, E., Dumas, C.: Study of deep learning techniques for side-channel analysis and introduction to ascad database. Cryptology ePrint Archive, Report 2018/053 (2018). https://eprint.iacr.org/2018/053

41. Rivest, R.L., Shamir, A., Adleman, L.: A method for obtaining digital signatures and public-key cryptosystems. Commun. ACM **21**(2), 120–126 (1978). https://doi.org/10.1145/359340.359342, http://doi.acm.org/10.1145/359340.359342

42. Rumelhart, D.E., Hinton, G.E., Williams, R.J.: Learning internal representations by error propagation. Technical report, California Univ San Diego La Jolla Inst for Cognitive Science (1985)

43. Shu, H., Zhu, H.: Sensitivity analysis of deep neural networks. In: Proceedings of the AAAI Conference on Artificial Intelligence, vol. 33, pp. 4943–4950 (2019). https://doi.org/10.1609/aaai.v33i01.33014943, http://dx.doi.org/10.1609/aaai.v33i01.33014943

44. Simonyan, K., Vedaldi, A., Zisserman, A.: Deep inside convolutional networks: visualising image classification models and saliency maps. Preprint, December 2013

45. Simonyan, K., Zisserman, A.: Very deep convolutional networks for large-scale image recognition. arXiv:1409.1556, September 2014

46. Srivastava, N., Hinton, G., Krizhevsky, A., Sutskever, I., Salakhutdinov, R.: Dropout: a simple way to prevent neural networks from overfitting. J. Mach. Learn. Res. **15**(56), 1929–1958 (2014). http://jmlr.org/papers/v15/srivastava14a.html

47. Standaert, F.-X., Malkin, T.G., Yung, M.: A unified framework for the analysis of side-channel key recovery attacks. In: Joux, A. (ed.) EUROCRYPT 2009. LNCS, vol. 5479, pp. 443–461. Springer, Heidelberg (2009). https://doi.org/10.1007/978-3-642-01001-9_26

48. Szegedy, C., Vanhoucke, V., Ioffe, S., Shlens, J., Wojna, Z.: Rethinking the inception architecture for computer vision, June 2016. https://doi.org/10.1109/CVPR.2016.308

49. Theis, L., Shi, W., Cunningham, A., Huszár, F.: Lossy image compression with compressive autoencoders. arXiv preprint arXiv:1703.00395 (2017)

50. Timon, B.: Non-profiled deep learning-based side-channel attacks with sensitivity analysis. IACR Trans. Cryptogr. Hardw. Embed. Syst. **2019**(2), 107–131 (2019). https://doi.org/10.13154/tches.v2019.i2.107-131

51. van der Valk, D., Picek, S., Bhasin, S.: Kilroy was here: the first step towards explainability of neural networks in profiled side-channel analysis. IACR Cryptol. ePrint Arch. 2019, 1477 (2019). https://eprint.iacr.org/2019/1477

52. Wang, D., Mao, K., Ng, G.W.: Convolutional neural networks and multimodal fusion for text aided image classification. In: 2017 20th International Conference on Information Fusion (Fusion), pp. 1–7. IEEE (2017)

53. Wegener, F., Moos, T., Moradi, A.: DL-LA: deep learning leakage assessment: a modern roadmap for SCA evaluations. IACR Cryptol. ePrint Arch. **2019**, 505 (2019)

54. Weissbart, L., Picek, S., Batina, L.: One trace is all it takes: machine learning-based side-channel attack on EdDSA. In: Bhasin, S., Mendelson, A., Nandi, M. (eds.) SPACE 2019. LNCS, vol. 11947, pp. 86–105. Springer, Cham (2019). https://doi.org/10.1007/978-3-030-35869-3_8

55. van Woudenberg, J.G.J., Witteman, M.F., Bakker, B.: Improving differential power analysis by elastic alignment. In: Kiayias, A. (ed.) CT-RSA 2011. LNCS, vol. 6558, pp. 104–119. Springer, Heidelberg (2011). https://doi.org/10.1007/978-3-642-19074-2_8

56. Wu, L., Picek, S.: Remove some noise: on pre-processing of side-channel measurements with autoencoders. IACR Trans. Cryptogr. Hardw. Embed. Syst. **2020**(4), 389–415 (2020). https://doi.org/10.13154/tches.v2020.i4.389-415

57. Yang, G., Li, H., Ming, J., Zhou, Y.: Convolutional neural network based side-channel attacks in time-frequency representations. In: Bilgin, B., Fischer, J.-B. (eds.) CARDIS 2018. LNCS, vol. 11389, pp. 1–17. Springer, Cham (2019). https://doi.org/10.1007/978-3-030-15462-2_1

58. Zaid, G., Bossuet, L., Habrard, A., Venelli, A.: Methodology for efficient CNN architectures in profiling attacks. IACR Trans. Cryptogr. Hardw. Embedd. Syst. **2020**(1), 1–36 (2019)

59. Zeiler, M.D., Fergus, R.: Visualizing and understanding convolutional networks. In: Fleet, D., Pajdla, T., Schiele, B., Tuytelaars, T. (eds.) ECCV 2014. LNCS, vol. 8689, pp. 818–833. Springer, Cham (2014). https://doi.org/10.1007/978-3-319-10590-1_53

60. Zhang, J., Zheng, M., Nan, J., Hu, H., Yu, N.: A novel evaluation metric for deep learning-based side channel analysis and its extended application to imbalanced data. IACR Trans. Cryptogr. Hardw. Embed. Syst. **2020**(3), 73–96 (2020). https://doi.org/10.13154/tches.v2020.i3.73-96

Artificial Neural Networks and Fault Injection Attacks

Shahin Tajik[✉] and Fatemeh Ganji

Worcester Polytechnic Institute, Worcester, USA
{stajik,fganji}@wpi.edu

Abstract. This chapter is on the security assessment of artificial intelligence (AI) and neural network (NN) accelerators in the face of fault injection attacks. More specifically, it discusses the assets on these platforms and compares them with those known and well-studied in the field of cryptography. This is a crucial step that must be taken in order to define the threat models precisely. With respect to that, fault attacks mounted on NNs and AI accelerators are explored.

1 Introduction

Physical attacks can threaten the confidentiality and integrity of the processed data in electronic embedded devices. Side-channel analysis and fault injection attacks are examples of such physical attacks. While most side-channel analysis techniques are considered passive, fault injection attacks involve an active adversary. In other words, the adversary attempts to observe a faulty behavior of the target platform by feeding faulty data or forcing it to operate in a physical condition, which is outside of the specified operating range. For instance, by manipulating the supplied voltage (a.k.a., voltage glitching), altering the frequency of the clock signal (a.k.a., clock glitching), or flipping bits in the memory with a laser beam the attacker can cause erroneous operation of the target device [3]. Fault injection attacks are usually considered a threat if the target platform is in possession of the adversary. Nevertheless, recent studies [2,12,15,20,38] have demonstrated that such fault attacks can also be carried out remotely on different platforms, without any physical access to the victim device.

The primary target of fault injection attacks has been cryptographic devices and secure hardware. For instance, by injecting faults into a finite state machine (FSM) implemented on a hardware platform, an adversary might be able to bypass some authentication states and get unauthorized access to some security-sensitive states. Moreover, by injecting faults into the cryptographic operations on a device and using mathematical tools, such as Differential Fault Analysis (DFA), an adversary might be able to recover the secret key by observing the generated faulty ciphertexts. Cryptographic hardware are not the only targets for fault attacks. The new victims are artificial intelligence (AI)-enabled hardware.

Hardware platforms specialized for AI tasks have been applied in various applications and services, offered in the whole spectrum from the cloud to edge, close to

L. Batina et al. (Eds.): Security and Artificial Intelligence, LNCS 13049, pp. 72–84, 2022.
https://doi.org/10.1007/978-3-030-98795-4_4

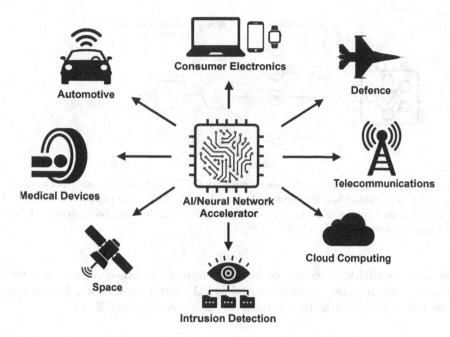

Fig. 1. Some applications of AI/neural network accelerators.

the consumer; therefore, such hardware platforms have made commercial, industrial, and defense products feasible. End-user devices, such as autonomous cars, smartphones, and robots, are a few examples of such products, see Fig. 1. While the benefits of AI in our lives are undeniable, there are several concerns regarding the security of AI hardware. Similar to cryptographic hardware, AI-enabled hardware could be potential target for physical attacks, such as fault attacks. The motivations behind physical attacks against the so-called AI/neural network accelerators is manyfold: accessing stored AI assets, IP piracy, obtaining unauthorized access to specific services, or simply disrupting the operation.

Consequently, a great deal of attention has to be paid to protect assets embedded in AI accelerators. On the positive side, it is known that the artificial neural networks (NNs), which are the most commonly-used AI algorithms implemented on the hardware, are - to some degree - tolerant to faults. This tolerance to faults might be used as an advantage to replace some of the current fault vulnerable hardware primitives by NNs to obtain a higher level of security against fault attacks, see, e.g., [1][1].

The aim of this chapter is mainly to review the *vulnerability* of the current AI accelerators and AI IP cores to fault attacks. The chapter is organized as follows. In Sect. 2, we review the threat models and assets on AI/neural network accelerators. In Sect. 3, we discuss the vulnerabilities of NNs to fault attacks. Section 4

---

[1] Note that fault tolerance is not an intrinsic feature of NNs and should be designed to be exhibited by the models [39].

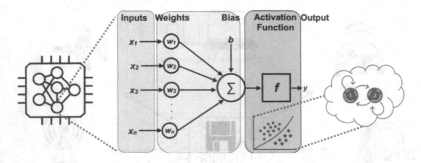

Fig. 2. A general architecture of a neural network (NN), with different abstraction level. The NN is pre-trained and implemented on an FPGA/ASIC. For this, the weights and biases are stored in the memory. The output layer of the NN can be represented by a finite state machine (FSM), cf. [2].

reviews the available AI/neural network accelerators and their security features. Potential fault injection techniques against AI/neural network accelerators are presented in Sect. 5. Finally, we conclude the chapter in Sect. 6.

2   Assets and Threat Models

In order to understand the threat of physical attacks against AI accelerators, we should first understand what the primary assets on AI/neural network accelerators are and how an adversary can benefit from attacking them. Note that to explore the assets, we should not limit ourselves to any specific class of physical attack (for a more detailed discussion about the impact of fault attack, please see Sect. 3). Besides, it is helpful to investigate how these assets differ from the conventional assets on cryptographic hardware, which are the traditional targets for fault attacks. In this regard, we briefly review a few examples of threat models and the main target assets in NNs. While there exist several learning algorithms that can be realized on hardware, we focus, in this chapter, mainly on artificial NN and its derivatives, since they have gained enormous popularity over the last decade due to their wide range of applications. An abstract model of NN architecture, which is realized by an FSM in hardware, can be seen in Fig. 2.

2.1   Attack Scenarios

In this subsection, we describe the possible attack scenarios against AI hardware and review the main target assets which have to be protected.

Training Data Extraction. One of the main assets of an AI system is the training data [40]. In some applications, such training data has to be stored during an enrollment phase on the chip to be compared later in an evaluation phase with the input data. A prime example of such a scenario is the biometrics data (e.g., fingerprints and face IDs), which are stored on smartphones [19]. In this case, if an adversary can get access to the training data, she can bypass authentication and get unauthorized access to specific services. Another example of training data is the medical data gathered from patients, which has to be kept confidential. Obtaining access to such data might lead to its misuse against the patients. Even in the cases that the training data is not sensitive, collecting such dataset still costs time and money for the designer of an AI system, e.g., the gathered data for self-driving cars. Therefore, an adversary can benefit from getting access to such dataset without investing time and money for its collection. Finally, the adversary can also tamper with the training data or spoof the training data to change the AI-based system's response.

Structure and Parameters Extraction. Another asset is the AI algorithm itself, such as trained neural networks (NNs) [4,7,17,41]. For several applications, it is time-consuming to train an NN with large training datasets. Since such training data is not available to everyone, replicating a similar NN with the same features and classification capabilities might be challenging, and therefore, it needs enormous research and development efforts. Therefore, to save time and compensate the lack of training data, it can be tempting for an adversary to attack the target AI platform to extract the architecture (e.g., number of layers and neurons) and parameters (e.g., weights, biases, and activation functions) of the trained IP. In this case, she can clone the IP and produce counterfeits. For instance, consider AI IP cores, which are used in self-driving cars. By purchasing one of such cars from a vendor, an adversary (e.g., an end-user or a competitor vendor) gets access to the deployed AI accelerator inside the car with unlimited time to attack and extract the IP and make a profit out of it. Moreover, in some cases, by knowing the architecture and parameters of an NN, one might be able to recover the used training data.

Disrupting Training and Classification Output. Many AI platforms are deployed in critical applications, such as intrusion detection systems, autonomous cars, medical devices, and defense systems. In these cases, any disruption in their performance might lead to irreparable damages or even loss of lives. It is conceivable that an adversary attempts to mount a physical attack to mislead the AI algorithms during training, inference, or classification phases or merely perform a denial-of-service (DoS) attack [2,6].

2.2 AI Assets vs Cryptographic Assets

As mentioned in Sect. 2.1, there are different types of assets on an AI platform, which need to be protected against physical attacks. In contrast to AI hardware, cryptographic hardware usually encompasses a single asset, i.e., the secret key, which needs to be protected. According to *Kerckhoffs's principle* [21,37], the main assumption is that the security of a device should not rely on the secrecy of its implementation details. In other words, even if details of a cryptographic implementation are entirely known to the adversary, she should not be able to extract the secret key from the device. Yet, in the case of an NN, the network structure is itself an asset, and therefore, needs protection. Besides, for breaking the security of a cryptographic algorithm (i.e., understanding the relation between inputs and outputs), it is needed to extract the exact secret key. However, an adversary can recover imprecise parameters retrieved from an NN and still generate the same output to a given input. This diversity of assets in AI hardware makes the security analysis of such systems more complicated than traditional cryptographic hardware.

3   Faults in Neural Network

NNs are generally assumed to be tolerant against faults and imprecision to a certain degree [26] due to their distributed structures and redundancy. In other words, NNs can be robust to noisy inputs and demonstrate a low sensitivity to the faults, and therefore, the result of the computation is not drastically affected. This phenomena is referred to *graceful degradation* in the literature [39]. However, a note of caution is needed here. Being fault-tolerant highly depends not on only the architecture and size of the NN, but also the training that the NN undergoes. For instance, small size NNs might not be fault-tolerant. Therefore, it cannot be claimed that NNs are in general fault-tolerant [39].

While the threat of fault attacks against NNs is a novel research direction in the field of security, the fault-tolerance feature of the NNs have been studied extensively for years in other areas, including hardware test and machine learning, see, e.g., [39]. The main motivation behind these studies in the test community has been the safety assessment of implemented NNs on hardware platforms, which are exposed to transient and permanent faults due to aging, thermal issues, voltage underscaling, and process variations in the very recent nano-scale technologies [5, 26, 27, 34–36, 42]. These faults can occur in all major parameters of an NN, such as weights, biases, inputs, etc. On the other hand, in the field of machine learning, several experimental studies have dealt with the concept of adversarial learning, where intentional faults are occurred mainly in the inputs of the NNs to affect the performance of the NN adversely [13].

It is indeed possible to inject intentional/adversarial faults in input, hidden, and output layers of an NN implementation (see Fig. 2). At each layer, the main functional and arithmetic components of each neuron and the parameters involved in the computation can be affected by faults, see Fig. 3. While manipulating the parameters needs a fault injection into the physical memory of an AI accelerator, e.g., through rowhammer attack [15], affecting multipliers, adders and activation functions, requires usually timing faults, e.g., caused by voltage glitching [2].

In this regard, the last two layers of NNs are of great interest to attackers aiming to induce misclassification without perturbing the inputs. One of the first studies on this has been conducted by Liu et al. to show that by changing some parameters, e.g., the biases, faults can be injected into an NN [25]. Since their results were based on simulations, a laser fault injection attack against NNs was introduced in [6] to show to what extent it is possible to obtain similar results in

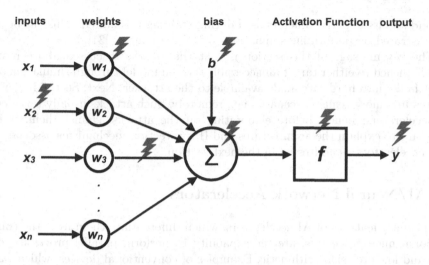

Fig. 3. The vulnerable components and parameters of a single neuron to fault injection, inspired by [7,39]

practice. In their experiments, various functions in an NN have been targeted, and it has been shown that multiple faults can be injected at the same time.

In another attempt, the attack introduced in [43] aims to inject faults into trained NNs with two aspects in mind: (1) keeping the classification of other inputs (in this case images), rather than the one targeted by the attacker, unchanged, and (2) minimizing the number of parameter modifications. The attack is enhanced by applying a systematic method to determine where a fault should be injected and which parameters (i.e., the biases and weights) can have a stronger influence on the performance of the attack. In practice, the issue with determining where the attack should be injected has become more commonly known and discussed in a number of studies. As an example, [15] has assessed the vulnerability of a large number of NNs to fault attacks and reported the interesting points to be targeted. This line of research has been pursued by Rakin et al. [31], suggesting to inject faults in memories used to store the weights. It has been further argued that by applying their proposed algorithm, it could be possible to identify the most vulnerable bits of weights saved in the memory to achieve a high-performance attack. For this purpose, and to verify that in practice, trained NNs have been employed to conduct simulations. Moreover, the attack has launched in a white-box fashion, i.e., full access to the weights and gradients is required. The same authors have shown that the above attack can be combined by an adversarial attack to launch a Trojan attack against NNs [32]. In doing so, when a trigger is enabled (i.e., giving a specially designed input) the network is forced to classify all inputs to a certain target class. It is expected that when following this procedure, an adversarial attack could become more efficient as solely a set of randomly sampled data is required to prepare the trigger. Additionally, access to neither the training data, nor the training method and its hyperparameters used during training is required. This has been demonstrated by performing simulation on NNs, similar to [31].

The key message of this section is that the attacks discussed above have been launched to either target an accessible trained model through simulation or inject faults into hardware made available to the attacker. Next, Sect. 5 reviews attacks in a more realistic scenario, i.e., remotely. Such attacks usually targeted AI accelerators; hence, before elaborating on the attacks against them, it is necessary to explain the architectures and IP protection mechanisms associated with accelerators as addressed in the next section.

4   AI/Neural Network Accelerators

The primary features of AI accelerators, which differentiate them from the conventional microprocessors, are the capability to perform parallel processing of data and low-precision arithmetic. Examples of conventional devices, which can fulfill these requirements include graphics processing units (GPUs) and field programmable gate arrays (FPGAs). Moreover, novel neural network processors are emerging to accelerate AI tasks on the edge devices. To assess the security of the AI IP cores and stored assets on these platforms, below, we briefly review their security.

4.1   GPUs

GPUs are designed primarily to run intensive computational tasks for image processing, which require parallelism. Since these platforms are offering parallel computing via several cores, they have been adapted for training and inference tasks in AI applications as well. GPUs are usually controlled by general purpose processors, such as x86 and ARM processors, in the same chip package. In this case, the security of stored AI IP cores and data is reduced to the security of the entire processor platform. An adversary, interested in extracting the NN structure or its parameters inside the memory, could attack the firmware protection schemes to obtain access to the IP. On the other hand, security features, such as ARM TrustZone or Intel SGX, are utilized to assure the confidentiality and integrity of the data in the memory of the chip during runtime. Naturally, the attacker can still mount physical attacks during the runtime on these platforms to interfere with the AI algorithm computation.

4.2   FPGAs

FPGAs provide the high parallelism of hardware with the reconfiguration flexibility of the software. FPGAs contain several thousands of configurable logic resources, a large number of dedicated digital signal processors, and dual-port RAMs. Hence, they are suitable for the realization of large parallel neural networks. Most FPGAs do not have any non-volatile memory (NVM) inside their packages to store their configuration data, the so-called, i.e., the so-called bitstream. Therefore, the bitstream has to be stored in an external NVM and transferred into the FPGA upon each power-on. The AI IP cores are also included in the bitstream. Hence, the confidentiality and integrity of AI IP cores and its parameters depend on the security of the bitstream encryption and authentication schemes. Moreover, an attacker can still tamper with the FPGA during runtime and mount physical attacks, such as fault attacks for reconfiguration of device, to influence the behavior of the AI algorithm.

4.3 Custom AI/Neural Network Accelerators

Instead of using a general-purpose processor or programmable logic, several research teams and vendors have started to design and fabricate their own AI/neural network/deep learning accelerators. DianNao [8], EIE [14], Eyeriss [9], Prime [10], and MAERI [22] are a few examples of such designed neural network accelerators by academia. On the other hand, products such as Google Tensor Product Unit (TPU) [18], Tesla Hardware 3 platform [33], and Apple Neural Engine [28] are examples of proprietary neural network accelerators designed by vendors. These co-processors contain dedicated neural network processors, which are specifically optimized for AI tasks. For instance, modules, such as activation functions, multiplication and addition operations, are realized in hardware to speed up the computation. These engines are integrated internally or externally to general-purpose processors based on ARM or x86 architectures. In this case, since the AI IP is included in the firmware, the confidentiality and integrity of the stored data and model is reduced to the security of the firmware protection schemes on these platforms. Since these accelerators are usually using compatible silicon-based digital logic and memory technologies, their vulnerability to fault attacks during the runtime is similar to other conventional platforms.

5 Fault Injection Attacks on AI Accelerators

As the threat of (passive) side-channel analysis, such as power analysis and cache attacks, against AI accelerators has been discussed extensively in the literature [4,11,17,40,41], here we focus on vulnerabilities of AI algorithms and accelerators to fault attacks.

In order to understand how an adversary can mount fault injection attack against an AI accelerator, we consider two different scenarios: (i) the adversary has physical access to the target, and hence, she can feed arbitrary inputs or operate the target in a non-valid condition (ii) the target is accessible only remotely, and the adversary can only interact with it by sending inputs and run her own code in a virtualized environment.

5.1 Traditional Fault Attack

In the case of traditional fault attacks, it is assumed that the adversary possesses the target. The neural network accelerators in the edge devices (e.g., smartphones, autonomous vehicles, or any other IoT device) are giving such access to end-users. Thus, based on the adversary's capability, different classes of fault attacks can be mounted on AI-enabled devices. The least expensive fault attacks are non-invasive fault injection attacks, e.g., voltage glitching [34,35], clock glitching [23,24], and electromagnetic faults, which can cause timing faults into the control and data path of the AI accelerator, and therefore, cause faulty computations or even erroneous outputs. More sophisticated fault attacks are based on more invasive techniques. The most prominent technique in this class is the laser fault injection attacks, which enables an adversary to not only influence the timing of the signal on the chip but precisely flip bits inside the memories, such as SRAMs. In this case, the attacker has potentially a higher control or manipulation capability over the AI co-processor's behavior [16].

5.2 Remote Fault Attacks

The assumption that the adversary has physical access to the target chip might be valid for edge devices. However, in other scenarios, where the chip is deployed, for instance, in the cloud, the adversary cannot perform the traditional fault injection attacks on the target. In this scenario, the adversary is usually able to rent shared resources (i.e., processing power and memory) on the cloud chips. Several studies have demonstrated that even with this limited access to the target chip, the adversary can perform fault injection attacks, see Fig. 4.

In the case of FPGAs, the resources of the chip can be spatially shared between several IP cores. The adversary can get partial access to a multi-tenant FPGA in a cloud to implant a hardware Trojan. The adversary's goal here is to remotely activate the hardware Trojan and inject a fault from her IP into other adjacent IP cores. The IP cores on multi-tenant FPGAs are separated by moats, and hence, there is no direct communication link between them. However, the Power Distribution Network (PDN) of the FPGA is shared between these IP cores. In order to bypass the isolation between IP cores and inject faults into neighboring IPs (e.g., an NN), the adversary has to load valid designs, which contain stealthy hardware Trojans capable of dropping the core voltage and overheating the chip, see Fig. 4. To avoid the detection carried out by bitstream security checks, the hardware Trojan has to be implanted in a valid configuration (i.e., a bitstream). RAM-Jam [2] is an example of such Trojans, which causes memory collisions in the dual-port RAMs of the FPGA and creates transient short circuits, leading to voltage drop and temperature increase on the chip. As a result, as one of the first attacks launched remotely[2], RAM-Jam can inject faults into pre-trained NN engines. For this purpose, the attack has targeted the hidden and the output layers of an NN by flipping bits (i.e., weights of NN) and bypassing the transitions between states representing the output classes.

Similarly, power waster circuits based on Ring-Oscillators and other valid power-hungry circuits [12,29,30] can cause severe voltage drops inside FPGAs. In

---

[2] In an independent study conducted in parallel with the one introducing RAM-Jam, Hong et al. have proposed their attack [15].

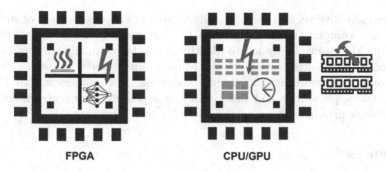

Fig. 4. Remote Fault Attacks on AI accelerators: Trojans inside an IP core (e.g., RAM-Jam and power waster circuits) can cause overheating and voltage drop inside FPGAs and cause timing faults into neural networks realized in adjacent IP cores. On processors, remote attacks, such as rowhammer can inject faults into DRAM modules and manipulates the NN parameters. Other attacks, e.g., clkscrew and v0ltpwn attacks, can cause timing faults into the NN computation.

both cases, the resulting voltage and temperature changes can cause timing faults in the neural network computations, running in parallel on the same FPGA, but owned by another user.

Similar to multi-tenant FPGAs, the deployed CPUs or GPUs as AI accelerators in the cloud are vulnerable to remote fault attacks as well. For instance, rowhammer attack [15] enables the attacker to flip bits in DRAM connected to the AI accelerators, responsible for storing the neural network parameters. Moreover, attacks, such as v0ltpwn [20] and clkscrew [38] can alter the voltage and clock frequency of the processor, respectively. As a result, timing faults can be injected into the operation of the neural network calculations, running in another virtual machine on the same processor. Note that most of these attacks are demonstrated on CPUs and have not been tested on GPUs yet. One reason could be the differences in the schedulers of GPUs, which decide on the resource allocation in real time. The uncertainty resulting from this real-time memory and computing core allocation makes fault attacks more challenging or ineffective. These schedulers are proprietary, and even though there are some reverse-engineering studies, the knowledge on how they work is limited.

6 Conclusion

This chapter reviewed the threat of physical attacks, especially fault injection attacks, against neural networks and their implementations on AI accelerators. We explored the primary assets of an AI system that needs to be protected against physical attacks. Moreover, we investigated the potential attack scenarios against an AI system both from theoretical and practical points of view, and how an adversary can benefit from such attacks.

Besides, we discussed and compared the assets on an AI accelerator with those on conventional cryptographic hardware. It became evident that the AI assets are more diverse, and therefore, the formal security assessment of such systems is more complicated. Consequently, further research on the impact of fault attacks on AI systems is needed to identify potential vulnerabilities and design proper countermeasures against them. Finally, since neural networks demonstrate some fault resiliency in specific scenarios, it is interesting to further evaluate the applicability and practicality of replacing fault vulnerable hardware/software primitives by a more fault-tolerant neural network.

References

1. Alam, M., et al.: Enhancing fault tolerance of neural networks for security-critical applications. arXiv preprint arXiv:1902.04560 (2019)
2. Alam, M.M., Tajik, S., Ganji, F., Tehranipoor, M., Forte, D.: RAM-jam: remote temperature and voltage fault attack on FPGAs using memory collisions. In: 2019 Workshop on Fault Diagnosis and Tolerance in Cryptography (FDTC), pp. 48–55. IEEE (2019)
3. Bar-El, H., Choukri, H., Naccache, D., Tunstall, M., Whelan, C.: The sorcerer's apprentice guide to fault attacks. Proc. IEEE **94**(2), 370–382 (2006)
4. Batina, L., Bhasin, S., Jap, D., Picek, S.: CSI NN: reverse engineering of neural network architectures through electromagnetic side channel. In: 28th USENIX Security Symposium (USENIX Security 19), pp. 515–532 (2019)
5. Bolt, G.: Fault models for artificial neural networks. In: [Proceedings] 1991 IEEE International Joint Conference on Neural Networks, pp. 1373–1378. IEEE (1991)
6. Breier, J., Hou, X., Jap, D., Ma, L., Bhasin, S., Liu, Y.: Practical fault attack on deep neural networks. In: Proceedings of the 2018 ACM SIGSAC Conference on Computer and Communications Security, pp. 2204–2206. ACM (2018)
7. Breier, J., Jap, D., Hou, X., Bhasin, S., Liu, Y.: SNIFF: reverse engineering of neural networks with fault attacks. arXiv preprint arXiv:2002.11021 (2020)
8. Chen, T., et al.: DianNao: a small-footprint high-throughput accelerator for ubiquitous machine-learning. ACM SIGARCH Comput. Archit. News **42**(1), 269–284 (2014)
9. Chen, Y.H., Emer, J., Sze, V.: Eyeriss: a spatial architecture for energy-efficient dataflow for convolutional neural networks. ACM SIGARCH Comput. Archit. News **44**(3), 367–379 (2016)
10. Chi, P., et al.: PRIME: a novel processing-in-memory architecture for neural network computation in ReRAM-based main memory. ACM SIGARCH Comput. Archit. News **44**(3), 27–39 (2016)
11. Dubey, A., Cammarota, R., Aysu, A.: MaskedNet: the first hardware inference engine aiming power side-channel protection. In: 2020 IEEE International Symposium on Hardware Oriented Security and Trust (HOST), pp. 197–208. IEEE (2020)
12. Gnad, D.R., Oboril, F., Tahoori, M.B.: Voltage drop-based fault attacks on FPGAs using valid bitstreams. In: 27th International Conference on Field Programmable Logic and Applications, pp. 1–7. IEEE (2017)
13. Goodfellow, I.J., Shlens, J., Szegedy, C.: Explaining and harnessing adversarial examples. arXiv preprint arXiv:1412.6572 (2014)
14. Han, S., Liu, X., Mao, H., Pu, J., Pedram, A., Horowitz, M.A., Dally, W.J.: EIE: efficient inference engine on compressed deep neural network. ACM SIGARCH Comput. Archit. News **44**(3), 243–254 (2016)

15. Hong, S., Frigo, P., Kaya, Y., Giuffrida, C., Dumitraş, T.: Terminal brain damage: exposing the graceless degradation in deep neural networks under hardware fault attacks. In: 28th USENIX Security Symposium (USENIX Security 2019), pp. 497–514 (2019)

16. Hou, X., Breier, J., Jap, D., Ma, L., Bhasin, S., Liu, Y.: Security evaluation of deep neural network resistance against laser fault injection. In: 2020 IEEE International Symposium on the Physical and Failure Analysis of Integrated Circuits (IPFA), pp. 1–6. IEEE (2020)

17. Hua, W., Zhang, Z., Suh, G.E.: Reverse engineering convolutional neural networks through side-channel information leaks. In: 2018 55th ACM/ESDA/IEEE Design Automation Conference (DAC), pp. 1–6. IEEE (2018)

18. Jouppi, N.: Google supercharges machine learning tasks with TPU custom chip. Google Blog May **18**, 1 (2016)

19. Wiggers, K.: Apple's A12 Bionic chip runs Core ML apps up to 9 times faster. Technical report. https://venturebeat.com/2018/09/12/apples-a12-bionic-chip-run-core-ml-apps-up-to-9-times-faster/

20. Kenjar, Z., Frassetto, T., Gens, D., Franz, M., Sadeghi, A.R.: V0LTpwn: attacking x86 processor integrity from software. In: 29th USENIX Security Symposium (USENIX Security 2020) (2020)

21. Kerckhoffs, A.: La cryptographie militaire, ou, Des chiffres usités en temps de guerre: avec un nouveau procédé de déchiffrement applicable aux systèmes à double clef. Librairie militaire de L, Baudoin (1883)

22. Kwon, H., Samajdar, A., Krishna, T.: MAERI: enabling flexible dataflow mapping over DNN accelerators via reconfigurable interconnects. ACM SIGPLAN Not. **53**(2), 461–475 (2018)

23. Liu, W., Chang, C.H., Zhang, F.: Stealthy and robust glitch injection attack on deep learning accelerator for target with variational viewpoint. IEEE Trans. Inf. Forensics Secur. **16**, 1928–1942 (2020)

24. Liu, W., Chang, C.H., Zhang, F., Lou, X.: Imperceptible misclassification attack on deep learning accelerator by glitch injection. In: 2020 57th ACM/IEEE Design Automation Conference (DAC), pp. 1–6. IEEE (2020)

25. Liu, Y., Wei, L., Luo, B., Xu, Q.: Fault injection attack on deep neural network. In: IEEE/ACM International Conference on Computer-Aided Design, pp. 131–138 (2017)

26. Mahdiani, H.R., Fakhraie, S.M., Lucas, C.: Relaxed fault-tolerant hardware implementation of neural networks in the presence of multiple transient errors. IEEE Trans. Neural Netw. Learn. Syst. **23**(8), 1215–1228 (2012)

27. Mehrotra, K., Mohan, C.K., Ranka, S., Chiu, C.T.: Fault tolerance of neural networks. Technical report, Syracuse Univ NY School of Computer and Information Science (1994)

28. Newsroom, A.: The future is here: iPhone X (2017). https://www.apple.com/newsroom/2017/09/the-future-is-here-iphone-x/. Accessed 8 Mar 2022

29. Provelengios, G., Holcomb, D., Tessier, R.: Characterizing power distribution attacks in multi-user FPGA environments. In: 2019 29th International Conference on Field Programmable Logic and Applications (FPL), pp. 194–201. IEEE (2019)

30. Provelengios, G., Holcomb, D., Tessier, R.: Power wasting circuits for cloud FPGA attacks. 2020 30th International Conference on Field Programmable Logic and Applications (FPL) (2020)

31. Rakin, A.S., He, Z., Fan, D.: Bit-flip attack: crushing neural network with progressive bit search. In: Proceedings of the IEEE International Conference on Computer Vision, pp. 1211–1220 (2019)
32. Rakin, A.S., He, Z., Fan, D.: TBT: targeted neural network attack with bit trojan. In: Proceedings of the IEEE/CVF Conference on Computer Vision and Pattern Recognition, pp. 13198–13207 (2020)
33. Review, A.: Tesla hardware 3 (full self-driving computer) detailed (2019). https://www.autopilotreview.com/tesla-custom-ai-chips-hardware-3/. Accessed 8 Mar 2022
34. Salami, B., et al.: An experimental study of reduced-voltage operation in modern FPGAs for neural network acceleration. In: 2020 50th Annual IEEE/IFIP International Conference on Dependable Systems and Networks (DSN), pp. 138–149. IEEE (2020)
35. Salami, B., Unsal, O.S., Kestelman, A.C.: On the resilience of RTL NN accelerators: fault characterization and mitigation. In: 2018 30th International Symposium on Computer Architecture and High Performance Computing (SBAC-PAD), pp. 322–329. IEEE (2018)
36. Sequin, C.H., Clay, R.: Fault tolerance in artificial neural networks. In: 1990 IJCNN International Joint Conference on Neural Networks, pp. 703–708. IEEE (1990)
37. Shannon, C.E.: Communication theory of secrecy systems. Bell Syst. Tech. J. **28**(4), 656–715 (1949)
38. Tang, A., Sethumadhavan, S., Stolfo, S.: CLKSCREW: exposing the perils of security-oblivious energy management. In: 26th USENIX Security Symposium (USENIX Security 2017), pp. 1057–1074 (2017)
39. Torres-Huitzil, C., Girau, B.: Fault and error tolerance in neural networks: a review. IEEE Access **5**, 17322–17341 (2017)
40. Wei, L., Luo, B., Li, Y., Liu, Y., Xu, Q.: I know what you see: power side-channel attack on convolutional neural network accelerators. In: Proceedings of the 34th Annual Computer Security Applications Conference, pp. 393–406 (2018)
41. Yan, M., Fletcher, C.W., Torrellas, J.: Cache telepathy: leveraging shared resource attacks to learn {DNN} architectures. In: 29th USENIX Security Symposium (USENIX Security 2020), pp. 2003–2020 (2020)
42. Zhang, J., Rangineni, K., Ghodsi, Z., Garg, S.: Thundervolt: enabling aggressive voltage underscaling and timing error resilience for energy efficient deep learning accelerators. In: Proceedings of the 55th Annual Design Automation Conference, pp. 1–6 (2018)
43. Zhao, P., Wang, S., Gongye, C., Wang, Y., Fei, Y., Lin, X.: Fault sneaking attack: a stealthy framework for misleading deep neural networks. In: 2019 56th ACM/IEEE Design Automation Conference (DAC), pp. 1–6. IEEE (2019)

Physically Unclonable Functions and AI
Two Decades of Marriage

Fatemeh Ganji[✉] and Shahin Tajik

Worcester Polytechnic Institute, Worcester, USA
{fganji,stajik}@wpi.edu

*"The design of cryptographic systems must be based
on firm foundations, whereas ad-hoc approaches and
heuristics are a very dangerous way to go."* [34]

Abstract. The current chapter aims at establishing a relationship
between artificial intelligence (AI) and hardware security. Such a connection between AI and software security has been confirmed and well-
reviewed in the relevant literature. The main focus here is to explore the
methods borrowed from AI to assess the security of a hardware primitive,
namely physically unclonable functions (PUFs), which has found applications in cryptographic protocols, e.g., authentication and key generation.
Metrics and procedures devised for this are further discussed. Moreover,
by reviewing PUFs designed by applying AI techniques, we give insight
into future research directions in this area.

1 Introduction

In order to realize a cryptographic protocol or primitive, the assumptions made
during design must hold. These assumptions relate in particular to secure key
storage and secure execution of the protocol/primitive, which have been proven
hard to attain in practice. The notion of root-of-trust has been introduced to deal
with this by providing adequate reasoning in relation to physical security, i.e.,
the guarantee to resist certain physical attack cf. [56]. In this regard, physically
unclonable functions (PUFs) have been identified as a promising solution to
secure key generation and storage issues [29,31].

The key premise of PUFs is that physical characteristics of the system
embodying the PUF can be tailored to derive an instance-specific feature of
that, which is inherent and *unclonable* [56] (see Fig. 1). Among the variants
of PUFs being considered in the literature are the so-called "intrinsic" PUFs,
where the above feature (1) is the result of the production process, and (2) can
be evaluated/measured internally [35]. A prime example of PUF families meeting these criteria is (some types of) silicon PUFs with manufacturing process
variations as the production process. One of the main advantages of these PUFs
is the easy-to-integrate aspect, enabling the direct application of the PUF in
integrated circuits (ICs). This is of great importance for ICs used in not only
every-day applications, but also cryptosystems.

© Springer Nature Switzerland AG 2022
L. Batina et al. (Eds.): Security and Artificial Intelligence, LNCS 13049, pp. 85–106, 2022.
https://doi.org/10.1007/978-3-030-98795-4_5

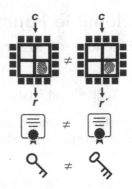

Fig. 1. A conceptual illustration of a PUF: For PUFs, the inevitable effect of manufacturing process variation is reinforced to enable PUF-based authentication systems and key generation. To this end, the PUF is given an input (i.e., a challenge) to generate a (statistically) different output (so-called response) depending on the physical characteristic of the IC embodying the PUF.

In the literature, a great number of research studies have been carried out to evaluate the properties of PUFs; at the heart of them is the unclonability. Obviously, if this property of a PUF is not fulfilled, neither the PUF nor the system encompassing that is secure. This chapter is devoted to the relationship between PUFs and AI, where the latter is used in a natural way to assess not only the security of PUFs, but also design PUFs. Among such approaches, if we focus on machine learning (ML)-enabled ones, the following interesting observation can be made.

For PUFs, as cryptographic primitives, one of the most effective techniques to assess their security lies at the intersection of cryptography and machine learning, namely provable ML algorithms. In addition to exploring the difference between such algorithms and ML algorithms commonly employed in various fields of studies, this chapter describes why provable ML algorithms should be considered when evaluating the security of PUFs. For this purpose, pitfalls in methods adopted to demonstrate the robustness of a PUF against ML attacks are explained. Besides, the metrics that have been defined to assess this are mentioned.

We put emphasis on the point that this chapter serves as neither an introduction to the concept of PUFs, nor their formalization and architectures. For these topics, we refer the reader to the seminal work and surveys published over the past decades, e.g., [2,27,56,57].

2   Background on PUFs

PUFs exploit the process variations and imperfections of metals and transistors in similar chips to provide a device-specific fingerprint. More formally, a PUF is a mathematical mapping generating virtually unique outputs (i.e., responses) to a given set of input bits (i.e., challenges). These responses can be used either to authenticate and identify a specific chip or as cryptographic keys for encryption/decryption. To use a PUF in an authentication scenario, the PUF has to go through the *enrollment* and *verification* phases. In the enrollment phase, the verifier creates a database of challenge-response-pairs (CRPs) for the PUF.

During the verification phase in the field, a set of challenges from the verifier is fed to the PUF, and the generated responses will be compared to the stored responses in the database for verification. In this phase, due to the natural noisy characteristics of PUFs, the verifier must resolve the noisy CRPs, i.e., for a given challenge, the response could be different, when the measurement is repeated (so-called the reliability problem). For this purpose, application of majority voting and *fuzzy extractors* are the prominent examples [12]. The latter is a sub-set of helper data algorithms, performing post-processing to meet key generation requirements: reproducibility, high-entropy, and control. For this purpose, such algorithms generate helper data that can be stored in insecure (off-chip) non-volatile memory (NVM), for instance, or by another party [11]. It is worth mentioning that the helper data is considered public. More importantly, this data inevitably leaks information about the PUF responses, leaving the door open for the cloning of PUFs.

PUF Instantiations. There are several ways to categorize PUFs. One of the most well-known ways to classify them is based on the amount of CRPs that they can provide. PUFs with a small number of CRPs are considered as weak PUFs, and PUFs with an exponential number of CRPs are considered strong PUFs. The most prominent examples of weak PUFs are SRAM PUF, Ring-Oscillator (RO) PUF, and Butterfly PUF. SRAM PUFs [40] exploits the random power-up pattern inside an SRAM to generate a unique fingerprint. Since the inverters inside each SRAM cell (Fig. 2(a)) have mismatches due to process variations, it is predictable at which logical value the cell is settled after power-up. In this case, the challenge to the PUF can be the address of memory cells, and the response is the value stored in each cell. The RO PUF, on the other hand, utilizes the intrinsic differences between frequencies of equal lengths ROs to produce the unique fingerprints. In the case of RO PUF [83], a pair of ROs is selected by a given challenge, and the response is a binary value based on the comparison of the RO frequencies, see Fig. 2(c).

The underlying principles of the strong PUFs are very similar to weak PUFs, i.e., exploiting bistable and delay-based circuits. However, in contrast to weak PUFs, the components of strong PUFs are tailored in a way that results in an exponential number of CRPs. The most prominent strong PUF is the Arbiter PUF family [53], where the intrinsic timing differences of two symmetrically designed paths, chosen by a challenge, are exploited to generate a binary response at the output of the circuit, see Fig. 2(b). It has become clear from the very beginning that the Arbiter PUF is vulnerable to machine learning attacks (see Sect. 3 for more details). Therefore, XOR Arbiter PUFs and other Arbiter-based PUFs have been proposed to mitigate the vulnerability of PUFs to machine learning attacks, see Fig. 2(d). Further research in the area of strong PUFs has

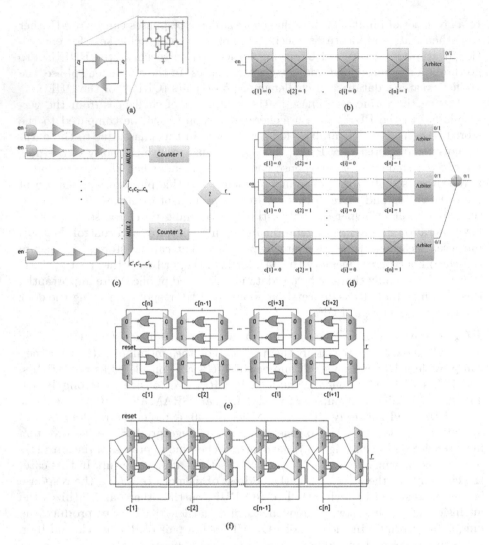

Fig. 2. PUF Architectures. (a) A cell of SRAM PUF along with its CMOS circuit [56]. (b) An Arbiter PUF. (c) A ring oscillator (RO) PUF. (d) An XOR Arbiter PUF with chains of Arbiter PUFs. (e) A bistable PUF (BR). (f) A twisted BR.

led to other strong PUFs constructions, which are inspired by bistable memory cells. The main instances of these classes are bistable-ring (BR) [8] and twisted bistable-stable (TBR) PUFs [81], see Fig. 2(e) and Fig. 2(f).

3   Attacks Against PUFs: Physical vs. Non-physical

In the same vein as other security primitives, designs have been coming hand in hand with attacks. Irrespective of the methods and means, through which an

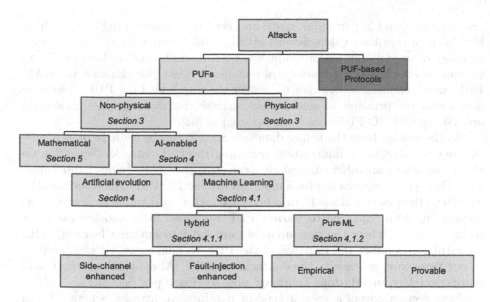

Fig. 3. The taxonomy of attacks launched against PUFs. This chapter mainly focuses on AI-enabled, non-physical attacks; however, some studies on the physical and mathematical analysis of PUFs are briefly discussed. Although attacks against PUF-based protocols are beyond the scope of this chapter, an interesting, AI-enabled example of such attacks is mentioned in Sect. 4.

attack is carried out, the goal of the adversary is to determine how the inputs are mapped to outputs of the PUF, thereby predicting the responses to unseen challenges. As broad as the range of PUF designs, attacks against PUFs have covered the whole spectrum in terms of different levels of destruction that they could cause. At one end of the spectrum, there are physical invasive attacks attempting to clone a PUF physically following a destructive procedure, e.g., through Focused Ion Beam (FIB) circuit edit[1] [38]. While fully-invasive attacks can arbitrarily alter the functionality of the circuit and disable any countermeasures, semi-invasive attacks with a lower level of destruction can be launched to extract the "secret" from the PUF cf. [65]. Here, secret extraction refers to the process of either reading-out the PUF responses [65] or measuring some parameters that can be further analyzed to characterize a PUF [84,85]. The latter is, of course, of greater interest to attackers as such attacks are not limited to memory-based PUFs. Interestingly, a group of semi-invasive attacks may not even damage the underlying PUF structure, see, e.g., [64]. Due to their nature, we categorize the above attacks as "physical attacks," see Fig. 3.

At the other end of the spectrum are physical non-invasive attacks, the adversary can observe/measure some challenge-response behavior-related parameters. The latter case is similar to that of side-channel attacks, widely studied in

---

[1] Note that through this chapter, to classify the attacks, the step taken to *clone* a PUF is considered.

cryptography, and in particular, hardware security. Not surprisingly, PUFs have also been susceptible to side-channel attacks, which is not limited to memory- or delayed-based PUFs. An attempt has been made by the authors of [70] to present an attack taking advantage of remanence decay side-channels in SRAM PUF, which enables the attacker to recover the response of the PUF. Additionally, under the principle of side-channel analysis, an electromagnetic emission analysis against RO PUFs has been reported in [63].

As the leakage from the helper data (see Sect. 2) can be thought of as a side-channel revealing some information regarding the PUF, attacks depending on this vulnerability are other particularly interesting examples of side-channel analysis. This type of attacks has been mounted against RO PUF constructions [15]. Similarly, the power leakage from a fuzzy extractor used to perform error correction has been exploited to recover PUF responses [44]. Another examples include attacks, where the measurements are fed into machine learning (ML) algorithms to predict the response of the PUF to unknown CRPs. Therefore, in our taxonomy, we classify these attacks into the "AI-enabled" category, and more concretely, in "Machine Learning" one, see Fig. 3 (see Sect. 4.1).

Next section covers a special type of non-invasive attacks, where AI - in particular, machine learning (ML) algorithms- enables the attacker to learn the challenge-response behavior of PUFs (see Fig. 3). These attacks either rely on the availability of some physical measurements (see Sect. 4.1) or perform learning solely based on available CRPs (see Sect. 4.1).

4   AI-Enabled Attacks

This class is composed of attacks enhanced by incorporating techniques borrowed from the field of AI. In this regard, the application of ML algorithm has become a prominent subject for research due to their availability and ease of use. Nonetheless, other AI methods could be beneficial, when it comes to the security assessment of PUFs. For PUFs, [72,75] are two of the first studies focusing on this by employing evolution strategies and genetic programming against feed-forward Arbiter PUFs and RO PUFs, respectively. In this context, the security of recently emerging PUF architectures, e.g., non-linear current mirror PUFs [49] has been compromised through genetic algorithms [36].

Further application of such algorithms has been observed in [5], where Becker et al. have applied an optimization technique relying on artificial evolution, in particular, covariance matrix adaptation evolution strategy (CMA-ES). In doing so, it has been shown that the security of an XOR Arbiter PUFs embedded in a real-world radio-frequency identification (RFID) tag can be compromised. Interestingly enough, to launch the attack, the reliability information[2] collected from the PUF, which can be thought of as a "side-channel", has been further exploited. A similar concept has been adopted against Feed-forward Arbiter PUFs and leakage current-based PUFs. However, fault injection has been performed to assist

---

[2] Repetition of the measurement by giving the same challenge results in different responses.

the evolutionary algorithm applied against these PUFs [48, 50]. Regardless of the issues raised about the convergence of the evolutionary strategies, see, e.g., [68], its scalability, and reliance on the side-channels/injected faults, these attacks have attracted a great deal of attention in the hardware security community. For instance, in addition to above-mentioned attacks against PUFs as hardware primitives, [10] has demonstrated that recent Arbiter PUF-based protocols are susceptible to attacks employing the CMA-ES algorithm.

Next, attacks have been explained that apply the concept of *learning* the challenge-response behavior of a PUF through ML algorithms (i.e., a subset of AI).

4.1 Machine Learning Attacks

As explained before, the main goal of the attacker is to mimic the challenge-response behavior of a PUF, preferably at a minimal cost. For this purpose, given the CRPs exchanged between the verifier and the chip, it is natural to think of ML attacks attempting to learn the mechanism underlying the response generation. In the early stages of introducing PUFs it was assumed that such attacks could not be successful [29]; however, soon after conjecturing that PUFs are hard to learn, it has been experimentally verified that learning Arbiter PUFs is indeed possible [31]. This result initiated a line of research, being pursued for almost two decades now and resulted in studies covering various types of ML algorithms applied against a wide variety of PUFs. Among the ML algorithms discussed in the PUF-related literature are empirical and provable techniques, which we briefly review in this section. Before elaborating on *pure* ML attacks, which are not refined by means of side-channels, we focus on hybrid, physical-ML attacks.

Hybrid Attacks. The basic premise, on which these attacks are based, is the presence of physical, measurable quantities that either can enhance the success rate of a ML attack against a PUF or, from another perspective, need to be analyzed through ML. While the latter is being widely studied in other hardware-security domains, e.g., side-channel analysis against cryptosystems, the former has become more popular for PUFs. This has been partially motivated by the existence of PUFs, which have been considered harder to learn. In this context, for XOR Arbiter PUFs, it has been proposed to incorporate the timing and power information as side-channels in order to improve the learning process [74]. Another example of such attacks has been explained in [6], where controlled PUFs composed of an Arbiter PUF and the lightweight block cipher PRESENT has come under power side-channel analysis. The practical feasibility of these attacks has been questioned as accurate timing and power measurements may not be available.

This problem can be overcome by combing the ML and fault injection attacks, although at the cost of being (semi-) invasive in some cases. XOR Arbiter PUFs have been attacked following this observation, where the fault is injected in a semi-invasive manner [86]. Nevertheless, fault injection procedures used to facilitate the learning process can be non-invasive as well; however, the famous examples of such attacks have not employed ML algorithms, but rather evolutionary strategies [6] and mathematical modeling [14] (see Sect. 5).

Pure ML Attacks. Following the way paved by [31] to show the vulnerability of Arbiter PUFs to the Perceptron algorithm, Lim has demonstrated that a support vector machine (SVM) algorithm can also be used to learn the challenge-response behavior of Arbiter PUFs [54]. This line of research has been pursued and has led to exploring the application of two groups of ML algorithms in the context of PUFs, namely empirical and provable ML approaches. The former is widely taken in various domains, including hardware security, whereas the latter has been identified as a "sister field" of the cryptography and linked to complexity theory [71]. A major success factor of the provable techniques, in particular, Valiant's probably approximately correct (PAC) framework, is the link established between the probability of successful learning (so-called, confidence level), the number of training examples and their distribution, the complexity of the model assumed for the unknown function under test, and the accuracy of the learned model [87]. Such relationships cannot be made for empirical ML algorithms, more concretely, (1) the probability of successful learning is not known and cannot be defined prior to the experiments, and (2) the number of training examples cannot be determined beforehand. Moreover, empirical ML algorithms can suffer from a lack of generalizability and reproducibility. While generalization refers to the ability of the model to adapt properly to unseen data, drawn from the same distribution as of that followed to create the model, reproducibility means that an experiment can be repeated to reach the same conclusion.

Although the above challenges are not specific to the security assessment of PUFs, this assessment may become impossible due to the lack of generalizability and reproducibility. To investigate the vulnerability of a PUF with instance-specific features and sensitivity to environmental changes, it is crucial to come up with ML approaches, making standardization and comparison feasible. For these purposes, provable ML algorithms seem promising. Next, a brief overview of empirical and provable attacks against PUFs is provided.

Empirical ML Methods. As mentioned before, along with the development of PUFs have come ML attacks [31]. These attacks have become more critical as Arbiter PUFs, XOR Arbiter PUFs, Lightweight Secure PUFs [60], and RO PUFs have been successfully targeted by applying logistic regression [73]. This work has been followed by numerous studies that aim to assess the security of various PUF families against different empirical ML algorithms. Table 1 summarizes some of these studies by focusing on PUFs and the ML algorithms discussed in those studies.

Table 1. Some of the attacks enabled by empirical ML algorithm, with a focus on PUFs under attack, and models for representing the internal functionality of the respective PUFs.

Ref.	PUF under attack	ML algorithm	Mathematical model
[31]	Arbiter PUFs	Perceptron	Linear combinations of delays
[54]	Arbiter PUFs	Support Vector Machines (SVMs)	Hyperplanes
[73]	Arbiter PUFs, XOR Arbiter PUFs, Lightweight Secure PUFs	Logistic regression	Hyperplanes
[73]	RO PUFs	Quick Sort	NA
[41]	Arbiter and XOR Arbiter PUFs	Artificial Neural Networks and Support Vector Machines	NA
[81]	Bistable Ring (BR) and twisted BR PUFs	Artificial Neural Networks	NA
[91]	BR PUFs	SVM	LTFs
[88]	Non-linear voltage transfer characteristics (VTC)	Tree classifiers and bagging and boosting techniques	NA
[4, 46]	Double Arbiter PUFs [55]	Deep learning	NA
[79]	XOR APUF, Lightweight Secure PUF, Multiplexer PUF and its variants	Deep learning	NA
[90]	Interpose PUF [69]	Logistic regression	Hyperplanes

Remarks: With regard to the attacks listed in Table 1, an interesting observation can be made: except for some of the studies, no model, describing the functionality of the PUF, has been taken into account[3]. Such models are viewed as "data transformation" in empirical ML-related literature. In the absence of these transformations, it is not straightforward to justify why an algorithm should be chosen to perform the learning task.

Note that without such a justification, it is impossible to generalize the results obtained for a given PUF to other instances from that PUF family. This, of course, does not undervalue the importance of research on empirical ML algorithms in the context of PUFs; however, we emphasize that the results achieved through using such algorithms should be interpreted with caution.

Another remark is that some of the PUFs listed in Table 1 were proposed as a remedy for ML attacks, but have been attacked by other algorithms. This raises the question of whether the resistance to ML should be defined as resistance to "known ML attacks", which is answered in Sect. 6. In line with this, another question is what to do to increase the security of PUFs targeted by ML attacks? An illustrative example is the XOR Arbiter PUFs, where adding non-linearity through using the XOR combination function is suggested.

---

[3] Next, we discuss that for some provable techniques, this information is not required.

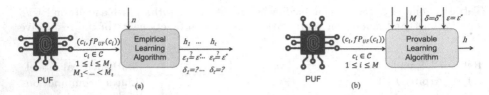

Fig. 4. Schematic illustrating the differences between a provable and an empirical ML algorithm applied in the context of PUFs cf. [18]. For an n-bit PUF, h denotes the model learned by the machine. ε^* is the desired minimum accuracy of h, whereas the acceptable confidence level δ^* is the probability of obtaining the desired model. On the contrary, for empirical ML algorithms, the latter parameter cannot be adjusted: it is not known if the algorithm converges to a model with the desired accuracy. In fact, after each learning phase, e.g., the jth round ($1 \leq j \leq t$), the accuracy of the model ε_j could be less than ε^*. Moreover, for provable ML algorithms, the maximum number of CRPs required for learning (M) can be computed as a function of ε^*, δ^*, which is not the case for empirical ML algorithms.

Nevertheless, to understand the effectiveness of such a countermeasure, it is *not enough* to rely on specific ML algorithms. Moreover, it is important to understand how and why ML algorithms could break the security of a PUF. Next, we discuss this in further detail.

Provable ML Methods. What can be understood from the above discussion is that attacks mounted by applying empirical ML algorithms depend largely on trial-and-error approaches. The importance of this problem becomes apparent as countermeasures designed to defeat them would also render ineffective. Moreover, since security assessment with regard to empirical ML algorithms is instance-, parameter-, and algorithm-dependent with no convergence guarantees, standardization and comparison between PUFs may not be feasible. In response to this, a provable ML framework, namely probably approximately correct (PAC) learning, has found application in studies on PUFs. Figure 4 presents the differences between an empirical algorithm and a provable one. It is worth noting here that ML attacks reported in the literature usually achieve an acceptable level of accuracy (e.g., 95%) regardless of employing an empirical or a provable algorithm. Hence, the main advantage of provable algorithms is not the accuracy of the model learned, but the possibility of defining the level of accuracy and confidence a priori.

PAC learning framework has been employed to launch provable ML attacks against PUFs. Families of PUFs targeted by PAC learning attacks include Arbiter [24], XOR Arbiter [23], RO [22][4], and BR and twisted BR PUFs [20,21]. These results have been extended to the cases where the noisy CRPs are available to learn a PUF [25].

---

[4] Note that although weak PUFs are not interesting targets from the point of view of ML attacks, their characteristics can be analyzed by applying provable methods and the metrics defined based on them cf. [18].

PAC learning of BR and twisted BR PUFs serves as a special example since no mathematical model describing their internal functionality has been known so far; hence, no data transformation, or so-called "representation" could be presented. Regardless of that, characteristics of these PUFs are formulated as Boolean functions, useful to launch the attack. In this case, it has been proven that, in general, the challenge bits have different amounts of influence on the response of a PUF to a given challenge.

Moreover, [21] has reintroduced property testing in the PUF-related literature. Property testing algorithms developed in ML theory examine whether properties of a specific class can be found in a given function, i.e., a PUF under test in our case. In doing so, if no representation is known for a PUF, it is at least possible to understand whether it can be represented by some functions. It could be a necessary step when looking for an appropriate, efficient ML algorithm to learn a PUF. Furthermore, if an incorrect representation is chosen without either knowing the internal functionality of a PUF or performing property tests, it is not possible to decide about the learnability of the PUF [17].

Remarks: We stress that when interpreting the above results, a great deal of attention should be paid to the setting of the PAC learning framework (access granted to the CRPs, distribution of the CRPs given to the machine, etc.) considered in a study. As explained in [17], this setting plays an important role when deciding if a PUF is provably (in)secure (see Sect. 6 for more details).

5 Mathematical Modeling

Mathematical modeling attacks do not fall within the category "AI-enabled" attacks, which is the main focus of this section; however, valuable lessons can be learned from these attacks. In this respect, one of the key messages to convey is that not every attack needs to be conducted with a view to adopting AI. In other words, security assessment of PUFs relying on AI, albeit a useful and important objective, should not be overstated as, in some cases, other mathematical methods can give more insight into the security of PUFs. This has been observed in a recent work of Zeitouni et al. [97], demonstrating that standard interpolation algorithms can be employed to predict the responses of (Rowhammer) DRAM-PUFs [80]. Another instance is the analysis performed in [13] that has not only resulted in a high-accuracy model of the PUF under test, namely Arbiter PUFs, but also linked the reliability of a PUF to CMOS (and interconnect) noise sources and further to the PUF model. As shown for Arbiter, RO and RO sum PUFs, the effectiveness of this attack can be enhanced by injecting fault through changes in environmental conditions [14].

Another example of such attacks concerns the so-called "cryptanalysis" of PUFs, where the adversary mounts computational attacks to predict the response to an unseen challenge with the probability higher than that of a random guess [66,77]. For this purpose, she can use the CRPs to partition the challenge-response space into subsets corresponding to the responses output by the PUF. To evaluate the effect of their attacks, the authors have targeted and successfully broken the security of RO PUFs with enhanced CRPs [59], composite PUFs [78] and the lightweight secure PUF [60], with multi-bit responses.

Within this category, the analysis presented in [92] plays a crucial role in understanding the mechanism of generating responses in BR PUFs. More specifically, by carrying out linear and differential cryptanalysis-inspired attacks, this study has shown that the response of a BR PUF can be determined by a few number of the challenge bits. This work motivates the study of provable techniques to quantify the influence of challenge bits on the responses of PUFs [18,20].

Finally, the attack presented in [19] can be considered, where a lattice basis-reduction method has been applied to XOR Arbiter PUFs with an arbitrarily large number of chains and controlled inputs and outputs, i.e., unknown challenges and responses from the adversary perspective. These methods have been first found in a number of cryptography problems, e.g., hidden subset sum problem (i.e.,a variant of the subset sum problem with the hidden set of summands). The similarity between this problem and controlled XOR Arbiter PUFs can become evident as the side-channel analysis is conducted to measure the accumulated delays at the output of the last stage of the Arbiter PUFs in the XOR Arbiter PUF. It has been demonstrated that this information is sufficient to reveal not only the hidden challenges and responses, but also model the PUF.

Remarks: Perhaps, the most important message of this section is that the failure of AI-enabled attacks per se should not be considered as a guarantee for the security of PUFs. As explained above, PUFs that are robust to some AI-enabled attacks, e.g., XOR Arbiter PUFs with a large number of chains, can be vulnerable to other families of attacks. These attacks can, of course, improve designers' understanding of mechanisms underlying the challenge-response behavior of PUFs, and consequently, results in developing more attack-resilient PUFs.

6   Resiliency Against ML Attacks

The attacks discussed in the previous section have posed serious challenges for the PUF designers and manufacturers. To tackle this issue, various countermeasures have been introduced in the literature, including controlled PUFs [62,95], re-configurable PUFs [62], PUFs with noise-induced CRPs [89,93,96], to name a few. "Controlled PUFs" is the umbrella term given to PUFs, where the adversary has restricted access to the CRPs through either obfuscating the challenges/responses [28,30] or mechanisms used to feed the challenges/collect the responses [16,45,52,52,62,94,95]. When it comes to re-configurability, PUFs with a mechanism to update the architecture of a PUF are devised [32,33,51,76].

When reviewing the papers mentioned above and in this section in general, it becomes evident that virtually all of the PUFs proposed in the literature have been designed having ML attacks in mind. This seems, however, paradoxical as attacks against PUFs, supposed to be ML attack-resilient, are being reported, see, e.g., [10,90]. The reason behind this can be the lack of (1) procedures to *prove* that the PUF exhibits this feature, and (2) metrics to assess whether a PUF is robust against ML attacks.

6.1 How to Prove the Security of a PUF Against ML Attacks

Proving the security of cryptographic primitives has been practiced for decades. For that, the security of the system must be defined, which is typically carried out through the definition of an adversary model and a security game. The former determines the power of the adversary in terms of, e.g., being uniform/non-uniform, interactive/non-interactive, etc. Adversary models also describe how the attacker interacts with the security game. This game further gives insight into the power of the adversary over the cryptosystem, i.e., her access to the systems and the conditions for considering an attack successful.

Definition of security from the perspective of information theory (e.g., "perfect secrecy") and computational complexity have been employed to argue about the security of cryptosystems. This is natural as an adversary (a.k.a., "codebreaker") has bounded computational resources. Consequently, designers attempt to make the codebreaking problem computationally difficult to ensure security. This definition of security in cryptography has been linked to machine theory in a seminal work of Rivest in 1991 [71]. Rivest observed the reliance of cryptography and machine learning on computational complexity, and further identified the similarities and differences between these two fields of study, including attack types and the queries required by an ML algorithm, exact versus approximate inference of an unknown target, etc.

To assess the security of a scheme against a learning algorithm, i.e., the adversary, the ML setting is specified in the PAC learning framework. In this regard, one can define a set of parameters including the number of examples given to the algorithm, the distribution from that they are drawn (if needed), a representative model of the target function (if any), and the accuracy of the approximation. Afterward, if *any* polynomial algorithm can learn the target function describing the cryptosystem, the security of the system is compromised. For PUFs, as cryptographic primitives, the same procedure can be followed; however, approaches proposed in the PUF-related literature have not pursued this.

In particular, it is common that the robustness of a newly designed PUF against ML attacks is evaluated by applying a couple of ML algorithms against the PUF. This is indeed not sufficient to claim that the PUF is robust against ML attacks in general. In the best case, if the experiment is repeated for numerous instances of a PUF to make the results statistically relevant, one can claim that the PUF is resilient to the specific ML algorithm applied in the experiment.

In contrast to such an ad-hoc process, the security of PUFs in the face of ML attacks have been analyzed rigorously in [26,37,39,95]. Specifically, [26] has dealt with this from the point of view of PAC learning and computational complexity. The security of a PUF proposed in [95] has been based upon a result previously obtained with regard to the PAC learning framework [23]. Herder et al. [39] have also designed their PUF on the basis of a reduction to a problem known to be hard to learn, namely learning parities with noise.

We sum up by quoting from Shannon's work that has argued against imprecise proof of security.

"In designing a good cipher [...] it is not enough merely to be sure none of the standard methods of cryptanalysis work- we must be sure that no method whatever will break the system easily. This, in fact, has been the weakness of many systems. [...] The problem of good cipher design is essentially one of finding difficult problems, subject to certain other conditions" [82] (see also [3]).

6.2 Metrics for Evaluating the Security of a PUF Against ML Attacks

In order to verify the robustness of a PUF against ML attacks in practice, a set of metrics should be provided that is well suited to various ML attacks. This task has been already accomplished for the purpose of verification that a PUF exhibits features relating to the quality. In this regard, a comprehensive set of metrics has been developed, which comprises cost, reliability, and security [43,47,58]. Nevertheless, metrics associated with the ML attacks have not been well studied in the literature. In the following paragraphs, some of such metrics proposed in the literature are discussed.

Entropy: One of the first attempts to define a metric indicating the ML attack-resiliency has been made in [61,62]. The authors have used entropy to quantify the unclonability, i.e., being resistant to reverse engineering and modeling (i.e., mainly non-physical attacks). Entropy of the PUF responses can be estimated by the uniqueness, or measured by inter-distance [47]. In more concrete terms, unclonability due to the ML attacks is translated to statistical prediction and measured by the Hamming distance between two challenges [61].

Strict Avalanche Criterion (SAC): It has been suggested that unpredictability can be achieved if the SAC property is satisfied: by flipping a bit in the challenge, each of the output bits flips with a probability of one half [62]. This has been further improved in [67], where the authors have shown that the distance between two challenges considered for computing the metric plays an important role.

Bias: In addition to the above metrics, it is obvious that the bias in the PUF responses can be beneficial to launch mathematical, in particular, machine learning attacks.

Noise Sensitivity: The study in [67] has presented a prime example illustrating the lack of firm foundations for evaluating of resiliency of PUFs to ML attacks. To address this issue, as provable ML methods applied against PUFs have become established, new metrics originating from Boolean and Fourier analyses have been introduced [18]. The notion of noise sensitivity is closely-related to the SAC property: the probability of flipping the output bit, when filliping each bit of the challenge with a pre-defined probability. It has been proved that the smaller and bounded the noise sensitivity is, the higher the probability of learning the PUF would be. More importantly, the algorithms for testing PUFs in terms of this metric have been made available cf. [18].

Expected Bias: Recent developments in the design and verification of PUFs with reliance on computational complexity result in adding a new metric to the list of formally-defined metrics: the expected bias [26]. The notion of the expected bias encompasses the average bias of a PUF in the presence of the noise, inherent to the design of the PUF due to, e.g., the effect of the routing, and/or having not sufficient deviation in the manufacturing process variations. These phenomena not only affect the responses of a PUF, but also induce correlation between two instances of a PUF implemented on a platform. Hence, the expected bias is a suitable measure to assess the security of PUFs, even ones composed of some PUF instances, e.g., XOR PUFs.

7 AI-Enabled Design of PUFs

Up until this point, we have focused on the interplay between the AI and PUFs from one point of view: applying ML to assess the security of PUFs. From another perspective, it is interesting to explore how AI can be employed to design PUFs. In the same way that ML-enabled attacks have been classified, this type of PUF design can be categorized into empirical and provable methods. In the first category, a PUF proposed in [1] can be considered, where weightless neural networks (WNNs) have been adopted to transform the challenges in the sense of controlled PUF. Another interesting example of such PUFs has been proposed in [9], where a weak PUF relying on the concept of asynchronous reset (ARES) behavior is designed. For this, a genetic algorithm has been employed with a fitness function defined based on the physical parameters of the transistors involved in the PUF circuit. In their scenario, the genetic algorithm automatically outputs an optimal PUF design for a given load.

On the other hand, in the second category, methods have been established that rely on the impossibility of learning specific functions. These impossibility results have been usually formulated in the PAC learning framework. Note that the impossibility taken into account here is not due to the setting chosen for the problem, e.g., representation, but the problem is inherently hard to learn. For instance, Herder et al. [39] have proposed a PUF relying on the hardness of learning parity with noise (LPN) problem. This problem remains open in computational learning theory, although it seems that the LPN problem is not as hard as NP-Hard problems [42].

Hammouri et al. [37] have presented one of the first studies on the application of PAC learning in the design of PUFs. For this, through reductions to problems that are known to be hard to learn, a proof of security has been suggested. This work has been followed by [95], where the design of the PUF is based upon a hardness problem proved for XOR Arbiter PUFs [23]. The study presented in [26] has demonstrated that a family of functions, known to be hard-to-predict (i.e., Tribes function) can be applied to amplify the hardness of somewhat hard PUFs. Their proof of security against ML attacks relies on the unpredictability of the proposed PUF, composed of PUFs with lower levels of unpredictability.

Interestingly, by adopting the concepts introduced in the context of PAC-learnability of PUFs, it has been shown that one could go one step further by devising an automated CAD framework to design a PUF, which can be provably ML attack-resilience [7].

Future Directions: Finally, we stress that compared to techniques originating in ML and used to attack PUF, not much effort has been invested in this topic. We expect that lessons learned from the AI-enabled attacks, and in particular, ML-based ones, become a tool for designing PUFs.

8   Conclusion

This chapter attempts to demonstrate how AI can offer the potential for verifying that security-related features of a PUF are met. In this regard, the application of AI is not limited to processing the data to, e.g., classify the seen input-output pairs of a PUF and predict the output associated with an unknown input (i.e., mounting an ML attack). On the contrary, when shifting our focus to a provable ML framework, it is possible to come up with security proofs in the sense of cryptography. This has been explained in detail in this chapter, along with countermeasures, developed to protect PUFs against ML attacks. Moreover, metrics and approaches to quantify the robustness of a PUF to such attacks have been described. Last but not least, a new line of research devoted to the design of PUFs through ML techniques is discussed.

Acknowledgements. We are deeply grateful for the guidance and support of our Ph.D. advisor, Jean-Pierre Seifert. Throughout our Ph.D. studies at the Technical University of Berlin, and after that, his insightful comments and advice have helped us to broaden our knowledge and expand our horizons. We are also very thankful to Domenic Forte for his guidance, tremendous support during our stay at the University of Florida, and encouragement, in particular, to make the tools (PUFmeter) publicly available.

References

1. de Araújo, L.S., et al.: Design of robust, high-entropy strong PUFs via weightless neural network. J. Hardw. Syst. Secur. **3**(3), 235–249 (2019). https://doi.org/10.1007/s41635-019-00071-z
2. Armknecht, F., Maes, R., Sadeghi, A.R., Standaert, F.X., Wachsmann, C.: A formalization of the security features of physical functions. In: 2011 IEEE Symposium on Security and Privacy, pp. 397–412. IEEE (2011)
3. Arora, S., Barak, B.: Computational Complexity: A Modern Approach. Cambridge University Press, Cambridge (2009)
4. Awano, H., Iizuka, T., Ikeda, M.: PUFNet: a deep neural network based modeling attack for physically unclonable function. In: 2019 IEEE International Symposium on Circuits and Systems (ISCAS), pp. 1–4. IEEE (2019)
5. Becker, G.T.: The gap between promise and reality: on the insecurity of XOR arbiter PUFs. In: Güneysu, T., Handschuh, H. (eds.) CHES 2015. LNCS, vol. 9293, pp. 535–555. Springer, Heidelberg (2015). https://doi.org/10.1007/978-3-662-48324-4_27

6. Becker, G.T., Kumar, R., et al.: Active and passive side-channel attacks on delay based PUF designs. IACR Cryptology ePrint Archive 2014, 287 (2014)
7. Chatterjee, D., Mukhopadhyay, D., Hazra, A.: PUF-G: a CAD framework for automated assessment of provable learnability from formal PUF representations. In: Proceedings of the 39th International Conference on Computer-Aided Design, pp. 1–9 (2020)
8. Chen, Q., Csaba, G., Lugli, P., Schlichtmann, U., Rührmair, U.: The bistable ring PUF: a new architecture for strong physical unclonable functions. In: 2011 IEEE International Symposium on Hardware-Oriented Security and Trust, pp. 134–141. IEEE (2011)
9. Chowdhury, S., et al.: A weak asynchronous RESet (ARES) PUF using start-up characteristics of null conventional logic gates. In: IEEE International Test Conference (ITC). IEEE (2020)
10. Delvaux, J.: Machine-learning attacks on PolyPUFs, OB-PUFs, RPUFs, LHS-PUFs, and PUF-FSMs. IEEE Trans. Inf. Forensics Secur. 14(8), 2043–2058 (2019)
11. Delvaux, J., Gu, D., Schellekens, D., Verbauwhede, I.: Helper data algorithms for PUF-based key generation: overview and analysis. IEEE Trans. Comput. Aided Des. Integr. Circuits Syst. 34(6), 889–902 (2014)
12. Delvaux, J., Gu, D., Verbauwhede, I., Hiller, M., Yu, M.-D.M.: Efficient fuzzy extraction of PUF-induced secrets: theory and applications. In: Gierlichs, B., Poschmann, A.Y. (eds.) CHES 2016. LNCS, vol. 9813, pp. 412–431. Springer, Heidelberg (2016). https://doi.org/10.1007/978-3-662-53140-2_20
13. Delvaux, J., Verbauwhede, I.: Side channel modeling attacks on 65nm arbiter PUFs exploiting CMOS device noise. In: 2013 IEEE International Symposium on Hardware-Oriented Security and Trust (HOST), pp. 137–142. IEEE (2013)
14. Delvaux, J., Verbauwhede, I.: Fault injection modeling attacks on 65 nm arbiter and RO sum PUFs via environmental changes. IEEE Trans. Circuits Syst. I Regul. Pap. 61(6), 1701–1713 (2014)
15. Delvaux, J., Verbauwhede, I.: Key-recovery attacks on various RO PUF constructions via helper data manipulation. In: 2014 Design, Automation & Test in Europe Conference & Exhibition (DATE), pp. 1–6. IEEE (2014)
16. Dubrova, E., Näslund, O., Degen, B., Gawell, A., Yu, Y.: CRC-PUF: a machine learning attack resistant lightweight PUF construction. In: 2019 IEEE European Symposium on Security and Privacy Workshops (EuroS&PW), pp. 264–271. IEEE (2019)
17. Ganji, F., Amir, S., Tajik, S., Forte, D., Seifert, J.P.: Pitfalls in machine learning-based adversary modeling for hardware systems. In: 2020 Design, Automation & Test in Europe Conference & Exhibition (DATE), pp. 514–519. IEEE (2020)
18. Ganji, F., Forte, D., Seifert, J.P.: PUFmeter a property testing tool for assessing the robustness of physically unclonable functions to machine learning attacks. IEEE Access 7, 122513–122521 (2019)
19. Ganji, F., Krämer, J., Seifert, J.P., Tajik, S.: Lattice basis reduction attack against physically unclonable functions. In: Proceedings of the 22nd ACM SIGSAC Conference on Computer and Communications Security, pp. 1070–1080 (2015)
20. Ganji, F., Tajik, S., Fäßler, F., Seifert, J.-P.: Strong machine learning attack against PUFs with no mathematical model. In: Gierlichs, B., Poschmann, A.Y. (eds.) CHES 2016. LNCS, vol. 9813, pp. 391–411. Springer, Heidelberg (2016). https://doi.org/10.1007/978-3-662-53140-2_19
21. Ganji, F., Tajik, S., Fäßler, F., Seifert, J.-P.: Having no mathematical model may not secure PUFs. J. Cryptogr. Eng. 7(2), 113–128 (2017). https://doi.org/10.1007/s13389-017-0159-4

22. Ganji, F., Tajik, S., Seifert, J.-P.: Let me prove it to you: RO PUFs are provably learnable. In: Kwon, S., Yun, A. (eds.) ICISC 2015. LNCS, vol. 9558, pp. 345–358. Springer, Cham (2016). https://doi.org/10.1007/978-3-319-30840-1_22

23. Ganji, F., Tajik, S., Seifert, J.-P.: Why attackers win: on the learnability of XOR arbiter PUFs. In: Conti, M., Schunter, M., Askoxylakis, I. (eds.) Trust 2015. LNCS, vol. 9229, pp. 22–39. Springer, Cham (2015). https://doi.org/10.1007/978-3-319-22846-4_2

24. Ganji, F., Tajik, S., Seifert, J.P.: Pac learning of arbiter PUFs. J. Cryptogr. Eng. **6**(3), 249–258 (2016)

25. Ganji, F., Tajik, S., Seifert, J.-P.: A Fourier analysis based attack against physically unclonable functions. In: Meiklejohn, S., Sako, K. (eds.) FC 2018. LNCS, vol. 10957, pp. 310–328. Springer, Heidelberg (2018). https://doi.org/10.1007/978-3-662-58387-6_17

26. Ganji, F., Tajik, S., Stauss, P., Seifert, J.-P., Tehranipoor, M., Forte, D.: Rock'n'roll PUFs: crafting provably secure pufs from less secure ones (extended version). J. Cryptogr. Eng. **11**(2), 105–118 (2020). https://doi.org/10.1007/s13389-020-00226-7

27. Gao, Y., Al-Sarawi, S.F., Abbott, D.: Physical unclonable functions. Nat. Electron. **3**(2), 81–91 (2020)

28. Gassend, B., Clarke, D., Van Dijk, M., Devadas, S.: Controlled physical random functions. In: Proceedings of 18th Annual Computer Security Applications Conference, pp. 149–160 (2002)

29. Gassend, B., Clarke, D., Van Dijk, M., Devadas, S.: Silicon physical random functions. In: Proceedings of the 9th ACM Conference on Computer and Communications Security, pp. 148–160 (2002)

30. Gassend, B., Dijk, M.V., Clarke, D., Torlak, E., Devadas, S., Tuyls, P.: Controlled physical random functions and applications. ACM Trans. Inf. Syst. Secur. (TISSEC) **10**(4), 1–22 (2008)

31. Gassend, B., Lim, D., Clarke, D., Van Dijk, M., Devadas, S.: Identification and authentication of integrated circuits. Concurr. Comput. Pract. Exp. **16**(11), 1077–1098 (2004)

32. Gehrer, S., Sigl, G.: Reconfigurable PUFs for FPGA-based SoCs. In: 2014 International Symposium on Integrated Circuits (ISIC), pp. 140–143. IEEE (2014)

33. Gehrer, S., Sigl, G.: Using the reconfigurability of modern FPGAs for highly efficient PUF-based key generation. In: 2015 10th International Symposium on Reconfigurable Communication-centric Systems-on-Chip (ReCoSoC), pp. 1–6. IEEE (2015)

34. Goldreich, O.: Foundations of Cryptography: Volume 1, Basic Tools. Cambridge University Press, Cambridge (2007)

35. Guajardo, J., Kumar, S.S., Schrijen, G.-J., Tuyls, P.: FPGA intrinsic PUFs and their use for IP protection. In: Paillier, P., Verbauwhede, I. (eds.) CHES 2007. LNCS, vol. 4727, pp. 63–80. Springer, Heidelberg (2007). https://doi.org/10.1007/978-3-540-74735-2_5

36. Guo, Q., Ye, J., Gong, Y., Hu, Y., Li, X.: Efficient attack on non-linear current mirror PUF with genetic algorithm. In: 2016 IEEE 25th Asian Test Symposium (ATS), pp. 49–54. IEEE (2016)

37. Hammouri, G., Öztürk, E., Sunar, B.: A tamper-proof and lightweight authentication scheme. Pervasive Mob. Comput. **4**(6), 807–818 (2008)

38. Helfmeier, C., Boit, C., Nedospasov, D., Seifert, J.P.: Cloning physically unclonable functions. In: 2013 IEEE International Symposium on Hardware-Oriented Security and Trust (HOST), pp. 1–6. IEEE (2013)

39. Herder, C., Ren, L., Van Dijk, M., Yu, M.D., Devadas, S.: Trapdoor computational fuzzy extractors and stateless cryptographically-secure physical unclonable functions. IEEE Trans. Dependable Secure Comput. **14**(1), 65–82 (2016)

40. Holcomb, D.E., Burleson, W.P., Fu, K.: Power-up SRAM state as an identifying fingerprint and source of true random numbers. IEEE Trans. Comput. **58**(9), 1198–1210 (2008)

41. Hospodar, G., Maes, R., Verbauwhede, I.: Machine learning attacks on 65nm arbiter PUFs: accurate modeling poses strict bounds on usability. In: 2012 IEEE International Workshop on Information Forensics and Security (WIFS), pp. 37–42. IEEE (2012)

42. Kalai, A.T., Mansour, Y., Verbin, E.: On agnostic boosting and parity learning. In: Proceedings of the Fortieth Annual ACM Symposium on Theory of Computing, pp. 629–638 (2008)

43. Kang, H., Hori, Y., Satoh, A.: Performance evaluation of the first commercial PUF-embedded RFID. In: Global Conference on Consumer Electronics, pp. 5–8. IEEE (2012)

44. Karakoyunlu, D., Sunar, B.: Differential template attacks on PUF enabled cryptographic devices. In: 2010 IEEE International Workshop on Information Forensics and Security, pp. 1–6. IEEE (2010)

45. Katzenbeisser, S., Kocabaş, Ü., Van Der Leest, V., Sadeghi, A.R., Schrijen, G.J., Wachsmann, C.: Recyclable PUFs: logically reconfigurable PUFs. J. Cryptogr. Eng. **1**(3), 177 (2011)

46. Khalafalla, M., Gebotys, C.: PUFs deep attacks: enhanced modeling attacks using deep learning techniques to break the security of double arbiter PUFs. In: 2019 Design, Automation & Test in Europe Conference & Exhibition (DATE), pp. 204–209. IEEE (2019)

47. Kim, I., Maiti, A., Nazhandali, L., Schaumont, P., Vivekraja, V., Zhang, H.: From statistics to circuits: foundations for future physical unclonable functions. In: Sadeghi, A.R., Naccache, D. (eds.) Towards Hardware-Intrinsic Security. Information Security and Cryptography, pp. 55–78. Springer, Heidelberg (2010). https://doi.org/10.1007/978-3-642-14452-3_3

48. Kumar, R., Burleson, W.: Hybrid modeling attacks on current-based PUFs. In: 2014 IEEE 32nd International Conference on Computer Design (ICCD), pp. 493–496. IEEE (2014)

49. Kumar, R., Burleson, W.: On design of a highly secure PUF based on non-linear current mirrors. In: 2014 IEEE International Symposium on Hardware-Oriented Security and Trust (HOST), pp. 38–43. IEEE (2014)

50. Kumar, Raghavan, Burleson, Wayne: Side-channel assisted modeling attacks on feed-forward arbiter PUFs using silicon data. In: Mangard, Stefan, Schaumont, Patrick (eds.) RFIDSec 2015. LNCS, vol. 9440, pp. 53–67. Springer, Cham (2015). https://doi.org/10.1007/978-3-319-24837-0_4

51. Kursawe, K., Sadeghi, A.R., Schellekens, D., Skoric, B., Tuyls, P.: Reconfigurable physical unclonable functions-enabling technology for tamper-resistant storage. In: 2009 IEEE International Workshop on Hardware-Oriented Security and Trust, pp. 22–29. IEEE (2009)

52. Lao, Y., Parhi, K.K.: Novel reconfigurable silicon physical unclonable functions. In: Proceedings of Workshop on Foundations of Dependable and Secure Cyber-Physical Systems (FDSCPS), pp. 30–36 (2011)

53. Lee, J.W., Lim, D., Gassend, B., Suh, G.E., Van Dijk, M., Devadas, S.: A technique to build a secret key in integrated circuits for identification and authentication applications. In: 2004 Symposium on VLSI Circuits. Digest of Technical Papers (IEEE Cat. No. 04CH37525), pp. 176–179. IEEE (2004)

54. Lim, D.: Extracting secret keys from integrated circuits. Ph.D. thesis, Massachusetts Institute of Technology (2004)

55. Machida, T., Yamamoto, D., Iwamoto, M., Sakiyama, K.: A new mode of operation for arbiter PUF to improve uniqueness on FPGA. In: 2014 Federated Conference on Computer Science and Information Systems, pp. 871–878. IEEE (2014)

56. Maes, R.: Physically Unclonable Functions: Constructions, Properties and Applications. Springer, Heidelberg (2013). https://doi.org/10.1007/978-3-642-41395-7

57. Maes, R., Verbauwhede, I.: Physically unclonable functions: a study on the state of the art and future research directions. In: Sadeghi, A.R., Naccache, D. (eds.) Towards Hardware-Intrinsic Security. Information Security and Cryptography, pp. 3–37. Springer, Heidelberg (2010). https://doi.org/10.1007/978-3-642-14452-3_1

58. Maiti, A., Gunreddy, V., Schaumont, P.: A systematic method to evaluate and compare the performance of physical unclonable functions. In: Athanas, P., Pnevmatikatos, D., Sklavos, N. (eds.) Embedded Systems Design with FPGAs, pp. 245–267. Springer, Heidelberg (2013). https://doi.org/10.1007/978-1-4614-1362-2_11

59. Maiti, A., Kim, I., Schaumont, P.: A robust physical unclonable function with enhanced challenge-response set. IEEE Trans. Inf. Forensics Secur. 7(1), 333–345 (2011)

60. Majzoobi, M., Koushanfar, F., Potkonjak, M.: Lightweight secure PUFs. In: 2008 IEEE/ACM International Conference on Computer-Aided Design, pp. 670–673. IEEE (2008)

61. Majzoobi, M., Koushanfar, F., Potkonjak, M.: Testing techniques for hardware security. In: 2008 IEEE International Test Conference, pp. 1–10. IEEE (2008)

62. Majzoobi, M., Koushanfar, F., Potkonjak, M.: Techniques for design and implementation of secure reconfigurable PUFs. ACM Trans. Reconfigurable Technol. Syst. (TRETS) 2, 1–33 (2009)

63. Merli, D., Heyszl, J., Heinz, B., Schuster, D., Stumpf, F., Sigl, G.: Localized electromagnetic analysis of RO PUFs. In: 2013 IEEE International Symposium on Hardware-Oriented Security and Trust (HOST), pp. 19–24. IEEE (2013)

64. Merli, D., Schuster, D., Stumpf, F., Sigl, G.: Semi-invasive EM attack on FPGA RO PUFs and countermeasures. In: Proceedings of the Workshop on Embedded Systems Security, pp. 1–9 (2011)

65. Nedospasov, D., Seifert, J.P., Helfmeier, C., Boit, C.: Invasive PUF analysis. In: 2013 Workshop on Fault Diagnosis and Tolerance in Cryptography, pp. 30–38. IEEE (2013)

66. Nguyen, P.H., Sahoo, D.P., Chakraborty, R.S., Mukhopadhyay, D.: Efficient attacks on robust ring oscillator PUF with enhanced challenge-response set. In: Proceedings of Design, Automation & Test in Europe Conference & Exhibition, pp. 641–646. EDA Consortium (2015)

67. Nguyen, P.H., Sahoo, D.P., Chakraborty, R.S., Mukhopadhyay, D.: Security analysis of arbiter PUF and its lightweight compositions under predictability test. ACM Trans. Design Autom. Electron. Syst. (TODAES) 22(2), 1–28 (2016)

68. Nguyen, P.H., Sahoo, D.P., Jin, C., Mahmood, K., van Dijk, M.: MXPUF: secure PUF design against state-of-the-art modeling attacks. IACR Cryptology ePrint Archive 2017, 572 (2017)

69. Nguyen, P.H., Sahoo, D.P., Jin, C., Mahmood, K., Rührmair, U., van Dijk, M.: The interpose PUF: Secure PUF design against state-of-the-art machine learning attacks. IACR Transactions on Cryptographic Hardware and Embedded Systems, pp. 243–290 (2019)
70. Oren, Y., Sadeghi, A.-R., Wachsmann, C.: On the effectiveness of the remanence decay side-channel to clone memory-based PUFs. In: Bertoni, G., Coron, J.-S. (eds.) CHES 2013. LNCS, vol. 8086, pp. 107–125. Springer, Heidelberg (2013). https://doi.org/10.1007/978-3-642-40349-1_7
71. Rivest, R.L.: Cryptography and machine learning. In: Imai, H., Rivest, R.L., Matsumoto, T. (eds.) ASIACRYPT 1991. LNCS, vol. 739, pp. 427–439. Springer, Heidelberg (1993). https://doi.org/10.1007/3-540-57332-1_36
72. Rührmair, U., Sehnke, F., Sölter, J., Dror, G., Devadas, S., Schmidhuber, J.: Modeling attacks on physical unclonable functions. In: Proceedings of the 17th ACM Conference on Computer and Communications Security, pp. 237–249. ACM (2010)
73. Rührmair, U., Sehnke, F., Sölter, J., Dror, G., Devadas, S., Schmidhuber, J.: Modeling attacks on physical unclonable functions. In: Proceedings of the 17th ACM Conference on Computer and Communications Security, pp. 237–249 (2010)
74. Rührmair, U., et al.: Efficient power and timing side channels for physical unclonable functions. In: Batina, L., Robshaw, M. (eds.) CHES 2014. LNCS, vol. 8731, pp. 476–492. Springer, Heidelberg (2014). https://doi.org/10.1007/978-3-662-44709-3_26
75. Saha, I., Jeldi, R.R., Chakraborty, R.S.: Model building attacks on physically unclonable functions using genetic programming. In: 2013 IEEE International Symposium on Hardware-Oriented Security and Trust (HOST), pp. 41–44. IEEE (2013)
76. Sahoo, D.P., Mukhopadhyay, D., Chakraborty, R.S., Nguyen, P.H.: A multiplexer-based arbiter PUF composition with enhanced reliability and security. IEEE Trans. Comput. 67(3), 403–417 (2017)
77. Sahoo, D.P., Nguyen, P.H., Mukhopadhyay, D., Chakraborty, R.S.: A case of lightweight PUF constructions: cryptanalysis and machine learning attacks. IEEE Trans. Comput. Aided Des. Integr. Circuits Syst. 34(8), 1334–1343 (2015)
78. Sahoo, D.P., Saha, S., Mukhopadhyay, D., Chakraborty, R.S., Kapoor, H.: Composite PUF: a new design paradigm for physically unclonable functions on FPGA. In: 2014 IEEE International Symposium on Hardware-Oriented Security and Trust (HOST), pp. 50–55. IEEE (2014)
79. Santikellur, P., Bhattacharyay, A., Chakraborty, R.S.: Deep learning based model building attacks on arbiter PUF compositions. Cryptology ePrint Archive, Report 2019/566 (2019)
80. Schaller, A., et al.: Intrinsic rowhammer PUFs: leveraging the rowhammer effect for improved security. In: 2017 IEEE International Symposium on Hardware Oriented Security and Trust (HOST), pp. 1–7. IEEE (2017)
81. Schuster, D., Hesselbarth, R.: Evaluation of bistable ring PUFs using single layer neural networks. In: Holz, T., Ioannidis, S. (eds.) Trust 2014. LNCS, vol. 8564, pp. 101–109. Springer, Cham (2014). https://doi.org/10.1007/978-3-319-08593-7_7
82. Shannon, C.E.: Communication theory of secrecy systems. Bell Syst. Tech. J. 28(4), 656–715 (1949)
83. Suh, G.E., Devadas, S.: Physical unclonable functions for device authentication and secret key generation. In: 2007 44th ACM/IEEE Design Automation Conference, pp. 9–14. IEEE (2007)
84. Tajik, S., et al.: Photonic side-channel analysis of arbiter PUFs. J. Cryptol. 30(2), 550–571 (2017). https://doi.org/10.1007/s00145-016-9228-6

85. Tajik, S., et al.: Physical characterization of arbiter PUFs. In: Batina, L., Robshaw, M. (eds.) CHES 2014. LNCS, vol. 8731, pp. 493–509. Springer, Heidelberg (2014). https://doi.org/10.1007/978-3-662-44709-3_27

86. Tajik, S., Lohrke, H., Ganji, F., Seifert, J.P., Boit, C.: Laser fault attack on physically unclonable functions. In: 2015 Workshop on Fault Diagnosis and Tolerance in Cryptography (FDTC), pp. 85–96 (2015)

87. Valiant, L.G.: A theory of the learnable. Commun. ACM **27**(11), 1134–1142 (1984)

88. Vijayakumar, A., Patil, V.C., Prado, C.B., Kundu, S.: Machine learning resistant strong PUF: Possible or a pipe dream? In: International Symposium on Hardware Oriented Security and Trust (HOST), pp. 19–24. IEEE (2016)

89. Wang, S.J., Chen, Y.S., Li, K.S.M.: Adversarial attack against modeling attack on PUFs. In: 2019 56th ACM/IEEE Design Automation Conference (DAC), pp. 1–6. IEEE (2019)

90. Wisiol, N., et al.: Splitting the interpose PUF: a novel modeling attack strategy. IACR Transactions on Cryptographic Hardware and Embedded Systems, pp. 97–120 (2020)

91. Xu, X., Rührmair, U., Holcomb, D.E., Burleson, W.: Security evaluation and enhancement of bistable ring PUFs. In: Mangard, S., Schaumont, P. (eds.) RFIDSec 2015. LNCS, vol. 9440, pp. 3–16. Springer, Cham (2015). https://doi.org/10.1007/978-3-319-24837-0_1

92. Yamamoto, D., Takenaka, M., Sakiyama, K., Torii, N.: Security evaluation of bistable ring PUFs on FPGAs using differential and linear analysis. In: 2014 Federated Conference on Computer Science and Information Systems (FedCSIS), pp. 911–918 (2014)

93. Yashiro, R., Hori, Y., Katashita, T., Sakiyama, K.: A deep learning attack countermeasure with intentional noise for a PUF-based authentication scheme. In: Simion, E., Géraud-Stewart, R. (eds.) SecITC 2019. LNCS, vol. 12001, pp. 78–94. Springer, Cham (2020). https://doi.org/10.1007/978-3-030-41025-4_6

94. Ye, J., Hu, Y., Li, X.: RPUF: physical unclonable function with randomized challenge to resist modeling attack. In: 2016 IEEE Asian Hardware-Oriented Security and Trust (AsianHOST), pp. 1–6. IEEE (2016)

95. Yu, M.D.M., Hiller, M., Delvaux, J., Sowell, R., Devadas, S., Verbauwhede, I.: A lockdown technique to prevent machine learning on PUFs for lightweight authentication. IEEE Trans. Multi-Scale Comput. Syst. **2**(3), 146–159 (2016)

96. Yu, M.D.M., Verbauwhede, I., Devadas, S., M'Raihi, D.: A noise bifurcation architecture for linear additive physical functions. In: 2014 IEEE International Symposium on Hardware-Oriented Security and Trust (HOST), pp. 124–129 (2014)

97. Zeitouni, S., Gens, D., Sadeghi, A.R.: It's hammer time: how to attack (rowhammer-based) DRAM-PUFs. In: 2018 55th ACM/ESDA/IEEE Design Automation Conference (DAC), pp. 1–6. IEEE (2018)

AI for Authentication and Privacy

Privacy-Preserving Machine Learning Using Cryptography

Christian Rechberger[1] and Roman Walch[1,2]([✉])

[1] Graz University of Technology, Graz, Austria
{christian.rechberger,roman.walch}@iaik.tugraz.at
[2] Know-Center GmbH, Graz, Austria

Abstract. Data scientists require an extensive training set to train an accurate and reliable machine learning model – the bigger and diverse the training set, the better. However, acquiring such a vast training set can be difficult, especially when sensitive user data is involved. The General Data Protection Regulation (GDPR) and similar regulations may prohibit the gathering and processing of this sensitive data. Privacy-preserving cryptographic protocols and primitives, like secure multi-party computation (MPC) and fully homomorphic encryption (FHE), may provide a solution to this problem. They allow us to perform calculations on private and unknown data and can, therefore, be used to classify and train on GDPR protected data sets. While still considered very inefficient, privacy-preserving machine learning using MPC and FHE has been heavily researched in recent years. In this chapter, we give an introduction to MPC and FHE, how they can be used, their limitations, and describe how state-of-the-art publications apply them to machine learning algorithms.

Keywords: MPC · FHE · Machine learning · Privacy

1 Introduction

In the age of big data, machine learning has proven to be a powerful tool to process the vast amount of data gathered. It can be used in several different domains, such as image recognition, recommendation systems, and classification of medical data, to name a few. In supervised learning, machine learning models are trained by using a large pre-classified training set, and the performance of the resulting model highly depends on the training data. Generally speaking, the bigger and diverse the data set used during training, the more accurate the model. However, collecting a suitable training set is no easy task at all and comes with several challenges. One particular problem is that in many applications, the training data consists of sensitive user data, such as medical records, images, and the user's voice, and collecting and using this data raises privacy concerns. Especially with new regulations, like the General Data Protection Regulation

© Springer Nature Switzerland AG 2022
L. Batina et al. (Eds.): Security and Artificial Intelligence, LNCS 13049, pp. 109–129, 2022.
https://doi.org/10.1007/978-3-030-98795-4_6

(GDPR)[1] and similar, new solutions are required to protect sensitive data when used in machine learning. These new solutions could potentially also allow several companies to combine their data set to produce better models, without revealing sensitive inputs to other companies.

But not only training of machine learning models is affected by these regulations. Some companies provide pre-trained models in machine-learning-as-a-service (MLaaS), where clients can upload data to get a prediction in exchange for a fee. But again, the client's upload can include private data, which needs to be protected. On the other hand, the pre-trained model can be considered to be a sensitive Intellectual Property (IP) and should, therefore, stay private as well.

To summarize, the realization of privacy-preserving machine learning requires the protection of sensitive data during the training of a model, of inputs to the classification process, and of the model used for prediction. With recent improvements in the area of privacy-preserving cryptography, protocols and primitives like secure multi-party computation (MPC) and fully homomorphic encryption (FHE) may provide a solution to these privacy problems. These protocols and primitives have been researched heavily in recent years and already became efficient enough for some practical use cases. As an example, we want to mention the publication *Mobile Private Contact Discovery at Scale* [36] by researchers from TU Graz and TU Darmstadt. In this work, the authors tackle the privacy issues when subscribing to mobile messenger services, like Signal and WhatsApp. These messengers perform a contact discovery, where the app automatically uploads the entire address book of the user to the service provider to find contacts who are already subscribed to the services. However, uploading the full address book, of course, leaks sensitive private information and should be avoided. The authors of the paper use a specially tailored two-party MPC protocol, called *private set intersection* (PSI) for unbalanced sets, to make the contact discovery private, but still efficient. The outcome of their protocol is that both parties, the user and the service provider, learn nothing more than the intersection of their address books. Their fastest protocol is able to compare 1024 client contacts to a database with 2^{28} entries in less than 3 s over a real WiFi connection.

Following the recent improvement in the performance of privacy-preserving cryptography, researches have now tried to apply them to machine learning applications. Since many of these applications involve complex tasks, straight forward usage of MPC and FHE often leads to too inefficient protocols. Thus, the main focus of the current research is to make MPC and FHE efficient enough for real-world privacy-preserving machine learning applications.

In this chapter, we aim to give an overview of privacy-preserving cryptography as it is used in machine learning applications. We first describe MPC and FHE, the cryptographic primitives used in state-of-the-art publications. Then we present different security models for which MPC or FHE protect sensitive information. In a nutshell, these security models define how many participating parties are corrupted and what they are allowed to do. Then we describe the different use cases in which we can use MPC and FHE to protect sensitive

---

[1] https://eur-lex.europa.eu/legal-content/EN/ALL/?uri=celex:32016R0679.

data, including federated learning on combined datasets, private classification, and machine learning as a service. We also give an overview of selected state-of-the-art privacy-preserving machine learning publications and describe their contribution. Finally, we describe some limitations we have to consider when using MPC and FHE in practice.

Remark 1. Besides using cryptography, many other techniques for preserving the privacy of models and datasets in machine learning applications have been proposed in the literature (f.e. differential privacy [23]). However, in this work, we want to focus on the cryptographic aspects in the realization of privacy-preserving machine learning. We refer the reader to, e.g., [43] for an overview of other proposed techniques.

2   Cryptographic Protocols and Primitives

In this section, we present secure multi-party computation and fully homomorphic encryption, cryptographic protocols, and primitives, which are the main tools to improve the privacy of machine learning algorithms.

2.1   Secure Multi-Party Computation (MPC)

The problem with outsourcing computations or sharing data is trusting other parties. Secure multi-party computation (MPC) protocols aim to get rid of the trust assumptions and allow several mutually distrusting parties $P_1, \ldots, P_n$ to jointly evaluate a public function f on their combined input $f(x_1, \ldots, x_n)$. During the execution of the protocol, the other parties learn nothing more than the output of the function, the inputs stay secret and will not be revealed. MPC protocols first were introduced by Yao in 1986 [61] and have been heavily researched and optimized since then. However, MPC protocols require large amounts of data to be communicated between parties during the private evaluation of the function f. This communication complexity is considered to be the main bottleneck of MPC protocols.

The number of parties participating in the MPC protocol has a significant impact on the performance, in particular in the communication required between the parties. In general, the exchanged amount of data grows quadratically in the number of parties involved. Furthermore, the number of parties also influences the choice of the underlying base protocols, since some protocols are optimized for the 2-party use case. In general, we distinguish 2-party (2PC) and multi-party protocols (MPC).

MPC Base Protocols. In this section, we describe the fundamental building blocks of MPC, which are Yao's Garbled Circuits (based on oblivious transfer) and different secret sharing schemes.

Oblivious Transfer (OT). Oblivious transfer [25,49] is a two-party protocol where one party (the sender) owns two secrets x_0 and x_1 and the other party (the receiver) has a selection bit $b \in \{0, 1\}$. The goal of OT is that the receiver gets the secret x_b, but b remains hidden from the sender, and the receiver also does not learn anything about x_{1-b}. We depict OT in Fig. 1. As shown by Kilian [38], this simple protocol can theoretically be used to implement any cryptographic task. OT protocols and various extensions are implemented in, e.g., the libOTe [52] library.

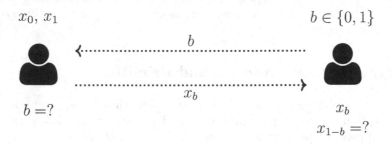

Fig. 1. Schematic depiction of oblivious transfer.

Yao's Garbled Circuits. One of the most widely known and used two-party protocol is Yao's Garbled Circuit protocol [61]. This protocol allows evaluating boolean circuits in algebraic normal form (i.e., consisting of AND-gates and XOR-gates) privately. In contrast to other MPC-protocols, Yao's Garbled Circuits require a constant number of communication rounds independent of the evaluated circuit. The main idea behind the protocol is that one party (the garbler) obfuscates the truth tables of each gate in the circuit by assigning a random value to each wire. Then the output values of the truth tables are encrypted with the corresponding input values, and the entries are randomly shuffled. The garbler then sends the garbled circuit to the other party (the evaluator) alongside the obfuscated values of the garbler's input. The evaluator then uses oblivious transfer to get the obfuscated values corresponding to his input, and he then is able to evaluate the whole circuit to produce the final result. We depict a small garbled circuit in Fig. 2. Many optimizations were proposed for Yao's Garbled Circuits, including point-and-permute [5], garbled row reduction [46], Free-XOR [40], and half-gate [62]. Applying them all results in a scheme, where AND gates only require two rows for their garbled truth tables, and XOR's do not require a garbled truth table at all. BMR [5] is a multi-party version of Yao's protocol, which also requires a constant number of communication rounds. Yao's garbled circuit protocol is implemented in, e.g., the emp-toolkit [60]. Furthermore, the TinyGarble project [57] provides synthesis tools for optimized garbled circuits based on the hardware description language Verilog.

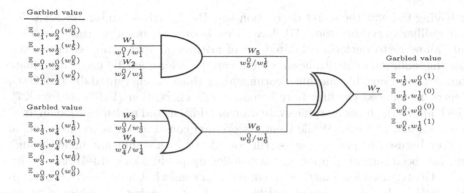

Fig. 2. Depiction of a small garbled circuit. Modified from [33].

Secret Sharing. Secret sharing is a simple, yet powerful primitive at the core of many MPC applications. In a (t, n)-secret sharing scheme, a secret s is split amongst n parties such that $\leq t-1$ of these shares do not reveal any information about the initial secret s. However, t of the shares are enough to reconstruct the secret s. Once a secret is shared, the parties can compute linear functions (additions and constant multiplications) on the shares locally, but require additional communication to compute non-linear functions (multiplications). In the end, they can combine their resulting shares to receive the final result of their computations. Popular secret sharing schemes are additive secret sharing and Shamir's secret sharing [56]. While additive secret sharing is a (n, n)-secret sharing scheme over a Ring where the shares x_i can be summed up to reconstruct the secret $x = \sum_i x_i$, Shamir's scheme uses polynomials $f(X) = \sum_{i=0}^{t-1} a_i X^i$ to construct a (t, n)-threshold sharing scheme. In contrast to Yao's garbled circuit, which is defined as a 2PC protocol, secret sharing schemes can be trivially extended to multiple parties. One popular secret sharing scheme, secure against malicious adversaries with dishonest majority (see Sect. 3), is SPDZ [20,21], which is implemented in the MP-SPDZ [37,58], SCALE-MAMBA [3], and FRESCO [2] libraries. The advantage of SPDZ is that it splits the protocol into an input-independent *offline phase* and an input-dependent *online phase*. The offline phase is costly in terms of computation and the amount of exchanged data, but it can be precomputed before the actual execution of the protocol. As a trade-off, the online phase, where the user inputs are used, is very efficient. To implement multiplications of shared data, SPDZ uses Beaver triples [4], pre-shared triples of the form $(c = a \cdot b)$, to linearize multiplications. One of the main tasks of the offline phase is to produce these beaver triples, one for each multiplication in the online phase.

2.2   Fully Homomorphic Encryption (FHE)

Homomorphic encryption (HE) schemes are cryptographic primitives that allow performing computations on encrypted data without having to decrypt them first or having to know the secret decryption key. Partial HE schemes, like RSA [53] and Paillier's cryptosystem [47], have been known for decades. However, they only allow us to perform a limited set of arithmetic operations (either homomorphic addition or multiplication) and can, therefore, not be used to evaluate complex functions, like machine learning algorithms, on encrypted data. In 2009, Gentry introduced the first fully homomorphic encryption (FHE) scheme [27], which allows the homomorphic evaluation of addition and multiplication an arbitrary amount of times. While Gentry's original construction is too impractical to ever be used in practice, it is still considered as a significant breakthrough and has been improved upon in many followup publications [13–16, 26]. In his work, Gentry used ideal lattices to construct a somewhat homomorphic encryption (SHE) scheme and introduced his novel bootstrapping procedure to transform it into an FHE scheme. Today's schemes follow Gentry's original blueprint and construct a bootstrapable SHE scheme. However, the security of modern schemes is based on the ring learning with errors (R-LWE) [44,50] hardness assumption from lattice-based cryptography. In these schemes, random noise is introduced during encryption, which grows during homomorphic operations. A homomorphic addition only adds negligible noise to the ciphertext. However, a homomorphic multiplication increases the noise level significantly and is often considered the limiting factor in those schemes. Once the noise has become too large, the ciphertext cannot be decrypted correctly anymore. The bootstrapping procedure aims to reduce the noise level by homomorphically re-encrypting the ciphertext. However, performing the bootstrapping procedure is very costly in terms of computational effort. Thus, in practice, we often try to avoid bootstrapping by choosing a large enough parameter set that supports the evaluation of the desired use case, i.e., we often use somewhat homomorphic encryption schemes.

At the time of writing, several different FHE schemes and their implementations in various libraries are used for several different use cases. Table 1 gives an overview of the schemes and their libraries. Since the CKKS scheme allows to (approximately) encrypt floating-point numbers, it has been used in many recent machine learning applications [6, 8, 9, 22].

Table 1. Overview of different FHE schemes.

Scheme	Used for	Libraries
BGV [14]	Integers modulo prime powers	HElib [29, 30], PALISADE [48]
BFV [13, 26]	Integers modulo t	SEAL [55], PALISADE [48]
CKKS[a] [15]	Floating point numbers	HElib [29, 30], SEAL [55], PALISADE [48]
TFHE [16]	Boolean circuits	TFHE [17]

[a] The CKKS scheme is often also called HEAAN in the literature.

SIMD Encoding. A big advantage of the BGV, BFV, and CKKS homomorphic encryption schemes is that they naturally allow encrypting of a vector of n plaintexts into only one ciphertext. Thereby, the size of the resulting ciphertext does not depend on the exact number ($\leq n$) of plaintexts encoded. Operations performed on the ciphertext then affect each of the slots of the encrypted plaintext vector independently, similar to single-instruction-multiple-data (SIMD) instructions on modern CPU's (AVX, SSE2, etc.). The supported SIMD operations include addition/subtraction, multiplication, and slot-rotation; however, directly accessing a specific slot is not possible. Using the SIMD encoding allows for more efficient implementations of the complex functions used in machine learning. For example, consider the classification of images using neural networks: On one hand, SIMD-batching can be used to classify several images at once and, therefore, maximize throughput. On the other hand, we can intelligently encode data into the SIMD-slots of the ciphertexts to minimize the classification latency of one image. SIMD encoding, for example, can be used to speed up matrix multiplication using the diagonal method introduced by Halevi and Shoup in [30].

3 Security Models

Privacy-preserving cryptographic primitives are defined to be secure in one of several different security models against adversaries with different capabilities. In this section, we will introduce some of the different security models.

3.1 MPC

Regarding the security of MPC protocols, we divide into several different notions of security in which we guarantee security against adversaries with different levels of power. As a rule of thumb: The fewer security guarantees the MPC protocol should provide, the more efficient the protocol becomes. Two major security notions are the *semi-honest* and *malicious* security models, which are both highly relevant in practice and whose application depends on the trust assumption of the scenario.

Semi-Honest Security. If there is enough trust between all the parties, we will choose an MPC protocol that is secure in the *semi-honest* (or honest-but-curious) model. In this security model, corrupt parties may try to learn the private input of other parties only using all the public information and the information they receive during the MPC protocol. Furthermore, the corrupted parties are allowed to collaborate by combining their received values. However, in this security model, no party is allowed to deviate from the predefined protocol, i.e., the parties always perform the correct computations and send correct values to others. The semi-honest model against this weaker (passive) adversaries allows implementing more efficient MPC protocols with acceptable overhead, which have already been successfully used in practice.

Malicious Security. In contrast, the *malicious* security model also allows corrupt parties to deviate from the protocol arbitrarily. They can, for example, try to send messages which would enable inferring more information on the inputs of other parties, or purposely falsify the result. This stronger security notion drastically reduces the level of trust needed between the parties. Protocols in this security notion usually either use zero-knowledge proofs, cut-and-choose procedures, or information-theoretically secure MACs [21] to detect malicious behavior of corrupt parties. However, the addition of these proofs is costly in terms of both communication and computational complexity. As a rule of thumb, going from *semi-honest* security to *malicious* to deal with the more flexible adversaries leads to a slowdown of approximately one order of magnitude. Furthermore, communication complexity is also expected to increase significantly. As a consequence, in practice one should always consider if there is a level of trust between the parties. If so, protocols that are only secure in the *semi-honest* model are reasonable, due to their substantial performance advantages.

Honest/Dishonest Majority. MPC protocols are not only divided into the two security models previously described, but they also differ in the number of allowed corrupted and colluding parties. In the literature, we distinguish between either having an *honest* or *dishonest majority* amongst all participating parties. This distinction has a direct impact on the efficiency of the protocol, where protection against a dishonest majority requires different approaches in which usually more computations and more communication between the parties is necessary. In a two-party protocol, one can never achieve an honest majority; however, in the multi-party setting, it is often reasonable to assume that an adversary can only corrupt less than half the parties.

3.2 FHE

In contrast to MPC, using fully homomorphic encryption only allows protecting the confidentiality of the encrypted data. Combining FHE with zero-knowledge proofs, for example, to enable detection of parties deviating from the agreed protocol (and, thus, achieve malicious security), is by the time of writing still an ongoing research topic. Therefore, using FHE is only secure in the semi-honest security model where parties do not learn anything from the information they receive during the execution of the protocol.

4 Settings

Using MPC and FHE in machine learning allows secure solutions for different scenarios, which we discuss in this section. We will discuss the actual state-of-the-art of secure machine learning application in Sect. 6.

4.1 MPC

In machine learning, we can use MPC in the following two scenarios.

Collaborative Learning on Combined Datasets. In machine learning, it is necessary to have a big and diverse dataset to produce accurate and reliable models. Especially small companies may struggle with creating such a big dataset. A solution would be to combine their datasets with those of other companies, but the companies may not be willing or allowed to share the data. MPC provides a solution to this problem: The parties can use secret sharing to share their dataset to the other parties securely, and they jointly compute the training algorithm. As a result, every party receives the trained model, but the inputs stay hidden from the other parties. We illustrate this collaborative learning process in Fig. 3.

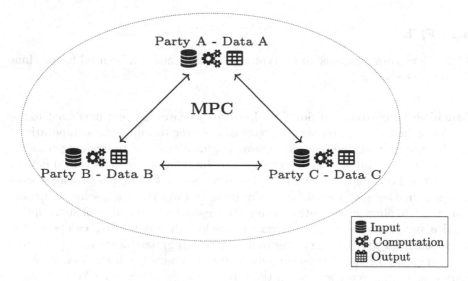

Fig. 3. Collaborative Learning using MPC

Keep in mind that the parties executing the MPC protocol can differ from the parties providing the data. In a more general solution, multiple parties secretly share their datasets to, for example, three computing servers, which do the actual MPC computations. This general scenario allows for multiple parties to participate in the protocol, avoiding the quadratic growth in communication complexity for each new party.

Private Classification. Another use case of MPC in machine learning is private classification. One party owns a model, and the other party wants to use this model to classify some input. The model may be seen as intellectual property and should stay private. The input of the other party may be protected by privacy regulations and should remain hidden as well. A 2PC protocol can, therefore, be used to classify the input using the model without revealing the model or the input. Depending on the used 2PC protocol, either only the client or both parties receive the classified output. We illustrate this private classification process in Fig. 4.

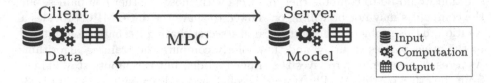

Fig. 4. Private Classification using MPC

4.2 FHE

FHE allows computations on encrypted data and thus can be used for machine learning as a service.

Machine Learning as a Service. In some use-cases, a client may want to use the know-how or the computing power of a server to outsource computations. In the case of machine learning, these computations can be training a model or classifying an input. These scenarios may be relevant for constrained devices with limited computing power (e.g., IoT-devices), or for using a private, corporate machine learning model for classification. In the latter case, some companies may want to allow classifications using their model as some kind of subscription service, but again clients may not want to disclose their data. FHE can be used in these scenarios to allow the server to do the training/classification on encrypted data to ensure privacy for user inputs. Figure 5 depicts these services. This scenario differs in several ways from the private classification using MPC scenario (Sect. 4.1): First of all, only the server performs the computation in the FHE scenario, contrary to the joint computation in the MPC use-case. Furthermore, the client sends all data in encrypted form to the server, and the server replies with an encrypted result. Only the client, who knows the secret decryption key, can decrypt the result, and thus, only the client receives the final output of the protocol.

5 Difficulties and Proposed Solutions

The usage of FHE and MPC in machine learning protocols comes with different practical limitations, which we evaluate in this section.

In secret sharing schemes, and when we want to use fully homomorphic encryption, we can only evaluate functions consisting of additions and multiplications, i.e., we can only evaluate polynomials. Therefore, if we want to privately compute other functions, like the commonly used ReLU and MaxPool, we either have to combine the sharing scheme with different protocols (e.g., edaBits [24])

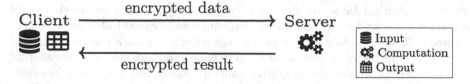

Fig. 5. Machine Learning as a Service using FHE

or we approximate the function by using Taylor series or Chebyshev polynomials [31]. This approximation will introduce an error into the computation.

Another thing to consider is that the efficiency of MPC and FHE depends on the number of multiplications in the evaluated circuit. In secret sharing schemes, a multiplication requires communication between all parties, while additions can be computed locally. As described in Sect. 2.1, in Yao's Garbled Circuit protocol, AND gates need to be garbled, contrary to XOR gates, which do not require a garbled truth table. Therefore, for MPC applications, the total number of multiplications (and AND gates) in the evaluated circuit significantly impacts the performance of the protocol. As already described above for FHE, the noise embedded in ciphertexts grows only slightly for addition, but significantly for multiplications. Hence, the number of consecutive multiplications, i.e., the multiplicative depth of the circuit, is limited before the noise becomes too large, and the ciphertext cannot be decrypted anymore. Furthermore, performing a homomorphic multiplication is also slower than computing a simple homomorphic addition. As a consequence, (consecutive) multiplications should be avoided if possible.

Another issue with the presented privacy-preserving tools is that comparison of secret data and branching programs can only be evaluated when working with boolean circuits (i.e., garbled circuits or TFHE) or integers in binary encoding. Comparing encrypted/secret-shared integers or branching on encrypted data is still an open research question. One approach to finding a solution for this problem is, for example, approximating an integer comparison by evaluation of a low degree polynomial [11].

6 State-of-the-Art

In this section, we discuss state-of-the-art publications in the area of privacy-preserving machine learning for deep learning and regression applications. Our survey is not exhaustive; we focus on fundamentally different approaches to give the reader an idea of some different techniques employed to make private training and classification more efficient.

6.1 MPC Training Algorithms

ABY3 - MPC-Framework. ABY3 [45] is a three-party computation (3PC) framework designed to switch between three different types of MPC protocols efficiently: **Arithmetic** secret sharing over a ring $\mathbb{Z}_{2^k}$, **Binary** secret sharing of vectors $x \in \mathbb{Z}_2^k$, and secret sharing of elements using keys suitable for a 3-party variant of **Y**aos's garbled circuit protocol. Such a framework can be effectively used in machine learning applications. On the one hand, arithmetic secret sharing is well suited for implementing matrix multiplications, but non-linear functions can only be approximated. On the other hand, binary secret sharing, and Yao's garbled circuits are inefficient for matrix multiplications, but they can be used to implement piecewise polynomial functions (e.g., ReLU) without the need of approximation.

Furthermore, the authors also describe novel techniques to implement fixed-point multiplications of shared floating-point values for the 3+-party case. They implemented their framework in the semi-honest security model with an honest majority, but also describe variants of each building block in the malicious security setting in their paper. To benchmark their library, they implemented training of linear regression, logistic regression, and deep neural networks for the collaborative learning use case described in Sect. 4.1. Their approach only differs from textbook implementations of these learning algorithms in the following ways:

– They have to approximate floating-point values with fixed-point integers and, consequently, secret share fix-point integers to the parties. They claim, however, that this has only little to no impact on the accuracy of the trained models.
– The logistic functions need to be approximated with their piecewise polynomial approach, which leads to a small drop in accuracy.

As a result, they were able to train a neural network for the MNIST dataset [42] with three fully connected layers (128, 128, and 10 nodes respectively) and a ReLU activation function between each layer for 15 epochs in 45 min, outperforming results of previous papers by several orders of magnitude.

SecureNN. One difficulty of using secret sharing MPC protocols for private collaborative neural network training is the efficient computation of involved nonlinearities, like ReLU and MaxPool. In the ABY3 framework, which we describe in the previous section, the authors use efficient switching protocols to be able to calculate the nonlinearities using Yao's garbled circuits. In SecureNN [59], Wagh et al. describe novel protocols to effectively calculate nonlinearities without approximations and without the need to switch from a secret-sharing scheme to a garbled circuit scheme and vice-versa. They describe novel 3-party and 4-party protocols to efficiently compute comparisons and MSB extractions on shared values, which they use to implement the ReLU and MaxPool functions and their derivatives. Their protocols are secure in the semi-honest security model with an honest majority. Similar to the ABY3 framework, their runtime of training a neural network for the MNIST dataset [42] with three fully connected layers (128, 128, and 10 nodes respectively) and a ReLU activation function between each layer for 15 epochs takes 52.8 min in the 3-party case and 46.8 min when four parties are involved.

HELEN. Most state-of-the-art MPC protocols are designed to provide security in the semi-honest security model. In the publication HELEN [63], Zheng et al. describe techniques to secure the collaborative training of a linear regression model in the malicious security setting against a dishonest majority. More specifically, their protocol guarantees that inputs of an honest party are never revealed, even if all other parties are corrupt. Zheng et al. use a combination of several different techniques to make their protocol practical but still guaranteeing security. 1) They leverage zero-knowledge proofs to ensure that parties follow the protocol 2) They use the distributed Alternating Direction Method of Multipliers (ADMM) [12] optimizer to reduce communication between the parties. 3) They use a singular value decomposition (SVD) of their inputs to simplify the zero-knowledge proofs. 4) They use an additive homomorphic encryption scheme to distribute intermediate results and the encrypted model to the other parties. 5) They use SPDZ to securely share the secret key of the additive homomorphic encryption scheme to all parties. Therefore, after finishing the learning process, all parties must participate in decrypting the final result by providing their share of the secret key.

As a result, Zheng et al. report a performance improvement of up to 5 orders of magnitude (depending on the specific use case) compared to previous state-of-the-art protocols.

6.2 MPC Classification

XONN. In XONN [51], Riazi et al. introduce an end-to-end framework for oblivious deep neural network inference based on Yao's garbled circuit protocol. They realize, that a vector dot product of neurons in a binarized neural network (BNN) with inputs and weights $x, w \in \{-1, 1\}$ is equivalent to an XNOR-PopCount operation on inputs and weights $x_b, w_b \in \{0, 1\}$. Similarly, a MaxPool operation can be modeled as a Boolean-OR operation in such a BNN. Remember that the XOR and XNOR operations are considered to be free in garbling protocols since they require no garbled truth table (see Sect. 2.1 above). Therefore, when using Yao's garbled circuits, Riazi et al. do not require any multiplication for the matrix multiplications in fully connected or convolution neural network layers. They use the sign function as the activation function in their BNN, which can also easily be implemented in garbled circuits by merely extracting the most significant bit (MSB) of the input. Another advantage of using Yao's garbled circuits is that there is always a constant number of interaction rounds between the server and the client, independent of the depth of the network.

They implement their framework in the semi-honest security model but claim that only standard techniques, like cut-and-choose, are required to make their framework secure in the malicious security setting as well. For easy usage, Riazi et al. provide a compiler to easily convert a KERAS [18] description of a neural network into a format compatible with their XONN framework. They evaluate the performance of their framework on binarized versions of several different neural networks. This includes a binarized Fitnet [54] with 21 layers for which they achieve a classification of a CIFAR-10 [41] sample in 16.78 s.

6.3   HE Training Algorithms

HE Logistic Regression Training. Bergamaschi et al. [6] have published an interesting example of HE involving the training of encrypted logistic regression data. Their implementation improves an iterative gradient descent method originally introduced by Kim et al. [39] and is based on the CKKS implementation in HElib. By exploiting the SIMD capabilities of the CKKS scheme, Bergamaschi et al. were able to train and homomorphically evaluate over 30.000 models in parallel on encrypted medical data within only 20 min. The parameters of all those models were packed into different entries of encrypted vectors and the elementwise operations of the CKKS SIMD scheme allowed to run the iterative procedure in such a bit-slice approach on all of them in parallel. CKKS naturally operates on complex values, and the authors successfully used this complex number plaintext to double the available SIMD slots. The sigmoid function was approximated following [39] using low-degree polynomials in a bound range around zero.

Since the authors omitted to bootstrap and, thus, used CKKS as a somewhat-homomorphic encryption scheme, the number of training iterations is very limited. Given averaged initial weights and an input ciphertext matrix, where each row corresponds to an input record, and each column corresponds to a model parameter, they were able to homomorphically compute the logistic regression of a considerable number of models in a reasonable amount of time.

6.4   HE Deep Learning Classification

FHE-DiNN. In the publication FHE-DiNN [10], Bourse et al. address the problem of implementing very deep neural networks with fully homomorphic encryption. More specifically, they use the TFHE scheme, which is optimized for binary circuits and fast bootstrapping. To apply TFHE to neural networks, Bourse et al. first discretize the neural network and use the *sign* function as activation. Therefore, propagating signals have values $\in \{0, 1\}$ and the network repeatedly computes the sign of a weighted ($w_i \in \{0, 1\}$) sum of ± 1 inputs. Furthermore, they adapt the base TFHE scheme to be capable of performing this multisum, and the sign operation is directly embedded in the bootstrapping procedure. With this adaptation, they reset the noise in the ciphertexts after each neuron by applying the bootstrapped sign function. With this approach, they achieve scale-invariant homomorphic neural network inference with the chosen TFHE parameters being independent of the network depth. Furthermore, the evaluation time of the network just grows linearly with the number of neurons, and the neurons in each layer can be computed in parallel. They achieve a single-threaded evaluation time of 1.65 s for 100 neurons. However, the authors describe that discretizing a pre-trained neural network leads to a drop in classification accuracy. Bourse et al. leave it to future work to directly train a discretized neural network.

E2DM. In the E2DM [34] framework, Jiang et al. focus on optimizing homomorphic matrix multiplications in the case where both matrices are homomorphically encrypted. Their methods can be used to homomorphically classify encrypted inputs using an encrypted neural network model as well. The main idea behind their algorithm is to split a matrix-matrix multiplication $A \cdot B$, with $A, B \in \mathbb{R}^{d \times d}$, into d entry wise multiplications $\odot$, such that $A \cdot B = \sum_{i=0}^{d-1} A_i \odot B_i$. They show how to efficiently construct A_i and B_i by using FHE friendly operations, like rotation and ciphertext-plaintext multiplications. As a result, their algorithm scales linearly with d (complexity $O(d)$) and has a depth of 2 ciphertext-plaintext multiplications and only one ciphertext-ciphertext multiplication. Furthermore, they generalize their methods to implement multiplication of rectangular matrices as well and also show to use the SIMD-encoding to perform multiple matrix multiplications in parallel. In modern FHE schemes, ciphertext-ciphertext multiplications are significantly more expensive in terms of runtime and noise increase than ciphertext-plaintext multiplications. However, in E2DM, they are still able to achieve an amortized classification speed for the CryptoNets [28] neural network on a MNIST [42] dataset sample of 26 ms.

CHET. Using fully homomorphic encryption for complex tasks, like deep neural network classification, is still a considerable challenge. It requires a lot of expertise and engineering effort to achieve the best possible performance. Several different options need to be considered: 1) Setting the optimal FHE parameters to maximize performance, but still provide correctness and security 2) Using sufficient precision for the floating-point arithmetic 3) Optimal usage of SIMD capabilities to either minimize latency or maximize throughput.

The CHET compiler [22] from Microsoft Research takes care of these considerations and automatically translates a tensor description of a deep neural network to an FHE circuit using the approximate homomorphic encryption scheme CKKS. Their compiler automatically calculates the depth of the resulting homomorphic circuit to choose the smallest parameters possible to achieve a security level of 128 bit, and therefore maximizes performance. It is designed to minimize latency for one classification by leveraging the SIMD capabilities of CKKS for speeding up the involved operations. It explores several different SIMD encodings and chooses the best performing according to a predefined cost model. Furthermore, it provides a profile-guided selection of the minimal required floating-point precision. As a result, they were able to classify a sample of the CIFAR-10 dataset [41] using the SqueezeNet [32] architecture in 164.7 s. It should be noted since CHET only relies on FHE for private deep neural network inference, it has to substitute the involved nonlinearities (ReLU, MaxPool) with more FHE friendly functions (polynomials, AveragePool) resulting in a small accuracy drop.

nGraph-HE. Modern machine learning libraries, like TensorFlow [1] use graph compilers, like Intel nGraph [19], to optimize deep learning models. These compilers express machine learning models in a graph-based intermediate representation, on which they can perform hardware-specific optimizations.

This approach allows machine learning engineers to describe their neural networks in a high-level description language without dealing with these hardware-based optimizations themselves. The core idea of nGraph-HE [9], and the followup work nGraph-HE2 [8], is to extend Intel nGraph to additionally consider homomorphic encryption as a separate hardware target to also perform graph-based optimizations specifically for FHE. This addition again hides the complexity of FHE-implementations from the machine learning engineers while also exploiting the extensive toolset build for plain machine learning libraries. In their publications, Boemer et al. claim that only adding one line to an existing TensorFlow implementation of a trained neural network would transform it into an FHE implementation using Microsoft SEAL as a backbone library. However, similar to the CHET compiler (see the previous section), a limitation of nGraph-HE is that it cannot deal with nonlinearities natively. That is why it either uses HE-friendly approximations of these functions, or it leverages the client to compute the nonlinearities in plain, possibly leaking information about the model weights. For the latter use case, the followup publication MP2ML [7] recently combined nGraph-HE with secure 2-party computation protocols to overcome this privacy issue. nGraph-HE's implementation of the CryptoNets [28] network can classify an MNIST [42] sample in 2.05 s, with SIMD encoding they achieve a throughput of 1998 images per second.

GAZELLE. In the publication GAZELLE [35], Juvekar et al. propose a framework for secure neural network inference based on a combination of FHE and MPC. The main idea behind their contribution is as follows: First, they use an additive homomorphic encryption scheme, similar to BFV, to encrypt the data, which should be classified using the neural network. The server then directly applies linear layers (fully connected layers and convolution layers) as matrix multiplication to the encrypted data. They leverage the SIMD encoding of the HE scheme to speed up matrix multiplication and, therefore, decrease latency for one inference. For non-linear functions, like the commonly used MaxPool and ReLU functions, they use garbled circuits. To this end, they propose an interactive switching scheme, which allows a translation of an FHE ciphertext into secret shares, which can be used to evaluate a function $y = f(x)$ using garbled circuits. The circuit is designed such that the result y is secretly shared amongst the two parties, i.e., $y = y_1 + y_2$ with party i receiving y_i. The client then encrypts his share $\mathcal{E}(y_1)$, and the server can produce the encrypted result by simply adding his share to the fresh ciphertext he receives from the client $\mathcal{E}(y) = \mathcal{E}(y_1) + y_2$. With this protocol, they achieve the following two advantages:

- In many MPC/FHE machine learning publications, the non-linear functions are approximated using polynomials. However, switching to a garbled circuit scheme allows implementing ReLU and MaxPool without approximations.
- The interactive switching scheme re-encrypts the FHE-ciphertext and can, therefore, be seen as interactive bootstrapping to reduce noise.

As a result, Juvekar et al. are able to achieve an classification latency for the CryptoNets [28] neural network on a MNIST [42] dataset sample of 30 ms.

7 Limitations

While the privacy-preserving primitives we discussed in this work are very promising, they come with several limitations and open research questions. The probably most severe limitation of these cryptographic primitives is the introduction of a huge computational and communicational overhead compared to performing the same computations in plain. Especially for complex tasks, like training a deep neural network, this overhead is often too large to be practical. The problem becomes even more severe when trying to secure the protocols in the malicious security setting. But using this security model might often be necessary in practice, since using the more efficient semi-honest security model would allow corrupt parties to cheat without being detected and, therefore, implies some trust between the parties.

MPC protocols require that all participating parties know the function they want to evaluate on the secret data. This implies that in the private classification setting described in Sect. 4.1, all parties know some hyperparameters of the secret model, like the number of layers and neurons in a neural network. Hiding these hyperparameters might also be of interest by companies that want to monetize their secret models and is an interesting question for future research.

MPC and FHE protect secret data during the computation of a function; however, they cannot protect against implicitly leaking confidential data by publishing the result of the computation. Think about the simple use case, where two parties engage in an MPC protocol to calculate the sum of their inputs, i.e., $y = x_1 + x_2$, where x_i belongs to party i. The computation does not leak x_i, but each party knowing the output y can calculate the input of the other party by subtracting their own secret input. Therefore, when applying MPC/FHE in practice, some additional mechansims, like differential privacy [23], might be required to protect the inputs of all parties.

Protocols secure in the malicious security setting prevent parties to deviate from the defined protocol. However, even this security model does not protect against using malicious input in the first place. Think about the collaborative learning use case in Sect. 3. One party may want to use a faulty dataset (e.g., labeling images of dogs as birds) with the intent to produce a wrong model. Additional steps would be required to protect against training on malformed inputs, e.g., securely test the input data of each party before engaging in the protocol.

Finally, data scientists often use knowledge of the dataset to finetune their machine learning models. However, this finetuning might also prove to be difficult when the inputs of the training phase are unknown to the scientists. The finetuning steps would also have to be modeled as a function that has to be computed with MPC or FHE as well.

8 Conclusion

In this chapter, we gave an overview of multi-party computation and fully homomorphic encryption, their security models, and how they can be used to protect sensitive data in the context of machine learning applications. We gave an overview of state-of-the-art publications and described their techniques to make privacy-preserving machine learning more efficient.

While MPC and FHE are promising techniques to compute on private data, and some simple tasks already profit from the security guarantees they achieve, there is still a lot of room for improvement. These techniques are still very inefficient in both computing time and data transmission, and especially in the strong malicious security setting, the computational and communicational overhead is too severe for many practical applications.

Acknowledgments. This work was supported by the "DDAI" COMET Module within the COMET – Competence Centers for Excellent Technologies Programme, funded by the Austrian Federal Ministry for Transport, Innovation and Technology (bmvit), the Austrian Federal Ministry for Digital and Economic Affairs (bmdw), the Austrian Research Promotion Agency (FFG), the province of Styria (SFG) and partners from industry and academia. The COMET Programme is managed by FFG.

References

1. Abadi, M., et al.: Tensorflow: large-scale machine learning on heterogeneous distributed systems. CoRR abs/1603.04467 (2016)
2. Alexandra Institute: FRESCO - a FRamework for Efficient Secure COmputation (2020). https://github.com/aicis/fresco
3. Aly, A., Keller, M., Rotaru, D., Scholl, P., Smart, N.P., Wood, T.: SCALE-MAMBA (2020). https://homes.esat.kuleuven.be/nsmart/SCALE/
4. Beaver, D.: Efficient multiparty protocols using circuit randomization. In: Feigenbaum, J. (ed.) CRYPTO 1991. LNCS, vol. 576, pp. 420–432. Springer, Heidelberg (1992). https://doi.org/10.1007/3-540-46766-1_34
5. Beaver, D., Micali, S., Rogaway, P.: The round complexity of secure protocols (extended abstract). In: STOC, pp. 503–513. ACM (1990)
6. Bergamaschi, F., Halevi, S., Halevi, T.T., Hunt, H.: Homomorphic training of 30,000 logistic regression models. In: Deng, R.H., Gauthier-Umaña, V., Ochoa, M., Yung, M. (eds.) ACNS 2019. LNCS, vol. 11464, pp. 592–611. Springer, Cham (2019). https://doi.org/10.1007/978-3-030-21568-2_29
7. Boemer, F., Cammarota, R., Demmler, D., Schneider, T., Yalame, H.: MP2ML: a mixed-protocol machine learning framework for private inference. In: ARES, pp. 14:1–14:10. ACM (2020)
8. Boemer, F., Costache, A., Cammarota, R., Wierzynski, C.: nGraph-HE2: a high-throughput framework for neural network inference on encrypted data. In: WAHC@CCS, pp. 45–56. ACM (2019)
9. Boemer, F., Lao, Y., Cammarota, R., Wierzynski, C.: nGraph-HE: a graph compiler for deep learning on homomorphically encrypted data. In: CF, pp. 3–13. ACM (2019)
10. Bourse, F., Minelli, M., Minihold, M., Paillier, P.: Fast homomorphic evaluation of deep discretized neural networks. In: Shacham, H., Boldyreva, A. (eds.) CRYPTO 2018. LNCS, vol. 10993, pp. 483–512. Springer, Cham (2018). https://doi.org/10.1007/978-3-319-96878-0_17
11. Bourse, F., Sanders, O., Traoré, J.: Improved secure integer comparison via homomorphic encryption. In: Jarecki, S. (ed.) CT-RSA 2020. LNCS, vol. 12006, pp. 391–416. Springer, Cham (2020). https://doi.org/10.1007/978-3-030-40186-3_17

12. Boyd, S.P., Parikh, N., Chu, E., Peleato, B., Eckstein, J.: Distributed optimization and statistical learning via the alternating direction method of multipliers. Found. Trends Mach. Learn. **3**(1), 1–122 (2011)
13. Brakerski, Z.: Fully homomorphic encryption without modulus switching from classical GapSVP. In: Safavi-Naini, R., Canetti, R. (eds.) CRYPTO 2012. LNCS, vol. 7417, pp. 868–886. Springer, Heidelberg (2012). https://doi.org/10.1007/978-3-642-32009-5_50
14. Brakerski, Z., Gentry, C., Vaikuntanathan, V.: (Leveled) fully homomorphic encryption without bootstrapping. In: ITCS, pp. 309–325. ACM (2012)
15. Cheon, J.H., Kim, A., Kim, M., Song, Y.: Homomorphic encryption for arithmetic of approximate numbers. In: Takagi, T., Peyrin, T. (eds.) ASIACRYPT 2017. LNCS, vol. 10624, pp. 409–437. Springer, Cham (2017). https://doi.org/10.1007/978-3-319-70694-8_15
16. Chillotti, I., Gama, N., Georgieva, M., Izabachène, M.: Faster fully homomorphic encryption: bootstrapping in less than 0.1 seconds. In: Cheon, J.H., Takagi, T. (eds.) ASIACRYPT 2016. LNCS, vol. 10031, pp. 3–33. Springer, Heidelberg (2016). https://doi.org/10.1007/978-3-662-53887-6_1
17. Chillotti, I., Gama, N., Georgieva, M., Izabachène, M.: TFHE: fast fully homomorphic encryption library (2016). https://tfhe.github.io/tfhe/
18. Chollet, F., et al.: Keras (2015). https://keras.io
19. Cyphers, S., et al.: Intel nGraph: an intermediate representation, compiler, and executor for deep learning. CoRR abs/1801.08058 (2018)
20. Damgård, I., Keller, M., Larraia, E., Pastro, V., Scholl, P., Smart, N.P.: Practical covertly secure MPC for dishonest majority – Or: breaking the SPDZ limits. In: Crampton, J., Jajodia, S., Mayes, K. (eds.) ESORICS 2013. LNCS, vol. 8134, pp. 1–18. Springer, Heidelberg (2013). https://doi.org/10.1007/978-3-642-40203-6_1
21. Damgård, I., Pastro, V., Smart, N., Zakarias, S.: Multiparty computation from somewhat homomorphic encryption. In: Safavi-Naini, R., Canetti, R. (eds.) CRYPTO 2012. LNCS, vol. 7417, pp. 643–662. Springer, Heidelberg (2012). https://doi.org/10.1007/978-3-642-32009-5_38
22. Dathathri, R., et al.: CHET: an optimizing compiler for fully-homomorphic neural-network inferencing. In: PLDI, pp. 142–156. ACM (2019)
23. Dwork, C.: Differential privacy. In: Bugliesi, M., Preneel, B., Sassone, V., Wegener, I. (eds.) ICALP 2006. LNCS, vol. 4052, pp. 1–12. Springer, Heidelberg (2006). https://doi.org/10.1007/11787006_1
24. Escudero, D., Ghosh, S., Keller, M., Rachuri, R., Scholl, P.: Improved primitives for MPC over mixed arithmetic-binary circuits. In: Micciancio, D., Ristenpart, T. (eds.) CRYPTO 2020. LNCS, vol. 12171, pp. 823–852. Springer, Cham (2020). https://doi.org/10.1007/978-3-030-56880-1_29
25. Even, S., Goldreich, O., Lempel, A.: A randomized protocol for signing contracts. Commun. ACM **28**(6), 637–647 (1985)
26. Fan, J., Vercauteren, F.: Somewhat practical fully homomorphic encryption. IACR Cryptol. ePrint Arch. **2012**, 144 (2012)
27. Gentry, C.: Fully homomorphic encryption using ideal lattices. In: STOC, pp. 169–178. ACM (2009)
28. Gilad-Bachrach, R., Dowlin, N., Laine, K., Lauter, K.E., Naehrig, M., Wernsing, J.: CryptoNets: applying neural networks to encrypted data with high throughput and accuracy. In: ICML. JMLR Workshop and Conference Proceedings, vol. 48, pp. 201–210. JMLR.org (2016)
29. Halevi, S., Shoup, V.: Design and implementation of a homomorphicencryption library (2013). https://github.com/homenc/HElib

30. Halevi, S., Shoup, V.: Algorithms in HElib. In: Garay, J.A., Gennaro, R. (eds.) CRYPTO 2014. LNCS, vol. 8616, pp. 554–571. Springer, Heidelberg (2014). https://doi.org/10.1007/978-3-662-44371-2_31
31. Hesamifard, E., Takabi, H., Ghasemi, M.: Deep neural networks classification over encrypted data. In: CODASPY, pp. 97–108. ACM (2019)
32. Iandola, F.N., Moskewicz, M.W., Ashraf, K., Han, S., Dally, W.J., Keutzer, K.: SqueezeNet: AlexNet-level accuracy with 50x fewer parameters and <1mb model size. CoRR abs/1602.07360 (2016)
33. Jean, J.: TikZ for Cryptographers. (2016) https://www.iacr.org/authors/tikz/
34. Jiang, X., Kim, M., Lauter, K.E., Song, Y.: Secure outsourced matrix computation and application to neural networks. In: CCS, pp. 1209–1222. ACM (2018)
35. Juvekar, C., Vaikuntanathan, V., Chandrakasan, A.: GAZELLE: a low latency framework for secure neural network inference. In: USENIX, pp. 1651–1669. USENIX Association (2018)
36. Kales, D., Rechberger, C., Schneider, T., Senker, M., Weinert, C.: Mobile private contact discovery at scale. In: USENIX. pp. 1447–1464. USENIX Association (2019)
37. Keller, M.: MP-SPDZ: a versatile framework for multi-party computation. In: CCS, pp. 1575–1590. ACM (2020)
38. Kilian, J.: Founding cryptography on oblivious transfer. In: STOC, pp. 20–31. ACM (1988)
39. Kim, A., Song, Y., Kim, M., Lee, K., Cheon, J.H.: Logistic regression model training based on the approximate homomorphic encryption. IACR Cryptol. ePrint Arch. **2018**, 254 (2018)
40. Kolesnikov, V., Schneider, T.: Improved garbled circuit: free XOR gates and applications. In: Aceto, L., Damgård, I., Goldberg, L.A., Halldórsson, M.M., Ingólfsdóttir, A., Walukiewicz, I. (eds.) ICALP 2008. LNCS, vol. 5126, pp. 486–498. Springer, Heidelberg (2008). https://doi.org/10.1007/978-3-540-70583-3_40
41. Krizhevsky, A.: The CIFAR-10 Dataset (2009). http://www.cs.toronto.edu/kriz/cifar.html
42. LeCun, Y., Cortes, C., Burges, C.: The MNIST Database of Handwritten Digits (2009). http://yann.lecun.com/exdb/mnist/
43. Liu, B., Ding, M., Shaham, S., Rahayu, W., Farokhi, F., Lin, Z.: When machine learning meets privacy: a survey and outlook. CoRR abs/2011.11819 (2020)
44. Lyubashevsky, V., Peikert, C., Regev, O.: On ideal lattices and learning with errors over rings. In: Gilbert, H. (ed.) EUROCRYPT 2010. LNCS, vol. 6110, pp. 1–23. Springer, Heidelberg (2010). https://doi.org/10.1007/978-3-642-13190-5_1
45. Mohassel, P., Rindal, P.: Aby^3: a mixed protocol framework for machine learning. In: CCS, pp. 35–52. ACM (2018)
46. Naor, M., Pinkas, B., Sumner, R.: Privacy preserving auctions and mechanism design. In: EC, pp. 129–139. ACM (1999)
47. Paillier, P.: Public-key cryptosystems based on composite degree residuosity classes. In: Stern, J. (ed.) EUROCRYPT 1999. LNCS, vol. 1592, pp. 223–238. Springer, Heidelberg (1999). https://doi.org/10.1007/3-540-48910-X_16
48. Polyakov, Y., Rohloff, K., Ryan, G., Cousins, D.: Palisade lattice cryptography library (2020). https://palisade-crypto.org/software-library/
49. Rabin, M.: How to exchange secrets by oblivious transfer. Technical report, TR-81, Aiken Computation Laboratory, Harvard University (1981)
50. Regev, O.: On lattices, learning with errors, random linear codes, and cryptography. In: STOC, pp. 84–93. ACM (2005)

51. Riazi, M.S., Samragh, M., Chen, H., Laine, K., Lauter, K.E., Koushanfar, F.: XONN: xnor-based oblivious deep neural network inference. In: USENIX, pp. 1501–1518. USENIX Association (2019)
52. Rindal, P.: libOTe: an efficient, portable, and easy to use Oblivious Transfer Library. https://github.com/osu-crypto/libOTe
53. Rivest, R.L., Shamir, A., Adleman, L.M.: A method for obtaining digital signatures and public-key cryptosystems. Commun. ACM **21**(2), 120–126 (1978)
54. Romero, A., Ballas, N., Kahou, S.E., Chassang, A., Gatta, C., Bengio, Y.: FitNets: hints for thin deep nets. In: ICLR (Poster) (2015)
55. Microsoft SEAL (release 3.6) (2020). https://github.com/Microsoft/SEAL. Microsoft Research, Redmond, WA
56. Shamir, A.: How to share a secret. Commun. ACM **22**(11), 612–613 (1979)
57. Songhori, E.M., Hussain, S.U., Sadeghi, A., Schneider, T., Koushanfar, F.: Tiny-Garble: highly compressed and scalable sequential garbled circuits. In: IEEE S&P, pp. 411–428. IEEE (2015)
58. University of Bristol: Multi-Protocol SPDZ (2020). https://github.com/data61/MP-SPDZ
59. Wagh, S., Gupta, D., Chandran, N.: SecureNN: 3-party secure computation for neural network training. Proc. Priv. Enhancing Technol. **2019**(3), 26–49 (2019)
60. Wang, X., Malozemoff, A.J., Katz, J.: EMP-toolkit: efficient MultiParty computation toolkit (2016). https://github.com/emp-toolkit
61. Yao, A.C.: How to generate and exchange secrets (extended abstract). In: FOCS, pp. 162–167. IEEE (1986)
62. Zahur, S., Rosulek, M., Evans, D.: Two halves make a whole. Reducing data transfer in garbled circuits using half gates. In: Oswald, E., Fischlin, M. (eds.) EUROCRYPT 2015. LNCS, vol. 9057, pp. 220–250. Springer, Heidelberg (2015). https://doi.org/10.1007/978-3-662-46803-6_8
63. Zheng, W., Popa, R.A., Gonzalez, J.E., Stoica, I.: Helen: maliciously secure coopetitive learning for linear models. In: IEEE S&P, pp. 724–738. IEEE (2019)

Machine Learning Meets Data Modification
The Potential of Pre-processing for Privacy Enchancement

Giuseppe Garofalo[1]([✉]), Manel Slokom[2], Davy Preuveneers[1], Wouter Joosen[1], and Martha Larson[2,3]

[1] imec-Distrinet, KU Leuven, Celestijnenlaan 200A, 3001 Heverlee, Belgium
{giuseppe.garofalo,davy.preuveneers,wouter.joosen}@cs.kuleuven.be
[2] Delft University of Technology, Delft, The Netherlands
m.slokom@tudelft.nl
[3] Radboud University, Nijmegen, The Netherlands
M.Larson@cs.ru.nl

Abstract. We explore how data modification can enhance privacy by examining the connection between data modification and machine learning. Specifically, machine learning "meets" data modification in two ways. First, data modification can protect the data that is used to train machine learning models focusing it on the intended use and inhibiting unwanted inference. Second, machine learning can provide new ways of creating modified data. In this chapter, we discuss data modification approaches, applied during data pre-processing, that are suited for online data sharing scenarios. Specifically, we define two scenarios "User data sharing" and "Data set sharing" and describe the threat models associated with each scenario and related privacy threats. We then survey the landscape of privacy-enhancing data modification techniques that can be used to counter these threats. The picture that emerges is that data modification approaches hold promise to enhance privacy, and can be used alongside of conventional cryptographic approaches. We close with an outlook on future directions focusing on new types of data, the relationship among privacy, and the importance of taking an interdisciplinary approach to data modification for privacy enhancement.

1 Introduction

The importance of data in for gaining insight and supporting decision making has long been appreciated. However, recently recognition has grown of other aspects of data, both positive and negative. On the positive side, data are useful for training machine learning (ML) models that guide the development of new products and enable new services. ML has lead to a growing demand for data by businesses and other organizations looking to create value, to reduce costs or to boost profits. On the negative side, data can be dangerous. Large, centralized collections are susceptible to breaches and give rise to privacy and security risks. Moreover, ML algorithms introduce novel attack surfaces, opening the door to function creep by service providers and putting privacy at risk.

© Springer Nature Switzerland AG 2022
L. Batina et al. (Eds.): Security and Artificial Intelligence, LNCS 13049, pp. 130–155, 2022.
https://doi.org/10.1007/978-3-030-98795-4_7

It has become apparent that we need to understand how to derive benefit from data without running serious risks. Conventional approaches use encryption, or multiple layers of system security, to protect data. Such approaches are effective, but also have specific drawbacks. They are technically complex to implement and must be continuously monitored for breaches. Approaches to protecting privacy that do not suffer these drawbacks would clearly be advantageous.

In this chapter, we take a look at a set of less conventional approaches that involve an alternative process: data modification. Data modification is the practice of changing raw data into a transformed form for the purpose of protection. One commonality between conventional approaches to data protection, is that they assume that data must be maintained in its original form in order to be useful. Although, this might be the case for some applications, with the rise of machine learning there are an increasing number of cases for which the original data is not necessarily. Approaches like machine learning that work probabilistically can tolerate variation in the data, especially in cases where that variation does not impact aspects of the data most important for the task at hand.

When data modification is integrated into a data pipeline, it is usually integrated as a pre-processing step. In contrast, conventional data protection approaches can be applied multiple places along the pipeline. We use the term "pre-processing" to refer to a transformation applied to raw data, possibly during the phases of cleaning or feature extraction. Data modification at the beginning of the pipeline can be combined with other forms of encryption or security anywhere along the pipeline to add extra protection. In this chapter, however, we focuses specifically on data modification.

The result of data modification is a data set that can be shared and further used without needing to reverse the modification, as opposed to encryption, where generally only decrypted data can be used in a meaningful way. After modification, data no longer offer a viable opportunity to threaten privacy or attack security. The overhead of managing encryption keys or of monitoring system level security can be spared. Data modification can protect against data misuse by an internal party and can limit the damage done by a breach.

This chapter discusses how ML and data modification are related, and how the modification of data is growing in importance as a method for privacy enhancement. The chapter follows two major themes, corresponding to two ways in which machine learning can be said to "meet" data modification. First, data modification protects the data fed into ML algorithms. Second, ML can be used to data in order to create protection. Our chapter provides a literature survey that covers work on data modification techniques that fit into these two themes. We argue that the relationship between ML and data modification is not static, but can be anticipated to evolve in the future. Specifically, interest in data modification is driven by the growth of ML, due to both the risks associated with ML as well as the specific opportunities that it presents. Next, we turn to further discuss this effect, in order to provide important background and motivation for the use of data modification for privacy enhancement.

1.1   Risks and Opportunities of Machine Learning

Growth and Uncertainty: Machine learning applications are trained using large amounts of data. The data are often collected from people, and contain detailed information reflecting those people's identities, attributes, activities, and habits. As ML becomes central to the way that businesses produce value, more and more data are collected. More data means not only more private information, but also greater challenges in data management and storage. Data must be transferred, stored remotely, and processed using cloud services, increasing the opportunities for privacy violations. It starts becoming uncertain how data can be found in the future from the moment the data are collected. Furthermore, Machine-learning-as-a-service (MLaaS) has recently emerged, making results generated by complex models available to a wide public. MLaaS interfaces are easy and cheap. However, widely exposing models increases the risk of inference of properties of the data used to train those models.

Conventional ways of protecting data often assume top-down planning of data management rather than organic expansion, or careful control over the use of the products of data. Data modification becomes increasingly interesting as a means of privacy enhancement in conditions that cannot be fully anticipated or controlled.

Shifting Incentive Structures: Data have long been valuable, but the rise of machine learning has seen a further increase in that value. This value changes the incentive structures surrounding data that have been collected by companies. Specifically, the temptation arises to use data in ways that were not intended when the data were collected. It is not always the case that the change that triggers data to be used for an unexpected new purpose is a sudden change. It may be that the purpose for which the data are used slowly evolves away from the original purpose, a process commonly referred to as *function creep*. These issues are described by an *honest-but-curious* party. This party has the right to use the data, but is driven by an incentive structure to use it in ways inconsistent with the original purpose. The concept of curiosity should be understood with a broad interpretation that covers both the situation of greed (because data can be used to create value) and the situation of neglect (because it is easier and less expensive than to take care of data properly).

The incentive is strong to cut corners when managing or processing data, as illustrated by recent high-profile scandals. The Cambridge Analytica scandal is an example of a failure of data control [52]. It serves to illustrate that complex data environments can give rise to new ways in which data can end up where they should not be, serving a purpose that they should not serve. Another issue is that the task remains the same, but the way that the data are processed suddenly changes. A recent inquiry showed how Amazon employees were instructed to perform manual inspection and transcription of voice signals [78].

The Purpose of Data: The rise of machine learning has seen a focus on the purpose of data. Companies that collect data have a business model and train machine learning models that help them to create value within that model. Moving forward, we expect that the collection of data will be more tightly linked to purpose. In Europe, the General Data Protection Regulations (GDPR) tackles the dangers of data by enforcing the *data minimization* principle: only data that are useful for the task to be carried out can be obtained, upon consent by the user, and for a limited time.

The rise of data sets with a purpose opens the door for a new kind of data modification: *purpose-aware modification*. Purpose-aware modification changes the data so that it is still useful for some purpose (training a particular type of model) but contains minimal privacy-sensitive information. Such data modification has the potential to be particularly effective by introducing changes along any dimensions that is (nearly) orthogonal to the relevant features. Furthermore, data minimization does not always imply removing data. Data minimization should also focus on reducing the information that the data contains. Understanding purpose-aware data modification will help us understand how to more effectively minimize data.

1.2   Scope and Outline

The data modification techniques that we cover in this chapter fulfill two prerequisites. First, they do not use cryptography. In other words, Fully Homomorphic Encryption (FHE) and Secure Multi-Party Computation (MPC) are out of scope. We refer to [86] for a thorough discussion of the crypto-oriented landscape of privacy-preserving ML.

Avoiding cryptography cuts computational requirements drastically, and avoids issues such as key management.

Second, we assume a centralized scenario. In other words, it is not possible to avoid that the modified data are at some point held by a single entity. Thus, we exclude scenarios of distributed training, also known as distributed machine learning (DML). An example is federated learning which consists of random nodes being assigned a small training task to be carried out locally. They will optimize the global model and send the gradient update to the central node for aggregation. Secure parameter aggregation, involving differential privacy (DP) and MPC, protects against the privacy leakage resulting from the loss of the model. [86] gives an overview of the privacy-preserving DML techniques in this area.

The next section in this chapter provides a characterization of two important scenarios in which data are used, "user data sharing" and "data set sharing". These scenarios are chosen because they illustrate the types of privacy risks that can be addressed by data modification. After describing the scenarios, we then provide threat models that capture the nature of the privacy risks. Then, we give an overview of the state of the art of data modification techniques that have been proposed to enhance privacy. The techniques have two distinct relations to machine learning: first, machine learning can be used to create data modification, and, second, the modified data can be used by machine learning algorithms.

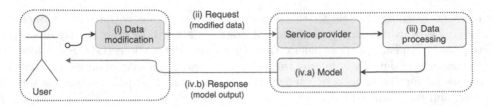

Fig. 1. Scenario 1: user data sharing.

These relations are highlighted in our overview. The chapter finishes with a discussion of challenges and open directions.

2 Scenarios and Requirements

Our data sharing scenarios are inspired by the growing interest in cloud computing technologies [15]. As data becomes cheap, both for centralized entities to collect and edge devices to share, novel business models are popping up that take advantage of this abundance. Considering this relationship between the user (at the edge) and the service provider (at the centre), we obtain abstractions of two scenarios for sharing data. Making reference to these two sharing scenarios allows us to focus on the specific challenges posed by the collection of data for ML pipelines in the context of existing regulatory frameworks [44], and the potential for pre-processing data prior to their release.

In the first scenario, a user shares sensitive data with a service provider (SP) to train a ML model, receive a prediction, or carry out an analysis. In the second scenario, a data-collector has received sensitive data and wants to enable third-parties to perform data analysis. We cannot assume that the channel by which data is shared is reliable. These scenarios allow for a more in-depth discussion on the threats and defenses covered throughout the chapter.

2.1 Scenario 1: User Data Sharing

In this scenario, the user sharing the data is the person who produced the data. The user shares the data in order to receive a certain output, but at the same time does not want the data to be used for a purpose that they do not approve of. The sharing of data serves to feed a ML model or to perform statistical data analysis. This scenario is important due to the rise of cloud-based computer vision APIs, which make it possible for any business/user to build a state-of-the-art model merely by sharing data [2]. This scenario allows a user to benefit from the model while controlling privacy risks. For example, a user can share an image on a social media platform, and agree that platform analyzes that image for the purpose of producing recommendations, but not agree that the platform uses it for other purposes, e.g., training a facial recognition system.

The ML pipeline that we identify as a final goal of this scenario is conventionally divided into modules, which are shown in Fig. 1. Data are first collected and pre-processed by the users themselves, then *Data modification* is performed. Performing modification right after collection is important for several reasons, including cleaning data and minimising storing and network requirements. Technically, modification could also be performed after sharing. However, we focus on applications that apply modification before sharing for privacy-preserving purposes. Next, a *Data processing* module carries out pre-processing and, if needed, extracts relevant features from the data. Feature extraction might be directly integrated into the machine learner, or be carried out as a separate step. For example, the machine learner might be a classifier that uses the data to learn how to label images of animals as *cat* or *dog*. The phase in which data is presented to the classifier for the purpose of learning is called "training". The phase in which a new, yet-unseen data sample is presented to the classifier to obtain a label and/or score is called "inference".

Combing the ML pipeline just described with the data sharing steps, we arrive at a scenario that describes how a *User* and a *Service provider (SP)* interact in a data-value exchange protocol. We divide the procedure in four main steps illustrated in Fig. 1:

i Data are generated/captured and processed to obtain a sample.
ii The sample is shared with the SP, typicality through an unreliable channel (the internet).
iii The sample is further (optionally) processed and fed to the ML model.
iv The SP returns an answer to the user.

In general, the two communicating parties have competing needs: one the one hand, the user wants to be protected; on the other hand, the SP aims to maximize utility. In line with the data quality principles of the GDPR (Art. 5), we define the following requirements:

1. Data confidentiality: by protecting data, we minimize the risks of sharing sensitive information with, generally untrustworthy, third-parties.
2. Data minimization: only data that is needed for the primary learning task is sent via the communication channel.
3. Purpose limitation: data collection and data processing are limited to used in a clearly defined ML task.
4. Usefulness: the ML process preserves the primary utility of the service and the value for the users.

2.2   Scenario 2: Data Set sharing

In this scenario, a pool of people, i.e., the *Data subjects*, have already shared sensitive data with a central node, i.e., the *Data collector*. This might be a hospital who collects the digital clinical diary of their patients [28]. The central node is trusted to be the only entity that is allowed to manage sensitive information,

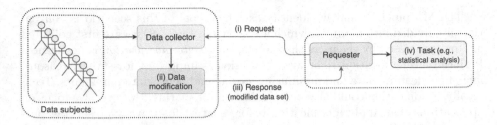

Fig. 2. Scenario 2: Data set sharing.

hence no other party is granted direct access permissions. An external entity, i.e., the *Requester*, performs an access request to obtain a modified version of the data set. The Requester might be a benign organization such as a research institute that aims to performs in-depth analysis or train a ML model.

The interaction between a requester and a data collector can be divided into four steps (Fig. 2):

i The *Requester* forwards a request to the data collector.
ii The data set is processed by the *Data collector*.
iii The modified version of the data set is shared to the *Requester*.
iv The *Requester* performs some defined tasks, e.g., statistical analysis, inference on the received data set.

In this scenario, the data collector manages highly sensitive data that must not be leaked to untrusted parties. Nonetheless, benign requesters can greatly benefit from the sharing of this asset. The main requirements that arise from this scenario include:

1. Data confidentiality: the original data can only be accessed by the *Data collector*.
2. Data privacy: the released data set has to remain anonymous for the *Requestor* and/or suppress sensitive attributes.
3. Usefulness: the usefulness of the released data set is preserved for the inferential task carried out by the *Requester*.

We can observe that two scenarios are similar in that they represent a relationship between a sharer and a receiver. However, they differ with respect to the information that is sent through the unreliable communication channel. In Scenario 1, the data are relevant to an individual, and in Scenario 2, they are relevant for an entire group. Additionally, in Scenario 1, the data is shared with a particular model with a particular function as the target. In Scenario 2, the use of the data is not necessarily limited to a single purpose. Keeping these differences in mind will make it easier to understand the structure of the landscape of threats and countermeasures.

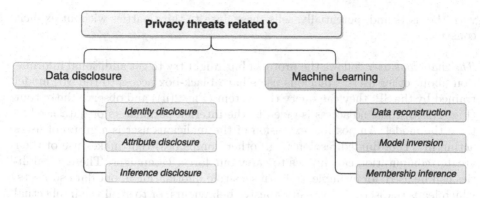

Fig. 3. Privacy threats specific to the contexts of data sharing and machine learning.

3   Threat Model

We define our threat actors based on a standard scheme used in the literature [70]. An attacker has a clear *goal* to carry out, the extent to which the goal is pursued, however, depends on the attacker's *resources*. The resources might include prior knowledge about the target as well as technological and economic resources. The resources deployed are dependent on the *risks* an attacker is willing to take and *countermeasures* used by the target. Based on this scheme, in this section, we model adversaries by presenting threat models that are related to our scenarios. The presentation of the threat models is followed by a description of the main privacy threats linked to our malicious users (Fig. 3).

3.1   Scenario 1 Threat Model

In Scenario 1, "User data sharing", we have two interacting entities: the *Service provider* (SP) and the *User*. Both stakeholders can act maliciously in order to maximize their value at the expense of other actors. Hence, we describe two malicious actors that are directly derived from the previous ones: the *honest-but-curious service provider*, and the *malicious user*.

The honest-but-curious service provider is the coordinator of the communication, i.e., the SP of Fig. 1. Its primary intent is to run the service smoothly while behaving honestly by following the protocol as expected. Accordingly, it receives requests (Fig. 1(ii)) and produces rightful answers (Fig. 1(iv.b)). However, it is *curious* in the sense that it aims at gathering as much information as possible about its users. Specifically, it can modify step (iii) of Fig. 1 to gain out-of-context knowledge that the *User* does not intend the SP to gain. As the SP can be a big corporation, we assume they have the power and resources to obtain additional knowledge about their customers, train large networks, and coordinate an attack between many subsidiaries if needed. In this context, data re-purposing poses a severe threat to the user. The SP performs a task beyond the original one agreed with the users and, potentially, sells these data to third-parties without explicit consent.

The malicious user follows the protocol but might try to get additional information about other users. Malicious users have black-box access to the ML model trained by the SP: they can query the system (Fig. 2(ii)) and observe the output (Fig. 2(iv.b)), but no access is given to the internal parameters or data used to train the model. An possible extension of the malicious user is a group of users acting in a coordinated fashion (e.g., other companies) that makes use of their greater computation capabilities to carry out larger campaigns. These capabilities can be used, for example, to learn sensitive information about data subjects, which leads to discriminative and abusive behaviours, or to steal the intellectual property of the SP (e.g., the ML model internals).

3.2   Scenario 2 Threat Model

Like Scenario 1, Scenario 2, "Data set sharing", is characterized by a two-party interactive exchange. The two main attackers, as before, are adversarial versions of the attackers participating in the exchange: the *malicious requester* and the *honest-but-curious data collector*.

The malicious requester aims to de-anonymize, de-obfuscate or carry out unwanted inference on the received data set. As a requester, it requests access to a data set (Fig. 2(i)) acting as a trustworthy party and obtains a modified version of the target data set (Fig. 2(iii)). At this point, it carries out the inference step (Fig. 2(iv)) targeting users' private attributes, having full access to the original data set. In the worst case, the malicious requester can be a powerful entity capable of obtaining further data about the victims – like the powerful malicious user of Scenario 1 – which enhances its knowledge about the target data distribution. Anonymization techniques could protect users' privacy in this setting. Unfortunately, data are easy to de-anonymize by harnessing correlations between variables and linking different data sources [60].

The honest-but-curious data collector is a *Data collector* (Fig. 2) that works on behalf of its data subjects. It may attempt to infer sensitive information about its customers based on the collected data combined with additional background knowledge. This actor partially overlaps with the honest-but-curious SP of Scenario 1 in that it behaves honestly but leverages its position to maximize its profits, e.g., by collecting and/or retaining data more than necessary. In order to avoid redundancy, we consider the data collector as a trustworthy entity that is required to protect the data before being released to third-parties (i.e., the *requester*).

3.3 Privacy Threats in the Context of ML

Next, we discuss the privacy threats that are related directly to the machine learning model (Fig. 3, right side). These can be understood as mainly related to Scenario 1, "User data sharing", in which we are concerned about the path traveled by the data of an individual user. These threats are related to data modification because data modification can be used to counter them. The gravity of the threat depends on the sensitivity of the data and the threat model of the attacker. We mention the following set of threats [8, 19]:

Data Reconstruction [7,8,72]. Several methods aim at reconstructing private data from a processed version of the data. For example, trying to reconstruct private information after the original data has been transformed into feature vectors. In data reconstruction, the attacker can exploit various levels of knowledge. A malicious user is constrained by the output returned by the SP and the information they know about other users. In contrast, an SP attempting to reconstruct data is constrained by the modification performed locally by the user, but has access to the internals of their own models. Assuming that data samples undergo a modification, the knowledge about the procedure represents an additional tool. The trade-off between the amount of distortion is the data and the usefulness that is preserved determines the amount of protection for both the user and the SP.

Model Inversion   [27]. A ML model can undercover statistical correlations between publicly known variables and sensitive attributes. Model inversion allows malicious users to query the system in order to infer sensitive attributes about a target user if they know something about the target user from another source. For example, given a picture of the target, which is usually available on social media, the attacker (a malicious user) requests the SP to output the probability that the target has of developing skin cancer. At the same time, the SP can abuse its power to sell sensitive data or the access to the model to third-parties interested in these valuable information.

Membership Inference [10,26,73]. The attacker seeks to infer whether an individual was a member of the training set used to build the ML model. In Scenario 1, the membership inference threat is the threat that malicious user aims to learn whether a target user's data was used in building SP's model. The malicious user queries the system and uses the received output to carry out an inferential analysis.

3.4 Privacy Threats in the Context of Data Sharing

Now, we move to discuss the privacy threats that are related directly to data disclosure (Fig. 3, left side). Again, these threats are related to data modification because data modification can be use to counter them. In the context of data set publishing, which falls under Scenario 2, a major threat is represented by the *disclosure* of sensitive information. However, data disclosure is also a threat for the user in Scenario 1. Generally, we distinguish three major types of disclosure [77,80]:

Identity Disclosure. Identity disclosure occurs when a malicious requester successfully links their target with data obtained from the Data collector. The linkage can be made using a small set of variables. If successful, the adversary has access to sensitive attributes in the shared data. An example of identity disclosure was the case of the Netflix Prize competition, where an anonymized data set was released where each record was a tuple containing an anonymous user ID, a movie, the rating given by the user to the movie and the date of the grade [12]. Using the Internet Movie Database as the source of background knowledge, this data set was successfully de-anonymized and Netflix records of known users were identified [60].

Attribute Disclosure. Attribute disclosure if some key variables about the user are already known, and a malicious requester is able to infer additional characteristics (attributes) of the targets from a data set leveraging these variables. In [77], authors used an example where every person with "race = black", "aged 50–60", "living in region ZIP = 1234" in the data set has the same sensitive variable "religion = roman/catholic". Therefore, if the adversary knows that an individual has the characteristics "race = black", "aged 50–60" and "ZIP = 1234", the sensitive variable "religion" is easily inferred.

Inference Disclosure. Sensitive information disclosure occurs when an malicious requester is able to determine characteristics of the target more accurately by making use of the released data [77] and the process of inference. With inference disclosure, individuals are threatened not merely due to the information in their records, but by statistical properties of the entire database [32]. An example would be when you are one of the two richest people in a country. The aggregated information on a survey regarding the income of everyone in the country has been released. You can now easily estimate the wealth of the other rich person by using the published information.

4   Overview of Data Modification Techniques

In this section, we provide an overview of the relevant techniques relevant to the scenarios in Sect. 2 and of use for countering the privacy threats presented in Sect. 3. We provide a categorization in Fig. 4, which summarizes the approaches covered throughout the section and indicates their relation to the scenarios. Many techniques are applicable to both reference scenarios some are more closely connected to Scenario 2, "Data set sharing".

Techniques to pre-process data before sharing can be divided into non-perturbative, perturbative, and synthetic data generation. Non-perturbative techniques achieve privacy protection by applying masks or generalizing given

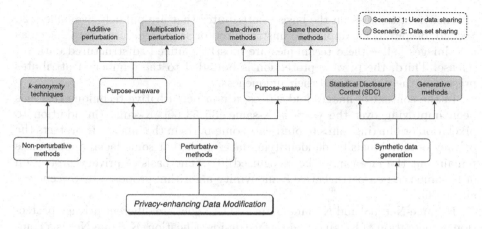

Fig. 4. Taxonomy of the landscape of privacy-enhancing data modification techniques. The boxes designating the methods are shaded to link them to our two scenarios.

attributes. Perturbative methods apply a transformation as a means to hide/obfuscate the sensitive attributes. A further division separates perturbative methods into techniques that apply indiscriminate noise, i.e., purpose-unaware, and techniques that incorporate some knowledge about what the data is to be used for, i.e., purpose-aware. Lastly, it is possible to generate synthetic data that preserve statistical properties of the target distribution while protecting the privacy of users whose data was in the original data set.

There are further differences related to the techniques that we present here that depend on the kind of data that is given as input. In the rest of the chapter, we differentiate between techniques appropriate for structured and for unstructured data. A *structured data set* corresponds to a set of records (rows) composed of well-defined attributes (columns). This data typically resides in a relational database. By contrast, an *unstructured data set* is not organized in a way that directly encodes meaningful relationships between data points. Unstructured data includes many forms of text, images, and audio. A *semi-structured data set* falls between the two. It defines hierarchies/groups of samples without being fundamentally tabular in nature, essentially adding semantic categorization on top of an unstructured data set.

4.1 Non-perturbative Techniques

Non-perturbative techniques adjust the original data so that it is less precise, but do not otherwise change the data [21]. Traditional indistinguishability approaches modify the data so as to prevent identification of individuals within a data set. By generalizing or suppressing specific attributes within a data set, we can achieve properties such as k-anonymization, t-closeness and l-diversity.

However, these approaches suffer from several shortcomings: First, they are not always suitable for releasing large data sets since they may allow the inference of sensitive attributes on the basis of attributes that are publicly available [12]. Second, despite being applied to unstructured or semi-structured data – such as face images [34] – these techniques are mostly confined to structured data set release. Third, the privacy protection is bounded to the number of attributes present in the data set and their uniqueness.

In the context of images and videos, a non-perturbative technique that has been improving over the years is K-same [35,53,66]. K-same (in addition to pixelation or blurring) aims to obfuscate some parts in the images. It protects the privacy of individuals by de-identifying faces such that some facial appearances remain but the face cannot be recognized [61]. The basis of privacy protection of K-same is a non-perturbative k-anonymity algorithm proposed by Sweeney et al. in [76].

K-Same-Net [53] and K-Same-Siamese-GAN [66] are different privacy protection amelioration of K-same against face de-identification. K-Same-Net is a combination of recent generative neural networks (GNN) with k-anonymity mechanisms. It generates synthetic surrogate face images by combining the characteristics of the identities used to form the model. K-Same-Siamese-GAN combines the power of K-same anonymity mechanism with generative adversarial network and hyperparameter tuning. We can consider K-Same-Siamese-GAN to combine non-perturbative methods and synthetic data generation.

4.2 Pertubative Techniques

Perturbative techniques introduce distortions into the data [21] and can be either purpose-unaware or purpose-aware. Purpose-unaware techniques aim to modify the data in a way that contributes to protecting privacy, while at the same time maintaining the usefulness of the data for general purposes. Purpose-aware techniques make use of advance knowledge of the function that the modified data is intended to serve, and modify the data the data in a way that maintains the usefulness of the data for that function.

Purpose-Unaware Techniques. Among traditional pertubative techniques, data swapping and rank swapping exchange confidential attributes between different records [21], data shuffling shuffles the values of the confidential variables among observations [59]. The perturbations are constrained such that the usefulness of the data is maintained. However, while these techniques are sufficient for simple, structured, data sets, they are not suited to address the limitations of large collections of unstructured data. In the following, we delve into recent work on additive and multiplicative perturbation as purpose-unaware techniques.

In the domain of *additive perturbation*, differential privacy (DP) is the de-facto standard for anonymization and attribute hiding [20]. DP, in its most basic form [25], defines formal privacy guarantees that a set of algorithms usually implement via noise addition. These are guarantees on the amount of sensitive information leaked by publishing two 'close' data sets. The privacy loss is measured by ϵ. DP has several advantages w.r.t. previous techniques. First, it makes it possible to quantify the privacy loss via ϵ and tune the utility-privacy trade-off accordingly. Second, it models a worst-case adversary whose aim is to learn a target variable of the target user. Third, because it is not property of the data set, like *k-anonymity*, but rather a property of the process [20], DP can be combined with several techniques and can be applied at different stages. In its *local* configuration, for example, DP permits the local processing of data before sharing with an untrusted party. Random noise addition, however, is a double-edged sword. It protects against reconstruction attacks but does not offer the possibility to balance privacy and usefulness in a satisfactory manner.

Within the ML landscape, DP can be applied at different stages of the pipeline: beyond the protection of input and output, several techniques target the training of a model. The goal is to train a model on sensitive data while guaranteeing DP. Abadi et al. [3] introduced a variation on the stochastic gradient descent (SGD) algorithm, commonly used to train deep neural networks. In particular, they propose to modify the gradient computation by clipping and adding noise. This method is also referred to as *Moments Accountant* since its formal guarantees originate from privacy loss being accounted for at each step of the training procedure. This randomization can be moved to users' devices, as proposed by Arachchige et al. [9]. We can achieve DP training of a deep learning model without trusting a central node, i.e., no sensitive data leave the device.

A second form of noise addition is based on random projections, i.e., *multiplicative perturbation*. Multi-dimensional projections can be used on structured input to preserve the distance between the samples in a lower-dimensional space [6]. This technique makes it possible to run analytics as well as train a regression or classification model on the modified data. Differently from DP-like techniques, projections are prone to reconstruction attacks and sensitive leakage. Recently, Jiang et al. [42] proposed a method to apply individual Gaussian random projections locally that also protect against common attacks. In contrast to previous techniques, they harness the capabilities of deep learning to learn complex patterns and find a projection that better suits semi-structured or unstructured data.

Purpose-Aware Techniques. Next we turn to discuss perturbative techniques that protect data, while maintaining usefulness for a particular function. This function (i.e., "purpose") is known before data modification is applied, and the process used to modify the data is specifically designed so that the modified data can still fulfill this function.

We start with an example that is well suited to illustrate the basic principle of purpose-aware techniques. The example is drawn from the area of recommender systems and is a close fit with Scenario 2 "Data set sharing". In this example, a company (acting as a *Data collector*) shares data with an external researcher (acting as a *Requester*), who is carrying out recommender system research (the *Task*). In this case, the data consists of a so-called user-item matrix in which each row corresponds to a user and contains information on the interactions that the user has had with a set of items, corresponding to the columns. Slokom

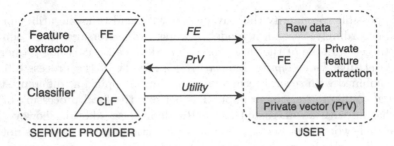

Fig. 5. The split between feature extraction and training in a user data sharing scenario [65]. The feature extractor can be trained with the utility of the classifier, i.e., purpose-aware, or being decoupled from the classifier, i.e., purpose-unaware, depending on the task at hand.

et al. [74] introduced a data masking approach called *Shuffling Non-Nearest-Neighbors* (Shuffle-NNN) that modifies the data so that it no longer contains precise information about which user has interacted with which item. At the same time, Shuffle-NNN aims to maintain the usefulness of the data for the purpose of training and testing recommender systems, which is necessary to carry out research. Shuffle-NNN generates a masked data set by changing a large portion of values of the preferences in a user's profile. Shuffle-NNN can be considered a Data-driven method used to create purpose-aware data modification, because it uses patterns in the data in order to decide which changes to make. Specifically, Shuffle-NNN aims to preserve item-item similarity information, based on the assumption that this information is the most important pattern that needs to be present in the data in order to train and test a recommender system algorithm and move forward recommender system research. Shuffle-NNN applies a data shuffling technique hides (i.e., changes) preferences of users for individual items. Shuffle-NNN occurs in two steps: neighborhood selection and value swapping. Neighborhood selection determines the neighborhoods of every item based on the K-nearest neighbor algorithm and then joins these neighborhoods in order to find a set of critical items. All items not in this set are considered "non-nearest neighbors" and are shuffled. The protection level is judged by the number of ratings that were hid.

Other purpose-aware approaches differ from this basic example along a number of different dimensions. First, they can modify feature representations extracted from the data, rather than the original data itself. Second, they can use machine learning to determine how to modify the data and/or how to preserve patterns in the data needed to maintain usefulness. Third, they can seek to provide privacy guarantees, whereby it is important to keep in mind that whether or not a guarantee holds depends on the threat model. We will now go on to cover series of more sophisticated purpose-aware techniques that exhibit these various dimensions.

Among approaches that use machine learning, techniques based on multi-objective optimization are important. Here, we discuss two examples of work that has investigated the possibility to perform data-driven data modification at the edge. Liu et al. [49] combine deep networks and noise to obtain the best trade-off between privacy and utility. They find a candidate subset of features for noise addition by harnessing a deep auto-encoder: an architecture comprising a compressing part (i.e., the encoder) and a reconstructing part (i.e., the decoder). On top of it, DP-noise is added to obtain measurable privacy guarantees.

Osia et al. [65] propose a hybrid framework in which a feature extractor is trained by a provider with privacy guarantees and shared with the user (cf. Fig. 5). The user can then derive a private representation that is shared with the provider, hence moving the privacy-preserving modification to the edge. The extracted features, or *private vector*, is designed to only contain relevant information for the primary learning task, thus adaptable on the learning task and the given privacy objective. The framework [65] makes use of a fine-tuning strategy. A cloud provider fine-tunes a pre-trained model with two objectives: the primary classification loss function and a contrastive loss. While the first term accounts for the utility of the process, the second one is directly applied to an intermediate layer, such that two samples with the same label end up being close in the feature space and two samples with different labels are separated as much as possible. After training, the classification block is discarded and the feature extractor is shared with the users. In this specific case, data are not shared by the user to perform training, rather for carrying out inference on a trained model.

Also among approaches using machine learning, an increasing among of work makes use of generative adversarial networks [33] (GANs). A GAN models a minmax game between a generator G and a discriminator D: while G is being trained to approximate a target data distribution, D tries to distinguish between a real sample and a generated one. Because a GAN realizes a minmax game, we refer to GAN-based data modification approaches as "Game theoretic methods". Normally, G and D are implemented using two deep neural networks that are trained *adversarially*. The output is a generator that (1) provides realistic data samples and (2) is able to deceive the discriminator. Adversarial learning overcomes the difficulty of modelling an underlying distribution. For this reason, it can be particularly useful when we cannot formally define our privacy objective, because it provides a data-driven way to characterize the private and the target variable distributions.

An ambitious line of work has considered the possibility of bridging the gap between generative networks, adversarial learning, and privacy guarantees. Huang et al. first proposed GAP [38]: a framework to achieve an optimal privacy mechanism inspired by GANs. Here, the generator becomes a *privatizer* that protects against attribute leakage, and the discriminator becomes the *adversary* competing with the latter by trying to infer the protected attribute. The learning strategy is defined as a constrained minmax optimization process that infers the distribution from the data set. This greatly improves the practicality of the approach compared to information-theoretic strategies based on Mutual Information (MI) – a measure of the dependence between two random variables – that is often deemed as an intractable problem.

The seminal work on GAN-based methods had been adapted to different domains in recent years. Different data distributions and different requirements on the private attributes that must be protected require different approaches, both from an architectural and an optimization perspective. Biometric data represent a tough challenge. Applications using biometric data require that the modified data is useful for a specify purpose, e.g., identifying a user. At the same time, sensitive attributes must be protected. The challenge arises because cues of identity and cues related to sensitive attributes are tightly tangled in the data. The information that must be maintained in the data, and the information that must be protected differs from use-case to use case, but the challenge arising from entanglement remains.

In the area of biometric data, some work has tackled the data anonymization problem [30,40,47,51,58,67] and other focused more on the selective compression of data to retain pre-determined attributes [16,31,56,63]. However, techniques working in image domain present substantial differences w.r.t. techniques applied to motion data from inertial sensors. Ren at al. [67] introduce a model trained with an adversarial regularizer and an action recognition network. This data-driven strategy aims at finding the right perturbation that preserves action recognition performance in videos. Li et al. [47] take a different approach by using a conditional generative networks (CGANs). The face is first identified and blurred. A CGAN then generates a new face image by fixing key features – such as the head pose. A similar approach based on GANs and swapping is presented in [40] where the head pose and the background are the only preserved attributes. Beyond identity obfuscation (or anonymization), Chhabra et al. [16] tackle the soft biometric privacy problem. Their proposed algorithm searches for a sub-optimal perturbation that preserves one attributes but hides multiple sensitive attributes. Similarly, PrivacyNet [57] uses a GAN-like training procedure to achieve controllable privacy w.r.t. several sensitive attributes – such as gender and age. In the context of motion sensor data, a few approaches have been proposed that tackle the anonymization of the input trace [51] or the selective hiding of private attributes [31].

Another application domain is online image sharing. Here, the goal is to maintain the usefulness of the images from the point of view of people looking at the images. Images should retain their quality after data modification. At the same time, modified images should offer privacy protection. Oh et al. [62] investigate person recognition, and propose a framework formulated as a game between a social media user and a recognizer. The user attempts to perturbs the image to protect the identity of the person it depicts and the recognizer attempts to break the protection using a countermeasure. Larson et al., [45] formulate a benchmarking task to encourage work on techniques that protect sensitive information in images going beyond faces in people, starting with protecting sensitive scene information in images. Whereas in [62], the assumption is made that the adversarial techniques will preserve the quality of the images, in [45], preserving image usefulness for sharing is specified explicitly as a goal of the data modification.

Zhao et al. [85] is an example of an approach that maintains quality and can be used to protect against unwanted inference of a classifier. Alternation between enlarging perturbations informed by the classification loss and minimizing perturbations informed by perceptual color distance is shown to result in efficient and effective adversarial examples. Shan et al. [71] propose Fawkes, which applies a cloak to images to protect users against unwanted face recognition. Fawkes attempts to move the latent representation of a user towards a second user. More work is needed on broadening the threat model under which such approaches offer protection, especially to include countermeasures deployed by the attacker. More information on adversarial examples can be found in [87].

Our main emphasis is on techniques that enhance privacy by striving to limit the information that can be derived from modified data. For completeness we mention another goal, namely, protecting data from being used in an unwanted fashion. Huang et al. [39] proposed a method for making user data unusable for training machine learning models. Whereas standard strategies seek to maximize error inducing noise, [39] pursues the strategy of finding small noise that minimizes the model's error via a min-min optimization process.

4.3 Synthetic Data Generation

Synthetic data preserves specific statistical properties or relationships between attributes in the original space, without exposing users. Synthetic data generation methods work by first constructing a model of the target data distribution and then generating synthetic surrogates. In this section, we discuss synthetic data generation going from statistical disclosure control [21, 79] to deep learning [4, 81, 83].

Synthetic data is first proposed for the Statistical Disclosure Control (SDC), or inference control methods. SDC seeks to protect the users' data from being disclosed/linked to a specific user [22, 41]. The main purpose of SDC is to release protected data to minimize *disclosure risk*, i.e., the risk that a malicious user uses data to determine sensitive variables of a victim user. To retain data utility, the statistical analysis on protected data and original data must yield similar results [41]. Synthetic data generation is one of the methods which can be used for SDC. Several approaches have been proposed in the literature for generating synthetic data for SDC, such as data distortion by probability distribution [48], synthetic data by multiple imputation [68] and synthetic data by Latin Hypercube Sampling [18]. Recent techniques for generating synthetic data fall into three basic categories [22, 24]: fully synthetic, partially synthetic and hybrid techniques.

Fully synthetic data sets keep the original data private since they are obtained as a replacement set created entirely anew. [22]. We note the disclosure risk for fully synthetic data sets is low, as all values are synthetic. Differently, partially synthetic data sets contain a mix of original and synthetic values [22]. Techniques to achieve partial synthesis replace only observed values for variables that bear a high risk of disclosure (i.e., key variables) [23]. The disclosure risk for partially synthetic data sets is higher than for fully synthetic data sets, since some true values remain in the data set. The disclosure risk significantly increases if the adversary knows which records are present in the data. However, partially synthetic data sets typically have a higher data utility compared to the fully synthetic data sets. Third, hybrid masking techniques generate masked data as a combination of original and synthetic data sets [18]. The value in the original data set is linearly matched with the value in the synthetic data set and are then added together or multiplied to create the published value [84]. This combination allows for better control over individual characteristics [18].

The difference between partially synthetic data sets and hybrid masking is the following: with partially synthetic data sets, an individual variable is either replaced by a synthetic record or the record is kept original, while in hybrid masking the values in each record are added or multiplied with the corresponding value in the synthetic data set.

The domain of synthetic data generation has been evolving over the years. A more recent line of research focuses on deep learning-based *synthetic data generation*. The generated data retains the same statistical properties as the original data while being private for the users. In [4], Abay et al. propose a generative deep learning technique that produces synthetic data from an original data while preserving the utility. An auto-encoder is used to partition the original data into groups. For each group, they build a private generative auto-encoder called *DP-SYN*. The auto-encoder first learns the latent representation for each group, and then uses the expectation maximization algorithm to simulate them. In [46], a variational auto-encoder (VAE) is used as a generative model. The first step is to feed the encoder with the original data and the model outputs a reconstructed data. The second step is to feed the decoder with Gaussian random data. Then, it generates new data from the Gaussian distribution. They showed that VAE succeeds to generate an artificial data that closely mimics the original data while maintaining good accuracy. In addition to auto-encoders and variational auto-encoders, generative adversarial network [33] (GAN) has been widely used for generating synthetic data [5,17,50,81,83]. As discussed above, GANs are composed of two networks: a generator and a discriminator. The generator attempts to produce a realistic looking data based on the learned data distribution and the discriminator seeks to differentiate between the real data from the original data and the synthetic data from the generator. Bindschaedler et al. [13] propose a new approach for releasing privacy preserving synthetic through plausible deniability data while maintaining statistical properties of the data. It is based on the fact that there are at least k ($k > 0$) input records that could have generated the observed output with similar probability. Plausible deniability has two main steps [13]: First, the *generative step* consists of constructing a utility preserving data model. Second, the *privacy test step* aims to protect the privacy of users whose data records are in the input data set. It ensures that every released output can be plausibly deniable.

5 Summary and Future Directions

In this chapter, we have provided an overview of data modification for privacy enhancement based on two main scenarios: user data sharing (Sect. 2.1) and data set sharing (Sect. 2.2). We discussed the related threat models, which describe risks and sources of privacy leakages. We then provided an overview of different approaches for privacy-enhancing data modification (Sect. 4). In the following, we point out important discussions and sketch directions for future work.

5.1 New Types of Data

Data are at the center of research on approaches to privacy enhancement. While structured data lend themselves to the use of traditional techniques based on k-anonymity or DP, semi-structured and unstructured data need a different set of approaches. Moving to new types of data requires careful attention to both the potential and the challenges that are related to the use of machine learning for data modification. Specifically, approaches that extract privacy representations are promising (cf. Sect. 4), but present a future challenge since machine learning research does not study feature extraction to the same depth across different types of data. Extracting features using a neural network is common for face images. However, for sensor data for activity recognition or fingerprint authentication it is generally necessary to rely on manual feature engineering for feature extraction [69]. In some contexts, static features provide a level of interpretability that is currently lacking when using dynamic features. This is important when outsourcing the feature extraction process (Fig. 5), since dynamic features can introduce a new attack surface. For example, it is non-trivial to define the relationship between 128 features extracted from a deep learning model for face recognition as it is to exactly define 64 statistical attributes derived from a motion trace. As a consequence, hand-crafted feature engineering aid the sanitation of data – by imposing constraints on the validity of the features – and can leverage human intelligence in a human-in-the-loop learning process [37]. Nonetheless, deep learning has been demonstrated to be a great ally in solving problems in which traditional ML falls short due to unstructured and complicated data [55], and model explanations can provide an adversary with additional information that hinder the privacy-preserving mechanisms [72].

5.2 Privacy and Fairness

Harmful social bias in machine learning can originate from data sets, algorithms, and processes. Recently, increasing amounts of research have been devoted to the analyses of discrimination and the embedding of fairness into the automatic decision making process [54]. In many cases, the attributes that are deemed sensitive for the user are the ones which drive the unwanted discrimination. Suppressing them, however, is not enough to obtain a fair representation. As with *sensitive attribute disclosure*, the correlation among variables retains the source of bias within our target data distribution, even after attribute suppression.

There is a substantial overlap between work investigating algorithmic fairness and private data modification. Beyond the overlap of sensitive attributes, techniques are applied at similar steps of the pipeline: prior to feeding the algorithm (pre-processing) [14,43], during processing [14] and post-processing [54]. Often, the obfuscation targets the membership in a *protected* group while preserving the utility, which can be modelled as the minmax optimization process seen with purpose-aware data modification. Recent efforts towards the realization of a framework for controllable and measurable fairness include open source libraries that implement the proposed techniques [11].

5.3   Interdisciplinarity

Currently, the domain of privacy-preserving techniques is fragmented across different research communities. Machine learning researchers might approach the problem from a learning perspective, focusing on the model and its optimization. By contrast, the privacy community relies on well-established formal definitions and thoroughly studied solutions. Privacy is a broad field encompassing objective metrics and legal requirements that are often either detached or incompatible [82]. This separation widens further if we consider that the formal techniques are applied in a multitude of systems and that specific domains, e.g., image classification vs. recommender systems, require domain-targeted solutions.

In order to advance research on data modification for privacy enhancement, it is important to bring different disciplines together. Examples of successful collaboration in related areas includes bridging the gap between science and society [64], ethics and big data [29,36], privacy and data quality [1,75]. Here we mention two reasons why we find interdiscplinary approaches to be particularly important. First, machine learning technology is developing rapidly. As a result, the ways in which machine learning meets data modification are constantly changing. Machine learning experts and privacy experts must work together to identify how data modification can address new threats of machine learning and also how machine learning can enable new methods for data modification. Second, data modification is often well-suited for general privacy enhancement, but not for well-defined guarantees of privacy protection in real-world use scenarios. Tackling this challenge will require development of threat models that help to define where data modification could be most helpful, and how it could be combined with other approaches. A benefit of data modification is that it can be used in a decentralized way, in other words, applied at the edge, i.e., on a user's personal device before the user shares the data. Such scenarios must also be incorporated into threat models. Research dedicated to developing the threat models must involve experts in machine learning, distributed systems, human factors, privacy, and the law.

Acknowledgements. This research is partially funded by the Research Fund KU Leuven, and by the Flemish Research Programme Cybersecurity.

References

1. This thing called fairness: disciplinary confusion realizing a value in technology. Proc. ACM Hum.-Comput. Interact. **3**(CSCW), 1–36 (2019)
2. Amazon Rekognition: Automate your image and video analysis with machine learning. (2020). https://aws.amazon.com/rekognition/. Accessed 07 Feb 2021
3. Abadi, M., et al.: Deep learning with differential privacy. In: Proceedings of the 2016 ACM SIGSAC Conference on Computer and Communications Security, pp. 308–318 (2016)
4. Abay, N.C., Zhou, Y., Kantarcioglu, M., Thuraisingham, B., Sweeney, L.: Privacy preserving synthetic data release using deep learning. In: Berlingerio, M., Bonchi, F., Gärtner, T., Hurley, N., Ifrim, G. (eds.) ECML PKDD 2018. LNCS (LNAI), vol. 11051, pp. 510–526. Springer, Cham (2019). https://doi.org/10.1007/978-3-030-10925-7_31
5. Acs, G., Melis, L., Castelluccia, C., De Cristofaro, E.: Differentially private mixture of generative neural networks. IEEE Trans. Knowl. Data Eng. **31**(6), 1109–1121 (2018)
6. Aggarwal, C.C., Philip, S.Y.: A survey of randomization methods for privacy-preserving data mining. In: Aggarwal, C.C., Yu, P.S. (eds.) Privacy-Preserving Data Mining. Advances in Database Systems, vol. 34, pp. 137–156. Springer, Boston (2008). https://doi.org/10.1007/978-0-387-70992-5_6
7. Al-Rubaie, M., Chang, J.M.: Reconstruction attacks against mobile-based continuous authentication systems in the cloud. IEEE Trans. Inf. Forensics Secur. **11**(12), 2648–2663 (2016)
8. Al-Rubaie, M., Chang, J.M.: Privacy-preserving machine learning: threats and solutions. IEEE Secur. Priv. **17**(2), 49–58 (2019)
9. Arachchige, P.C.M., Bertok, P., Khalil, I., Liu, D., Camtepe, S., Atiquzzaman, M.: Local differential privacy for deep learning. IEEE Internet Things J. **7**(7), 5827–5842 (2019)
10. Backes, M., Berrang, P., Humbert, M., Manoharan, P.: Membership privacy in microRNA-based studies. In: Proceedings of the ACM SIGSAC Conference on Computer and Communications Security, pp. 319–330 (2016)
11. Bellamy, R.K., et al.: AI fairness 360: an extensible toolkit for detecting, understanding, and mitigating unwanted algorithmic bias. arXiv preprint arXiv:1810.01943 (2018)
12. Bennett, J., Lanning, S., et al.: The Netflix prize. In: Proceedings of the Annual Knowledge Discovery and Data Mining Cup and Workshop, p. 35 (2007)
13. Bindschaedler, V., Shokri, R., Gunter, C.A.: Plausible deniability for privacy-preserving data synthesis. Proc. Very Large Data Base Endow. **10**(5), 481–492 (2017)
14. Calmon, F.P., Wei, D., Vinzamuri, B., Ramamurthy, K.N., Varshney, K.R.: Optimized pre-processing for discrimination prevention. In: Proceedings of the 31st International Conference on Neural Information Processing Systems, pp. 3995–4004. Curran Associates Inc. (2017)
15. Chen, D., Zhao, H.: Data security and privacy protection issues in cloud computing. In: The IEEE International Conference on Computer Science and Electronics Engineering, vol. 1, pp. 647–651 (2012)
16. Chhabra, S., Singh, R., Vatsa, M., Gupta, G.: Anonymizing k-facial attributes via adversarial perturbations. In: Proceedings of the 27th International Joint Conference on Artificial Intelligence, pp. 656–662 (2018)

17. Choi, E., Biswal, S., Malin, B., Duke, J., Stewart, W.F., Sun, J.: Generating multi-label discrete patient records using generative adversarial networks. Proc. Mach. Learn. Res. **68**, 286–305 (2017)
18. Dandekar, R.A., Cohen, M., Kirkendall, N.: Sensitive micro data protection using latin hypercube sampling technique. In: Domingo-Ferrer, J. (ed.) Inference Control in Statistical Databases. LNCS, vol. 2316, pp. 117–125. Springer, Heidelberg (2002). https://doi.org/10.1007/3-540-47804-3_9
19. De Cristofaro, E.: An overview of privacy in machine learning. arXiv preprint arXiv:2005.08679 (2020)
20. Desfontaines, D., Pejó, B.: SoK: differential privacies. Proc. Priv. Enhanc. Technol. **2020**(2), 288–313 (2020)
21. Domingo-Ferrer, J.: A survey of inference control methods for privacy-preserving data mining. In: Aggarwal, C.C., Yu, P.S. (eds.) Privacy-Preserving Data Mining. Advances in Database Systems, vol. 34, pp. 53–80. Springer, Boston (2008). https://doi.org/10.1007/978-0-387-70992-5_3
22. Drechsler, J.: Synthetic Datasets for Statistical Disclosure Control: Theory and Implementation, vol. 201. Springer, Heidelberg (2011). https://doi.org/10.1007/978-1-4614-0326-5
23. Drechsler, J., Bender, S., Rässler, S.: Comparing fully and partially synthetic datasets for statistical disclosure control in the German IAB establishment panel. Trans. Data Priv. **1**(3), 105–130 (2008)
24. Drechsler, J., Reiter, J.P.: An empirical evaluation of easily implemented, non-parametric methods for generating synthetic datasets. Comput. Stat. Data Anal. **55**(12), 3232–3243 (2011)
25. Dwork, C., Roth, A.: The algorithmic foundations of differential privacy. Found. Trends® Theor. Comput. Sci. **9**(3–4), 211–407 (2014)
26. Dwork, C., Smith, A., Steinke, T., Ullman, J., Vadhan, S.: Robust traceability from trace amounts. In: 2015 IEEE 56th Annual Symposium on Foundations of Computer Science, pp. 650–669 (2015)
27. Fredrikson, M., Jha, S., Ristenpart, T.: Model inversion attacks that exploit confidence information and basic countermeasures. In: Proceedings of the 22nd ACM SIGSAC Conference on Computer and Communications Security, pp. 1322–1333 (2015)
28. Fung, B.C.M., Wang, K., Chen, R., Yu, P.S.: Privacy-preserving data publishing: a survey of recent developments. ACM Comput. Surv. **42**(4), 1–53 (2010)
29. Gambs, S.: Privacy and ethical challenges in big data. In: Zincir-Heywood, N., Bonfante, G., Debbabi, M., Garcia-Alfaro, J. (eds.) FPS 2018. LNCS, vol. 11358, pp. 17–26. Springer, Cham (2019). https://doi.org/10.1007/978-3-030-18419-3_2
30. Garofalo, G., Van hamme, T., Preuveneers, D., Joosen, W.: A siamese adversarial anonymizer for data minimization in biometric applications. In: IEEE European Symposium on Security and Privacy Workshops, pp. 334–343 (2020)
31. Garofalo, G., Preuveneers, D., Joosen, W.: Data privatizer for biometric applications and online identity management. In: Friedewald, M., Önen, M., Lievens, E., Krenn, S., Fricker, S. (eds.) Privacy and Identity 2019. IAICT, vol. 576, pp. 209–225. Springer, Cham (2020). https://doi.org/10.1007/978-3-030-42504-3_14
32. Gomatam, S., Karr, A.F., Reiter, J.P., Sanil, A.P.: Data dissemination and disclosure limitation in a world without microdata: a risk-utility framework for remote access analysis servers. Stat. Sci. **20**, 163–177 (2005)
33. Goodfellow, I., et al.: Generative adversarial Nets. In: Ghahramani, Z., Welling, M., Cortes, C., Lawrence, N.D., Weinberger, K.Q. (eds.) Advances in Neural Information Processing Systems, vol. 27, pp. 2672–2680. Curran Associates, Inc. (2014)

34. Gross, R., Airoldi, E., Malin, B., Sweeney, L.: Integrating utility into face de-identification. In: Danezis, G., Martin, D. (eds.) PET 2005. LNCS, vol. 3856, pp. 227–242. Springer, Heidelberg (2006). https://doi.org/10.1007/11767831_15
35. Gross, R., Sweeney, L., De la Torre, F., Baker, S.: Model-based face de-identification. In: International Computer Vision and Pattern Recognition Workshop, p. 161 (2006)
36. Hagendorff, T.: The ethics of AI ethics: an evaluation of guidelines. Minds Mach. **30**, 1–22 (2020)
37. Holzinger, A.: Interactive machine learning for health informatics: when do we need the human-in-the-loop? Brain Inform. **3**(2), 119–131 (2016). https://doi.org/10.1007/s40708-016-0042-6
38. Huang, C., Kairouz, P., Chen, X., Sankar, L., Rajagopal, R.: Context-aware generative adversarial privacy. Entropy **19**(12), 656 (2017)
39. Huang, H., Ma, X., Erfani, S.M., Bailey, J., Wang, Y.: Unlearnable examples: making personal data unexploitable. In: International Conference on Learning Representations (2021)
40. Hukkelås, H., Mester, R., Lindseth, F.: DeepPrivacy: a generative adversarial network for face anonymization. In: Bebis, G., et al. (eds.) ISVC 2019. LNCS, vol. 11844, pp. 565–578. Springer, Cham (2019). https://doi.org/10.1007/978-3-030-33720-9_44
41. Hundepool, A., et al.: Statistical Disclosure Control. Wiley, Hoboken (2012)
42. Jiang, L., Tan, R., Lou, X., Lin, G.: On lightweight privacy-preserving collaborative learning for internet-of-things objects. In: Proceedings of the International Conference on Internet of Things Design and Implementation, pp. 70–81 (2019)
43. Kamiran, F., Calders, T.: Data preprocessing techniques for classification without discrimination. Knowl. Inf. Syst. **33**(1), 1–33 (2012)
44. Kop, M.: Machine learning & EU data sharing practices. Stanford-Vienna Transatlantic Technology Law Forum, Transatlantic Antitrust (2020)
45. Larson, M., Liu, Z., Brugman, S., Zhao, Z.: Pixel privacy. Increasing image appeal while blocking automatic inference of sensitive scene information. In: Working Notes Proceedings of the MediaEval Workshop (2018)
46. Li, S.C., Tai, B.C., Huang, Y.: Evaluating variational autoencoder as a private data release mechanism for tabular data. In: 24th IEEE Pacific Rim International Symposium on Dependable Computing, pp. 198–1988 (2019)
47. Li, T., Lin, L.: AnonymousNet: natural face de-identification with measurable privacy. In: Proceedings of the IEEE Conference on Computer Vision and Pattern Recognition Workshops (2019)
48. Liew, C.K., Choi, U.J., Liew, C.J.: A data distortion by probability distribution. ACM Trans. Database Syst. **10**(3), 395–411 (1985)
49. Liu, C., Chakraborty, S., Mittal, P.: DEEProtect: enabling inference-based access control on mobile sensing applications. arXiv preprint arXiv:1702.06159 (2017)
50. Lu, P.H., Wang, P.C., Yu, C.M.: Empirical evaluation on synthetic data generation with generative adversarial network. In: Proceedings of the 9th International Conference on Web Intelligence, Mining and Semantics, pp. 1–6 (2019)
51. Malekzadeh, M., Clegg, R.G., Cavallaro, A., Haddadi, H.: Mobile sensor data anonymization. In: ACM Proceedings of the International Conference on Internet of Things Design and Implementation, pp. 49–58 (2019)
52. McNamee, R., Parakilas, S.: The Facebook breach makes it clear: data must be regulated. The Guardian (2018). https://www.theguardian.com/commentisfree/2018/mar/19/facebook-data-cambridge-analytica-privacy-breach. Accessed 07 Feb 2021

53. Meden, B., Emeršič, Ž, Štruc, V., Peer, P.: K-same-net: K-anonymity with generative deep neural networks for face deidentification. Entropy **20**(1), 60 (2018)
54. Mehrabi, N., Morstatter, F., Saxena, N., Lerman, K., Galstyan, A.: A survey on bias and fairness in machine learning. arXiv preprint arXiv:1908.09635 (2019)
55. Miotto, R., Wang, F., Wang, S., Jiang, X., Dudley, J.T.: Deep learning for healthcare: review, opportunities and challenges. Brief. Bioinform. **19**(6), 1236–1246 (2018)
56. Mirjalili, V., Raschka, S., Ross, A.: Gender privacy: an ensemble of semi adversarial networks for confounding arbitrary gender classifiers. In: the 9th IEEE International Conference on Biometrics Theory, Applications and Systems, pp. 1–10 (2018)
57. Mirjalili, V., Raschka, S., Ross, A.: PrivacyNet: semi-adversarial networks for multi-attribute face privacy. IEEE Trans. Image Process. **29**, 9400–9412 (2020)
58. Mirjalili, V., Raschka, S., Namboodiri, A., Ross, A.: Semi-adversarial networks: convolutional autoencoders for imparting privacy to face images. In: International Conference on Biometrics, pp. 82–89. IEEE (2018)
59. Muralidhar, K., Sarathy, R.: Data shuffling: a new masking approach for numerical data. Manage. Sci. **52**(5), 658–670 (2006)
60. Narayanan, A., Shmatikov, V.: Robust de-anonymization of large sparse datasets. In: IEEE Symposium on Security and Privacy, pp. 111–125 (2008)
61. Newton, E.M., Sweeney, L., Malin, B.: Preserving privacy by de-identifying face images. IEEE Trans. Knowl. Data Eng. **17**(2), 232–243 (2005)
62. Oh, S.J., Fritz, M., Schiele, B.: Adversarial image perturbation for privacy protection – a game theory perspective. In: International Conference on Computer Vision (ICCV) (2017)
63. Oleszkiewicz, W., Kairouz, P., Piczak, K., Rajagopal, R., Trzciński, T.: Siamese generative adversarial privatizer for biometric data. In: Jawahar, C.V., Li, H., Mori, G., Schindler, K. (eds.) ACCV 2018. LNCS, vol. 11365, pp. 482–497. Springer, Cham (2019). https://doi.org/10.1007/978-3-030-20873-8_31
64. Olhede, S.C., Wolfe, P.J.: The growing ubiquity of algorithms in society: implications, impacts and innovations. Philos. Trans. R. Soc. A: Math. Phys. Eng. Sci. **376**(2128), 20170364 (2018)
65. Osia, S.A., et al.: A hybrid deep learning architecture for privacy-preserving mobile analytics. IEEE Internet Things J. **7**, 4505–4518 (2020)
66. Pan, Y.L., Haung, M.J., Ding, K.T., Wu, J.L., Jang, J.S.: k-Same-Siamese-GAN: k-same algorithm with generative adversarial network for facial image deidentification with hyperparameter tuning and mixed precision training. In: IEEE proceedings of the 16th International Conference on Advanced Video and Signal Based Surveillance, pp. 1–8 (2019)
67. Ren, Z., Jae Lee, Y., Ryoo, M.S.: Learning to anonymize faces for privacy preserving action detection. In: Proceedings of the European Conference on Computer Vision, pp. 620–636 (2018)
68. Rubin, D.B.: Discussion statistical disclosure limitation. J. Off. Stat. **9**(2), 461 (1993)
69. Rui, Z., Yan, Z.: A survey on biometric authentication: toward secure and privacy-preserving identification. IEEE Access **7**, 5994–6009 (2018)
70. Salter, C., Saydjari, O.S., Schneier, B., Wallner, J.: Toward a secure system engineering methodolgy. In: Proceedings of the 1998 Workshop on New Security Paradigms, pp. 2–10. ACM (1998)

71. Shan, S., Wenger, E., Zhang, J., Li, H., Zheng, H., Zhao, B.Y.: Fawkes: protecting personal privacy against unauthorized deep learning models. In: Proceeding of USENIX Security (2020)
72. Shokri, R., Strobel, M., Zick, Y.: Privacy risks of explaining machine learning models. arXiv preprint arXiv:1907.00164 (2019)
73. Shokri, R., Stronati, M., Song, C., Shmatikov, V.: Membership inference attacks against machine learning models. In: Symposium on Security and Privacy, pp. 3–18. IEEE (2017)
74. Slokom, M., Larson, M., Hanjalic, A.: Data masking for recommender systems: prediction performance and rating hiding. In: Late Breaking Results, in Conjunction with the 13th ACM Conference on Recommender Systems (2019)
75. Srivastava, D., Scannapieco, M., Redman, T.C.: Ensuring high-quality private data for responsible data science: vision and challenges. J. Data Inf. Qual. **11**(1), 1–9 (2019)
76. Sweeney, L.: Achieving k-anonymity privacy protection using generalization and suppression. Internat. J. Uncertain. Fuzziness Knowl.-Based Syst. **10**(05), 571–588 (2002)
77. Templ, M.: Statistical Disclosure Control for Microdata: Methods and Applications in R. Springer, Heidelberg (2017). https://doi.org/10.1007/978-3-319-50272-4
78. Tim, V., Denny, B., Lente, V.H., Ruben, V.D.H.: Google employees are eavesdropping, even in your living room VRT NWS has discovered (2019). https://www.vrt.be/vrtnws/en/2019/07/10/google-employees-are-eavesdropping-even-in-flemish-living-rooms/. Accessed 07 Feb 2021
79. Torra, V.: Privacy in data mining. In: Maimon, O., Rokach, L. (eds.) Data Mining and Knowledge Discovery Handbook, pp. 687–716. Springer, Boston (2009). https://doi.org/10.1007/978-0-387-09823-4_35
80. Torra, V.: Masking methods. In: Torra, V. (ed.) Data Privacy: Foundations, New Developments and the Big Data Challenge. Studies in Big Data, vol. 28, pp. 191–238. Springer, Cham (2017). https://doi.org/10.1007/978-3-319-57358-8_6
81. Tripathy, A., Wang, Y., Ishwar, P.: Privacy-preserving adversarial networks. In: 57th IEEE Annual Allerton Conference on Communication, Control, and Computing, pp. 495–505 (2019)
82. Wu, F.T.: Defining privacy and utility in data sets. Univ. Colorado Law Rev. **84**, 1117 (2013)
83. Xu, L., Skoularidou, M., Cuesta-Infante, A., Veeramachaneni, K.: Modeling tabular data using conditional GAN. In: Wallach, H., Larochelle, H., Beygelzimer, A., dÁlché-Buc, F., Fox, E., Garnett, R. (eds.) Advances in Neural Information Processing Systems, vol. 32, pp. 7335–7345 (2019)
84. Yu, T., Jajodia, S.: Secure Data Management in Decentralized Systems, vol. 33. Springer, Boston (2007). https://doi.org/10.1007/978-0-387-27696-0
85. Zhao, Z., Liu, Z., Larson, M.: Towards large yet imperceptible adversarial image perturbations with perceptual color distance. In: Proceedings of the IEEE/CVF Conference on Computer Vision and Pattern Recognition (CVPR), June 2020
86. Rechberger, C., Walch, R.: Privacy-preserving machine learning using cryptography. In: Batina, L., Bäck, T., Buhan, I., Picek, S. (eds.) Security and Artificial Intelligence. LNCS, vol. 13049, pp. 109–129. Springer, Cham (2022)
87. Hernández-Castro, C.J., Liu, Z., Serban, A., Tsingenopoulos, I., Joosen, W.: Adversarial machine learning. In: Batina, L., Bäck, T., Buhan, I., Picek, S. (eds.) Security and Artificial Intelligence. LNCS, vol. 13049, pp. 287–312. Springer, Cham (2022)

AI for Biometric Authentication Systems

Tim Van hamme, Giuseppe Garofalo[✉], Sander Joos, Davy Preuveneers,
and Wouter Joosen

imec-Distrinet, KU Leuven, Celestijnenlaan 200A, 3001 Heverlee, Belgium
{tim.hamme,giuseppe.garofalo,sander.joos,davy.preuveneers,
wouter.joosen}@cs.kuleuven.be

Abstract. Biometric authentication is currently one of the most attractive authentication methodologies, as it is very user friendly and is the most secure option for consumer grade mobile device authentication. Furthermore, biometric authentication can provide unique security properties, as it is the only authentication factor that is hard to share or steal. Machine learning has further advanced biometric authentication performance and helps detect well known attack vectors such as spoofing attacks. Sadly, the use of machine learning enlarges the already elaborate attack surface of biometric authentication systems. We further explore the how, pros and cons of machine learning for – the interesting security problem – biometric authentication.

1 Introduction

Authentication involves verifying the authenticity of a proof of identity. One of the earliest and most well known examples of (biometric) authentication are hand written signatures. Signatures are widely used to sign legally binding documents, even though these signatures are rarely verified, nor its authenticity is often disputed. For example, how many people check the signature on the ID card of the signing party or even on their credit card in the chip and sign payment paradigm? Moreover, signatures are easy to forge, reducing their level of security even further. Yet, signatures work well in the real world, probably due to the physical context as well as a strong legislation against forgery. Thus, even though hand written signatures are a great example of a biometric authentication modality, they cannot be adopted in a digital and/or remote authentication scenario. Still, institutions like banks have a great interest in systems for automatic signature validation due to their pervasiveness.

In online authentication systems, passwords were a much better alternative as they are easier to input and easier to match for a machine. Passwords, however, have become a nuisance for users, as well as a security burden. Users develop password headaches due to increasing password lengths and a growing number of password protected accounts. Additionally, long passwords are troublesome for mobile devices. Furthermore, system providers do not store passwords safely, as password database breaches have become the new 'normal' [36]. Hence, passwords have become a security risk, as they are often breached or easily phished

© Springer Nature Switzerland AG 2022
L. Batina et al. (Eds.): Security and Artificial Intelligence, LNCS 13049, pp. 156–180, 2022.
https://doi.org/10.1007/978-3-030-98795-4_8

due to password reuse. Furthermore, streaming service providers are pestered by credential sharing, which circumvents the personal service they deliver.

Security researchers have been searching for alternative authentication schemes for the past twenty years [8]. Biometric technologies have great potential, as they are able to recognize the user in a near frictionless manner. However, the adoption of biometrics is still low because recognition performance, security and privacy need to be improved collectively.

Recent advances in machine learning drastically increased recognition performance and this aids in securing the biometric system itself. In this chapter, we show where machine learning technology is applied in the biometric authentication pipeline. However, the blade cuts both ways, as the use of machine learning enlarges the attack surface of biometric recognition systems.

This book chapter mainly deals with biometric authentication. Biometric systems are also used for more controversial topics such as surveillance and law enforcement, which are out of scope of this chapter. Recently, big biometric recognition vendors – such as IBM, Amazon and Microsoft – are refusing to sell their biometric recognition products to law enforcement and even openly question whether this research direction should be pursued [33,35,61]. The pretext is recent work by Buolamwini et al. [9] that showed that biometric recognition performance differs for different gender and skin color. This discrimination of biometric systems is probably due to human bias introduced by system designers.

2   Biometric System

In this section we familiarize the reader with the main concepts in biometrics: we first describe the main building blocks [10] and introduce the two main phases: the *enrollment* and *query* phases. Second, we map the biometric system on a typical ML pipeline. Third, we identify the attack surface. Last, we introduce the evaluation metrics.

2.1   System Design

A biometric system can operate as a *verification* or a *identification* system. The verifier performs a 1-to-1 matching between the query sample that is presented at the input and the enrollment sample stored under the user's profile. Differently, the identifier carries out a 1-to-many matching, which compares the query biometric to a database of enrolment samples. Thus, the tasks answer two different questions: in the first case, we want to verify whether the user is who they claim to be. In the latter case, we are looking for an unknown person within a set of known identities.

Figure 1 shows the typical building blocks in a biometric system, however, in the real world boundaries are blurred and components might overlap. The first step in the chain acquires a biometric measurement. Sensors – such as fingerprint scanners – measure the unique biometric signal and act as the interface between

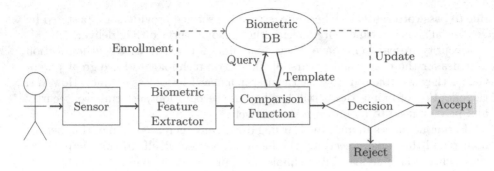

Fig. 1. Architecture of a biometric authentication system [10]

the user and the system. This can require cooperation by the user, e.g. active measurement in face recognition on mobile devices, or happen in the background without prompting any command, e.g. passive analysis of gait patterns via cameras or motion sensors.

The signal is then forwarded to the biometric feature extraction module. Here, the relevant features for user identification are extracted. Prior to biometric feature extraction, the measured signal might undergo pre-processing or a sanity check. These biometric features are stored in a database and retrieved during matching. The biometric template, is constructed from the set of biometric features.

The database is populated during the *enrollment phase*. The user presents their biometric trait several times to the sensor. The templates are extracted, encrypted, and stored. The enrollment phase is typically short and does not allow to capture samples in many different contexts. The length of the enrollment phase is limited by usability and security: an enrollment phase that lasts for weeks is not user friendly. Furthermore, the enrollment phase happens in a special security context as it is a trusted phase. Thus, the input obtained during enrollment has a significant impact on the integrity of the system.

After a user is enrolled in the system, their identity can be verified. During the *query phase* the newly obtained query sample is compared with the biometric template. In a verification scenario, the user claims an identity which is used to query, or index, the database. In case of identification, the database is scanned to search for a match between the query sample and the biometric templates that populate the database.

The matching is performed within the *comparison function* block, and, based on its output, a decision is made on whether to grant or deny the user access to the protected environment, i.e. accept or reject the user. Optionally, to deal with changes in biometric traits, a second decision block can decide to add the query sample to the enrollment samples in the biometric database [4].

The pipeline can be implemented *online* or *offline*, maintaining its structure. However, the separation between the client and the server is often subtle. We can draw a separation between the sensor and the biometric feature extraction

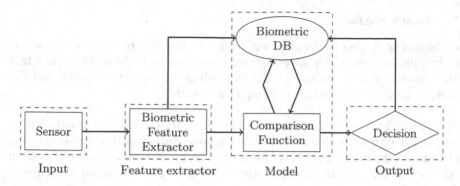

Fig. 2. Machine learning pipeline and related blocks in the biometric authentication pipeline.

step or choose to extract biometric features locally. Depending on the situation, appropriate measure to store the biometric template in a secure and private fashion applies.

2.2 ML-Enabled Biometric Authentication

Recent developments in machine learning (ML) have boosted biometric recognition accuracy. Depending on the chosen modality, ML can be more or less integrated in the different steps described in Sect. 2.1. For example, feature extraction is commonly performed by means of automated algorithms, which has been demonstrated to bring better performance than statistical and manually-engineered features.

We can look at a ML model as a parametric function $f_\theta(x)$, where θ are the parameters of the model and x is the input vector. Pre-processing and manual feature engineering are usually performed before feeding x to the model. Therefore, training is reduced to a search for the best set of parameters w.r.t. a pre-defined evaluation metric that drives the training phase.

We can draw a parallel between the ML pipeline and the biometric pipeline as depicted in Fig. 2. The sensor measuring the biometric signal outputs the input x. A set of relevant features for the given task is extracted by the subsequent module, i.e. the *feature extractor*. As outlined before, pre-processing and signal refinement are, optionally, carried out between these two steps. The *model* can incorporate the decision function as well as the template database. We can learn a model that encodes the identity of a pre-defined set of users as an alternative to traditional distance function, like computing the *Hamming distance*. Finally, a decision is made based on the output of the model.

By looking at the biometric pipeline as a ML pipeline, we introduce new vulnerabilities that are inherited from the nature of the ML system itself. These can be divided in threats affecting the input of the system, the model, and the output.

2.3   Attack Surface

As a biometric system is complex, with different building blocks, its attack surface is quite extensive. An adversary can target every building block in Fig. 2 or the interfaces between them [65]. Depending on the attack point and the attacker's goal different attack techniques are used [5].

Input Level. The sensor captures the biometric trait. This raw input data is transformed into a machine comparable representation during pre-processing and feature extraction. Therefore, we define the input level as the combination of the sensor and the biometric feature extractor. Depending on the current state of the system – *enrollment* or *query* phase – the input data is stored in the biometric database or processed by the comparison function. The following attack techniques target the input level:

1. *Spoofing or presentation attack.* This type of attack presents fabricated biometric traits to the sensor. Defenses – presentation attack detection or liveness checks – aim to verify whether the submitted data is real or fake.
2. *Replay.* Replay attacks are launched at the interfaces between the building blocks. Not only raw sensor data, for example an image found on social media, can be replayed. An attacker can operate one step later and replay extracted feature vectors. Defenses rely on secure encrypted communication channels that implement some sort of challenge response protocol, however, this does not defend against insider threats.

Biometric DB Level. Attacks on this level focus on corrupting the database or stealing the templates. Biometric templates are valuable as they contain sensitive information (function creep), or can later be used to perform replay attacks or craft spoofing samples.

1. *Adversarial examples.* Adversarial examples are not only a threat to the comparison function, but to the biometric database as well. As mentioned before, in some biometric authentication schemes the biometric template is a machine learning model, with other words, the biometric database contains a personalized comparison function. Adversarial examples that target the comparison function level are injected during query phase, while those that target the biometric database are injected during enrollment phase, or during query phase. Examples that are injected during query phase target the automated update strategy. A secure enrollment phase is paramount in defending against these attacks. Defenses for the update strategy focus on detection [43].
2. *Hill climbing.* The goal of hill climbing attacks is to extract the biometric templates from the template database. The attacker injects arbitrary samples at the interface, which they change depending on (fine-grained) output from the authentication system. As these attacks also target the interfaces between the building blocks, the same defenses as for replay attacks apply.
3. *Insertion, deletion and theft.* Inserting or deleting elements in the biometric database allows the attacker to manipulate the outcome of the authentication

system. Alternatively, an attacker can steal the templates to perform replay attacks, to craft spoofing material or to extract private information from the template. Defenses consist of biometric template protection [64] such as secure sketches, fuzzy commitment schemes [72] or cancelable biometrics [66,83].

Decision Level. During query phase, the comparison function provides a score that encapsulates the likeliness that the query sample originates from the same person as the enrollment samples. As discussed above, this function takes input that is generated with the aid of machine learning or is a machine learning algorithm itself. Attacks on this level manipulate the output of the comparison function:

1. *Adversarial examples.* The attacker crafts special examples that fool a machine learning component to manipulate the output of the comparison function. These examples are injected prior to arriving at the comparison function, thus either at the interfaces or at the sensor itself. Defenses against this type of attacks focus either on detection or robustness of ML algorithms.
2. *Malware infection.* An attacker or insider manipulates the node that runs the comparison function to thwart the outcome of the comparison function. Good security practices – secure code, end-point security, input sanitation, etc. – defend against this threat. We do not further explore this threat, as it is not a specific biometric system vulnerability.

Depending on the attacker's goal, knowledge and capabilities they will apply one of the aforementioned attack techniques. In general, the attacker has the capability to influences either the query phase or the enrollment phase. If the system allows for template updating, the attacker can try to influence this mechanism instead of the enrollment phase. An attacker that acts during the query phase aims to evade the system either through spoofing [76] or generating physical realizable adversarial examples [77,98]. Alternatively that attacker can launch a hill climbing attack [57] to violate biometric template privacy. Contrary, influencing updates or enrollment leads to *poisoning* attacks. In a poisoning attack [4,43], the attacker compromises the biometric template to either violate system integrity or its availability, i.e. rendering it useless.

2.4   Evaluation Metrics

Biometric authentication performance is measured with the equal error rate (EER). As illustrated in Fig. 3, the EER occurs at the threshold where false acceptance rate (FAR), also called false match rate (FMR), equals the false rejection rate (FRR), also called false non-match rate (FNMR).

$$FAR = \frac{FP}{FP + TN} \tag{1}$$

$$FRR = \frac{FN}{FN + TP} \tag{2}$$

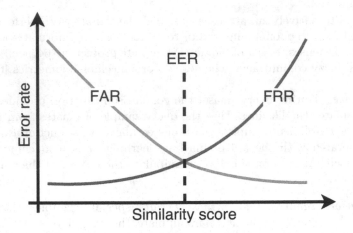

Fig. 3. The equal error rate is defined by the similarity score at which the FAR and FRR are equal to each other.

Determining the threshold for EER post factum is incorrect. In a real system the threshold for the authentication decision is determined upfront, typically on the validation set. The EER threshold from the validation set is then used in the test set, which determines the FAR and FRR. To express recognition performance as one number the half total error rate is defined as:

$$HTER = \frac{FAR + FRR}{2} \tag{3}$$

When setting the accept threshold in a real system, the system designer can opt for more security, by setting the threshold more strict (typically higher). A more strict threshold however, leads to more false rejects, which penalizes usability.

3   Biometric Feature Extraction

A biometric system deals with biometric feature vectors and biometric templates. Biometric feature vectors are obtained during enrollment and compared with the stored enrollment templates during verification. In this section we discuss all steps necessary to obtain these biometric feature vectors and templates. They are acquired by first capturing the biometric trait with a biometric sensor. Then, the raw biometric data is transformed through pre-processing, and finally the biometric feature vector is extracted through feature extraction.

3.1   Sensors

The sensor is the interface between the physical world and the digital biometric authentication system. It captures the biometric trait and presents the digital signal – typical a multivariate time-series, a 2D image or a video – to the feature extractor. The nature of the sensor – the type of data captured, sampling rate, resolution, etc. – impacts the performance of the system drastically, but also its security, as some traits are inherently more costly to forge, for example face authentication with 2D or 3D images [38]. Fusing sensors further enhances the security without hindering authentication accuracy [14].

Since the sensor provides the input to the system, the integrity of the system is highly dependent on the trust placed in the sensor to adequately provide signals originating from a real biometric trait. If the sensor can be circumvented, arbitrary input can be given to the system, which leads to a variety of attacks. Therefore biometric systems are often implemented as trusted end-to-end pipelines where the identity verifier controls all building blocks [7], e.g. physical access and local authentication on smart devices. In remote authentication scenario's however, the pipeline is not fully under control of the verifier as sensing is done locally and (some of) the other building blocks are implemented on a remote server. The degree of trust w.r.t. the input depends on the system design, however, for all types of systems trusted input is paramount for integrity. Therefore, trust in sensor input can be enhanced by relying on secure hardware modules [30], sensor authentication by leveraging physically unclonable functions (PUFs) [13] or sensor authentication by profiling unique sensor noise with ML [16,17,47,86].

A sensor that measures a biometric signal will always capture very personal information that can be used for other purposes than authentication [18]. Therefore, a user should trust that the sensor does not leak the raw biometric data, and that the obtained biometric signal or a derivative will not be misused further down the biometric authentication chain [70].

3.2 Pre-processing

Pre-processing is paramount for recognition performance. In this step the quality of the signal is checked and improved by removing noise and performing alignment. For this end pre-processing leverages ordinary signal processing such as denoising, as well as machine learning. A good example can be found in IMU based gait authentication where the signal is segmented in steps, this removes phase shifts, as well as provides a single coherent unit to extract features from. Furthermore, IMU based gait authentication systems need to account for variations in sensor orientation, e.g. the multivariate time series signal is transformed into gait dynamic image (GDIs) [103] by estimating the angle between the acceleration vectors on distinct time steps.

Face recognition is another example of a biometric modality with a vast body of literature. Older methods, subdivide the pre-processing pipeline of face authentication systems in four steps: face detection [95,97,101], pose estimation [50], landmark detection and finally face alignment based on these landmarks. Face alignment procedures are typically categorized either as *template fitting* [104] or *regression based* [12]. The downside of these older methods is that they rely on manual feature extraction methods that try to extract shapes, which is challenging in unconstrained environments with varying lightning conditions, occlusions, radical face poses and different facial expressions. Convolutional neural networks (CNNs) seem to perform a lot better in these real world environments. Therefore the most recent face alignment systems rely on deep learning technology. One of the most well known examples is MTCCN [99] which is used among others in the more recent implementations of FaceNet [74]. Still, alignment of faces remains challenging under different poses. Recently GANs have been proposed to deal with poses by performing pose estimation, pose correction and finding a pose-invariant representation [85]. Thus, more recent methods no longer subdivide face alignment in different steps and perform the operation in one go.

We provide a last example in fingerprint authentication. As fingerprint matching happens mainly based on the coordinates of extracted minutiae, a correct alignment is important. Recent work by Shuch et al. correct for rotations by leveraging a siamese networks architecture built on top of CNNs [75].

3.3   Feature Extraction

The feature extraction phase aims to find a low-dimensional – compared to the original input signal – representation of the input data such that inter-person similarity is minimized and intra-person similarity maximized. Finding a discriminate feature set is paramount for recognition performance. Before the introduction of deep learning, feature extraction was performed manually by statistically describing the signal or extracting discriminating features in different domains, e.g. time-domain, frequency-domain, ... Deep learning improved upon this situation by automatically extracting discriminate representations of highly complex signals. Therefore, in most biometric modalities deep learning is used to find a discriminate representation of the biometric data, a note worthy counter example are fingerprints, where most systems still rely on minutiae for matching [60]. Even though minutiae are handcrafted features, due to poor image quality, skin conditions, and other sources of noise minutiae benefits from deep learning [19, 53, 73, 82].

Hand-Crafted Features. Robust feature extraction depends heavily on a good pre-processing phase. For example, IMU based gait authentication is highly depended on robust step segmentation [22, 28, 46, 69]. A user's step characteristics are represented by a length normalized time sequence that captures one step. Matching is then performed by dynamic time warping of the average of the enrollment samples and the query sample.

Step segmentation however is hard, therefore later approaches no longer segment steps and extract statistical features derived from sliding or tumbling windows over the accelerometer and gyroscope traces [44, 93]. Statistical features are powerful to describe the general characteristics of a signal, but often fail to adequately capture spatial-temporal relations. Hidden markov models can capture these temporal relations by relying on the cyclic nature of gait patterns [54, 87]. HMMs work well in lab conditions, however, they seem to lack expressiveness to function well in less constrained environments.

Automated Feature Extraction. In the visual domain CNNs and RNNs have been applied successfully to capture spatial-temporal relations in complex data. IMU based gait authentication also benefits from these techniques. CNNs have been applied successfully on segmented steps [27], gait dynamic images [102] and variable length sequences [88]. Alternatively RNNs have been adopted in a similar manner, both on segmented [25] steps and windowed signals [96]. Even when deep learning techniques are applied, signals are pre-processed and different representations of the signals are fed to the system, e.g. gait dynamic images [103] and the extraction of roll and pitch [88] to accommodate for changes in sensor orientation; or steps segmentation is performed to align the phase of the signal. With other words, unnecessary sources of noise are removed.

3.4 Attacks and Defenses

As mentioned in Sect. 2.3, an attacker can try to attack the system by presenting something different than the real biometric trait to the sensor, i.e. presentation attack or by injecting forged or observed samples at the interfaces between the different components, i.e. replay attack. For example, in face recognition, presentation – also known as spoofing [76] – attacks are performed by presenting a mugshot, a video or a mask to the camera. Alternatively, fingerprint sensors can be tricked by fakes made from wood glue or print outs with conductive ink [11]. To perform a replay attack, an adversary needs to obtain access to the interfaces between the different components, for example by physically opening devices or by breaking 'secured' communication channels – insider attacks.

Some authentication modalities are more robust to spoofing as it is more costly to produce a fake. 2D face authentication is by far the cheapest to spoof, as personal images are found all over the internet and high quality print outs are relatively cheap. 3D face authentication is more expensive to spoof, as it requires a mask to be built. On top of that, obtaining an accurate 3D representation of a face without the real model is harder.

Presentation attack detection – also known as liveness detection – is an unsolved problem in the biometrics community. The topic has dedicated tracks on the major biometrics conferences: IEEE International Conference on Biometrics: Theory Applications and Systems (BTAS), IAPR International Conference on Biometrics (ICB) and International Joint Conference on Biometrics (IJCB); and a biyearly competition LivDet [1,49]. Typically liveness detection is done either by adding additional hardware or in software by looking for specific characteristics of spoofs. Software based liveness checks rely on ML, the 2015 LivDet competition winner [56] adopts CNNs to detect spoofs. They show that their method is superior to earlier proposed solutions that rely on manually engineered features such as local binary pattern (LBP) extraction and more traditional ML methods like SVMs. Raja et al. [63] further explored the difference in expressiveness between manually engineered features – texture based, LBP, etc. – and automated features learned by a deep learning model and confirm the earlier observation: PAD benefits from deep learning based features, because they are more robust and lead to better recognition performance. Sadly attackers can also leverage the power of machine learning to produce new attack vectors, for example, due to the recent successes in speech synthesis, arbitrary speech, i.e. authentication systems that do not rely on a fixed keyphrase, have become easy to spoof. Luckily, recent work by Yan et al. [94] showed that it is possible to characterize the difference of sound generated by humans and machines.

Defences against replay attacks are typically implemented in one of two ways: a *challenge response system* or by correlating the biometric signal with an *additional out-of-band signal* received from another sensor. The challenge response system relies on applying a signal that is beyond the control of the attacker, and then retrieving this same signal from within the biometric data. For example one can use the screen of a smartphone to produce a color coded signal during face authentication. If the reflections match the applied pattern one can be fairly sure that the biometric trait is not replayed [78,81]. Alternatively some biometrics rely on applying a changeable signal, the biometric system can thus observe the unique reaction to the signal, i.e. the biometric used for matching, and the signal itself for PAD, an example of such system is hand geometry [41]. EEG is an example of a more complex biometric with the same potential.

Defences based on out-of-band signal correlation obtain two signals, one with the biometric and another via a different communication channel and different sensor. Both signals are correlated since they capture a similar pattern. For example, the heart rate can be obtained in a recording of a face as well as through a PPG sensor or a finger held to the camera [80]. Another example requires to move the camera during face authentication. The movements from the video are then matched to the ones observed by the IMU sensor [42]. We want to point out that most of the replay prevention methods also defend against spoofing attacks as they defend against a stronger attacker.

4 Biometric DB

Storing a feature vector in a biometric DB threatens the user's privacy as well as the integrity of the whole authentication system. Therefore, modification are applied to transform a feature vector into a *template*, which is retrieved for matching at verification time. We discuss here the requirements for a secure and private template storage, the techniques that ensure its protection, and the attacks that aim to alter it.

4.1 Template Enrollment

The template enrollment phase populates the template DB (cfr. Fig. 1). Depending on the given modality, these representations can vary greatly and present different implementation challenges. The stored template can be either a (set of) feature vector(s) or a model function. Furthermore, these templates can be self-updatable or static.

Static templates are usually updated on-demand, as per request of the user or the service provider. Differently, self-adapting templates deal with changes in appearance applying continuous updates. The system can simply harness the samples provided by the user at verification time, thus becoming invisible to the users themselves. Self-updating strategies help to cope with natural and artificial modifications of one's biometric trait – such as a haircut or old age wrinkles for face images. In practice, the decision made at verification time is fed back to the biometric DB to update the stored template based on a specific update policy (cfr. Fig. 1).

The storage step is highly sensitive, since losing these biometric information, e.g. following a data breach, threatens the availability and integrity of the system. Moreover, biometric templates are unique per user and non-renewable. Hence failing to securely store them jeopardize users' privacy.

4.2 Template Matching

Template matching is performed in the *Comparison Function* module. This module however does not always apply its own function. If the template consists of a ML model, for example OneClass-SVM, the matching function is embedded in the template itself. Thus, the comparison function itself is passed to the *Comparison Function* module. Contrary, if the template is a (set of) feature vector(s), matching happens based on the function defined in the comparison function, which is often some sort of distance function.

4.3 Attacks and Defenses

In real-world applications, a template should not be stored in plain-text to prevent breaches and the permanent loss of users' identity. Encrypting the reference template protects against data breaches by preventing their reconstruction. However, the template is recovered for matching, thus can potentially be stolen at each new authentication attempt. Therefore, biometric template protection (BTP) schemes apply a transformation that does not require the raw biometric during the query phase. BTP schemes instead store derived artefacts which comply with the following three requirements (ISO/IEC FCD 24745):

1. *Irreversibility:* It should be computationally hard to reconstruct the reference template.
2. *Unlinkability:* It should not be possible to link different templates derived from the same biometric sample.
3. *Revocability:* The reference template should be revocable in a way that the original biometric sample is re-usable across services.

By allowing the reuse of a single sample across different services, BTP prevents cross-matching and minimizes the risks associated to unauthorized breaches. The transformation requires a secret key that is provided first during enrolment. At authentication time, the features and the key are used to compute a reference template that is matched with the stored one. Thus, the matching happens in the transformed domain.

Irreversibility and revocability are achieved by using cryptographic-alike one-way functions. The most delicate step of the process is the management of the keys. In BTPs, this is done in two ways [68]: (1) biometric cryptosystems bind a key to or generate a key from a biometric feature vector. The retrieval and the generation is driven by the so-called *helper data*, which is provided by the user during both operational phases. (2) Cancelable biometrics apply a transformation that can be invertible or non-invertible. The key that is used to perform the given transformation is protected via a second factor that can be, e.g., a password or a second biometric trait.

Key challenges of BTPs include [51]:

– *Take into account advances in the feature extraction process.* Templates derived from fingerprints and face images usually yield a high accuracy due to being easy to transform into a binary and consistent representation. A common example is the use of bloom filters [67]. However, face images are bounded to deep learning algorithms that extract feature that might be unsuitable to existing template protection schemes. Moreover, voice recognition is one example of a biometric trait that is unsuitable to traditional transformations. In fact, it has been proven to be less consistent and yield pure result, therefore relying on a *model* rather than a *template* for authentication [52].
– *Bridge the gap between performance and security.* Estimating the biometric distribution is key to trade-off between privacy and accuracy. However, this is rarely achieved in practice.
– *Address the unlinkability of biometric templates.* Unlinkability evaluation is an unsolved problem in BTP schemes. This is due to the schemes being often bounded to the use of a second factor [6]. General frameworks exist to evaluate the unlinkability of templates generated using different keys [32]. A different approach to prevent this problem is to work in the encrypted domain by harnessing Fully Homomoprhic Encryption (FHE) [84]. On the one hand, FHE has the advantage of preventing degradation of data, since the operation are performed in the encrypted domain but on the original, unmodified, sample. On the other hand, only a limited set of operations are possible, and a substantial computational overhead applies.

Privacy Leakages. BTP schemes are effective against *data breaches*. A stolen template can be revoked, thereby reducing the risk of theft and loss. However, other blocks of the system still leak sensitive data about the user [62]. The attacker might harness the verification output to gain knowledge about the system and the user. The amount of information varies based on the output received from the system: it can be a binary response (accepted/rejected) or a score (e.g. model output). In the latter case, we talk about Hill-Climbing attacks [57,58]. Hill-Climbing has been used to uncover encrypted face images from observing a quantized output [2]. An input is presented to the system and compared to a reference target template. Based on the output matching score, modifications are applied. Throughout the process, only modifications yielding an higher matching score are retained.

To counteract information leakage, output randomization could be used. This protects the model and the templates by preventing or hindering reconstruction attacks. These attacks are usually performed as a first step before carrying out other attacks for which knowledge is key (e.g. adversarial attacks).

Adversarial ML: Poisoning. Poisoning attacks aim to inject a set of malicious samples within a target training set. The adversary targets the self-update strategy of the ML model, such that every re-training steps moves the function learned by the model in the direction specified by the adversary. This contamination leads to two threats: a denial of service, which disrupt the service, and a careful modification of the model function that selectively grant or deny access to a target user.

In the context of biometric authentication, this attack targets self-adapting templates during the enrollment phase. The goal of the adversary can be either to find the best modification to be authenticated as a rightful user (untargeted attack) or deny authentication to a predefined victim (targeted attack). In the target poisoning case, Biggio et al. [4] have analyzed the resilience of a biometric template under white box access to the model and no further protection layer. Garofalo et al. [29] have investigated the poisoning setting for a OneClass-SVM model authenticating a single user. This last attack relies on strong assumptions on the adversaries capabilities. The adversarial sample needs to comply with the following three features: (1) it can by-pass the PAD layer, (2) it is accepted as a sample for the victim user, (3) is able to trigger a template update (i.e. accepted with a high certainty) and (4) acts within a realistic budget in terms of number of queries. The aforementioned assumptions are relaxed by Lovisotto et al. [43], who perform an attack on biometric systems during the query phase, leveraging template updating.

5   Comparison Functions

Authentication/identification tasks are comparisons between (a subset of) previously enrolled features (biometric template), and the biometric features originating from the new query sample. In this section we give more details on the most used comparison functions and the attacks against them.

5.1   Distance Functions

There are a few different options for the actual comparison function. If one wants to work with simple distance functions between features, the choice usually depends on the model the features were derived from [91]. For example, in facial authentication systems, the current state-of-the-art feature extractors are variant of the well-known cross entropy loss, which has an inherent angular component [21]. Therefore the features derived from those models should be compared with an angular distance loss. On the other end, some feature extractors for facial authentication systems are trained on losses that are explicitly trained to emit features that are separated in L_2 distance [74], which leads obviously to the use of Euclidean distance functions to compare features in subsequent authentication attempts.

Regardless of which distance function is used, some different schemes for which two vectors to compare exist. Since using only one of the enrolled features is not a good representative of the enrolled person, the new feature vector is usually compared against a weighted combination of enrolled feature vectors, called the centroid. The weighting scheme can be simple where each feature vector is weighted equally. Alternatively, a higher weight is given to the most recent feature vectors. These are a few of the often used options, but many more exist [3].

Another variable to play with is which subset of the feature vectors to take into account. The intuitive option is to use every enrolled feature vector in the centroid. This option is intuitive because the more feature vectors are used in the centroid, the better the centroid should be an approximation of the actual centroid of the target identity. But different schemes exist that offer different trade-offs. One could for example use only a subset of the feature vectors, namely those that correspond to the feature vectors that have the highest distance to the new feature vector. Intuitively this makes the system more resilient to false accepts, since the hardest comparison is chosen, and should not make a difference for benign comparisons. Again, multiple different options exist, each suited for different system designs and trading off security, usability and other metrics.

These distance functions are often used in open-ended systems and therefore usable for both identification and verification. For verification, it is simple to query the desired centroid from the template database, calculate the feature vector from the authentication attempt and make the decision whether or not it is authenticated (based on some threshold, e.g. EER). For identification this is much the same, except that instead of making a binary classification against one specific centroid, the distance between all centroids (identities) is calculated, and the identity with the closest match is returned. A variant of this does also return the closest identity, but only if the distance falls below a specified centroid. This to ensure that returning the "least negative" isn't detrimental to the security of the system, and can be thought of as having a "other" type of class.

5.2   Learned Functions

SVM are also a common decision function in biometric authentication. Since authentication can't be modelled as a binary classification task (it is hard to model the negative set, since all other users belong to it), one-class SVMs are used [27, 29]. They are commonly used to model e.g. smartphone access, or other systems where there is only one legitimate user. They are then trained on feature vectors from that legitimate user which form the positive set. They are then able to discern between new feature vectors from that user, where the user is authenticated if the new feature vector is classified as positive by the one-class SVM.

Another way to perform open set recognition is by calculating the loglikelihood ratio of the probability of the biometric sample under a universal background model (UBM) and under a personal adapted model [72,87]. These universal background models used to consist of gaussian mixture models (GMMs), however, in speaker verification they found a more discriminate low dimension representation called i-vectors (identity-vectors). I-vectors are compared by the use of linear discriminant analysis (LDA) [20].

5.3   Attacks and Defenses

Attacks Against Classic Distance Functions. Since the classic distance functions only rely on the new feature vector, it is the specific model that is the weak link in this case. If the model can be tricked into emitting a feature vector that is close enough to an intended feature vector, the attack is successful. This is easily doable with the now well-known adversarial examples.

Adversarial ML. While using machine learning has been very beneficial for authentication systems, it has introduced additional attack vectors for attackers to exploit. Evasion attacks in this context are defined as making the decision function output the wrong decision, to the benefit of the attacker. There exist a few variations under the umbrella of evasion attacks. These variations consist of specifics such as: flipping the decision in binary cases (e.g. authenticated vs not authenticated) versus a claimed identity, or changing the final classification of closed-ended system [5,77]. The latter is not common since authentication systems are better suited for open-ended systems.

Another important distinction in evasion attacks depends on the intended classification. For binary cases this is self-evident, but for open-ended systems there are two variations. Either an attacker can trick the decision function to identify as a specified target (targeted evasion attacks) [39,98], or as any target that is not the original (untargeted evasion attacks). In the case of verification, where matching is performed against a chosen identity, the target is usually chosen (for obvious reasons). In the case of verification, both attacks are valid options, dependent on the goal of the attacker.

Defenses. Defenses against adversarial input focus on improving the robustness of the machine learning classifier during training [34,71,92] or on detecting adversarial input [15]. The two main strategies to improve model robustness are adversarial training or adapting the loss function to obtain better separated and more condensed classes in feature space. Detection systems look for adversarial noise, which is typically constraint in order to be physically realizable.

6   Summary

Biometric authentication might just be the future for authentication systems. They are more user friendly and offer unique security properties. Machine learning plays a massive roll in improving recognition performance by constructing more complex comparison functions or providing more discriminate presentations of highly complex biometric data. Furthermore, machine learning aids in solving some of the security problems such as spoofing and replay attacks. Machine learning however, does also enlarge the attack surface introducing new attack vectors that can be exploited.

To study the impact of machine learning on biometric authentication, we introduced the different building blocks of such system. We then showed how these biometric building blocks map upon a machine learning pipeline. Within this comprehensive model we discussed the security and privacy challenges of the biometric authentication system. Thereby providing the reader with a comprehensive model to further study the application of machine learning for biometric system security. To end this chapter we summarize how biometric authentication is best modelled as a machine learning problem; why deep learning does not only provide benefits, but also introduces new threats; and what (research) challenges still remain.

6.1   Biometric Authentication as an Open Set Problem

Biometric authentication, i.e. the verification of a claimed identity, is within the security community sometimes modelled as a closed-world binary classification problem [79,89,100], however, this has several disadvantages: (1) from a practical perspective it makes it hard to train your classifier as the data set is highly unbalanced due to short enrollment phases. Thus, there is a limited amount of positive data – you –, while there is a lot of data necessary to represent the negative class – not you. (2) it is close to impossible to represent the negative class accurately. The classification of a previously unseen person will depend heavily on the population used to represent the negative class. If that specific user has traits more similar to the positive class then any of negative classes, that person will be authenticated. (3) Zhao et al. [100] proved that closed world binary classifiers do not sufficiently constrain their decision boundaries, which leads to worse then expected performance.

All of the biometric authentication work discussed in the previous sections model the verification problem as an open-world problem. This better corresponds with the limited amount of enrollment data that is available in real biometric systems. Furthermore, an open-world assumption is a more realistic problem representation, as not the whole population can be seen at training time. The most used open-world techniques are: dynamic time warping, which measures the similarity of two temporal sequences; one-class support vector machines; universal background models and few shot learning with siamese networks or other deep learning based feature extractors.

6.2   Threats Linked to New Factors and Deep Learning

Deep learning has paved the way for the use of novel bio- and behavior-metrics for authentication, like finger-vein [40], ECG [37], hand geometry [41], EEG or eye movement [24,45], however, these techniques enlarge the attack surface.

The use of deep learning in critical infrastructure sparked a whole new domain of research, i.e. adversarial examples. Additionally, human bias is represented in machine learning algorithms, which leads to unfair algorithms. Due to this human bias, security levels of authentication systems are different depending on skin color, ethnicity and gender [9,55]. Lastly, due to deep learning function creep has become a bigger threat, because more complex functions can be learned, thus also functions that map biometric feature vectors to soft biometrics or even the raw biometric data [31,48]. In general, due to deep learning any form of personal data has become more sensitive, as the amount of leakage is unclear. The other way round, as deep learning enables to estimate biometric features from other biometric traits, sharing any kind of personal data poses a security risk for biometric authentication [23].

6.3 Future Directions

Biometric authentication systems still have a long way to go before they become a satisfactory authentication methodology that can be applied in a wide set of use cases. More research is needed to further reduce user interaction, limit the attack surface and ensure that biometric authentication does not violate user privacy. Ross et al. [70] described the future directions for biometrics in general. We focus here on biometric authentication specifically.

To make biometric authentication systems fully frictionless they should be able to run unobtrusively in the background, constantly monitoring the user context and natural human-computer interactions. Biometrics must help drive the shift from the current single shot authentication paradigm to a paradigm with continuous authentication. As a biometric modality that fits all use cases does not exist, the future biometric authentication system will most probably leverage many different biometric modalities and sensors [26]. Such system should be adaptive and deal with missing modalities, temporal discrepancies and decide when to perform step-up authentication at the penalty of user interaction [90].

Throughout this book chapter we've shown the elaborate attack surface of biometric authentication systems. The vast body of literature on presentation attack detection still does not describe the holy-grail. We are in need of anti-spoofing methods that generalize over different attack types and datasets [59]. Defenses that are successful against replay attacks and spoofing rely on challenge-response methodologies [41,81] or correlate different biometric signals [80]. However, these techniques add more friction or are not universally applicable. Lastly, the use of deep learning introduces new threats such as deep fooling, back door attacks – where the model is learnt to react differently for pre-defined input patterns – and model stealing – where the expensive machine learning model is stolen. New research can focus on either showing the extent of the treats or coming up with novel detection strategies.

Biometric authentication keeps struggling with privacy threats [58]. More research is necessary to better understand the extent to which private attributes are leaked and how to limit this leakages without sacrificing recognition performance. Alternatively, future research could focus on the security threat for biometric authentication due to the sharing of biometric traits in other context, for example, medical data, fitness trackers, social media, online DNA tests, etc.

Acknowledgements. This research is partially funded by the Research Fund KU Leuven, and by the Flemish Research Programme Cybersecurity.

References

1. Livdet. https://livdet.org. Accessed 11 June 2020
2. Adler, A.: Images can be regenerated from quantized biometric match score data. In: Canadian Conference on Electrical and Computer Engineering 2004 (IEEE Cat. No. 04CH37513), vol. 1, pp. 469–472. IEEE (2004)
3. Biggio, B., Didaci, L., Fumera, G., Roli, F.: Poisoning attacks to compromise face templates. In: 2013 International Conference on Biometrics (ICB), pp. 1–7. IEEE (2013)
4. Biggio, B., Fumera, G., Roli, F., Didaci, L.: Poisoning adaptive biometric systems. In: Gimel'farb, G., et al. (eds.) SSPR /SPR 2012. LNCS, vol. 7626, pp. 417–425. Springer, Heidelberg (2012). https://doi.org/10.1007/978-3-642-34166-3_46
5. Biggio, B., Russu, P., Didaci, L., Roli, F., et al.: Adversarial biometric recognition: a review on biometric system security from the adversarial machine-learning perspective. IEEE Signal Process. Mag. **32**(5), 31–41 (2015)
6. Blanton, M., Aliasgari, M.: Analysis of reusability of secure sketches and fuzzy extractors. IEEE Trans. Inf. Forensics Secur. **8**(9), 1433–1445 (2013)
7. Blasco, J., Chen, T.M., Tapiador, J., Peris-Lopez, P.: A survey of wearable biometric recognition systems. ACM Comput. Surv. **49**(3), 1–35 (2016). https://doi.org/10.1145/2968215
8. Bonneau, J., Herley, C., v. Oorschot, P.C., Stajano, F.: The quest to replace passwords: a framework for comparative evaluation of web authentication schemes. In: 2012 IEEE Symposium on Security and Privacy, pp. 553–567 (2012)
9. Buolamwini, J., Gebru, T.: Gender shades: intersectional accuracy disparities in commercial gender classification. In: Conference on Fairness, Accountability and Transparency, pp. 77–91 (2018)
10. Campisi, P.: Security and Privacy in Biometrics, vol. 24. Springer, Heidelberg (2013). https://doi.org/10.1007/978-1-4471-5230-9
11. Cao, K., Jain, A.K.: Hacking mobile phones using 2D printed fingerprints. Michigan State University, Department of Computer Science and Engineering (2016)
12. Cao, X., Wei, Y., Wen, F., Sun, J.: Face alignment by explicit shape regression. Int. J. Comput. Vision **107**(2), 177–190 (2014). https://doi.org/10.1007/s11263-013-0667-3
13. Cao, Y., Zhang, L., Zalivaka, S.S., Chang, C., Chen, S.: CMOS image sensor based physical unclonable function for coherent sensor-level authentication. IEEE Trans. Circuits Syst. I Regul. Pap. **62**(11), 2629–2640 (2015)
14. Chen, S., Pande, A., Mohapatra, P.: Sensor-assisted facial recognition: an enhanced biometric authentication system for smartphones. In: Proceedings of the 12th Annual International Conference on Mobile Systems, Applications, and Services, pp. 109–122 (2014)
15. Chou, E., Tramèr, F., Pellegrino, G., Boneh, D.: SentiNet: detecting physical attacks against deep learning systems. arXiv preprint arXiv:1812.00292 (2018)

16. Cozzolino, D., Marra, F., Gragnaniello, D., Poggi, G., Verdoliva, L.: Combining PRNU and noiseprint for robust and efficient device source identification. EURASIP J. Inf. Secur. **2020**(1), 1–12 (2020). https://doi.org/10.1186/s13635-020-0101-7

17. Cozzolino, D., Verdoliva, L.: Noiseprint: a CNN-based camera model fingerprint. IEEE Trans. Inf. Forensics Secur. **15**, 144–159 (2019)

18. Dantcheva, A., Elia, P., Ross, A.: What else does your biometric data reveal? Survey Soft Biometrics **11**(3), 441–467 (2016)

19. Darlow, L.N., Rosman, B.: Fingerprint minutiae extraction using deep learning. In: IEEE International Joint Conference on Biometrics, IJCB 2017, 22–30 January 2018 (2018). https://doi.org/10.1109/BTAS.2017.8272678

20. Dehak, N., Kenny, P.J., Dehak, R., Dumouchel, P., Ouellet, P.: Front-end factor analysis for speaker verification. IEEE Trans. Audio Speech Lang. Process. **19**(4), 788–798 (2011)

21. Deng, J., Guo, J., Xue, N., Zafeiriou, S.: ArcFace: additive angular margin loss for deep face recognition. In: Proceedings of the IEEE Conference on Computer Vision and Pattern Recognition, pp. 4690–4699 (2019)

22. Derawi, M.O., Bours, P., Holien, K.: Improved cycle detection for accelerometer based gait authentication. In: 2010 Sixth International Conference on Intelligent Information Hiding and Multimedia Signal Processing, pp. 312–317 (2010). https://doi.org/10.1109/IIHMSP.2010.84

23. Eberz, S., Lovisotto, G., Patanè, A., Kwiatkowska, M., Lenders, V., Martinovic, I.: When your fitness tracker betrays you: quantifying the predictability of biometric features across contexts. In: 2018 IEEE Symposium on Security and Privacy (SP)m, pp. 889–905 (2018)

24. Eberz, S., Lovisotto, G., Rasmussen, K.B., Lenders, V., Martinovic, I.: 28 blinks later: tackling practical challenges of eye movement biometrics. In: Proceedings of the 2019 ACM SIGSAC Conference on Computer and Communications Security, CCS '19, pp. 1187–1199. Association for Computing Machinery, New York (2019). https://doi.org/10.1145/3319535.3354233

25. Fernandez-Lopez, P., Liu-Jimenez, J., Kiyokawa, K., Wu, Y., Sanchez-Reillo, R.: Recurrent neural network for inertial gait user recognition in smartphones. Sensors (Switzerland) **19**(18), 1–16 (2019). https://doi.org/10.3390/s19184054

26. Fridman, L., et al.: Multi-modal decision fusion for continuous authentication. Comput. Electr. Eng. **41**, 142–156 (2015)

27. Gadaleta, M., Rossi, M.: IDNet: smartphone-based gait recognition with convolutional neural networks. Pattern Recognit. **74**, 25–37 (2018). https://doi.org/10.1016/j.patcog.2017.09.005. http://www.sciencedirect.com/science/article/pii/S0031320317303485

28. Gafurov, D., Snekkenes, E., Bours, P.: Improved gait recognition performance using cycle matching. In: 24th IEEE International Conference on Advanced Information Networking and Applications Workshops, WAINA 2010, pp. 836–841 (01 2010)

29. Garofalo, G., Rimmer, V., Preuveneers, D., Joosen, W., et al.: Fishy faces: crafting adversarial images to poison face authentication. In: 12th {USENIX} Workshop on Offensive Technologies ({WOOT} 18) (2018)

30. Gilchrist, G., Viavant, S.D.: Trusted biometric client authentication (2000). uS Patent 6,167,517

31. Gomez-Barrero, M., Galbally, J.: Reversing the irreversible: a survey on inverse biometrics. Comput. Secur. **90**, 101700 (2020)

32. Gomez-Barrero, M., Galbally, J., Rathgeb, C., Busch, C.: General framework to evaluate unlinkability in biometric template protection systems. IEEE Trans. Inf. Forensics Secur. **13**(6), 1406–1420 (2017)
33. Greene, J.: Microsoft won't sell police its facial-recognition technology, following similar moves by Amazon and IBM. https://www.washingtonpost.com/technology/2020/06/11/microsoft-facial-recognition/. Accessed 15 June 2020
34. Hafemann, L.G., Sabourin, R., Oliveira, L.S.: Characterizing and evaluating adversarial examples for offline handwritten signature verification. IEEE Trans. Inf. Forensics Secur. **14**(8), 2153–2166 (2019)
35. Hamilton, I.A.: Outrage over police brutality has finally convinced Amazon, Microsoft, and IBM to rule out selling facial recognition tech to law enforcement. Here's what's going on. https://www.businessinsider.com/amazon-microsoft-ibm-halt-selling-facial-recognition-to-police-2020-6?r=US&IR=T. Accessed 15 June 2020
36. Hunt, T.: haveibeenpwnd. https://haveibeenpwned.com/. Accessed 15 June 2020
37. Karimian, N., Woodard, D., Forte, D.: ECG biometric: spoofing and countermeasures. IEEE Trans. Biometrics Behav. Identity Sci. **2**, 257–270 (2020)
38. Komkov, S., Petiushko, A.: AdvHat: real-world adversarial attack on ArcFace face id system. arXiv preprint arXiv:1908.08705 (2019)
39. Kreuk, F., Adi, Y., Cisse, M., Keshet, J.: Fooling end-to-end speaker verification with adversarial examples. In: 2018 IEEE International Conference on Acoustics, Speech and Signal Processing (ICASSP), pp. 1962–1966 (2018)
40. Kuzu, R.S., Piciucco, E., Maiorana, E., Campisi, P.: On-the-fly finger-vein-based biometric recognition using deep neural networks. IEEE Trans. Inf. Forensics Secur. **15**, 2641–2654 (2020)
41. Li, J., Fawaz, K., Kim, Y.: Velody: nonlinear vibration challenge-response for resilient user authentication. In: Proceedings of the 2019 ACM SIGSAC Conference on Computer and Communications Security, CCS '19, pp. 1201–1213. Association for Computing Machinery, New York (2019). https://doi.org/10.1145/3319535.3354242
42. Li, Y., Li, Y., Yan, Q., Kong, H., Deng, R.H.: Seeing your face is not enough: an inertial sensor-based liveness detection for face authentication. In: Proceedings of the 22nd ACM SIGSAC Conference on Computer and Communications Security, pp. 1558–1569 (2015)
43. Lovisotto, G., Eberz, S., Martinovic, I.: Biometric backdoors: a poisoning attack against unsupervised template updating (2019)
44. Lu, H., Huang, J., Saha, T., Nachman, L.: Unobtrusive gait verification for mobile phones. In: Proceedings of the 2014 ACM International Symposium on Wearable Computers, ISWC '14, pp. 91–98. ACM, New York (2014). https://doi.org/10.1145/2634317.2642868
45. Luo, S., Nguyen, A., Song, C., Lin, F., Xu, W., Yan, Z.: OcuLock: exploring human visual system for authentication in virtual reality head-mounted display. In: Proceedings 2020 Network and Distributed System Security Symposium. Internet Society (2020)
46. Mantyjarvi, J., Lindholm, M., Vildjiounaite, E., Makela, S.M., Ailisto, H.A.: Identifying users of portable devices from gait pattern with accelerometers. In: Proceedings, (ICASSP '05). IEEE International Conference on Acoustics, Speech, and Signal Processing, vol. 2, pp. ii/973-ii/976 (2005). https://doi.org/10.1109/ICASSP.2005.1415569

47. Marra, F., Poggi, G., Sansone, C., Verdoliva, L.: Blind PRNU-based image clustering for source identification. IEEE Trans. Inf. Forensics Secur. **12**(9), 2197–2211 (2017)
48. Matovu, R., Serwadda, A.: Your substance abuse disorder is an open secret! gleaning sensitive personal information from templates in an EEG-based authentication system. In: 2016 IEEE 8th International Conference on Biometrics Theory, Applications and Systems (BTAS), pp. 1–7 (2016)
49. Mura, V., et al.: LivDet 2017 fingerprint liveness detection competition 2017. In: 2018 International Conference on Biometrics (ICB), pp. 297–302. IEEE (2018)
50. Murphy-Chutorian, E., Trivedi, M.M.: Head pose estimation in computer vision: a survey. IEEE Trans. Pattern Anal. Mach. Intell. **31**(4), 607–626 (2008)
51. Nandakumar, K., Jain, A.K.: Biometric template protection: bridging the performance gap between theory and practice. IEEE Signal Process. Mag. **32**(5), 88–100 (2015)
52. Nautsch, A., et al.: Preserving privacy in speaker and speech characterisation. Comput. Speech Lang. **58**, 441–480 (2019)
53. Nguyen, D.L., Cao, K., Jain, A.K.: Robust minutiae extractor: integrating deep networks and fingerprint domain knowledge. In: Proceedings - 2018 International Conference on Biometrics, ICB 2018, pp. 9–16 (2018). https://doi.org/10.1109/ICB2018.2018.00013
54. Nickel, C., Busch, C., Rangarajan, S., MÃbius, M.: Using hidden Markov models for accelerometer-based biometric gait recognition. In: 2011 IEEE 7th International Colloquium on Signal Processing and its Applications, pp. 58–63 (2011). https://doi.org/10.1109/CSPA.2011.5759842
55. NIST: Face recognition vendor test (FRVT). https://www.nist.gov/programs-projects/face-recognition-vendor-test-frvt-ongoing. Accessed 15 June 2020
56. Nogueira, R.F., de Alencar Lotufo, R., Campos Machado, R.: Fingerprint liveness detection using convolutional neural networks. IEEE Trans. Inf. Forensics Secur. **11**(6), 1206–1213 (2016)
57. Pagnin, E., Dimitrakakis, C., Abidin, A., Mitrokotsa, A.: On the leakage of information in biometric authentication. In: Meier, W., Mukhopadhyay, D. (eds.) INDOCRYPT 2014. LNCS, vol. 8885, pp. 265–280. Springer, Cham (2014). https://doi.org/10.1007/978-3-319-13039-2_16
58. Pagnin, E., Mitrokotsa, A.: Privacy-preserving biometric authentication: challenges and directions. Security and Communication Networks 2017 (2017)
59. Patel, K., Han, H., Jain, A.K.: Cross-database face antispoofing with robust feature representation. In: You, Z., et al. (eds.) CCBR 2016. LNCS, vol. 9967, pp. 611–619. Springer, Cham (2016). https://doi.org/10.1007/978-3-319-46654-5_67
60. Peralta, D., et al.: A survey on fingerprint minutiae-based local matching for verification and identification: taxonomy and experimental evaluation. Inf. Sci. **315**, 67 – 87 (2015). https://doi.org/10.1016/j.ins.2015.04.013. http://www.sciencedirect.com/science/article/pii/S0020025515002819
61. Peters, J.: IBM will no longer offer, develop, or research facial recognition technology. https://www.theverge.com/2020/6/8/21284683/ibm-no-longer-general-purpose-facial-recognition-analysis-software. Accessed 15 June 2020
62. Punithavathi, P., Subbiah, G.: Can cancellable biometrics preserve privacy? Biometric Technol. Today **2017**(7), 8–11 (2017)

63. Raja, K.B., Raghavendra, R., Venkatesh, S., Gomez-Barrero, M., Rathgeb, C., Busch, C.: A study of hand-crafted and naturally learned features for fingerprint presentation attack detection. In: Marcel, S., Nixon, M.S., Fierrez, J., Evans, N. (eds.) Handbook of Biometric Anti-Spoofing. ACVPR, pp. 33–48. Springer, Cham (2019). https://doi.org/10.1007/978-3-319-92627-8_2

64. Rane, S., Wang, Y., Draper, S.C., Ishwar, P.: Secure biometrics: concepts, authentication architectures, and challenges. IEEE Signal Process. Mag. **30**(5), 51–64 (2013). https://doi.org/10.1109/MSP.2013.2261691

65. Ratha, N.K., Connell, J.H., Bolle, R.M.: Enhancing security and privacy in biometrics-based authentication systems. IBM Syst. J. **40**(3), 614–634 (2001). https://search.proquest.com/docview/222418906?accountid=17215. copyright - Copyright International Business Machines Corporation 2001; Last updated - 2012-02-17; CODEN - IBMSA7; SubjectsTermNotLitGenreText - United States; US

66. Rathgeb, C., Breitinger, F., Busch, C., Baier, H.: On application of bloom filters to iris biometrics. IET Biometrics **3**(4), 207–218 (2014)

67. Rathgeb, C., Gomez-Barrero, M., Busch, C., Galbally, J., Fierrez, J.: Towards cancelable multi-biometrics based on bloom filters: a case study on feature level fusion of face and iris. In: 3rd International Workshop on Biometrics and Forensics (IWBF 2015), pp. 1–6. IEEE (2015)

68. Rathgeb, C., Uhl, A.: A survey on biometric cryptosystems and cancelable biometrics. EURASIP J. Inf. Secur. **2011**(1), 3 (2011)

69. Rong, L., Jianzhong, Z., Ming, L., Xiangfeng, H.: A wearable acceleration sensor system for gait recognition. In: 2007 2nd IEEE Conference on Industrial Electronics and Applications, pp. 2654–2659 (2007). https://doi.org/10.1109/ICIEA.2007.4318894

70. Ross, A., et al.: Some research problems in biometrics: the future beckons. In: Proceedings of 12th IAPR International Conference on Biometrics (ICB) (2019)

71. Rozsa, A., Günther, M., Rudd, E.M., Boult, T.E.: Facial attributes: accuracy and adversarial robustness. Pattern Recognit. Lett. **124**, 100–108 (2019). https://doi.org/10.1016/j.patrec.2017.10.024. http://www.sciencedirect.com/science/article/pii/S0167865517303926. Award Winning Papers from the 23rd International Conference on Pattern Recognition (ICPR)

72. Rúa, E.A., Maiorana, E., Luis, J., Castro, A., Campisi, P., Member, S.: Biometric template protection using universal background models: an application to online. Signature **7**(1), 269–282 (2012)

73. Sankaran, A., Pandey, P., Vatsa, M., Singh, R.: On latent fingerprint minutiae extraction using stacked denoising sparse autoencoders. In: IEEE International Joint Conference on Biometrics, pp. 1–7 (2014)

74. Schroff, F., Kalenichenko, D., Philbin, J.: FaceNet: a unified embedding for face recognition and clustering. In: Proceedings of the IEEE Conference on Computer Vision and Pattern Recognition, pp. 815–823 (2015)

75. Schuch, P., May, J.M., Busch, C.: Unsupervised learning of fingerprint rotations. In: 2018 International Conference of the Biometrics Special Interest Group (BIOSIG), pp. 1–6 (2018)

76. Schuckers, S.: Presentations and attacks, and spoofs, oh my. Image Vision Comput. **55**, 26–30 (2016). https://doi.org/10.1016/j.imavis.2016.03.016. http://www.sciencedirect.com/science/article/pii/S026288561630052X.   Recognizing future hot topics and hard problems in biometrics research

77. Sharif, M., Bhagavatula, S., Bauer, L., Reiter, M.K.: Accessorize to a crime: real and stealthy attacks on state-of-the-art face recognition. In: Proceedings of the 2016 ACM SIGSAC Conference on Computer and Communications Security, pp. 1528–1540 (2016)
78. Smith, D.F., Wiliem, A., Lovell, B.C.: Face recognition on consumer devices: reflections on replay attacks. IEEE Trans. Inf. Forensics Secur. **10**(4), 736–745 (2015)
79. Solano, J., Tengana, L., Castelblanco, A., Rivera, E., Lopez, C.E., Ochoa, M.: A few-shot practical behavioral biometrics model for login authentication in web applications (2020)
80. Spooren, J., Preuveneers, D., Joosen, W.: PPG2Live: Using dual PPG for active authentication and liveness detection. In: Proceedings of the 12th IAPR International Conference on Biometrics (ICB 2019). IEEE (2019)
81. Tang, D., Zhou, Z., Zhang, Y., Zhang, K.: Face flashing: a secure liveness detection protocol based on light reflections. In: 25th Annual Network and Distributed System Security Symposium, NDSS 2018, San Diego, California, USA, 18–21 February 2018. The Internet Society (2018). http://wp.internetsociety.org/ndss/wp-content/uploads/sites/25/2018/02/ndss2018_03B-5_Tang_paper.pdf
82. Tang, Y., Gao, F., Feng, J., Liu, Y.: FingerNet: an unified deep network for fingerprint minutiae extraction. IEEE International Joint Conference on Biometrics, IJCB 2017 2018-January, pp. 108–116 (2018). https://doi.org/10.1109/BTAS.2017.8272688
83. Teoh, A.B., Kuan, Y.W., Lee, S.: Cancellable biometrics and annotations on BioHash. Pattern Recogn. **41**(6), 2034–2044 (2008)
84. Torres, W.A.A., Bhattacharjee, N., Srinivasan, B.: Effectiveness of fully homomorphic encryption to preserve the privacy of biometric data. In: Proceedings of the 16th International Conference on Information Integration and Web-based Applications & Services, pp. 152–158 (2014)
85. Tran, L., Yin, X., Liu, X.: Disentangled representation learning GAN for pose-invariant face recognition. In: Proceedings of the IEEE Conference on Computer Vision and Pattern Recognition, pp. 1415–1424 (2017)
86. Valsesia, D., Coluccia, G., Bianchi, T., Magli, E.: User authentication via PRNU-based physical unclonable functions. IEEE Trans. Inf. Forensics Secur. **12**(8), 1941–1956 (2017)
87. Van hamme, T., Rúa, E.A., Preuveneers, D., Joosen, W.: Gait template protection using HMM-UBM. In: 2018 International Conference of the Biometrics Special Interest Group (BIOSIG), pp. 1–8 (2018)
88. Van hamme, T., Garofalo, G., Argones Rúa, E., Preuveneers, D., Joosen, W.: A systematic comparison of age and gender prediction on IMU sensor-based gait traces. Sensors **19**(13), 2945 (2019). https://doi.org/10.3390/s19132945
89. Van hamme, T., Preuveneers, D., Joosen, W.: Improving resilience of behaviometric based continuous authentication with multiple accelerometers. In: Livraga, G., Zhu, S. (eds.) DBSec 2017. LNCS, vol. 10359, pp. 473–485. Springer, Cham (2017). https://doi.org/10.1007/978-3-319-61176-1_26
90. Van hamme, T., Preuveneers, D., Joosen, W.: Managing distributed trust relationships for multi-modal authentication. J. Inf. Secur. Appl. **40**, 258 – 270 (2018). https://doi.org/10.1016/j.jisa.2018.01.003. http://www.sciencedirect.com/science/article/pii/S2214212617304180
91. Wang, M., Deng, W.: Deep face recognition: a survey (2019)
92. Wang, Y., Wu, C., Zheng, K., Wang, X.: Improving reliability: user authentication on smartphones using keystroke biometrics. IEEE Access **7**, 26218–26228 (2019)

93. Wu, M.M.A., Schneider, O.S., Karuei, I., Leong, L., MacLean, K.: Introducing GaitLib: a library for real-time gait analysis in smartphones (2014)
94. Yan, C., Long, Y., Ji, X., Xu, W.: The catcher in the field: a fieldprint based spoofing detection for text-independent speaker verification. In: Proceedings of the 2019 ACM SIGSAC Conference on Computer and Communications Security, CCS '19, pp. 1215–1229. Association for Computing Machinery, New York (2019). https://doi.org/10.1145/3319535.3354248
95. Yang, M.H., Kriegman, D.J., Ahuja, N.: Detecting faces in images: a survey. IEEE Trans. Pattern Anal. Mach. Intell. **24**(1), 34–58 (2002)
96. Yao, S., Hu, S., Zhao, Y., Zhang, A., Abdelzaher, T.: DeepSense: a unified deep learning framework for time-series mobile sensing data processing. In: Proceedings of the 26th International Conference on World Wide Web, WWW '17, pp. 351–360. International World Wide Web Conferences Steering Committee, Republic and Canton of Geneva, Switzerland (2017). https://doi.org/10.1145/3038912.3052577
97. Zhang, C., Zhang, Z.: A survey of recent advances in face detection (2010)
98. Zhang, G., Yan, C., Ji, X., Zhang, T., Zhang, T., Xu, W.: DolphinAttack: inaudible voice commands. In: Proceedings of the 2017 ACM SIGSAC Conference on Computer and Communications Security, pp. 103–117 (2017)
99. Zhang, K., Zhang, Z., Li, Z., Qiao, Y.: Joint face detection and alignment using multitask cascaded convolutional networks. IEEE Signal Process. Lett. **23**(10), 1499–1503 (2016). https://doi.org/10.1109/LSP.2016.2603342
100. Zhao, B.Z.H., Asghar, H.J., Kaafar, M.A.: On the resilience of biometric authentication systems against random inputs. In: Proceedings 2020 Network and Distributed System Security Symposium (2020). https://doi.org/10.14722/ndss.2020.24210
101. Zhao, W., Chellappa, R., Phillips, P.J., Rosenfeld, A.: Face recognition: a literature survey. ACM Comput. Surv. (CSUR) **35**(4), 399–458 (2003)
102. Zhao, Y., Zhou, S.: Wearable device-based gait recognition using angle embedded gait dynamic images and a convolutional neural network. Sensors **17**(3) (2017). https://doi.org/10.3390/s17030478. http://www.mdpi.com/1424-8220/17/3/478
103. Zhong, Y., Deng, Y.: Sensor orientation invariant mobile gait biometrics. In: IEEE International Joint Conference on Biometrics, pp. 1–8 (2014). https://doi.org/10.1109/BTAS.2014.6996246
104. Zhu, X., Ramanan, D.: Face detection, pose estimation, and landmark localization in the wild. In: 2012 IEEE Conference on Computer Vision and Pattern Recognition, pp. 2879–2886. IEEE (2012)

Machine Learning and Deep Learning for Hardware Fingerprinting

Carlos Javier Hernandez-Castro[✉]

Complutense University, Madrid, Spain
chernandez@ucm.es

Abstract. Device or machine fingerprinting is the process of collecting information on a (part of a) device for its identification. This can be done under different scenarios and using information from different hardware and software layers of the device. Hardware fingerprinting typically refers to device fingerprinting using information collected from the hardware layer. Hardware fingerprinting can have nefarious usages related to privacy abuse, as well as many positive ones such as *soft authentication*, indoor positioning systems, and others. Here we introduce some of the uses of hardware fingerprinting, with special emphasis on those related to commonly available devices, and explain how machine learning and deep learning have enabled and/or improved them. Additionally, we discuss some of their limitations and possibilities for improvement.

1 Introduction

Let's start defining hardware device fingerprinting as the process by which a hardware (HW) device is partially or completely identified by its remotely observable characteristics. Alternatively, it is possible to use these characteristics to identify the context of the device. These measures, or fingerprints, are based on any type of information emanating from the device. However, here we will focus on those features based on the physical characteristics of the device. We will also comment on other features that originate at higher layers (data link, message content, application behaviour). The reason to focus on the low-level features is that, in general, the closer that our fingerprint is to the physical layer, the harder it is considered to fake or replicate. This is so because these low-level fingerprints typically measure deviations that are inadvertently created during production, and that is considered difficult to replicate. This might not always be the case: when the data extracted from the device is not under our control (for example, the case described in Sect. 4.3), forgery of the fingerprint might still be possible.

Overall, the ability to HW fingerprint a device has both a positive connotation and a negative connotation. On the positive side, HW fingerprinting can allow for a non-Cryptographic authentication, sometimes referred to as *soft authentication*. On the negative, it can constitute an unintended privacy leak. Thus, depending on the context, we might want to increase the difficulty of HW fingerprinting of some devices, particularly when they are used in the open and

© Springer Nature Switzerland AG 2022
L. Batina et al. (Eds.): Security and Artificial Intelligence, LNCS 13049, pp. 181–213, 2022.
https://doi.org/10.1007/978-3-030-98795-4_9

can leak private information about their users - or, on the opposite, we might want to allow for a HW fingerprint to be as precise as possible. Both cases have in common that we are interested in measuring our ability to use different techniques to fingerprint a device reliably, as well as the ability of an attacker to forge that fingerprint.

Veridically, HW device fingerprinting is in some cases related to side-channel attacks, as it can use side-channel leaks to gather extra information from the origin of a signal, message or data. Contrary to side-channel attacks, HW device fingerprinting does not intend to learn anything about the internal state of a particular device, but only to be able to identify a device or family of devices from the rest, or a property related to it. In this sense, we can see HW fingerprinting as a side-channel attack on the identity and context of the devices.

Eke, the rest of the chapter is organised as follows: In Sect. 2, we present a short background in HW fingerprinting, followed by Sect. 3, where we discuss its main use-cases. In Sect. 4, we discuss in detail some of the domains of application of HW fingerprinting, along with recent advances in their areas. This is by no means a comprehensive review, as that would require much more than a book chapter. In Sect. 5, we discuss some of the challenges of HW fingerprinting while using machine learning (ML) and deep learning (DL). Finally, we present a short Sect. 6, which summarises the main aspects of the application of ML and DL to HW device fingerprinting.

2   Background

Distinctively, the concept of fingerprinting, as applied to computer systems, originates with the use of software (SW) fingerprints to remotely detect the operating system (OS), patches and application servers installed in a system. Remote OS identification is possible because each transport control protocol/Internet protocol (TCP/IP) stack has OS-dependent characteristics that can be seen in header fields, like default values, and as enabled options [134]. Later, it expanded to the ability to identify a particular device even if its TCP/IP attributes changed [73].

Mainly, the notion of fingerprinting can be applied in very different scenarios. For example, it might be possible to fingerprint applications based on network traffic, even if it is encrypted [68], or when the collected data is susceptible to noise. The gathering of the data can be passive or active, and can be done either remotely (typically) or locally. The processing of the collected data can vary from gathering simple statistical metrics to training and applying deep learning models. We will see examples of all these scenarios in the following sections.

HW and SW Fingerprinting. HW device and running SW fingerprinting share some similarities. Both typically use side-channel information to identify a device or family of devices. Both also have to be resilient to noise in the measurements. Similarly, both are typically used in a remote context. There are some other aspects in which they contrast:

- SW fingerprinting is typically centred in obtaining some information regarding a remote working piece of SW, but not uniquely identifying it, as the same SW is replicated and used several times. HW device fingerprinting, on the other side, can give some information about a device (brand, model) but sometimes also uniquely identify it.
- As the measurements in SW fingerprinting originate in the SW layer, they are not considered as difficult to replicate as low-level HW device fingerprinting measurements.

There is an interesting confluence of HW and SW fingerprinting in which the HW capabilities are reported or measured at some local SW layer using some widespread API. As this capabilities allow to identify each device, these measurements are enough for a high-level HW fingerprint. Some examples of this confluence are OS and cross-browser fingerprints based on different HW and SW-level capabilities (as installed graphics cards, central processing unit (CPU) cores, audio cards, installed fonts, etc.) [30] or characteristics (as the battery capacity in a mobile device [91] or other sensors accessible using HTML5 [48,72,88]).

Relationship with Other Cryptographic and Cyber Security Techniques. Fingerprints are not new to Cryptography nor Cyber Security. Cryptographic hash functions have been long used for fingerprinting file contents. Machine code *signatures* have been used in malware detection. Biometry is a branch of Cyber Security that deals with finding robust fingerprints and measurements that are typically used for identity verification, for example, in access control. In this sense, it is natural that the same idea is applied to SW and HW devices, and with similar intentions. The main difference is that in many cases, SW and especially HW fingerprinting can be used remotely, without physical access to the device to be fingerprinted, as we can use radio-frequency (RF) signals that emanate from the devices.

Historical Background. In 2005, researchers showed that transport control protocol (TCP) timestamps could be used to calculate the clock skew of a device remotely [73]. This allowed several attack possibilities, as detecting whether a device is a virtual guest and which ones are on the same host (possibly part of a virtual honeynet), or tracking a device as it connects to different servers on the Internet, even if it is using different networks, etc.

This work was followed by others fingerprinting both HW and device drivers for 802.11 devices [47,51] using characteristics dependent on both the node hardware and the driver behaviour.

These ideas were later used in other wireless technologies and expanded to other features. The feature set used to create the fingerprint is indeed linked to the use case scenario:

- If we are performing passive fingerprinting as a way to track a network device passively, sometimes we can assume that the device is unaware of the tracking and that it is not using any anti-fingerprinting mechanism. If this is the case, we can use any characteristic available, as we are assuming that the device will no try to fake them.

- When we want to use fingerprinting to authenticate a remote device that might be used in an attack (for example, a fake 802.11 access point), we cannot assume that any measurements that can be easily faked by an attacker (because, for example, they are SW dependent) will be valid.
- When using fingerprinting for forensic device identification, what we can consider legit as a fingerprint depends on several factors related to the plausible adversarial attacks to the fingerprints.
- If fingerprinting is used to learn about the context of a device (typically, its location), typically all actors are interested in it to work, so we can use any characteristic available. Note, though, that even in some of these cases, it is conceivable that attackers might be interested in altering the fingerprints.

In summary, when proposing and testing a HW device fingerprinting mechanism, it is important to specify its use case and threat model.

In order to uniquely distinguish over time some devices through their fingerprints, the fingerprints must be both sufficiently diverse and sufficiently stable. In practice, neither diversity nor stability is fully attainable, and improving one tends to impact the other adversely. For example, the assimilation of a new browser setting into the browser fingerprint would usually increase diversity. However, it would also reduce stability, because if a user changes that setting, then the browser fingerprint would change as well.

3   Use Cases

In this section, we will present and briefly discuss some of the use cases of HW device fingerprinting. We will also comment on cost and implementation considerations affecting the usability of the solutions in each case.

3.1   Reconnaissance

Several security tools include the capacity to check the SW vendor and version of a system in order to use tailored attacks against it [19]. Similarly, the discovery of several HW and SW vulnerabilities in 802.11 devices [29] and the apparition of exploit tools [28] sparked an interest to fingerprint each particular device.

This does not apply only to 802.11 technology. In general, the ability to perform a detailed reconnaissance of the HW and SW targets is interesting from a security point of view.

3.2   Authentication

Cryptography allows for several different ways in which to implement strong authentication protocols. Nevertheless, these ways have their drawbacks, which typically can be related to:

- The complexity of algorithms and implementations, that can lead to design and programming errors.
- The need to securely produce, store, use and manage a set of private keys. This can increase the deployment and operational cost of the key management system (KMS).
- The lack of compatibility with previous technologies to which Cryptographic solutions are retrofitted (for example, with controller-area network (CAN) bus solutions [89]).
- The cost of the hardware to properly implement secure storage, secure key control, and others. This is more important when we are designing low-cost solutions that are going to be mass-produced, for example in the Internet of things (IoT) or the automotive market.

Thus, in some environments, especially those in which we use low-cost embedded devices (as typically is the case in IoT), a Cryptographic solution might not be the best alternative from the business point of view. In these circumstances, we can use HW device fingerprinting as a way of attaining *soft authentication*. In some scenarios, the fingerprint can be measured and checked by a single monitor that is installed in a node that already has more processing resources (for example, an access point (AP), a bus gateway, etc.) that controls access to the media, restricting it only to known devices. In other scenarios, the clients can check the fingerprint of the connection provider (again, typically an AP) to check that this is not a fake one set-up by an attacker.

We can leverage this authentication mechanism to prevent message spoofing, network jamming, AP impersonation, lateral network movements, etc. It can also be implemented in a layered fashion in combination with a Cryptographically-insecure protocol, like the truncated MAC used in AUTOSAR Secure Onboard Communication [121].

3.3 Attacks to Privacy

The ability to remotely fingerprint a HW device also allows an attacker to gain information regarding its user. Even in protocols that are designed to be privacy-aware, low-level HW fingerprinting can allow for breaking all privacy protections implemented at a higher level [16,114].

This can be especially problematic, as low-level HW device fingerprints are pervasive, affecting all of the device actions, measures and data produced.

3.4 Indoor Positioning Systems

Global navigation satellite system do not provide accurate positioning indoors due to attenuation. The need for accurate indoor location has been fueled by industry, and initially addressed by tailored systems able to a high localization accuracy but with a high cost. Following that phase, the use of the sensors inside smartphones for indoor location gained widespread use [118]. This usage, though, is not as accurate, and given the complex and noisy scenarios involved, typically requires a ML algorithm to process the features and estimate the device location.

3.5   Forensic Device Identification

From a legal point of view, it is of interest to be able to show that a particular HW device was used to commit a crime. Some examples can be identifying:

- A wireless card used in an attack leveraging a fake AP.
- A global system for mobile communications (GSM) base-station used in an attack to gather metadata, clone subscriber identity module (SIM) cards, etc.
- A GSM jamming device.
- A radio station transmitting without a license.
- A mobile phone or digital camera used to capture certain photos.
- A computer used to browse some sites while using privacy-protecting techniques like using a virtual machine, privacy-protecting browser, the ToR network [115] and/or virtual private network (VPN)s.

In all of these and other cases, different HW device identification techniques can be used to relate with a high accuracy a physical device to its recorded illegal activity, thus providing strong evidence relating a device to an action. Note that, in these cases, it is important to show that the fingerprint is unique and stable enough to make a clear identification. This process, requiring a broad dataset to test, can be very time consuming and difficult - but it is typically only needed once per device type.

4   Domains of Use of ML and DL for HW Fingerprinting

HW device fingerprinting can be done in a variety of scenarios, and using both intended results from the hardware (as the result data, for example, an image captured from a camera) as well as unintended, secondary products (as RF emanations from a computer monitor). In this section, we will present and comment on some of the scenarios in which HW fingerprinting has been used, focusing on the different HW fingerprinting targets, technologies, and applications of ML or DL to the fingerprinting process. Note that this is not intended as a comprehensive review of fingerprinting techniques using ML or DL, as that would require a full book. Thus, some important application of fingerprinting technologies, as to global navigation satellite system (GNSS) [50,124], GSM [57,114], Bluetooth (BT) [55] and physically unclonable function (PUF)s [44,62,69,105,112] are not discussed.

4.1   Radio Fingerprinting

Radio device fingerprinting consists on remotely analyzing the emitted radio signal from a radio device to find differences (often subtle) that allow identifying the device (partially or totally) and, possibly, additional contextual data (typically, its physical location).

Radio device fingerprinting can be both active and passive. Active methods interact with the device over the radio channel, typically sending some special input to create the desired output. Passive methods monitor the radio channel and analyze the received signals without any interaction.

A radio device, like any other networked device, can be analysed and fingerprinted at different network layers: physical, link, network, etc. Here we will focus on features calculated over the physical layer, that is, without decoding and analyzing other higher-level characteristics of the message.

Some of the challenges of radio device fingerprinting are:

- Noise and signal distortion: radio signals are prone to attenuation, additive noise and multi-path components (from both single-bounce and multiple-bounce scattering). These distortions imply that the received signal will lose several aspects from the original, and will depend not only on the distance to the transmitter but also on the local propagation.
- Fingerprint stability: the decided fingerprinting method has to consider that the signal might vary over time due to propagation differences and also device differences. Among the device differences, the temperature, the input current and others can affect the generated signal.
- Transferability of the fingerprinting technique: sometimes, especially in the case of techniques using ML and more so using DL, the model is a black-box where we do not have a good understanding of its function. This implies that a model that works well for a certain scenario (and dataset) might not work in a different setting. Transferability tests should be in place in these cases.
- Required hardware: while some fingerprinting techniques use consumer radio devices to interact or monitor the channels, others use universal software radio peripheral (USRP) devices that are more expensive. This means that, for those proposals to be implemented, a dedicated node has to be included, augmenting the price of the solution.

In the following sections, we will present some of the radio fingerprinting techniques for several radio technologies, presenting their different use cases. Some of these technologies have underwent a lengthy analysis of different fingerprinting techniques. In those cases, we will focus on the approaches that use ML or DL. Note that this is not an exhaustive list of the different RF network technologies and their device fingerprinting techniques: such analysis would take much more space than the we have available.

802.11 (WiFi). Two of the primary use cases of 802.11 device fingerprinting are:

- Pre-attack reconnaissance: knowing the type of AP in an 802.11 network allows an attacker to realize targeted attacks on 802.11 platforms (an example is [29]).
- AP impersonation: tools as rglueap or rfakeap [28] allow an attacker to set-up a fake AP that mimics the MAC address, BSSID and SSID of the real AP, allowing to implement many (MiTM) attacks.

The combination of both threat models means that ideally, we would like to find a way in which we can fingerprint 802.11 devices (both AP and clients) for authentication, but without revealing information valuable for an attacker, like device brand and model.

Seminal works on 802.11 device fingerprinting showed that both HW and device drivers could be identified in some circumstances, using characteristics dependent on both the node hardware and driver programming. The author of [47] presents both active and passive fingerprinting methods. The active identification looks at differences in the implementation of the 802.11 association using specially crafted association and authentication reply frames. The passive approach examines the duration field of the 802.11 frames, reaching 97% accuracy when using a set of 13 wireless cards.

In [51], the authors use statistical analysis (mean and standard deviation) of the distribution of inter-frame times during probing for other nodes. The behaviour during probing is not part of the 802.11 standard, so it is left for the driver programmers to determine. Depending on distance and signal propagation conditions, they get accuracies between 77% and 96% - with no signal obstructions and at a distance of 38 cm. This approach has some limitations, including the inability to distinguish some driver versions, and the difficulty of fingerprinting when the drivers are programmed using a Hardware Abstraction Layer - with happened in 2006 with most wireless cards containing the Atheros chipset. Additionally, it is possible to avoid the detection of the driver, for example allowing configurable probing, adding automated noise, or by driver code modification or patching.

Remote calculation of clock skews has been one of the earliest techniques used in HW device fingerprinting [73]. The authors of [65] apply it to 802.11 in order to detect fake APs. They do so using the time synchronization function (TSF), used for the timestamps in the beacon/response frames. Correct time synchronization is important in frequency-hopping networks like 802.11, because all nodes must change frequency channels in a coordinated pattern. The TSF is a local timer based on a 1-MHz clock. Beacon frames are used to periodically announce the value of the TSF to other nodes in the network. The authors test that for several APs, clock skews remain consistent over time for the same APs but vary significantly among different APs. They create estimations of the different clock skews using linear regression (least-squares fitting), and are able to identify all tested APs with as low as 50 to 100 packets. The authors of [13] find that it is possible to attack this fingerprint by patching a particular device driver[1] so that it updates its TSF with the ones sent by the real AP that is being impersonated. In any case, they propose an update to [65] by measuring the line-fitting error as a proxy of a detector of this attack. This detection algorithm works better when the time interval between AP beacon frames is shorter.

Another of the earlier approaches to active 802.11 fingerprinting used the responses of the APs and clients to specially crafted messages [26]. The use case, again, is to detect the chipsets and drivers, in this case to detect the presence

---

[1] The *MadWiFi* driver, present in many Atheros chipsets.

of fake APs. In order to create this classifier, the authors use the decision-list learning algorithm [104], as its result is human readable and possible to tweak by hand.

Many of the earlier 802.11 fingerprinting approaches where using some kind of ML model to do the classification of the fingerprint. This trend continued and increased through the years. With the popularity of DL since 2012, researchers started looking at the possible benefits of using it for 802.11 fingerprinting. We will comment now on some of these works.

One of the advantages of DL is to benefit from more quantities of data, either directly or using data augmentation techniques. In [53], they apply DL to the sampled complex signals of both 802.11 and automatic dependent surveillance-broadcast (ADS-B) devices with the intent to exploit *"hardware imperfections unique to each device"*. The authors use 400 signal samples per each of the 100 ADS-B devices, and 300 samples per each of the 19 WiFi devices. The authors use a 1-dimensional convolutional neural network (CNN) with two convolutional layers (five layers in total) trained on the preamble of the signals. The authors are able to achieve 99.5% accuracy using 19 WiFi devices, and 81.6% accuracy for 100 ADS-B devices, improving the results of using only the real component of the signal (97.8% and 75% accordingly). They also test their approach using additive Gaussian noise as a data augmentation step, and find that the addition of noise makes the neural network (NN) much more resilient to low signal-to-noise ratio (SNR) scenarios. Other similar approaches use different DL models for classification, like long short-term memory (LSTM)s [130], or a mix of real and complex-valued NNs and CNNs [116]. The authors of [111] are able to fingerprint 140 802.11 devices using the raw IQ samples from the physical layer, using a 16-node USRP X310 SDR testbed, and a CNN network architecture with four layers: two convolutional layers and two fully connected layers. They achieve over 99% accuracy.

As we can see, while traditional ML-based approaches have focused on specific features of the behaviour of the devices, DL allows for a direct analysis of the sampled signal without the need for feature selection, allowing for very accurate results. On the other side, it is difficult to estimate the transferability of the DL solutions to other datasets, as well as their overall accuracy when using them for forensic fingerprinting.

ZigBee. Institute of Electrical and Electronics Engineers (IEEE) 802.15 is a working group of the IEEE 802 standards committee that deals with local-area network (LAN)s and metropolitan area network (MAN)s. IEEE 802.15 is concerned with personal area network (WPAN) standards. IEEE 802.15.4 in particular is designed for low-rate wireless personal area network (LR-WPAN)s, attractive for low-power, close-range, low-bandwidth, low-cost applications of wireless networking. These networks are of special interest for industrial control and embedded systems.

ZigBee is a Layer 3 (network layer) specification often used on top of the 802.15.4 layers. It is typically employed in home automation, *smart* meters, medical device data collection, and other IoT scenarios. Its transmission distance is between 10 and 100 m in line-of-sight conditions, although it can transmit data in a mesh fashion over longer distances. It uses 16 channels and a 16-bit cyclic redundancy code (CRC). It has a set rate of 250 Kbit/s.

It is challenging to deploy large numbers of ZigBee devices [117]. It is not clear whether a typical public-key infrastructure (PKI)-based mutual authentication solution can be practical in some of these scenarios. Being able to fingerprint a ZigBee device as belonging to a particular vendor can be an important component in a layered security approach. Also, ZigBee device fingerprinting can allow for authentication of the communication devices. This is a cheap way of implementing another mechanism for access control to the network, that can be part of a layered security system. Even using Cryptography for authentication, the implementation of the key storage and management can become problematic. Having an additional security layer can provide further assurance.

There have been several successful proposals to fingerprint ZigBee devices. [66] presents a way in which to fingerprint each device using only commodity radio interfaces and open-source software. [85] train a CNN using the complex baseband error signal. The authors are able to achieve 92% identification accuracy when using seven devices, also through an ample range of SNRs. [132] are able to outperform this work by both using a general denoising auto-encoder (denoising auto-encoder (DAE)) and combining the semi-steady and steady-state signals of ZigBee devices. Their proposal improves the identification accuracy to 23.5% (by 14%) at low SNRs (from −10 dB to 5 dB simulated with Gaussian noise). At 10 dB, the identification accuracy is 97.5%, when identifying 27 devices. This is an interesting result, as the proliferation of low-power IoT devices generates interest in improving the identification accuracies at low SNR. Note though that these last two results were achieved using an USRP radio as the receiver.

Indoor Positioning Systems. An accurate and easy to use indoor positioning systems (IPS) can help users navigate in large, unfamiliar indoor buildings as airports, shopping centres or festivals. It can also be used to enable location-based services as targeted promotions and advertisements. In a production environment, manufacturers can use IPS to improve asset tracking and production-flow. This is why IPS based on RF fingerprints have received significant attention in recent years. This is problematic due to the attenuation of satellite signals (used by GNSS) inside or near buildings. In contrast, nowadays it is common to find several 802.11 APs in and near buildings. This has led to another use-case of ML and DL: 801.11 signal fingerprinting for indoor location. We can use features like the visibility and strength of the beacon frames of the different APs to create a fingerprint that varies according to each location inside the building.

Even though this is not a security application of fingerprinting, it has security implications, as estimated location can be used in different security scenarios, for example, to restrict or allow access to the 802.11 network, or to monitor personnel and HW movements while indoors. It also has implications in responding to emergencies and monitoring critical infrastructures. To that extent, different attacks have been designed [17,32,35,79–81,131], including poisoning crowd-sourced indoor location databases [126], and countermeasures have been devised for these and other attacks [133].

Typically, the features used for location fingerprinting are based on one or a combination of:

- Fine-grained channel state information (CSI) from the physical layer.
- Coarse-grained received signal strength indicator (RSSI) measurements.
- Mid-grained spatial beam SNRs.

For some applications, we want to obtain the exact user location inside a building. In other occasions however, we just need to estimate at room or area levels. Smartphone-based indoor location systems which rely on fingerprinting can be used for both. If we need to estimate the exact location, it is required an exhaustive sampling of the locations for training the system. If we need less resolution, we can train the system using fewer examples. There are different approaches to select the locations to fingerprint and use for training and testing:

- The most exhaustive one consists of using a complete grid of points which cover the entire part of the building where users are to be located [67]. This requires the biggest amount of time to take the training fingerprints, and the maximum computational cost and execution time needed to run the location algorithms. This can be a major drawback if we want to cover large areas.
- A less exhaustive one consists of using a randomly distributed set of points for training and testing [83]. This adaptive approach allows the user to focus in certain areas of interest and to relieve the requirements on the rest of the areas. This approach can be of interest when only room-level or area-level resolution is required.
- Also intended for room-level accuracy, [92] propose to only measure the points in the border of each room without taking fingerprints from their interior.

As the number of points to fingerprint can be significant, most approaches focus on using ML or DL to train a classifier that predicts the location. Many different models have been proposed and tested. Euclidean distance between feature vectors seems like a plausible metric for location estimation. That is why one of the earliest ML algorithms tried was K-Nearest Neighbor (KNN), used in algorithms such as Redpin [25]. Other models, such as support vector machines (SVM), Bayesian modeling, NNs [27], Gaussian mixture model (GMM)s [31], KNNs revisited [137], ADTree, BFTree, Decision Stump, FT, J-48, J-48graft, LADTree, LMT, NBTree, Random Forest, Random Tree, REPTree and Naïve Bayes have also been tried [92] with different requirements and in different scenarios. To have an idea of the attainable resolution, the accuracy of systems using a KNN approach is of a few meters approximately.

The use of DL has had special impact improving the state-of-the-art of indoor location. [103] use a DL approach to learn CSI features stable over time, that are later fed to a KNN classifier for location estimation. [74] are able to use DL to improve accuracy from a root mean-square error (RMSE) of 28.7 cm to 11.1 cm.

ZigBee devices have also been used for indoor location fingerprinting. [71] use the received signal strength (received signal strength (RSS)) of radio signals of 802.11 WiFi access points (APs) measured on multiple ZigBee channels, as there is an overlap in the frequencies used. A feature vector with the RSS of multiple APs is used for machine-learning based fingerprinting localization. The are able to achieve over 90% success rate with a window of 5×5 m.

Similarly, Bluetooth low energy (BLE) has been tested for indoor location. The deployment costs of BLE beacons is low, and they can run on batteries for prolonged periods of time. Typically, KNN is used to find the closest or closer feature vectors and infer the location from them. There have been several approaches to BLE indoor location [40, 126, 138]. Among them, [139] is of greater practical interest, as it does not need to know the beacon location nor the user location during the training phase. Their proposed method can estimate both the beacon positions and the reference fingerprinting map (RFM) using graph-based optimization. The authors experiment in two scenarios: a *dense* scenario, with 0.0144 beacons per square-meter, and sparse one, with half the population of beacons. They attain a mean error of fingerprinting-based positioning of 2.78 m for dense beacon situation and about 4.11 m for sparse beacon situation.

Radio-Frequency Identification. Radio-frequency identification tags are used everywhere: from e-passports, to animal identification tags, factory data collection, smart cards, defense applications (with active tags), railroads, public transport, electronic toll systems, among many others. An active element is the one providing the energy, and a passive element receives the energy from a RF field and is able to use it to turn on, compute and transmit back.

The low-power requirements of radio-frequency identification (RFID) mean that it can be used in combination with lightweight Cryptography, allowing for authentication and confidentiality, but many of the proposed approaches have important vulnerabilities [1–12, 58–61, 93–100, 106–109].

One of the earliest works on RFID RF fingerprinting was [42]. Its authors try four different active transmissions: standard initiation of communications, initiation of communications using carrier frequencies out of the specifications, bursts of RF energy, and non-modulated carrier linear sweeps from 100 Hz to 15 MHz. They create fingerprints based on both modulation-shape features (Hilbert transformation and starting time of the modulation) and spectral features (down-sampled Fourier transform (FFT) further reduced in dimensionality using principal component analysis (PCA)). The feature set is built from N captured samples from each transponder. The distance between fingerprints is calculated using the Mahalanobis distance. The authors test their approach using 50 *identical* devices, JCOP NXP 4.1 smart cards that contain NXP RFID transponders, as well as 8 electronic passports from 3 different countries. Combining all possible classification strategies, they reach an equivalent error-rate (ERR) of 2.43%. Further note that this is achieved using a simple 1-neighbour KNN classifier.

Note that the RFID chip present in e-passports allows for additional ways of achieving fingerprinting [15].

The authors of [22] apply RF fingerprinting to RFID devices. The authors use typical statistical measurements on the RF signals: variance, kurtosis, skewness, and Shannon entropy. They collect large sets of RFID RF samples, and train two different classifier models on them: KNN and SVM. They reach up to 99% classification accuracy.

Note that many of these approaches apply also to near-field communications (NFC), which is also based on the RFID protocols. A NFC device can act as a reader and also as a tag, and operate on the same frequency as high-frequency radio-frequency identification (HF-RFID) (13.56 MHz), thus allowing for some shared fingerprinting techniques, especially those that are based on the RF signal at low-level.

Vehicle to Everything. Vehicle to everything refers to the abilities of upcoming vehicles to directly communicate with its surroundings, both with other vehicles (vehicle to vehicle (V2V)) and with the surrounding transport infrastructure (vehicle to infrastructure (V2I)). There are two possible candidate technologies on which vehicle to everything (V2X) is being implemented: cellular networks (in particular, 5 generation (5G)) and direct local-range radio links operating at 5.9GHz and with a range of about 1000 metres (dedicated short range communications (DSRC)).

Cellular-network based V2X (or C-V2X) can work with current long-term evolution (LTE) networks, but it is being designed by the 5G Automotive Association (5GAA) to benefit from 5G networks. 5G networks have well known privacy issues that allow an attacker to easily fingerprint devices at the application layer [114].

In DSRC, each vehicle sends its location, heading and speed 10 times per second. Surrounding vehicles that receive the message can calculate the risk imposed by the transmitting vehicle. DSRC has been designed aiming for a high degree of cybersecurity and privacy. Messages are authenticated, and pseudonym certificates are used for short times so that they cannot be easily used to track a vehicle, therefore not violating the driver privacy. These protections are implemented at higher layers, but even though the possibility of radio device fingerprinting was raised [101], it was not researched until [16].

The authors of [16] chose an initial set of statistical features typically used for RF fingerprinting, composed by variance, entropy, skewness, and kurtosis. They use feature selection based on the sequential forward selection (SFS) method, in which features are sequentially added to an candidate set until the verification accuracy does not increase. They use a SVM classifier with a radial basis function (RBF) kernel, as it has proven to work well in other RF fingerprinting scenarios [57]. They perform hyperparameter tuning, in particular, the scaling factor and box constraint, using 10-fold cross-validation (CV). In the initial, ideal scenario, the authors are able to reach an average verification accuracy of 99.5%.

To simulate more realistic scenario, the authors simulate noise by adding Gaussian noise and also simulate multipath fading. This has a significant impact on the feature values and then, in the accuracy of the classifier. In the worst case, the accuracy falls to 24% for a SNR of -10 dB.

Contrary, the speed of the vehicles is not a problem. The authors study the potential loss of accuracy when the observation time is decreased, so less samples can be collected. Even with a number of samples in the 10 to 200 range, the accuracy is always in the 93.5 to 95.5 range, proving that the speed of the vehicle is not a significant factor for RF fingerprinting.

4.2   Bus Fingerprinting

This fingerprinting technique has many similarities to the previous one for radio signals, although here the signals propagate in a physical/logical bus topology, changing the propagation characteristics and allowing for other possibilities based on timing.

CAN Transceiver Fingerprinting. Automotive vehicles have electronic control unit (ECU)s controlling their different sensors, actuators, and interfaces. These ECUs are interconnected using different bus technologies, being CAN (or its newer version CAN-FD) the earliest and nowadays the most common. It is nowadays common to find *more than* 100 ECUs communicating inside a single vehicle [89].

Several attacks have been proposed and demonstrated over vehicles [33,75, 87]. These attacks can be both local (with physical access to the CAN bus or a local interface) or remote, leveraging both LANs (as 802.11 or BlueTooth) and wide-area network (WAN)s (typically, data over cellular networks).

If the attacker wants to have control over the physical aspects of the vehicle, it needs to either control or impersonate the ECUs that are related to them - braking, acceleration, engine control, etc. As a regular CAN bus does not provide authentication mechanisms, impersonating an ECU can be as simple as sending a message with one of the IDs from that ECU. These IDs are typically related to the priority and content of the message.

Thus, many of these attacks require, at some point, the ability to impersonate an ECU from another ECU or gateway. Message authentication has been proposed to prevent these attacks. Even though several Cryptographic techniques have been proposed [20,54,56,77,82,90,113,123,125,128,129], most have not been implemented due to different practical factors [89]. There are three non-cryptographic alternatives to ECU source message authentication: Timed CAN (TCAN) [23], clock-skew detection [36] and electrical signal fingerprinting [14,39]. These non-cryptographic methods have the important advantages of not requiring key creation, distribution nor management, nor requiring the presence of an embedded hardware security module (HSM) nor secure key storage. These imply no bus overhead and backward compatibility with existing devices.

TCAN, a promising proposal, has not been implemented yet. A robust TCAN implementation might have to deal with challenges due to signal degradation and non-linear bus topologies. Clock-skew only applies to periodic messages and, although they constitute most[2] of the messages over CAN, it has been found not robust against attack [110]. Electrical signal fingerprinting has been demonstrated in the laboratory, and although its current results are not yet good enough for production level, it is promising and has room for improvements (Fig. 1).

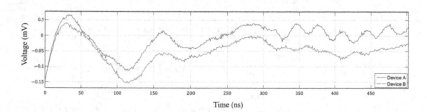

Fig. 1. An example of variations in signaling from different ECUs. Example from [39].

The authors of [39] generate electrical signal fingerprints using CAN extended frames, in which 18 bits of the IDs are fixed and out of the arbitration[3], thus free of signal interference. They calculate eight time-domain features and nine frequency-domain features, computed on the data gathered using an oscilloscope with a 1GHz band-with and 2.5GS/s sampling rate. The sum of the 17 features represent the whole fingerprint of a signal.

Three different classifiers are trained on the data to predict the corresponding ECU that sent each message. To this extent, the authors create a data-set of 900 signals sent from 12 different ECUs. This number of ECUs is consistent with the number of ECUs typically present on a CAN sub-network. The authors try three different models as classifiers using different hand-picked hyper-parameters: a SVM with linear and RBF kernels, a NN with 1, 50 and 100 hidden neurons, and a boosted decision trees (BDT) with 10, 50 and 100 trees. The metric they use for the selection is the accuracy, obtained using 10-fold CV.

Table 1 shows the confusion matrix for identifying ECUs for the different ML models: SVM, NN and BDT are, respectively. Note that the intra-class differentiation is class-dependent, with the biggest trouble to differentiate between $ECU6$ and $ECU11$, independently of the model used.

The model that achieves best accuracy depends on the pattern selected for the 18 ID bits, but in general, most achieved accuracies stay over 94%, with them topping at 96.48% for NN with 100 hidden nodes.

In a similar fashion, in [14] the author selects 40 features from the signals (both in the time-domain and frequency-domain), and performs feature selection

---

[2] Periodic CAN messages can typically constitute around 90% of CAN bus messages, although this varies by vehicle platform and operating conditions.

[3] The CAN bus arbitrates priority based on the ID of the messages colliding. Using extended identifiers when there is no need, it is possible to fix 18 bits of the ID for all ECUs.

Table 1. Confusion matrix for identifying ECUs when SVM, NN, and BDT are used, respectively. Table from [39].

	ECU1	ECU2	ECU3	ECU4	ECU5	ECU6	ECU7	ECU8	ECU9	ECU10	ECU11	ECU12
ECU1	98.22 / 98.33 / 97.78	0/0/0	0/0/0	0.67 / 0.33 / 0.22	1.11 / 1.22 / 1.89	0/0/0	0/0/0	0 / 0.11 / 0	0/0/0	0/0/0	0/0/0	0/0/0
ECU2	0/0/0	95.89 / 95.11 / 95.89	0/0/0	4.11 / 4.89 / 4.11	0/0/0	0/0/0	0/0/0	0/0/0	0/0/0	0/0/0	0/0/0	0/0/0
ECU3	0/0/0	0/0/0	99.33 / 98.78 / 98.67	0.67 / 1.00 / 1.33	0 / 0.22 / 0	0/0/0	0/0/0	0/0/0	0/0/0	0/0/0	0/0/0	0/0/0
ECU4	0.78 / 0.44 / 0.44	6.78 / 4.78 / 6.33	0.56 / 1.00 / 0.89	91.67 / 93.78 / 91.67	0.22 / 0 / 0.67	0/0/0	0/0/0	0/0/0	0/0/0	0/0/0	0/0/0	0/0/0
ECU5	1.44 / 1.33 / 2.11	0/0/0	0.11 / 0.11 / 0.11	0 / 0.78 / 0	98.33 / 98.44 / 97.00	0/0/0	0/0/0	0 / 0.11 / 0	0.11 / 0 / 0	0/0/0	0/0/0	0/0/0
ECU6	0/0/0	0/0/0	0/0/0	0/0/0	0/0/0	86.33 / 85.00 / 86.33	0/0/0	0.44 / 0.56 / 0.44	0/0/0	0/0/0	13.22 / 14.44 / 13.22	0/0/0
ECU7	0/0/0	0/0/0	0/0/0	0/0/0	0/0/0	0/0/0	99.78 / 99.78 / 99.56	0/0/0	0/0/0	0.22 / 0.22 / 0.44	0/0/0	0/0/0
ECU8	0/0/0	0/0/0	0/0/0	0/0/0	0/0/0	1.89 / 1.22 / 1.56	0/0/0	97.00 / 97.56 / 95.22	0/0/0	0/0/0	1.11 / 1.22 / 3.22	0/0/0
ECU9	0/0/0	0/0/0	0/0/0	0/0/0	0/0/0	0/0/0	0/0/0	0/0/0	100 / 99.89 / 99.44	0 / 0.11 / 0.56	0/0/0	0/0/0
ECU10	0/0/0	0/0/0	0/0/0	0/0/0	0/0/0	0/0/0	0 / 0.22 / 0	0/0/0	0 / 0 / 0.11	100 / 100 / 99.00	0/0/0	0 / 0 / 0.67
ECU11	0/0/0	0/0/0	0/0/0	0/0/0	0 / 0.11 / 0	13.22 / 12.44 / 14.22	0/0/0	1.89 / 1.67 / 2.78	0/0/0	0/0/0	84.89 / 85.78 / 83.00	0/0/0
ECU12	0/0/0	0/0/0	0/0/0	0/0/0	0/0/0	0/0/0	0/0/0	0/0/0	0/0/0	0 / 0.22 / 0	0/0/0	100 / 100 / 99.78

based on the joint mutual information criterion, finally selecting 11 of them. The author uses four CAN transceivers, driven by their respective microcontrollers. He also tests using different CAN cable qualities and lengths. As a classifier, a NN using 20 hidden nodes is selected, achieving an accuracy of 98.3%. Note that the higher result, compared to [39], might be related to the lower number of classes.

Note that accurate electric signal fingerprinting might also allow for device identification, thus preventing tampering by avoiding the use of counterfeit parts, another important problem in the automotive industry [127].

4.3 Data Fingerprinting

In this section we will focus on the analysis of the data that is produced by a device, typically some type of a sensor. Sensors have manufacturing differences that can potentially be used for unique HW device fingerprinting. In this scenario, we do not extract the data from the device ourselves, but it is the device who produces the data. Additionally, in some of these scenarios, we do not have direct access to the data produced, but someone else does. This implies that this data might have gone through additional processing steps that might potentially have lowered the amount of unique identifying information that can be extracted from it. It also means that the person providing the data might be an attacker, a possibility that we need to consider in our threat model.

We can distinguish two main scenarios:

- Active: in this scenario, the attacker can control the input that will be processed by the device, thus choosing the input that allows to extract the most information. The control might be total (ideal case) or partial (with noise, etc.).
- Passive: in this scenario, the attacker is only able to eavesdrop on the output of the devices to be fingerprinted. She has no control on the input.

We will introduce now some cases pertaining to both scenarios, classified by the sensor or device from which the data originates.

Camera Fingerprinting. Digital cameras are increasingly widespread, and more capable ones are embedded into other widespread devices such as mobile phones or autonomous driving vehicles. There is an ample research in camera fingerprinting. Here, we will summarise some interesting proposals as well as the ML and DL methods used in them.

There are several ways in which a digital camera can be partially identified (brand and possibly model) or completely identified:

- Lens: lenses introduce aberrations, some of which can be used for camera identification. This does not apply to cameras that have an interchangeable lens, like digital single lens reflex (DSLR)s.
- Colour filter array: cameras that do not have a different sensor for each color, have a colour filter array (CFA) that filters light components for each pixel. To obtain all the pixels in all colours, typically an interpolation algorithm is used. This algorithm depends on the camera producer, and sometimes, the model.
- Dust: DSLR cameras allow for users to change lenses. In that process, some dust and other particles might be deposited on the sensor. There are issues with the stability of this fingerprint, as some cameras have an automatic sensor cleaning system, and some users regularly clean their camera sensors. Plus, additional dust can be deposited over time.

- Sensor pattern noise: the sensor pattern noise (SPN) is derived from some imperfections in the manufacturing of the camera sensor and the other devices interacting with it. There are two main components of the SPN: the fixed pattern noise (FPN) and the sensor pattern noise (PRNU). While the FPN is caused by electrical currents that are static and do not depend on the input light, the PRNU is derived from the different sensitivity of pixels to light, so its effect is multiplicative with the input light, as explained in Eq. 1, where I^O is the noise-free camera input, K represents the PRNU and γ represents the FPN.
- White balance: this processing is included in all digital cameras. It allows to achieve a constant color reproduction for images, independently of the light source type. Identifying the algorithm used can allow to identify the brand and possibly the model of the camera.
- Media format: most cameras allow to store their outputs in different media formats. The particularities of these formats, as chosen by the manufacturer, can allow for brand and model identification. As an example, many cameras allow to save the captured images as Joint Photographic Experts Group (JPEG) files. JPEG allows for lossy compression by compressing with less accuracy the high frequency parts of the image. This is achieved through the quantization matrix, applied to the frequency coefficients from the discrete cosine transform (DCT). JPEG allows manufacturers to design their own quantization matrices, that are included in each produced JPEG file. Similar techniques are used in some video formas, such as Moving Picture Experts Group (MPEG).
- *Blind*: in this case, a whole camera (lens, CFA, sensor and processing) is considered as a black-box. Different models are created and trained over the data, that allow for later identification of the cameras used. As the whole camera is modelled, fingerprint stability can be an issue.
- Feature fusion: this is not a pure method in itself, but a combination some of the features obtained from the previous approaches into a more comprehensive feature vector.
- DL: some DL proposals try direct camera identification, somehow similarly to the *blind* approach, but recently, many DL approaches try to extract the SPN by removing the scene content.

$$I = I^O \times (1 + K) + \gamma \tag{1}$$

We will focus on those methods that allow for device identification: lens, SPN, feature fusion and DL. We will not consider the dust detection method, as it only applies to DSLR cameras, nor the *blind* methods, as their stability is not yet known.

Lens identification has been tested through the estimation of radial distortion, which maps straight lines into curves. In [38], the straight lines are detected using Devernay's straight line method [45], computing the aberration coefficients as a lens fingerprint. On a small three-camera dataset, the authors achieved 91%

camera identification accuracy. The same authors test different focus lengths for a five-camera dataset, finding that the accuracy drops for longer focal lengths [37].

Sensor pattern noise has been broadly studied. [78] were the first to consider FPN for camera classification. [70] were among the first to use the SPN for camera classification. They used 34 hand-picked features to train a SVM classifier. SPN has shown to have a good stability and allow for unique fingerprints. Unfortunately, SPN have some limitations:

- Extraction: the typical way to extract the SPN is using an adaptive low-pass filter. This means that high-frequency components of an image, like edges, can be mistaken as part of the SPN.
- Low image compression: JPEG and other lossy image compression algorithms pay less attention to high frequency components (pixel-level detail). The main components of the SPN are high-frequency. Thus, images compressed with high compression ratios (>90%) erase much of this information.
- Image cropping: if an image is a cropped version of a full photograph, chances are that the deleted parts are important contributors to the SPN.
- Fingerprint copy attack: it is possible to extract the SPN from one or several public images, and apply it to images taken using a different device, thus forging the SPN of another camera. Some researchers have analysed this from a game-theory perspective [135], or using asymmetric information to create *fragile* fingerprints that are erased upon compression [102].

The authors of [49] use feature fusion to propose a classifier based on SPN, lens characteristics, CFA and format features. They plan to test it using 32 devices from seven vendors. Fingerprints are matched using a cross-correlation ranking.

There are many recent proposals for camera fingerprinting based on DL. In [18], they do so creating a Deep Neural Network (DNN) that has a high-pass filter in its first layer. [136] uses residual learning to substract the scene. [41] designed a Siamese CNN that extracts the camera artifacts. [84] propose a combination of a feature extractor and a similarity network to determine whether two image patches contain the same traces or not. [21] use a similar approach, but considering whole images and thus learning the spatial locality as well as the SPN.

High dynamic range images pose a different problem, as they are created from several low dymamic range (LDR) images using different algorithms. This might affect the presence and extraction of a SPN. In [63], the authors train a CNN to detect different high dynamic range (HDR) image types. Still, the identification of camera sources from HDR images is an open problem.

Even though there has been many great advances, there are several challenges in camera fingerprinting that restrict it to certain scenarios and also limit their ability as evidence-facilitating forensic tools. The recent surge in DL approaches to the problem has the potential to allow for wide-scale implementations, if some of these limitations can be overcame. Yet, the black-box approach typical of DL, as well as its own security problems such as adversarial examples, or their ability to detect forged SPNs, might limit their suitability to a forensic scenario.

Accelerometer Fingerprinting. An accelerometer is a sensor that measures the acceleration force that is applied to the device along three orthogonal physical axes. This acceleration is measured in m/s^2. Nowadays, most smartphones contain an accelerometer.

In [24], they analyse the accelerometer calibration errors. To do so, they repeatedly query the accelerometer, detect when it is idle, and check its estimation of the Earths gravity by solving an optimization problem. The six resulting values (two for each dimension) are the sensor fingerprint. They achieve a 58% accuracy when combining this measurement with the user-agent string.

The authors of [46] conduct experiments on 107 different accelerometer chips and devices including them under laboratory conditions. They devise a series of features, eight in the time-domain and ten in the frequency-domain, that can be used for accelerometer fingerprinting both at the model and device level.

In [64], their authors check whether these features can be used in practice by checking their uniqueness and robustness using a data-set of over eight million accelerometer events from 5.000 devices. In their set-up, the device needs to stay still for a few seconds during registration (30 s according to [46]). This allows for them to measure the sensors' manufacturing imperfections. As such, the registration process is crucial and needs to be further secured. The authors try five different ML algorithms (SVM, KNN, bagging tree, RF and ensembles of trees). They also combine these features with similar ones for other sensors typically embedded with accelerometers: gyroscopes, magnetic field detector, orientation sensor, gravity sensor, linear acceleration sensor and rotation vector. While they achieve 78% accuracy using accelerometers, other sensors provide better accuracy, like the rotation vector (99.8%). Combining all sensors raw data, they achieve 99.995% device identification accuracy.

The authors of [122] use the accelerometer as a second way of authenticating an user logging into an identity access management (IAM). To do so, they first record the response of the accelerometer to the phone vibration. Note that both can be done through JavaScript. To counter spoofing attacks, when an user first registers, several traces are collected, each having different length vibration chunks. The authors expect that each chunk will have a different vibration behavior due to the difference in vibration length. Upon login, the IAM system extracts the same features and compares them to the features from the corresponding chunk at registration. For each vibration chunk, eight time-domain features are used: mean, standard deviation, average deviation, skewness, kurtosis, RMS amplitude, minimum and maximum. The authors perform some tests and conclude that the short chunks contain more entropy than the long chunks, and that the features are unique and robust enough. They proceed to test the authentication algorithm using 15 mobile phones. Each login trace of the users device is checked by the matching algorithm, that outputs a positive or negative response. The authors find a true positive rate (TPR) of $0,74$ and false positive rate (FPR) of $0,09$ for chunks, and $0,80$ and $0,02$ for full traces (sets of chunks), concluding that it is a suitable algorithm for two-factor authentication (2FA). They implement their solution in OpenAM.

Speaker and Microphone Fingerprinting. In [43], the authors study different features for fingerprinting the sound system of a mobile phone, both partially -speaker and microphone independently- and as a whole. As ML algorithms, the authors explore KNN and GMM. They use 52 devices from five makers (eight different models in total), and collect their sound production using the in-built microphone of a laptop computer. They also try using different audio excerpts: instrumental music (as ringtones), human speech, and songs (both music and speech). With this setup, they try the following experiments:

- Speaker fingerprint: use the mobile phones to play the different audio excerpts and record the sound with the laptop, for further analysis.
- Microphone fingerprint: use the mobile phones to record the audio clips played with the laptop.
- Sound system fingerprint: use the mobile phones to play and record audio at the same time.

The authors are able to correctly classify brand and model with 100% accuracy in all these scenarios. They test device identification using 15 devices with the same brand and model. Here, the authors are able to classify the device using the speaker with a f_1-score between 0.94 and 0.98 (depending on the audio type excerpt), using the microphone with a f_1-score between 0.95 and 1, and using both with a f_1-score of 1 for all audio excerpt type.

In [24] they check not only the accelerometer as a sensor to fingerprint each device, but also the microphone, characterizing its response to different frequencies. To do so, they play an audio signal at a given intensity using the speaker, and they record it using the microphone (as in [43]). They calculate the ratio between the amplitude of the recorded intensity over the original signal. They measure this feedback ratio for different frequencies. A novelty of their study is that they check on the practical problem that the feedback ratio for a device is similar, but not identical, for different surfaces on which it might be. To measure the efficiency of this fingerprint, they use 16 similar devices (brand and model) over three different surfaces. They match the different ratios using maximum-likelihood, assuming that for each device, its response at a certain frequency is a normally distributed random variable. Using this scheme, the authors are able to correctly identify the 16 devices with 100% accuracy. The authors also devise another method in which they play several non-harmonic frequencies simultaneously, and use the amplitude at each as a feature vector for 17 devices. When using KNN, they reach 95% identification accuracy. A similar active approach has been proposed by companies, claiming to *emit and receive inaudible sound-waves* [119]. Some of these sound fingerprinting techniques are already being used in the Internet [48].

The authors of [34] use the same idea to propose *S2M*, an authentication protocol in which two devices with speakerphones and microphones can authenticate each other.

Microphones are not always necessary to capture audio from a mobile device [86]. Note that this opens the door for another fingerprinting loop, based on the speaker and the gyroscope, or just the gyroscope.

5   Challenges

Although the use of ML and DL has allowed HW device fingerprinting to improve its results, both regarding its strengths - for example, analysing low-level signals efficiently and create hard-to-reproduce fingerprints [39] - and its capabilities - for example, improving indoor location accuracy [92] -, the use of ML and DL brings its own challenges to HW device fingerprinting. In the following sections, we will comment on some of them.

Scale. As we have seen in this chapter, in a number of fingerprinting approaches, we use classifiers to determine the identity of the HW device to which a fingerprint pertains. Classifiers try to detect inter-class variance, without being affected by intra-class variance. Assuming these two values are independent on the number of classes to be distinguished, it is probabilistically easier to distinguish between a lesser number of classes.

This will be dependent on the relationship between inter-class and intra-class variation. An estimation, using a medium-size dataset, can be visualized with the CIFAR 10 vs. the CIFAR 100 image datasets [76], the last one with 10 times as classes as the first one. While the current state of the art for CIFAR 10 image classification is 99% accuracy, it is just 93.51% for CIFAR 100.

This is an important challenge when trying to fingerprint several thousands or even millions of devices. It is also very important for forensic evidence, as the rate of false positives should be low enough as to constitute proper judicial evidence.

Transferability. Transferability, or the ability to use a trained model on a different data distribution, is a very well studied problem in both ML and DL. Typically, ML models that are based on hand-picked features have a known transferability, as this will depend on how well the features represent not only the training dataset but the whole population distribution, and this can sometimes be assessed. DL approaches, on the other hand, have less understood transferability properties, given that they learn the low level features used for classification from the training data. Thus, the risk that these low-level features are tailored to the particular training dataset, and not to the whole population, is greater and less understood than in ML models. Depending on the amount of data from the new population, we might be able to retrain the whole DL model, or only apply transfer learning, retraining only the higher layers of the DL model. In this case, the model performance is typically not as good as with the original training dataset.

Data Distribution Dependency. When using ML, and more so when using DL, data plays a central role to any project. In particular, we need to consider:

- Cost: how many fingerprints do we need for our project? From how many different devices? How many of them for each device? This will affect the HW acquisition cost and the fingerprint elaboration cost.

- Data vs. model: ML and DL models perform differently depending on the specifics of the data. What metric are we using for the model type selection and hyper-parameter search? Is this metric reliable if the data changes drastically? Can we test whether the model selection is resilient to expected changes in the data?
- Distribution drift: there are different causes for drifts in data distribution. We can classify them as unintended, and possibly related to real HW and fingerprint drifts, or intended, and related to active antagonists producing an attack (as, for example, added noise for trying to mask a fingerprint).

Resilience to Noise and Transformations. The problem of noise (or low SNR), attenuation and multi-path propagation is paramount in RF fingerprinting. Noise and attenuation also happen in bus propagation, like the CAN bus. Similarly, the problem of image transformations is key in digital camera fingerprinting.

Most techniques using ML for fingerprinting try to model some of these transformations and check their robustness against them. In some cases, it is possible to find features that are not much affected by these transformations, but typically this is the case only for a small subset of the initial features, rendering the resulting classifier less performing.

Typically, DL approaches to fingerprint directly add these transformations to the data in a *data augmentation* phase that increases the model robustness to them, and sometimes even the model performance in noise-free scenarios. In some scenarios, it is unknown though whether these noise models are stable and cover all aspects.

Adversarial Techniques. Masking the device signal or the result data, or changing it in an adversarial way (including the use of adversarial examples [52,120]), can be used to try to fool the classifier not being able to link the data to a device entity or worse, into thinking that the identity of the device is a different one. This is of crucial importance in forensic analysis, and all classifiers used in this scenario should assess their resilience to different kinds of known adversarial attacks. Note that this assessment is far from trivial. Although this assessment cannot cover all the possible adversarial attacks, but at least, it can give a rate of resilience to the known ones.

6 Summary

The main approach of using ML for HW device fingerprinting is to use either very simple models as linear regression or 1-neighbour KNN when the fingerprint is based on just one or a homogeneous set of a few features. When the feature set is larger and/or more heterogeneous, more capable models as SVM, RF and others are chosen. In some cases, dimensionality reduction algorithms (such as PCA) and feature-set selection algorithms are used.

In a few scenarios, these ML approaches lead to classifiers that have a good enough accuracy and resilience for production environments. Some examples are [22], who achieve 99% classification accuracy identifying RFID devices; [16], who achieve over 99% classification accuracy identifying V2X DSRC modules, although this accuracy decreases markedly with lower SNRs; [39], who get up to 96% message classification accuracy for 12 ECUs, which might be enough for a network intrusion detection system (NIDS), but possibly are not sufficient for a network intrusion prevention system (NIPS); [64], who use the rotation sensor in many mobile devices to fingerprint them with 99.8% accuracy, and combine features from all typical sensors on mobile devices to fingerprint these devices with 99.995% accuracy; and [24], who use the speaker and microphone of 16 mobile devices to classify them with 100% accuracy. Note that typically, these accuracies are reported for a small number of classes, even though in some of these scenarios [39], such small numbers are realistic assumptions.

In other scenarios, there is not a clear set of features to use, or the approaches based on hand-picked features do not attain the desired behaviour under realistic conditions of noise, transformations, or adversarial attacks. In these cases, different DL approaches have been tested. There are several examples of this situation: [53] and [111] for 802.11 device fingerprinting with over 99% accuracy; [132] for fingerprinting ZigBee devices with over 97% accuracy; and [74] use DL to improve IPS accuracy to 11.1 cm. Note that some of them have used typical DNN architectures with little or no modification, while others have created architectures more tailored to the problem at hand. If larger datasets are published, it is conceivable that better tailored DL architectures will show better results. Thus, we can expect to see further improvements, which will arrive faster if big raw datasets are published.

Forensic analysis is possibly the most demanding fingerprinting scenario, as it requires certain assurances that are not typically considered when designing a ML algorithm or DL architecture. These requirements are: proof of good behaviour over the entire data population[4], stability of the fingerprint, and measurable resilience to adversarial techniques, including forged fingerprints and adversarial examples. Although there has been important advances on model explainability and also resilience to adversarial examples, both still remain open problems. Furthermore, model explainability and resilience to adversarial examples do not cover all robustness requirements. It would be interesting to exhaustively discuss the requirements of ML and DL models regarding forensic fingerprinting, and create a framework to check the suitability of the models regarding these requirements. This could also work as an incentive for the ML community to contribute to hardening such models.

---

[4] Note that ML and DL algorithms aim for this, but typically can only test the behaviour in a particular test dataset.

References

1. Abdolmaleki, B., Baghery, K., Akhbari, B., Aref, M.R.: Cryptanalysis of two EPC-based RFID security schemes. In: International ISC Conference on Information Security and Cryptology - ISCISC2015, pp. 1–6. IEEE, September 2015
2. Abdolmaleki, B., Baghery, K., Akhbari, B., Reza Aref, M.: Attacks and improvements on two new-found RFID authentication protocols. In: International Symposium on Telecommunications - IST 2014, pp. 1–6, July 2014
3. Aghili, S.F., Bagheri, N., Gauravaram, P., Safkhani, M., Sanadhya, S.K.: On the security of two RFID mutual authentication protocols. In: Hutter, M., Schmidt, J.-M. (eds.) RFIDSec 2013. LNCS, vol. 8262, pp. 86–99. Springer, Heidelberg (2013). https://doi.org/10.1007/978-3-642-41332-2_6
4. Ahmadian, Z., Salmasizadeh, M., Aref, M.R.: Desynchronization attack on RAPP ultralightweight authentication protocol. Cryptology ePrint Archive, Report 2012/490 (2012)
5. Ahmadian, Z., Salmasizadeh, M., Aref, M.R.: Recursive linear and differential cryptanalysis of ultralightweight authentication protocols. Cryptology ePrint Archive, Report 2012/489 (2012)
6. Ain, Q.U., Mahmood, Y., Mujahid, U., Najam-ul islam, M.: Cryptanalysis of mutual ultralightweight authentication protocols: SASI and RAPP. In: International Conference on Open Source Systems and Technologies - ICOSST 2014, Lahore, Pakistan, pp. 136–145, December 2014
7. Akgün, M., Bayrak, A.O., Çağlayan, M.U.: Attacks and improvements to chaotic map-based RFID authentication protocol. Secur. Commun. Netw. 8, 4028–4040 (2015)
8. Akgun, M., Caglayan, M.U.: Weaknesses of two RFID protocols regarding desynchronization attacks. In: International Wireless Communications and Mobile Computing Conference IWCMC - 2015, Dubrovnik, Croatia, August 2015
9. Akgün, M., Çağlayan, M.U.: On the security of recently proposed RFID protocols. Cryptology ePrint Archive, Report 2013/820 (2013)
10. Akgün, M., Çağlayan, M.U.: Providing destructive privacy and scalability in RFID systems using PUFs. Ad Hoc Networks, February 2015
11. Alavi, S.M., Abdolmaleki, B., Baghery, K.: Vulnerabilities and improvements on HRAP⁺, a hash-based RFID authentication protocol. Adv. Comput. Sci. Int. J. 3(6), 51–56 (2014)
12. Alavi, S.M., Baghery, K., Abdolmaleki, B.: Security and privacy flaws in a recent authentication protocol for EPC C1 G2 RFID tags. Adv. Comput. Sci. Int. J. 3(5), 44–52 (2014)
13. Arackaparambil, C., Bratus, S., Shubina, A., Kotz, D.: On the reliability of wireless fingerprinting using clock skews, pp. 169–174, January 2010. https://doi.org/10.1145/1741866.1741894
14. Avatefipour, O.: Physical-fingerprinting of electronic control unit (ECU) based on machine learning algorithm for in-vehicle network communication protocol "can-bus" (2017)
15. Avoine, G., Beaujeant, A., Hernandez-Castro, J., Demay, L., Teuwen, P.: A survey of security and privacy issues in ePassport protocols. ACM Comput. Surv. 48, 1–37 (2016). https://doi.org/10.1145/2825026
16. Baldini, G., Giuliani, R., Cano, E.: An analysis of the privacy threat in vehicular ad hoc networks due to radio frequency fingerprinting. Mob. Inf. Syst. 2017, 1–13 (2017). https://doi.org/10.1155/2017/3041749

17. Bauer, K., Mccoy, D., Anderson, E., Breitenbach, M., Grunwald, G.G.D.: The directional attack on wireless localization: how to spoof your location with a tin can. In: Proceedings of IEEE Conference on Global Telecommunications, pp. 4125–4130 (2009)
18. Bayar, B., Stamm, M.: A deep learning approach to universal image manipulation detection using a new convolutional layer, pp. 5–10, June 2016. https://doi.org/10.1145/2909827.2930786
19. Beale, J., Meer, H., van der Walt, C., Deraison, R.: Nessus Network Auditing: Jay Beale Open Source Security Series. Elsevier (2004)
20. Bellare, M., Rogaway, P.: Entity authentication and key distribution. In: Stinson, D.R. (ed.) CRYPTO 1993. LNCS, vol. 773, pp. 232–249. Springer, Heidelberg (1994). https://doi.org/10.1007/3-540-48329-2_21
21. Bennabhaktula, G., Alegre, E., Karastoyanova, D., Azzopardi, G.: Device-based image matching with similarity learning by convolutional neural networks that exploit the underlying camera sensor pattern noise, April 2020
22. Bertoncini, C., Rudd, K., Nousain, B., Hinders, M.: Wavelet fingerprinting of radio-frequency identification (RFID) tags. IEEE Trans. Ind. Electron. **59**(12), 4843–4850 (2011)
23. Biham, E., Bitan, S., Gavril, E.: TCAN: authentication without cryptography on a can bus based on nodes location on the bus. In: Embedded Security in Cars - ESCAR Europe 2018 Conference. ESCAR (2018)
24. Bojinov, H., Michalevsky, Y., Nakibly, G., Boneh, D.: Mobile device identification via sensor fingerprinting. arXiv abs/1408.1416 (2014)
25. Bolliger, P.: Redpin-adaptive, zero-configuration indoor localization through user collaboration. In: Proceedings of the First ACM International Workshop on Mobile Entity Localization and Tracking in GPS-Less Environments, pp. 55–60 (2008)
26. Bratus, S., Cornelius, C., Kotz, D., Peebles, D.: Active behavioral fingerprinting of wireless devices. In: Proceedings of the ACM Conference on Wireless Network Security (WiSec), pp. 56–61. ACM, March 2008. https://doi.org/10.1145/1352533.1352543. https://www.cs.dartmouth.edu/~kotz/research/bratus-fingerprint/index.html
27. Brunato, M., Battiti, R.: Statistical learning theory for location fingerprinting in wireless LANs. Comput. Netw. **47**(6), 825–845 (2005)
28. Butti, L.: Raw wireless tools homepage (2006). http://rfakeap.tuxfamily.org/
29. Butti, L., Tinnés, J.: Discovering and exploiting 802.11 wireless driver vulnerabilities. J. Comput. Virol. **4**, 25–37 (2008). https://doi.org/10.1007/s11416-007-0065-x
30. Cao, Y., Li, S., Wijmans, E.: (Cross-)browser fingerprinting via OS and hardware level features, January 2017. https://doi.org/10.14722/ndss.2017.23152
31. Carlotto, A., Parodi, M., Bonamico, C., Lavagetto, F., Valla, M.: Proximity classification for mobile devices using Wi-Fi environment similarity. In: Proceedings of the First ACM International Workshop on Mobile Entity Localization and Tracking in GPS-Less Environments, pp. 43–48 (2008)
32. Chang, N., Rashidzadeh, R., Ahmadi, M.: Robust indoor positioning using differential Wi-Fi access points. IEEE Trans. Consum. Electron. **56**(3), 1860–1867 (2010)
33. Checkoway, S., et al.: Comprehensive experimental analyses of automotive attack surfaces. In: Proceedings of the 20th USENIX Conference on Security, SEC 2011, p. 6. USENIX Association (2011)

34. Chen, D., et al.: S2M: a lightweight acoustic fingerprints-based wireless device authentication protocol. IEEE Internet Things J. **4**(1), 88–100 (2017)
35. Chen, Y., Kleisouris, K., Li, X., Trappe, W., Martin, R.: A security and robustness performance analysis of localization algorithms to signal strength attacks. TOSN **5**, 1–37 (2009). https://doi.org/10.1145/1464420.1464422
36. Cho, K.T., Shin, K.G.: Fingerprinting electronic control units for vehicle intrusion detection. In: Proceedings of the 25th USENIX Conference on Security Symposium, SEC 2016, pp. 911–927. USENIX Association (2016)
37. Choi, K., Lam, E., Wong, K.: Automatic source camera identification using the intrinsic lens radial distortion. Opt. Express **14**, 11551–11565 (2006). https://doi.org/10.1364/OE.14.011551
38. Choi, K., Lam, E., Wong, K.: Source camera identification using footprints from lens aberration. In: Proceedings of the SPIE, vol. 6069, February 2006. https://doi.org/10.1117/12.649775
39. Choi, W., Jo, H., Woo, S., Chun, J., Park, J.: Identifying ECUs using inimitable characteristics of signals in controller area networks. IEEE Trans. Veh. Technol. **67**, 4757–4770 (2016). https://doi.org/10.1109/TVT.2018.2810232
40. Cinefra, N.: An adaptive indoor positioning system based on Bluetooth low energy RSSI (2013)
41. Cozzolino, D., Verdoliva, L.: Noiseprint: a CNN-based camera model fingerprint. IEEE Trans. Inf. Forensics Secur. **15**, 144–159 (2019). https://doi.org/10.1109/TIFS.2019.2916364
42. Danev, B., Heydt-Benjamin, T.S., Čapkun, S.: Physical-layer identification of RFID devices. In: Proceedings of the 18th Conference on USENIX Security Symposium, SSYM 2009, pp. 199–214. USENIX Association (2009)
43. Das, A., Borisov, N., Caesar, M.: Do you hear what I hear? Fingerprinting smart devices through embedded acoustic components. In: Proceedings of the 2014 ACM SIGSAC Conference on Computer and Communications Security, CCS 2014, pp. 441–452. Association for Computing Machinery, New York (2014). https://doi.org/10.1145/2660267.2660325
44. Delvaux, J.: Machine-learning attacks on PolyPUFs, OB-PUFs, RPUFs, LHS-PUFs, and PUF–FSMs. IEEE Trans. Inf. Forensics Secur. **14**, 2043–2058 (2019). https://doi.org/10.1109/TIFS.2019.2891223
45. Devernay, F., Faugeras, O.: Automatic calibration and removal of distortion from scenes of structured environments. In: Proceedings of the SPIE, vol. 2567, July 1995. https://doi.org/10.1117/12.218487
46. Dey, S., Roy, N., Xu, W., Choudhury, R., Nelakuditi, S.: AccelPrint: imperfections of accelerometers make smartphones trackable, January 2014. https://doi.org/10.14722/ndss.2014.23059
47. Ellch, J.P.: Fingerprinting 802.11 devices (2006). https://calhoun.nps.edu/handle/10945/2592
48. Englehardt, S., Narayanan, A.: Online tracking: a 1-million-site measurement and analysis, pp. 1388–1401, October 2016. https://doi.org/10.1145/2976749.2978313
49. Ferrara, P., Beslay, L.: Multimodal fingerprinting of imaging devices -inception report project AVICAO - authors and victims identification of child abuse on-line, December 2016. https://doi.org/10.2760/751517
50. Foruhandeh, M., Mohammed, A.Z., Kildow, G., Berges, P., Gerdes, R.: Spotr: GPS spoofing detection via device fingerprinting (2020)

51. Franklin, J., McCoy, D., Tabriz, P., Neagoe, V., Van Randwyk, J., Sicker, D.: Passive data link layer 802.11 wireless device driver fingerprinting. In: Proceedings of the 15th Conference on USENIX Security Symposium, USENIX-SS 2006, vol. 2015. USENIX Association (2006)

52. Goodfellow, I.J., Shlens, J., Szegedy, C.: Explaining and harnessing adversarial examples. arXiv:1412.6572 (2014)

53. Gopalakrishnan, S., Cekic, M., Madhow, U.: Robust wireless fingerprinting via complex-valued neural networks (2019)

54. Groza, B., Murvay, S., van Herrewege, A., Verbauwhede, I.: LiBrA-CAN: a lightweight broadcast authentication protocol for controller area networks. In: Pieprzyk, J., Sadeghi, A.-R., Manulis, M. (eds.) CANS 2012. LNCS, vol. 7712, pp. 185–200. Springer, Heidelberg (2012). https://doi.org/10.1007/978-3-642-35404-5_15

55. Hall, J., Barbeau, M., Kranakis, E.: Detecting rogue devices in Bluetooth networks using radio frequency fingerprinting, pp. 108–113, January 2006

56. Hartkopp, O., Schilling, R.M.: Message authenticated CAN. In: Escar Conference, Berlin, Germany (2012)

57. Hasse, J., Gloe, T., Beck, M.: Forensic identification of GSM mobile phones. In: Proceedings of the First ACM Workshop on Information Hiding and Multimedia Security, pp. 131–140 (2013)

58. Hernandez-Castro, J.C., Estevez-Tapiador, J.M., Peris-Lopez, P., Quisquater, J.J.: Cryptanalysis of the SASI ultralightweight RFID authentication protocol with modular rotations. In: International Workshop on Coding and Cryptography - WCC 2009, Ullensvang, Norway, May 2009

59. Hernandez-Castro, J.C., Peris-Lopez, P., Phan, R.C.-W., Tapiador, J.M.E.: Cryptanalysis of the David-Prasad RFID ultralightweight authentication protocol. In: Ors Yalcin, S.B. (ed.) RFIDSec 2010. LNCS, vol. 6370, pp. 22–34. Springer, Heidelberg (2010). https://doi.org/10.1007/978-3-642-16822-2_3

60. Hernandez-Castro, J.C., Tapiador, J.E., Peris-Lopez, P., Clark, J.A., Talbi, E.G.: Metaheuristic traceability attack against SLMAP, an RFID lightweight authentication protocol. In: Proceedings of the 23rd IEEE International Parallel and Distributed Processing Symposium - IPDPS 2009, Rome, Italy. IEEE Computer Society, May 2009

61. Hernandez-Castro, J.C., Peris-Lopez, P., Aumasson, J.-P.: On the key schedule strength of PRESENT. In: Garcia-Alfaro, J., Navarro-Arribas, G., Cuppens-Boulahia, N., de Capitani di Vimercati, S. (eds.) DPM/SETOP -2011. LNCS, vol. 7122, pp. 253–263. Springer, Heidelberg (2012). https://doi.org/10.1007/978-3-642-28879-1_17

62. Hospodar, G., Maes, R., Verbauwhede, I.: Machine learning attacks on 65nm arbiter PUFs: accurate modeling poses strict bounds on usability. In: 2012 IEEE International Workshop on Information Forensics and Security (WIFS), pp. 37–42 (2012)

63. Huo, Y., Zhu, X.: High dynamic range image forensics using CNN (2019)

64. Hupperich, T., Hosseini, H., Holz, T.: Leveraging sensor fingerprinting for mobile device authentication. In: Caballero, J., Zurutuza, U., Rodríguez, R.J. (eds.) DIMVA 2016. LNCS, vol. 9721, pp. 377–396. Springer, Cham (2016). https://doi.org/10.1007/978-3-319-40667-1_19

65. Jana, S., Kasera, S.: On fast and accurate detection of unauthorized wireless access points using clock skews, vol. 9, pp. 104–115, January 2008. https://doi.org/10.1109/TMC.2009.145

66. Jenkins, I.R., Shapiro, R., Bratus, S., Speers, R., Goodspeed, T.: Fingerprinting IEEE 802.15.4 devices with commodity radios. Technical report. TR2014-746, Dartmouth College, Computer Science, Hanover, NH, March 2014. http://www. cs.dartmouth.edu/reports/TR2014-746-rev2.pdf

67. Kaemarungsi, K., Krishnamurthy, P.: Modeling of indoor positioning systems based on location fingerprinting. In: IEEE Infocom 2004, vol. 2, pp. 1012–1022. IEEE (2004)

68. Karagiannis, T., Papagiannaki, K., Faloutsos, M.: BLINC: multilevel traffic classification in the dark, vol. 35, pp. 229–240, January 2005

69. Khalafalla, M., Gebotys, C.: PUFs deep attacks: enhanced modeling attacks using deep learning techniques to break the security of double arbiter PUFs. In: 2019 Design, Automation Test in Europe Conference Exhibition (DATE), pp. 204–209 (2019)

70. Kharrazi, M., Sencar, H.T., Memon, N.: Blind source camera identification. In: 2004 International Conference on Image Processing, ICIP 2004, vol. 1, pp. 709–712 (2004)

71. Kimoto, R., Ishida, S., Yamamoto, T., Tagashira, S., Fukuda, A.: MuCHLoc: indoor zigbee localization system utilizing inter-channel characteristics †. Sensors (Basel, Switzerland) **19**, 1645 (2019)

72. Kobusinska, A., Brzezinski, J., Pawulczuk, K.: Device fingerprinting: analysis of chosen fingerprinting methods. In: IoTBDS (2017)

73. Kohno, T., Broido, A., Claffy, K.C.: Remote physical device fingerprinting. In: 2005 IEEE Symposium on Security and Privacy (S&P 2005), pp. 211–225 (2005)

74. Koike-Akino, T., Wang, P., Pajovic, M., Sun, H., Orlik, P.V.: Fingerprinting-based indoor localization with commercial MMWave WiFi: a deep learning approach. IEEE Access **8**, 84879–84892 (2020)

75. Koscher, K., et al.: Experimental security analysis of a modern automobile. In: 2010 IEEE Symposium on Security and Privacy, pp. 447–462. IEEE (2010)

76. Krizhevsky, A., Nair, V., Hinton, G.: CIFAR datasets (2000). https://www.cs. toronto.edu/~kriz/cifar.html

77. Kurachi, R., Matsubara, Y., Takada, H., Adachi, N., Miyashita, Y., Horihata, S.: CaCAN-centralized authentication system in can (controller area network). In: 14th International Conference on Embedded Security in Cars (ESCAR 2014) (2014)

78. Kurosawa, K., Kuroki, K., Saitoh, N.: CCD fingerprint method-identification of a video camera from videotaped images. In: Proceedings 1999 International Conference on Image Processing (Cat. 99CH36348), vol. 3, pp. 537–540 (1999)

79. Kushki, A., Plataniotis, K.N., Venetsanopoulos, A.N.: Sensor selection for mitigation of RSS-based attacks in wireless local area network positioning. In: 2008 IEEE International Conference on Acoustics, Speech and Signal Processing, pp. 2065–2068 (2008)

80. Li, X., Chen, Y., Yang, J., Zheng, X.: Designing localization algorithms robust to signal strength attacks, pp. 341–345, April 2011. https://doi.org/10.1109/ INFCOM.2011.5935178

81. Li, Z., Trappe, W., Zhang, Y., Nath, B.: Robust statistical methods for securing wireless localization in sensor networks. In: Fourth International Symposium on Information Processing in Sensor Networks, IPSN 2005, pp. 91–98 (2005)

82. Lin, C.W., Sangiovanni-Vincentelli, A.: Cyber-security for the controller area network (CAN) communication protocol. In: 2012 International Conference on Cyber Security, pp. 1–7. IEEE (2012)

83. Lin, H., Zhang, Y., Griss, M., Landa, I.: WASP: an enhanced indoor locationing algorithm for a congested Wi-Fi environment. In: Fuller, R., Koutsoukos, X.D. (eds.) MELT 2009. LNCS, vol. 5801, pp. 183–196. Springer, Heidelberg (2009). https://doi.org/10.1007/978-3-642-04385-7_13

84. Mayer, O., Stamm, M.C.: Forensic similarity for digital images. IEEE Trans. Inf. Forensics Secur. **15**, 1331–1346 (2020)

85. Merchant, K., Revay, S., Stantchev, G., Nousain, B.: Deep learning for RF device fingerprinting in cognitive communication networks. IEEE J. Sel. Top. Signal Process. **12**(1), 160–167 (2018)

86. Michalevsky, Y., Boneh, D., Nakibly, G.: Gyrophone: recognizing speech from gyroscope signals. In: 23rd USENIX Security Symposium (USENIX Security 2014), San Diego, CA, pp. 1053–1067. USENIX Association, August 2014. https://www.usenix.org/conference/usenixsecurity14/technical-sessions/presentation/michalevsky

87. Miller, C., Valasek, C.: Remote exploitation of an unaltered passenger vehicle. Black Hat USA **2015**, 91 (2015)

88. Nakibly, G., Shelef, G., Yudilevich, S.: Hardware fingerprinting using HTML5, March 2015

89. Nowdehi, N., Lautenbach, A., Olovsson, T.: In-vehicle can message authentication: an evaluation based on industrial criteria. In: 2017 IEEE 86th Vehicular Technology Conference (VTC-Fall), pp. 1–7 (2017)

90. Nürnberger, S., Rossow, C.: – vatiCAN – vetted, authenticated CAN Bus. In: Gierlichs, B., Poschmann, A.Y. (eds.) CHES 2016. LNCS, vol. 9813, pp. 106–124. Springer, Heidelberg (2016). https://doi.org/10.1007/978-3-662-53140-2_6

91. Olejnik, L., Acar, G., Castelluccia, C., Díaz, C.: The leaking battery - a privacy analysis of the HTML5 battery status API. IACR Cryptology ePrint Archive **2015**, 616 (2015)

92. Organero, M., Brito-Pacheco, C.: Improving accuracy and simplifying training in fingerprinting-based indoor location algorithms at room level. Mob. Inf. Syst. **2016** (2016). https://doi.org/10.1155/2016/2682869

93. Peris-Lopez, P., Hernandez-Castro, J.C., Estevez-Tapiador, J.M., Li, T., Li, Y.: Vulnerability analysis of RFID protocols for tag ownership transfer. Comput. Netw. **54**(9), 1502–1508 (2010)

94. Peris-Lopez, P., Hernandez-Castro, J.C., Tapiador, J.M.E., Li, T., van der Lubbe, J.C.A.: Weaknesses in two recent lightweight RFID authentication protocols. In: Bao, F., Yung, M., Lin, D., Jing, J. (eds.) Inscrypt 2009. LNCS, vol. 6151, pp. 383–392. Springer, Heidelberg (2010). https://doi.org/10.1007/978-3-642-16342-5_28

95. Peris-Lopez, P., Hernandez-Castro, J.C., Estevez-Tapiador, J.M., van der Lubbe, J.C.A.: Security flaws in a recent ultralightweight RFID protocol. In: Workshop on RFID Security - RFIDSec Asia 2010. Cryptology and Information Security, Singapore, Republic of Singapore, vol. 4, pp. 83–93. IOS Press, February 2010

96. Peris-Lopez, P., Hernandez-Castro, J.C., Estevez-Tapiador, J.M., Palomar, E., van der Lubbe, J.C.A.: Cryptographic puzzles and distance-bounding protocols: practical tools for RFID security. In: IEEE International Conference on RFID - IEEE RFID 2010, Orlando, Florida, USA, pp. 45–52. IEEE Computer Society, April 2010

97. Peris-Lopez, P., Hernandez-Castro, J.C., Estevez-Tapiador, J.M., Ribagorda, A.: RFID systems: a survey on security threats and proposed solutions. In: Cuenca, P., Orozco-Barbosa, L. (eds.) PWC 2006. LNCS, vol. 4217, pp. 159–170. Springer, Heidelberg (2006). https://doi.org/10.1007/11872153_14

98. Peris-Lopez, P., Hernandez-Castro, J.C., Estevez-Tapiador, J.M., Ribagorda, A.: Cryptanalysis of a novel authentication protocol conforming to EPC-C1G2 standard. In: Workshop on RFID Security - RFIDSec 2007, Malaga, Spain, July 2007
99. Peris-Lopez, P., Hernandez-Castro, J.C., Phan, R.C.-W., Tapiador, J.M.E., Li, T.: Quasi-linear cryptanalysis of a secure RFID ultralightweight authentication protocol. In: Lai, X., Yung, M., Lin, D. (eds.) Inscrypt 2010. LNCS, vol. 6584, pp. 427–442. Springer, Heidelberg (2011). https://doi.org/10.1007/978-3-642-21518-6_30
100. Peris-Lopez, P., Hernandez-Castro, J.C., Tapiador, J.M., van der Lubbe, J.C.: Cryptanalysis of an EPC class-1 generation-2 standard compliant authentication protocol. Eng. Appl. Artif. Intell. **24**(6), 1061–1069 (2011)
101. Petit, J., Schaub, F., Feiri, M., Kargl, F.: Pseudonym schemes in vehicular networks: a survey. IEEE Commun. Surv. Tutor. **17**(1), 228–255 (2014)
102. Quiring, E., Kirchner, M., Rieck, K.: On the security and applicability of fragile camera fingerprints, July 2019
103. Rao, X., Li, Z., Yang, Y.: Device-free passive wireless localization system with transfer deep learning method. J. Ambient. Intell. Hum. Comput. **11**(10), 4055–4071 (2020). https://doi.org/10.1007/s12652-019-01662-y
104. Rivest, R.L.: Learning decision lists. Mach. Learn. **2**(3), 229–246 (1987)
105. Rührmair, U., Sölter, J.: PUF modeling attacks: an introduction and overview. In: 2014 Design, Automation Test in Europe Conference Exhibition (DATE), pp. 1–6 (2014)
106. Safkhani, M., Bagheri, N., Peris-Lopez, N., Mitrokotsa, A., Hernandez-Castro, J.C.: Weaknesses in another Gen2-based RFID authentication protocol. In: IEEE International Conference on RFID-Technology and Applications - IEEE RFID TA 2012, Nice, France. IEEE Press, IEEE, November 2012
107. Safkhani, M., Peris-Lopez, P., Badheri, N., Naderi, M., Hernandez-Castro, J.C.: On the security of Tan et al. serverless RFID authentication and search protocols. In: Workshop on RFID Security - RFIDSec 2012, Nijmegen, Netherlands, June 2012
108. Safkhani, M., Peris-Lopez, P., Hernandez-Castro, J.C., Bagheri, N.: Cryptanalysis of the Cho et al. protocol: a hash-based RFID tag mutual authentication protocol. J. Comput. Appl. Math. **259**, 571–577 (2013)
109. Safkhani, M., Peris-Lopez, P., Hernandez-Castro, J.C., Bagheri, N., Naderi, M.: Cryptanalysis of Cho et al'.s protocol, a hash-based mutual authentication protocol for RFID systems. Cryptology ePrint Archive, Report 2011/311 (2011)
110. Sagong, S., Ying, X., Clark, A., Bushnell, L., Poovendran, R.: Cloaking the clock: emulating clock skew in controller area networks, pp. 32–42, April 2018. https://doi.org/10.1109/ICCPS.2018.00012
111. Sankhe, K., Belgiovine, M., Zhou, F., Riyaz, S., Ioannidis, S., Chowdhury, K.: Oracle: optimized radio classification through convolutional neural networks. In: IEEE INFOCOM 2019 - IEEE Conference on Computer Communications, pp. 370–378 (2019)
112. Santikellur, P., Bhattacharyay, A., Chakraborty, R.S.: Deep learning based model building attacks on arbiter PUF compositions. IACR Cryptology ePrint Archive 2019, 566 (2019)
113. Schweppe, H., Roudier, Y., Weyl, B., Apvrille, L., Scheuermann, D.: Car2x communication: securing the last meter-a cost-effective approach for ensuring trust in car2x applications using in-vehicle symmetric cryptography. In: 2011 IEEE Vehicular Technology Conference (VTC Fall), pp. 1–5. IEEE (2011)

114. Shaik, A., Borgaonkar, R., Park, S., Seifert, J.P.: New vulnerabilities in 4G and 5G cellular access network protocols: exposing device capabilities. In: Proceedings of the 12th Conference on Security and Privacy in Wireless and Mobile Networks, WiSec 2019, pp. 221–231. Association for Computing Machinery, New York (2019). https://doi.org/10.1145/3317549.3319728
115. Shields, C., Levine, B.N.: A protocol for anonymous communication over the internet. In: Proceedings of the 7th ACM Conference on Computer and Communications Security, pp. 33–42 (2000)
116. Smith, L., et al.: Classifying WiFi "physical fingerprints" using complex deep learning. In: Hammoud, R.I., Overman, T.L., Mahalanobis, A. (eds.) Automatic Target Recognition XXX, vol. 11394, pp. 82–96. International Society for Optics and Photonics, SPIE (2020). https://doi.org/10.1117/12.2557933
117. Smith, S.: Cryptographic scalability challenges in the smart grid, pp. 1–3, January 2012. https://doi.org/10.1109/ISGT.2012.6175564
118. Subbu, K.P., Zhang, C., Luo, J., Vasilakos, A.V.: Analysis and status quo of smartphone-based indoor localization systems. IEEE Wirel. Commun. **21**(4), 106–112 (2014)
119. Subramaniam, N.: Google buys slicklogin: this is how its sound-based password system works (2014). https://www.firstpost.com/tech/news-analysis/google-buys-slicklogin-heres-sound-based-password-system-works-3647955.html
120. Szegedy, C., et al.: Intriguing properties of neural networks. arXiv:1312.6199 (2013)
121. Tromba, D., Huber, J.: Assessment and guidance for autosar secure onboard communication application. In: 17th Escar Europe: Embedded Security in Cars (Konferenzveröffentlichung). (Extended Abstract) (2019)
122. Van Goethem, T., Scheepers, W., Preuveneers, D., Joosen, W.: Accelerometer-based device fingerprinting for multi-factor mobile authentication. In: Caballero, J., Bodden, E., Athanasopoulos, E. (eds.) ESSoS 2016. LNCS, vol. 9639, pp. 106–121. Springer, Cham (2016). https://doi.org/10.1007/978-3-319-30806-7_7
123. Van Herrewege, A., Singelee, D., Verbauwhede, I.: CANAuth-a simple, backward compatible broadcast authentication protocol for CAN bus. In: ECRYPT Workshop on Lightweight Cryptography, vol. 2011, p. 20 (2011)
124. Wang, H., Cheng, W., Xu, C., Zhang, M., Hu, L.: Method for identifying pseudo GPS signal based on radio frequency fingerprint. In: 2018 10th International Conference on Communications, Circuits and Systems (ICCCAS), pp. 354–358 (2018)
125. Wang, Q., Sawhney, S.: Vecure: a practical security framework to protect the can bus of vehicles. In: 2014 International Conference on the Internet of Things (IOT), pp. 13–18. IEEE (2014)
126. Wang, Y., Yang, X., Zhao, Y., Liu, Y., Cuthbert, L.: Bluetooth positioning using RSSI and triangulation methods. In: 2013 IEEE 10th Consumer Communications and Networking Conference (CCNC), pp. 837–842 (2013)
127. Weimerskirch, A.: Automotive and industrial data security. In: Cybersecurity and Cyber-physical Systems Workshop (2012)
128. Weisglass, Y., Oren, Y.: Authentication method for can messages. Escar Europe (2016)
129. Woo, S., Jo, H.J., Lee, D.H.: A practical wireless attack on the connected car and security protocol for in-vehicle can. IEEE Trans. Intell. Transp. Syst. **16**(2), 993–1006 (2014)
130. Wu, Q., et al.: Deep learning based RF fingerprinting for device identification and wireless security. Electron. Lett. **54**(24), 1405–1407 (2018)

131. Yang, J., Chen, Y., Lawrence, V.B., Swaminathan, V.: Robust wireless localization to attacks on access points. In: 2009 IEEE Sarnoff Symposium, pp. 1–5 (2009)
132. Yu, J., et al.: Radio frequency fingerprint identification based on denoising autoencoders, July 2019
133. Yuan, L., Hu, Y., Li, Y., Zhang, R., Zhang, Y., Hedgpeth, T.: Secure RSS-fingerprint-based indoor positioning: attacks and countermeasures. In: 2018 IEEE Conference on Communications and Network Security (CNS), pp. 1–9 (2018)
134. Zalewski, M.: p0f (2012). http://lcamtuf.coredump.cx/p0f3/
135. Zeng, H., Liu, J., Yu, J., Kang, X., Shi, Y., Wang, Z.: A framework of camera source identification Bayesian game. IEEE Trans. Cybern. **47**, 1–12 (2016). https://doi.org/10.1109/TCYB.2016.2557802
136. Zhang, K., Zuo, W., Chen, Y., Meng, D., Zhang, L.: Beyond a Gaussian denoiser: residual learning of deep CNN for image denoising. IEEE Trans. Image Process. **26**(7), 3142–3155 (2017)
137. Zhou, C., Xie, H., Shi, J.: Wi-Fi indoor location technology based on k-means algorithm. In: Zhang, Z., Shen, Z.M., Zhang, J., Zhang, R. (eds.) LISS 2014, pp. 765–770. Springer, Heidelberg (2015). https://doi.org/10.1007/978-3-662-43871-8_110
138. Zhuang, Y., Yang, J., Li, Y., Qi, L., El-Sheimy, N.: Smartphone-based indoor localization with Bluetooth low energy beacons. Sensors **16**(5), 596 (2016)
139. Zuo, Z., Liu, L., Zhang, L., Fang, Y.: Indoor positioning based on Bluetooth low-energy beacons adopting graph optimization. Sensors **18**, 3736 (2018). https://doi.org/10.3390/s18113736

AI for Intrusion Detection

Intelligent Malware Defenses

Azqa Nadeem[1(✉)], Vera Rimmer[2], Wouter Joosen[2], and Sicco Verwer[1]

[1] Delft University of Technology, Delft, The Netherlands
{azqa.nadeem,s.e.verwer}@tudelft.nl
[2] imec-DistriNet, KU Leuven, Leuven, Belgium
{vera.rimmer,wouter.joosen}@cs.kuleuven.be

Abstract. With rapidly evolving threat landscape surrounding malware, intelligent defenses based on machine learning are paramount. In this chapter, we review the literature proposed in the past decade and identify the state-of-the-art in various related research directions—malware detection, malware analysis, adversarial malware, and malware author attribution. We discuss challenges that emerge when machine learning is applied to malware. We also identify the key issues that need to be addressed by the research community in order to further deepen and systematize research in the malware domain.

1 Introduction

Over the past two decades, malicious software (malware) has emerged as one of the biggest security threats. AV-test, a security research institute, has reported detecting more than 1000 Million malware samples in 2019[1]. According to Accenture, a malware attack on a company can cost $2.4M on average and can take 50 days to resolve[2]. Anti-Viruses (AVs) are considered to be the first line of defense. However, according to a survey by Ponemon Institute, 69% organizations do not believe that AVs can block the threats that they monitor. Given these staggering numbers, classical rule-based malware detectors can simply not be expected to detect the large influx of malware variants. The main problem with rule-based defenses is that they are reactive, where a rule is added only *after* experiencing an attack.

Machine Learning (ML) has become a promising ally for malware detection. The security community has been investigating ways to incorporate machine learning for intelligent malware detection, profiling, and analysis. Figure 1 shows a typical pipeline for malware defense and the opportunities to introduce machine learning in it. It is noteworthy that machine learning is also useful for attackers: Due to the intrinsic adversarial nature of the threat landscape, machine learning has not only been used to build intelligent defenses, but it has also been used to develop intelligent attacks that evade detection. In the past decade alone, this arms-race has resulted in more than 20,000 research articles.

---

[1] https://www.av-test.org/en/statistics/malware/.
[2] https://www.accenture.com/us-en/insight-cost-of-cybercrime-2017.

© Springer Nature Switzerland AG 2022
L. Batina et al. (Eds.): Security and Artificial Intelligence, LNCS 13049, pp. 217–253, 2022.
https://doi.org/10.1007/978-3-030-98795-4_10

In this chapter, we conduct a systematic survey of the literature published in the past decade to establish a taxonomy of the main research themes. For an unbiased literature review, we select peer-reviewed papers containing a combination of fixed search queries that are highly cited in their domain. We summarize the state-of-the-art in various sub-fields of intelligent malware defenses, *i.e.,* malware detection, malware analysis, adversarial malware, and malware author attribution. The literature is greatly dominated by *malware detection* approaches with the aim of developing scalable behavioral signatures. Approaches from other domains have been applied to perform malware detection, such as natural language processing, image visualization, graph mining, and bioinformatics. We categorize the research in this domain according to the data source and feature representation used for their classifiers. *Malware analysis* is another research direction that develops tools that provide the necessary insights to improve malware detection. We discuss approaches that aim to increase interpretability, and provide smarter ways to collect behavioral traces. *Adversarial machine learning* has recently gained popularity, not only for machine learning-based offensive security, but also for hardening machine learning classifiers. Finally, *malware author attribution* aims to associate malware to its author(s), a field that is mainly driven by law enforcement agencies. Although not a very active area, it serves as a powerful use-case for interdisciplinary research. Figure 2 shows the literature overview in a chronological order, divided across the aforementioned research directions.

We discuss important considerations that emerge when machine learning is applied to malware, such as resilience against concept drift and evasion, handling imbalanced datasets, using appropriate evaluation metrics, and providing privacy and performance guarantees. We have observed that the absence of toy problems, representative datasets, explainable approaches, and the usage of noisy ground truth has limited the reproducibility of available research. Specifically, explainable approaches are necessary for debugging existing techniques and developing newer ones based on obtained insights. These issues need to be addressed by the research community in order to encourage systematized research in the intelligent malware defenses domain.

This chapter is organized as follows. Section 2 serves as a roadmap for the rest of the chapter: it identifies the feature sources and representations that have been used to characterize malware in the literature, including several feature engineering modes. Section 3 discusses the vast literature that explores effective and efficient malware detection methods. We expand the discussion on malware research in Sect. 4 by covering relevant areas, *i.e.,* malware analysis, adversarial malware, and author attribution. Section 5 enumerates the main challenges unique to machine learning-based malware defenses. Section 6 highlights the four key issues that should be addressed to enable reproducible research in the intelligent malware defenses domain. Finally, we conclude our discussion in Sect. 7.

2   Malware Characterization

The success of machine learning classifiers lies in finding the data that appropriately characterizes malware. Determining these data and the input features

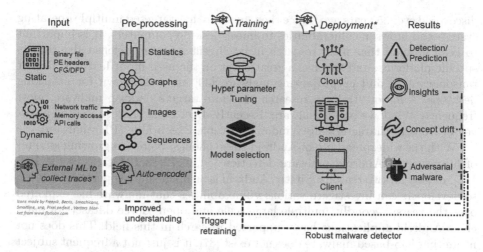

Fig. 1. Machine learning pipeline for malware defense: Raw input data gets transformed into features during pre-processing, which are given as input for model training. The raw data may be collected using ML-based sandboxing. Features may be automatically learned using auto-encoders. Depending on the problem, the model may be deployed at different locations, and the output may be used in several ways: Malware detection typically raises alerts; Insights obtained from malware analysis can lead to improved malware characterization; Detecting changes in data distribution can trigger model retraining; Incorporation of adversarial malware in the training process can lead to robust models.

required for machine learning is a difficult task since they will be used to detect new malware samples that may behave in unexpected ways. Anderson *et al.* [10] suggest that effective feature engineering, including features obtained from domain experts, plays a key role in classifier performance. There exists a myriad of literature exploring the various features that can be used to characterize different types of malware [122,132]. In this chapter, we provide an overview of the past ten years of intelligent malware defenses from a technical machine learning perspective, grounded in the types of features used to characterize malware: statistical, graphs, images, and sequences. The type of input feature greatly influences which machine learning technology can be employed. Other important considerations are: (a) the target platform of the malware, (b) how to collect data from a malware, and (c) how to extract features from such data. We briefly introduce these other considerations below but will not go into detail.

2.1   Platform-Specific Malware and Defenses

Malware often targets consumer devices, like desktop computers and handheld devices. The first malware was a PC-based virus, called Elk Cloner[3],

---

[3] https://en.wikipedia.org/wiki/Elk_Cloner.

discovered over 35 years ago. Since then, malware has targeted multiple operating system and browser vulnerabilities to infect desktop computers. It is important to keep in mind that most research in intelligent malware defense also targets specific platforms, and this has a great effect on the used input features. Recent ransomware [4] and cryptojacking malware [30] are well-known for attacking desktops. A major strain in research therefore targets desktop malware, most frequently Windows-based malware. Recently, Ucci *et al.* [122] presented a survey of features characterizing Windows Portable Executable (PE) malware.

With the widespread use of Android smartphones, there is a growing amount of literature on Android malware detection [54,66,72,83,104,118,119,134,144, 145], mainly for two reasons: Firstly, Android is an open-source operating system, so developers can investigate various vulnerabilities that malware has exploited over the years; Secondly, multiple large-scale and open-source datasets of malicious Android applications have supported research in this field. This does not mean that iOS-based malware does not exist [87], it is just not a frequent subject of research.

Nowadays consumer devices are increasingly becoming equipped with Internet connectivity, known as the *Internet of Things (IoT)*. This comes with new risks culminating in a novel strain of malware specifically targeting IoT devices [131]. IoT devices are commonly made available on the Internet with their default configurations, which makes them an easy target for the attackers. Since IoT devices have limited computational resources, their built-in security is significantly inferior to other internet-connected devices, making it an ideal use-case for intelligent malware defenses. Several recent works have proposed to enhance IoT security using ML-based malware detection [13,40]. In this chapter, we try to avoid this distinction between platforms, instead focusing on technological differences. However, often the platform and technologies are tightly linked, and solutions are typically not directly applicable to other platforms.

2.2   Feature Sources

There are two major approaches for analyzing malware: (i) static analysis, and (ii) dynamic analysis. Machine learning has been applied successfully in both approaches. For static analysis, *static features* are extracted from a malware's code, *i.e.*, without executing it. For dynamic analysis, features are extracted by running malware and monitoring its behavior. These features can be obtained from two sources: standard *dynamic features* are generated on the host device, typically by interacting with the operating system, while *network features* are created from network traffic generated by hosts in a network.

Static Features. The source code of a malware, often obtained by decompiling its binary, is the most reliable artefact to identify its objective. Early studies on malware detection have mainly characterized malware using features extracted from its code. These features are often obtained by doing a comparative analysis of goodware (benign software) and malware features, and selecting the ones that are observed more frequently in malware. PE headers are commonly used for Windows malware [3,33,47,59,107], while some works extract features directly from the malware binary itself [56,60,96]. Most of the recent literature from static analysis comes from the smartphone domain (*i.e.*, Android), where the features are extracted from either the APK's manifest file or the disassembled Dalvik bytecode for signature generation. Shabtai *et al.* [111] is one of the earlier works on Android malware detection that uses features from the Dalvik byte-code in order to perform binary classification (*i.e.*, malware vs. goodware). One of their major contributions is to apply a myriad of classification algorithms and select the one that achieves the highest accuracy. Other features, such as Opera-tional Codes (OpCodes) [40,72] and function API calls [1,5,54,105,134], are also commonly used for malware detection. Existing works also analyze the amount and types of permissions that applications request to measure their malicious-ness [63,104,134,144]. For a higher-level semantic analysis, features from Control flow graphs [104,137] and Data flow graphs [39] have also been used.

Dynamic Features. With the widespread use of code obfuscation tools to evade detection and to generate malware variants, syntactic analysis has become increasingly more difficult. Additionally, there has been a spike in fileless malware infections[4], where the malware code resides purely in the victim host's memory without leaving any code fingerprints. Hence, dynamic analysis is more popular for malware detection. In dynamic analysis, malware is executed in a controlled environment and its behavior is monitored [94]. Information such as, system API calls [19,34,75,141], memory access patterns [55,74], and running processes [20] are common sources for feature selection. Some works consider inter-file relation-ships between files present on a system for malware detection [95,120]. There also exist hybrid approaches, where static analysis guides dynamic analysis for thorough code coverage [117].

Network Features. Network traffic analysis is popular because it can be per-formed remotely and presents lower overhead than its system-activity counter-part. However, machine learning has been slow to materialize in the network security domain because of noisy ground truth and non-stationary data distri-bution [10]. Existing sandboxes also have limited support for handling network requests due to the risk of lateral movement, *i.e.*, when the attacker who has gained access to the network spreads their reach to other hosts [45]. Nevertheless, the use of HTTP header fields [27,66,93] and traffic connections [83] is common for malicious traffic detection. Privacy concerns have also been addressed in network security. Boukhtouta *et al.* [18] evaluate the differences between Deep Packet Inspection (DPI) based methods and IP-header based methods for classi-fying malicious network traffic. They conclude that IP-header features make the machine learning model generalizable and can achieve higher accuracy due to the independence from packet payloads. They also suggest that using IP-header features can help fingerprint zero-day malware, *i.e.*, malware never seen before.

---

[4] https://www.cybereason.com/blog/fileless-malware.

2.3   Feature Engineering Modes

Most of the existing works perform manual feature engineering, where the features are initially obtained from domain experts and are further cherry-picked based on a classifier's accuracy [1,5,33,40,54,59,72,93,96,105,107,134]. The downside to manually engineering features is that it is a laborious and (potentially) subjective process, which may need to be repeated in case of concept drift, for example. The malware threats also need to be fully scoped-out before arriving at the optimal feature-set. Nevertheless, knowing the features beforehand helps with explaining and debugging a classifier's decisions.

In the recent years, deep neural networks have gained tremendous traction, making automated feature engineering through representation learning (*e.g.,* with auto-encoders) a popular choice. Pascanu *et al.* [89] propose a recurrent neural network approach, specifically Echo State Networks, for automatically extracting time-domain features. They use these features in a Logistic Regression (LR) model for malware classification, and achieve better performance than a trigram based manual feature engineering approach. David *et al.* [28] propose a system that uses Deep Belief Networks (DBN), which are a type of generative graphical deep neural network that can perform unsupervised learning, with a deep stack of de-noising auto-encoders to automatically generate behavioral signatures. Yuxin *et al.* [137] have also used DBNs as auto-encoders to automatically extract features from malware executables.

A common critique faced by features that are automatically learned from deep neural networks is that they are uninterpretable, and hence undesirable for building explainable solutions. Building interpretable deep learning models is an open area of research. Zhu *et al.* [145] have recently proposed an interesting approach that automatically engineers features by mimicking human analysts' feature engineering processes. Their system mines academic documents and synthesizes their knowledge into interpretable features that are later used for Android malware classification. They report comparable results to state-of-the-art manual feature engineering approaches.

2.4   Feature Representation

After having selected the data source and features to use, the next step is to determine how to process these data. We identify four different kinds of feature representations in this chapter, *i.e.,* statistical, graphs, images, and sequences. Note that feature representation means the format of the input given to a ML classifier, not the intermediate representations from representation learning.

Represent as Statistics. The most common representation for features in the literature is statistical [1,3,5,10,16,20,34,63,66,73,77,93,97,99,104–107,119,134,144]. Feature values are collapsed using aggregates or correlations. Some statistical features also capture the temporal aspect of the behavior without having to deal with sequential data, *e.g.,* the Power Spectral Density of the FFT of the Command & Control communication [121].

Represent as Graphs. One branch of literature represents malware using graphs, *e.g.,* to represent the hosts a malware connects with, as an abstraction over the original feature-set to get a high-level view of malware's behavior. Graphs are used to either ease analysis [139] or to extract semantic features for malware detection [32,42,95,120]. Graphs are also used to perform malware causality analysis [68,70,140].

Represent as Images. Another branch of literature explores various visualization methods in order to characterize malware. A malware binary can be converted into an image by encoding the raw values of the binary as the color intensity of pixels [2,50,56,84,114,130]. The intuition here is that a malware family may share similar code pieces, which will appear as similar motifs in the image. Visualizing malware, and hence exposing these similarities to the human eye, can potentially aid manual malware analysis. Furthermore, research has also applied standard image classification techniques to perform efficient and reasonably accurate malware detection. Despite these encouraging initial results, we note that image representation for malware classification should be considered with caution, as discussed in more detail in Sect. 3.3.

Represent as Sequences. There is an increasing amount of literature that is investigating the use of sequential data in behavior characterization. Although sequential features capture the temporal aspect of behavior, machine learning algorithms with inherent support for sequences are rare. The main difficulty lies in appropriately measuring the distance between two sequences in the presence of noise, delays and misalignments. Methods from other fields, such as *sequence alignment* adopted from bioinformatics [26,57], and *n-grams* adopted from natural language processing [22,35,40,47,52] have been utilized to that end. Increasingly more approaches are using deep neural networks because they have good support for sequences, *e.g.,* Long Short Term Memory networks (LSTM) [75,141], Recurrent Neural Networks (RNN) [43,59,112] and Word2Vec [9,21,54].

Fig. 2. Overview of ML-based malware defenses proposed over the past decade.

Table 1. Literature according to feature source and representation.

Representation	Source		
	Static	Dynamic	Network
Statistical	[1,5,63,73,77,104–107,119,134,144]	[19,20,34,77,99]	[10,16,66,77,93,97,121]
Graphs	[32,42,104]	[68,70,95,120]	[140]
Images	[2,50,56,60,84,114,130]	–	[125]
Sequences	[13,21,22,26,28,33,40,47,54,59,72,73,89,96,137,145]	[57,75,141]	[36,91]

3   Malware Detection

A central objective of malware research is to develop behavioral signatures that can automatically detect future malware variants. We make a distinction between two major strains of research in the malware domain: *Detection-based* (this section) and *Analysis-based* (Sect. 4.1).

Most of the existing literature is about malware detection and signature generation, with the end-goal of optimizing metrics, such as classifier accuracy and F1-scores [16,36,77,91,93,97,121]. To this end, a plethora of research has been conducted over the past ten years that explores various features, representations, and machine learning algorithms. LeDoux *et al.* [61] summarize the research on malware detection, particularly on code-reuse detection, using machine learning. They also enumerate malware analysis problems that machine learning *is* equipped to solve. The vast literature on feature extraction and data mining techniques for malware detection is comprehensively described by Ye *et al.* [132]. Souri *et al.* [116] evaluate various signature- and behavior-based intelligent malware detectors.

We survey malware detection methods by focusing on the feature representations used by the applied machine learning or data mining technology. Both supervised and unsupervised machine learning techniques have been used in the literature. We categorize them into three classes: (i) *Binary classification*: Determine whether an unlabeled software is goodware or malware, (ii) *Multi-class classification*: Given a set of unlabeled malware samples and a set of known malware family names, perform malware family attribution, and (iii) *Clustering*: Given a set of unlabelled software, categorize them into distinct classes based on structural/behavioral differences. Table 1 summarizes the malware detectors reviewed in this chapter, categorized according to the feature source (*i.e.*, static, dynamic, network) and input representation (*i.e.*, statistical, graph, image, sequence) that they employ.

3.1   Statistical Approaches

An aggregated feature-set is the most widespread feature representation used in literature. Statistical features are fast to compute and simple to incorporate in a machine learning classifier.

Experiments have shown that the prevalence of certain feature values is a decent indicator of malware. Naturally, binary classification proves to be more successful under this setting than multi-class classification. Hence, even if the experimental dataset is composed of malware from multiple families, earlier works considered them together as one 'malicious' class. Alazab *et al.* [5] perform binary classification for the task of 'zero-day' malware detection. They use the frequency of static API calls to characterize Windows binaries, and show that it is indeed possible to distinguish between malware and goodware using this characterization. Aafer *et al.* [1] propose a light-weight Android malware detector based on the frequency of static API calls. They use K-Nearest Neighbors (KNN) to detect and alert the user of malicious applications. Sahs *et al.* [104] characterize Android applications using a binary vector of used permissions. Because there exist significantly more benign applications than malicious ones, they utilize a one-class Support Vector Machine (SVM) which characterizes benign applications well, and helps detect Android malware. Yerima *et al.* [134] use Bayesian classification to detect malware. They characterize applications using API call- and permission-frequencies.

Santos *et al.* [106] utilize the frequency of OpCode occurrence in executables to detect malware. They show that Polynomial Kernel classifiers and Random Forests achieve the best performance, which is not surprising because these algorithms have a long history of performing well in text classification. Suarez *et al.* [119] extract statistical features from Control Flow Graph (CFG) code blocks, such as the number and redundancy of code chunks, and common and discriminant code chunks. These text-based features are used for multi-class classification. Earlier deep learning approaches have also characterized malware using aggregates. For example, Saxe *et al.* [107] propose a malware detection system that uses a feature-set of byte histograms and frequency of PE import calls.

Although statistical features have been applied successfully in a supervised manner, there are assumptions that may be difficult to realize in practice. For example, AV-assigned family labels are noisy and novel threats are common. In contrast, unsupervised learning can be used independently to identify novel threats. In the binary classification setting, an anomaly detection approach is often used to model the benign class and anomalies are labelled as malicious, giving the capability to detect novel threats. For example, Burguera *et al.* [19] built a malware detection system using K-Means clustering to identify anomalous system events by finding deviations from one 'normal' cluster. For the multi-class setting, clustering is used to identify different threat classes. Perdisci *et al.* [93] present one of the first unsupervised clustering approaches to detect HTTP-based malware. They propose multi-step clustering to enable large-scale malware behavioral signature generation. Unsupervised machine learning is also often used in combination with supervised approaches to improve detection capabilities. Rieck *et al.* [99] propose an incremental analysis approach for malware family identification: by first performing clustering to identify *novel malware classes*, and then classifying unknown malware samples by assigning them to these discovered classes. Burnap *et al.* [20] have recently developed an unsupervised learning method based on Self Organizing Feature Maps (SOMs) that cluster similar malware behavior. They use the clusters of similar behavior as features for later classification tasks. The key benefit of this approach is an added layer of abstraction for improved classification—instead of using raw features for classification, the system allows fuzzy boundaries that can map new samples onto the existing decision boundary. David *et al.* [28] use Deep Belief Networks, a type of unsupervised model, to automatically generate malware behavioral signatures. Finally, Li *et al.* [66] build a network traffic-based malware classifier that utilizes both supervised and unsupervised classifiers to improve classification accuracy.

Effective malware detectors provide stable and trustworthy results. Since statistical features provide an aggregated view, a malicious application may appear similar to a benign application from this point of view. Hence, the choice of feature representation plays a crucial role in a classifier's robustness. Recently, Milosevic *et al.* [73] compared two text-mining approaches for Android malware detection—using statistical features (*i.e.,* permissions) and sequential features (*i.e.,* bag-of-words of decompiled Dex code). Their experiments show that the bag-of-words approach performs better due to better malware characterization, indicating that statistical features may not be the optimal choice in all cases. Another way to improve the robustness of malware detectors is to use *Ensemble learning, i.e.,* a learning paradigm that combines the decisions of multiple classifiers to arrive at the final decision. Ensemble models, such as Random Forests have been shown to be robust to non-stationary data distribution, such as network traffic [10]. Recently, Zhu *et al.* [144] proposed an ensemble Rotation Forests model to classify Android malware. Rotation Forests [100] are an ensemble of Decision Trees where diversity through rotated principal components is given emphasis, resulting in more stable decisions.

3.2 Graph-Mining Approaches

Graph-mining approaches have been used to represent malware's relationships in a graphical format, in order to provide an added abstraction layer. Malware literature adopts scalable graph mining approaches to perform fast detection.

Security products often have to mark files as malicious or benign based on a partial view of the host's file system. Approaches using inter-file relationships have emerged as a solution. Chau *et al.* [95] perform malware detection using large-scale graph inference. They consider files as malware based on *guilt-by-association*—they exploit the inter-file relationships present on multiple systems to compute reputation scores for unlabelled files. They use Belief Propagation algorithm to mark files with low reputation as malware. They evaluate their approach on a 60 terabyte dataset composed of a Billion-node graph, and show significant improvement over existing approaches. Acar *et al.* [120] also use a similar approach to detect malware, with the additional use of Locality Sensitive Hashing (LSH) for efficiently binning similar files.

Hou *et al.* [42] build the first approach that uses a Structured Heterogeneous Information Network (HIN) to characterize API-relatedness. The HIN edges are used to measure the semantic similarity between API calls, that is used to measure maliciousness of an application using multi-kernel learning. Fan *et al.* [32] improve upon the previous approach using a *meta-graph* to determine inter-file relationships for malware detection. For cost-effectiveness, they use *MetaGraph2Vec* to learn low-dimensional representations for the HIN that preserves its structure and semantics. *MetaGraph2Vec* is a meta-graph approach that has shown competitive performance for heterogeneous graph-mining tasks such as node classification and clustering.

Using graphs to perform causality analysis is also an area of interest. Zhang *et al.* [140] detect malware by performing *causality analysis* on its network traffic. They build Triggering Relation Graphs (TRG) that show the inter-dependency of various network events. The TRGs show an absence of dependency between legitimate and malicious network events, hence making it easier to detect malicious activities. Liu *et al.* [68] build a backward- and forward-causality graph to detect abnormal system events, based on their rareness and location in the causality graph.

3.3   Image Visualization Approaches

Malware visualization has opened a new research direction that uses ML-based image classification to detect malware. These approaches rely on converting a malware binary into an image which is then provided to an image classifier, either as a raw image or as a set of extracted features. The key assumptions for these methods are: (a) *malware families have similar images because of code reuse,* and (b) *malware images are significantly different from goodware images.*

In 2011, Nataraj *et al.* [84] proposed a straightforward method to convert malware into an image: a malware executable represented as a binary vector is reshaped into a matrix of an arbitrary width and is viewed as a grey-scale image. The authors observed that malware binaries belonging to the same family were visually similar in both layout and texture. They extracted textural features from these images and applied K-Nearest-Neighbors to perform malware family identification. This approach proved to be very efficient and achieved high accuracy, close to prior methods that used static features such as n-grams. Furthermore, they showed that malware belonging to one family packed with the same packer, or containing sections encrypted with polymorphic engines, are still categorized together as the same family, indicating some level of resilience to *naïve* obfuscation. Motivated with the initial positive results, several follow-up studies [2,56] expanded the research by investigating different types of image feature extractors and machine learning classifiers. Approaches to malware classification based on image similarity were confirmed to be effective on the commonly used Kaggle Microsoft Malware dataset [101].

Recent work has started applying deep neural networks for the classification task, inspired by their encouraging performance in the image classification domain. Kalash *et al.* [50] successfully perform malware family identification with a two-dimensional Convolutional Neural Network (CNN) architecture, and Singh *et al.* [114] convert malware binaries into colored-images to classify obfuscated malware with a `ResNet-50` architecture, *i.e.,* a CNN architecture with shortcut connections providing superior performance. Yakura *et al.* [130] applied a CNN with attention mechanism [128] that allows to explain which areas of an image contribute to particular classification decisions. Le *et al.* [60] have recently proposed a fully automated malware classification approach for non-domain experts. They represent raw binary files as grey-scale images using the approach by Nataraj et al. [84]. The images are given to a hybrid network, i.e., CNN with Bi-directional LSTM model, which outperforms a traditional CNN model.

Despite promising performance on benchmark datasets, representing binaries as images for malware detection comes with several limitations. Apart from some empirical results, there appears to be little evidence to strongly support the aforementioned underlying assumptions of malware classification based on visual similarity of binaries. Some studies have encountered images from different malware families that exhibited such similar patterns that they were classified in one class [2]. Naturally, only previously seen malware can be identified, while zero-day malware which is structurally different will likely evade detection [56]. Even for known malware, a common case of false negatives is observed when malicious content of relatively small size is embedded within a goodware, such that the resulting image remains very similar to other benign examples. Additionally, when global image features are used, merely relocating sections in a binary or adding large sections with redundant data may be sufficient to alter the image texture and mislead a classifier. These issues illustrate that generalizability of this approach, beyond particular datasets, remains an open question.

While image representations allow large-scale malware classification in a computationally feasible way, deep neural networks do not necessarily require this intermediate transformation. One-dimensional CNN architectures and sequential deep neural networks are directly applicable to raw one-dimensional binaries. Meanwhile, reshaping an initially one-dimensional binary sequence to a two-dimensional image with an arbitrarily chosen width introduces artificial spatial relations that are not present in the original file. Additionally, this representation does not appear stable, as adding or removing binary data in one location may completely change the positional relations in the vertical direction of the converted image [130]. Such artefacts may obscure naturally occurring patterns in data and negatively impact classification. This line of reasoning may also apply to a few studies that attempt to use CNN on dynamic features, such as malicious network traffic: Wang et al. [125] perform malware detection by representing network traffic as images. In any case, it is very challenging to make such two-dimensional CNNs capable of recognizing the temporal dependencies required for processing traffic data.

3.4   Sequence Learning Approaches

Sequential pattern mining has emerged as a promising approach for malware detection due to increasingly better-performing sequential ML classifiers.

Earlier sequence learning works utilize n-grams to characterize temporal behavior. Jain et al. [47] represent PE files as n-grams (with varying values for n) to perform binary classification. They select the prominent n-grams using Class-wise Document Frequency method. Their experiments show that trigrams with Random Forests give the best malware detection performance. Similarly,

Canfora *et al.* [22] use n-grams generated from OpCode sequences to detect malware families. They show that bigrams with Random Forests give the best performance. We believe these differences exist due to different datasets and feature selection approaches. Fan *et al.* [33] uses function call sequences and an All-Nearest Neighbors (ANN) classifier for PE-malware detection. ANN is a modification of K-Nearest Neighbors algorithm that makes a decision based on *all* neighbors. ANN makes a compromise on run-time efficiency for the sake of robustness.

In recent works, deep learning-based approaches have dominated malware detection using sequence learning. Convolutional Neural Networks (CNN) are used due to their ability to detect complex and non-linear patterns in data. Raff *et al.* [96] build a CNN framework that takes an entire PE binary as input for automated feature engineering and malware detection. Their method consumes the entire executable as opposed to only the PE-header to avoid over-fitting on the header features. However, their results do not show significant improvement over their baseline—a byte n-gram model. Mclaughlin *et al.* [72] perform Android malware detection using a CNN framework that utilizes raw OpCode sequences. Azmoodeh *et al.* [13] also use OpCode sequences to perform binary classification on IoT malware that is specifically used for military purposes. They reduce the feature dimensions using Principle Component Analysis (PCA) by providing only the first two components to the classifier. Recently, Cakir *et al.* [21] have used Word2Vec feature embedding on OpCode sequences to characterize malware. They use Gradient Boosting, which is a type of ensemble learner, for binary classification of malware. Karbab *et al.* [54] use CNN and Word2Vec feature embedding on API call sequences for malware family identification. They evaluate their system on multiple datasets, such as the MalGenome dataset [143], the Drebin dataset [12], and benign applications from Google Play[5]. Kolosnjaji *et al.* [59] perform multi-class classification using hybrid deep learning, *i.e.,* Convolutional and Recurrent Neural Networks (CNN/RNN), for Windows malware family identification.

Recently, Haddadpajouh *et al.* [40] have explored various configurations of Long Short Term Memory networks (LSTMs) for IoT malware classification. They characterize binaries by their OpCode sequences, and then choose the features that maximize the Information Gain (IG). However, it is unclear how generalizable their results are as they only use ~500 binaries for the classification task. Zhang *et al.* [141] use so-called behavior chains based on API call sequences to characterize malware's behavior. They use LSTMs to perform binary classification and report a false positive rate of less than 2% (in the best case). Mishra *et al.* [75] use deep learning and the sequence of dynamic system calls for malware classification in the cloud environment. Their system uses two layered approach – CNN for feature engineering and Bi-directional LSTMs for malware detection. They evaluate their system on a university's network traffic and show promising results.

Sequential features are a common occurrence in bioinformatics. As computer viruses attain their characterization from similarity to natural viruses,

---

[5] https://play.google.com/store/apps.

bioinformatics-inspired solutions have also been proposed to detect malware variants. A common approach to detect similar DNA sequences is through the use of sequence alignment algorithms, such as the Smith-Waterman algorithm. Sequence alignment methods work by assigning a score based on matches, mismatches and gaps. These values are embedded in a substitution matrix. Domain-specific substitution matrices exist for bioinformatics applications. Chen et al. [26] map malware's binary code to Amino acid characters, and use the so-called Residue substitution matrix, while Naidu et al. [82] report that the PAM-350 substitution matrix performs the best for malware variant detection. Chen et al. [26] also develop a multiple sequence alignment method that uses neural networks to classify viruses and worms. They show that alignment-based methods allow classifiers to find similarities with more ease compared to other methods.

3.5   Performance Optimizations

Malware detectors need to be efficient to cope with the exponential increase in malware attacks. Hence, some works propose extensions to existing works for improving the performance of traditional malware detectors.

Feature Reduction. A classifier's performance is directly dependent on the quality of features used for model learning. The key idea is to select the least number of features that maximally characterize a malware. Hence, a straightforward optimization is to conduct a feature reduction step that eliminates redundant features. Li et al. [63] develop a fast Android malware detector using an SVM classifier. As a feature reduction step, they perform 'significant permissions' analysis, that selects only the permissions that distinguish between malicious and benign applications with high confidence. Their results achieve up to 32 times speed-up compared to two competing approaches, i.e. Drebin [12] and Permission-induced Risk Malware Detection [124]. Similarly, Yerima et al. [134] select only the features with maximum Mutual Information (MI) to speed up their malware detector. Firdausi et al. [34] demonstrate elevated performance of their malware detector after conducting a best-first feature selection process.

Hardware-Assisted Detection. Hardware-assisted Malware Detection (HMD) has emerged as an alternative for improving malware detection using Hardware Performance Counters (HPC). HMDs are light-weight detectors that live on the microprocessor to provide a first-line of defense, and to reduce overhead on software-based detectors. Khasawneh et al. [55] show that hardware-detectors reduce performance overhead by up to 11 times compared to software-only detectors. Xu et al. [129] propose a novel HMD that monitors system calls' memory access patterns, which are used to classify malware, e.g., kernel rootkits.

Existing studies suggest that HMDs execute a malware sample multiple times in order to collect the required data, due to the limited number of HPCs available on microprocessors. Most of the methods propose to use an ensemble of light-weight classifiers to resolve this issue. Khasawneh et al. [55] propose an ensemble of *specialized* LR classifiers to improve the performance of HMDs, while only inducing minimal additional overhead on the cycle-time and power consumption. *Specialized classifiers* are malware-family specific classifiers, *i.e.,* one classifier is trained for one class of malware. They use LR due to its cheap and simple implementation on the microprocessor. Sayadi *et al.* [110] propose ensemble learning to collect the required data while using even less HPCs. Their results show that ensemble learning approach using only 4 HPCs can match the robustness and performance of standard classifiers that use 16 HPCs. In a recent work, Sayadi *et al.* [109] demonstrate that the performance of HMDs is directly related to the number of available HPCs. They propose a feature reduction step in order to select the most significant HPCs. They propose a two-step classification approach: a *course-grained classifier* that categorizes a software as either goodware or one of the malicious classes (*i.e.,* rootkit or trojan); followed by a *fine-grained specialized classifier* (*i.e.,* one for each type of malicious class). To further reduce the run-time, they utilize ensemble learning in the coarse-grained classifiers and show that using merely 4 HPCs outperforms state-of-the-art classifiers with 8 HPCs by a factor of 1.31.

3.6 Trend

There is a growing interest towards alternative approaches for malware detection, such as causality-based, and ant-colony optimization-based approaches [44], and a more targeted focus on Android malware detection. The use of sequence learning is growing, especially due to superior performance of recurrent neural networks, such as LSTMs, but also due to sequences being better equipped to characterize behavior. For example, Amer *et al.* [9] have used a combination of Word2Vec and Markov chains to establish the relationship between malware API call sequences. Despite that, works on network-traffic based sequential models are meagre due to the difficulty of handling non-stationary and noisy sequences. There is also a growing concern for the brittle nature of neural networks, to be discussed in Sect. 4.2, which is driving research towards better interpretability of such models' output.

4   Additional Research Directions

Although malware detection is a central research objective, there are additional research directions that have been gaining traction lately. *Malware analysis*, as opposed to detection, aims to improve malware understandability rather than to optimize detection rates [17,78,119]. *Adversarial machine learning* techniques have gained particular popularity in recent years in relation to detecting evasive malware. Finally, *attributing malware* to its author(s) is also an area of interest, mainly driven by law enforcement agencies. In this section, we discuss the seminal works in these three popular research themes.

4.1   Malware Analysis

Malware analysis methods aim to improve malware understandability, and provide essential insights that can improve malware detection methods. Although malware analysis and detection are often seen together in literature, below we present approaches that: (a) aim to improve malware understandability, *e.g.*, by providing insights into malware relationships, and (b) enable malware analysis, *e.g.*, by collecting traces and building analysis environments.

Ucci *et al.* [122] present a recent survey on ML-based malware analysis techniques. The survey provides a taxonomy of research objectives, features and ML algorithms used for Windows PE malware. They identify topical trends on malware triage. They also present the concept of *Malware Analysis Economics* that studies the trade-off between detection accuracy and the resources required for detection.

Increasing Interpretability. Malware analysts have to frequently monitor large-scale network traffic, which is a laborious task. Zhang *et al.* [139] propose a framework to visualise the causal relationships between network requests to help detect abnormal events. Their user studies reveal that visualising network traffic in this way enhances analysts' malware detection capabilities. Mariconti *et al.* [70] perform causality analysis on user actions that trigger a malware infection. They characterize malware samples by the trigger-actions commonly performed by users. Their method can successfully infer relations between, *e.g.*, information-stealing malware and web pages asking for user credentials. Suarez *et al.* [119] build a dendrogram of malware families showing overlapping code snippets, which helps them to generate evolution-invariant signatures.

Smith *et al.* [115] have pointed towards the semantic gap between the machine learning and malware analysis communities. One of their proposals is to reposition the task from *identifying malware* to *identifying behavior*, making it possible to understand what a malware is doing. Along these lines, Nadeem *et al.* [81] have proposed the use of behavioral profiles to describe malware samples as opposed to using black-box family names. They develop MalPaCA, a clustering-based framework that discovers distinct behaviors present in network traffic and uses the cluster membership information to generate a profile for each malware sample.

Collecting Traces. Collecting malware traces, especially for dynamic analysis, is a challenging problem due to the difficulty of finding live malware samples and setting up sandboxes. Burguera *et al.* [19] addresses the unavailability of malware datasets by setting up a crowd-sourcing system to collect system traces from unlimited number of real smartphone users. Secondly, effective features for malware are often not shared among the security community. Gu *et al.* [39] address this issue by introducing a consortium blockchain framework. The blockchain is used as a database of malware-characterizing features. Their classifier consumes the blockchain for malware family identification. Recently, Shibahara *et al.* [112] have proposed a machine learning-based data collection method for efficient dynamic analysis. Typically, malware traces are collected for a fixed amount of time before moving on to executing the next sample. The method proposed in [112] treats network traces as natural language, and uses the communication pattern as a heuristic to suspend analysis. They use RNN to learn the underlying objective of communication and to detect when a change in purpose occurs. They suspend analysis when a malware has stopped its activities. With this approach, they report a reduction of 67.1% analysis time.

Sandboxing. Multiple works have proposed sandboxes that can forcefully trigger malware functionality in order to provide more holistic behavioral logs, but very few have used machine learning to do so. There also exist other approaches that use search-based algorithms to improve code coverage of malware samples, e.g., Wang et al. [126] propose a fuzzing-based approach to forcefully trigger malware's hidden behaviors. Among the literature that uses machine learning is the work by Spreitzenbarth et al. [117]. They propose an end-to-end analysis environment for Android malware where applications are executed, traces are collected and a clustering algorithm categorizes them as malware or goodware. However, they only use machine learning to *post-process* behavioral traces. Additionally, their sandbox does not support latest Android versions. Yerima et al. [133] have recently proposed a machine learning based malware analysis framework. They learn a state machine of each Android application using code's static analysis. They use insights from the state machine to guide the so-called *stateful event generation*. They also compare with an existing approach based on random event-generation and show that the guided behavior-triggering approach results in better data collection.

An orthogonal research objective is *sandbox evasion*, where a malware uses machine learning to detect whether it is being executed in a sandbox or on a live system. When malware detects the presence of a sandbox, it either shuts down, or starts sending garbage data to mislead analysis. Yokoyama et al. [135] show that it is possible for attackers to use straightforward machine learning algorithms to differentiate between a sandbox and a live system based on leaking characteristics of Windows-based sandboxes. Miramirkhani et al. [74] propose sandbox evasion techniques based on the natural 'wear and tear' of a real system compared to that of a sandbox. They exploit the past usage of a system to determine its age and degree of use. They show that a simple decision tree classifier can differentiate between a sandbox and a real system with a very high accuracy.

Trend. The security community appears to be heavily biased towards detection-based solutions. Analysis is most often conducted as a precursor for detection methods, or as a part of Systematization of Knowledge studies. Recently, there has been a push towards using explainable machine learning for the malware domain, which specifically allows to reason about classifier decisions. Fan et al. [31] have evaluated various explanation techniques for malware analysis, and conclude that LIME [98] and SHAP [69] provide the most robust and stable explanations. Also, machine learning has not yet been applied to malware lineage—how a certain malware family evolves over time in terms of structure, behavior and its target. Most of the work in this domain is manual and requires a deep understanding of the evolving threat landscape: e.g., Black et al. [17] perform an in-depth analysis of banking malware families, and Moubarak *et al.* [78] discuss the structural relationship between several potentially state-sponsored malware. Evidently, the success of this research is dependent on the quality and size of the used dataset.

4.2   Adversarial Malware

The security of machine learning is an active area of research that has been gaining increasing popularity in the recent years. This theme addresses the arms-race between crafting evasive malware samples (offensive security) and developing robust methods to detect said samples (defensive security). Although the threat landscape is already adversarial in nature, many approaches in this area have been borrowed from the computer vision domain, where adversarial ML was pioneered. Biggio *et al.* [15] provide an overview of the developments in adversarial machine learning in the past ten years. An open problem in this area is using machine learning to craft adversarial malware samples where the perturbations are big enough to mimic goodware while preserving malicious functionality.

Offensive Security. While evasive malware has existed for a long time, latest research applies machine learning to automatically craft these samples. These techniques work by performing small perturbations on a malware sample to create a variant that leads to a misclassification by the ML model. Most of the proposed attacks are gradient-based, as they target deep neural networks. White-box techniques require some knowledge of the target, such as the structure and weights of the target model, while black-box techniques do not assume any knowledge of the targeted classifier.

There are two main concerns in creating adversarial malware samples: (a) the perturbations are performed in the continuous domain, while malware binaries exist in the discrete domain; and (b) the frameworks often create perturbations that break functionality of the executable. Anderson *et al.* [11] have proposed a reinforcement learning-based method to guide the search for functionality-preserving perturbations. However, since their method is quite general, they report modest evasion rates. Grosse *et al.* [38] propose a method for crafting adversarial examples that operates in the discrete domain and preserves functionality. They craft adversarial Android malware by adding constraints to the perturbations—they only allow changes in the manifest file that adds a single line of code to the application. They use the adversarial examples on Drebin [12] and report a misclassification (evasion) rate of 69%. Hu *et al.* [43] target RNN models based on sequential API features. They learn a local substitute (surrogate) model of the victim RNN that propagates the gradients to a generative RNN that produces sequential adversarial examples. Their results show that more than 90% of the adversarial examples result in misclassifications. Kolosnjaji *et al.* [58] target a sequential model that learns from raw malware bytes. They craft adversarial examples using a gradient-based attack modifying the last 1% of the bytes that achieve misclassifications. They report a maximum evasion rate of 60%. Al-Dujaili *et al.* [3] adapt the saddle-point optimization problem from the continuous domain to generate adversarial examples in the discrete domain. They present a framework that discovers adversarial examples and incorporates them in the training process to harden the learnt classifier. They conclude that the randomized rounding technique helps discover four times as many adversarial examples. Chen *et al.* [25] craft adversarial Android malware by optimally perturbing the Dalvik byte code to target semantic features. They show the effectiveness of their adversarial examples by using them on two famous Android malware detectors, MaMaDroid [86] and Drebin [12], where they report an evasion rate of 100%. Recently, Verwer *et al.* [123] used [3] to develop GRAMS, which is a greedy approach that randomly flips bits to obtain functionality-preserving high-quality adversarial examples in the discrete domain. GRAMS was successful in crafting evasive malware and defending against competitors' evasion attempts during the robust malware detection challenge[6].

Poisoning attacks are another important concern for machine learning classifiers. Poisoning attacks refer to an attacker's capability to inject adversarial examples during classifier *training phase*, such that it learns to classify malicious entities as benign. For example, Biggio *et al.* [14] poison behavioral malware clustering and Muñoz-González *et al.* [79] propose a poisoning algorithm for deep learning classifiers. Chen *et al.* [24] have specified attacker models for poisoning attacks in the malware domain: (a) a *weak attacker* who injects malicious code in the non-logical part of the application, such as manifest file; (b) a *strong attacker* who injects malicious code in resources, such as jar or jpg; and (c) a *sophisticated attacker* who uses Dynamic Code Loading via Reflection for injecting malicious code at run-time. Having concrete attacker models provides terminology to develop more streamlined defenses, and to compute resilience guarantees.

Defensive Security. One approach for forensic malware analysis is to categorize malware based on similar evasion strategies. Kirat *et al.* [57] propose a bioinformatics-inspired solution to generate and analyze evasion signatures—they cluster similar evasive behavior among malware samples. They use a sequence alignment algorithm to measure similarity among different system call sequences. Then, they extract evasion signatures from the behavioral clusters. These signatures can be used to detect when a future malware sample attempts to evade detection in a similar way.

One of the key benefits of adversarial machine learning is that it hardens the security of an adversarially trained model [38]. When adversarial examples are part of the training process, they allow to discover samples in the so-called *blind spots* of the malicious domain, increasing its robustness to unseen evasive samples. Recently, there has been a lot of interest in developing ML-based adversary-aware approaches. The main difference from malware detectors previously discussed in Sect. 3 is that these approaches actively anticipate evasion attempts. Demontis *et al.* [29] propose a so-called *secure-learning* paradigm that

---

[6] https://github.com/ALFA-group/malware_challenge.

suggests having the feature weights more evenly distributed in order to bound linear classifiers' sensitivity to feature changes. They also propose attacker models based on their capabilities, knowledge and skills. Zhang *et al.* [138] propose an adversary-aware feature selection method, since the choice of features may also be a factor in adversarial robustness. Their wrapper-based framework makes assumptions about the adversary and simulates evasion attacks at each step of the training phase. The framework chooses the features that maximize the classifier's generalizability in the absence of adversarial examples and minimize the classifier's impact against evasion attempts. Chen *et al.* [23] present a robust malware detection system based on two key components: (a) a *feature selection method* that picks features that maximize attacker's evasion costs, and (b) an *ensemble learning method* with diverse classifiers that incorporate a major part of the feature space. Li *et al.* [62] investigate the resilience of ensemble classifiers and the effectiveness of ensemble attacks. Their experiments show that while adversarial training for ensemble classifiers promotes robustness, they are unfortunately no match for adversarial examples learned through ensemble methods.

Another way to harden classifiers without explicit adversarial training is through the special handling of suspicious files. Chen *et al.* [24] have developed a self-adaptive learning scheme for detecting poisoning attacks. They introduce a so-called *camouflage detector* that finds suspicious false negatives by performing similarity analysis with the most-benign and most-malicious looking samples, and sends such *camouflaged samples* back to the training phase as malicious examples.

Trend. At the moment of writing, the security community seems to have a strong affinity towards offensive security research. Naturally, conducting defensive research is especially challenging due to the strict requirements that a defensive framework is expected to fulfill. In case of malware defenses, provable robustness to evasion is a major milestone that cannot be reached by the community without public datasets of evasive malware. We believe that adversarial learning for defensive model hardening is an unfolding but promising research field.

4.3   Malware Author Attribution

In general, authorship attribution can be considered from two perspectives: (i) *code authorship attribution* – attributing a software to its author(s); and (ii) *family attribution* – identifying code similarities between unlabelled software pieces. In malware research, the latter problem appears as *malware family identification*, which involves multi-class classification already covered in Sect. 3. Hence, here we discuss the code authorship attribution problem.

Code authorship attribution has a rich history in the Software Engineering literature. The aim of this research is to extract features that capture an author's programming style. Existing work can also be found in related fields, such as forgery and plagiarism detection where the goal is to extract distinguishing stylistic or fingerprinting attributes from a software that identifies where the code was copied from. Source code attribution is the simplest variant since the author's stylistic features can be relatively easily extracted. One such work is proposed by Alsulami *et al.* [8] who extract features from the Abstract Syntax Tree (AST) of source code collected from Google Code Jam (GCJ). In fact, GCJ and Github are popular sources of experimental data for authorship attribution, in general [6,7,103,113].

In many real-world settings however, source code is not directly available, rendering aforementioned techniques ineffective. It is also commonly believed that the compilation process removes most of the stylistic features. Rosenblum *et al.* [103] perform one of the first attempts to address this problem by using a ML approach that identifies the surviving stylistic features for binary authorship attribution.

It is noteworthy that code authorship attribution for malware is significantly more difficult because the authors have strong incentives to hide their identity. Using machine learning to solve the attribution problem is also tricky because code samples from known malware authors that are required to train a classifier are rarely available. Additionally, the availability of malware-as-a-service indicates that samples are authored by multiple developers in a malware's lifetime. Hence, research in this area is scarce because of the difficulty of establishing a ground truth.

Saxe *et al.* [108] have written an introductory book on big data analysis for malware detection. They show the usage of static and dynamic analysis for performing *shared code analysis* with the aim of identifying similar adversary groups. Alrabaee *et al.* [6] propose a multi-layered approach to improve malware binary authorship attribution by conducting both syntax- and semantic- analysis. They attempt to reconstruct the source code from malware binaries, which they compare with code-based signatures of other families. They also extract semantic features, such as the way registers are manipulated, to establish strong evidence for attribution. Rosenberg *et al.* [102] use deep neural networks for the attribution of nation-state Advanced Persistent Threats (APTs). They observe that nation-state APTs have different styles and objectives, which makes their classification feasible. To that end, they take raw dynamic logs as input to the neural network that learns a high-level abstraction of the APTs. Their system is evaluated on two major nation-state malware families and show it to be effective for the purpose.

Natural Language Processing has also been proposed for attribution purposes after its success in attributing cyber-stalkers [35]. Kalgutkar *et al.* [52] build an Android malware detection system based on 'malware author' signatures. Their system leverages strings extracted from the malware binaries to generate profiles of malware authors, with the expectation that future malware samples authored by the same person will match the profiles. They use n-grams for feature representation and Support Vector Machine for APK classification.

Research related to adversarial attacks also exists in code authorship attribution. Simko *et al.* [113] propose adversarial stylometry attacks to defeat source code attribution classifiers. They demonstrate that current code attribution classifiers are not robust to adversarial attacks, even when they are executed by non-experts. The authors claim that although not fool-proof, augmenting machine learning classifiers with human analysts proves to be more resilient against adversarial attacks, especially when they are warned about potential forgeries in the code. They analyze C/C++ programs and conclude that semantic features, such as those extracted from ASTs are more resilient to forgery attacks.

Alrabaee *et al.* [7] present a literature survey of existing techniques for malware binary attribution. The survey also lists features that can be used for author attribution because they survive compilation, *e.g.*, compiler information, system calls, and the usage of particular strings may characterize coding styles. Additionally, certain type of bugs in the code may also point to semantic hints that can be used for author attribution. They also note that a key research challenge is feature selection that captures author's style rather than functionality of the program. Following this, Murenin *et al.* [80] have used LIME to understand the role of selected features in source code attribution for Android malware.

Iqbal *et al.* [46] have recently published a book on authorship attribution and cyber forensics using machine learning in which they comprehensively describe research into authorship identification and attribution using few training samples, authorship characterization and verification. Kalgutkar *et al.* [51] show how the field has evolved from basic software matching techniques to sophisticated methods based on API calls and dependency graphs. They conclude that although there is no one-size-fits-all solution yet for malware attribution, the existing work on varying levels of abstraction has brought us one step closer to the solution. Nevertheless, this field still has many open problems that are yet to be explored.

Trend. The popularity of the malware attribution field is impacted by the adversarial and ad-hoc nature of the threat landscape. Unavailability of open datasets further complicates realistic evaluation. Further, having a narrow target audience (*e.g.*, law enforcement, intelligence agencies) means that the works do not get highly cited and thus remain undiscovered. We believe that this field can get a new life with explainable approaches, open benchmark datasets and access to ground truth.

5   Challenges in ML-Applied Malware Defenses

The malware domain presents unique challenges for machine learning application. After years of research, the security community has made a significant headway in highlighting the proper usage of machine learning for malware defenses. As a result, additional problems have emerged that require further investigation. Souri *et al.* [116] and Ye *et al.* [132] identify several unsolved problems in the data-mining based malware detection domain. One must remember that machine learning is not a silver bullet that can solve all malware-related problems [51]. In this section, we describe common pitfalls and challenges that emerge when ML is used for malware detection, which should be accounted for when designing and evaluating such methods.

Robustness Against Time-Decay. Some of the existing work is filled with unrealistic simplifying assumptions about the malware landscape. One of the most prevalent assumptions is the *closed-world assumption*, which assumes that training data is fully representative of all categories of samples that may appear at test-time. However, as malware is an ever-evolving threat, static training data will inevitably become outdated. Consequently, researchers have shown that ML-classifiers' performance degrades over time [92,107]. Recent works have incorporated *concept drift detection* in their ML classifiers for handling non-stationary data population. These classifiers continually re-learn the changing concepts in order to maintain an acceptable detection accuracy. Jordaney *et al.* [48] and Wang *et al.* [127] use P-values that can proactively detect concept drift before the classifier's performance starts to degrade. There is also a growing interest in semantic features that are less affected by malware evolution and hence slow down the aging of malware detectors [142].

Robustness Against Evasion. Evasion resilience is an important characteristic for deployable classifiers. A misleading expectation from ML classifiers is that they should be *fully and provably evasion resilient*. To this end, defensive adversarial machine learning has emerged as a promising solution for evasion resilient classifiers, which has been previously discussed in Sect. 4.2. The purpose of defensive adversarial ML is to explore additional search space in order to harden models against evasion attempts. However, this search is still bounded by the Independent and Identically Distributed data (i.i.d) assumption. As a consequence, out-of-distribution adversarial examples prevalent in the open world are unlikely to be detected by an adversarially trained ML classifier.

Imbalanced Training-Set. Benign examples occur significantly more frequently than malicious ones. Failure to incorporate this trait in the training dataset creates a so-called *spatial-bias* [92] in the classifier. Existing works have often used unrealistic class distribution, *e.g.,* the use of inverted class distribution [83] and equal class distribution [90,136]. Chen *et al.* [27] propose a solution for imbalanced network traffic classification to perform accurate Android malware detection. They experiment with various combinations of imbalanced classification algorithms, such as Synthetic Minority Oversampling Technique (SMOTE) with SVM, SVM cost-sensitive and C4.5 cost-sensitive. They also develop Simplex Imbalanced Data Gravitation-based Classification (S-IDGC) that works faster while maintaining the stability of IDGC. In the deep learning domain, Le *et al.* [60] use the class re-balance sampling procedure in bidirectional LSTMs to address the class imbalance problem.

Evaluation Metrics. The usage of appropriate evaluation metrics is an underrated challenge. For example, using accuracy to measure a classifier's performance when it is trained with a highly imbalanced dataset results in misleading conclusions. Similarly, precision and recall values can also be altered based on the choice of empirical thresholds and dataset-specific parameters. Meanwhile, evaluating approaches using such varied metrics limits objective analysis, and the obtained results become incomparable. Jordaney et al. [49] demonstrate that traditional evaluation metrics show misleading information about classifiers' performance. They propose two metrics based on non-conformity measures for evaluating a classifiers' performance. *Credibility* measures the homogeneity of a given label compared to others of the same class, and *Confidence* measures the separation between a given label and other classes. Pendlebury et al. [92] have recently identified experimental biases in existing Android malware classifiers, namely (a) *spatial bias* due to unrealistic class distribution in training and testing data, and (b) *temporal bias* due to incorrect time splits causing impossible configurations. They propose a new metric, namely Area Under Time (AUT), to characterize classifier robustness when time decay is present.

Privacy Concerns. Machine learning classifiers typically perform better with fine-grained contextual features. In an attempt to perform large-scale classification, classifiers have access to both benign and malicious data. Privacy concerns arise as the feature-set becomes more and more fine-grained. For example, DPI-based approaches analyze the payload of each packet, which may contain privacy sensitive information. With data protection laws being widely enforced, such methods are tricky to deploy at large-scale. There are a couple of solutions for being privacy-aware: (i) selecting abstract features that do not violate the privacy of user actions, while still being able to characterize malicious behavior; (ii) deploying a distributed classifier, as in the case of federated learning, that trains on local data provided by multiple clients [85]. In the latter solution, secure multi-party computation (SMC) and differential privacy (DP) are required to provide privacy guarantees.

Performance Optimizations. Malware infections are a widespread security threat faced by all network-connected devices. Classical machine learning solutions are often not ideal for fending off millions of malware infections each day. Effective intelligent defenses should be fast, proactive and evolve with the changing threat landscape. Hence, a dedicated research direction exists that designs online, optimized classifiers capable of detecting malware in real-time. Federated learning, discussed earlier as a possible solution to privacy issues, provides a distributed infrastructure that enables efficient large-scale detection. Other works are discussed in Sect. 3.5.

6 Open Problems in ML–Based Malware Defenses

In this section, we discuss what we believe are the key problems that the research community should address. At the heart lies the problem of reproducible research: the absence of *toy problems* and *representative datasets* makes the results from different papers incomparable. Furthermore, the results often cannot be taken at their face value because malware *ground truth* is inherently inconsistent and unreliable. Crucially, many solutions eagerly emphasize metric optimization but overlook *explainability*, providing little new insight into the problem of malware detection. We believe that these four issues hinder fair assessment of new contributions in the intelligent malware defenses domain. It is very difficult to objectively compare new methods against state-of-the-art solutions for the same problem, using the same data, and the same ground truth. An alarming side-effect is the lack of meaningful contributions to the field even though many new papers are published each year.

Toy Problems. Toy problems are important in the early development of a research field. These are simplified challenges that can help develop and test methodologies that solve a more challenging problem. Computer science in general and artificial intelligence in particular have established traditional toy problems that are still used to develop newer methodologies. However, malware research has always aimed to solve real-world threats. We observe that limited access to data and resources that are necessary for the evaluation of proposed methodologies has constrained systematic and open academic research. Moreover, building fool-proof methodologies in malware detection is an especially challenging problem, because the adversaries keep evolving rapidly. Since malware is constantly evolving, the research is driven by the availability of newer threats, and is reactive in nature. In light of these inevitable issues, we urge the community to introduce standardized toy problems, which could act as a starting point for developing new methods in a more synchronized and proactive manner. Toy problems would allow the assessment of proposed algorithms in isolation from the general practical limitations of malware detection. Ultimately, as the algorithms become more mature, they should be enhanced for deployment—practical feasibility should not be fully discarded at the envisioning stage.

Representative Datasets. The biggest hurdle in ML-based malware analysis research is the absence of representative datasets. These datasets are crucial for the development of usable and generalizable defensive solutions. However, with the rapid evolution of malware, any available dataset becomes obsolete in a matter of years, *e.g.,* the well-known VX Heavens dataset [41] from 2010, the Drebin dataset [12] from 2010–2012, and the MalGenome dataset [143] from 2012 are arguably no longer representative. Since most of the available datasets are not representative, the trained models only describe part of the real threat landscape. This is not to say that open-source datasets are not available. In fact, the Stratosphere IPS project[7] has published large-scale network traffic, *e.g.,* the CTU-13 dataset [37] captures traffic for 13 botnet scenarios, and the recently published IoT-23 dataset [88] captures 20 IoT malware scenarios and 3 benign ones. The Kaggle Microsoft Malware dataset [101] was also widely used in multiple works. Other works have also released their private datasets for reproducibility [67,105]. Nevertheless, one promising way for the academic community to gain access to reliable and representative data is to establish a long-term collaboration with industry partners who directly monitor the threat landscape and can provide updated threat intelligence for the development of robust machine learning solutions. This is an excellent way to keep up with

---

[7] https://www.stratosphereips.org/datasets-overview.

the rapidly changing threat landscape. The downside is that the data often contains highly sensitive information that cannot be released to the public, thus exacerbating problems of reproducibility.

Noisy Ground Truth. Existing literature has repeatedly shown that AV-provided malware family labels are inconsistent. These labels are used as ground truth by researchers to evaluate newer malware detection methods, making the results unreliable. Popular tools, such as VirusTotal[8], run multiple AV scanners and return an array of labels predicted by each scanner, without any indication as to which is correct. There is also an absence of a common vocabulary that all security companies can follow to label malware samples. Research has shown that the consensus reached by AV scanners regarding the labeling of a single malware sample is no better than a coin-toss (around 50%) [76]. Machine learning has also been slow to materialize in network security domain due to non-stationary data and noisy ground truth [10]. Unsupervised ML can already provide a foundation to address this issue. However, in practice, existing unsupervised ML approaches often use some form of ground truth for evaluation. For example, Perdisci *et al.* [93] evaluate their malware clustering by introducing a notion of AV graphs that depict the agreement between AV vendors as a measure of cluster cohesion and separation. Yuping *et al.* [65] use majority-voted family labels from 25 AV vendors as their ground truth to evaluate malware clustering. Li *et al.* [64] have advised caution when deciphering highly accurate clustering results as they can be impacted by spatial bias: performing majority voting on AV-provided labels is hazardous, since if most of the AV vendors are in agreement, it typically indicates that the families are already easy to detect. Hence, we either need better ground truth [53] or purely data-driven unsupervised evaluation approaches.

Explainable Solutions. In recent works, deep learning based malware detectors have surpassed the performance of traditional ML classifiers. They have also automated the detection pipeline for the most part. However, deep neural networks are inherent black-boxes that provide limited interpretability. It is also alarming how brittle deep learning is to adversarial attacks. Alternatively, non-deep learning approaches are not much more interpretable—they are frequently packed with complicated filtering steps to maximise performance [77], which also turns them into black-boxes. This concern has motivated research on explainable machine learning. Explainable models enable identification of bias in raw data, debug errors in trained models, enable model optimization, and allow analysts to extrapolate advanced results, *i.e.,* to get detailed insights from data instead of simply reading off detection rates. Without explainability, such extrapolation will be difficult and error-prone. Mathews *et al.* [71] provide a summary of explainable ML techniques for malware classification, including both intrinsic and post-hoc methods. The research trend shows that moving forward, special emphasis will be given to explainable and human-in-the-loop solutions.

---

[8] https://www.virustotal.com/.

7   Summary

Machine learning has emerged as a promising ally for developing intelligent malware defenses. However, the research in this area is scattered across different venues and domains. In this chapter, we identify the key research themes and assemble the state-of-the-art literature that has been proposed in the past decade. In doing so, we highlight trends in these research themes.

The literature is greatly dominated by *malware detection* approaches with the aim of developing scalable behavioral signatures. We categorize the research in this domain according to the data source and feature representation used for their classifiers. The trends in the literature suggest that sequence learning and explainable machine learning are considered promising areas of research. *Malware analysis* is another research direction that develops tools that provide the necessary insights to improve malware detection. *Adversarial machine learning* has recently gained popularity to harden machine learning classifiers. Also, *malware author attribution* proves to be a challenging field with limited progress due to the unavailability of datasets, and an absence of concrete problem statements that data-driven methods can realistically address.

We have discussed important considerations that emerge when machine learning is applied in the malware domain, such as resilience against concept drift and evasion, handling imbalanced datasets and using appropriate evaluation metrics. We have also identified key issues that need to be addressed in our opinion by the research community in order to encourage systematized research in the malware domain: toy problems, representative datasets, noisy ground truth, and explainable solutions. Without overcoming these issues, limited progress can be made due to the inability to compare research results.

It is evident that intelligent malware defenses will continue to grow. However, understanding the unique challenges that the malware domain brings to the table is absolutely essential for developing effective machine learning enabled solutions that can withstand the test of time.

References

1. Aafer, Y., Du, W., Yin, H.: DroidAPIMiner: mining API-level features for robust malware detection in Android. In: Zia, T., Zomaya, A., Varadharajan, V., Mao, M. (eds.) SecureComm 2013. LNICST, vol. 127, pp. 86–103. Springer, Cham (2013). https://doi.org/10.1007/978-3-319-04283-1_6
2. Ahmadi, M., Ulyanov, D., Semenov, S., Trofimov, M., Giacinto, G.: Novel feature extraction, selection and fusion for effective malware family classification. In: Proceedings of the Sixth ACM Conference on Data and Application Security and Privacy, pp. 183–194 (2016)
3. Al-Dujaili, A., Huang, A., Hemberg, E., O'Reilly, U.M.: Adversarial deep learning for robust detection of binary encoded malware. In: 2018 IEEE Security and Privacy Workshops (SPW), pp. 76–82. IEEE (2018)
4. Al-rimy, B.A.S., Maarof, M.A., Shaid, S.Z.M.: Ransomware threat success factors, taxonomy, and countermeasures: a survey and research directions. Comput. Secur. **74**, 144–166 (2018)

5. Alazab, M., Venkatraman, S., Watters, P., Alazab, M., et al.: Zero-day malware detection based on supervised learning algorithms of API call signatures. In: 2011 Australasian Data Mining Conference (AusDM 11) (2010)
6. Alrabaee, S., Saleem, N., Preda, S., Wang, L., Debbabi, M.: OBA2: an onion approach to binary code authorship attribution. Digit. Investig. **11**, S94–S103 (2014)
7. Alrabaee, S., Shirani, P., Debbabi, M., Wang, L.: On the feasibility of malware authorship attribution. In: Cuppens, F., Wang, L., Cuppens-Boulahia, N., Tawbi, N., Garcia-Alfaro, J. (eds.) FPS 2016. LNCS, vol. 10128, pp. 256–272. Springer, Cham (2017). https://doi.org/10.1007/978-3-319-51966-1_17
8. Alsulami, B., Dauber, E., Harang, R., Mancoridis, S., Greenstadt, R.: Source code authorship attribution using long short-term memory based networks. In: Foley, S.N., Gollmann, D., Snekkenes, E. (eds.) ESORICS 2017. LNCS, vol. 10492, pp. 65–82. Springer, Cham (2017). https://doi.org/10.1007/978-3-319-66402-6_6
9. Amer, E., Zelinka, I.: A dynamic windows malware detection and prediction method based on contextual understanding of API call sequence. Comput. Secur. **92**, 101760 (2020)
10. Anderson, B., McGrew, D.: Machine learning for encrypted malware traffic classification: accounting for noisy labels and non-stationarity. In: Proceedings of the 23rd ACM SIGKDD International Conference on Knowledge Discovery and Data Mining, pp. 1723–1732 (2017)
11. Anderson, H.S., Kharkar, A., Filar, B., Roth, P.: Evading machine learning malware detection. Black Hat (2017)
12. Arp, D., Spreitzenbarth, M., Hubner, M., Gascon, H., Rieck, K., Siemens, C.: Drebin: effective and explainable detection of Android malware in your pocket. In: NDSS, vol. 14, pp. 23–26 (2014)
13. Azmoodeh, A., Dehghantanha, A., Choo, K.K.R.: Robust malware detection for internet of (battlefield) things devices using deep eigenspace learning. IEEE Trans. Sustain. Comput. **4**(1), 88–95 (2018)
14. Biggio, B., et al.: Poisoning behavioral malware clustering. In: Proceedings of the 2014 Workshop on Artificial Intelligent and Security Workshop, pp. 27–36 (2014)
15. Biggio, B., Roli, F.: Wild patterns: ten years after the rise of adversarial machine learning. Pattern Recogn. **84**, 317–331 (2018)
16. Bilge, L., Balzarotti, D., Robertson, W., Kirda, E., Kruegel, C.: Disclosure: detecting botnet command and control servers through large-scale netflow analysis. In: ACSAC, pp. 129–138. ACM (2012)
17. Black, P., Gondal, I., Layton, R.: A survey of similarities in banking malware behaviours. Comput. Secur. **77**, 756–772 (2017)
18. Boukhtouta, A., Mokhov, S.A., Lakhdari, N.E., Debbabi, M., Paquet, J.: Network malware classification comparison using dpi and flow packet headers. J. Comput. Virol. Hacking Tech. **12**(2), 69–100 (2016)
19. Burguera, I., Zurutuza, U., Nadjm-Tehrani, S.: CrowDroid: behavior-based malware detection system for Android. In: Proceedings of the 1st ACM Workshop on Security and Privacy in Smartphones and Mobile Devices, pp. 15–26 (2011)
20. Burnap, P., French, R., Turner, F., Jones, K.: Malware classification using self organising feature maps and machine activity data. Comput. Secur. **73**, 399–410 (2018)
21. Cakir, B., Dogdu, E.: Malware classification using deep learning methods. In: Proceedings of the ACMSE 2018 Conference, pp. 1–5 (2018)

22. Canfora, G., De Lorenzo, A., Medvet, E., Mercaldo, F., Visaggio, C.A.: Effectiveness of opcode ngrams for detection of multi family Android malware. In: 2015 10th International Conference on Availability, Reliability and Security, pp. 333–340. IEEE (2015)
23. Chen, L., Hou, S., Ye, Y.: SecureDroid: enhancing security of machine learning-based detection against adversarial Android malware attacks. In: Proceedings of the 33rd Annual Computer Security Applications Conference, pp. 362–372 (2017)
24. Chen, S., et al.: Automated poisoning attacks and defenses in malware detection systems: an adversarial machine learning approach. Comput. Secur. **73**, 326–344 (2018)
25. Chen, X., et al.: Android HIV: a study of repackaging malware for evading machine-learning detection. IEEE Trans. Inf. Forensics Secur. **15**, 987–1001 (2019)
26. Chen, Y., Narayanan, A., Pang, S., Tao, B.: Malicioius software detection using multiple sequence alignment and data mining. In: 2012 IEEE 26th International Conference on Advanced Information Networking and Applications, pp. 8–14. IEEE (2012)
27. Chen, Z., et al.: Machine learning based mobile malware detection using highly imbalanced network traffic. Inf. Sci. **433**, 346–364 (2018)
28. David, O.E., Netanyahu, N.S.: Deepsign: deep learning for automatic malware signature generation and classification. In: 2015 International Joint Conference on Neural Networks (IJCNN), pp. 1–8. IEEE (2015)
29. Demontis, A., et al.: Yes, machine learning can be more secure! a case study on Android malware detection. IEEE Trans. Dependable Secure Comput. **16**, 711–724 (2017)
30. Eskandari, S., Leoutsarakos, A., Mursch, T., Clark, J.: A first look at browser-based cryptojacking. In: 2018 IEEE European Symposium on Security and Privacy Workshops (EuroS&PW), pp. 58–66. IEEE (2018)
31. Fan, M., Wei, W., Xie, X., Liu, Y., Guan, X., Liu, T.: Can we trust your explanations? Sanity checks for interpreters in Android malware analysis. IEEE Trans. Inf. Forensics Secur. **16**, 838–853 (2020)
32. Fan, Y., Hou, S., Zhang, Y., Ye, Y., Abdulhayoglu, M.: Gotcha-sly malware! scorpion a metagraph2vec based malware detection system. In: Proceedings of the 24th ACM SIGKDD International Conference on Knowledge Discovery & Data Mining, pp. 253–262 (2018)
33. Fan, Y., Ye, Y., Chen, L.: Malicious sequential pattern mining for automatic malware detection. Expert Syst. Appl. **52**, 16–25 (2016)
34. Firdausi, I., Erwin, A., Nugroho, A.S., et al.: Analysis of machine learning techniques used in behavior-based malware detection. In: 2010 Second International Conference on Advances in Computing, Control, and Telecommunication Technologies, pp. 201–203. IEEE (2010)
35. Frommholz, I., Al-Khateeb, H.M., Potthast, M., Ghasem, Z., Shukla, M., Short, E.: On textual analysis and machine learning for cyberstalking detection. Datenbank-Spektrum **16**(2), 127–135 (2016)
36. Garcia, S.: Modelling the network behaviour of malware to block malicious patterns. The stratosphere project: a behavioural IPS. Virus Bulletin (2015)
37. Garcia, S., Grill, M., Stiborek, J., Zunino, A.: An empirical comparison of botnet detection methods. Comput. Secur. **45**, 100–123 (2014)
38. Grosse, K., Papernot, N., Manoharan, P., Backes, M., McDaniel, P.: Adversarial examples for malware detection. In: Foley, S.N., Gollmann, D., Snekkenes, E. (eds.) ESORICS 2017. LNCS, vol. 10493, pp. 62–79. Springer, Cham (2017). https://doi.org/10.1007/978-3-319-66399-9_4

39. Gu, J., Sun, B., Du, X., Wang, J., Zhuang, Y., Wang, Z.: Consortium blockchain-based malware detection in mobile devices. IEEE Access **6**, 12118–12128 (2018)
40. HaddadPajouh, H., Dehghantanha, A., Khayami, R., Choo, K.K.R.: A deep recurrent neural network based approach for internet of things malware threat hunting. Futur. Gener. Comput. Syst. **85**, 88–96 (2018)
41. VX Heaven: VX heaven virus collection, 15 May 2010. http://vxheaven.org/
42. Hou, S., Ye, Y., Song, Y., Abdulhayoglu, M.: HinDroid: an intelligent Android malware detection system based on structured heterogeneous information network. In: Proceedings of the 23rd ACM SIGKDD International Conference on Knowledge Discovery and Data Mining, pp. 1507–1515 (2017)
43. Hu, W., Tan, Y.: Black-box attacks against RNN based malware detection algorithms. In: Workshops at the Thirty-Second AAAI Conference on Artificial Intelligence (2018)
44. Huang, H., Deng, H., Sheng, Y., Ye, X.: Accelerating convolutional neural network-based malware traffic detection through ant-colony clustering. J. Intell. Fuzzy Syst. (Preprint) **37**, 1–15 (2019)
45. Ijaz, M., Durad, M.H., Ismail, M.: Static and dynamic malware analysis using machine learning. In: 2019 16th International Bhurban Conference on Applied Sciences and Technology (IBCAST), pp. 687–691. IEEE (2019)
46. Iqbal, F., Debbabi, M., Fung, B.C.: Machine Learning for Authorship Attribution and Cyber Forensics. Springer, Heidelberg (2020)
47. Jain, S., Meena, Y.K.: Byte level n–gram analysis for malware detection. In: Venugopal, K.R., Patnaik, L.M. (eds.) ICIP 2011. CCIS, vol. 157, pp. 51–59. Springer, Heidelberg (2011). https://doi.org/10.1007/978-3-642-22786-8_6
48. Jordaney, R., et al.: Transcend: detecting concept drift in malware classification models. In: 26th USENIX Security Symposium (USENIX Security 2017), pp. 625–642 (2017)
49. Jordaney, R., Wang, Z., Papini, D., Nouretdinov, I., Cavallaro, L.: Misleading metrics: on evaluating machine learning for malware with confidence. Technical report (2016)
50. Kalash, M., Rochan, M., Mohammed, N., Bruce, N.D., Wang, Y., Iqbal, F.: Malware classification with deep convolutional neural networks. In: 2018 9th IFIP International Conference on New Technologies, Mobility and Security (NTMS), pp. 1–5. IEEE (2018)
51. Kalgutkar, V., Kaur, R., Gonzalez, H., Stakhanova, N., Matyukhina, A.: Code authorship attribution: methods and challenges. ACM Comput. Surv. (CSUR) **52**(1), 1–36 (2019)
52. Kalgutkar, V., Stakhanova, N., Cook, P., Matyukhina, A.: Android authorship attribution through string analysis. In: Proceedings of the 13th International Conference on Availability, Reliability and Security, pp. 1–10 (2018)
53. Kantchelian, A., et al.: Better malware ground truth: techniques for weighting anti-virus vendor labels. In: Proceedings of the 8th ACM Workshop on Artificial Intelligence and Security, pp. 45–56 (2015)
54. Karbab, E.B., Debbabi, M., Derhab, A., Mouheb, D.: MalDozer: automatic framework for Android malware detection using deep learning. Digit. Investig. **24**, S48–S59 (2018)
55. Khasawneh, K.N., Ozsoy, M., Donovick, C., Abu-Ghazaleh, N., Ponomarev, D.: Ensemble learning for low-level hardware-supported malware detection. In: Bos, H., Monrose, F., Blanc, G. (eds.) RAID 2015. LNCS, vol. 9404, pp. 3–25. Springer, Cham (2015). https://doi.org/10.1007/978-3-319-26362-5_1

56. Kirat, D., Nataraj, L., Vigna, G., Manjunath, B.: SigMal: a static signal processing based malware triage. In: Proceedings of the 29th Annual Computer Security Applications Conference, pp. 89–98 (2013)
57. Kirat, D., Vigna, G.: MalGene: automatic extraction of malware analysis evasion signature. In: Proceedings of the 22nd ACM SIGSAC Conference on Computer and Communications Security, pp. 769–780 (2015)
58. Kolosnjaji, B., et al.: Adversarial malware binaries: evading deep learning for malware detection in executables. In: 2018 26th European Signal Processing Conference (EUSIPCO), pp. 533–537. IEEE (2018)
59. Kolosnjaji, B., Zarras, A., Webster, G., Eckert, C.: Deep learning for classification of malware system call sequences. In: Kang, B.H., Bai, Q. (eds.) AI 2016. LNCS (LNAI), vol. 9992, pp. 137–149. Springer, Cham (2016). https://doi.org/10.1007/978-3-319-50127-7_11
60. Le, Q., Boydell, O., Mac Namee, B., Scanlon, M.: Deep learning at the shallow end: malware classification for non-domain experts. Digit. Investig. **26**, S118–S126 (2018)
61. LeDoux, C., Lakhotia, A.: Malware and machine learning. In: Yager, R.R., Reformat, M.Z., Alajlan, N. (eds.) Intelligent Methods for Cyber Warfare. SCI, vol. 563, pp. 1–42. Springer, Cham (2015). https://doi.org/10.1007/978-3-319-08624-8_1
62. Li, D., Li, Q.: Adversarial deep ensemble: evasion attacks and defenses for malware detection. IEEE Trans. Inf. Forensics Secur. **15**, 3886–3900 (2020)
63. Li, J., Sun, L., Yan, Q., Li, Z., Srisa-an, W., Ye, H.: Significant permission identification for machine-learning-based Android malware detection. IEEE Trans. Ind. Inf. **14**(7), 3216–3225 (2018)
64. Li, P., Liu, L., Gao, D., Reiter, M.K.: On challenges in evaluating malware clustering. In: Jha, S., Sommer, R., Kreibich, C. (eds.) RAID 2010. LNCS, vol. 6307, pp. 238–255. Springer, Heidelberg (2010). https://doi.org/10.1007/978-3-642-15512-3_13
65. Li, Y., Jang, J., Hu, X., Ou, X.: Android malware clustering through malicious payload mining. In: Dacier, M., Bailey, M., Polychronakis, M., Antonakakis, M. (eds.) RAID 2017. LNCS, vol. 10453, pp. 192–214. Springer, Cham (2017). https://doi.org/10.1007/978-3-319-66332-6_9
66. Li, Z., Sun, L., Yan, Q., Srisa-an, W., Chen, Z.: DroidClassifier: efficient adaptive mining of application-layer header for classifying Android malware. In: Deng, R., Weng, J., Ren, K., Yegneswaran, V. (eds.) SecureComm 2016. LNICST, vol. 198, pp. 597–616. Springer, Cham (2017). https://doi.org/10.1007/978-3-319-59608-2_33
67. Lindorfer, M., Neugschwandtner, M., Weichselbaum, L., Fratantonio, Y., Van Der Veen, V., Platzer, C.: Andrubis-1,000,000 apps later: a view on current Android malware behaviors. In: 2014 Third International Workshop on Building Analysis Datasets and Gathering Experience Returns for Security (BADGERS), pp. 3–17. IEEE (2014)
68. Liu, Y., et al.: Towards a timely causality analysis for enterprise security. In: NDSS (2018)
69. Lundberg, S.M., Lee, S.I.: A unified approach to interpreting model predictions. In: Advances in Neural Information Processing Systems, vol. 30, pp. 4765–4774 (2017)
70. Mariconti, E., Onaolapo, J., Ross, G., Stringhini, G.: The cause of all evils: assessing causality between user actions and malware activity. In: 10th USENIX Workshop on Cyber Security Experimentation and Test (CSET 2017) (2017)

71. Mathews, S.M.: Explainable artificial intelligence applications in NLP, biomedical, and malware classification: a literature review. In: Arai, K., Bhatia, R., Kapoor, S. (eds.) CompCom 2019. AISC, vol. 998, pp. 1269–1292. Springer, Cham (2019). https://doi.org/10.1007/978-3-030-22868-2_90

72. McLaughlin, N., et al.: Deep Android malware detection. In: Proceedings of the Seventh ACM on Conference on Data and Application Security and Privacy, pp. 301–308 (2017)

73. Milosevic, N., Dehghantanha, A., Choo, K.K.R.: Machine learning aided Android malware classification. Comput. Electr. Eng. **61**, 266–274 (2017)

74. Miramirkhani, N., Appini, M.P., Nikiforakis, N., Polychronakis, M.: Spotless sandboxes: evading malware analysis systems using wear-and-tear artifacts. In: 2017 IEEE Symposium on Security and Privacy (SP), pp. 1009–1024. IEEE (2017)

75. Mishra, P., Khurana, K., Gupta, S., Sharma, M.K.: VMAnalyzer: malware semantic analysis using integrated CNN and bi-directional LSTM for detecting VM-level attacks in cloud. In: 2019 Twelfth International Conference on Contemporary Computing (IC3), pp. 1–6. IEEE (2019)

76. Mohaisen, A., Alrawi, O., Larson, M., McPherson, D.: Towards a methodical evaluation of antivirus scans and labels. In: Kim, Y., Lee, H., Perrig, A. (eds.) WISA 2013. LNCS, vol. 8267, pp. 231–241. Springer, Cham (2014). https://doi.org/10.1007/978-3-319-05149-9_15

77. Mohaisen, A., Alrawi, O., Mohaisen, M.: AMAL: high-fidelity, behavior-based automated malware analysis and classification. Comput. Secur. **52**, 251–266 (2015)

78. Moubarak, J., Chamoun, M., Filiol, E.: Comparative study of recent MEA malware phylogeny. In: 2017 2nd International Conference on Computer and Communication Systems (ICCCS), pp. 16–20. IEEE (2017)

79. Muñoz-González, L., et al.: Towards poisoning of deep learning algorithms with back-gradient optimization. In: Proceedings of the 10th ACM Workshop on Artificial Intelligence and Security, pp. 27–38 (2017)

80. Murenin, I., Novikova, E., Ushakov, R., Kholod, I.: Explaining Android application authorship attribution based on source code analysis. In: Murenin, I., Novikova, E., Ushakov, R., Kholod, I. (eds.) NEW2AN/ruSMART -2020. LNCS, vol. 12525, pp. 43–56. Springer, Cham (2020). https://doi.org/10.1007/978-3-030-65726-0_5

81. Nadeem, A., Hammerschmidt, C., Gañán, C.H., Verwer, S.: Beyond labeling: using clustering to build network behavioral profiles of malware families. In: Stamp, M., Alazab, M., Shalaginov, A. (eds.) Malware Analysis Using Artificial Intelligence and Deep Learning, pp. 381–409. Springer, Cham (2021). https://doi.org/10.1007/978-3-030-62582-5_15

82. Naidu, V., Narayanan, A.: Using different substitution matrices in a string-matching technique for identifying viral polymorphic malware variants. In: 2016 IEEE Congress on Evolutionary Computation (CEC), pp. 2903–2910. IEEE (2016)

83. Narudin, F.A., Feizollah, A., Anuar, N.B., Gani, A.: Evaluation of machine learning classifiers for mobile malware detection. Soft. Comput. **20**(1), 343–357 (2014). https://doi.org/10.1007/s00500-014-1511-6

84. Nataraj, L., Karthikeyan, S., Jacob, G., Manjunath, B.S.: Malware images: visualization and automatic classification. In: Proceedings of the 8th International Symposium on Visualization for Cyber Security, pp. 1–7 (2011)

85. Nguyen, T.D., Marchal, S., Miettinen, M., Fereidooni, H., Asokan, N., Sadeghi, A.R.: Dïot: a federated self-learning anomaly detection system for IoT. In: 2019 IEEE 39th International Conference on Distributed Computing Systems (ICDCS), pp. 756–767. IEEE (2019)

86. Onwuzurike, L., Mariconti, E., Andriotis, P., Cristofaro, E.D., Ross, G., Stringhini, G.: MaMaDroid: detecting Android malware by building Markov chains of behavioral models (extended version). ACM Trans. Privacy Secur. (TOPS) 22(2), 1–34 (2019)

87. Pajouh, H.H., Dehghantanha, A., Khayami, R., Choo, K.K.R.: Intelligent OS X malware threat detection with code inspection. J. Comput. Virol. Hacking Tech. 14(3), 213–223 (2018)

88. Parmisano, A., Garcia, S., Erquiaga, M.J.: Stratosphere laboratory. A labeled dataset with malicious and benign IoT network traffic (2020). https://www.stratosphereips.org/datasets-iot23

89. Pascanu, R., Stokes, J.W., Sanossian, H., Marinescu, M., Thomas, A.: Malware classification with recurrent networks. In: 2015 IEEE International Conference on Acoustics, Speech and Signal Processing (ICASSP), pp. 1916–1920. IEEE (2015)

90. Peiravian, N., Zhu, X.: Machine learning for Android malware detection using permission and API calls. In: 2013 IEEE 25th International Conference on Tools with Artificial Intelligence, pp. 300–305. IEEE (2013)

91. Pellegrino, G., Lin, Q., Hammerschmidt, C., Verwer, S.: Learning behavioral fingerprints from netflows using timed automata. In: IFIP, pp. 308–316. IEEE (2017)

92. Pendlebury, F., Pierazzi, F., Jordaney, R., Kinder, J., Cavallaro, L.: TESSERACT: eliminating experimental bias in malware classification across space and time. In: 28th USENIX Security Symposium (USENIX Security 2019), pp. 729–746 (2019)

93. Perdisci, R., Lee, W., Feamster, N.: Behavioral clustering of http-based malware and signature generation using malicious network traces. In: NSDI, vol. 10 (2010)

94. Pirscoveanu, R.S., Hansen, S.S., Larsen, T.M., Stevanovic, M., Pedersen, J.M., Czech, A.: Analysis of malware behavior: type classification using machine learning. In: 2015 International Conference on Cyber Situational Awareness, Data Analytics and Assessment (CyberSA), pp. 1–7. IEEE (2015)

95. "Polo" Chau, D.H., Wright, A., Nachenberg, C., Faloutsos, C., Wilhelm, J.: Polonium: tera-scale graph mining and inference for malware detection. In: Proceedings of the SIAM International Conference on Data Mining, pp. 131–142. Society for Industrial and Applied Mathematics (2011)

96. Raff, E., Barker, J., Sylvester, J., Brandon, R., Catanzaro, B., Nicholas, C.K.: Malware detection by eating a whole exe. In: Workshops at the Thirty-Second AAAI Conference on Artificial Intelligence (2018)

97. Rafique, M.Z., Caballero, J.: FIRMA: malware clustering and network signature generation with mixed network behaviors. In: Stolfo, S.J., Stavrou, A., Wright, C.V. (eds.) RAID 2013. LNCS, vol. 8145, pp. 144–163. Springer, Heidelberg (2013). https://doi.org/10.1007/978-3-642-41284-4_8

98. Ribeiro, M.T., Singh, S., Guestrin, C.: "Why should I trust you?" explaining the predictions of any classifier. In: Proceedings of the 22nd ACM SIGKDD International Conference on Knowledge Discovery and Data Mining, pp. 1135–1144 (2016)

99. Rieck, K., Trinius, P., Willems, C., Holz, T.: Automatic analysis of malware behavior using machine learning. J. Comput. Secur. 19(4), 639–668 (2011)

100. Rodriguez, J.J., Kuncheva, L.I., Alonso, C.J.: Rotation forest: a new classifier ensemble method. IEEE Trans. Pattern Anal. Mach. Intell. **28**(10), 1619–1630 (2006)
101. Ronen, R., Radu, M., Feuerstein, C., Yom-Tov, E., Ahmadi, M.: Microsoft malware classification challenge. arXiv preprint arXiv:1802.10135 (2018)
102. Rosenberg, I., Sicard, G., David, E.O.: DeepAPT: nation-state APT attribution using end-to-end deep neural networks. In: Lintas, A., Rovetta, S., Verschure, P.F.M.J., Villa, A.E.P. (eds.) ICANN 2017. LNCS, vol. 10614, pp. 91–99. Springer, Cham (2017). https://doi.org/10.1007/978-3-319-68612-7_11
103. Rosenblum, N., Zhu, X., Miller, B.P.: Who wrote this code? Identifying the authors of program binaries. In: Atluri, V., Diaz, C. (eds.) ESORICS 2011. LNCS, vol. 6879, pp. 172–189. Springer, Heidelberg (2011). https://doi.org/10.1007/978-3-642-23822-2_10
104. Sahs, J., Khan, L.: A machine learning approach to Android malware detection. In: 2012 European Intelligence and Security Informatics Conference, pp. 141–147. IEEE (2012)
105. Sami, A., Yadegari, B., Rahimi, H., Peiravian, N., Hashemi, S., Hamze, A.: Malware detection based on mining API calls. In: Proceedings of the 2010 ACM Symposium on Applied Computing, pp. 1020–1025 (2010)
106. Santos, I., Brezo, F., Ugarte-Pedrero, X., Bringas, P.G.: Opcode sequences as representation of executables for data-mining-based unknown malware detection. Inf. Sci. **231**, 64–82 (2013)
107. Saxe, J., Berlin, K.: Deep neural network based malware detection using two dimensional binary program features. In: 2015 10th International Conference on Malicious and Unwanted Software (MALWARE), pp. 11–20. IEEE (2015)
108. Saxe, J., Sanders, H.: Malware Data Science: Attack Detection and Attribution. No Starch Press (2018)
109. Sayadi, H., et al.: 2SMaRT: a two-stage machine learning-based approach for runtime specialized hardware-assisted malware detection. In: 2019 Design, Automation & Test in Europe Conference & Exhibition (DATE), pp. 728–733. IEEE (2019)
110. Sayadi, H., Patel, N., PD, S.M., Sasan, A., Rafatirad, S., Homayoun, H.: Ensemble learning for effective run-time hardware-based malware detection: a comprehensive analysis and classification. In: 2018 55th ACM/ESDA/IEEE Design Automation Conference (DAC), pp. 1–6. IEEE (2018)
111. Shabtai, A., Fledel, Y., Elovici, Y.: Automated static code analysis for classifying Android applications using machine learning. In: 2010 International Conference on Computational Intelligence and Security, pp. 329–333. IEEE (2010)
112. Shibahara, T., Yagi, T., Akiyama, M., Chiba, D., Yada, T.: Efficient dynamic malware analysis based on network behavior using deep learning. In: 2016 IEEE Global Communications Conference (GLOBECOM), pp. 1–7. IEEE (2016)
113. Simko, L., Zettlemoyer, L., Kohno, T.: Recognizing and imitating programmer style: adversaries in program authorship attribution. Proc. Priv. Enhancing Technol. **2018**(1), 127–144 (2018)
114. Singh, A., Handa, A., Kumar, N., Shukla, S.K.: Malware classification using image representation. In: Dolev, S., Hendler, D., Lodha, S., Yung, M. (eds.) CSCML 2019. LNCS, vol. 11527, pp. 75–92. Springer, Cham (2019). https://doi.org/10.1007/978-3-030-20951-3_6
115. Smith, M.R., et al.: Mind the gap: on bridging the semantic gap between machine learning and malware analysis. In: Proceedings of the 13th ACM Workshop on Artificial Intelligence and Security, pp. 49–60 (2020)

116. Souri, A., Hosseini, R.: A state-of-the-art survey of malware detection approaches using data mining techniques. HCIS **8**(1), 1–22 (2018). https://doi.org/10.1186/s13673-018-0125-x
117. Spreitzenbarth, M., Schreck, T., Echtler, F., Arp, D., Hoffmann, J.: Mobile-sandbox: combining static and dynamic analysis with machine-learning techniques. Int. J. Inf. Secur. **14**(2), 141–153 (2015)
118. Suarez-Tangil, G., Dash, S.K., Ahmadi, M., Kinder, J., Giacinto, G., Cavallaro, L.: DroidSieve: fast and accurate classification of obfuscated Android malware. In: Proceedings of the Seventh ACM on Conference on Data and Application Security and Privacy, pp. 309–320 (2017)
119. Suarez-Tangil, G., Tapiador, J.E., Peris-Lopez, P., Blasco, J.: Dendroid: a text mining approach to analyzing and classifying code structures in Android malware families. Expert Syst. Appl. **41**(4), 1104–1117 (2014)
120. Tamersoy, A., Roundy, K., Chau, D.H.: Guilt by association: large scale malware detection by mining file-relation graphs. In: Proceedings of the 20th ACM SIGKDD International Conference on Knowledge Discovery and Data Mining, pp. 1524–1533. Association for Computing Machinery, New York (2014). https://doi.org/10.1145/2623330.2623342
121. Tegeler, F., Fu, X., Vigna, G., Kruegel, C.: BotFinder: finding bots in network traffic without deep packet inspection. In: CoNEXT, pp. 349–360. ACM (2012)
122. Ucci, D., Aniello, L., Baldoni, R.: Survey of machine learning techniques for malware analysis. Comput. Secur. **81**, 123–147 (2019)
123. Verwer, S., Nadeem, A., Hammerschmidt, C., Bliek, L., Al-Dujaili, A., O'Reilly, U.M.: The robust malware detection challenge and greedy random accelerated multi-bit search. In: Proceedings of the 13th ACM Workshop on Artificial Intelligence and Security, pp. 61–70 (2020)
124. Wang, W., Wang, X., Feng, D., Liu, J., Han, Z., Zhang, X.: Exploring permission-induced risk in Android applications for malicious application detection. IEEE Trans. Inf. Forensics Secur. **9**(11), 1869–1882 (2014)
125. Wang, W., Zhu, M., Zeng, X., Ye, X., Sheng, Y.: Malware traffic classification using convolutional neural network for representation learning. In: 2017 International Conference on Information Networking (ICOIN), pp. 712–717. IEEE (2017)
126. Wang, X., Yang, Y., Zhu, S.: Automated hybrid analysis of Android malware through augmenting fuzzing with forced execution. IEEE Trans. Mob. Comput. **18**(12), 2768–2782 (2018)
127. Wang, Z., Tian, M., Jia, C.: An active and dynamic botnet detection approach to track hidden concept drift. In: Qing, S., Mitchell, C., Chen, L., Liu, D. (eds.) ICICS 2017. LNCS, vol. 10631, pp. 646–660. Springer, Cham (2018). https://doi.org/10.1007/978-3-319-89500-0_55
128. Xu, K., et al.: Show, attend and tell: neural image caption generation with visual attention. In: International Conference on Machine Learning, pp. 2048–2057 (2015)
129. Xu, Z., Ray, S., Subramanyan, P., Malik, S.: Malware detection using machine learning based analysis of virtual memory access patterns. In: Design, Automation & Test in Europe Conference & Exhibition (DATE), pp. 169–174. IEEE (2017)
130. Yakura, H., Shinozaki, S., Nishimura, R., Oyama, Y., Sakuma, J.: Malware analysis of imaged binary samples by convolutional neural network with attention mechanism. In: Proceedings of the Eighth ACM Conference on Data and Application Security and Privacy, pp. 127–134 (2018)
131. Yang, Y., Wu, L., Yin, G., Li, L., Zhao, H.: A survey on security and privacy issues in internet-of-things. IEEE Internet Things J. **4**(5), 1250–1258 (2017)

132. Ye, Y., Li, T., Adjeroh, D., Iyengar, S.S.: A survey on malware detection using data mining techniques. ACM Comput. Surv. (CSUR) **50**(3), 1–40 (2017)
133. Yerima, S.Y., Alzaylaee, M.K., Sezer, S.: Machine learning-based dynamic analysis of Android apps with improved code coverage. EURASIP J. Inf. Secur. **2019**(1), 4 (2019)
134. Yerima, S.Y., Sezer, S., McWilliams, G., Muttik, I.: A new Android malware detection approach using Bayesian classification. In: 2013 IEEE 27th International Conference on Advanced Information Networking and Applications (AINA), pp. 121–128. IEEE (2013)
135. Yokoyama, A., et al.: SandPrint: fingerprinting malware sandboxes to provide intelligence for sandbox evasion. In: Monrose, F., Dacier, M., Blanc, G., Garcia-Alfaro, J. (eds.) RAID 2016. LNCS, vol. 9854, pp. 165–187. Springer, Cham (2016). https://doi.org/10.1007/978-3-319-45719-2_8
136. Yuan, Z., Lu, Y., Xue, Y.: DroidDetector: Android malware characterization and detection using deep learning. Tsinghua Sci. Technol. **21**(1), 114–123 (2016)
137. Yuxin, D., Siyi, Z.: Malware detection based on deep learning algorithm. Neural Comput. Appl. **31**(2), 461–472 (2017). https://doi.org/10.1007/s00521-017-3077-6
138. Zhang, F., Chan, P.P., Biggio, B., Yeung, D.S., Roli, F.: Adversarial feature selection against evasion attacks. IEEE Trans. Cybern. **46**(3), 766–777 (2015)
139. Zhang, H., Sun, M., Yao, D., North, C.: Visualizing traffic causality for analyzing network anomalies. In: Proceedings of the 2015 ACM International Workshop on International Workshop on Security and Privacy Analytics, pp. 37–42 (2015)
140. Zhang, H., Yao, D.D., Ramakrishnan, N., Zhang, Z.: Causality reasoning about network events for detecting stealthy malware activities. Comput. Secur. **58**, 180–198 (2016)
141. Zhang, H., Zhang, W., Lv, Z., Sangaiah, A.K., Huang, T., Chilamkurti, N.: MALDC: a depth detection method for malware based on behavior chains. World Wide Web **23**, 991–1010 (2019)
142. Zhang, X., et al.: Enhancing state-of-the-art classifiers with API semantics to detect evolved Android malware. In: Proceedings of the 2020 ACM SIGSAC Conference on Computer and Communications Security, pp. 757–770 (2020)
143. Zhou, Y., Jiang, X.: Dissecting Android malware: characterization and evolution. In: 2012 IEEE Symposium on Security and Privacy, pp. 95–109. IEEE (2012)
144. Zhu, H.J., You, Z.H., Zhu, Z.X., Shi, W.L., Chen, X., Cheng, L.: DroidDet: effective and robust detection of Android malware using static analysis along with rotation forest model. Neurocomputing **272**, 638–646 (2018)
145. Zhu, Z., Dumitraş, T.: FeatureSmith: automatically engineering features for malware detection by mining the security literature. In: Proceedings of the 2016 ACM SIGSAC Conference on Computer and Communications Security, pp. 767–778 (2016)

Open-World Network Intrusion Detection

Vera Rimmer[1]($\boxtimes$), Azqa Nadeem[2], Sicco Verwer[2], Davy Preuveneers[1],
and Wouter Joosen[1]

[1] imec-DistriNet, KU Leuven, Leuven, Belgium
{vera.rimmer,davy.preuveneers,wouter.joosen}@cs.kuleuven.be
[2] Delft University of Technology, Delft, The Netherlands
{azqa.nadeem,s.e.verwer}@tudelft.nl

Abstract. This chapter contributes to the ongoing discussion of strengthening security by applying AI techniques in the scope of intrusion detection. The focus is set on open-world detection of attacks through data-driven network traffic analysis. This research topic is complementary to the earlier chapter on intelligent malware detection.

In this chapter, we revisit the foundations of machine learning-based solutions for network security, which aim to make network defense tools more autonomous, adaptive, proactive and responsive. Specifically, we give a comprehensive introduction to the research on anomaly detection for network intrusion detection – that is, defensive schemes that do not assume complete prior knowledge of malicious patterns and instead learn the notion of normality from benign traffic. Along with outlining the recent advances in the field, we provide insights and reflect on the current limitations and research challenges. Therefore, this chapter presents compelling research opportunities to advance machine learning techniques in network security and push the boundaries of open-world network intrusion detection.

1 Introduction

Intrusion detection is an integral part of securing information systems. Detection tools stem from the early realization of the computer security community that full and provable protection of an ICT infrastructure is practically infeasible, if not impossible. Attempts to compromise the system can emerge from within the infrastructure as well as from its adversarial environment. An intrusion detection system (IDS) therefore aims at detecting exploitation attempts and active misuse both within the perimeter and from outside of it.

Continuous monitoring of the system and accurate detection of malicious behavior constitute the first step of the incident response process. For this fundamental step, an IDS performs acquisition of relevant data streams that represent operation of the system and its internal and external communication. Through an in-depth real-time analysis of these monitored data, an IDS searches for any signs of a potential misuse of the system. If such evidence is detected with high enough confidence, an alert is raised which is then propagated to security analysts, or to a Security Information and Event Management (SIEM) system. SIEM

© Springer Nature Switzerland AG 2022
L. Batina et al. (Eds.): Security and Artificial Intelligence, LNCS 13049, pp. 254–283, 2022.
https://doi.org/10.1007/978-3-030-98795-4_11

systems are used mostly in larger networks to aggregate and correlate alerts and other security events. This way the incident response team can analyze the data from IDS and other sources (network logs, firewalls, servers, antivirus software, etc.) in one place to construct a full picture of threats in the network before taking measures.

In essence, an IDS is responsible for intelligent automated decision making that can, depending on the correctness of those decisions, either safeguard or disrupt normal operation of the infrastructure. Reliable intrusion detection is indispensable, but despite the world-wide efforts of the last 40 years, IDSs regularly generate false alarms, at times fail to prevent intrusions, and thus end up jeopardizing system and data security with high recovery costs. A vast amount of research and development has gone into creating dedicated tools and algorithms in order to bring intelligent and reliable intrusion detection into reality. Among the possible solutions, artificial intelligence (AI) has always been a compelling component for automated knowledge retrieval that aids in efficient detection of ever-changing attacks, with a varying level of complexity and involvement. Especially in light of recent advances in the machine learning (ML) and deep learning domains, the solution space is evolving so rapidly that it has become challenging to keep track of major changes.

With this chapter, we aim to revise the intrinsic factors that continue to pose challenges for research on machine learning based solutions for network security. As AI algorithms are ubiquitously used across all possible data sources and points of IDS deployment, for the purpose of a more contained discussion we will focus on *network intrusion detection* as one particularly prominent and highly representative application of machine learning in network security. Specifically, we will explore *network traffic* as the primary data source for detection. Network intrusion detection systems can detect attacks either through *misuse detection*, i.e. matching observed traffic to a known malicious traffic signature, or through *anomaly detection*, i.e. detecting suspicious patterns as indicators of malicious activity by comparing traffic to a previously established *benign baseline*. While both directions present unique research challenges, in this chapter we highlight traffic anomaly detection as a particularly promising approach which does not rely on the knowledge of malicious signatures, but instead detects earlier unseen attack patterns. This intrinsic ability of anomaly detection to discover novel attack types respects the *open-world* nature of intrusion detection where attacks are continuously evolving. Therefore, we dedicate our discussion to *open-world network intrusion detection*, a highly compelling and indispensable paradigm in network security that can be empowered with machine learning capabilities.

The chapter is organized as follows. In Sect. 2, we introduce the IDS domain and its core concepts. After reviewing the problem statement and the threat model of a network-based IDS, we move on to outlining the principal machine learning techniques and their underlying assumptions in Sect. 3. Finally, in Sect. 4, we analyze open challenges, specifically in relation to the usage of machine learning for open-world detection on network traffic. As these challenges were revealed through a long and potent line of research, an important question remains as to which recent advances have been made to address them. We conclude our reflections on the current state of the domain in Sect. 5.

2   Network Intrusion Detection

Malicious attempts to invade an ICT infrastructure must be detected and localized while in progress. This objective implies performing real-time analysis of continuous streams of data from various sources and locations in search for indicators of compromise. Traditionally, the process of intrusion detection has been split between network-based (NIDS) and host-based (HIDS) systems, that serve complementary purposes by monitoring malicious activities at different levels. HIDS runs on internal nodes, carrying the ability to closely monitor their individual behavior. It primarily relies on host-specific data sources, such as system and kernel-level activity traces, program analysis, audit logs, files and documents. Maintaining a fine-grained access to activities on individual hosts enables a HIDS to precisely localize misuse, e.g. an active malware. For further information on HIDSs and the diverse data types they utilize to detect attacks, we refer the reader to the recent survey [17].

The holy grail of intrusion detection is to recognize threats as early as possible before the system and its data get compromised. Since the most common way for intruders to enter an infrastructure is through the network, a NIDS – being placed at the edge of the network – analyses inbound and outbound network traffic and thus acts as the first line of defense. As opposed to the host-based level of monitoring, a network-based approach gives a more expansive view over the network, allowing for an early detection of attacks, including those that target multiple hosts at once. NIDSs can be also freely deployed within the perimeter, enabling them to monitor traffic traversing inside the network and to detect internal attacks. Today, security is moving beyond traditional perimeter-based solutions: the growth in cloud, mobile and edge computing and connected devices makes network borders and access points much less defined. The *Zero Trust* paradigm has been introduced [55] to address the gaps in traditional network design by (i) not trusting any entities inside or outside the organization network, and by (ii) segmenting the network and thus providing only limited access required to perform specific tasks, even after verification. From perspective of network intrusion detection, this entails that all network traffic is treated as untrusted, increasing the workload for NIDSs deployed at choke points in the zero-trust network.

AI-powered traffic analysis and network defense tools are becoming ubiquitous across ICT infrastructures, being adopted to diverse network architectures, points of NIDS deployment and data sources. Before diving into the data-driven approach used to enhance network intrusion detection, we establish a general threat model under which a NIDS operates.

2.1   Network Threats

Cyberthreats targeted by a NIDS are either executed over a network, or communicate with external parties over a network. A NIDS mirrors the entire network traffic that is permitted by a firewall, being able to distinguish attacks across the OSI stack, from Layer 2 (Data Link) potentially all the way up to Layer 7 (Application). Very broadly, these threats can be categorized into passive and active attacks.

Passive attacks do not involve any meaningful interaction with nodes in a target network and do not alter any data. Instead, the purpose is to *probe* the system – obtain useful information which can be efficiently collected through, for instance, *network scanning* or *port scanning*. Network scanning allows to detect accessible nodes, while probing open ports allows to identify services running on these nodes, exposing their vulnerabilities. As such, a passive attack does not leave any traces in the system and is by itself a preparatory step before a more aggressive intervention. Detecting a passive attack in real-time gives a defender an opportunity to proactively identify an adversary and prevent their intrusion.

The types of *active attacks*, however, vary greatly. These are the network attacks that aim at compromising integrity, confidentiality and availability of target systems. Without being exhaustive, we list some of the most prominent attack scenarios.

The most basic way to *penetrate* the network would be by brute forcing credentials of a legitimate user, which is characterized by an overwhelming series of unsuccessful logins rather noticeable in the inbound network traffic. More advanced attackers penetrate a protected network by carefully exploiting vulnerabilities found in its perimeter and thus gaining unauthorized, potentially privileged access to the system in a more stealthy manner. These can be misconfigurations or vulnerabilities in firmware of entry-level network devices, or web and software vulnerabilities of publicly accessible hosts, such as buffer overflows, cross-site scripting (XSS) and SQL injections. Similar to brute force attacks, these exploits can also be launched over the network, carried in incoming network packets' payloads. However, due to traffic encryption and a number of other considerations to be discussed further, malicious payloads even of well-known exploits are not guaranteed to be detected.

Apart from penetration attacks, another large family of network threats is *denial of service* (DoS) attacks, which aim at disrupting normal functioning of target hosts and deny their availability to legitimate users. This goal can be achieved through flooding the victim node or resource with superfluous requests in an attempt to overload both the network bandwidth and the system, possibly also targeting its IDS. There are many variations of a DoS attack, including SYN flooding, ICMP flooding, smurf and others, which differ in mechanics and final effects. A distributed DoS attack (DDoS) is launched from numerous sources at once, often automated by a whole network of compromised computers – bots. Today, *botnets* are seen as the largest network security threat and remain one of the key research topics in intrusion detection. Bots become disguised as legitimate actors through infecting privately owned systems. Their automated illegitimate activities can have various malicious impact, ranging from spam and click fraud campaigns to identity theft, DoS attacks and malware infections. Remote command-and-control (C&C) servers send instructions to the compromised cluster of computers and receive back reports and leaked information. Even though botnets generate a lot of communication, detecting them through traffic analysis or other means is a serious challenge for any type of IDS, as bots continue to evolve and find better disguises.

While botnets are rather stealthy and can cause extremely damaging consequences, there is an attack class that surpasses others in evasiveness, sophistication and severity – *advanced persistent threats* (APTs). These threats are human-driven attacks targeted against a specific infrastructure and aimed at gaining an ongoing access for a long period of time in order to exfiltrate sensitive valuable data – this could be, for instance, intellectual property of organizations, trade secrets, or customer information. It is especially difficult to detect an APT at the moment of perimeter penetration or privilege escalation, since advanced attackers may use unknown exploits or social engineering tricks to infiltrate an infrastructure. Afterwards, an APT only infects a few chosen hosts to get closer to valuable resources of the network, effectively staying under the radar. They rarely contact remote C&C servers, and when they do, they use encryption or obfuscation techniques, complicating traffic analysis by a NIDS. However, the *data exfiltration* process – a common goal of an APT – may be well observable in outbound network traffic, which grants a crucial defensive role to a NIDS.

2.2   Network Traffic Monitoring

Network traffic became a universal data source for intrusion detection thanks to standardization and ubiquity of network protocols, which makes NIDSs adaptable to a wide range of platforms and applications. A NIDS collects and inspects network traffic in different modes, mostly either on a packet level or on a flow level. These approaches to traffic monitoring differ in informational content and practicality, and selecting one, or a combination, depends on the environment and the threat model.

Packet-Level Inspection. Capturing traffic from the network by a NIDS for monitoring and analysis purposes is achieved with promiscuous access to *copies* of network packets, and therefore without interference in communication. Full packet captures are usually made in the *pcap* file format, a widely used and portable format for packet inspection. Pcap files can be processed with Deep Packet Inspection (DPI), which performs both packet header and payload analysis. DPI can provide extensive information about communication, exposing malicious payloads to a NIDS. One of the earliest IDS tools that performs application-level DPI is Snort [80], an open-source signature-based detector. Snort matches observed packets with known malicious patterns using regular expressions (e.g., for a linux web server, a pattern could be an HTTP request containing 'etc./passwd'). A more recent open-source NIDS called Suricata [1] improves scalability of Snort [5]. Such signature-based NIDS strongly rely on a rich database of malicious payloads. For anomaly-based NIDS, one prominent example is the Zeek [2] tool (formerly known as Bro [73]). Zeek constructs benign baseline profiles for an application's usage based on predefined policy scripts and flags deviations from these profiles. For instance, it was shown to effectively detect web attacks, such as reflected XSS injection and SQL injection, by inspecting strings in the HTTP-request parameters [98]. With access to payloads, these attacks are straightforwardly detected due to presence of unusual characters in the request body.

Despite all these advantages, processing full packet captures comes with some considerable practical issues. The sheer volume of packets in modern high speed communication networks is overwhelming, making DPI inefficient or even infeasible in real-time. Moreover, storing full captures for further network forensics is a highly limited resource. Captures of very large packets are often incomplete or even limited to header information, largely omitting the most informative parts. And finally, two fundamental limitations to performing DPI are (i) invasion of privacy through accessing and storing benign packets' content, and (ii) traffic encryption. Packet-level inspection on TLS-encrypted traffic can be realized through man-in-the-middle solutions that decrypt and re-encrypt payloads, thereby violating end-to-end security guarantees, which can be both unsafe and computationally intensive for a particular environment. An ongoing line of research explores DPI over encrypted traffic through matching encrypted tokens with encrypted rules [70,84]. Currently this approach requires computationally intensive setup phases for every network connection, and, without the aid of decryption, supports only a limited number of IDS rules.

In view of the above circumstances – high data rates, computationally demanding processing, privacy and encryption concerns – DPI for intrusion detection is arguably becoming increasingly obsolete in modern environments. Nevertheless, there exist numerous network intrusion detection datasets with full packet captures, as packet-level analysis has proven to be highly beneficial for research purposes.

Flow-Level Inspection. Rather than inspecting and storing all individual incoming and outgoing packets, a NIDS may group relevant packets together in a *flow* and collect their aggregated information on a flow level. A traffic flow is commonly defined as a series of bidirectional packets exchanged between two hosts that share a five-tuple – source and destination IP addresses, source and destination ports, and a protocol – collected over a certain period of time. This may correspond to a duration of one complete network connection, or to a predefined time window (until a timeout is reached). Flow-level information is aggregated across all the packets belonging to one flow – typically this includes timestamps of start and finish, number of packets and bytes, arrival times, certain packet header attributes, etc. These traffic flow meta-data provide a high-level description of communication between source and destination hosts which can be very telling about its benign or malicious nature [90]. As a result, flow-based inspection does not take into account traffic content, but instead reveals informative high-level communication patterns, while greatly reducing the size of data to be analyzed.

Packet counts are recorded when packets cross network router interfaces. Most often, flow data aggregation is performed through Netflow [21] – a network monitoring protocol that is well integrated in modern network environments. Since Netflow counters are mostly generated directly on the network equipment, performance of the network may be affected. The overhead can be limited by performing traffic aggregation at the hardware level or even by decoupling traffic routing and flow computation by passively copying traffic data, similar to the case of packet inspection. As opposed to the packet-level inspection, which mostly provides signature-based analysis, an advantage of flow-based inspection is that it supports anomaly detection approach, as we describe in Sect. 3. Furthermore, network aggregates are applicable in the context of end-to-end encryption or privacy constraints of a particular environment, because they omit packet payloads from analysis. This property facilitates public availability of real traffic data aggregated in the form of flows, which is extremely valuable for open network intrusion detection research. A NIDS can also implement a hybrid approach that combines DPI and traffic flow analysis in a number of variations, mostly relying on the flow-based analysis complemented with an occasional payload inspection of suspicious traces.

3   A Data Analysis Approach

Monitored traffic traces – in the form of full captures or aggregated flows – are analyzed to find indicators of potential attacks. In the early days, review of monitored activities for intrusion detection was performed manually by security analysts or system administrators. They used to devise and manually adjust rules and heuristics that would help to find harmful packets and identify suspicious behavior. The volume and increasing complexity of monitored data has long deemed any such manual efforts insufficient and prompted the community to introduce automation. Already in the 1990s, progress in AI research enabled investigation of ML techniques[1] in application to intrusion detection. The power of data analysis is in interpreting large amounts of data and automatically discovering new relevant knowledge – a highly valuable capability in the ever-growing and ever-changing security landscape.

A ML-based IDS employs a data-driven approach to intrusion detection – it uses ML methods to autonomously learn characteristic rules and patterns from previously observed data. For the case of network intrusion detection, the abundance of network traffic data creates an opportunity to apply data-driven techniques. A ML-based NIDS configured for *misuse detection* can detect variants of known attacks by finding patterns sufficiently similar to previously seen malicious traffic. On the other hand, a ML-based NIDS that performs *anomaly*

---

[1] Machine learning is defined as a subfield of AI that focuses on data-driven modeling of concepts, while deep learning is a subfield of machine learning that uses a particular family of techniques – artificial neural networks with representation learning.

detection can model 'normal' behavior of the system by learning from benign network traffic, and catches anomalous patterns that deviate significantly from the baseline. In the context of high non-stationarity and strong heterogeneity of network traffic, another strength of ML is its ability to dynamically adapt to changes in the network when exposed to new data.

The prolific use of AI cannot be merely attributed to impressive automation capabilities of ML algorithms, as it also relies heavily on expert involvement. In order to benefit from the advantages offered by ML, the designer of a ML-based NIDS applies their domain expertise to create an appropriate learning system. First and foremost, an in-depth understanding of the network environment and the threat model are required in the *data representation* phase that converts monitored traffic data into a suitable format for ML. Applying ML methods directly to raw monitoring data, such as full pcap files, is not only hardly computationally feasible, but also does not usually yield useful results. The reason is that the numerous values in their original form are not equally relevant to the learning problem, which is especially true for data of such complex structure and overwhelming volume as network traffic. Therefore, an IDS designer leverages expert knowledge to find a compact representation of raw traffic which conveys characteristics that are most relevant to the task of misuse or anomaly detection. This step is known as *feature extraction* – a transformation that converts an initial set of input data into derived values, or *features*, that capture its underlying structure and complexity. As a result, information-rich raw data is represented as a *feature vector* containing compact, non-redundant information that is appropriate for subsequent learning and inference. The goal of the feature extraction process is to compose such features that describe patterns in data which, during inference, can *generalize* to previously unseen samples drawn from the same distribution. Today there exist two major general approaches to extracting features: (i) *feature engineering & selection* – hand-crafting and selecting most salient features based on practical experience and intuition about the problem, and (ii) *feature learning* – automated feature extraction with the use of learning algorithms.

The quality of features constructed from input data is one of the most influential factors that define the effectiveness of a ML algorithm. For optimal performance, it is crucial to keep the feature set up-to-date with the ongoing changes in the learning problem – a concern especially present in network security. Therefore, in NIDS domain, both approaches to feature extraction are continuously revised and improved: while the former has traditionally played a predominant role, the latter is receiving increasing attention lately in light of recent progress in deep learning (DL) research.

Feature Engineering and Selection. When engineering features for network intrusion detection, and other related traffic analysis tasks [16], it is important to consider the characteristics of the learning problem and define the level of granularity of features. In networking, an analyst can choose from the wide range of packet-level, flow-level, session- or connection-level, and multi-flow features, with increasing level of granularity. On each level, a statistical description of data, such as distributions of attributes or groups of attributes, can be formed:

– *Packet-level* features are extracted or derived from collected packets: payload information, packet-specific header attributes and packet-level statistics, e.g. mean and variance of packet sizes and inter-arrival times.
– *Flow-level* description includes simple aggregated statistical features such as mean flow duration, mean number of packets per flow, mean number of bytes per flow, bytes transmitted per second, and more. The latest versions of Net-Flow compute very basic features of traffic flows in real time, including bytes per packet and packets per flow, which are further used to derive flow-based statistics. Despite the simplicity, statistical features turn out to be highly informative of the nature of a particular communication, as they are quite effective in revealing traffic anomalies and particular known malicious patterns. For instance, a basic DoS attack is a volumetric attack that is commonly characterized by sending many packets in one direction within a short time period, making flow statistics well-suited for detection.
– *Connection-level* features are extracted from the transport layer and include information about the particular network connection (which may be split into several flows). For TCP connections, these additional features may include advertised window sizes in TCP headers and the throughput distributions.
– *Multi-flow* features appear especially valuable for security applications such as network intrusion detection. For some types of intrusions, meaningful revealing information can be only derived through aggregation across multiple flows/connections. For instance, for a particular flow, number of recent connections from the same source or to the same destination can be relevant. These aggregated measurements are highly instrumental, for instance, in detecting attacks executed over multiple connections, be that from different sources against the same victim, or against different nodes in the network. Probe attacks, DDoS attacks and bot communication are obvious examples, where one flow in isolation might appear harmless, while the overall behavior is more indicative. *Temporal statistical features* is another example of feature extraction approach that aims to solve the problem of a narrow one-flow view by aggregating traffic information over time across multiple flows, thereby respecting temporal dependencies between them [64].

The set of engineered features is often further optimized through automatic *feature selection* in order to discard redundant or irrelevant features and reduce dimensionality of voluminous data. In this way, feature selection may decrease computational overhead while maintaining accuracy, and also help to avoid *overfitting* of a ML model to the training data of high complexity, i.e. memorizing the data instead of deriving the underlying patterns. For different approaches to composing and reducing the feature set, we refer the reader to the corresponding surveys [16,26,68].

The resulting new set of high-quality manually extracted features forms feature vectors that are compact, non-redundant, informative and generalized, and possibly *interpretable*, having clear semantics for each vector dimension. Arriving at high quality representations is a challenging iterative manual process, involving experimentation with many techniques in combination with domain expertise and intuition about the problem. *Feature learning* aims at automating the process of feature extraction, relaxing the need for close expert involvement.

Feature Learning. As ML approaches struggle with high-dimensional inputs and manual feature extraction, *deep neural networks* have recently been embraced for dimensionality reduction and feature/representation learning. DL approaches are able to automatically extract discriminative internal representations of the input through a series of non-linear transformations upon observing sufficient amounts of data. Several studies applied *deep belief networks* for misuse and anomaly detection in order to obviate manual engineering of traffic flow features [6,32,41,86]. Automatically learned representations have proven to be more robust to irrelevant deviations in data and thus contributed to higher generalizability of ML models to earlier unseen patterns. The immediate drawback of automatically learned abstract features is that, as opposed to hand-crafted feature vectors, they do not provide clear semantics. Decisions of DL-based NIDS are, therefore, hardly directly interpretable. This calls for additional methods to verify that a trained DL-based feature extractor has learned appropriate meaningful traffic patterns and to explain a model's decisions to security analysts [7,69]. Therefore, more automation implies less interpretability – a trade-off that a NIDS designer has to balance.

3.1 Machine Learning for NIDS

When selecting an appropriate ML model, it is crucial to understand how to leverage the properties of the features and relationship between them. For instance, streaming data represented as a time series consists of temporal features, which are best interpreted with a model capable of recognizing temporal dependencies. The choice of a learning algorithm, however, starts with defining a concrete ML problem statement that most accurately represents the task of intrusion detection, be it misuse- or anomaly-based. This encapsulates at the very least such influential factors as (i) expected input and output of the system, (ii) assumption about the knowledge of all existing data categories, and (iii) availability of annotated training data.

Input and Output. The expected input implies the data representation, i.e. the types and dimensionality of extracted and selected features. The expected output of the model is a design choice of how to present the inferred information about the event for further analysis and response. In general, for a given test instance, the output can be a *label*: malicious vs. benign or anomaly vs. benign. For anomaly detection in particular, it can also be an anomaly score that indicates significance of the detected anomaly for further investigation. Optionally, the model can also provide its confidence score for each decision.

Closed-World and Open-World Assumptions. The assumption about the knowledge of all data categories is what largely drives the choice between misuse and anomaly detection in the first place. A misuse detector is typically deployed under a *closed-world* assumption, which implies that all possible data categories, i.e. types of intrusions, have been seen at the training stage of the model. A common closed-world NIDS employs a ML *classifier* that learns to recognize a traffic instance as benign or belonging to one or another attack class, thus performing *intrusion recognition*. Closed-world detection has been thoroughly researched in the network security domain, and has been traditionally favored by industry due to predictability and high detection rates. However, in operation, such a model can only detect known malicious behaviors and assumes that no unexpected attack type may appear.

In reality, a network environment operates under a much more challenging threat model that includes known attacks, new variants of known attacks and completely novel, earlier unseen cyber-threats, comprising an *open world* of possibilities (hence the title of this chapter). In order to enable open-world detection, a ML problem statement has to change from standard classification to either *open-world recognition* [11] (also called open-set recognition/classification), or *anomaly detection* [20] (also called outlier detection). An open-world classifier performs its originally intended task, but also leverages additional mechanisms to be able to identify novel patterns as instances that cannot be confidently classified as one of the learned attack types. Anomaly detection algorithms, however, are inherently open-world: as was explained earlier, anomaly detection exclusively relies on knowledge of benign data (normal, background traffic), and flags any sufficiently deviant pattern as a potential intrusion attempt of unknown nature. Therefore, in operation, an anomaly-based NIDS is an open-world detector as it targets both known and unknown attacks, although it can similarly use patterns of earlier seen attacks for model evaluation at the design stage. A core drawback of employing anomaly detection for defensive purposes is its dependence on the notion of 'normality' – as a consequence, a pattern that deviates from normal data for benign reasons is also flagged as potentially malicious, usually causing a high number of false alerts that need to be investigated. Further in Sect. 4, we zoom in on the challenges of traffic anomaly detection.

There are many studies in the literature that join anomaly detection with misuse detection in an attempt to combine the strengths of both paradigms: improve the detection rate and minimize the rate of false alerts. In fact, commercial platforms very rarely use anomaly detection in isolation, but rather adopt the *hybrid* approach [54]. The mismatch between the promises of anomaly detection and its actual adoption in industry is what demands a more explicit academic focus on anomaly-based IDS research.

Supervised and Unsupervised Learning. Another fundamental distinction between ML approaches relates to availability of annotated/*labeled* data. *Supervised* ML, such as classification, is a learning mode that relies on labeled training data. Namely, a classifier requires a significant number of representative labeled training examples from all the considered classes. Therefore, a classifier-based misuse detector works with a continuously updated database of known malicious patterns that need to be well represented in training data for a NIDS.

Acquiring labeled malicious data is expensive, as it requires either manual investigation by network experts, or development of automated labeling algorithms, which essentially create a chicken and egg problem. Moreover, supervised learning is in general highly sensitive to *class imbalance* in data, demanding equal representation of every class. Otherwise, a classifier trained with imbalanced data becomes biased towards the majority class and largely ignores instances belonging to the minority class of interest. Since in network environments benign traffic is predominant, the benign class outweighs malicious traffic classes in labeled training data, causing a much lower representation of attacks. This undermines the sole purpose of intrusion detection, since the most interesting and inherently rare intrusions become overlooked. The issue can be addressed by using specialized techniques to increase importance of the minority attack classes [97]. Another solution is attack simulation performed to generate more malicious traffic for training under an assumption of its representativeness of real intrusions. However, for simulated benchmark datasets, the class imbalance problem is not unheard of, either.

Unsupervised ML paradigm obviates the need for labeled data altogether. A general example is *clustering*, which performs exploratory data analysis to draw inferences and find hidden patterns and correlations in unlabeled data. Clusters are automatically formed with the use of a similarity measure between instances. Unsupervised approaches generally do not assume any a priori knowledge on the data distribution and labels, which corresponds to a realistic NIDS scenario. In practice, though, *semi-supervised* anomaly detection is often applicable under the assumption of availability of labeled normal data. As the shortage of malicious labeled traffic is the main issue, both supervised and semi-supervised approaches pose the biggest interest for NIDS research.

While supervised NIDS approaches are widely utilized and thoroughly studied in the literature, they either violate the open-world context of network security, or extensively rely on manual data labeling, or both. In recent years, unsupervised and semi-supervised techniques in application to NIDS are gaining more traction; however, the research is largely ongoing. The community have composed a number of excellent surveys on the topic that provide detailed taxonomies and analyses of existing ML-based approaches to NIDS. For the closed-world misuse detection research, we refer the reader to the corresponding expansive literature that surveys supervised classification methods [12,18]. Further in our discussion, we elaborate on the open-world NIDS research, specifically, unsupervised or semi-supervised anomaly-based ML paradigms, which we believe deserve more attention in the field of network security. Hence, our aim is to complement the existing surveys [4,34,42,96], which provide in-depth analyses of individual techniques, with a broad overview of the current solution space and the key remaining challenges.

3.2   Anomaly Detection for Open-World NIDS

An *anomaly* is commonly defined as a rare pattern that does not conform to expected behavior. In machine learning, an anomaly is detected as an outlier with respect to the region representing normal data. In intrusion detection, different types of anomalies are typically mapped to different types of malicious behavior:

1. *Point anomalies* – individual data observations that lie outside of the normal behavioral boundaries (relative to the rest of the data). For instance, sophisticated network exploits that aim to gain unauthorized access or escalate privileges, such as buffer overflow attacks or web attacks, can be carefully deployed through one packet payload, or one traffic flow. Simple probing attacks, launched through malformed packets, incomplete connections or with incorrect combinations of header attributes, also form a point anomaly.

2. *Contextual anomalies* – individual data observations that are anomalous in a given context. One example of a contextual anomaly are stealthy probing attack [91], where each individual packet and the whole connection may correspond to normal traffic. However, given the context of systematic information collection without meaningful interaction, the connection becomes anomalous. Some botnet traffic can also arguably be considered a contextual anomaly: while communication with the C&C server can by itself form a benign connection, its timestamp may point to suspicious behavior.

3. *Collective anomalies* – multiple data observations occurring together that differ from normal behavior. The key here is the collective occurrence of those observations, as each single instance is not anomalous by itself. A common example is a DoS attack, where only one connection is legitimate, but the abundance of similar connections becomes anomalous as they overwhelm the target system. Another example is the brute force network attacks, where a single incorrect log-in attempt is not yet suspicious, but a sequence of frequent attempts makes them collectively anomalous.

For anomaly-based network intrusion detection to be effective, the following assumptions have to hold:

- *Benign data assumption* – there exists a region with well-defined boundaries that encompasses all the normal traffic data.
- *Clean training data* (for semi-supervised approaches) – benign training data acquired by collecting live background traffic is attack-free.
- *All attacks are rare and anomalous* – traffic generated by malicious actions related to network intrusions deviates sufficiently from the normal traffic and will only constitute a small fraction of monitored data.
- *All anomalies are malicious* – whenever a deviant pattern is observed, it presents evidence of a potential intrusion.
- *Attacks are universal* – given correct modeling of normal data, all types of attacks are detected equally well.

Naturally, the extent to which these properties can be safely assumed differs from one environment to another and strongly depends on the threat model of a NIDS. For instance, it is already clear that a system tailed to detection of one of the three types of anomalies is not a universal detector for all attack types. We elaborate more on the implications of these assumptions in the next section.

Major anomaly detection techniques explored in application to intrusion detection can be grouped in four categories.

Statistical Approaches. Statistical anomaly-detection works based on the principles of the statistical theory to model the distinction between normal and anomalous. A common solution for anomaly-based NIDS is Principle Component Analysis (PCA) – a dimensionality reduction approach that projects high-dimensional data onto a normal and anomalous subspace. PCA does not assume any statistical distribution and is known for low computational complexity. Lakhina et al. explored the use of PCA on network traffic [57]; however, further studies revealed sensitivity of PCA to such aspects as the level of traffic aggregation and small noises in the normal subspace [79], which the state-of-the-art solutions aim to overcome [35,36].

Clustering Approaches. Clustering groups unlabeled traffic based on a chosen similarity metric, e.g. a Euclidean distance, and flag outliers as potential intrusions. Plenty of clustering algorithms have been applied to NIDS. More recent works utilize k-means with optimizations [52], Gaussian mixture model [15], incremental grid clustering [28] and novel affinity propagation clustering [102]. The advantages of clustering usually are stable performance and the possibility of incremental updates. On the other hand, clustering is not intrinsically optimized for anomaly detection, can be time-consuming and heavily depends on distance measures and tuning.

One-Class Classification. A semi-supervised adaptation of classification is called one-class classification, as it only utilizes negative examples in training, i.e. benign data. A data instance that falls outside of the learned class, depending on a chosen threshold, is considered anomalous. One-class Naive Bayes [94] and one-class Support Vector Machine (SVM) [54] are recent examples of traditional ML approaches used for anomaly-based NIDS. While we already discussed deep learning approaches for feature learning and dimensionality reduction, deep neural networks are also being employed as sole anomaly detectors. Deep belief networks [37], variational autoencoders [69] and ensembles of light-weight shallow autoencoders [64] have been successfully used for anomaly detection on network data, demonstrating good generalization abilities and self-adaptive nature of neural networks. A lingering issue of DL-based anomaly detectors is that by themselves, they are not optimized for anomaly detection, therefore selecting appropriate thresholds and tuning the architecture is challenging.

Time-Series Forecasting. Forecasting is a semi-supervised predictive anomaly detection approach specifically tailed for sequential inputs (including data with high seasonality), as they are capable of detecting temporal anomalies in complex scenarios [3]. The idea is to perform rolling predictions based on observed normal data and compare them with new observations. Strong deviation from predictions thus indicates an anomaly. While there exist numerous advanced time-series modeling and forecasting techniques, from traditional exponential smoothing [95] to more modern ones such as recurrent neural networks [60], their application to network traffic anomaly detection has thus far been limited. This approach does not only heavily rely on unpolluted training benign data and clear observable trends, but also struggles with high-dimensionality and categorical inputs. In light of remarkable performance by recurrent neural networks in anomaly detection on multi-dimensional time-series, we expect new forecasting NIDS approaches to appear in near future.

In the remainder of this chapter, we give a fresh look on the state of open-world NIDS research in terms of main challenges and recent contributions.

4   Challenges and Advances in Open-World NIDS Research

Machine learning algorithms, and anomaly detection in particular, have gained a lot of attention in network intrusion detection research because of its compelling potential in detecting novel attacks. A decade ago, the community brought into the spotlight the intrinsic challenges of open-world network intrusion detection [42,43,88,96]. It turned out that most of the conducted research explored ML-based IDS solutions under numerous unrealistic assumptions. In reality, with these wishful assumptions dropped, the effectiveness of ML-based solutions in detecting novel and known attacks falls way down below the estimated performance. In the context of a NIDS, ML algorithms are tasked with search for the unknown, while costs for mistakes in a security-critical environment are high. A fundamental question was raised as to how appropriate ML algorithms are to such defensive applications, and which guarantees they can give for operation in sensitive environments.

Since then, the security domain grew significantly, with attacks becoming more sophisticated and resourceful. A wide spectrum of cutting-edge machine learning techniques, including deep learning and big data analytics, have been proposed for a variety of applications. New benchmark NIDS datasets have been jointly developed and evaluated [78]. In general, today we observe a closer collaboration between the AI and the security community. In light of the new developments, we revisit the primary conceptual and practical issues of ML-based NIDS.

4.1   Original Premise of Anomaly Detection

The underlying assumptions of machine learning underpin open-world ML-based NIDS solutions. To enable the full potential of ML, these assumptions have to align with domain-specific characteristics, which in the case of securing dynamic and modern network environments is not a trivial question. For anomaly detection specifically, the community is actively attempting to address some of the following fundamental questions:

Can normal data be modeled? Most of the studies attempt to model benign traffic; however, not all benign behaviors follow a common distribution. It is overwhelmingly hard to completely capture the notion of 'normality', so the safest assumption to make is that the model cannot describe all the possible benign instances. Hence, false alerts and missed attacks are unavoidable, and adjustment to novel benign patterns is necessary, which we discuss further in the section.

Is it possible to acquire clean training data? The current consensus is that normal traffic collected in a live environment is never attack-free without additional (manual) sanitization.

Are attacks rare? Certain illegitimate activities in the network (e.g., scanning) have become so common that they comprise a large fraction of background traffic [103]. Durumeric et al. [30] revealed that DDoS cannot be considered anomalous in most networks. However, even though large-scale attacks are not rare, these are not of the biggest interest for detection. More sophisticated intrusions such as APTs are still manifested in rare events.

Are attacks anomalous? The answer directly relates to the vague definition of traffic 'normality'. Due to the noisy and highly varied nature of traffic, attack features may in practice appear as variations of benign traffic. Iglesias et al. [50] have recently conducted an analytical study to assess the 'outlierness' of malicious traffic. They confirmed that network attacks have higher global distance-based outlierness averages; however, attack and normal traffic distributions strongly overlap. One can choose the feature space that maximizes the separation of benign and malicious traffic, which indicates that understanding the nature of target anomalies in a certain scenario is instrumental for anomaly detection. Another known issue is that attackers may attempt to make traffic features indistinguishable from normal traffic. We elaborate on the associated risks further in the section.

Are attacks universal and equally detectable? Taking everything into account, there is little ground in assuming that different types of intrusions can be detected in one common manner. Moreover, the very definition of what is malicious differs across environments. Indeed, we observe the trend of developing NIDSs tailored to specific threat models. This includes, e.g., works that focus on botnet detection [58,81], DDoS detection [92], and especially APT detection [61], where data exfiltration through the network can be a target anomaly. It is quite unlikely that such targeted detectors generalize to other types of intrusions, but perhaps that should not be the initial goal. We advocate for deeper insight in target malicious activities even for open-world anomaly detectors, in order to adopt the most suitable strategies.

Is a detected anomaly an attack? Nowadays, it is commonly acknowledged that an anomaly detected by a NIDS is most probably a false alert. Even correctly detected anomalies are not always malicious: sometimes, deviations happen due to noise, changes in the underlying infrastructure or changes in the benign data distribution. Therefore, additional processing is required to investigate the issue, as monitoring and detection is just the earliest stage in the complex process of incident management. Additional analysis, attack correlation and response planning is a prerogative of Security Information and Event Management (SIEM) platforms [14]. While researchers have mainly focused on developing effective solutions for detection, studies on automatic intrusion response are still limited. The main challenge is in providing an accurate and informative description of the detected anomaly, including *interpretation* of the ML model's decision to raise an alert.

4.2 High Error Rates and Performance Estimation

Among the main problems with adoption of anomaly detection in mainstream security systems, high *false positive rate* (FPR) is an immediate candidate. For an enterprise IDS, manual investigation and interpretation of alerts consumes expensive analyst time. Given the large volumes of processed data and a low *base rate* of attacks of interest, even a very small fraction of false alerts generated by a nearly-perfect model yields an unacceptably large absolute number, effectively rendering a NIDS unusable in the operational setting. This issue of *base rate fallacy* was raised two decades ago [9], and is seen today as an inevitable pitfall of open-world detection: *precision of an IDS will always be determined by both the base rate of different attacks and the FPR.* Regretfully, however, we lack historical statistics for the base rates of attacks in real computer infrastructures, and measuring them reliably is still considered beyond present capabilities [71].

As the tolerance for errors in the application domain is critically low, researchers started advocating for placing more emphasis on constraining the FPR while preserving high detection rates [88]. Since then, more studies have targeted this specific problem. We observe that the solution space can be mainly branched into five complementary directions: (i) further developing more precise learning algorithms to lower the FPR [4,34]; (ii) post-processing alerts with the use of context or prior knowledge in the system [45,104], in order to aid in manual diagnostics and potentially understand the nature of an anomaly; (iii) employing a *hybrid* approach by combining anomaly detectors with misuse detectors [46], which cannot detect novel attacks but are considered less prone to mispredictions. (iv) tuning model parameters and detection thresholds in order to obtain optimal trade-offs in success rates and false alerts [89]; (v) modeling a realistic network environment in a structured manner and choosing appropriate metrics to correctly estimate the FPR and the overall performance.

While the first four objectives are gradually unfolding in present research, the last one is fundamental and largely remains an open question. It relates to the inherent difficulties with evaluating an open-world detector, which started being actively discussed more than ten years ago [42,43,88] and still hold today. With more progress in this direction, future NIDS studies should adopt an appropriate evaluation methodology and correct metrics that correspond to an actual operational usage of the target system. This requirement encapsulates such a crucial issue as validating and testing the model on data that resembles real-world ratios of benign vs. attack data – which again relates to the base rate fallacy. Without satisfying these goals, performance numbers and errors rates achieved in lab conditions will remain hardly reliable or comparable. The issue is especially pronounced for unsupervised methods, which learn from distributions and spaces drawn from the observed data. Note that even modern benchmark datasets are not said to be representative of an actual ratio of normal and attack traffic, therefore they are most often not directly applicable for (unsupervised) open-world evaluation schemes. We detail on the representativeness of existing datasets further below.

All in all, the research on decreasing the FPR while preserving performance in a general NIDS setting is still unfolding. Despite some studies emphasizing the post-processing stage of predictions, there is generally not enough investigation being made on the nature of false alerts, while most of the works solely focus on increasing the detection rates instead. Even though anomaly detectors with manageable error rates are allegedly becoming more widely adopted in industry, these solutions are often designed for specific scenarios and their internals are rarely publicly available [4,42,48], preventing direct comparison. The field appears to be in the urgent need of a common comprehensive methodology for estimating and comparing performance and error rates of an open-world NIDS.

4.3   Representative Datasets and Ground Truth

In IDS research, evaluation on benchmark datasets primarily serves a two-fold purpose: (i) *real-world performance estimation* of a particular algorithm, and (ii) *consistent comparison* between different approaches. In this respect, quality of data has a decisive influence on valid outcome of both objectives. Unfortunately, benchmark datasets do not always adequately represent the real problem of network intrusion detection, discrediting the performance numbers achieved in laboratory conditions. As a response, over the last 10 years the community has collectively devised the criteria that reliable research traffic data should meet [31,67,83,85,96,101], which encapsulate the following dataset properties: (i) realistic w.r.t. real production environments; (ii) valid w.r.t. completeness of traces; (iii) labeled; (iv) correctly labeled w.r.t. benign training data for anomaly-detection; (v) highly variant and diverse w.r.t. used services, protocols, benign behaviors and attacks; (vi) correctly implemented w.r.t. real attack scenarios; (vii) easily updatable with new services and attacks; (viii) reproducible for periodical updates and performance comparisons; (ix) shareable/non-sensitive; (x) well-documented. Despite this recently achieved consensus and clarity in guidelines, a lot of fundamental limitations of the task hamper both creation and publication of a corresponding proper dataset. Consequentially, many researchers have kept using the existing suboptimal datasets for the sake of comparison with prior work. Unfortunately, the usage of outdated or even novel but flawed datasets may lead to unreliable ML evaluations, as has been recently shown by Engelen et al. [31]. Nevertheless, the research community is making tangible progress in this direction by exploring both possibilities to contribute a new dataset: (i) generate synthetic traffic, and (ii) collect real traffic in a production environment.

Generation of synthetic datasets provides the luxury of a controlled environment, clean labels and no privacy concerns. The main challenge, however, is in simulation of realistic background traffic, lately attempted through statistically modeling user behavior [82,85] or more recently through modeling relevant traffic communication scenarios with input randomization [22,23]. Even though creators of modern synthetic datasets strive to satisfy the requirements and min-imize occurrence of *simulation artifacts*, the practice of evaluating a novel IDS on a synthetic dataset solely, however, is often criticized as insufficient. While it can be reasonable to compare different frameworks on synthetic data, evaluation on diverse network traffic collected in a live environment over a lengthy period of time is becoming the desired norm in NIDS research.

Real traffic, on the other hand, should be stripped of confidential data, care-fully labeled and rigorously sanitized in order to meet the established criteria. Several studies contributed approaches to sanitization of traffic [13,25,47,100] in order to not only label embedded attacks and benign traces, but also to pre-select the most representative instances. Automated sanitization uses such methods as entropy analysis and signature-based attack labeling, which may result in erroneous ground-truth. Manual sanitization hardly scales and is prone to human bias, which threatens reliability and representativeness of the dataset, respectively. However, manual supervision in labeling seems unavoidable when it comes to zero-day network attacks.

All in all, it is unclear whether a perfectly sanitized real traffic-based dataset can be obtained. Hence, learning algorithms that are robust to the inevitably occurring noise in labels would give a strong advantage from the operational point of view. Promising examples for anomaly detection on imperfectly labeled traffic include, e.g., robust PCA algorithms [62,72] and a convex combination of anomaly detectors' outputs [44].

Another suggestion for creation of an open, real NIDS dataset was voiced by Gates et al. [43], who promoted a community-based approach. One promi-nent example is the MAWILab dataset [39] – a public repository for automated labeling and performance estimation that has since been continuously updated and collectively labeled with the use of state-of-the-art anomaly detectors. While anomaly detection solutions on these data are still scarce [19], we believe that such collective efforts establish a strong foundation for open-world detection research.

4.4   Concept Drift

In dynamic environments, events undergo gradual and abrupt changes over time, which cause a shift in data distribution known as the *concept drift* [74]. When developing data-driven real-time defensive solutions such as ML-based IDSs, it is crucial to account for concept drift, otherwise the model's performance is unpredictably and heavily impacted. For an anomaly detector, this implies the need to track drift in the data in order to continuously adjust to the new definition of normal behavior, instead of erroneously flagging these changes as anomalies. A direct way to re-adapt the system accordingly is to re-train the model on new data, as is strongly recommended in the literature [42,63,88]. In anomaly detection literature, the problem of detecting newly emerging pat-terns is referred to as *novelty detection*, when previously unobserved detected patterns in data are incorporated into the normal model. In time-series analy-sis, a similar idea is defined as *change point detection* [10] that aims to detect points in a time-series from which the data distribution changes. Conventional approaches often suggested for ML-based defenses aim to detect concept drift by recognizing model's performance degradation on streaming data and identifying the appropriate moment for a model update. Naturally, the crucial trade-off emerges between the detection delay and the detection quality. Some families of ML algorithms such as neural networks can adapt through a continuous retraining mechanism known as *online/incremental learning*, exemplified by a DL-based IDS that analyzes log data [29]. By incorporating the most recent changes in system logs into the DNN model, a DL-based IDS can adjust to the newly emerging patterns in a timely manner. Incremental learning can also be applied for traditional ML algorithms, albeit with high computational complexity. For instance, Rassam et al. [76] utilize an adaptive principal component classifier-based anomaly detector that tracks dynamic normal changes in real sensor data. However, effectiveness and practicality of incremental learning or re-training for an anomaly IDS on network traffic – non-stationary streaming data – largely remain unexplored. Raza et al. [77] developed a theoretical approach that addresses detection of covariate shifts in generic non-stationary environments and can potentially aid in IDS concept drift. One promising approach to an autonomic anomaly NIDS was proposed by Wang et al. [102], who use novel clustering algorithms to label new data and dynamically adapt to normal behavior. They show efficacy of their algorithm on a private dataset of real HTTP traffic streams. Zhang et al. [106] employ a competing approach specifically tailored to high-dimensional streaming data. To account for concept drift, they perform adaptive subspace analysis that fully relies on human feedback to prune away irrelevant subspaces of anomalies. As this novel algorithm is only evaluated on the KDD'99 dataset, its ability to generalize to real traffic and scale to live environments is unknown. Dong et al. [27] developed a batch-based adaptation approach that utilizes an SVM classifier and incorporates human feedback to determine when re-training is necessary. Their evaluation is limited to malicious web requests, and they use a public dataset with HTTP traffic.

Currently, a thorough investigation of concept drift detection and adaptation techniques for open-world NIDSs is pending, and the lack of public representative benchmark datasets that contain labeled shifts in traffic has been one of the largest roadblocks. A notable recent contribution is the UGR'16 dataset [59] – real anonymized Netflow data for adaptive NIDS research that includes long-term traffic evolution and periodicity.

4.5 Real-Time Detection

In the era of growing risk and severity of cyber-attacks, an effective NIDS is expected to detect potential threats immediately as they occur in the network. An ideal *real-time* detector processes and analyzes a continuous stream of data in its natural sequential form and makes immediate decisions online [66]. Anomaly detection is regarded as indispensable in early open-world detection of novel, unusual behaviors, and yet the existing approaches are not effective enough in real-time detection [4] and still largely resort to offline analysis, or batch processing at best, allowing some intrusions to go unnoticed for days. In the meantime, the bar for real-time processing capabilities is only increasing: not only does the internet traffic double each year, but in addition to that, the growth of the Internet of Things (IoT), sensors, smart cities, mobile clouds, autonomous vehicles, and other emerging technologies has unleashed enormous amounts of generated network data. Cisco has reported [40] that by 2022, the omnipresent non-PC devices are estimated to drive 81% of global internet traffic, opening the gate for more large-scale network attacks against small connected devices. The network data of today is already characterized by huge volume, velocity, variety and veracity, fulfilling the definition of *big data*. Traditional ML-enabled NIDS have not been developed to handle big data, but largely aimed at enhancing learning algorithms, which mostly results in increasing the computational complexity and processing time [4,18,34], further hindering real-time analysis.

As the demand for effective security monitoring raises higher by day, novel solutions are required to facilitate large-scale, real-time detection. Hoplaros et al. [49] explored *data summarization* techniques that mine patterns in summaries of network traffic to approximate final decisions and improve efficiency of detection. Since this approach effectively allows to cut offline detection runtimes, the authors propose to develop stream data summarization and distributed summarization methods for online detection. The downside is that complex summarization on big data contributes to opacity of model predictions, while threat analysis benefits from more granularity and transparency in decision-making.

Collaborative intrusion detection systems that employ several distributed monitors for collection and analysis of traffic pose an alternative to the bottleneck stand-alone anomaly detectors. A collaborative NIDS is considered to be much more efficient in analysis of numerous data streams traversing through large networks and IT ecosystems. Vasilomanolakis et al. [99] provide a taxonomy and a detailed survey on the topic, including possible topologies and threat models for a collaborative NIDS. Zarpelao et al. [105] presented a survey of stand-alone and collaborative IDS solutions specifically for IoT infrastructures. Crucially, most of the modern NIDS research on large-scale networks, IoT in particular, does not provide enough details for reproducibility and use private specifically chosen testbeds or simulation tools. Moreover, the internal mechanisms of existing commercial products are also hardly available. All in all, a thorough investigation on public data with a standardized evaluation strategy is required to assess effectiveness of a collaborative NIDS in real-time detection of sophisticated attacks in modern network environments.

Suthaharan et al. [93] were among the first to highlight the challenging big data properties associated with network monitoring for security. They advocated incorporating known big data frameworks, e.g. Hadoop [87], into a ML-based NIDS framework, in order to combine *big data processing* tailored to real-time analytics with supervised ML classifiers and representation-learning techniques. This integration requires to rethink implementations of ML algorithms in general and introduce *parallelization* by either dividing data into separately processed subsets, or dividing a ML algorithm into concurrently performed steps. Later on, the discussion was extended to anomaly-based NIDS in order to enable real-time open-world detection on large streaming data [19,33,64,65,75]. Recently, Habeeb et al. [48] have thoroughly reviewed real-time network anomaly detection algorithms and discussed the aspects and challenges of their application to big network traffic data. Despite the promise of big data frameworks widely deployed in other domains, in network security we still observe a premature state of big data processing capabilities. Efficient model and parameter selection, automation of data filtering and curation, dynamic resource allocation, reduction of power and memory consumption are only a few associated future research directions. With these enhancements, advance anomaly detection in combination with modern big data tools should be adequate to handle large-scale real-time detection, feature extraction and selection, labeling, and model retraining.

4.6   Adversarial Robustness

Attackers have always had great incentives and tools to evade detection by a NIDS. Knowing the blind spots of a detector, an adaptive attacker chooses the optimal strategy that fools a NIDS into thinking that the passing traffic is legitimate. Misuse-based detectors that inspect traffic on the packet level are traditionally evaded through such means as encryption, obfuscation and packet fragmentation, which make sure that malicious traffic does not match a known signature. A general anomaly-based detector is vulnerable to *mimicry attacks*, which modify malicious traffic in such a way that it corresponds to normal traffic patterns [38,53]. Besides, any type of a NIDS is susceptible to various DoS attacks, which can overload the detector with meaningless connections to create a bottleneck, so that the actual malicious connection comes through unnoticed. The security analysis of novel NIDS solutions with respect to adaptive attackers is regarded as a crucial research angle.

In the last decade, more attention was brought specifically to evasion of ML-enabled defenses. When placing a ML model at the core of a defensive system, one will always involuntarily introduce a new attack vector of undetermined severity. *Adversarial machine learning* is a set of techniques that exploit specific vulnerabilities of ML algorithms in order to trigger an incorrect output. These vulnerabilities arise from the same aspect that makes ML models unadapted to concept drift: ML models that are initially designed and evaluated in a stationary environment without any external influences assume a certain data distribution with static priors. The guarantees provided by this evaluation are only valid for the expected inputs to the model, i.e. the datapoints generated from the same data distribution that was considered during training and testing. NIDSs, however, are deployed in *non-stationary adversarial environments*, where attackers may choose to purposefully alter and perturb the input data to force the ML model to fail, thus inducing *adversarial drift* [51]. Adaptive attacks that specifically target vulnerabilities and assumptions of ML algorithms are referred to in the literature as *adversarial attacks*.

Corona et al. [24] describe a general adaptive threat model for a NIDS and review studies of one particular category of adversarial attacks – *poisoning* attacks. In case of ML models that are designed to automatically adapt to changes in normal traffic – either through online learning or retraining –, an attacker can poison the model by inserting adversarial noise in seemingly benign traffic that is consequently used for training. After compromising the learning process in this way, the attacker can bypass the poisoned model by manipulating input samples in accordance with the new decision boundary. Essentially, as a result of a poisoning attack, an attacker establishes a *backdoor* in the ML model that allows to evade detection. For instance, Kloft and Laskov [56] explored poisoning attacks against centroid anomaly detection and confirmed its effectiveness on feature vectors representing real HTTP traffic.

The second, most known type of adversarial attacks is *evasion*, where an attacker constructs a malicious *adversarial example* by introducing carefully crafted minor perturbations in input traffic that cause a desired output of the target model. In case of a targeted attack, an adversary attempts to influence the exact outcome of prediction at inference time. Meanwhile, an untargeted attack succeeds as long as any misprediction occurs. To construct adversarial examples that effectively evade detection, an adversary should either have direct access to some of the target's model properties (architecture, parameters, training data, input features, etc.), or simply be able to continuously query the model as an oracle and analyze its output. These threat models are referred to as *white-box* and *black-box* respectively, with the latter assuming minimal knowledge about the target NIDS. While the black-box scenario is more appropriate in network security, white-box approaches to generation of adversarial examples are also applicable assuming a local surrogate ML model whose decision boundary is close to that of the target.

Although all these approaches are algorithmically feasible in terms of mathematical formulations, their practicality and impact on security of real network environments are just starting to be comprehensively researched. Preliminary research results on closed-world systems (e.g., evasion of botnet classifiers trained on Netflow features [8]) indicate that ML algorithms used behind NIDSs are indeed not robust to perturbations. However, at this point, it remains unclear whether adversarial attacks against open-world network intrusion detection systems can withstand domain-specific practical constraints. One of the obstacles to investigating this question is the absence of dedicated research datasets that include sophisticated ML-specific evasion attempts in raw network traffic. Another more fundamental concern is the overall utility of adversarial learning in this context, that is how compelling this approach would be for a network attacker. While introducing ML into a NIDS pipeline undeniably creates additional tangible threats, other more conventional attack vectors – such as the above-mentioned mimicry attacks or DoS attacks that overload the detector – appear much less costly or complex to perform than adversarial attacks against ML. As the practicality and impact of adversarial attacks in the operational scenario of a NIDS remain unknown, and other challenges in using ML effectively keep affecting operational performance of NIDSs, hardening detectors used in actual services and infrastructures against adversarial perturbations has not yet gained the envisioned priority.

5   Conclusion

Machine learning for network intrusion detection is an extremely intriguing and potent research direction, which – despite its strong theoretical base – is still lacking devoted attention in defensive security. Today, the community acknowledges the non-stationarity and adversarial nature of security applications, promoting thoughtful and realistic evaluation of effective and adaptable ML-based defenses. We had to face the hard truths about domain-specific properties and limitations of ML in open dynamic environments. While we cannot create a silver-bullet solution to network intrusion detection, we can deepen our understanding of the underlying issues and provide fundamentally sound ML techniques for NIDS.

In this chapter, we reviewed the wide spectrum of impressive research efforts in the area of anomaly-based NIDS and highlighted the main challenges that should become the focus of the future research. Our analysis encompasses the domain misalignment with the original assumptions of anomaly detection, high error rates, the problem of performance estimation and comparison, availability of realistic datasets and reliable ground truth, adaptability to concept drift, feasibility of real-time detection, and adversarial impact. From our discussion, it becomes evident that there is no clear-cut separation between various challenges or desired properties of open-world detection systems. Moreover, the undeniable benefits of using ML in security context come together with a number of concerns and even incompatibilities between the techniques and the problem at hand. It is the balance between entrusting security tasks to ML and yet being aware of its potential pitfalls that may bring out the most reliable and fruitful solutions.

Therefore, we hope that the future research will reason about network intrusion detection in a more principled way that considers all important aspects in conjunction and allows to systematically assess how they affect each other. To achieve that, we encourage the community to collectively devise appropriate ML methodologies to develop and evaluate realistic open-world network intrusion detectors in different environments and threat models. As this is a tough task for the years to come, we need to scale research by composing benchmarking scenarios under a common set of assumptions to compare novel methods in a fair and informative way. To this end, the coordinated effort and the open science approach to NIDS research – i.e., new open realistic datasets and open-source implementations – deserve the highest priority.

Acknowledgments. This research is partially funded by the Research Fund KU Leuven, and by the Flemish Research Programme Cybersecurity.

References

1. Suricata IDS (2010). https://suricata-ids.org/. Accessed 1 June 2020
2. Zeek IDS (2018). https://zeek.org/. Accessed 12 July 2020
3. Ahmad, S., Lavin, A., Purdy, S., Agha, Z.: Unsupervised real-time anomaly detection for streaming data. Neurocomputing **262**, 134–147 (2017)
4. Ahmed, M., Mahmood, A.N., Hu, J.: A survey of network anomaly detection techniques. J. Netw. Comput. Appl. **60**, 19–31 (2016)
5. Albin, E., Rowe, N.C.: A realistic experimental comparison of the Suricata and Snort intrusion-detection systems. In: 2012 26th International Conference on Advanced Information Networking and Applications Workshops, pp. 122–127. IEEE (2012)
6. Alrawashdeh, K., Purdy, C.: Toward an online anomaly intrusion detection system based on deep learning. In: 2016 15th IEEE International Conference on Machine Learning and Applications (ICMLA), pp. 195–200. IEEE (2016)
7. Amarasinghe, K., Kenney, K., Manic, M.: Toward explainable deep neural network based anomaly detection. In: 2018 11th International Conference on Human System Interaction (HSI), pp. 311–317. IEEE (2018)
8. Apruzzese, G., Colajanni, M.: Evading botnet detectors based on flows and random forest with adversarial samples. In: 2018 IEEE 17th International Symposium on Network Computing and Applications (NCA), pp. 1–8. IEEE (2018)
9. Axelsson, S.: The base-rate fallacy and its implications for the difficulty of intrusion detection. In: Proceedings of the 6th ACM Conference on Computer and Communications Security, pp. 1–7 (1999)
10. Basseville, M., Nikiforov, I.V., et al.: Detection of Abrupt Changes: Theory and Application, vol. 104. Prentice Hall Englewood Cliffs (1993)
11. Bendale, A., Boult, T.: Towards open world recognition. In: Proceedings of the IEEE Conference on Computer Vision and Pattern Recognition, pp. 1893–1902 (2015)
12. Berman, D.S., Buczak, A.L., Chavis, J.S., Corbett, C.L.: A survey of deep learning methods for cyber security. Information **10**(4), 122 (2019)
13. Bermúdez-Edo, M., Salazar-Hernández, R., Díaz-Verdejo, J., García-Teodoro, P.: Proposals on assessment environments for anomaly-based network intrusion detection systems. In: Lopez, J. (ed.) CRITIS 2006. LNCS, vol. 4347, pp. 210–221. Springer, Heidelberg (2006). https://doi.org/10.1007/11962977_17
14. Bhatt, S., Manadhata, P.K., Zomlot, L.: The operational role of security information and event management systems. IEEE Secur. Priv. **12**(5), 35–41 (2014)
15. Bigdeli, E., Mohammadi, M., Raahemi, B., Matwin, S.: Incremental anomaly detection using two-layer cluster-based structure. Inf. Sci. **429**, 315–331 (2018)
16. Boutaba, R., et al.: A comprehensive survey on machine learning for networking: evolution, applications and research opportunities. J. Internet Serv. Appl. **9**(1), 1–99 (2018). https://doi.org/10.1186/s13174-018-0087-2
17. Bridges, R.A., Glass-Vanderlan, T.R., Iannacone, M.D., Vincent, M.S., Chen, Q.: A survey of intrusion detection systems leveraging host data. ACM Comput. Surv. (CSUR) **52**(6), 1–35 (2019)
18. Buczak, A.L., Guven, E.: A survey of data mining and machine learning methods for cyber security intrusion detection. IEEE Commun. Surv. Tutor. **18**(2), 1153–1176 (2015)
19. Casas, P., Soro, F., Vanerio, J., Settanni, G., D'Alconzo, A.: Network security and anomaly detection with Big-DAMA, a big data analytics framework. In: 2017

IEEE 6th International Conference on Cloud Networking (CloudNet), pp. 1–7. IEEE (2017)

20. Chandola, V., Banerjee, A., Kumar, V.: Anomaly detection: a survey. ACM Comput. Surv. (CSUR) **41**(3), 1–58 (2009)

21. Claise, B., Sadasivan, G., Valluri, V., Djernaes, M.: Cisco systems netflow services export version 9 (2004)

22. Clausen, H., Aspinall, D.: Examining traffic microstructures to improve model development. In: 2021 IEEE Security and Privacy Workshops (SPW), pp. 19–24. IEEE (2021)

23. Clausen, H., Flood, R., Aspinall, D.: Controlling network traffic microstructures for machine-learning model probing. In: Garcia-Alfaro, J., Li, S., Poovendran, R., Debar, H., Yung, M. (eds.) SecureComm 2021. LNICST, vol. 398, pp. 456–475. Springer, Cham (2021). https://doi.org/10.1007/978-3-030-90019-9_23

24. Corona, I., Giacinto, G., Roli, F.: Adversarial attacks against intrusion detection systems: taxonomy, solutions and open issues. Inf. Sci. **239**, 201–225 (2013)

25. Cretu, G.F., Stavrou, A., Locasto, M.E., Stolfo, S.J., Keromytis, A.D.: Casting out demons: sanitizing training data for anomaly sensors. In: 2008 IEEE Symposium on Security and Privacy (SP 2008), pp. 81–95. IEEE (2008)

26. Davis, J.J., Clark, A.J.: Data preprocessing for anomaly based network intrusion detection: a review. Comput. Secur. **30**(6–7), 353–375 (2011)

27. Dong, Y., et al.: An adaptive system for detecting malicious queries in web attacks. Sci. China Inf. Sci. **61**(3), 1–16 (2018). https://doi.org/10.1007/s11432-017-9288-4

28. Dromard, J., Roudière, G., Owezarski, P.: Online and scalable unsupervised network anomaly detection method. IEEE Trans. Netw. Serv. Manag. **14**(1), 34–47 (2016)

29. Du, M., Li, F., Zheng, G., Srikumar, V.: DeepLog: anomaly detection and diagnosis from system logs through deep learning. In: Proceedings of the 2017 ACM SIGSAC Conference on Computer and Communications Security, pp. 1285–1298 (2017)

30. Durumeric, Z., Bailey, M., Halderman, J.A.: An internet-wide view of internet-wide scanning. In: 23rd USENIX Security Symposium (USENIX Security 2014), pp. 65–78 (2014)

31. Engelen, G., Rimmer, V., Joosen, W.: Troubleshooting an intrusion detection dataset: the cicids2017 case study. In: 2021 IEEE Security and Privacy Workshops (SPW), pp. 7–12 (2021)

32. Erfani, S.M., Rajasegarar, S., Karunasekera, S., Leckie, C.: High-dimensional and large-scale anomaly detection using a linear one-class SVM with deep learning. Pattern Recogn. **58**, 121–134 (2016)

33. Feng, W., Zhang, Q., Hu, G., Huang, J.X.: Mining network data for intrusion detection through combining SVMs with ant colony networks. Futur. Gener. Comput. Syst. **37**, 127–140 (2014)

34. Fernandes, G., Rodrigues, J.J.P.C., Carvalho, L.F., Al-Muhtadi, J.F., Proença, M.L.: A comprehensive survey on network anomaly detection. Telecommun. Syst. **70**(3), 447–489 (2018). https://doi.org/10.1007/s11235-018-0475-8

35. Fernandes, G., Jr., Carvalho, L.F., Rodrigues, J.J., Proença, M.L., Jr.: Network anomaly detection using IP flows with principal component analysis and ant colony optimization. J. Netw. Comput. Appl. **64**, 1–11 (2016)

36. Fernandes, G., Jr., Rodrigues, J.J., Proenca, M.L., Jr.: Autonomous profile-based anomaly detection system using principal component analysis and flow analysis. Appl. Soft Comput. **34**, 513–525 (2015)

37. Fiore, U., Palmieri, F., Castiglione, A., De Santis, A.: Network anomaly detection with the restricted Boltzmann machine. Neurocomputing **122**, 13–23 (2013)
38. Fogla, P., Sharif, M.I., Perdisci, R., Kolesnikov, O.M., Lee, W.: Polymorphic blending attacks. In: USENIX Security Symposium, pp. 241–256 (2006)
39. Fontugne, R., Borgnat, P., Abry, P., Fukuda, K.: MAWILab: combining diverse anomaly detectors for automated anomaly labeling and performance benchmarking. In: ACM CoNEXT 2010, Philadelphia, PA, December 2010
40. Global Mobile Data Traffic Forecast: Cisco visual networking index: Global mobile data traffic forecast update, 2017–2022. Update **2017**, 2022 (2019)
41. Gao, N., Gao, L., Gao, Q., Wang, H.: An intrusion detection model based on deep belief networks. In: 2014 Second International Conference on Advanced Cloud and Big Data, pp. 247–252. IEEE (2014)
42. Garcia-Teodoro, P., Diaz-Verdejo, J., Maciá-Fernández, G., Vázquez, E.: Anomaly-based network intrusion detection: techniques, systems and challenges. Comput. Secur. **28**(1–2), 18–28 (2009)
43. Gates, C., Taylor, C.: Challenging the anomaly detection paradigm: a provocative discussion. In: Proceedings of the 2006 Workshop on New Security Paradigms, pp. 21–29 (2006)
44. Grill, M., Pevný, T.: Learning combination of anomaly detectors for security domain. Comput. Netw. **107**, 55–63 (2016)
45. Grill, M., Pevný, T., Rehak, M.: Reducing false positives of network anomaly detection by local adaptive multivariate smoothing. J. Comput. Syst. Sci. **83**(1), 43–57 (2017)
46. Guo, C., Ping, Y., Liu, N., Luo, S.S.: A two-level hybrid approach for intrusion detection. Neurocomputing **214**, 391–400 (2016)
47. Guo, C., Zhou, Y.J., Ping, Y., Luo, S.S., Lai, Y.P., Zhang, Z.K.: Efficient intrusion detection using representative instances. Comput. Secur. **39**, 255–267 (2013)
48. Habeeb, R.A.A., Nasaruddin, F., Gani, A., Hashem, I.A.T., Ahmed, E., Imran, M.: Real-time big data processing for anomaly detection: a survey. Int. J. Inf. Manag. **45**, 289–307 (2019)
49. Hoplaros, D., Tari, Z., Khalil, I.: Data summarization for network traffic monitoring. J. Netw. Comput. Appl. **37**, 194–205 (2014)
50. Iglesias, F., Hartl, A., Zseby, T., Zimek, A.: Are network attacks outliers? A study of space representations and unsupervised algorithms. In: Cellier, P., Driessens, K. (eds.) ECML PKDD 2019. CCIS, vol. 1168, pp. 159–175. Springer, Cham (2020). https://doi.org/10.1007/978-3-030-43887-6_13
51. Kantchelian, A., et al.: Approaches to adversarial drift. In: Proceedings of the 2013 ACM Workshop on Artificial Intelligence and Security, pp. 99–110 (2013)
52. Karami, A., Guerrero-Zapata, M.: A fuzzy anomaly detection system based on hybrid PSO-Kmeans algorithm in content-centric networks. Neurocomputing **149**, 1253–1269 (2015)
53. Kayacik, H.G., Zincir-Heywood, A.N.: Mimicry attacks demystified: what can attackers do to evade detection? In: 2008 Sixth Annual Conference on Privacy, Security and Trust, pp. 213–223. IEEE (2008)
54. Kim, G., Lee, S., Kim, S.: A novel hybrid intrusion detection method integrating anomaly detection with misuse detection. Expert Syst. Appl. **41**(4), 1690–1700 (2014)
55. Kindervag, J., et al.: Build security into your network's DNA: the zero trust network architecture. Forrester Research Inc., pp. 1–26 (2010)

56. Kloft, M., Laskov, P.: Online anomaly detection under adversarial impact. In: Proceedings of the Thirteenth International Conference on Artificial Intelligence and Statistics, pp. 405–412 (2010)
57. Lakhina, A., Crovella, M., Diot, C.: Diagnosing network-wide traffic anomalies. ACM SIGCOMM Comput. Commun. Rev. **34**(4), 219–230 (2004)
58. Le, D.C., Zincir-Heywood, A.N., Heywood, M.I.: Data analytics on network traffic flows for botnet behaviour detection. In: 2016 IEEE Symposium Series on Computational Intelligence (SSCI), pp. 1–7. IEEE (2016)
59. Maciá-Fernández, G., Camacho, J., Magán-Carrión, R., García-Teodoro, P., Therón, R.: UGR '16: a new dataset for the evaluation of cyclostationarity-based network IDSs. Comput. Secur. **73**, 411–424 (2018)
60. Malhotra, P., Vig, L., Shroff, G., Agarwal, P.: Long short term memory networks for anomaly detection in time series. In: Proceedings, vol. 89. Presses universitaires de Louvain (2015)
61. Marchetti, M., Pierazzi, F., Colajanni, M., Guido, A.: Analysis of high volumes of network traffic for advanced persistent threat detection. Comput. Netw. **109**, 127–141 (2016)
62. Mardani, M., Mateos, G., Giannakis, G.B.: Dynamic anomalography: tracking network anomalies via sparsity and low rank. IEEE J. Sel. Top. Signal Process. **7**(1), 50–66 (2012)
63. Maxion, R.A., Tan, K.M.: Benchmarking anomaly-based detection systems. In: Proceeding International Conference on Dependable Systems and Networks, DSN 2000, pp. 623–630. IEEE (2000)
64. Mirsky, Y., Doitshman, T., Elovici, Y., Shabtai, A.: Kitsune: an ensemble of autoencoders for online network intrusion detection. arXiv preprint arXiv:1802.09089 (2018)
65. Mirsky, Y., Shabtai, A., Shapira, B., Elovici, Y., Rokach, L.: Anomaly detection for smartphone data streams. Pervasive Mob. Comput. **35**, 83–107 (2017)
66. Mukherjee, B., Heberlein, L.T., Levitt, K.N.: Network intrusion detection. IEEE Netw. **8**(3), 26–41 (1994)
67. Nehinbe, J.O.: A critical evaluation of datasets for investigating IDSs and IPSs researches. In: 2011 IEEE 10th International Conference on Cybernetic Intelligent Systems (CIS), pp. 92–97. IEEE (2011)
68. Nguyen, H.T., Franke, K., Petrovic, S.: Feature extraction methods for intrusion detection systems. In: Threats, Countermeasures, and Advances in Applied Information Security, pp. 23–52. IGI Global (2012)
69. Nguyen, Q.P., Lim, K.W., Divakaran, D.M., Low, K.H., Chan, M.C.: Gee: a gradient-based explainable variational autoencoder for network anomaly detection. In: 2019 IEEE Conference on Communications and Network Security (CNS), pp. 91–99. IEEE (2019)
70. Ning, J., Poh, G.S., Loh, J.C., Chia, J., Chang, E.C.: PrivDPI: privacy-preserving encrypted traffic inspection with reusable obfuscated rules. In: Proceedings of the 2019 ACM SIGSAC Conference on Computer and Communications Security, pp. 1657–1670 (2019)
71. van Oorschot, P.C.: Intrusion detection and network-based attacks. In: van Oorschot, P.C. (ed.) Computer Security and the Internet. ISC, pp. 309–338. Springer, Cham (2021). https://doi.org/10.1007/978-3-030-83411-1_11
72. Pascoal, C., De Oliveira, M.R., Valadas, R., Filzmoser, P., Salvador, P., Pacheco, A.: Robust feature selection and robust PCA for internet traffic anomaly detection. In: 2012 Proceedings IEEE Infocom, pp. 1755–1763. IEEE (2012)

73. Paxson, V.: Bro: a system for detecting network intruders in real-time. Comput. Netw. **31**(23–24), 2435–2463 (1999)
74. Quionero-Candela, J., Sugiyama, M., Schwaighofer, A., Lawrence, N.D.: Dataset Shift in Machine Learning. The MIT Press, Cambridge (2009)
75. Ramamoorthi, A., Subbulakshmi, T., Shalinie, S.M.: Real time detection and classification of DDoS attacks using enhanced SVM with string kernels. In: 2011 International Conference on Recent Trends in Information Technology (ICRTIT), pp. 91–96. IEEE (2011)
76. Rassam, M.A., Maarof, M.A., Zainal, A.: Adaptive and online data anomaly detection for wireless sensor systems. Knowl.-Based Syst. **60**, 44–57 (2014)
77. Raza, H., Prasad, G., Li, Y.: EWMA model based shift-detection methods for detecting covariate shifts in non-stationary environments. Pattern Recogn. **48**(3), 659–669 (2015)
78. Ring, M., Wunderlich, S., Scheuring, D., Landes, D., Hotho, A.: A survey of network-based intrusion detection data sets. Comput. Secur. **86**, 147–167 (2019)
79. Ringberg, H., Soule, A., Rexford, J., Diot, C.: Sensitivity of PCA for traffic anomaly detection. In: Proceedings of the 2007 ACM SIGMETRICS International Conference on Measurement and Modeling of Computer Systems, pp. 109–120 (2007)
80. Roesch, M., et al.: Snort: lightweight intrusion detection for networks. In: Lisa, vol. 99, pp. 229–238 (1999)
81. Sakib, M.N., Huang, C.T.: Using anomaly detection based techniques to detect http-based botnet c&c traffic. In: 2016 IEEE International Conference on Communications (ICC), pp. 1–6. IEEE (2016)
82. Sharafaldin, I., Gharib, A., Lashkari, A.H., Ghorbani, A.A.: Towards a reliable intrusion detection benchmark dataset. Softw. Netw. **2018**(1), 177–200 (2018)
83. Sharafaldin, I., Lashkari, A.H., Ghorbani, A.A.: Toward generating a new intrusion detection dataset and intrusion traffic characterization. In: ICISSP, pp. 108–116 (2018)
84. Sherry, J., Lan, C., Popa, R.A., Ratnasamy, S.: BlindBox: deep packet inspection over encrypted traffic. In: Proceedings of the 2015 ACM Conference on Special Interest Group on Data Communication, pp. 213–226 (2015)
85. Shiravi, A., Shiravi, H., Tavallaee, M., Ghorbani, A.A.: Toward developing a systematic approach to generate benchmark datasets for intrusion detection. Comput. Secur. **31**(3), 357–374 (2012)
86. Shone, N., Ngoc, T.N., Phai, V.D., Shi, Q.: A deep learning approach to network intrusion detection. IEEE Trans. Emerg. Top. Comput. Intell. **2**(1), 41–50 (2018)
87. Shvachko, K., Kuang, H., Radia, S., Chansler, R.: The Hadoop distributed file system. In: 2010 IEEE 26th Symposium on Mass Storage Systems and Technologies (MSST), pp. 1–10. IEEE (2010)
88. Sommer, R., Paxson, V.: Outside the closed world: on using machine learning for network intrusion detection. In: 2010 IEEE Symposium on Security and Privacy, pp. 305–316. IEEE (2010)
89. Sperotto, A., Mandjes, M., Sadre, R., de Boer, P.T., Pras, A.: Autonomic parameter tuning of anomaly-based IDSs: an SSH case study. IEEE Trans. Netw. Serv. Manag. **9**(2), 128–141 (2012)
90. Sperotto, A., Schaffrath, G., Sadre, R., Morariu, C., Pras, A., Stiller, B.: An overview of IP flow-based intrusion detection. IEEE Commun. Surv. Tutor. **12**(3), 343–356 (2010)
91. Staniford, S., Hoagland, J.A., McAlerney, J.M.: Practical automated detection of stealthy portscans. J. Comput. Secur. **10**(1–2), 105–136 (2002)

92. Su, M.Y.: Real-time anomaly detection systems for denial-of-service attacks by weighted k-nearest-neighbor classifiers. Expert Syst. Appl. **38**(4), 3492–3498 (2011)
93. Suthaharan, S.: Big data classification: problems and challenges in network intrusion prediction with machine learning. ACM SIGMETRICS Perform. Eval. Rev. **41**(4), 70–73 (2014)
94. Swarnkar, M., Hubballi, N.: OCPAD: one class Naive Bayes classifier for payload based anomaly detection. Expert Syst. Appl. **64**, 330–339 (2016)
95. Szmit, M., Szmit, A.: Usage of modified holt-winters method in the anomaly detection of network traffic: case studies. J. Comput. Netw. Commun. **2012**, 1–5 (2012). Article ID: 192913
96. Tavallaee, M., Stakhanova, N., Ghorbani, A.A.: Toward credible evaluation of anomaly-based intrusion-detection methods. IEEE Trans. Syst. Man Cybern. Part C (Appl. Rev.) **40**(5), 516–524 (2010)
97. Thomas, C.: Improving intrusion detection for imbalanced network traffic. Secur. Commun. Netw. **6**(3), 309–324 (2013)
98. Varadarajan, G.K., Santander Peláez, M.: Web application attack analysis using bro IDs. SANS Institute **90**, 1–22 (2012)
99. Vasilomanolakis, E., Karuppayah, S., Mühlhäuser, M., Fischer, M.: Taxonomy and survey of collaborative intrusion detection. ACM Comput. Surv. (CSUR) **47**(4), 1–33 (2015)
100. Velarde-Alvarado, P., Vargas-Rosales, C., Martinez-Pelaez, R., Toral-Cruz, H., Martinez-Herrera, A.F.: An unsupervised approach for traffic trace sanitization based on the entropy spaces. Telecommun. Syst. **61**(3), 609–626 (2015). https://doi.org/10.1007/s11235-015-0017-6
101. Viegas, E.K., Santin, A.O., Oliveira, L.S.: Toward a reliable anomaly-based intrusion detection in real-world environments. Comput. Netw. **127**, 200–216 (2017)
102. Wang, W., Guyet, T., Quiniou, R., Cordier, M.O., Masseglia, F., Zhang, X.: Autonomic intrusion detection: adaptively detecting anomalies over unlabeled audit data streams in computer networks. Knowl.-Based Syst. **70**, 103–117 (2014)
103. Xu, K., Zhang, Z.L., Bhattacharyya, S.: Profiling internet backbone traffic: behavior models and applications. ACM SIGCOMM Comput. Commun. Rev. **35**(4), 169–180 (2005)
104. Yue, W.T., Çakanyıldırım, M.: A cost-based analysis of intrusion detection system configuration under active or passive response. Decis. Support Syst. **50**(1), 21–31 (2010)
105. Zarpelão, B.B., Miani, R.S., Kawakani, C.T., de Alvarenga, S.C.: A survey of intrusion detection in internet of things. J. Netw. Comput. Appl. **84**, 25–37 (2017)
106. Zhang, J., Li, H., Gao, Q., Wang, H., Luo, Y.: Detecting anomalies from big network traffic data using an adaptive detection approach. Inf. Sci. **318**, 91–110 (2015)

Security of AI

Adversarial Machine Learning

Carlos Javier Hernández-Castro[1], Zhuoran Liu[2], Alex Serban[2],
Ilias Tsingenopoulos[3]([✉]), and Wouter Joosen[3]

[1] Complutense University, Madrid, Spain
[2] Radboud University, Nijmegen, The Netherlands
[3] imec-Distrinet, KU Leuven, Leuven, Belgium
ilias.tsingenopoulos@cs.kuleuven.be

Abstract. Recent innovations in machine learning enjoy a remarkable
rate of adoption across a broad spectrum of applications, including
cyber-security. While previous chapters study the application of machine
learning solutions to cyber-security, in this chapter we present adversarial machine learning: a field of study concerned with the security of
machine learning algorithms when faced with attackers. Likewise, adversarial machine learning enjoys remarkable interest from the community,
with a large body of works that either propose attacks against machine
learning algorithms, or defenses against adversarial attacks. In particular, adversarial attacks have been mounted in almost all applications
of machine learning. Here, we aim to systematize adversarial machine
learning, with a pragmatic focus on common computer security applications. Without assuming a strong background in machine learning, we
also introduce the basic building blocks and fundamental properties of
adversarial machine learning. This study is therefore accessible both to
a security audience without in-depth knowledge of machine learning and
to a machine learning audience.

1 Introduction

While previous chapters discuss the applications of machine learning (ML) to
security, it is also compelling to reflect on the vulnerabilities of ML algorithms.
In this chapter, we provide a broad introduction to adversarial ML – a field of
study concerned with failure modes of ML algorithms when faced with adversarial attackers. In particular, we focus on adversarial ML for security-oriented
practical cases, where the failure of ML algorithms to satisfy the intended functionality represents a security vulnerability. In such cases a well-thought and
practical threat model is essential. This contrasts the recent increase in popularity of adversarial ML for deep learning (DL), where the focus is on the algorithmic robustness of computer vision and natural language processing. While
adversarial ML may pose security risks for some applications of computer vision,

C. J. Hernández-Castro, Z. Liu, A. Serban and I. Tsingenopoulos—Equal contributions,
authors ordered alphabetically.

© Springer Nature Switzerland AG 2022
L. Batina et al. (Eds.): Security and Artificial Intelligence, LNCS 13049, pp. 287–312, 2022.
https://doi.org/10.1007/978-3-030-98795-4_12

e.g., autonomous driving, this does not entail that computer vision is a powerful attack vector for malicious attackers to exploit.

These contrasting views emerge due to two causes. First, the lack of thorough threat models leads to the false impression that some vulnerabilities of ML algorithms, such as the sensitivity to small perturbations in the input space, have immediate security consequences [41]. Second, the economics of creating defenses against adversarial attacks are often disregarded. The importance of protecting against adversarial threats is evident in ML-based security applications, for instance in malware detection. At the same time, solving vulnerabilities for some seemingly non-critical applications, like object detection in cloud image storage, can also prove crucial under a convincing threat model.

In this chapter, we take a practical approach and present the most important developments in applications of ML. Our presentation is focused on understanding the basic building blocks of adversarial ML and on showcasing different use cases where adversarial ML raises security concerns. The rest of this chapter is organized as follows. We begin with background information on ML and introduce adversarial ML from a historical perspective (Sect. 2). Next we discuss the elements for threat modeling (Sect. 3) and use them to present white-box attacks (Sect. 4) and black-box attacks (Sect. 5). Afterwards, we introduce defenses and a protocol for evaluating adversarial defenses (Sect. 6). We continue with a presentation of adversarial ML in different domains (Sect. 7) and concluding remarks (Sect. 8).

2   Background

Whenever not mentioned otherwise, we use the task of supervised classification to support our presentation. Mitchell describes the general task of learning from experience w.r.t to a task and a performance measure if the performance on the task increases with experience [86]. Given a set of training examples defined on an input space $\mathcal{X}$ and corresponding labels defined on an output space $\mathcal{Y}$, sampled from a fixed probability distribution over the space $\mathcal{Z} = \mathcal{X} \times \mathcal{Y}$, an algorithm seeks to uncover a mapping $f : \mathcal{X} \to \mathcal{Y}$ which maximizes the performance measure (i.e., minimizes the error rate). The error rate is measured by a loss function $l : \mathcal{Y} \times \mathcal{Y} \to \mathbb{R}$ which is positive whenever there is an error and zero otherwise. During learning, an algorithm selects a function f^* from the space $\mathcal{F}$ (also called the hypothesis space) such that the expected loss $r(f) = \mathbb{E}_{(x,y\sim\mathcal{D})}[l(f(x,\theta),y)]$ is minimal: $f^* = \arg\min_{f\in\mathcal{F}} r(f)$, where θ are the parameters of f. However, at training time the full distribution $\mathcal{P}$ of the data is unknown. Instead, only a set of samples drawn from $\mathcal{P}$, $\mathcal{D} = \{(x_i, y_i)\}_{i=1}^n$ is available for training. Therefore, the empirical loss is used to approximate the expected loss:

$$\hat{f} = \arg\min_{f\in\mathcal{F}} \quad \mathbb{E}_{(x,y)\sim\mathcal{D}}[l(f(x,\theta),y)], \tag{1}$$

where $f(x,\theta)$ can be any mapping from $\mathcal{X}$ to $\mathcal{Y}$ such as a neural network or a linear function. The choice of $\mathcal{F}$ represents a bias induced by the algorithm developers and can lead to over-fitting when $\mathcal{F}$ is too expressive or under-fitting when $\mathcal{F}$ is not expressive enough.

Fundamental Assumptions of ML. Two fundamental assumptions underpin the ML framework introduced above. Firstly, the data used both at training and test time is sampled identically from the same probability distribution P, and the samples are mutually independent (also called the i.i.d assumption). Secondly, since the input space X can be very large (in most applications of ML the input is high-dimensional), ML algorithms assume that most of this space consists of invalid inputs and that interesting inputs (together with all their variations) lie in a collection of lower dimensional manifolds.

Both assumptions have critical consequences for the security of ML algorithms because once any of the assumptions is broken, the algorithms become vulnerable. For example, if a malicious attacker uses at test time an input sampled from another distribution than P, the algorithm is expected to fail because it was not designed to work with data outside P. Similarly, if the test inputs lie off the training data manifold, the algorithms are unlikely to perform well.

2.1 Related Work

Research in adversarial ML began around 2004, when Dalvi et al. [28], followed by Lowd and Meek [82] targeted linear models for spam detection, and managed to construct viable adversarial attacks. Later on, Barreno et al. [9] introduced a taxonomy for attacks and defenses in adversarial settings, which was refined in [8]. This early taxonomy defined common ML threat models, and was comprehensive enough to encompass modern attacks. In particular, Barreno et al. made a clear distinction between attacks at *training time* – which assume attackers can manipulate the training data – and attacks at *test time* – which assume attackers can only query already trained models.

This classification shaped future work, where a large body of publications discussed adversarial attacks against ML models at both training [14,97] and test time [43,82] while defense mechanisms were devised against such attacks [18,69]. In parallel to developing attacks and defenses, several works proposed methods to evaluate the security of ML models against adversarial attacks [8,13].

With the burgeoning field of DL, a renewed wave of interest in adversarial ML is observed. The seminal work that sparked this interest was a publication for test time attacks in DL by Szegedy et al. [114]. The discovery that deep neural networks (DNNs) are susceptible to small perturbations in the input space – also called adversarial examples – triggered an impressive body of publications that analyze the phenomenon from different angles, with a focus on computer vision algorithms. Several overviews and taxonomies on this topic can be found in the works of [2,76,103,112]. While many of these publications claim security consequences of adversarial examples and hypothesize that deployment of ML algorithms may be delayed until these vulnerabilities are solved, other publications show these claims are spurious as they lack explicit security threats [41]. Biggio and Roli [15] draw a parallel between the evolution of adversarial ML and the rise of DL. They observe that publications which focus on DL seem unaware of early research in adversarial ML and miss important details for security, especially regarding threat modeling.

More recently, the interest on adversarial ML has overflowed to other types of attacks, such as train time attacks [56], model inversion [66] or model extraction [117]. These directions are meant to complement the research in adversarial examples and explore the full spectrum of adversarial ML.

Besides the works presented above, several publications present broad overviews of adversarial ML. The book by Joseph et al. [68] offers a comprehensive introduction to the field, tackling multiple topics of interest. Similarly, Vorobeychik and Kantarcioglu [119] published a book to introduce adversarial ML, while literature reviews [23,103] with slightly different focuses have been published.

3   Threat Modeling and Taxonomy of Adversarial Machine Learning

Before describing adversarial attacks and defenses, we introduce the threat modeling elements which can be used to characterize them. For any discussion about security it is mandatory to have a description of a threat model, also called an attack model. The attack model describes what an attacker aims to achieve (the attacker's goal) together with a description of the attacker's knowledge and capability. These form a description of the resources needed to mount the attack and achieve the goals.

Similarly, when designing a defense, the defenders choose a model in which the defense works. This model involves the critical assumptions a defense makes, the processing step where the defense is applied, the resources needed to develop and deploy it and the resources needed to break or bypass it. The latter can be either an attempt to break the defense, or to disprove the claims necessary to develop it and although important, it is often overlooked [21,116].

3.1   Attacks

We characterize adversarial attacks using three dimensions corresponding both to early taxonomies [8] and with recent updates [15,68,92]: (1) the attacker's influence, (2) the attacker's goal or specificity and (3) the attacker's knowledge of the model under attack. A fourth dimension concerns the security or privacy violation that can map to the confidentiality, integrity, availability (CIA) triad [68]. However, in the chapter we obviate its use as it is not a prevailing approach in the related work.

Based on the assets influenced during the attack, attacks are classified in:

- *Train time attacks* – also called causative or training *data poisoning* attacks [15,68]; these attacks manipulate the *training data* and influence the training process.
- *Test time attacks* – also called inference or exploratory attacks [68]; these attacks manipulate only the data used at *test time* and do not alter the training process.

Formally, assuming the available data set $\mathcal{D}$ for learning is divided in a training $\mathcal{D}_{train}$ and a testing $\mathcal{D}_{test}$ data set, the train time attacks assume knowledge of

$\mathcal{D}_{train}$ and the capacity to alter or corrupt inputs or labels in order to bias the outcome of $f(\boldsymbol{\theta})$. In classification, we can picture a scenario in which a fraction of $\mathcal{D}_{train}$ is corrupted such that any examples from class c_1 will be classified as c_2. Similarly, test time attacks presume access only to $\mathcal{D}_{test}$. This type of attacks can only be mounted after training and assumes that test examples can be altered in order to achieve the attacker's goals.

Further on, based on the attacker's goals, attacks are classified in:

- *Targeted attacks* – focus on *one input*.
- *Untargeted attacks* – also called indiscriminate attacks, focus on a *set of inputs*.

In the supervised classification scenario introduced in Sect. 2, targeted attacks can also be interpreted as inducing a misclassification of an example towards a *specific class*. Conversely, untargeted attacks can be interpreted as inducing a *random* misclassification. Formally, given a sample $\boldsymbol{x}$, targeted attacks aim to find a perturbation η, $\boldsymbol{x}' = \boldsymbol{x} + \eta$ such that $f(\boldsymbol{x}') = \hat{y}$ where $\hat{y} \neq y$ is a label selected by the attacker and y is the true label. Similarly, in untargeted attacks $\hat{y}$ is any label not equal with y: $f(\boldsymbol{x}') = \hat{y}, \forall \hat{y} \neq y$.

Based on the attacker's knowledge, attacks are classified in:

- *White-box attacks* – attackers have complete knowledge of the model under attack, the training and the test data and can completely replicate the model.
- *Black-box attacks* – attackers do not have any knowledge of the model under attack, but can query it as an oracle.

Formally, white-box attacks presume the attacker has full access to $\mathcal{D}$ and $f(\boldsymbol{\theta})$, while black-box attacks only have access to $\boldsymbol{x}'$ and y, with $y = f(\boldsymbol{x}', \boldsymbol{\theta})$. An illustration of white-box and black-box attacks is provided in Fig. 1.

Biggio and Roli [15] also consider a gray box scenario in which the attacker has partial knowledge about the model under attack. However, this attack type is an instance of the black-box attack where the attacker has some restrictions [21].

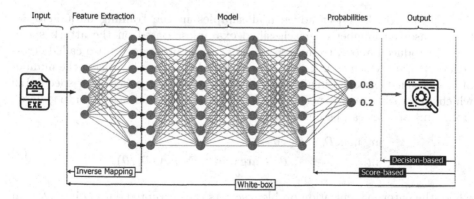

Fig. 1. The components of an abstract malware detection model, that form a pipeline from sample input to output. Below the model are the various levels of access an adversary can have.

3.2   Defenses

Defenders can *react* and improve the system in response to new attacks or act in advance and *proactively* design the ML algorithms with security in mind. This corresponds to two types of defenses, namely *reactive* and *proactive* [14,76].

Moreover, defenses can be classified based on the step of the processing pipeline in which they are deployed, in [103]:

- *Guards* – guards act as a preprocessing step before malicious inputs reach a ML models. These methods try to detect adversarial inputs or apply input transformations to reduce their impact. Formally, guards can be defined as a function $g(\phi)$ that processes the input before the ML model: $f(g(x,\phi),\theta)$. In some cases, $g(\phi)$ can choose to discard the input altogether.
- *Defenses by design* – also called model hardening. These defenses consist of new models, new regularization techniques or new training procedures that alleviate the impact of adversarial inputs.
- *Certified defenses* – defenses which use formal methods to certify that models cannot be attacked within some bounds. Certified defenses can only provide certificates for the training data set (and not for the testing data set).

4   White-Box Attacks

Although the scenario in which attackers have complete knowledge of the model under attack is not probable in security sensitive contexts, understanding white-box attacks can help in many ways. For example, white-box attacks enhance the algorithms' designers power to evaluate and understand the models developed [19]. Moreover, white-box attacks can be used to create powerful defenses [84]. In this section we present the basics of white-box attacks, using the assets influenced during the attack, introduced in Sect. 3.

4.1   Train Time White-Box Attacks

Train time attacks inject adversarial samples in the training data in order to increase the number of misclassified examples. Based on the attack specificity introduced above, train time attacks can be untargeted (also called error-generic [15]) in which an attacker cause a denial of service by raising the number of misclassified examples in all classes, and targeted (also called error-specific) in which an attacker causes specific misclassifications, e.g., for one class. In general, train time attacks can be defined as:

$$
\begin{aligned}
&\arg\max \mathcal{D}_c \quad f'(\cdot,\theta^*) \\
&s.t. \qquad\qquad \theta^* \in \arg\min_{\theta} \; l(\mathcal{D}_{\text{train}} \cup \mathcal{D}_c, \theta),
\end{aligned}
\tag{2}
$$

where the outer maximization problem selects the corrupted data points $\mathcal{D}_c$ that will lead to the best outcome, based on an attacker's defined $f'(\cdot)$. The inner minimization problem retrains the ML model with these data points [67]. In all cases, attackers are interested in minimizing the number of samples $\mathcal{D}_c$ that have to be corrupted in order to achieve their goals.

Particularly interesting for train time attacks is the scenarios of online learning, where algorithms learn on the fly, as new data becomes available. A landmark example of train time attacks is the Tay Twitter bot launched by Microsoft, which quickly learned to post offensive Tweets, looking at other comments.

4.2   Test Time White-Box Attacks

At test time, an attacker can change a sample in order to induce a desired behavior for the model under attack. In classification, the problem can be framed as finding a sample x' derived from a natural input x such that $f(x', \theta) = \hat{y}$, where $\hat{y}$ can be any label different than the original label y in the untargeted scenario or a specific label in the targeted scenario.

Finding x' can be framed as an optimization problem where we seek to discover the minimum change $\eta = d(x' - x)$ s.t. $\hat{y} \neq y$:

$$
\begin{aligned}
\min. \quad & d(x' - x), \\
\text{s.t.} \quad & f(x', \theta) = \hat{y},
\end{aligned}
\tag{3}
$$

where $d(\cdot)$ is a distance function defined on the (metric) input space $\mathcal{X}$. The choice of $d(\cdot)$ is context dependent and influences x'. For example, in object recognition or image classification $d(\cdot)$ is commonly a p-norm, with $p \in \{1, 2, \infty\}$. Research on human visual perception-aware adversarial images also consider geometric transformation [31,123], textural-aware p-norm [27,83,131] color transformation [10,57,73,105,132], and existing perceptual metrics [96,121,133]. Choosing different values for p influences the size of the perturbation η. In other contexts, such as malware detection, $d(\cdot)$ can be the number of bits that can be flipped s.t. the binary still compiles. Similarly, for spam detection $d(\cdot)$ can be the number of characters that have to be changed in a document in order to bypass a detector.

With full knowledge of the parameters θ, Eq. 3 can be solved with algorithms like L-BFGS [114] or genetic algorithms [4]. However, in contexts where it is needed to solve Eq. 3 fast, attackers cannot rely on classical solvers. For example, if we wish to strengthen the model under attack using adversarial samples in training, a fast method to generate adversarial examples is needed. Conversely, if one sample suffices for the attacker – think of malware detection, where one sample that passes a detector is sufficient for a successful attack – attackers can rely on classical solvers.

In order to overcome the computational disadvantage of classical solvers, researchers have developed fast methods to generate adversarial examples. The most popular attack, called FGSM [46] takes one step towards maximizing the loss function (assuming the loss is differentiable): $\eta = \epsilon \text{sign} \left(\nabla_x l(f(x, \theta), y) \right)$, which corresponds to a step towards the sign of the gradient. In order to strengthen this attack, it can be applied iteratively, and the outcome can be projected on the space defined by $d(\cdot)$ [84]. This iterative attack called projected gradient descent (PGD) is one of the most popular, that also stood the test of time [84].

Other types of attacks mounted at test time use modified samples in order to check if an input was used during training, i.e., model inversion [66] or for trying to reverse engineer the model under attack, i.e., model extraction [117]. In all cases the problem can be framed as an optimization problem or as solving a system of equations [117].

5   Black-Box Attacks

In comparison to white-box attacks, black-box attacks are more likely in security-critical applications. For example, a cloud ML service, an online malware analysis tool, a network intrusion detection system, or a CAPTCHA test are scenarios in which an attacker can only observe the decisions of a model.

Black-box attacks against ML models are delineated by two main assumptions: (1) queries to the model under attack can be submitted consistently and (2) the model responds with its decisions, without any further access to the specifics behind it. Services like Google Cloud Vision AI[1] or VirusTotal[2], which offer image classification and malware detection APIs respectively, have been shown to be susceptible to black-box attacks [6,64]. Even in such restricted environments, the mere decisions that a model makes are sufficient to mount adversarial attacks.

Based on the underlying method, the query requirements, and the underlying assumptions, we can classify black-box attacks in:

- *Score-based Attacks* – use gradient-free optimization methods to approximate the gradient of a black-box loss function and generate adversarial examples.
- *Transfer-based Attacks* – use a substitute model, trained by selectively querying the black-box model. Afterwards the substitute model is used to generate adversarial examples in a white-box setting.
- *Decision-based (also called Boundary) Attacks* – the attacks use only the final, hard-label decision of the model.

5.1   Score-Based Attacks

A black-box ML model means that attackers do not have access to the analytical expression that defines it. Therefore, score-based attacks use the class probabilities that a model outputs, as a way to estimate the gradient of its loss function. One of the first papers to propose gradient estimation as a way to attack ML models was by Chen et al. [25], where they approximate the gradient using the finite differences method $df/dx \approx (f_2 - f_1)/\Delta x$. However, for a complex model, e.g., Inception-v3 for object classification, approximating the gradient of only

---

[1]   https://cloud.google.com/vision.
[2]   https://www.virustotal.com/gui/home/upload.

one sample x with the finite differences method requires more than 500,000 queries.

While interesting in nature, this approach has limited practical implications because it faces scalability issues. Subsequent publications [64,65] expand on it, using bayesian optimization or natural evolution strategies to reduce the number of queries.

The class probabilities generated by the black-box model can also be used differently. Alzantot et al. [5] use this score as the degree of fitness of the adversarial perturbations. The candidate solutions are constructed around an initial input example x by applying independent and uniformly distributed random noise to every dimension of the input vector. They evaluate the fitness of a generation's members to select parents, then crossover and mutation are performed to form the next generation until a successful adversarial example is discovered.

Score-based attacks can have a high success rate because the gradient estimation is calculated and refined directly on the underlying black-box function (the model under attack), and they can function irrespective to the model family being attacked. At the same time they have a high query budget and they construct single-use, conditional on a specific sample perturbations.

5.2 Transfer-Based Attacks

Transfer-based attacks stem from the observation that adversarial examples crafted on one model can also transfer to other models, regardless on the algorithms used [114]. These attacks restrict or completely eschew the number of queries submitted to the model under attack. In order to mount transfer-based attacks, an attacker requires information about the data used for training, as their effectiveness relies considerably on the degree of access to the training set. Liu et al. [78] performed a comprehensive evaluation of transfer-based attacks, between and within model families. They showed that transferability is more prominent when three conditions hold: a) examples are transferred between models of the same family, e.g., between convolutional neural networks, b) when the training data are described by the same distribution, c) when the hyperparameters used to train the model are similar or comparable in magnitude. Conceptually it is evident why: the intention is for the substitute model to learn a decision boundary as close to the black-box model as possible.

Another approach in training substitute models for black-box attacks involves generative adversarial networks (GANs). To further increase the utility of queries, Xiao et al. [122] utilize generative models in order to generate perturbations conditional on input. Their pivotal idea is that instead of learning the ground-truth labels the goal of the GAN discriminator is to fit the black-box detector, by replacing the ground-truth labels with the black-box model output. Hu et al. [59] formulate a similar attack methodology against a malware classifier. Moreover, if the adversary's capabilities allow it, and in order for adversarial examples to be more robust and transferable, they can be created against an ensemble of diverse substitute models.

5.3   Decision-Based Attacks

Decision-based attacks rely solely on the final decision of the model, i.e., the class output of a classifier. These attacks can be considered a constrained version of score-based attacks, where the only informative signal is the final output.

The first to propose effective decision-based attacks were Brendel et al. [17], which introduced a novel approach to generate adversarial examples. Instead of starting from the original example, the authors initiate the attack from an example belonging to the target class (i.e. one with a potentially large perturbation) and minimize this perturbation by moving the example closer to ones in the original class. The strength of this approach is that an attacker has access to a continuous and more informative signal while minimizing this distance.

In order to discover better adversarial examples, i.e., with minimal perturbation, decision-based attacks have to look for perturbation directions that take a step away from the decision boundary. The overall query efficiency depends significantly on the proposed distribution of directions to explore. In Brunner et al. [20] the number of queries needed is reduced through biased sampling of this distribution, while Chen et al. [24] have further improved the efficiency by replacing this exploratory step with an improved estimation of the gradient direction. Vulnerability to decision-based attacks is essential to evaluate for two key reasons: (1) conceptually they correspond to many realistic use-cases, where the model exposes an interface and is attacked in real time (rather than pre-calculating a perturbation on a substitute model), and (2) they can be more efficient compared to attacks with access to more information, and this efficiency is steadily improving. To better visualize the various threat models, an abstract malware detection model is depicted in Fig. 1.

6   Defenses

Although a plethora of defenses against adversarial attacks have been proposed over time, the landscape of *effective* adversarial defenses remains scarce. Particularly because the correct evaluation of adversarial defenses proves difficult [21,116]. For example, many defenses against test time attacks induce a phenomenon called "gradient masking" [7], in which the gradient used by attackers to generate adversarial examples is obscured. Such defenses provide a misleading sense of security, while in fact the models remain vulnerable to other types of attacks that do not use gradients.

Similarly, many defenses which propose to use distinct training objectives in order to achieve robustness (defenses by design, Sect. 3) induce a comparable phenomenon [116]. However, instead of hiding the gradient information these defenses are evaluated against classical attacks (e.g., PGD) that are not catered to accommodate the new loss functions. This evaluation can lead to illusive results, showing the models are robust when in fact they are not. Tramer et al. [116] showed recently that many defenses published at top tier conferences in ML suffer from this phenomenon.

Moreover, while appealing because they can give formal guarantees, certified defenses [63] can provide the guarantees only for the training data set. In case the training data is not representative for the data generation distribution, certified defenses will render the models vulnerable to data sampled from the same distribution, but distinct from the training data.

In light of this, we consider it futile to introduce state-of-the art defenses which are not proven to stand the test of time or cannot provide guarantees for test data. Instead, we only briefly discuss some defenses that proved effective over time and comment on a protocol of evaluating defenses in Sect. 6.1.

The most common defense against attacks at training time is to perform outlier detection or input sanitization before training [113]. In this case, the quality of the outlier detection mechanism employed will dictate the strength of the defense.

Conversely, the most common defense against attacks at test time, which is also considered one of the most successful, is adversarial training. This defense adds adversarial examples in the training data set and changes the training objective to: $\tilde{l}(\cdot) = \alpha l(f(\boldsymbol{x}, \boldsymbol{\theta}), y) + (1 - \alpha)l(f(\boldsymbol{x}', \boldsymbol{\theta}), y)$, where α controls the influence of adversarial examples during training. When $\alpha = 0$, training is performed only with adversarial examples. If the method to generate adversarial examples manages to approximate well the space we want to provide robustness to (defined by $d(\cdot)$), adversarial training can, in principle, provide robustness for this space. For example, pairing the PGD attack to approximate the space around an input with adversarial training, is known to be an effective defense. However, since PGD follows an iterative procedure, the training time is substantially increased. Moreover, although effective, adversarial training has not succeeded to fully protect a model in practice. New training procedures partially alleviate some of these issue by accumulating perturbations during training and reducing the number of iterations [104], but most adversarially trained models remain vulnerable to adversarial attacks.

The overall dynamics of defenses change in realistic black-box scenarios, where we consider the black-box model as a deployed interface that accepts queries and responds with decisions. This opens the opportunity for a complementary defense, beyond building a priori more robust models, through observing and adapting the system behavior as the attack unfolds. For example, Chen et al. [26] have proposed a stateful detection methodology for an image classification model. Their approach keeps track of the history of submitted queries in order to detect if a query is part of an attack or benign. Each query attributed to a uniquely identified actor is mapped to a lower dimensional space using an encoder. The encoder is pre-trained to map visually similar queries close to each other, even if adversaries have used transformations like rotation and translation to obfuscate their activity. The lower dimensional mapping contributes also to the efficiency of searching the history of queries per actor and to the scalability of the approach.

6.1   On the Evaluation of Adversarial Defenses

As mentioned above, the evaluation of adversarial defenses is not trivial because the effects of a defense – e.g., if the defense hides some information or actually protects a model – are hard to determine. Therefore, there is no standard way to test adversarial defenses. The general recommendation is to test a defense rigorously, against a wide variety of attacks that can be adapted and catered to specific characteristics of the defense, i.e., to custom loss functions or regularization terms. Until now, the most detailed protocol for evaluating adversarial defenses is the work of Carlini et al. [21]. Moreover, the lessons learned from [7] and [116], which succeeded in breaking a variety of defenses can contribute to strengthen the evaluation protocols.

Similarly, it is recommended to design and think of tests for data out of the training distribution [40] (see Sect. 2) and adapt traditional and practical security techniques such as red teaming [19] in order to constantly evaluate ML models and develop a sense of skepticism about their robustness.

From a theoretical perspective, it is rather unlikely that completely robust ML models can be built in the near future, without trading other resources. For example, in some learning settings, developing robust models requires a trade-off between accuracy and robustness [100], a phenomenon which was also observed empirically in other settings [118]. A way to overcome such trade-offs is to collect more training data. However, the upper bounds on the data set sizes needed to develop robust models are not realistic in practice [100]. We recommend following the standard procedures defined in [21,116] when designing or evaluating ML models in adversarial settings.

7   Domains of Adversarial Machine Learning

Adversarial examples can be built for any applications of ML & DL. However, each application domain has a particular type of input being processed. Initial techniques for creating adversarial examples assumed a continuous domain – even though the input was quantized. Conversely, many practical applications have a discrete input space that has to comply with data formats (e.g., a PDF file, PE executable, etc.). More restrictions on the input data, such that some important characteristic of the input-related semantics are preserved impose new constraints on the methods used to mount adversarial attacks.

For example, in some domains (others than computer vision), the feature extraction is a separate step preceding the input to the model, and it is usually neither invertible nor differentiable (see Fig. 1). As a consequence, inverse-mapping the necessary perturbations from the feature space, that is the representation of an example that a ML model accepts, to the problem space, that is the actual example as it occurs, is a non-trivial process. This process is aggravated further if we consider that despite any adversarial perturbation, the mapping has to guarantee that the semantics of the original unperturbed sample are preserved.

In this section we discuss practical domain where adversarial ML poses security risks, and scenarios in which the two steps mentioned above are separated.

7.1 Malware Detection

The rise of polymorphic malware and its spread meant that manual detection rules (or *signatures*[3]) could not keep up with the number of new malware [72]. Therefore, the detection of malware moved from hand-crafted heuristics to hand-crafted features and ML [102]. This was the case for both static analysis, in which the binary code is examined, and dynamic analysis, in which the code behavior is examined - typically by looking at which OS or API functions it calls, its network behavior, and additional information from the anti-virus clouds.

Malware detection using ML or DL has some particular requirements:

- Interpretability – when a false positive or a false negative occurs, it is desirable to be able to understand whether there is a problem in the model, or the data, making it easier to correct its behavior.
- Low FPR – false positives should be extremely low in order to make the application usable. For this, some companies use a model ensemble that allows them to fix false positives without a whole model retraining [72].
- Dataset size and diversity: when using DL, large data-sets are required. These should include representative malware and benign files, produced with different compilers, libraries, etc.
- Adaptability – ML algorithms typically assume a fixed distribution, or one that changes slightly over time. In the case of malware, algorithms are up against active adversaries that evolve and change their malware to avoid detection. At the same time, companies produce new types and versions of executables that are benign.

Prior to DL, the feature set was always handcrafted, which requires domain expertise. In a more recent example of hand-crafting features, [62] created 114 higher concepts from API call sequences and combined them with their inputs (as tri-grams) to build a malware detector and a malware family classifier. By combining both outputs, they improved the performance of both classifiers. Also for the identification of the malware family other authors proposed a DL solution: using dynamic analysis, they used the sequence of API calls (from a group of 60 selected) of a malware and analyzed them using convolutional and recurrent neural networks [71]. These solutions still relied on hand-crafted features though.

One of the first proposals that did not use hand-crafted features is MalConv, a convolutional neural network proposed by [94] that analyzes executable files in PE format up to several million bytes. It does not rely on any kind of feature engineering. Even so, and just using static analysis, is able to reach state-of-the-art performance or surpass it (depending on the metric).

---

[3] These signatures typically consisted on code fragments, file properties, hashes of the file or fragments, and combinations of these.

Kolosnjaji et al. [70] proposes an attack against MalConv based on appending bytes, calculated using gradient descend (similar to the FGSM attack described in Sect. 4), with a success rate of 60%. In order to protect against these attacks, Al-Dujail et al. [3] propose an adversarial training framework samples generated with this method are included in the training data set.

Hu and Tan [58] also focus on the PE format, but on classifiers using RNNs applied to sequences of API calls. The authors train an RNN that approximates the detector, and then train another RNN to generate successful adversarial examples, with non-detection rates over 96%.

A different way to create adversarial malware is by training a Reinforcement learning (RL) agent [6]. This is a fully black-box attack, where only the final decision of the classifier is observed. The authors train the agent by doing functionality-preserving operations directly on the executable, a non-trivial approach to execute and often overlooked in adversarial machine learning research. The agent learns which sequences of actions are likely to result in evading the classifier, by selecting the optimal one from a closed set at each step. Actions that the authors considered was adding a function to the import address table that is never used, manipulating existing section names, creating new (unused) sections, creating a new entry point, manipulating debug info, and so forth.

Note that these works are academic and typically do not fully resemble the more complex DL architectures used in production environments. For example, [72] proposes a model based on similarity hashing, and then fine-grained analysis of each hash bucket depending on its classification difficulty using either an static label or a ML model. They also use an exemplar network [29] to classify targeted attacks, of which there are one or a few examples.

Grosse et al. [47] present one of the earlier works on the creation of adversarial examples for malware detection on Android applications. Using the DREBIN data set, the authors create an state-of-the-art classifier, and later use it to craft adversarial examples. As the input is discrete (a machine code program, or binary vector), so are changes to the input. In order not to alter the malware functionality, changes are restricted to certain instruction additions and changes in the *AndroidManifest.xml* file. Even with these restrictions, the authors achieve a miss-classification rate of over 60% with as little as an average of 14 binary changes to the input. Liu et al. [77] solve the same task using genetic algorithms.

These are not the only binary formats attacked. Other binary formats attacked with adversarial examples are PDF files [12], in order to inject undetected malware through adversarial examples. They also did it by appending new features to the PDF. Their work was followed by Xu et al. [126], who use genetic algorithms to fool two PDF malware detectors (PDFrate and Hidost).

7.2 Authentication

Biometric authentication refers to the process of ensuring that individuals are who they claim to be, by matching their physical or behavioral biometrics to an existing template. As a paradigm it is becoming widespread in various domains like law enforcement, border control, civil identification, but also physical and logical access.

On account of their performance, DNNs have been adopted in face recognition systems. Sharif et al. [107] were the first to attack such a system with a physically realizable adversarial attack, by constraining the adversarial perturbation only within a fixed frame around the eyes. Thus the adversary has the ability to 3D print the perturbation as wearable glasses and subsequently wear them in order to bypass detectors. In an attempt to make the attack general and to take into account potential environment discrepancies like pose or lighting, they follow a universal adversarial approach by computing perturbations on a range of the adversary's images. The attack is highly successful (over 80%) against common face recognition systems.

In [11], Biggio et al. comprehensively explore the attack surface of biometric authentication systems and showcase the vulnerabilities a self-updating system introduces. The physically realizable attacks can potentially exploit this vulnerability, called template poisoning. For a user to get authenticated, the extracted representation of their biometrics is compared to a template database. This comparison results in a confidence score that, if larger than a threshold, authenticates the user and the sample is enrolled in the template database. The authors in [81] show that adversaries can take advantage of this self-updating system and use adversarial glasses not only to authenticate, but through successive attempts to also move the template closer to them so that in the future they can authenticate without any accessories.

This property holds in every other context where systems learn and update themselves in a continuous and online manner. Attacks in these contexts can carry a dual, more insidious nature: able to evade and poison a system at the same time.

7.3   CAPTCHAs

Over twenty years ago CAPTCHAs, or Completely Automated Public Turing test to tell Computers and Humans Apart, were conceived as tests to detect humans from robots online [87]. The principle by which CAPTCHAs function is by presenting problems or puzzles that are difficult for AI but easy for humans to solve.

Unfortunately, CAPTCHAs have been unsuccessful in delivering robust security, either due to shortcomings in design or due to resourceful attacks [35–39, 48–54, 88, 127, 135]. The most pertinent design criteria that such a test should embody are:

- Easy to construct and to grade for a machine.
- Easy for a human to solve.
- Difficult for an algorithm to guess the correct solution, even at very low success rates (<1%).
- Public, so that their security should not be based on the obscurity of the algorithms used.
- Time-proof, or resilient to the advances in ML & DL.

Text-based CAPTCHAs in particular had enjoyed widespread adoption and a long evolution, but were ultimately defeated by a combination of apt feature extraction and ML [39]. Some implementations, like reCAPTCHA, started by using their own set of hard image-recognition problems as tests, only to later realize that their own DNNs were able to solve them [45,108]. reCAPTCHA also offered speech recognition tasks, that were either too simple for algorithms [98, 99,115], or too difficult for humans [16].

The interest in using image recognition as a CAPTCHA has steadily increased while algorithms have maintained the ability to solve them, both prior to the rise of DL [30,44], and after [110,134]. There have been several proposals to make CAPTCHAs more resilient with little success so far. Using trap images has been shown to be prone to statistical analysis [55], while more recent proposals that create tests by using adversarial examples [91] and the transferability property show more promise. Lately, the area of bot identification has moved towards the security by obscurity paradigm in what some companies call *behavioral CAPTCHAs*, thus obviating the public part of the acronym. These detection mechanisms are based on user and client (browser) fingerprinting, as well as *possibly* more evolved algorithms that observe user behavior in order to correctly classify unknown clients.

While behavioral CAPTCHAs have not worked particularly well so far [109, 111,120], they are still largely ongoing by virtue of being adaptable to attackers. Image-based CAPTCHAs are still used when the behavioral algorithm is unable to predict a new client with certainty.

7.4   Computer Vision

Adversarial examples for computer vision algorithms have dominated the scene, with multiple applications ranging from object detection, object classification, image segmentation or depth estimation [125]. Nonetheless, the range of application where computer vision algorithms are used in security (and safety) critical systems is smaller [41].

A line of research concerned with autonomous driving makes extensive use of DL-based computer vision algorithms, which are highly susceptible to adversarial attacks. For instance, adversarial examples can be encountered in traffic sign recognition [33]. However, as safety and security are paramount concerns in autonomous vehicles, it is unlikely that the information from computer vision algorithms will not be double checked with other information sources, such as high definition maps. As far as we are concerned, traffic signs are designed for humans, which cannot maintain accurate maps of all the traffic signs. Nevertheless, computers do not suffer from this weakness, and mobile applications for driving assistance already integrate traffic signs. Therefore, although it is theoretically possible to endanger autonomous vehicles with adversarial attacks, in practice this attack vector may not lead to effectively realized attacks.

A related line of work is concerned with object detection and their removal from videos [32]. If computer vision algorithms are used for object tracking, in surveillance or other applications, security risks can emerge. However, in critical applications other sensors (e.g., infra-red) are also used to detect objects, as they are considered more reliable. Albeit appealing in theory, these applications are as well less susceptible to effective adversarial attacks.

Nonetheless, research in adversarial computer vision has contributed a plethora of compelling results and it is currently leading the field of adversarial ML, as well as being the benchmark environment and context where almost the entirety of fundamentally new attacks and defenses are evaluated on.

7.5   Speech Recognition

Automatic Speech recognition (ASR) enables machines to transform human speech information into text, in order to improve human-machine interactions. There have been a large number of voice controllable systems (VCS) that are based on ASR techniques, for instance, voice-based search, personal assistance of smartphones, home interaction systems, and in-vehicle infotainment systems [129]. Recently, DL-based ASR has achieved unprecedented developments, but adversarial ML also make ASR one of the most vulnerable applications.

Authentication (see also Sect. 7.2) is one security critical application of ASR, where people's voice is used as the biometric to identify individuals [1]. Note that compared with other biometrics, speech information is easily accessible. From the point of system availability [8], adversarial examples can be used to increase the false negative rate of the ASR system in order to make it unreliable. From the point of system integrity [8], adversasrial examples can be generated to resemble any voice.

VCS is another important application that is susceptible to adversarial examples, and it is widely deployed in commercial services, e.g., Siri, Google Assistant, Alexa, etc. By injecting voice commands that are inaudibility to human listeners, adversaries can manipulate the VCS-supported devices to achieve some malicious goals. For example, DolphinAttack [130] can manipulate the navigation system in an Audi automobile by modulating voice commands on ultrasonic carriers, which may influence the driver and cause severe results. And SurfingAttack [128] leverages ultrasonic guided wave to mount non-line-in-sight attack. Adversarial examples in DL-based ASR was comprehensively explored by Carlini et al. [22], where they analyzed hidden voice commands attacks that are unintelligible to human listeners and proposed detection and mitigation strategies against such attacks.

One characteristic of audio adversarial examples is "over-the-air", which indicates whether the adversarial voice is still effective after playing the adversarial audio on a speaker and record them with a microphone. Another characteristic of adversarial examples in ASR is inaudibility, which indicates whether human listeners can precept the adversarial voice. Inaudibility is equivalent to *imperceptibility* of adversarial images [114]. Instead of l_∞ norm in images, psychoacoustics were leveraged to achieve the goal of inaudibility [93, 101].

7.6   Reinforcement Learning

Besides the supervised classification example introduced with Sect. 2, adversarial examples also manifest in RL. The objective in RL is for an agent to learn an optimal behavior or decision-making in an environment, by optimizing a reward function. RL solutions have been adopted in a wide range of domains, including many in cybersecurity such as cyber-physical systems [34], network attacks [85], smart grid security [89] and mobile edge caching [124].

Moreover, RL relates to adversarial machine learning in two ways:

1. RL can be used to create adversarial attacks to other ML models, that in turn, can be RL agents.
2. RL can be attacked using adversarial ML.

A RL approach for adversarial attacks has already been discussed in the malware Subsect. 7.1.

Parameterizing RL agents with DNNs introduces the same vulnerabilities that DNNs have, as it is possible to craft adversarial examples that fool the estimation of the state or the output of policy network. Huang et al. [60] have demonstrated that black-box attacks against RL agents are possible. For example, adversarial inputs on RL agents transfer to other agents as long as the goal remains the same. The authors tested three well-known RL algorithms – namely DQN, TRPO and A3C – using the FGSM attack (Sect. 4). In case they do not know which algorithm they are attacking, they calculate a proxy using the aforementioned RL algorithms. They discover that some adversarial input strategies are more transferable than others: for instance, when the adversary is constrained to a single pixel perturbation in the input image, the attack is particularly transferable.

Note that the input does not need to be adversarial constantly in order to fool an agent. Lin et al. [75] show that it is possible to time the adversarial input in order to diminish the reward of the agent. In particular, they attack both DQN and A3C in a white-box setting using two different approaches: the strategically-timed attack, where they choose the best moment to push the agent to select the least likely action (minimum reward), and the enchanting attack, where with a sequence of adversarial inputs they lead the agent to a pre-defined target state.

Being able to modify an agent's observation during training time is a strong assumption. To this end, Gleave et al. [42] introduce another adversarial agent in the environment instead of directly manipulating the input. The second agent learns how to fool the first one by discovering an adversarial policy, resulting from a zero-sum game. They evaluate the approach in a number of two-player games in robotics environments that include simulated physics and visual interaction (MuJoCo). The adversarial agent is able to learn policies that force the other agent to fail at its task.

In order to have a realistic evaluation of how robust are RL policies in adversarial settings, the policy of every agent must be determined through adversarial training, in the presence of adversarial agents. The authors demonstrated than an attacker can learn to produce close to natural observations, that are adversarial.

7.7   Other Domains

We aimed to cover adversarial examples in the most prominent security applications. As ML methodologies have proliferated widely, it is not possible to be exhaustive, while also focusing on the fundamentals of adversarial ML. One such domain that we do not tackle is intrusion detection systems that are always a target of evasion attacks. Even though the construction of adversarial examples in the feature space proved to be feasible, and ML solutions are gradually being adopted in network intrusion detection systems, the effectiveness and practicality of adversarial examples in the context of live network environments remains an open question. For more information we refer to the Open-World Network Intrusion Detection chapter.

As a rule of thumb and irrespective of the domain, if a system is based on or uses ML, it is vulnerable to adversaries and adversarial examples. Therefore, it is imperative, as a user, engineer or system designer, to be aware and well-informed about the vulnerabilities that ML models can exhibit. Note that, in contrast to all malicious adversarial attacks we have discussed, adversarial examples can have beneficial applications, like being used for privacy protections against unauthorized ML [61, 74, 79, 80, 90, 95, 106]. We refer readers interested in privacy protection to the Privacy Enhancement chapter.

8   Conclusions

We provided a brief introduction to adversarial machine learning (ML) – a field of study concerned with failure modes of ML algorithms when faced with adversarial attackers. We focused on presenting the range of attacks grouped by threat models and explaining the basic formulation for the attacks. We hope this information can help practitioners to understand how to construct and protect against adversarial inputs for their models. Furthermore, we introduced a considerable range use cases in security critical applications, where adversarial ML is mature and practiced.

We acknowledge that given the space constraints, this presentation can not be exhaustive. Whenever possible, we give pointers to literature offering more comprehensive overviews. We note that adversarial ML is an active research field, and that vulnerabilities to adversaries are inherent to the way current ML models are built. Up to this moment, no ML model is robust against adversaries and no defense is known to protect against adversarial inputs. While the arms race between attacks and defenses accelerates, proofs of robust behavior are ever more challenging and ultimately ephemeral. This opens many research avenues and also raises concerns about the deployment of ML algorithms in security critical contexts without prior and extensive consideration.

Acknowledgements. This research is partially funded by the Research Fund KU Leuven, and by the Flemish Research Programme Cybersecurity.

References

1. Automatic speaker verification spoofing and countermeasures challenge. http://www.asvspoof.org/
2. Akhtar, N., Mian, A.: Threat of adversarial attacks on deep learning in computer vision: a survey. IEEE Access **6**, 14410–14430 (2018)
3. Al-Dujaili, A., Huang, A., Hemberg, E., O'Reilly, U.M.: Adversarial deep learning for robust detection of binary encoded malware. In: S&P Workshops, pp. 76–82. IEEE (2018)
4. Alzantot, M., Balaji, B., Srivastava, M.: Did you hear that? adversarial examples against automatic speech recognition. In: NIPS Workshop on Machine Deception (2018)
5. Alzantot, M., Sharma, Y., Chakraborty, S., Zhang, H., Hsieh, C.J., Srivastava, M.B.: Genattack: practical black-box attacks with gradient-free optimization. In: Proceedings of the Genetic and Evolutionary Computation Conference, pp. 1111–1119. ACM (2019)
6. Anderson, H.S., Kharkar, A., Filar, B., Evans, D., Roth, P.: Learning to evade static PE machine learning malware models via reinforcement learning. arXiv:1801.08917 (2018)
7. Athalye, A., Carlini, N., Wagner, D.: Obfuscated gradients give a false sense of security: circumventing defenses to adversarial examples. In: ICLR (2018)
8. Barreno, M., Nelson, B., Joseph, A.D., Tygar, J.D.: The security of machine learning. Mach. Learn. **81**(2), 121–148 (2010). https://doi.org/10.1007/s10994-010-5188-5
9. Barreno, M., Nelson, B., Sears, R., Joseph, A.D., Tygar, J.D.: Can machine learning be secure? In: CCS, pp. 16–25. ACM (2006)
10. Bhattad, A., Chong, M.J., Liang, K., Li, B., Forsyth, D.A.: Unrestricted adversarial examples via semantic manipulation. In: ICLR (2020)
11. Biggio, B., Russu, P., Didaci, L., Roli, F.: Adversarial biometric recognition?: a review on biometric system security from the adversarial machine-learning perspective. IEEE Sig. Process. Mag. **32**(5), 31–41 (2015)
12. Biggio, B., et al.: Evasion attacks against machine learning at test time. In: Blockeel, H., Kersting, K., Nijssen, S., Železný, F. (eds.) ECML PKDD 2013. LNCS (LNAI), vol. 8190, pp. 387–402. Springer, Heidelberg (2013). https://doi.org/10.1007/978-3-642-40994-3_25
13. Biggio, B., Fumera, G., Roli, F.: Security evaluation of pattern classifiers under attack. IEEE Trans. Knowl. Data Eng. **26**(4), 984–996 (2013)
14. Biggio, B., Nelson, B., Laskov, P.: Poisoning attacks against support vector machines. In: ICML, pp. 1467–1474 (2012)
15. Biggio, B., Roli, F.: Wild patterns: ten years after the rise of adversarial machine learning. Pattern Recogn. **84**, 317–331 (2018)
16. Bigham, J.P., Cavender, A.C.: Evaluating existing audio CAPTCHAs and an interface optimized for non-visual users. In: CHI, pp. 1829–1838. ACM (2009)
17. Brendel, W., Rauber, J., Bethge, M.: Decision-based adversarial attacks: reliable attacks against black-box machine learning models. In: ICLR (2018)
18. Brückner, M., Kanzow, C., Scheffer, T.: Static prediction games for adversarial learning problems. J. Mach. Learn. Res. **13**(10), 2617–2654 (2012)
19. Brundage, M., et al.: Toward trustworthy AI development: mechanisms for supporting verifiable claims. arXiv:2004.07213 (2020)

20. Brunner, T., Diehl, F., Le, M.T., Knoll, A.: Guessing smart: biased sampling for efficient black-box adversarial attacks. In: ICCV, pp. 4958–4966 (2019)
21. Carlini, N., et al.: On evaluating adversarial robustness. arXiv:1902.06705 (2019)
22. Carlini, N., et al.: Hidden voice commands. In: USENIX Security, pp. 513–530 (2016)
23. Chakraborty, A., Alam, M., Dey, V., Chattopadhyay, A., Mukhopadhyay, D.: Adversarial attacks and defences: a survey. arXiv:1810.00069 (2018)
24. Chen, J., Jordan, M.I., Wainwright, M.J.: Hopskipjumpattack: a query-efficient decision-based attack. In: S&P, pp. 668–685 (2020). IEEE
25. Chen, P.Y., Zhang, H., Sharma, Y., Yi, J., Hsieh, C.J.: Zoo: zeroth order optimization based black-box attacks to deep neural networks without training substitute models. In: Proceedings of the 10th ACM Workshop on Artificial Intelligence and Security, pp. 15–26. AISec 2017. ACM (2017)
26. Chen, S., Carlini, N., Wagner, D.: Stateful detection of black-box adversarial attacks. arXiv:1907.05587 (2019)
27. Croce, F., Hein, M.: Sparse and imperceivable adversarial attacks. In: ICCV, pp. 4724–4732 (2019)
28. Dalvi, N., Domingos, P., Sanghai, S., Verma, D., et al.: Adversarial classification. In: KDD, pp. 99–108. ACM (2004)
29. Dosovitskiy, A., Fischer, P., Springenberg, J.T., Riedmiller, M., Brox, T.: Discriminative unsupervised feature learning with exemplar convolutional neural networks. IEEE Trans. Pattern Anal. Mach. Intell. **38**(9), 1734–1747 (2015)
30. Elson, J., Douceur, J.R., Howell, J., Saul, J.: Asirra: a CAPTCHA that exploits interest-aligned manual image categorization. In: CCS, pp. 366–374. ACM (2007)
31. Engstrom, L., Tran, B., Tsipras, D., Schmidt, L., Madry, A.: A rotation and a translation suffice: fooling CNNs with simple transformations. In: NIPS 2017 Workshop on Machine Learning and Computer Security (2017)
32. Eykholt, K., et al.: Physical adversarial examples for object detectors. arXiv:1807.07769 (2018)
33. Eykholt, K., et al.: Robust physical-world attacks on deep learning visual classification. In: CVPR, pp. 1625–1634 (2018)
34. Ferdowsi, A., Challita, U., Saad, W., Mandayam, N.B.: robust deep reinforcement learning for security and safety in autonomous vehicle systems. In: IEEE Conference on Intelligent Transportation Systems, Proceedings, ITSC, pp. 307–312 (2018)
35. Fritsch, C., Netter, M., Reisser, A., Pernul, G.: Attacking image recognition CAPTCHAs. In: Katsikas, S., Lopez, J., Soriano, M. (eds.) TrustBus 2010. LNCS, vol. 6264, pp. 13–25. Springer, Heidelberg (2010). https://doi.org/10.1007/978-3-642-15152-1_2
36. Gao, H., Lei, L., Zhou, X., Li, J., Liu, X.: The robustness of face-based CAPTCHAs. In: 2015 IEEE International Conference on Computer and Information Technology; Ubiquitous Computing and Communications; Dependable, Autonomic and Secure Computing; Pervasive Intelligence and Computing, pp. 2248–2255 (2015)
37. Gao, H., Wang, W., Fan, Y.: Divide and conquer: an efficient attack on Yahoo! CAPTCHA. In: IEEE International Conference on Trust, Security and Privacy in Computing and Communications, pp. 9–16 (2012)
38. Gao, H., Wang, W., Qi, J., Wang, X., Liu, X., Yan, J.: The robustness of hollow CAPTCHAs. In: CCS, pp. 1075–1086. ACM (2013)
39. Gao, H., et al.: A simple generic attack on text captchas. NDSS, pp. 21–24 (2016)

40. Geirhos, R., et al.: Shortcut learning in deep neural networks. Nature Mach. Intell. **2**(11), 665–673 (2020)
41. Gilmer, J., Adams, R.P., Goodfellow, I., Andersen, D., Dahl, G.E.: Motivating the rules of the game for adversarial example research. arXiv:1807.06732 (2018)
42. Gleave, A., Dennis, M., Wild, C., Kant, N., Levine, S., Russell, S.: Adversarial policies: attacking deep reinforcement learning. In: ICLR (2019)
43. Globerson, A., Roweis, S.: Nightmare at test time: robust learning by feature deletion. In: ICML (2006)
44. Golle, P.: Machine learning attacks against the Asirra captcha. In: SOUPS. ACM (2009)
45. Goodfellow, I.J., Bulatov, Y., Ibarz, J., Arnoud, S., Shet, V.D.: Multi-digit number recognition from street view imagery using deep convolutional neural networks. In: ICLR (2014)
46. Goodfellow, I.J., Shlens, J., Szegedy, C.: Explaining and harnessing adversarial examples. In: ICLR (2015)
47. Grosse, K., Papernot, N., Manoharan, P., Backes, M., McDaniel, P.: Adversarial examples for malware detection. In: Foley, S.N., Gollmann, D., Snekkenes, E. (eds.) ESORICS 2017. LNCS, vol. 10493, pp. 62–79. Springer, Cham (2017). https://doi.org/10.1007/978-3-319-66399-9_4
48. Hernández-Castro, C.J., R-Moreno, M.D., Barrero, D.F.: Using JPEG to measure image continuity and break capy and other puzzle CAPTCHAs. IEEE Internet Comput. **19**(6), 46–53 (2015)
49. Hernandez-Castro, C.J., Ribagorda, A., Hernandez-Castro, J.C.: On the strength of EGglue and other logic CAPTCHAs. In: SECRYPT, pp. 157–167 (2011)
50. Hernandez-Castro, C.J., Ribagorda, A.: Pitfalls in captcha design and implementation: the math captcha, a case study. Comput. Secur. **29**(1), 141–157 (2010)
51. Hernandez-Castro, C.J., Barrero, D.F., R-Moreno, M.D.: A machine learning attack against the civil rights captcha. In: International Symposium on Intelligent Distributed Computing (IDC) (2014)
52. Hernandez-Castro, C.J., Hernandez-Castro, J.C., Stainton-Ellis, J.D., Ribagorda, A.: Shortcomings in CAPTCHA design and implementation: Captcha2, a commercial proposal. In: International Network Conference (INC) (2010)
53. Hernández-Castro, C.J., R-moreno, M.D., Barrero, D.F.: Side-channel attack against the Capy HIP. In: International Conference on Emerging Security Technologies (EST), pp. 99–104. IEEE (2014)
54. Hernandez-Castro, C.J., Ribagorda, A., Saez, Y.: Side-channel attack on labeling captchas. In: SECRYPT (2010)
55. Hernández-Castro, C., Li, S., R-Moreno, M.: All about uncertainties and traps: statistical oracle-based attacks on a new captcha protection against oracle attacks. Comput. Secur. **92**, 101758 (2020)
56. Hong, S., Chandrasekaran, V., Kaya, Y., Dumitraş, T., Papernot, N.: On the effectiveness of mitigating data poisoning attacks with gradient shaping. arXiv:2002.11497 (2020)
57. Hosseini, H., Poovendran, R.: Semantic adversarial examples. In: CVPR Workshops, pp. 1614–1619 (2018)
58. Hu, W., Tan, Y.: Black-box attacks against RNN based malware detection algorithms. In: AAAI Workshops (2017)
59. Hu, W., Tan, Y.: Generating adversarial malware examples for black-box attacks based on GANs. arXiv:1702.05983 (2017)
60. Huang, S., Papernot, N., Goodfellow, I., Duan, Y., Abbeel, P.: Adversarial attacks on neural network policies. In: ICLR (2017)

61. Huang, W.R., Geiping, J., Fowl, L., Taylor, G., Goldstein, T.: Metapoison: practical general-purpose clean-label data poisoning. In: NeurIPS (2020)
62. Huang, W., Stokes, J.W.: MtNet: a multi-task neural network for dynamic malware classification. In: Caballero, J., Zurutuza, U., Rodríguez, R.J. (eds.) DIMVA 2016. LNCS, vol. 9721, pp. 399–418. Springer, Cham (2016). https://doi.org/10.1007/978-3-319-40667-1_20
63. Huang, X., et al.: Safety and trustworthiness of deep neural networks: a survey. arXiv:1812.08342 (2018)
64. Ilyas, A., Engstrom, L., Athalye, A., Lin, J.: Black-box adversarial attacks with limited queries and information. In: ICML, pp. 2137–2146 (2018)
65. Ilyas, A., Engstrom, L., Madry, A.: Prior convictions: black-box adversarial attacks with bandits and priors. In: ICLR (2019)
66. Jagielski, M., Carlini, N., Berthelot, D., Kurakin, A., Papernot, N.: High accuracy and high fidelity extraction of neural networks. In: USENIX Security (2019)
67. Jagielski, M., Oprea, A., Biggio, B., Liu, C., Nita-Rotaru, C., Li, B.: Manipulating machine learning: poisoning attacks and countermeasures for regression learning. In: S&P, pp. 19–35. IEEE (2018)
68. Joseph, A.D., Nelson, B., Rubinstein, B.I., Tygar, J.: Adversarial Machine Learning. Cambridge University Press, Cambridge (2018)
69. Kołcz, A., Teo, C.H.: Feature weighting for improved classifier robustness. In: CEAS (2009)
70. Kolosnjaji, B., et al.: Adversarial malware binaries: evading deep learning for malware detection in executables. In: EUSIPCO, pp. 533–537. IEEE (2018)
71. Kolosnjaji, B., Zarras, A., Webster, G., Eckert, C.: Deep learning for classification of malware system call sequences. In: Kang, B.H., Bai, Q. (eds.) AI 2016. LNCS (LNAI), vol. 9992, pp. 137–149. Springer, Cham (2016). https://doi.org/10.1007/978-3-319-50127-7_11
72. Labs, K.: Machine learning methods for malware detection (2020). https://media.kaspersky.com/en/enterprise-security/Kaspersky-Lab-Whitepaper-Machine-Learning.pdf
73. Laidlaw, C., Feizi, S.: Functional adversarial attacks. NeurIPS (2019)
74. Larson, M., Liu, Z., Brugman, S., Zhao, Z.: Pixel privacy: increasing image appeal while blocking automatic inference of sensitive scene information. In: Working Notes Proceedings of the MediaEval Workshop (2018)
75. Lin, Y.C., Hong, Z.W., Liao, Y.H., Shih, M.L., Liu, M.Y., Sun, M.: IJCAI, p. 3756–3762. AAAI Press (2017)
76. Liu, Q., Li, P., Zhao, W., Cai, W., Yu, S., Leung, V.C.: A survey on security threats and defensive techniques of machine learning: a data driven view. IEEE Access 6, 12103–12117 (2018)
77. Liu, X., Du, X., Zhang, X., Zhu, Q., Wang, H., Guizani, M.: Adversarial samples on android malware detection systems for IoT systems. Sensors 19(4), 974 (2019)
78. Liu, Y., Chen, X., Liu, C., Song, D.: Delving into transferable adversarial examples and black-box attacks. In: ICLR (2017)
79. Liu, Z., Zhao, Z., Larson, M.: Pixel privacy 2019: protecting sensitive scene information in images. In: Working Notes Proceedings of the MediaEval Workshop (2019)
80. Liu, Z., Zhao, Z., Larson, M.: Who's afraid of adversarial queries? the impact of image modifications on content-based image retrieval. In: ICMR (2019)
81. Lovisotto, G., Eberz, S., Martinovic, I.: Biometric backdoors: a poisoning attack against unsupervised template updating. In: Euro S&P (2019)

82. Lowd, D., Meek, C.: Adversarial learning. In: KDD, pp. 641–647. ACM (2005)
83. Luo, B., Liu, Y., Wei, L., Xu, Q.: Towards imperceptible and robust adversarial example attacks against neural networks. In: AAAI, vol. 32 (2018)
84. Madry, A., Makelov, A., Schmidt, L., Tsipras, D., Vladu, A.: Towards deep learning models resistant to adversarial attacks. In: ICLR (2018)
85. Malialis, K., Kudenko, D.: Distributed response to network intrusions using multiagent reinforcement learning. Eng. Appl. Artif. Intell. **41**, 270–284 (2015)
86. Mitchell, T.M., et al.: Machine learning. McGraw Hill, Burr Ridge, IL, vol. 45, no. 37, pp. 870–877 (1997)
87. Naor, M.: Verification of a human in the loop or Identification via the Turing Test (1996). http://www.wisdom.weizmann.ac.il/~naor/PAPERS/human.ps
88. Nguyen, V.D., Chow, Y.-W., Susilo, W.: Attacking animated CAPTCHAs via character extraction. In: Pieprzyk, J., Sadeghi, A.-R., Manulis, M. (eds.) CANS 2012. LNCS, vol. 7712, pp. 98–113. Springer, Heidelberg (2012). https://doi.org/10.1007/978-3-642-35404-5_9
89. Ni, Z., Paul, S.: A multistage game in smart grid security: a reinforcement learning solution. IEEE Transactions on neural networks and learning systems **30**(9), 2684–2695 (2019)
90. Oh, S.J., Fritz, M., Schiele, B.: Adversarial image perturbation for privacy protection a game theory perspective. In: ICCV, pp. 1491–1500 (2017)
91. Osadchy, M., Hernandez-Castro, J., Hernandez, J., Gibson, S., Dunkelman, O., Pérez-Cabo, D.: No bot expects the DeepCAPTCHA! introducing immutable adversarial examples, with applications to CAPTCHA generation. IEEE Trans. Inf. Forensics Secur. **12**(11), 2640–2653 (2016)
92. Papernot, N., McDaniel, P., Sinha, A., Wellman, M.: Towards the science of security and privacy in machine learning. arXiv:1611.03814 (2016)
93. Qin, Y., Carlini, N., Cottrell, G., Goodfellow, I., Raffel, C.: Imperceptible, robust, and targeted adversarial examples for automatic speech recognition. In: ICML, pp. 5231–5240 (2019)
94. Raff, E., Barker, J., Sylvester, J., Brandon, R., Catanzaro, B., Nicholas, C.K.: Malware detection by eating a whole exe. In: AAAI (2018)
95. Rajabi, A., Bobba, R.B., Rosulek, M., Wright, C.V., Feng, W.c.: On the (im) practicality of adversarial perturbation for image privacy. In: Proceedings on Privacy Enhancing Technologies, pp. 85–106 (2021)
96. Rozsa, A., Rudd, E.M., Boult, T.E.: Adversarial diversity and hard positive generation. In: CVPR Workshops, pp. 25–32 (2016)
97. Rubinstein, B.I., et al.: Antidote: understanding and defending against poisoning of anomaly detectors. In: ACM SIGCOMM Conference on Internet Measurement, pp. 1–14. ACM (2009)
98. Sano, S., Otsuka, T., Okuno, H.G.: Solving Google's continuous audio CAPTCHA with HMM-based automatic speech recognition. In: Sakiyama, K., Terada, M. (eds.) IWSEC 2013. LNCS, vol. 8231, pp. 36–52. Springer, Heidelberg (2013). https://doi.org/10.1007/978-3-642-41383-4_3
99. Santamarta, R.: Breaking gmail's audio captcha. http://blog.wintercore.com/?p=11 (2008). http://blog.wintercore.com/?p=11. Accessed 13 Feb 2010
100. Schmidt, L., Santurkar, S., Tsipras, D., Talwar, K., Madry, A.: Adversarially robust generalization requires more data. In: NeurIPS, pp. 5014–5026 (2018)
101. Schönherr, L., Kohls, K., Zeiler, S., Holz, T., Kolossa, D.: Adversarial attacks against automatic speech recognition systems via psychoacoustic hiding. In: NDSS (2019)

102. Schultz, M.G., Eskin, E., Zadok, F., Stolfo, S.J.: Data mining methods for detection of new malicious executables. In: S&P, pp. 38–49. IEEE (2001)
103. Serban, A., Poll, E., Visser, J.: Adversarial examples on object recognition: a comprehensive survey. ACM Comput. Surv. (CSUR)
104. Shafahi, A., et al.: Adversarial training for free! In: NeurIPS, pp. 3353–3364 (2019)
105. Shamsabadi, A.S., Sanchez-Matilla, R., Cavallaro, A.: Colorfool: semantic adversarial colorization. In: CVPR, pp. 1151–1160 (2020)
106. Shan, S., Wenger, E., Zhang, J., Li, H., Zheng, H., Zhao, B.Y.: Fawkes: protecting privacy against unauthorized deep learning models. In: USENIX Security, pp. 1589–1604 (2020)
107. Sharif, M., Bhagavatula, S., Bauer, L., Reiter, M.K.: Accessorize to a crime: real and stealthy attacks on state-of-the-art face recognition. In: CCS, pp. 1528–1540. ACM (2016)
108. Shet, V.: Street view and reCAPTCHA technology just got smarter (2014). https://security.googleblog.com/2014/04/street-view-and-recaptcha-technology.html. Accessed 14 Aug 2017
109. Sidorov, Z.: Rebreakcaptcha: Breaking google's recaptcha v2 using google (2017). https://east-ee.com/2017/02/28/rebreakcaptcha-breaking-googles-recaptcha-v2-using-google/
110. Sivakorn, S., Polakis, I., Keromytis, A.D.: I am robot: (deep) learning to break semantic image captchas. In: Euro S&P, pp. 388–403. IEEE (2016)
111. Sivakorn, S., Polakis, J., Keromytis, A.D.: I'm not a human : breaking the google reCAPTCHA (2016)
112. Smith, L.N.: A useful taxonomy for adversarial robustness of neural networks. arXiv:1910.10679 (2019)
113. Steinhardt, J., Koh, P.W.W., Liang, P.S.: Certified defenses for data poisoning attacks. In: NeurIPS, pp. 3517–3529 (2017)
114. Szegedy, C., et al.: Intriguing properties of neural networks. In: ICLR (2013)
115. Tam, J., Simsa, J., Hyde, S., von Ahn, L.: Breaking Audio Captchas, pp. 1625–1632. Curran Associates, Inc. (2008)
116. Tramèr, F., Carlini, N., Brendel, W., Madry, A.: On adaptive attacks to adversarial example defenses. In: NeurIPS (2020)
117. Tramèr, F., Zhang, F., Juels, A., Reiter, M.K., Ristenpart, T.: Stealing machine learning models via prediction APIs. In: USENIX Security, pp. 601–618 (2016)
118. Tsipras, D., Santurkar, S., Engstrom, L., Turner, A., Madry, A.: Robustness may be at odds with accuracy. In: ICLR (2019)
119. Vorobeychik, Y., Kantarcioglu, M.: Adversarial machine learning. Synth. Lect. Artif. Intell. Mach. Learn. 12(3), 1–169 (2018)
120. Wang, D., Moh, M., Moh, T.S.: Using Deep Learning to Solve Google ReCAPTCHA v2's Image Challenges, pp. 1–5 (2020)
121. Wong, E., Schmidt, F., Kolter, Z.: Wasserstein adversarial examples via projected sinkhorn iterations. In: ICML, pp. 6808–6817 (2019)
122. Xiao, C., Li, B., yan Zhu, J., He, W., Liu, M., Song, D.: Generating adversarial examples with adversarial networks. In: IJCAI, pp. 3905–3911 (2018)
123. Xiao, C., Zhu, J.Y., Li, B., He, W., Liu, M., Song, D.: Spatially transformed adversarial examples. In: ICLR (2018)
124. Xiao, L., Wan, X., Dai, C., Du, X., Chen, X., Guizani, M.: Security in mobile edge caching with reinforcement learning. IEEE Wirel. Commun. 25(3), 116–122 (2018)
125. Xie, C., Wang, J., Zhang, Z., Zhou, Y., Xie, L., Yuille, A.: Adversarial examples for semantic segmentation and object detection. In: ICCV, pp. 1369–1378 (2017)

126. Xu, W., Qi, Y., Evans, D.: Automatically evading classifiers: a case study on pdf malware classifiers. In: NDSS (2016)
127. Yan, J., Ahmad, A.S.E.: A low-cost attack on a microsoft captcha. In: CCS, pp. 543–554. ACM (2008)
128. Yan, Q., Liu, K., Zhou, Q., Guo, H., Zhang, N.: Surfingattack: interactive hidden attack on voice assistants using ultrasonic guided wave. In: NDSS (2020)
129. Yu, D., Deng, L.: Automatic Speech Recognition. SCT, Springer, London (2015). https://doi.org/10.1007/978-1-4471-5779-3
130. Zhang, G., Yan, C., Ji, X., Zhang, T., Zhang, T., Xu, W.: Dolphinattack: Inaudible voice commands. In: CCS, pp. 103–117. ACM (2017)
131. Zhang, H., Avrithis, Y., Furon, T., Amsaleg, L.: Smooth adversarial examples. EURASIP J. Inf. Secur. 2020(1), 1–12 (2020)
132. Zhao, Z., Liu, Z., Larson, M.: Adversarial color enhancement: generating unrestricted adversarial images by optimizing a color filter. In: BMVC (2020)
133. Zhao, Z., Liu, Z., Larson, M.: Towards large yet imperceptible adversarial image perturbations with perceptual color distance. In: CVPR, pp. 1039–1048 (2020)
134. Zhou, Y., Yang, Z., Wang, C., Boutell, M.: Breaking google reCAPTCHA v2. J. Comput. Sci. Coll. 34(1), 126–136 (2018)
135. Zhu, B.B., et al.: Attacks and design of image recognition captchas. In: CCS, pp. 187–200. ACM (2010)

Deep Learning Backdoors

Shaofeng Li[1(✉)], Shiqing Ma[2], Minhui Xue[3], and Benjamin Zi Hao Zhao[4]

[1] Shanghai Jiao Tong University, Shanghai, China
shaofengli@sjtu.edu.cn
[2] Rutgers University, New Brunswick, USA
shiqing.ma@rutgers.edu
[3] The University of Adelaide, Adelaide, Australia
jason.xue@adelaide.edu.au
[4] Macquarie University, Sydney, Australia

Abstract. In this chapter, we will give a comprehensive survey on backdoor attacks, mitigation and challenges and propose some open problems. We first introduce an attack vector that derives from the Deep Neural Network (DNN) model itself. DNN models are trained from gigantic data that may be poisoned by attackers. Different from the traditional poisoning attacks that interfere with the decision boundary, backdoor attacks create a "shortcut" in the model's decision boundary. Such a "shortcut" can only be activated by a trigger known by the attacker itself, while it performs well on benign inputs without the trigger. We then show several mitigation techniques from the frontend to the backend of the machine learning pipeline. We finally provide avenues for future research. We hope to raise awareness about the severity of the current emerging backdoor attacks in DNNs and attempt to provide a timely solution to fight against them.

1 Introduction to Backdoors in Deep Neural Networks

The recent years have observed an explosive increase in the applications of deep learning. Deep neural networks have been proven to outperform both traditional machine learning techniques and human cognitive capacity in many domains. Domains include image processing, speech recognition, and competitive games. Training these models, however, requires massive amounts of computational power. Therefore, to cater to the growing demands of machine learning, technology giants have introduced Machine Learning as a Service (MLaaS) [40], a new service delivered through cloud platforms. Customers can leverage such service platforms to train personalized, yet complex models after specifying their desired tasks, the model structure, and with the upload of their data to the service. Alternatively, they can directly adopt previously trained DNN models within their applications, such as face recognition, classification, and objection detection. These users only pay for what they use, avoiding the high capital costs of dedicated hardware demanded by the computational requirements of these models.

However, there is little transparency of the training process of models produced by MLaaS or pre-trained models open-sourced on the Internet. These models may have

---

B. Z. H. Zhao—The authors are listed in alphabetical order.

© Springer Nature Switzerland AG 2022
L. Batina et al. (Eds.): Security and Artificial Intelligence, LNCS 13049, pp. 313–334, 2022.
https://doi.org/10.1007/978-3-030-98795-4_13

been compromised by Backdoor Attacks [14,29], which are aimed at fooling the model with pre-mediated inputs. Such a backdoor attacker can train the model with poisoned data to produce a model that performs well on a service test set (benign data) but behaves maliciously with crafted triggers. Similarly, a malicious MLaaS can covertly launch backdoor attacks by providing clients with models poisoned with backdoors.

Intuitively, a backdoor attack against Deep Neural Networks (DNNs) is to inject hidden malicious behaviors into DNNs such that the backdoor model behaves legitimately for benign inputs, yet invokes a predefined malicious behavior when its input contains a malicious trigger. The trigger can take a plethora of forms, including a special object present in the image (e.g., a yellow pad), a shape filled with custom textures (e.g., logos with particular colors) or even image-wide stylizations with special filters (e.g., images altered by Nashville or Gotham filters). These filters can be applied to the original image by replacing or perturbing a set of image pixels.

Formally, for a given benign model $\mathcal{F} : \mathcal{X} \mapsto \mathcal{Y}$, for a selected malicious output prediction result (the predefined malicious behavior) R, a backdoor attack is to generate: 1) a backdoor model $\mathcal{G} : \mathcal{X} \mapsto \mathcal{Y}$, 2) a backdoor trigger generator $\mathcal{T} : \mathcal{X} \mapsto \mathcal{X}$, which alters a benign input to a malicious input such that:

$$\mathcal{G}(x) = \begin{cases} \mathcal{F}(x), & \text{if } x \in \{ \mathcal{X} - \mathcal{T}(\mathcal{X}) \} \\ R, & \text{if } x \in \mathcal{T}(\mathcal{X}). \end{cases}$$

2 Backdoor Attacks

In this section, we firstly introduce the threat model of backdoor attacks. According to the attacker's capability, we demonstrate three types of threat models, *white-box*, *grey-box*, and *black-box* attack settings. After that, we survey several works about trigger stealthiness to improve the practice of the backdoor attacks in a human inspector scenario. Finally, we listed the backdoor attacks that are adopted in a range of application areas.

2.1 Threat Model

Consider an example scenario of deploying a traffic identification DNN model for autonomous vehicles, such DNN models can be trained on images of traffic signs, learn what stop signs and speed limit signs looks like, and then be deployed as part an autonomous car [16]. An adversary can inject Trojan behaviors into DNN models by compromising the training pipeline, or by directly corrupting the model's weights. An attacker can compromise the training pipeline by presenting additional augmented training samples with untouched training data when incrementally training the deployed DNN model. An example augmented image could be images of stop signs with yellow squares on them, each labeled as "speed limit sign", instead of "stop sign". With the backdoor trojan present, the adversary can trick the vehicle into running through stop signs by putting a sticky note (yellow square) on it.

On other hand, pre-trained models released by untrusted third-parties may have such trojans inserted. The attacker inserts the trojan into the DNN model, then pushes the poisoned model to online repositories (e.g. GitHub or model zoo for open access). When an victim downloads this backdoored DNN model for their task, the attacker can compromise the output of the model with the trigger known only to themselves. Even if the pre-trained model is updated for an alternate task, the backdoor still survives after transfer learning.

There are two ways to create backdoored DNN models. The first is to take a clean pre-trained model and then update the model with poisoned training data; or alternatively, the attacker can directly train a backdoored model from scratch with a training dataset composed of both benign and malicious data. The latter attack, however, will need access to the full original train dataset, While the former attacker will only need a small set of clean training data for retraining.

In regards to the attacker's capability, there are three types of threat models, *white-box*, *grey-box*, and *black-box* attack settings.

2.2 White-Box Setting

A white-box attack setting provides an attacker with the strongest attack assumptions: the attacker has full access to the target DNN models and full access to the training set.

BadNets. Gu et al. [14] propose BadNets which injects a backdoor by poisoning the training set. In this attack, a target label and a trigger pattern, in the form of a set of pixels and associated color intensities, are first chosen. Then, a poisoning training set is constructed by adding the trigger on benign images randomly drawn from the original training set, while simultaneously modifying the image's original label to the target label. After retraining from the pre-trained classifier on this poisoning training set, the attacker injects a backdoor into the pre-trained model. Gu et al.'s experiments provide insights into how the backdoor attack operates and tests the extreme scenario where the trigger is only a single pixel. Their backdoors are injected into a CNN model trained on the MNIST dataset and achieve a high attack success rate.

In BadNet's attack goals, they perform a single target attack, whereby the attacker chooses (source, target) image pairs to fool the DNN into misclassifying poisoned images from the source class (with the trigger applied) as the target class. We shall call this type of attack a "partial backdoor". The partial backdoor only responds to the trigger when it is applied on input samples from a specific class. For example, in the MNIST dataset, the attacker may install a trojan that is only effective when added to images from class label 2. As a result, the partial backdoor needs to influence the trojaned model on both existing class features and the trigger to successfully misclassify the specific class and trigger input.

Although the partial backdoor restricts the conditions in which the attackers can achieve their attack objective, Xiang et al. [47] note that this type of attack strategy can evade backdoor detection methods [12,43] which assume the trigger is input agnostic for all classes. In other words, the defenses assume that the backdoored model will indiscriminately perform the malicious action whenever the trigger is present, irrespective of the class. Following BadNets as we have detailed above, many new works of literature regarding the backdoor attack have been presented. To name a few, Dumford and Scheirer [11] inject a backdoor into a CNN model by perturbing its weights; Tan and Shokri [41] use indistinguishable latent representation for benign and adversarial data points via regularization to bypass the backdoor detection.

Dynamic Backdoor. Dynamic backdooring, as proposed by Salem et al. [36], features a technique whereby triggers for a specific target label have dynamic patterns and locations. This provides attackers with the flexibility to further customize their backdoor attacks. Salem et al. use *random backdoors* to demonstrate a naive attack, where triggers are sampled from a uniform distribution. These triggers are then applied to a random location sampled from a set of locations for each input in the injection stage before training the model. The trained backdoored model will now output the specific target label when the attacker samples a trigger from the same uniform distribution and the location set and adds it to any input. Evolving beyond the naive attack, Salem et al. construct a *backdoor generating network (BaN)* to produce a generative model (similar to the decoder of VAE [34] or generator of GANs [31]) that can transform latent prior distributions (i.e., Gaussian or Uniform distribution) into triggers. The parameters of this BaN is trained jointly with the backdoor model. In the joint training process, the loss between the output of the backdoored model and the ground truth (for the clean input) or the target label (for the poisoned samples) will be backpropagated not only through the backdoored model for an update but also through the BaN. Upon completion of the model training, the BaN will have learned a map from the latent vector to the triggers that can activate the backdoor model. Salem et al.'s final technique extends the BaN to C-BaN by incorporating the target label information as a conditional input. These changes result in inputs whereby the target label does not need to have its own unique trigger locations, and the generated triggers for different target labels can appear at any location on the input.

2.3 Grey-Box Setting

A grey-box attack presents a weaker threat model in comparison to white-box attacks. Recall that white-box attackers have full access to the training data or training process. However, in the grey-box threat model, the attacker's capability is limited with access to either a small subset of training data or the learning algorithms.

Poisoning Training Datasets. In the former grey-box setting, Chen et al. [6] propose a backdoor attack which injects a backdoor into DNNs by adding a small set of poisoned samples into the training dataset, without directly accessing the victim learning system. Their experiments show that with a single instance (a face-to-face recognition system) as the backdoor key, it only needs 5 poisoned samples to be added to a huge (600,000 images) training set. If the trigger is in the form of a pattern (e.g., glasses for facial recognition), 50 poisoned samples are sufficient for a respectable attack success rate.

Trojaning NN. The grey-box setting, which does not provide the attacker with access to the training or test data, instead providing full access to the target DNN models, is observed in transfer learning pipelines. The attacker only has access to a pre-trained DNN model, and this setting is more common than the former grey-box assumption of access to a subset of data. Liu et al.'s Trojaning attacker [28] has both a clean pre-trained model and a small auxiliary dataset generated by reverse engineering the model.

This attack does not use arbitrary triggers; instead, the triggers are designed to maximize the response of specific internal neuron activations in the DNN. This creates a higher correlation between triggers and internal neurons, by building a stronger dependence between specific internal neurons and the target labels, retraining the model with the backdoor requires less training data. Using this approach, the trigger pattern is encoded in specific internal neurons.

2.4   Black-Box Setting

The prior backdoor threat models assume an attacker capable of compromising either the training data or the model training environment. Such threats are unlikely in many common ML use-case scenarios. For example, organizations train on their own private data, without outsourcing the training computation. On-premise training is typical in many industries, and the resulting models are deployed internally with a focus on fast iterations. Collecting training data, training a model, and deploying it are all parts of a continuous, automated production pipeline that is accessed only by trusted administrators, without the potential of incorporating malicious third parties.

Compromising Code. Bagdasaryan and Shmatikov [3] propose a code-only backdoor attack in which the adversary does not need to access the training data or the training process directly. Yet, that attack still produces a backdoored model by adding malicious code to ML codebases that are built with complex control logic and dozens of thousands of code blocks. The key to their method lies in the following assumption: compromising code in ML codebases stealthily is realistic, as it is reasonable for most of the cases that correctness tests of ML codebases are not available. For example, the three most popular PyTorch repositories on GitHub, fairseq, transformers and fastai, all include multiple loss computations and complex model architectures. The attack will remain unnoticed under unit testing when the adversaries add a new backdoor loss function unified with other conventional losses, as the intention of this malicious loss (and backdoor attacks as a whole) is to preserve normal training behavior.

Specifically, they model backdoor attacks through the lens of multi-objective optimization (*w.r.t.* multiple loss functions). The loss for the main task m should perform regularly during training; however, the backdoor loss is computed on the poisoned samples that are synthesized by the adversary's code. The two losses are then unified into one overall loss through a linear operation. The authors solve their multi-objective optimization problem via Multiple Gradient Descent Algorithm (MGDA) [10].

Live Trojan. Costales et al. [8] propose a live backdoor attack that patches model parameters in system memory to achieve the desired malicious backdoor behavior. The attack setting assumes that the attacker can modify data in the victim process's address space (/proc/[PID]/map, /proc/[PID]/mem). Countless possibilities exist to enable this power. For example, trojaning a system library, or remapping memory between processes with a malicious kernel module, which has been proved effective in Stuxnet [20]. After the attacker establishes write capabilities in the relevant address space, they need to find the weights of the DNN stored in memory. The proposal suggests either Binwalk [15] or Volatility [24] to find signatures of the networks by detecting a large swath of binary storing weights. Once the malware has scanned the memory and the weights of

DNNs located, *masked retraining* is used to modify only the selected parameters which are the most significant neurons of the DNNs to perform as the backdoor behavior. In identifying the parameters of the model which will yield a high attack success rate, the attacker will compute the average gradient for a continuous subset of parameters on one layer with a window size across the entire poisoned dataset. Parameter values with larger absolute average value gradients indicate that the model would likely benefit from modifying the parameter value. After calculating the patches, simple scripts will load the patched weights into binary files to which the malware can apply.

Although this attack needs knowledge of the DNN's architecture, an attack can take a snapshot of the victim's system, extract the system image, and use forensic and/or reverse-engineering tools to achieve this indirectly and run code on the victim system. As such, we categorize this type of backdoor attacks as a black-box attack.

2.5 Trigger Stealthiness

We define the operator $\mathscr{T} : \mathscr{X} \mapsto \mathscr{X}$ mixes a clean input $x \in \mathscr{X}$ with the trigger τ to produce a trigger output $\mathscr{T}(x, \tau) \in \mathscr{X}$, i.e. the operator output remains in the same image space $\mathscr{X}$ as the input. Typically, the trigger τ consists of two parts: a mask $m \in \{0,1\}^n$, and a pattern $p \in \mathscr{X}$. Formally, the trigger embedding operator is defined as:

$$\mathscr{T}(x, \tau) = (1 - m) \odot x + m \odot p$$

When poisoning the training data, the attacker also mislabels the compromised training data with a target label t. This trigger or mislabelling is likely to be detected should a human manually inspect these samples. One potential approach to inject trojans into DNNs in a stealthy manner is to attach the triggers to poisoned data in an imperceptible way. Recent works propose hidden backdoor attacks, where the attached triggers is imperceptible to humans [23,53]. On other hand, with most backdoor attacks requiring the mislabeling of poisoned data to a target label t. Such a requirement is not necessarily practical in security-critical applications where the input data will be audited by human inspectors. Recent proposals introduce clean-label backdoor attacks, where the labels of poisoned samples are semantically consistent with the poisoned data [5,35,42]. Both approaches can improve the stealthiness of backdoor attacks, however a perfect combination of both still remains elusive.

Hiding Triggers. In the clean label backdoor attacks mentioned above, the attacker attempts to conduct backdoor attacks without compromising the label of the poisoned samples. On the other hand, it is also desirable to make the trigger patterns indistinguishable when mixed with legitimate data in order to evade human inspection.

Liao et al. [53] propose two approaches to make the triggers invisible to human users. The first is a small static perturbation with a simple pattern built upon empirical observations. As Liao et al. describe in [53], this method is limited due to the increased difficulty for pre-trained models to memorize these trigger features, regardless of the content or classification model. Consequently, this method of trigger hiding is only practical during the training stage, with access to large proportions of the dataset. The second trigger hiding method is inspired by the universal adversarial attack [32]. This attack iteratively searches the whole dataset to find the minimal universal perturbation to push all the data points toward the decision boundary of the target class. For each data point, an incremental perturbation Δv_i will be applied to push this data point towards the target decision boundary. Note that in the second method, although the smallest perturbation (trigger) can be found through a universal adversarial search, the method still needs to apply the trigger on the data points to poison the training set, and retrain the pre-trained model. In their work, the indistinguishability of Trojan trigger examples is attained by a magnitude constraint on the perturbations to craft such examples [30].

Li et al. [23] demonstrate the trade-off between the effectiveness and stealth of Trojans. Li et al. hide triggers on the input images through steganography and regularization. In the first backdoor attack, the adoption of steganography techniques involves the modification of the *least significant bits* to embed textual triggers into the inputs. Additionally, in Li et al.'s regularization approach, they develop an optimization algorithm involving $\mathscr{L}_p$ ($p = 0, 2, \infty$) regularization to effectively distribute the trigger throughout the target image. When compared to trigger patterns used by Saha et al. [35] (which are visually exposed during the attack phase), the triggers generated by Li et al.'s attack are invisible for human inspectors during both injection and attack phases.

Clean Label. Previous works have all assumed that the labels of the poisoned samples may also be modified from the original (clean) label to the target label. However, this change greatly hurts the stealthiness of the attack, as a human inspector would easily identify an inconsistency between the contents of the poisoned samples and their labels, irrespective of a unseen trigger. Particularly in security-critical scenarios, it is reasonable to assume that the dataset is checked by first pre-processing the data to identify outliers. This could be manual inspection by a human. This problem has seen the proposal of clean-label backdoor attacks, where the labels of poison samples aim to be semantically correct [5,35,42].

Marni et al. [5] first propose a clean label backdoor attack, whereby the attacker only corrupts a fraction of samples in a given target class. Thus, in this setting, the attacker does not need to change the labels of the corrupted samples. However, the penalty incurred is a need to corrupt a larger portion of the training samples. In Marni et al.'s experiments, the minimum poisoning rate of the target class training samples exceeds 30%; to achieve a sufficient attack success rate this value exceeded 40%. Turner et al. [42] also consider this setting and prove that when restricting the adversary to only poison a small proportion of samples in the target class (less than 25%), the attack becomes virtually non-existent. Turner et al. reasons that this observation is a result of the poisoned samples from the target class containing enough information for the classifier to correctly identify the samples as the target class without the influence of the trigger pattern. Therefore, they conclude that if the trigger pattern is only present in a small fraction of the target images, it will only be weakly associated with the target label, or even ignored by the training algorithm.

Consequently, in [42], Turner et al. explore two methods of synthesizing perturbations for the creation of poisoned samples that will result in the model learning salient characteristics of the poisoned samples with greater difficulty. This increased learning difficulty forces the model to rely more heavily on the backdoor pattern to make a correct prediction, overriding the influence of features from the original image, successfully introducing the backdoor. In their first method, A Generative Adversarial Network

(GAN) [13] embeds the distribution of the training data into a latent space. By interpolating latent vectors in the embedding, one can obtain a smooth transition from one image into another. To this end, they first train a GAN on the training set, producing a generator $G : \mathscr{R}^d \rightarrow R^n$. Then given a vector z in the d-dimensional latent vector generator, $\mathscr{G}$ will generate an image $\mathscr{G}(z)$ in the n-dimensional pixel space. Secondly, they optimize over the latent space to find the optimal reconstruction encoding that produces an image closest to the target image x in l_2 distance. Formally, the optimal reconstruction encoding of a target image x using $\mathscr{G}$ is

$$\mathscr{E}_{\mathscr{G}}(x) = \arg\min_{z \in \mathscr{R}^d} ||x - \mathscr{G}(z)||_2.$$

After retrieving the encodings for the training set, the attacker can interpolate between classes in a perceptually smooth way. Given a constant τ, they define the interpolation $\mathscr{I}_{\mathscr{G}}$ between images x_1 and x_2 as

$$\mathscr{I}_{\mathscr{G}}(x_1, x_2, \tau) = \mathscr{G}(\tau z_1 + (1 - \tau)z_2), \text{ where } z_1 = \mathscr{E}_{\mathscr{G}}(x_1), z_2 = \mathscr{E}_{\mathscr{G}}(x_2).$$

Finally, the attacker searches for a value of τ, large enough to make the salient characteristics of the interpolated image useless, however, small enough to ensure the content of the interpolation image $\mathscr{I}_{\mathscr{G}}(x_1, x_2, \tau)$ still agrees with the target label for humans. In their second approach, Turner et al. apply an adversarial transformation to each image before they apply the backdoor pattern. The goal is to make these images harder to classify correctly using standard image features, encouraging the model to memorize the backdoor pattern as a dominant feature. Formally, given a fixed classifier $\mathscr{C}$ with loss $\mathscr{L}$ and input x, they construct the adversarial perturbations as

$$x_{adv} = \arg\max_{||x'-x||_p \leq \varepsilon} \mathscr{L}(x'),$$

for some l_p-norm and bound ε. Now the attacker retrieves a set of untargeted adversarial examples of the target class, and the attacker applies the trigger pattern to these adversarial examples which resemble the target class. Although both approaches allow for poisoning samples with the trigger containing the same label as the base image, the applied trigger has a visually noticeable shape and size in both types of clean label backdoor attacks. Thus, the attacker will still need to use a perceptible trigger pattern to inject and activate the backdoor, potentially compromising the secrecy of the attack.

Saha et al. [35] propose a clean label backdoor attack, whereby the attacker hides the trigger in the poisoned data and maintains secrecy of the trigger until test time. Saha et al. first define a trigger pattern p with a binary mask m (i.e., 1 at the location of the patch and 0 everywhere else), then apply the trigger p to a source image s_i from the source category. The patched source image $\tilde{s}_i$ is

$$\tilde{s}_i = s_i \odot (1 - m) + p \odot m,$$

where $\odot$ is for element-wise product. After retrieving the poisoned source image, the attacker solves an optimization problem over an image from the target class as the poisoned image such that the l_2 distance of the patched source image $\tilde{s}$ is close to the poisoned image z in the feature space, meanwhile, the l_∞ distance between the poisoned image and its initial image t is maintained less than a threshold ε. Formally, a poisoned image z can be defined as:

$$\arg\min_{z} ||f(z) - f(\tilde{s})||_2^2$$

$$st. \quad ||z - t||_\infty < \varepsilon, \tag{1}$$

where $f(\cdot)$ is the intermediate features of the DNN and ε is a small value that ensures the poisoned image z is not visually distinguishable from the initial target image t. The optimization mentioned above only generates a single poisoned sample given a pair of images from source and target classes as well as a fixed location for the trigger. One can add this poisoned data with the correct label to the training data and train a backdoor model. However, such a model will only have the backdoor triggered when the attacker places the trigger at the same location on the same source image, limiting the practicality of the attack.

To address this shortcoming, Saha et al. [35] propose manipulating the poisoned images to be closer to the cluster of patched source images rather than being close to only the single patched source image. Inspired by universal adversarial examples [33], Saha et al. [35] minimize the expected value of the loss in Eq. (2) over all possible trigger locations and source images. In their extension, the attacker first samples $\mathcal{K}$ random images t_k from the target class and initializes poisoned images z_k with t_k; second, $\mathcal{K}$ random images s_k is sampled from the source class and patched with triggers at randomly chosen locations to obtain $\tilde{s}_k$. For a given z_k in the poisoned image set, they search for a $s_{\tilde{a}(k)}$ in the patched image set which is close to z_k in the feature space $f(\cdot)$, as measured by Euclidean distance. Next, the attacker creates a one-to-one mapping $a(k)$ for the poisoned images set and the patched images set. Finally, the attacker performs one iteration of mini-batch projected gradient descent as follows:

$$\arg\min_{z} \sum_{k=1}^{\mathcal{K}} ||f(z_k) - f(s_{\tilde{a}(k)})||_2^2$$

$$st. \quad \forall k : ||z_k - t_k||_\infty < \varepsilon. \tag{2}$$

Using the method above, the backdoor trigger samples are given the correct label and only used at test time.

2.6 Application Areas

Most backdoor attacks and defenses select the image classification task to demonstrate the effectiveness of their attacks and defenses. However, other learning systems also are vulnerable to backdoor attacks in a range of application areas, e.g., object detection [14, 45], Natural Language Processing (NLP) [7,9,19,25,28], graph classification [46,51], Reinforcement Learning (RL) [18,44,49] and Federated Learning (FL) [4,48]. We will briefly survey how backdoors can be used to manipulate these learning systems.

Object Detection. Differing from image classification, object detection seeks to both detect the position of specific physical objects in an input image and predict the detected object's label with some probability. Gu et al. [14] implemented their backdoor attack on a traffic sign detection and classification system in which images captured from a car-mounted camera. In their work, a stop sign is maliciously mis-classified as a speed-limit sign by the backdoored model. Hwoever, we note that the detected position of the signs remain unchanged, only the labels are mis-identified when triggers are present on the detected traffic signs. Wenger et al. [45] propose a credible backdoor attack against facial recognition systems in practice, in which 7 physical objects can trigger a change in an individual's identity.

Natural Language Processing (NLP). There are several backdoor attacks against NLP systems [7,9,19,22,25,28]. Most of these works only explore the task of text classification, e.g. sentiment analysis on movie reviews [2], or hate speech detection on online social data [17]. Liu et al. [28] demonstrate the effectiveness of their backdoor attack on sentence attitude recognition. They use a crafted sequence of words at a fixed position as the trojan trigger. Dai et al. [9] inject the trojan into a LSTM-based sentiment analysis task. In this attack, the poisoned sentences need to be inserted into all positions of the given paragraph. Chen et al. [7] extend the trigger's granularity from the sentence-level to a character level and word level. Lin et al. [25] compose two sentences that are dramatically different in semantics as triggers. Kurita et al. [19] introduce a trojan to pre-trained language models, whereby for different target classes, the attackers need to replace the token embedding of the triggers with their handcrafted embeddings.

Li et al. [22] propose two novel hidden backdoor attacks, the *homograph attack* and the *dynamic sentence attack*, applicable against three major NLP tasks, including toxic comment detection, neural machine translation, and question answering. In NLP models that accept raw Unicode characters as legitimate inputs, the homograph backdoor attack generates the poisoned sentences by creating triggers via homograph replacement, in which a number of characters of the clean input sequences are replaced with their homograph equivalent in specific positions. In a more rigorous data-collection setting could remedy the process; for example, poisoned sentences may be filtered by word error checkers in a pre-processing stage. They propose a dynamic sentence backdoor attack, in which trigger sentences are generated by Language Models are context-aware and more natural than static approaches.

Graph Classification. Zhang et al. [51] propose a subgraph based backdoor attack to Graph Neural Networks (GNNs), in which a GNN classifier predicts an attacker-chosen target label for a testing graph once a predefined subgraph is injected to the testing graph. Xi et al. [46] present a graph-oriented backdoor attack where triggers are defined as specific subgraphs including both topological structures and descriptive features.

Reinforcement Learning. Yang et al. [49] propose methods to discreetly introduce and exploit backdoor attacks within a sequential decision-making agent, by training multiple benign and malicious policies within a single long short-term memory (LSTM) network. Wang et al. [44] explore backdoor attacks on deep reinforcement learning based autonomous vehicles, where the malicious action include vehicle deceleration and acceleration to induce stop-and-go traffic waves to create traffic congestion. Kiourti et al. [18] present a tool for exploring and evaluating backdoor attacks on deep reinforcement learning agents, they evaluate their methods on a broad set of DRL benchmarks and show that after poisoning as little as 0.025% of the training data, the attacker can successfully inject the trojans into DRL models.

Federated Learning. In comparison to the traditional centralized machine learning setting, Federated Learning (FL) mitigates many systemic privacy risks and distributes computational costs. This has produced an explosive growth of federated learning research. The purpose of backdoor attacks in FL is that an attacker who controls one or several participants may manipulate their local models to simultaneously fit the clean and poisoned training samples. With the aggregation of local models from participants into a global model at the server, the global model will have been influenced by the malicious models to behave maliciously on compromised inputs. Bagdasaryan et al. [4] are the first to mount a single local attacker backdoor attack against a FL platform via *model replacement*. In their attack, the attacker proposes a target backdoored global model $\mathcal{X}$ they want the server to be in the next round. The attacker then scales up his local backdoored model to ensure it can survive the averaging step to ensure the global model is substituted by $\mathcal{X}$.

On the other hand, Xie et al. [48] propose a distributed backdoor attack (DBA) which decomposes a global trigger pattern into separate local patterns and uses these local patterns to inject into the training sets of different local adversarial participants. Figure 1 illustrates the intuition of the DBA. As we can see, the attackers only need to inject a piece of the global trigger to poison their local models, such that the collective trigger is learned by the global model. Surprisingly, DBA can use a global trigger pattern to activate the ultimate global model as well as a centralized attack does. Xie et al. find that although no singular adversarial party had been poisoned by the global trigger under DBA, the DBA indeed can still behave maliciously as a centralized attack.

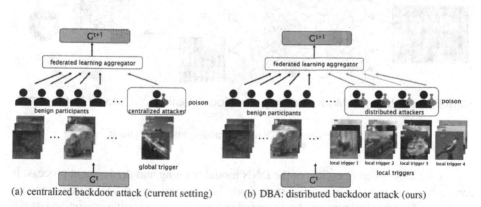

(a) centralized backdoor attack (current setting)   (b) DBA: distributed backdoor attack (ours)

Fig. 1. Intuition of the distributed backdoor attack (DBA) [48]. An attacker (orange) will poison a subset of his training data using only the trigger pattern located in the orange areas. The same reasoning applies to the remaining green, yellow, and blue marked attackers. (Color figure online)

3   Detecting and Defending Backdoors

Attacks from white- to black-box settings have been developed to subvert the machine learning model to include backdoored behavior. However, any model trainer or holder may take proactive steps to detect and defend their models against this threat. This section will describe at length how this attack may be thwarted. Overall, the task of detecting and defending against a backdoor attack can be divided into three key sub-tasks:

1. **Task 1:** *Detecting the existence of the backdoor.* For a given model, it is difficult to know if the model is compromised (i.e., a model with a backdoor) or not. The first step of detecting and defending against the backdoor attack is to analyze the model and determine if there is a backdoor present in this model.
2. **Task 2:** *Identifying the backdoor trigger.* When a backdoor is detected in a model, the second step is usually to identify which pattern (including its size, location, texture, and so on) is used as the trigger.
3. **Task 3:** *Mitigating the backdoor attack.* After identifying the existence of a backdoor, the mitigation of such an attack is to remove the backdoor behavior from the model. Note that backdoor models can be made to be robust against transfer learning or fine-tuning [50].

Note that not all detection and defense techniques will support all three sub-tasks. As some may assume prior knowledge that a backdoor has already been detected, and the proposal only contains techniques to recover the trigger or mitigate the attack.

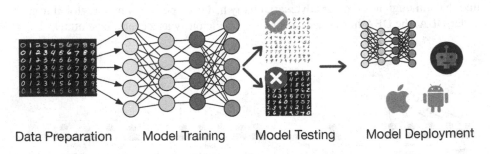

Data Preparation   Model Training   Model Testing   Model Deployment

Fig. 2. Overview of DNN model training and deployment.

Figure 2 shows an overview of the DNN model training and deployment process. It can be broken up into four general steps from data preparation, model training, model testing, and model deployment. As discussed in Sect. 2, most existing poisoning attacks target the model training (or model retraining) step. Thus, investigating if the model contains a backdoor, reconstructing potential triggers, and/or mitigating any backdoor attacks must occur after this training step. Thus, mitigation strategies will be employed either during model testing (i.e., pre-deployment) or at the model's runtime (i.e., post-deployment), and hence, depending on when the inspection occurs, existing detection and defense techniques can be divided into two categories: pre-deployment techniques or post-deployment techniques.

3.1 Pre-deployment Techniques

No Inspections. There exists work [26,52] attempting to directly mitigate the backdoor attack without inspecting the model behavior. The key technique behind these methods is to compress the model (e.g., by model pruning or similar techniques) or fine-tune the model with benign inputs to alter the model behavior hoping that the backdoor behavior is eliminated. Specifically, Zhao et al. [52] found that model pruning can remove some behaviors of a trained model, and potentially it can remove the backdoor of the model if pruning is purely using benign data.

Liu et al. [26] observe that pruning the model alone does not guarantee the removal of the model backdoor behavior. This is because the malicious model may use the same neuron to demonstrate both benign and malicious behaviors. Thus, if the neuron is removed, the model accuracy will be lower than that of the original model. This would be an undesirable consequence even though the model backdoor is removed. However, if this neuron is not pruned, the backdoor behavior is retained and the model continues to be malicious, also undesirable. Similarly, fine-tuning the model does not necessarily remove the model backdoor, as some attacks [50] target transfer learning scenarios where fine-tuning is needed. To solve this problem, Yao et al. propose Fine-Pruning, which combines the strengths of both fine-tuning and pruning to effectively nullify backdoors in DNN models. Fine-Pruning first removes backdoor neurons using pruning and fine-tuning the model in order to restore the drop in classification accuracy on clean inputs (which is introduced in the previous pruning procedure).

There are some limitations to these types of defenses. Firstly, model pruning itself has unknown effects on the model. Even though model accuracy after pruning does not decrease too much, many other important model properties, such as model bias (sometimes known as fairness) and model prediction performance, are not guaranteed to be the same. Using such models may potentially lead to severe consequences. Secondly, these mitigation techniques assume access to the training process and clean inputs, which conflicts with poisoning-based attacks.

Pre-deployment Model Inspections. Before the model is deployed, it is possible to check whether the model has been backdoored directly. This kind of strategy works without the running of the model, so it is also called static detection. For these types of techniques, some will require a large set of benign inputs to identify backdoors, such as Neural Cleanse (NC) [43], whereas others do not require much data (i.e., a limited number or even zero samples), such as ABS [27].

Neural Cleanse. Wang et al. [43] propose Neural Cleanse (NC), a pre-deployment technique to inspect DNNs, identify backdoors, and mitigate such attacks. Figure 3 illustrates the key observation that enables NC. The top figure shows a clean model with three output labels. If we want to perturb inputs belonging to C to A, more modification is needed to move samples across decision boundaries. The bottom figure shows the infected model, where the backdoor changes decision boundaries leading to a small perturbation value for changing inputs belonging to B and C to A.

Based on this observation, NC proposes to first compute a universal perturbation, which is the minimized amount of change to make the model predict a given target

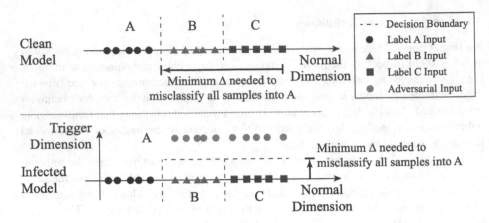

Fig. 3. Intuition of NC [43].

label. If the perturbation is small enough (i.e., smaller than a given threshold), NC considers it as one trigger. It then verifies this by adding this trigger to a large number of benign inputs and tests if it is really a trigger and tries to optimize it based on prediction results. After identifying the trigger, it can mitigate the attack by either using a filter (i.e., to detect images with such a trigger pattern) or patching the DNN by removing the corresponding behaviors by pruning the neural network.

NC has a number of limitations. First, NC makes an incorrect assumption that if pixels in a small region have a strong influence on the output result, they are treated as backdoor triggers. This results in NC confusing triggers with strong benign features. In many tasks, there exist strong local features, where a region of pixels is important for one output label, for example, the antlers of deers in CIFAR-10. Secondly, NC assumes that the trigger has to be small and in the corner areas. These are heuristics, which do not hold for many attacks. For example, Salem et al. [36] propose a dynamic attack, where triggers can be added to different places and can successfully bypass NC. Thirdly, NC requires a significant number of testing samples to determine if a backdoor exists in a model or not. In real-world scenarios, such a large number of benign inputs may not exist. Lastly, it is designed purely for input space attacks, and it does not work for feature space attacks, such as using Nashville and Gotham filters as triggers [27].

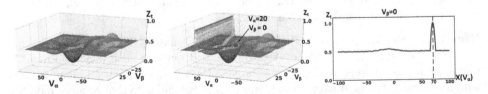

Fig. 4. Overview of ABS observations [27]. The left figure shows the feature surface of a benign model. The middle figure shows the feature surface of a model with a backdoor. The right figure shows a slice of surface for the backdoored model. The red dot in the middle figure shows a state where the attack happens, and it corresponds to the dashed line in the right figure. (Color figure online)

ABS. ABS is built on top of two key observations. The first is that successful attacks entail compromised neurons. In existing attacks, the backdoored model recognizes the trigger as a strong feature of the target label to achieve a high attack success rate. Such a feature is represented by a set of inner neurons, which are referred to as *compromised neurons*. The second observation is that compromised neurons represent a subspace for the target label that cutcrosses the whole space. This idea is shown in Fig. 4. The feature space surfaces of a benign model (left figure in Fig. 4) and that of a backdoored model are noticeably different. For a backdoored model, there exists a cut of the surface that is significantly different from the benign model due to the injected backdoor. As it works for all inputs, it will affect every prediction results once it is activated. Thus, it will interact with the whole interface. The phenomenon is demonstrated in the right figure of Fig. 4. When a neuron value is assigned to a special value, i.e., the trigger pixel value, the output will significantly deviate from normal.

Based on these observations, Liu et al. [27] propose Artificial Brain Stimulation (ABS). For any given input, ABS first predicts its label using the neural network. Then, it enumerates all neurons and performs a brain stimulation process. Namely, for each neuron, it tries to change its activation value to all possible values and simultaneously observes the value changes in the output. If there is one neuron whose behavior is similar to the right figure in Fig. 4, ABS treats it as a backdoor. To reconstruct the backdoor trigger, ABS then performs a reverse engineering process, which will try to find an input pattern that can strongly activate these compromised neurons and trigger the attack.

ABS also introduces a new type of backdoor attack, which is the feature space attack. Namely, the trigger is no longer an input pattern (i.e., a region with specific pixel values), but feature space patterns represent high-level features (e.g., an image filter). However, this attack also has its own limitations. Firstly, it assumes one backdoor for each class. This may not hold in practice, and backdoors have been shown to be dynamic [36]. Secondly, it currently enumerates neurons one by one, assuming the presence of a strong correlation between one neuron and the backdoor behavior, which may be hidden or overridden by more advanced attacks.

3.2 Post-deployment Techniques

In addition to static approaches functioning before models are deployed, there is also work that monitors the model at runtime and determines if the model has a backdoor and more importantly, if it has been triggered by an input or not. In this setting, the defense or detection system can inspect individual inputs, offering a focused means of directly reconstructing the trigger by inspecting the attack input.

STRIP. Gao et al. [12] propose STRong Intentional Perturbation (STRIP), a run-time trojan attack detection system. The workflow of STRIP is shown in Fig. 5. Firstly, STRIP will perturb each input by adding benign samples drawn from the test samples to obtain a list of perturbed inputs $X^{P_1}, X^{P_2}, ..., X^{P_N}$. These inputs are the overlap of a benign input and the given input. Next, it will feed all these inputs to the DNN model. Note that if the input contains a trigger, it is highly likely that a majority of the perturbed inputs will also yield predictions with the malicious output label result (due

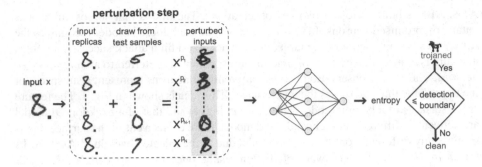

Fig. 5. Overview of STRIP [12].

to the existence of the trigger), whereas for a benign input, the results are closer to random. As a result, STRIP only needs to examine every prediction result, and can then make a judgment on if the input will trigger the backdoor or not.

STRIP can effectively detect backdoor models and inputs that trigger the backdoor if the trigger lies in the corners of the image or at least does not overly overlap with the main contents. Such an example is shown in Fig. 5). However, if the trigger does overlap with the contents (e.g., overlap with digits in Fig. 5), the detection will fail because the texture of the trigger will also be changed by the perturbations. Salem et al.'s [36] proposed a dynamic backdoor attack that uses triggers that can be in the middle of the image.

4 Applications of Backdoors

4.1 Watermarking

Digital Watermarking conceals information in a piece of media (e.g., sound, video, or images) to enable a party to verify the authenticity or the originality of the media. This watermark, however, must also be resilient to tampering and other actors seeking to subvert the legitimate piece of media.

Adi et al. [1] propose an IP protection method for DNNs by applying the backdoor to watermark DNNs. They present cryptographic modeling for both tasks of watermarking and backdooring DNNs, and show that the former can be constructed from the latter (through a cryptographic primitive known as *commitment*) in a black-box manner. The definition of the backdoor attack that Adi et al. provided in a cryptographic framework is as follows: Given a trigger set T and a labeling function T_L, the backdoor shall be termed as $b = (T, T_L)$. The backdooring algorithm $Backdoor(O^f, b, M)$ is a probabilistic polynomial-time (PPT) algorithm that receives as input an oracle to f (ground-truth labeling function $f : D \rightarrow L$, where D is input space, L is output space), the backdoor b and a model M, and outputs $\hat{M}$. $\hat{M}$ is considered *backdoored* if

$$Pr_{x \in \bar{D} \setminus T}[f(x) \neq Classify(\hat{M}, x)] \leq \varepsilon,$$
$$Pr_{x \in T}[T_L(x) \neq Classify(\hat{M}, x)] \leq \varepsilon,$$

$$(3)$$

where $\bar{D}$ is the meaningful input, $Classify(M,x)$ is a deterministic polynomial-time algorithm that, for an input $x \in D$ outputs a value $M(x) \in L\backslash\{\bot\}$, and $\bot$ is an undefined output label. This definition presents two ways to embed a backdoor. The first is that the backdoor is implanted into a *pre-trained model*. The second is the adversary can train a new model from scratch.

A watermarking scheme can be split into three key components.

1. Generation of the secret "marking" key mk. This key will be embedded as the watermark. A public verification key vk is also generated and will be used later to detect the watermark. In watermarking via backdoors, the backdoor is the marking key, while a commitment (the cryptographic primitive) used to generate the backdoor is the verification key.
2. Embedding the watermark (a backdoor b) into a DNN model. Through poisoned training data or retraining, as previously described in Sect. 2.1, the watermark (backdoor) can be embedded.
3. Verifying the presence of the watermark. Provided mk, vk, for a backdoor test $b = (T, T_L)$. If $\forall t^{(i)} \in T : T_L^{(i)} \neq f(t^{(i)})$, proceed to the next step, otherwise, the verification fails. Despite the detection of the watermark, one must verify the integrity of the commitment, i.e., if it was tampered or not. In the final step, the accuracy of the algorithm is verified. For all $i \in 1,..,n$, if more than $\varepsilon|T|$ elements from T does not satisfy $Classify(t^{(i)}, M) = T_L^{(I)}$, then the verification fails, otherwise the commitment has been successfully verified.

Adi et al. [1] prove their method upholds the properties of:

- *Functionality-preserving*: the prediction accuracy of the model should not be negatively influenced by the presence of the watermark.
- *Unremovability*: an adversary with full knowledge of the watermark generation process should not be able to remove the watermark from the model.
- *Unforgeability*: an adversary with only the verification key should not be able to demonstrate ownership of the marking key.
- *non-trivial ownership*: with knowledge of the watermark generation algorithm, a third party should not be able to generate marker and verification key pairs, and claim models for future models.

Li et al. [21], however, observe that the watermarking system proposed by Adi et al. [1] makes the assumption that only one backdoor (watermark) may be inserted into the model. For example, Salem et al. [36]'s Dynamic Backdoors contain multiple backdoors. The existence of multiple backdoors would result in multiple valid watermarks, and thus void the *Unforgeability* claim. The insertion of multiple backdoors would also impact the *Unremovability* of the original backdoor, otherwise termed as the persistence of the watermark. In response, Li et al. leverage two data preprocessing techniques that use out-of-bound values and null-embedding to improve the persistence of the watermark against other attackers and limit the effects of retraining in the event that another backdoor is to be injected on top of the existing backdoor. Li et al. also introduce *wonder filters*, a primitive to enable the embedding of bit-sequences (from the marker key) into the model.

The largest hurdle to overcome in the application of the backdoor attack as a means to watermark DNNs, is that neural networks are fundamentally designed to be tuned and trained incrementally. Li et al. propose a *model piracy* attack setting whereby an adversary wants to stake its own ownership claims on the model, or destroy the original owner's claims. To defend against this attack, Li et al. design a DNN watermarking system based on wonder filters that strongly authenticates owners by embedding (into the DNN) a filter described by the owner's private key. Where Li et al.'s work differs from Adi et al. is in the *wonder filter W*, which is a two-dimensional digital filter that can be applied to any input image. This filter will have 3 possible permutations for each pixel, transparent, positive change, or negative change, with a majority of filter pixels being transparent. Thus, W is defined by the position, size, and values of a $0/1$ bit pattern block.

When Li et al. apply *out-of-bound values*, they translate the $0/1$ bit pattern of W as out-of-bound values in the input images. A set of training data is processed with the filter. They then flip the values of the *wonder filter* to create an *inverted wonder filter* W^-. The *inverted filter* W^- is then applied to the same set of training data processed by W The set of images filtered by W are labeled as the target class label, while the W^- filtered data is labeled as the original class label before the data is used to train the backdoored model. As for the normal and null embeddings approach, the normal and null embeddings serve complementary objectives. The normal embedding injects the desired marker into the model, while the null embedding "locks down" the model, so no additional watermarks may be added.

Li et al.'s process of watermarking the image is similar to Adi er al's process, with the same three key processes of generating the secret "marking", or in this instance, the wonder filter W, embedding the watermark (and/or additionally locking down the model), and finally, the process of verifying the watermark, by using the image to compute W and an associated label. After applying W to a random set of images, it is expected that an authentic watermark should yield a majority of the target class label, instead of a random assortment of classes as expected from a random set of images, without W.

Li et al. also provide a security analysis to prove that their approach can uphold the requirements of *reliability, no false positives, unforgeability,* and *persistence*, whereby *Reliability* describes that for a given input x, a poisoned input ($x \oplus W$, or $x \oplus W^-$), the backdoored DNNs will produce the predefined output in a deterministic manner. *No False Positives* denotes that a verifier should not be capable of judging a clean model as the watermarked model. *unforgeability* ensures that the watermark injected on a DNN has a strong association with its owner, and *Persistence* guarantees that the watermark embedded cannot be corrupted or removed by an adversary.

4.2 Adversarial Example Detection

In Gotta Catch [39], Shan et al. observe that the backdoor attack will alter the decision boundary of the DNN models. Following the injection of a backdoor, the decision boundary of the original clean model will mutate. The mutation will result in triggers establishing shortcuts in the decision boundary of the backdoored model.

On the contrary, there is a common approach of adversarial attacks to find adversarial examples; for example, universal adversarial attacks [32,37], will try to iteratively search the whole dataset to find similar shortcuts to use as their universal adversarial examples. Based on this observation, the shortcut created by a backdoor can act as a trapdoor to capture the adversarial attacker's optimization process, detect, and/or recover from the adversarial attack [38]. The trapdoor implementation uses techniques similar to those found in BadNets backdoor attacks [14]. The authors define the trapdoor perturbation (the trigger) from multiple dimensions, e.g., mask ratio, size, pixel intensities, and relative locations.

4.3 Open Problems

- *Fair comparison of methods including attacks and defenses.* We have observed experimental settings (e.g. models and datasets) vary greatly across studies of different domains. Consequently to inspect the potential of AI Trojans in a standardized manner, The Intelligence Advanced Research Projects Activity (IARPA) has recently launched a program (and competition), Trojans in Artificial Intelligence (TrojAI) [16].
- *Persisting through fine-tuning in transfer learning.* A model backdoor can be made ineffective after only a few fine-tuning layers [14,50]. Unfortunately, this limits the practicality of the backdoor attack in the transfer learning setting. More advanced backdoor attacks that can persist through such fine-tuning processes remains a challenge.
- *Combining hidden triggers and clean labels.* To inject trojans into DNNs by poisoning the training data, the most stealthy method is to attach the triggers on the poisoned data in an imperceptible way, in addition to a correctly annotated label. Existing attacks either visually hide the triggers but retain an clearly poisoned label or correctly annotate the label with noticeable triggers. The combination of these stealth tactics, to produce poisoned data with an invisible trigger and clean labels still remains a challenge.
- *Accessing training data.* There are a variety of backdoor attacks, however only a small set has access to clean samples. In most security-sensitive cases, the attacker can only access a pre-trained model. The injection of a trojan by directly compromising the model weights without requiring access to the clean original training data still remains challenge.
- *Adaptiveness of Attacks and Defenses.* Existing attacks and defenses often discuss their effectiveness against reactive (dynamic) attack or defense countermeasures in a superficial and heuristic way, without including the adversary's possible countermeasures as a part of their works. These adaptive attacks and defenses can adaptively take optimal strategies when responding to an adversary's countermeasures, will provide improved practicality in realistic settings, but still remains an open challenge.

References

1. Adi, Y., Baum, C., Cissé, M., Pinkas, B., Keshet, J.: Turning your weakness into a strength: watermarking deep neural networks by backdooring. In: 27th USENIX Security Symposium, USENIX Security 2018, Baltimore, MD, USA, 15–17 August 2018, pp. 1615–1631 (2018)
2. Alzantot, M., Sharma, Y., Elgohary, A., Ho, B., Srivastava, M.B., Chang, K.: Generating natural language adversarial examples. In: Riloff, E., Chiang, D., Hockenmaier, J., Tsujii, J. (eds.) Proceedings of the 2018 Conference on Empirical Methods in Natural Language Processing, Brussels, Belgium, 31 October–4 November 2018, pp. 2890–2896. Association for Computational Linguistics (2018)
3. Bagdasaryan, E., Shmatikov, V.: Blind backdoors in deep learning models. arXiv preprint arXiv:2005.03823 (2020)
4. Bagdasaryan, E., Veit, A., Hua, Y., Estrin, D., Shmatikov, V.: How to backdoor federated learning. In: International Conference on Artificial Intelligence and Statistics, pp. 2938–2948 (2020)
5. Barni, M., Kallas, K., Tondi, B.: A new backdoor attack in CNNs by training set corruption without label poisoning. In: 2019 IEEE International Conference on Image Processing (ICIP), pp. 101–105. IEEE (2019)
6. Chen, X., Liu, C., Li, B., Lu, K., Song, D.: Targeted backdoor attacks on deep learning systems using data poisoning. arXiv preprint arXiv:1712.05526 (2017)
7. Chen, X., Salem, A., Backes, M., Ma, S., Zhang, Y.: BadNL: backdoor attacks against NLP models. arXiv preprint arXiv:2006.01043 (2020)
8. Costales, R., Mao, C., Norwitz, R., Kim, B., Yang, J.: Live trojan attacks on deep neural networks. In: Proceedings of the IEEE/CVF Conference on Computer Vision and Pattern Recognition Workshops, pp. 796–797 (2020)
9. Dai, J., Chen, C., Li, Y.: A backdoor attack against LSTM-Based text classification systems. IEEE Access **7**, 138872–138878 (2019)
10. Désidéri, J.-A.: Multiple-gradient descent algorithm (MGDA) for multiobjective optimization. C.R. Math. **350**(5–6), 313–318 (2012)
11. Dumford, J., Scheirer, W.J.: Backdooring convolutional neural networks via targeted weight perturbations. In: 2020 IEEE International Joint Conference on Biometrics, IJCB 2020, Houston, TX, USA, 28 September–1 October 2020, pp. 1–9. IEEE (2020)
12. Gao, Y., Xu, C., Wang, D., Chen, S., Ranasinghe, D.C., Nepal, S.: Strip: a defence against trojan attacks on deep neural networks. In: Proceedings of the 35th Annual Computer Security Applications Conference, pp. 113–125 (2019)
13. Goodfellow, I., et al.: Generative adversarial nets. In: Advances in Neural Information Processing Systems, pp. 2672–2680 (2014)
14. Gu, T., Dolan-Gavitt, B., Garg, S.: BadNets: identifying vulnerabilities in the machine learning model supply chain. IEEE Access **7**, 47230–47244 (2019)
15. Heffner, C.: Binwalk: firmware analysis tool (2010). https://code.google.com/p/binwalk/. Accessed 03 Mar 2013
16. IARPA. Trojans in artificial intelligence (TrojAI)
17. Kaggle. Toxic comment classification challenge (2020). https://www.kaggle.com/c/jigsaw-toxic-comment-classification-challenge/. Accessed 24 June 2020
18. Kiourti, P., Wardega, K., Jha, S., Li, W.: TrojDRL: evaluation of backdoor attacks on deep reinforcement learning. In: 2020 57th ACM/IEEE Design Automation Conference (DAC), pp. 1–6 (2020)
19. Kurita, K., Michel, P., Neubig, G.: Weight poisoning attacks on pretrained models. In: Proceedings of the 58th Annual Meeting of the Association for Computational Linguistics (Online, July 2020), pp. 2793–2806. Association for Computational Linguistics (2020)

20. Langner, R.: Stuxnet: dissecting a cyberwarfare weapon. IEEE Secur. Priv. **9**(3), 49–51 (2011)
21. Li, H., Willson, E., Zheng, H., Zhao, B.Y.: Persistent and unforgeable watermarks for deep neural networks. arXiv preprint arXiv:1910.01226 (2019)
22. Li, S., et al.: Hidden backdoors in human-centric language models. In: Kim, Y., Kim, J., Vigna, G., Shi, E. (eds.) 2021 ACM SIGSAC Conference on Computer and Communications Security, Virtual Event, CCS 2021, Republic of Korea, 15–19 November 2021, pp. 3123–3140. ACM (2021)
23. Li, S., Xue, M., Zhao, B., Zhu, H., Zhang, X.: Invisible backdoor attacks on deep neural networks via steganography and regularization. IEEE Trans. Dependable Secure Comput. **18**, 2088–2105 (2020)
24. Ligh, M.H., Case, A., Levy, J., Walters, A.: The Art of Memory Forensics: Detecting Malware and Threats in Windows, Linux, and Mac Memory. Wiley, Hoboken (2014)
25. Lin, J., Xu, L., Liu, Y., Zhang, X.: Composite backdoor attack for deep neural network by mixing existing benign features. In: Proceedings of the 2020 ACM SIGSAC Conference on Computer and Communications Security, pp. 113–131 (2020)
26. Liu, K., Dolan-Gavitt, B., Garg, S.: Fine-pruning: defending against backdooring attacks on deep neural networks. In: Bailey, M., Holz, T., Stamatogiannakis, M., Ioannidis, S. (eds.) RAID 2018. LNCS, vol. 11050, pp. 273–294. Springer, Cham (2018). https://doi.org/10.1007/978-3-030-00470-5_13
27. Liu, Y., Lee, W.-C., Tao, G., Ma, S., Aafer, Y., Zhang, X.: Abs: scanning neural networks for back-doors by artificial brain stimulation. In: Proceedings of the 2019 ACM SIGSAC Conference on Computer and Communications Security, pp. 1265–1282 (2019)
28. Liu, Y., et al.: Trojaning attack on neural networks. In: The Network and Distributed System Security Symposium (NDSS) (2017)
29. Liu, Y., et al.: Trojaning attack on neural networks. In: 25nd Annual Network and Distributed System Security Symposium, NDSS 2018, San Diego, California, USA, 18–21 February 2018. The Internet Society (2018)
30. Liu, Y., et al.: A survey on neural trojans. IACR Cryptology ePrint Archive 2020/201 (2020)
31. Mirza, M., Osindero, S.: Conditional generative adversarial nets. arXiv preprint arXiv:1411.1784 (2014)
32. Moosavi-Dezfooli, S., Fawzi, A., Fawzi, O., Frossard, P.: Universal adversarial perturbations. In: 2017 IEEE Conference on Computer Vision and Pattern Recognition, CVPR 2017, Honolulu, HI, USA, 21–26 July 2017, pp. 86–94 (2017)
33. Moosavi-Dezfooli, S.-M., Fawzi, A., Fawzi, O., Frossard, P.: Universal adversarial perturbations. In: Proceedings of the IEEE Conference on Computer Vision and Pattern Recognition, pp. 1765–1773 (2017)
34. Rezende, D.J., Mohamed, S., Wierstra, D.: Stochastic backpropagation and approximate inference in deep generative models. arXiv preprint arXiv:1401.4082 (2014)
35. Saha, A., Subramanya, A., Pirsiavash, H.: Hidden trigger backdoor attacks. In: The Thirty-Fourth AAAI Conference on Artificial Intelligence, AAAI 2020, New York, NY, USA, 7–12 February 2020, pp. 11957–11965. AAAI Press (2020)
36. Salem, A., Wen, R., Backes, M., Ma, S., Zhang, Y.: Dynamic backdoor attacks against machine learning models. arXiv preprint arXiv:2003.03675 (2020)
37. Shafahi, A., Najibi, M., Xu, Z., Dickerson, J.P., Davis, L.S., Goldstein, T.: Universal adversarial training. In: The Thirty-Fourth AAAI Conference on Artificial Intelligence, AAAI 2020, New York, NY, USA, 7–12 February 2020, pp. 5636–5643. AAAI Press (2020)
38. Shan, S., Wenger, E., Wang, B., Li, B., Zheng, H., Zhao, B.Y.: Gotta catch'em all: using honeypots to catch adversarial attacks on neural networks. In: Proceedings of the 2020 ACM SIGSAC Conference on Computer and Communications Security, CCS (2020)

39. Shan, S., Wenger, E., Wang, B., Li, B., Zheng, H., Zhao, B.Y.: Gotta catch'em all: using honeypots to catch adversarial attacks on neural networks. In: 2020 ACM SIGSAC Conference on Computer and Communications Security, Virtual Event, CCS 2020, USA, 9–13 November 2020, pp. 67–83. ACM (2020)
40. Shokri, R., Stronati, M., Song, C., Shmatikov, V.: Membership inference attacks against machine learning models. In: IEEE Symposium on Security and Privacy, pp. 3–18. IEEE (2017)
41. Tan, T.J.L., Shokri, R.: Bypassing backdoor detection algorithms in deep learning. In: IEEE European Symposium on Security and Privacy, EuroS&P 2020, Genoa, Italy, 7–11 September 2020, pp. 175–183. IEEE (2020)
42. Turner, A., Tsipras, D., Madry, A.: Clean-label backdoor attacks
43. Wang, B., et al.: Neural cleanse: identifying and mitigating backdoor attacks in neural networks. In: 2019 IEEE Symposium on Security and Privacy (SP), pp. 707–723. IEEE (2019)
44. Wang, Y., Sarkar, E., Maniatakos, M., Jabari, S.E.: Stop-and-go: exploring backdoor attacks on deep reinforcement learning-based traffic congestion control systems. arXiv preprint arXiv:2003.07859 (2020)
45. Wenger, E., Passananti, J., Yao, Y., Zheng, H., Zhao, B.Y.: Backdoor attacks on facial recognition in the physical world. arXiv preprint arXiv:2006.14580 (2020)
46. Xi, Z., Pang, R., Ji, S., Wang, T.: Graph backdoor. In: 30th USENIX Security Symposium, USENIX Security 2021 (2021)
47. Xiang, Z., Miller, D.J., Kesidis, G.: Revealing backdoors, post-training, in DNN classifiers via novel inference on optimized perturbations inducing group misclassification. In: IEEE International Conference on Acoustics, Speech and Signal Processing (ICASSP) (2020)
48. Xie, C., Huang, K., Chen, P.-Y., Li, B.: DBA: distributed backdoor attacks against federated learning. In: International Conference on Learning Representations (2019)
49. Yang, Z., Iyer, N., Reimann, J., Virani, N.: Design of intentional backdoors in sequential models. CoRR abs/1902.09972 (2019)
50. Yao, Y., Li, H., Zheng, H., Zhao, B.Y.: Latent backdoor attacks on deep neural networks. In: Proceedings of the 2019 ACM SIGSAC Conference on Computer and Communications Security, pp. 2041–2055 (2019)
51. Zhang, Z., Jia, J., Wang, B., Gong, N.Z.: Backdoor attacks to graph neural networks. arXiv preprint arXiv:2006.11165 (2020)
52. Zhao, B., Lao, Y.: Resilience of pruned neural network against poisoning attack. In: 2018 13th International Conference on Malicious and Unwanted Software (MALWARE), pp. 78–83. IEEE (2018)
53. Zhong, H., Liao, C., Squicciarini, A.C., Zhu, S., Miller, D.J.: Backdoor embedding in convolutional neural network models via invisible perturbation. In: Tenth ACM Conference on Data and Application Security and Privacy, CODASPY 2020, New Orleans, LA, USA, 16–18 March 2020, pp. 97–108. ACM (2020)

On Implementation-Level Security of Edge-Based Machine Learning Models

Lejla Batina[1], Shivam Bhasin[2], Jakub Breier[3], Xiaolu Hou[4],
and Dirmanto Jap[2(✉)]

[1] Radboud University, Nijmegen, The Netherlands
[2] Nanyang Technological University, Singapore, Singapore
djap@ntu.edu.sg
[3] Silicon Austria Labs, TU-Graz SAL DES Lab,
Graz University of Technology, Graz, Austria
[4] Slovak University of Technology, Bratislava, Slovakia

Abstract. In this chapter, we are considering the physical security of Machine Learning (ML) implementations on Edge Devices. We list the state-of-the-art known physical attacks, with the main attack objectives to reverse engineer and misclassify ML models. These attacks have been reported for different target platforms with the usage of both passive and active attacks. The presented works highlight the potential threat of stealing an intellectual property or confidential model trained with private data, and also the possibility to tamper with the device during the execution to cause misclassification. We also discus possible counter-measures to mitigate such attacks.

1 Introduction

Security evaluation labs are facing new challenges every day as the adversaries are becoming more powerful considering the resources available and more advanced in terms of methods and techniques they use. Thus, machine learning (ML) is becoming indispensable for secure cryptographic implementations and ML methods are becoming mandatory in security evaluations. This aspect of AI for physical attacks is elaborated in more detail in [58,59].

We are also witnessing an increase in intellectual property (IP) preserving strategies for various industries such as media content protection (Netflix and Spotify), automotive, wearables (such as watches and wristbands) etc. Basically, for those cases when optimized neural networks are of commercial interest, model details are often kept undisclosed. There are many reasons for keeping the neural network architectures secret. Often, those pre-trained models might provide additional information regarding the training data, which can be very sensitive. One critical example, is that if the model was trained on medical records of patients [19], confidential information could be encoded into the network during the training phase. Another use case of a neural net as an IP is in products using

L. Batina et al. (Eds.): Security and Artificial Intelligence, LNCS 13049, pp. 335–359, 2022.
https://doi.org/10.1007/978-3-030-98795-4_14

deep learning for high definition maps and cameras e.g. in automotive applications. As those markets are very competitive; the more efficient and effective neural networks are, the more successful companies selling them become.

Hence, determining the layout of the network with e.g. trained weights is a desirable target for an attacker. There are several ways to do it. First, the attacker might try to train new models, providing he/she has the access to target neural nets and training data. Second, the attacker could reverse engineer the neural nets of interest by using some additional information that becomes available while the device under attack is operating. This additional information is often physical and provided as a side channel e.g. timing, electromagnetic emanation (EM), or as a result of an active manipulations such as through fault injection responses and similar.

Relevant previous works on reverse engineering neural nets via side channels showed a lot of promise for this kind of research [4,5]. It was demonstrated that a side-channel attacker is capable of reverse engineering proprietary information from an ARM Cortex-M3 microcontroller, which is a platform often used in edge devices using neural networks such as wearables, surveillance cameras etc. Other works considering fault injection techniques and the information learned from this kind of attacks followed [6].

1.1   Machine Learning for Edge Devices

In this chapter, we are focusing on Edge devices that can be used in applications like automotive, security cameras, wristbands, smart factory etc. Edge devices are those that collect, process and store data, close to the things/edges/sensors where the information is produced and gathered. This paradigm on computing saves a lot on latency and enables real time processing, as compared to the cloud based alternatives. With time edge devices have been strengthened with enhanced capabilities like artificial intelligence (AI) to provide decision making power to them. This integration of AI or in particular machine learning capabilities to edge devices is popularly known as EdgeML [14]. These devices can range from general purpose hardware like an Arm CortexM3 microcontroller, or those with dedicated hardware support for ML processing like Nvidia Jetson, Intel neural compute stick etc.

1.2   Attacks on Machine Learning

Security and reliability of machine learning has been a rising matter of concern in recent years. Here we briefly discuss some of the most prominent types of attacks which have been reported.

Model extraction attacks were reported targeting machine learning algorithms. The main idea behind such attacks is to query a victim model as a black box, with chosen/known input data and try to construct another model which mimics the victim model in prediction and performance. Such attacks are widely popular in the Machine learning as a Service (MLaaS) paradigm, where an API of the victim model is available to the adversary on a pay per use basis [51] and the adversary aims to recover an equivalent model with minimum number of queries. Apart from model extraction, known attacks were extended to the recovery of training data by techniques like membership inference and model inversion. Shokri *et al.* [45] reported the leakage of sensitive information from machine learning models about individual data records used for training. They show that such models are vulnerable to membership inference attacks. Details about training data can also be leaked through model inversion as presented by Fredrikson *et al.* [18].

Other kinds of attacks compromising the reliability of machine learning were reported. These attacks systematically lead a trained model to predict an incorrect output, resulting in a so-called an evasion attack [48]. The modus operandi of this attack involves small changes in the input that push the model to cross the decision boundaries during the classification. This effectively changes the resulting output class. The perturbed inputs were later called *"adversarial examples"* and can be used for various different purposes, including targeted and untargeted misclassification, denial of service, etc.

All such attacks target the model behavior and run independent of implementation style. Normally, such an API model would be hosted on the cloud. As the attacks appeared, appropriate mitigation were also proposed, for example, against model extraction attacks [30,35], evasion [11] and adversarial attacks [12].

With the adoption of machine learning for edge devices under EdgeML paradigm, new vulnerabilities arose. The computation of resource intensive machine learning algorithms leaves a non-negligible physical signature for every execution. This physical signature depends on the model parameters and inputs. If the adversary who controls the inputs can measure this physical signature, it is possible to learn information about otherwise black box model. The physical signature can be in form of timing, power consumption, cache access patterns etc. A survey of side-channel based attacks on machine learning discussion on mitigation techniques is reported in Sect. 2.

EdgeML also exposes the machine learning computation to active adversary which are capable of disturbing the computation through intentional perturbations. The introduced disturbances to the computation may often lead the trained model to predict an incorrect output. From the higher level, these attack are similar to evasion attacks with adversarial attacks. However, an advanced adversary capable of fault injection can be much more powerful as the perturbations can potentially be inserted at an arbitrary point of the computation, giving a more precise control to the adversary. Further modification of these attacks can also lead to model extraction or denial of service. A survey of fault-injection based attacks on machine learning and discussion on mitigation techniques is reported in Sect. 3.

2   Overview Side Channel Threats to Machine Learning

With the systematic deployment of ML models on edge devices, unprecedented physical access to those models has lead to new security vulnerabilities. While classically these ML models are considered a black box, physical access permits different adversaries to snoop direct or indirect information about the internal execution. In this section, we provide an overview of recent works which used side-channel analysis to compromise ML models.

Side-channel attacks (SCA) are passive attacks that observe physical quantities related to computation of sensitive variables (dependent on secret data) and exploit it to gain confidential information. SCA have been widely studied in the community of information security and cryptography over the past two decades to demonstrate vulnerabilities in implementations of various security and cryptographic algorithms including both symmetric and asymmetric key primitives. They exploit physical traits like power consumption, computation time, cache access patterns, electromagnetic (EM) emanation, etc. Typical attacks relying on statistical methods are Differential Power Analysis (DPA) or Differential ElectroMagnetic Analysis (DEMA). Application of SCA on cryptographic primitives and recent advances with application of ML is previously discussed in [58,59].

When a given implementation of ML model is executed, it generates a physical signature. This physical signature, although unintentional, exists in various forms. Let us take an example of execution time of a neural network. This execution time will depend on structural parameters of the network like the number of layers, number of neurons, etc. Even inside a single neuron, the choice of the activation function influences the execution time, as shown in [5]. Activation functions like *ReLU* are a lot less resource intensive compared to *sigmoid* or *tanh* that involve complex operations like exponentiation. Moreover, the input-dependent execution time of exponentiation can reveal information about the input to an adversary who has access to detailed timing patterns. Similar vulnerabilities can also be exploited by an adversary who has access to other physical signatures.

Those side channels have been demonstrated to leak sensitive parameters of a ML model like number of layers, number of neurons, activation functions, secret weights, filter size etc. The leakage can be exploited in several scenarios. We identified three attack scenarios presented in the literature, which are as follows:

- *Model Extraction:* The adversary aims to recover parameters of the target model with as much precision as possible. Such attacks are relevant for the IP theft scenario where adversary has cost benefits to recover secret black box model and evade payment for additional licences. Precise knowledge of the model can also be exploited to learn information on training data, which can be sensitive and critical in certain settings like healthcare.
- *Substitute Model Extraction:* This is a weaker version of the model extraction attack where an adversary aims at recovering a model that performs similarly to the target black box model. The performance can be expressed in metrics like testing accuracy.
- *Input Recovery:* For certain applications, where the input to a model is privacy sensitive, appropriate security measures like encryption are used to not communicate the sensitive input in plaintext over an open communication channel. However, for inference tasks, the input must be decrypted before any processing by the ML model. Side-channel leakage of interactions between the

model and the secret input can also be exploited to learn information about the input. Most, if not all attacks in this class exploit the processing of the input in the first layer where processing is done on raw inputs.

2.1 State-of-the-Art

Previous works demonstrating vulnerabilities of ML models against side-channel attacks have looked into the following physical quantities:

- *Timing Side Channel:* The vulnerabilities under this class exploit the fact that the time of internal computation relates to the parameters of the target model. Previous research has shown that both, execution time and the time to access the model parameters can leak critical information.
- *Power/EM Side Channel:* Power consumption or EM emanations of internal operations can be exploited to gain information on involved sensitive values. Vulnerabilities in this class typically target, but are not limited to, basic operations like weight multiplication or CONV filters.
- *Microarchitectural Side Channel:* Executing ML models on commodity hardware like high-end CPU or GPU results in leakage at the microarchitectural level. Most known works have exploited cache access patterns in terms of timing related to cache hit or cache miss.

Table 1 provides the summary of recent attacks that have been reported. In the rest of this section, we will provide more details on relevant previous works.

Table 1. Summary of the state-of-the-art SCA for DL

Work	Side-channel	Attack model	Network	Target device
[27]	Timing, memory	Model extraction (first layer)	AlexNet, SqueezeNet	CNN Accelerator
[17]	Timing	Substitute model extraction	VGG	Intel CPU
[53]	Power	Input recovery	Binarized CNN	FPGA based CNN accelerator
[5]	EM	Input recovery	MLP, CNN	ARM microprocessor
[15]	Power, timing	Input recovery	MLP	Atmel microprocessor
[4]	EM	Model extraction	MLP, CNN	AVR and ARM microprocessors
[56]	EM, timing	Model extraction	Binarized ConvNet, VGG, LeNet, AlexNet	PYNQ board
[16]	Power	Model extraction (weight recovery)	BNN	FPGA accelerator
[54]	Cache	Substitute model extraction	VGG, ResNet	CPU
[24]	Cache	Substitute model extraction	VGG, ResNet, DenseNet, Inception, MobileNet, Xception	CPU
[26]	Cache	Model extraction	ResNet	NVDIA GPU

Timing Side-Channel. One of the earliest works on reverse engineering targeting Convolution Neural Networks (CNN) with Side-Channel Attacks (SCA) was proposed by Hua *et al.* [27]. The work acknowledges the sensitivity of the model and assumes standard protection like executing model computation in secure enclaves like Intel Software Guard Extensions (SGX). It exploits information leakage through timing (and memory) side-channels targeting CNN accelerators running in a secure enclave. The secure enclave prevents an adversary from accessing information of the execution, however, the off-chip memory accesses are still observable, which eventually allows reverse engineering of CNN structure and weights. Owing to the huge size of CNN models, it is not possible to store all weights/parameters on the on-chip memory, rather off-chip memory stores the parameters and is accessed when required in the computation. Memory access patterns reveal information of accessed memory locations and read/write patterns. The information leakage on access patterns remains available even if the memory is encrypted. As a result, Hua *et al.* demonstrate the retrieval of key network parameters like the number of layers, input/output sizes of each layer, size of filters, data dependencies among layers, etc. This allows an attacker to infer a small set of possible network structures by exploiting the execution time of a computation on a CNN accelerator.

Two commonly popular networks were successfully targeted, AlexNet [33] and SqueezeNet [28]. Once the network structure is recovered, the proposed attack can be extended to reverse engineer the secret weights of the CNN. The attack assumes usage of dynamic zero pruning in the CNN architecture and exploits it for weight recovery, with knowledge of the inputs. However, the exploited memory access patterns are available under a strong assumption like hardware Trojan, physical memory bus probing or compromised OS. Activation functions like *ReLU* which converts any negative input to zero, result in a large number of zeros in intermediate results of an inference. These extra zeros can be pruned to optimize storage. However, this memory optimization leaks the number of zero-valued pixels pruned by the activation function, which can then be exploited to retrieve information on weight and bias, in particular their ratio. The knowledge of ratio significantly reduces the entropy of weights. The authors demonstrated the recovery of the weight and the bias for the first layer of AlexNet. Weight recovery attacks on deeper layers were not investigated.

Duddu *et al.* [17] proposed a timing based attack on neural networks. The attack can target different hardware architectures or dedicated accelerators as long as the victim and the adversary use copies of the same hardware. The timing information under the black box model is used to determine the network depth under a fixed number of queries. With the information on network depth, the authors generate a substitute model of comparable accuracy to the original model. Reinforcement learning is used to reconstruct a substitute architecture. The attack is demonstrated on VGG [46]-like deep architectures on an Intel Xeon Gold 5115 platform, and the authors argue that the proposed method can be extended to any other hardware accelerator as well. The test accuracy of the substitute model is within 5% error margin from the targeted model architecture. Note that this method does not allow model extraction but finds a substitute network.

Power and EM Side-Channel. Batina *et al.* [4] proposed a full reverse engineering of neural network parameters based on power/EM side-channel analysis. The proposed attack is able to recover key parameters i.e., activation function, pre-trained weights, number of hidden layers and neurons in each layer, without access to any training data. The adversary uses a combination of simple power/EM analysis, differential power/EM analysis and timing analysis to recover different parameters. In the following, we describe in brief how different parameters are recovered.

The attack targets a trained model of a feed-forward neural network deployed on an embedded device for testing. The adversary feeds known random inputs in a form of floating point real numbers and observes side channels. Fixed point numbers make the attack easier. The measurement setup is shown in Fig. 1(a). A sample EM trace is shown in Fig. 1(b) for a 4-layer Multilayer Perceptron (MLP) with (50, 30, 20, 50) neurons. One can easily distinguish each of the 4-layers. Moreover, it is shown in [4], that the adversary can zoom into each neuron and observe each multiplication and activation function. In other words, the adversary can collect a large amount of traces in one go and reuse individual parts of the traces for recovering different parameters of the network.

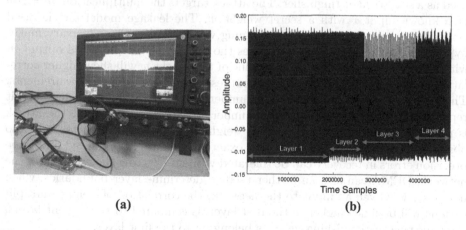

(a)   (b)

Fig. 1. (a) Experimental EM side-channel measurement setup, (b) Pattern of a 4-layer MLP network with (50, 30, 20, 50) neuron in each layer [4].

The first step is to recover the activation function for each neuron. The activation function is a non-linear component in the neural network processing and normalizing its complex implementation results in a non-constant time execution. Note that the adversary does not need new timing measurements. The EM traces provides precise timing patterns for each activation function in each neuron. Table 2 shows minimum, maximum and mean execution times of *sigmoid*, *tanh* and *ReLU* activation functions which can be matched to a pre-characterized profile for recovery. The pre-characterized timing profile of the activation functions, when compared with unlabeled timing profile of target activation function, will reveal the function with high probability. Even though some functions may have similar timing profiles like *sigmoid* and *tanh*, still with enough test samples, the two functions are easily distinguishable from each other owing to different mean timing and corresponding ranges (see Table 2).

Table 2. Minimum, Maximum, and Mean computation times (in ns) for different activation functions as measured from the EM trace.

Activation function	Minimum	Maximum	Mean
ReLU	9 767	9 837	9 801
Sigmoid	142 902	179 151	163 449
Tanh	157 693	220 790	208 231

The next step is to recover the individual weights. The weights are recovered using differential power/EM analysis and the Pearson correlation coefficient is used as a statistical distinguisher. The attack targets the multiplication $m = x \cdot w$ of a known input x with a secret weight w. The leakage model for the used embedded microcontroller is the Hamming weight (HW). The adversary makes hypothesis on the weight and correlates the activity of the predicted output m with measured traces t. The correct value of the weight w will show higher correlation compared to all other wrong hypotheses w^*, given enough measurements. The attack was demonstrated in real numbers in IEEE 754 format, where 32-bit representation is used. To keep the number of hypothesis in check, the attack is performed byte-wise and the 32-bit weight is recovered in 4 parts. It is also observed, that unlike in cryptography, exact weights are not required and some precision errors in recovery can be tolerated without affecting the accuracy of the network. DEMA can also be further used to determine layer boundaries, when not possible. Given an input to the network, the correlation of weight multiplications will be much higher in the first layer as compared to subsequent layers, thus allowing distinguishing neurons belonging to the first layer.

The full network is recovered in an iterative manner with a combination of these developed techniques. The network is recovered from input to output, neuron by neuron and layer by layer. The attack scales linearly with the size of the network and the same set of traces can be reused for various steps of the attack limiting the measurement effort.

Dubey *et al.* [16] proposed a power-based side-channel attack on a Binarized Neural Networks (BNN) to recover secret parameters such as weights and biases.

In contrast to Batina *et al.* [4], the target platform is parallel hardware accelerators running a 7-series FPGA board mounted on a SAKURA-X board. They exploit power leakage and perform a basic correlation attack on 4-bit of the weights and demonstrate a successful weight recovery with 200 measurements only. Authors further propose design of BNN accelerators that can resist DPA using countermeasures like masking.

Yu *et al.* [56] proposed a model extraction attack based on combination of EM side-channel measurement and adversarial active learning to recover the Binarized Neural Networks (BNNs) architecture on popular large-scale NN hardware accelerators. The network architecture is first inferred through EM leakage, and then, the parameters are estimated with adversarial learning. For the layer topology reverse engineering, the attacker observes the average timing behavior from the EM traces. This is based on the observation that different layers will result in different execution times. For example, the pooling layer typically requires a shorter time than a convolution one, and a fully-connected layer is observed to have the longest execution time, since it requires most of the sequential XNOR computations. Thus, by observing the timing profile, the adversary could reconstruct the network architecture. In the adversarial learning setting, the attacker crafts malicious inputs for the query, which could be used to identify the decision boundary for the trained model. For the attack, the adversary is assumed to be incapable of accessing the training data or knowing the model. The attack shown through the experiment could recover 96–99% in comparison to the black box model.

Considering input recovery attack using power/EM side-channel, the first attack was reported by Wei *et al.* [53]. Authors demonstrate recovery of the input image from FPGA based CNN accelerator. The proposed attack exploits a specific design choice, i.e., the line buffer in a convolution layer of a CNN. Two attack scenarios were presented considering different adversarial capabilities. The first one is the passive model, where the adversary eavesdrops the power consumption during the execution. Assuming that if the processed data is unchanged between cycles, the internal transitions will be limited, resulting in lower power consumption, and thus, by monitoring the power leakage, the adversary could determine if the pixels share similar values, whether they belong to the background of the image. The other is the active model, where the adversary is profiling the correlation between power signals, by building a power template. The power template characterizes the mapping between pixel values and the corresponding power leakage, under different kernels. The experiment conducted on a MNIST dataset reported a recovery success of 89%.

Batina *et al.* [5] also reported an input recovery attack on embedded platforms. They consider known or commonly used networks where the weights are either public or independently recovered using one of the reverse engineering techniques. Only the first layer weights are crucial for this attack which targets the multiplication between secret input and known weights. This attack is similar to the previous attack on multiplication proposed in [4]. The attack targets the multiplication $m = x \cdot w$ of a secret input x with a known weight w. The issue in this case is that each input is only processed once and thus must be recovered in a single measurement. To overcome this limitation, an adversary can exploit individual weight multiplications in different neurons, captured on different part of the same trace. Thus, EM measurements corresponding to a fixed unknown input and several known weights are present in the same measurement, which can be broken into short independent traces to conduct a classical correlation-based attack. This kind of attacks which exploit different computations in the same measurements are popularly known as horizontal attacks. For bigger networks with a large input layer, the amount of individual multiplications available to an adversary increases, thus allowing a bigger measurement set to perform the attack. The recovery was shown on MNIST images with a precision error of 2 decimal places resulting in almost no visual differences between original and recovered images. The attack also applies on CNN, where a single input value might be processed several times (due to convolution operation). A similar vulnerability as shown in [5] was exploited through timing side-channel by Dong et al. [15] to recover input MNIST images with 96% accuracy on 4-layer MLP running on an 8-bit Atmel XMEGA128 microprocessor. They exploit the fact that input multiplication with constant weights will result in a variable time floating point multiplication. The precise timing of the multiplication can be recovered by observing power side-channel trace.

Microarchitectural Side-Channel. Recently, some works based on microarchitectural attacks have also been proposed for the reverse engineering of Deep Learning (DL). Yan et al. [54] have proposed the Cache Telepathy method. The observation is that, for typical NN , the multiplication operation depends on GEMM (Generalized Matrix Multiply). In this case, the architecture parameters of the network will determine how many times the GEMM is called or the dimension of the matrices, which can be revealed through cache side-channel. The attack is based on common cache-based SCA, Flush+Reload [55] and Prime+Probe [36]. The target networks are VGG-16 [46] and ResNet-50 [22]. Using the proposed method, the search space for the architecture can be significantly reduced. In this work, the attack could reveal matrix multiplication related parameter such as convolutional or fully connected layers, and for others such as activation and pooling layers, it might be harder to recover.

Similarly, the authors of [24] proposed DeepRecon, an attack methodology based on cache side-channel that exploits Flush+Reload to reconstruct the Deep Neural Network (DNN) architecture. In their attack model, rather than accessing the target model directly like in other side-channel based attack, the adversary runs a co-located process on the host machine, in which the victim's model is also running. Similar to earlier work [54], the proposed attack does not generalize to computations on hardware other than a CPU. Also, they find that based on how the matrix multiplication is implemented, they are unable to estimate the inputs and parameters of a victim's model. As such, they hypothesize that this might be the limit of cache-based SCA on DNN.

Hu et al. [26] proposed an attack targeting GPU platform and highlighted some of the potential issues arising in contrast to other works. The attack is using the bus snooping technique, exploiting the off-chip memory address traces and PCIe events. The idea used in this work is that inter-layer DNN architecture features will be considered as string of "sentences", so by considering this instead of individual "word", it might maximize the likelihood of a correct match far more effectively than character-by-character approaches. To perform the experiment, they consider the Long short-term memory (LSTM) model, a common neural network, with CTC (Connectionist Temporal Classification) decoder, which is commonly used in Automatic Speech Recognition. The attack only requires the assumption that the adversary can observe the architectural side-channel over time. It also assumes the adversary can feed specific input and observe the results. The experiments are conducted on off-the-shelf Nvidia GPU running CNN, in a parallel manner, and the victim's model is ResNet-18 [22].

2.2 Countermeasures

The success of SCA on ML models can be mainly attributed to the naïve implementation of the model. Previously, ML models were rarely seen in hostile environments with adversaries benefiting from physical access. However, with IoT and edge-based devices, the threats have become real as highlighted by the range of works mentioned above. Thus, countermeasures must be investigated. As such, there is a wide research on SCA countermeasures against cryptographic implementations which can be also applied on ML models. However, direct application of countermeasures would result in a non-negligible overhead. In the following, we discuss some directions for countermeasures considering different physical side-channels.

Timing Side-Channel. It has been shown by multiple works that the execution time depends on network parameters which eventually leak sensitive information to the adversary. To overcome this problem, the designer can take two approaches. The first approach is to have constant time implementations of basic functions [43]. This can solve some issues where the value of the input is determined from the execution time but other issues like distinguishing between components (e.g. *sigmoid* vs. *ReLU*) may still be possible. The other approach is to randomize the execution timing in a way that it becomes independent of the sensitive information executed preventing an adversary to learn by observing timing information. This would require access to a good source of randomness and techniques like jitter and dummy operations can be used [38].

Power/EM Side-Channel. Hiding and Masking are the two typical types of countermeasures used against power/EM side-channel. Hiding aims at reducing the signal to noise ratio in a measurement, making attacks difficult. Masking uses randomization by mixing computation with random data to remove any correlation between sensitive variables and power/EM signature. Dubey *et al.* [16] proposed the first countermeasure for DNN against SCA. The countermeasure, referred to as MaskedNet, is based on masking. The resulting design uses novel masked components such as masked adder trees for fully-connected layers and masked Rectifier Linear Units for activation functions. They even use hiding countermeasure, like Wave Differential Dynamic Logic (WDDL) [49], to protect the sign-bit computation. The proposed protection increases the latency and area-cost by 2.8 and 2.3 times, respectively. When tested against first-order DPA, the attack against masking fails even when using 100k traces, however second-order DPA on masking can still break it with just 3.7 k traces. When analyzing the Difference-of-Means (DoM) test on the sign-bit computation, after 40k of traces, bit 0 and bit 1 can be distinguished. The argument for this is in the low noise platform used.

Microarchitectural Side-Channel. Much like timing and power/EM side-channel, hiding or randomizing cache activity of ML model execution can prevent such attacks. However, unsurprisingly, any of those choices result in performance overheads. Alam and Mukhopadhyay [3] proposed a countermeasure against microarchitectural side-channel attacks on ML models by observing the Hardware Performance Counter (HPC). During the execution of CNN, an evaluator, who does not know the detail of the implementation but can monitor various HPC events, conducts statistical hypothesis testing on the distribution of the data that can detect an attack. The evaluator throws an alarm when there is an anomaly in the distribution signifying potential side-channel leakage.

Thus, as a general observation, ML models do suffer from side-channel vulnerabilities and existing countermeasures stem from either hiding or masking families of countermeasures. In practice, a combination of various countermeasures is more likely deployed. However, for modern architectures, the network architecture can easily grow to millions of parameters, and such, the countermeasure overhead might make it impractical to implement. Thus, ML friendly countermeasures in terms of the overhead in cost must be investigated.

3   Overview of Fault Injection Threats to Machine Learning

In this section, we focus on a special class of physical attacks known as fault attacks, which have become a common practice owing to decreasing prices and increasing expertise required to mount such attacks [21]. Fault attacks are active attacks on a given implementation which try to perturb the internal computations by external means. Such attacks are commonly used for mounting secret key recovery attacks in cryptography or for violating/bypassing security checks [29]. Recently, fault attacks have been applied to neural networks to achieve misclassification or reverse engineering.

The rest of this section is organized as follows. Subsection 3.1 provides some necessary background on fault injection attacks and the possible threats they pose to neural network models. Subsection 3.2 outlines the current state-of-the-art and gives details on the most prominent works in this area. Finally, Subsect. 3.3 discusses possible countermeasures to protect neural networks against faults.

3.1   Background

Fault Injection Attacks (FIA) disrupt the device during the computation task, providing in this way some benefit to the attacker. Generally, this benefit can be anything from denial of service and privilege escalation, to the secret data recovery.

For example, in case of FIA on cryptographic circuits, the goal is typically to get the information on the secret key used during the encryption [29]. These attacks mostly exploit the scenario where the attacker has access to the device and can tamper with it, which is often the case for edge devices. However, there exist also techniques that can flip bits remotely, such as Rowhammer [31].

Multiple types of fault attacks and their outcomes on hardware devices are possible, resulting in various ways to affect the target device. These are often referred to as *fault models.* The most commonly deployed fault models in the literature are:

- *Bit flips:* allow the attacker to target a certain bit of the processed data and invert its value.
- *Stuck-at faults:* allow the attacker to set or reset the value of a certain bit of the processed data.
- *Random faults:* allow the attacker to change the value of a data structure (in register, memory, bus, etc.) to a random value.
- *Instruction skips:* allow the attacker to skip the execution of one or more instructions in the instruction sequence.
- *Instruction changes:* allow the attacker to change the executed instruction into another instruction – this can be achieved by faulting the instruction opcode.

In the pre-attack phase, the attacker needs to determine what kind of the fault model is realistic for the target device under test with the usage of specific fault injection equipment. After this knowledge is obtained and classified, the attacker can identify a fault analysis method that works fitting the given model.

When it comes to deployment of machine learning models in the field, there are many AI accelerators offering small size, low power consumption and low cost (e.g. Nvidia Jetson Nano, Google Coral, etc.). It was shown that small IoT devices like Raspberry Pi devices are also capable of running deep learning models [52]. These devices are ideal targets for fault injection attacks, as they might be physically accessible to the attacker and their complexity is low, thus allowing precise fault injection.

There are several attack scenarios affecting neural network models that can be achieved by fault attacks, mainly:

- *Denial of service:* faults can disturb the device in a way that it is not able to respond to a user's queries, leading to denial of service [40]. This can be either a permanent or a transient state.
- *Evasion:* classic evasion attack on ML models aims at misclassification of the input by adding adversarial perturbations in the input. In the evasion attack

by faults, the attacker disturbs the computation of the model resulting in the misclassification [37].

– *Model extraction:* it was shown that faults can help in recovering the confidential parameters of neural networks, such as weights and biases, allowing higher precision compared to other methods [9].

3.2   State-of-the-Art

The seminal work in the field of adversarial fault injection was published by Liu et al. in 2017 [37]. They introduced two types of attacks: *single bias attack* changes the bias value in either one of the hidden layers (in case of *ReLU* or similar activation function) or output layer of the network to achieve the misclassification; while *gradient descent attack* works in a similar way like Fast Gradient Sign Method [20], but changes the internal parameters instead of the input to the network. For more details on both types see below.

Practical fault injection by using a laser technique was shown by Breier et al. in 2018 [6]. They were able to disturb the instruction execution inside the general-purpose microcontroller to achieve the change of the neuron output. In their paper, they focused on behavior of three activation functions: in case of sigmoid and tanh, the fault resulted to inverted output, while in case of *ReLU*, the output was forced to be always zero.

Zhao et al. [57] proposed a *fault sneaking attack* on DNN models. The main goal is to cause misclassification to labels specified by the attacker, while keeping the fault injection stealthy. The stealthiness is achieved by keeping the accuracy of the faulted network as close to the original accuracy as possible. According to their results, they were able to keep the model accuracy loss to 0.8% for MNIST database and 1% for CIFAR database.

Breier et al. [9] analyzed reverse engineering in the context of transfer learning. The parameters from the teacher network are assumed to be known to the attacker. With the fault attack, the attacker can then recover the weights and biases of the new layers in the student network.

A survey on error tolerance of neural networks, published in 2017 [50], examines the effects of faults on DNN models.

In the rest of the section, we will provide more details on selected works.

Single Bias Attack and Gradient Descent Attack. Liu et al. [37] proposed the first work analyzing the effects of fault attacks on deep neural networks to achieve misclassification. They investigated two attack methods:

– *Single bias attack (SBA)* aims to achieve misclassification by modifying only one parameter in the neural network.
– *Gradient descent attack (GDA)* aims to achieve misclassificaiton for a targeted input pattern while keeping the accuracy for other input patterns.

As a threat model, they considered a white-box attack, where the attacker has knowledge of the structure, parameters as well as low-level implementation details of the targeted DNN. They also assumed that the practical attack is achievable by using current techniques so that the attacker can modify any parameter in DNN to an arbitrary value in the valid range of the used arithmetic format.

They considered *ReLU*-like activation functions, which are defined as follows

$$g(u) = \begin{cases} u & u \geq 0 \\ \alpha u & u < 0 \end{cases},$$

where $\alpha > 0$. They named DNN using *ReLU*-like activation function in the hidden layers as *ReLU*-like DNN.

To analyze the single bias attack, they give the following definition:

Definition 1. *[37] Given two variables x and y, if there exist two constants ε and δ such that $\frac{dy}{dx} = \delta$ when $x > \varepsilon$, we say y is one side linear to x and the one side linear slope is δ.*

With the notion of one side linearity, they prove the following result:

Theorem 1. *1. Let $y_1, y_2, \ldots, y_n$ variables, which are all one side linear to variable x with slopes $\delta_1, \delta_2, \ldots, \delta_n$ respectively. If $\delta_n > \delta_i, \forall i \neq n$, there exists a constant ε_{sink} such that $y_n > y_i, \forall i \neq n$ when $x > \varepsilon_{sink}$.*
2. In ReLU-like DNN, for a bias m in hidden layers, every output neuron is one side linear to m.

Thus, to achieve a single bias attack that misclassifies any input to the target class, the attacker analyzes the network structure to find a bias m in the hidden layer such that the targeted class has the largest one side linear slope w.r.t. m among all the output neurons. Then, by increasing m using fault the attacker would finally make the DNN's output converge at the target class.

They presented evaluation of SBA on a CIFAR model [47] which is a *ReLU*-like DNN. They achieved the highest attack accuracy of 57.23% by targeting the 6th layer of the network.

For the gradient descent attack, the authors aim at maximizing the following objective function by changing the parameters of only one single layer, denoted by θ,

$$J(\theta) = F^i(\theta, x) - |\theta - \theta_b|,$$

where θ_b denote original parameter values for a single layer, F^i represents the output for neuron corresponding to class i, and λ is an L1-norm regulator.

During the gradient descent, they proposed "modification compression" – at each iteration step, they replaced the element with the smallest absolute value in θ by 0. They showed by experiements that conducting modification compression can significantly reduce the number of modified parameters, by about 90%. The experiments with MNIST model [13] and CIFAR model [47] showed that GDA can achieve classification accuracy 95.20% and 81.66%, and degrades the benign accuracy by 3.86% and 2.35%, respectively.

Practical Attack on Microcontrollers and Activation Function. To the best of our knowledge, the only practical fault attack on neural network models was published in [6], where the authors used a laser to induce faults in a general purpose microcontroller. Next, we provide more details on this attack.

Attack Equipment Setup. The main component of the experimental laser fault injection station was the diode pulse laser with a wavelength of 1064 nm and pulse power of 20 W. This power was further reduced to 8 W by a 20 times objective lens which reduced the spot size to 15×3.5 μm^2.

As the device under test (DUT), `ATmega328P` microcontroller was used and mounted on `Arduino UNO` development board. The package of this chip was opened so that there is a direct visibility on a back-side silicon die with a laser. The board was placed on an `XYZ` positioning table with a step precision of 0.05 μm in each direction. A trigger signal was sent from the device at the beginning of the computation so that the injection time could be precisely determined. After the trigger signal was captured by the trigger and control device, a specified delay was inserted before laser activation. Laser activation timing was also checked by a digital oscilloscope for a greater precision. This setup is depicted in Fig. 2.

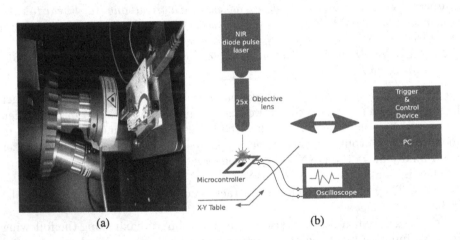

Fig. 2. Experimental laser fault injection setup – (a) device under test, (b) setup components.

DNN Activation Function Fault Analysis. To evaluate different activation functions, three simple 3-layer neural networks were implemented, with sigmoid, *ReLU* and tanh as the activation function for the second layer. The activation function for the last layer was set to be softmax. The neural networks were implemented in C programming language, which were further compiled to AVR assembly and uploaded to the DUT.

The activation functions in the second layer were surrounded with a trigger signal that raised a voltage on a selected Arduino board pin to 5 V, to help determine the laser timing.

As an instruction skip/change are one of the most basic attacks on micro-controllers, with high repeatability rates [8], this fault model was used in the experiments. The used microcontroller clock was 16 MHz, therefore one instruction took 62.5 ns. Some of the activation functions took over 2 000 instructions to execute. To check what are the vulnerabilities of the implementations, the timing of the laser glitch was varied from the beginning until the end of the function execution so that every instruction would be eventually targeted.

After a successful misclassification was observed, vulnerable instructions could be determined by visual inspection of the compiled assembly code and by checking the timing of the laser in that particular fault injection instance. With a laser power of 4.5% it was possible to disturb the algorithm execution, when tested with reference codes. More details on the behavior on this particular microcontroller under laser fault injection can be found in [8].

In this exploratory study, a random neural network was implemented, consisting of 3 layers, with 19, 12, and 10 neurons in input layer, hidden layer, and output layer, respectively. The fault attack was always targeting the computation of one of the activation functions in hidden layer. In the following, the experimental results on different activation functions will be explained in more detail.

ReLU was implemented in C as follows:

```
if (Accum > 0) {
    HiddenLayerOutput[i] = Accum;}
else {
    HiddenLayerOutput[i] = 0;}
```

where i loops from 1 to 12 so that each loop gives one output of the hidden layer. Accum is an intermediate variable that stores the input of the activation function for each neuron. The assembly code inspection showed that the result of the successful attack was executing the statement after else such that the output would always be 0. The corresponding assembly code is as follows:

```
1          ldi r1, 0        ;load 0 to r1
2          cp r1, r15       ;compare MSB of Accum to r1
3          brge else        ;jump to else if 0 >= Accum
4          movw r10, r15    ;HiddenLayerOutput[i] = Accum
5          movw r12, r17    ;HiddenLayerOutput[i] = Accum
6          jmp end          ;jump after the else statement
7  else:   clr r10          ;HiddenLayerOutput[i]= 0
8          clr r11          ;HiddenLayerOutput[i]= 0
9          clr r12          ;HiddenLayerOutput[i]= 0
10         clr r13          ;HiddenLayerOutput[i]= 0
11 end:    ...              ;continue the execution
```

where each float number is stored in 4 registers. For example, Accum is stored in registers r15,r16,r17,r18 and HiddenLayerOutput[i] is stored in r10,r11,r12,r13. Lines 4, 5 execute the equation HiddenLayerOutput[i] = Accum.

The attack was skipping the "jmp end" instruction that would normally avoid the part of code setting HiddenLayerOutput[i] to 0 in case Accum > 0. Therefore, such change in control flow renders the neuron inactive no matter what is the input value.

Sigmoid is implemented by a following code in C:

```
HiddenLayerOutput[i] = 1.0/(1.0 + exp(-Accum));
```

After the assembly code inspection, it was observed that the successful attack was taking advantage of skipping the negation in the exponent of exp() function, which compiles into one of the two following codes, depending on the compiler version:

```
A) neg r16        ;compute negation r16
B) ldi r15, 0x80 ;load 0x80 into r15
   eor r16, r15  ;xor r16 with r15
```

Laser experiments showed that both **neg** and **eor** could be skipped, and therefore, significant change to the function output was achieved.

Hyperbolic tangent was implemented by a following code in C:

```
HiddenLayerOutput[i] = 2.0/(1.0 + exp(-2*Accum)) - 1;
```

Similarly to sigmoid, the experiments showed that the successful attack was exploiting the negation in the exponential function, leading to an impact similar to sigmoid.

Softmax. It was unable to obtain any successful misclassification. There were only two different outputs as a result of the fault injection: either there was no output at all, or the output contained invalid values. This lack of valid output prevented further fault analysis to derive the actual fault model that happened in the device.

The summary of the results, showing the original and the faulted activation functions is depicted in Fig. 3, with the solid line depicting the original functions and dotted lines depicting the faulted functions.

Authors pointed out that it would make sense to explore different fault models, such as single bit flips that were experimentally achieved by laser in [1]. The first application of such attack would be to target the IEEE754 floating point representation for the weights. The representation follows 32-bit pattern $(b_{31}...b_0)$: 1 sign bit (b_{31}), 8 exponent bits $(b_{30}...b_{23})$ and 23 mantissa (fractional) bits $(b_{22}...b_0)$. The represented number is given by $(-1)^{b_{31}} \times 2^{(b_{30}...b_{23})_2 - 127} \times (1.b_{22}...b_0)_2$. A bit flip attack on the sign bit or on the exponent bits would make significant influence on the weight. This idea was later adopted in [25] to explore single bit upsets on the network parameters. We detail this work in the next part.

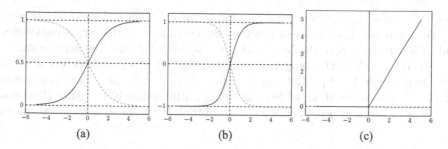

Fig. 3. (a) Sigmoid, (b) Hyperbolic tangent, and (c) *ReLU* functions. Solid lines indicate original function, dotted lines indicate faulted ones.

Single Bit-Flip Attack. A comprehensive evaluation of bitwise corruptions on various deep learning models was presented by Hong et al. in 2019 [25]. They showed that most models have at least one parameter such that if there is a bit-flip introduced in its bitwise representation, it will cause an accuracy loss of over 90%. The assumed attacker model is remote fault injection by using Rowhammer [31].

The main goal of [25] is to provide an investigation on how much damage can be achieved by minimal changes to the network caused by fault injection. The results are presented on popular image datasets – MNIST [34], CIFAR10 [32], and ImageNet [44]. Analysis is provided on 19 different DNN models, including newly generated architectures, and publicly available networks, such as VGG16 and AlexNet. To measure the impact, they defined a new metric called *Relative Accuracy Drop (RAD)*:

$$RAD = \frac{Acc_{pristine} - Acc_{corrupted}}{Acc_{pristine}},$$

where $Acc_{pristine}$ is the classification accuracy of the original (pristine) model and $Acc_{corrupted}$ is the classification accuracy of the corrupted model. For the experiments in the paper, they set $RAD > 0.1$ to be the criterion for indiscriminate damage to the model. For models working on MNIST dataset, it was possible to exhaustively flip every bit of every model parameter and measure RAD on the entire validation set. However, for larger models, this was not possible due to the number of parameters, as such experiment would require significant amount of time and/or processing power. Therefore, for CIFAR10 and ImageNet they defined three types of heuristics – the first one samples 10% of the validation set, the second one flips only the most significant bits of the numbers in IEEE754 floating-point representation, and the third one, used for ImageNet models, samples a fixed number of 20,000 parameters to attack. Several different types of impact were characterized:

- **Impact of number format representation:** impact of the bit-flip position, flip direction, and parameter sign;
- **Impact of the model:** impact of the layer width, activation function, dropout and normalization, model architecture.

Two different scenarios were considered in terms of attacker knowledge: surgical attack, where the adversary can precisely flip certain bit of the target parameter, and blind attack, where the bit position of the target parameter is random.

The results show that approximately 40–50% of DNN parameters are vulnerable to single bit-flips and can lead to ≈10% drop in accuracy. If a strong adversary is considered, capable of inducing faults remotely by using Rowhammer, it is possible to reach accuracy drop of 99% in the blind attacker scenario.

3.3 Countermeasures

Fault injection countermeasures can be deployed at different levels of the design – model architecture, software implementation, and hardware layer. In this part, we will discuss each of these in more detail.

Model Architecture. Neural networks contain vast amount of interconnected nodes. Because of their working principle, not all of them are activated for every input. Therefore, if faults are injected into nodes that are unused in the current execution, there will not be any outcome [41]. This behavior is known as partial fault tolerance and it was shown that neural network implementations of cryptographic operations can make them more resistant to faults than standard implementations [2]. The more redundancy is in the network, the better fault tolerance can be achieved, at the cost of higher memory usage and computation complexity.

Software Implementation. Redundancy and checks can be added in the model computation on the software level. A naïve approach would be to repeat the computation two or more times and then compare the results. If they are not equal, the device might have been tampered with. Redundant instruction sequences can protect against pre-defined number of faults [39]. Data within the instructions can be arranged in a redundant way that will protect against both data corruption and instruction skips [42]. Non-linear codes can be used to implement the operations that allow protection against multiple bit faults per operation [7].

Hardware Layer. Error detection and correction codes can be efficiently implemented in hardware. Computational circuits, or parts of them can be implemented in parallel and majority voting can be utilized to prevent outputting the faulty result [10]. Additional circuits can be deployed to detect voltage variations caused by fault injection. These circuits can raise an alarm and a pre-defined action to prevent the information leakage or release of incorrect output can be taken [23].

Additionally, there are physical measures that can be applied to prevent tampering, such as special shielding of the chip or erasing of memory if the chip package is damaged.

4   Conclusion

We have surveyed known physical attacks used for the purpose of reverse engineering ML models on a range of platforms and discussed possible countermeasures. The results published so far demonstrate that stealing the models in this way (as possible IP) is a clear and present threat. Specific use cases and applications on various edge and IoT devices should be carefully examined against those threats and accordingly protected.

5 Open Research Problems

Powerful adversaries today include those exploiting side-channel leakage from implementations on ML models and the ability to actively disturb the device's operations. Combining the two poses even more challenge to the engineering efforts in designing adequate defenses. The countermeasures considered so far are mainly from the crypto/security applications, which makes them suboptimal. On top, typical overheads in resources such as power/energy makes those defenses often unsuitable for low-end devices. As the adversaries are becoming ever more powerful and knowledgeable, it is necessary to revisit the design cycle and make it open at various phases such that the results of preliminary security evaluation can still be fed back to the implementations.

We see future works going more into directions of ML-specific countermeasures and new frameworks to evaluate the leakages before the models are put into the field.

Acknowledgement. This project has received funding from the European Union's Horizon 2020 Research and Innovation Programme under the Programme SASPRO 2 COFUND Marie Sklodowska-Curie grant agreement No. 945478.

References

1. Agoyan, M., Dutertre, J.M., Mirbaha, A.P., Naccache, D., Ribotta, A.L., Tria, A.: How to flip a bit? In: On-Line Testing Symposium (IOLTS), 2010 IEEE 16th International, pp. 235–239. IEEE (2010)
2. Alam, M., Bag, A., Roy, D.B., Jap, D., Breier, J., Bhasin, S., Mukhopadhyay, D.: Enhancing fault tolerance of neural networks for security-critical applications. arXiv preprint arXiv:1902.04560 (2019)
3. Alam, M., Mukhopadhyay, D.: How secure are deep learning algorithms from side-channel based reverse engineering? In: Proceedings of the 56th Annual Design Automation Conference 2019, DAC 2019, Las Vegas, NV, USA, 02–06 June 2019, p. 226. ACM (2019). https://doi.org/10.1145/3316781.3322465
4. Batina, L., Bhasin, S., Jap, D., Picek, S.: CSI NN: reverse engineering of neural network architectures through electromagnetic side channel. In: Heninger, N., Traynor, P. (eds.) 28th USENIX Security Symposium, USENIX Security 2019, Santa Clara, CA, USA, 14–16 August 2019, pp. 515–532. USENIX Association (2019). https://www.usenix.org/conference/usenixsecurity19/presentation/batina
5. Batina, L., Bhasin, S., Jap, D., Picek, S.: Poster: recovering the input of neural networks via single shot side-channel attacks. In: Cavallaro, L., Kinder, J., Wang, X., Katz, J. (eds.) Proceedings of the 2019 ACM SIGSAC Conference on Computer and Communications Security, CCS 2019, London, UK, 11–15 November 2019, pp. 2657–2659. ACM (2019). https://doi.org/10.1145/3319535.3363280

6. Breier, J., Hou, X., Jap, D., Ma, L., Bhasin, S., Liu, Y.: Practical fault attack on deep neural networks. In: Proceedings of the 2018 ACM SIGSAC Conference on Computer and Communications Security, pp. 2204–2206 (2018)
7. Breier, J., Hou, X., Liu, Y.: On evaluating fault resilient encoding schemes in software. IEEE Trans. Dependable Secur. Comput. **18**(3), 1065–1079 (2019)
8. Breier, J., Jap, D., Chen, C.N.: Laser profiling for the back-side fault attacks: with a practical laser skip instruction attack on AES. In: Proceedings of the 1st ACM Workshop on Cyber-Physical System Security, pp. 99–103. ACM (2015)
9. Breier, J., Jap, D., Hou, X., Bhasin, S., Liu, Y.: Sniff: reverse engineering of neural networks with fault attacks. arXiv preprint arXiv:2002.11021 (2020)
10. Breier, J., Khairallah, M., Hou, X., Liu, Y.: A countermeasure against statistical ineffective fault analysis. IEEE Trans. Circuits Syst. II Express Briefs **67**(12), 3322–3326 (2020)
11. Cao, X., Gong, N.Z.: Mitigating evasion attacks to deep neural networks via region-based classification. In: Proceedings of the 33rd Annual Computer Security Applications Conference, Orlando, FL, USA, 4–8 December 2017, pp. 278–287. ACM (2017). https://doi.org/10.1145/3134600.3134606
12. Chakraborty, A., Alam, M., Dey, V., Chattopadhyay, A., Mukhopadhyay, D.: Adversarial attacks and defences: a survey. arXiv preprint arXiv:1810.00069 (2018)
13. Ciresan, D.C., Meier, U., Masci, J., Gambardella, L.M., Schmidhuber, J.: Flexible, high performance convolutional neural networks for image classification. In: Twenty-Second International Joint Conference on Artificial Intelligence (2011)
14. Dennis, D.K., et al.: Edgeml: machine learning for resource-constrained edge devices (2020). https://github.com/Microsoft/EdgeML
15. Dong, G., Wang, P., Chen, P., Gu, R., Hu, H.: Floating-point multiplication timing attack on deep neural network. In: 2019 IEEE International Conference on Smart Internet of Things (SmartIoT), Tianjin, China, 9–11 August 2019, pp. 155–161. IEEE (2019). https://doi.org/10.1109/SmartIoT.2019.00032
16. Dubey, A., Cammarota, R., Aysu, A.: Maskednet: a pathway for secure inference against power side-channel attacks. CoRR abs/1910.13063 (2019). http://arxiv.org/abs/1910.13063
17. Duddu, V., Samanta, D., Rao, D.V., Balas, V.E.: Stealing neural networks via timing side channels. CoRR abs/1812.11720 (2018). http://arxiv.org/abs/1812.11720
18. Fredrikson, M., Jha, S., Ristenpart, T.: Model inversion attacks that exploit confidence information and basic countermeasures. In: Proceedings of the 22nd ACM SIGSAC Conference on Computer and Communications Security, pp. 1322–1333 (2015)
19. Gilad-Bachrach, R., Dowlin, N., Laine, K., Lauter, K.E., Naehrig, M., Wernsing, J.: Cryptonets: applying neural networks to encrypted data with high throughput and accuracy. In: Balcan, M., Weinberger, K.Q. (eds.) Proceedings of the 33nd International Conference on Machine Learning, ICML 2016, New York City, NY, USA, 19–24 June 2016. JMLR Workshop and Conference Proceedings, vol. 48, pp. 201–210. JMLR.org (2016). http://proceedings.mlr.press/v48/gilad-bachrach16.html
20. Goodfellow, I.J., Shlens, J., Szegedy, C.: Explaining and harnessing adversarial examples. arXiv:1412.6572 (2014)
21. Guillen, O.M., Gruber, M., De Santis, F.: Low-cost setup for localized semi-invasive optical fault injection attacks. In: Guilley, S. (ed.) COSADE 2017. LNCS, vol. 10348, pp. 207–222. Springer, Cham (2017). https://doi.org/10.1007/978-3-319-64647-3_13

22. He, K., Zhang, X., Ren, S., Sun, J.: Deep residual learning for image recognition. In: 2016 IEEE Conference on Computer Vision and Pattern Recognition, CVPR 2016, Las Vegas, NV, USA, 27–30 June 2016, pp. 770–778. IEEE Computer Society (2016). https://doi.org/10.1109/CVPR.2016.90

23. He, W., Breier, J., Bhasin, S., Miura, N., Nagata, M.: An FPGA-compatible PLL-based sensor against fault injection attack. In: 2017 22nd Asia and South Pacific Design Automation Conference (ASP-DAC), pp. 39–40. IEEE (2017)

24. Hong, S., et al.: Security analysis of deep neural networks operating in the presence of cache side-channel attacks. CoRR abs/1810.03487 (2018). http://arxiv.org/abs/1810.03487

25. Hong, S., Frigo, P., Kaya, Y., Giuffrida, C., Dumitra, T.: Terminal brain damage: exposing the graceless degradation in deep neural networks under hardware fault attacks. In: 28th USENIX Security Symposium (USENIX Security 19), pp. 497–514 (2019)

26. Hu, X., et al.: Neural network model extraction attacks in edge devices by hearing architectural hints. CoRR abs/1903.03916 (2019). http://arxiv.org/abs/1903.03916

27. Hua, W., Zhang, Z., Suh, G.E.: Reverse engineering convolutional neural networks through side-channel information leaks. In: Proceedings of the 55th Annual Design Automation Conference, DAC 2018, San Francisco, CA, USA, 24–29 June 2018, pp. 4:1–4:6. ACM (2018). https://doi.org/10.1145/3195970.3196105

28. Iandola, F.N., Han, S., Moskewicz, M.W., Ashraf, K., Dally, W.J., Keutzer, K.: Squeezenet: Alexnet-level accuracy with 50x fewer parameters and <0.5mb model size. arXiv:1602.07360 (2016)

29. Joye, M., Tunstall, M.: Fault Analysis in Cryptography, vol. 147. Springer, Heidelberg (2012)

30. Juuti, M., Szyller, S., Dmitrenko, A., Marchal, S., Asokan, N.: PRADA: protecting against DNN model stealing attacks. CoRR abs/1805.02628 (2018). http://arxiv.org/abs/1805.02628

31. Kim, Y., et al.: Flipping bits in memory without accessing them: an experimental study of dram disturbance errors. ACM SIGARCH Comput. Archit. News **42**(3), 361–372 (2014)

32. Krizhevsky, A., et al.: Learning multiple layers of features from tiny images (2009)

33. Krizhevsky, A., Sutskever, I., Hinton, G.E.: Imagenet classification with deep convolutional neural networks. In: Bartlett, P.L., Pereira, F.C.N., Burges, C.J.C., Bottou, L., Weinberger, K.Q. (eds.) Advances in Neural Information Processing Systems 25: 26th Annual Conference on Neural Information Processing Systems 2012. Proceedings of a Meeting Held, 3–6 December 2012, Lake Tahoe, Nevada, United States, pp. 1106–1114 (2012). https://proceedings.neurips.cc/paper/2012/hash/c399862d3b9d6b76c8436e924a68c45b-Abstract.html

34. LeCun, Y.: The mnist database of handwritten digits (1998). http://yann.lecun.com/exdb/mnist/

35. Lee, T., Edwards, B., Molloy, I., Su, D.: Defending against neural network model stealing attacks using deceptive perturbations. In: 2019 IEEE Security and Privacy Workshops, SP Workshops 2019, San Francisco, CA, USA, 19–23 May 2019, pp. 43–49. IEEE (2019). https://doi.org/10.1109/SPW.2019.00020

36. Liu, F., Yarom, Y., Ge, Q., Heiser, G., Lee, R.B.: Last-level cache side-channel attacks are practical. In: 2015 IEEE Symposium on Security and Privacy, SP 2015, San Jose, CA, USA, 17–21 May 2015, pp. 605–622. IEEE Computer Society (2015). https://doi.org/10.1109/SP.2015.43

358   L. Batina et al.

37. Liu, Y., Wei, L., Luo, B., Xu, Q.: Fault injection attack on deep neural network. In: Proceedings of the 36th International Conference on Computer-Aided Design, pp. 131–138. IEEE Press (2017)
38. Mentens, N., Gierlichs, B., Verbauwhede, I.: Power and fault analysis resistance in hardware through dynamic reconfiguration. In: Oswald, E., Rohatgi, P. (eds.) CHES 2008. LNCS, vol. 5154, pp. 346–362. Springer, Heidelberg (2008). https://doi.org/10.1007/978-3-540-85053-3_22
39. Moro, N., Heydemann, K., Encrenaz, E., Robisson, B.: Formal verification of a software countermeasure against instruction skip attacks. J. Cryptogr. Eng. 4(3), 145–156 (2014). https://doi.org/10.1007/s13389-014-0077-7
40. Murvay, P.S., Groza, B.: Dos attacks on controller area networks by fault injections from the software layer. In: Proceedings of the 12th International Conference on Availability, Reliability and Security, pp. 1–10 (2017)
41. Neggaz, M.A., Alouani, I., Niar, S., Kurdahi, F.: Are cnns reliable enough for critical applications? an exploratory study. IEEE Des. Test 37(2), 76–83 (2019)
42. Patrick, C., Yuce, B., Ghalaty, N.F., Schaumont, P.: Lightweight fault attack resistance in software using intra-instruction redundancy. In: Avanzi, R., Heys, H. (eds.) SAC 2016. LNCS, vol. 10532, pp. 231–244. Springer, Cham (2017). https://doi.org/10.1007/978-3-319-69453-5_13
43. Reparaz, O., Balasch, J., Verbauwhede, I.: Dude, is my code constant time? In: Atienza, D., Natale, G.D. (eds.) Design, Automation & Test in Europe Conference & Exhibition, DATE 2017, Lausanne, Switzerland, 27–31 March 2017, pp. 1697–1702. IEEE (2017). https://doi.org/10.23919/DATE.2017.7927267
44. Russakovsky, O., et al.: Imagenet large scale visual recognition challenge. Int. J. Comput. Vis. 115(3), 211–252 (2015)
45. Shokri, R., Stronati, M., Song, C., Shmatikov, V.: Membership inference attacks against machine learning models. In: 2017 IEEE Symposium on Security and Privacy, SP 2017, San Jose, CA, USA, 22–26 May 2017, pp. 3–18. IEEE Computer Society (2017). https://doi.org/10.1109/SP.2017.41
46. Simonyan, K., Zisserman, A.: Very deep convolutional networks for large-scale image recognition. In: Bengio, Y., LeCun, Y. (eds.) 3rd International Conference on Learning Representations, ICLR 2015, San Diego, CA, USA, 7–9 May 2015, Conference Track Proceedings (2015). http://arxiv.org/abs/1409.1556
47. Springenberg, J.T., Dosovitskiy, A., Brox, T., Riedmiller, M.: Striving for simplicity: The all convolutional net. arXiv preprint arXiv:1412.6806 (2014)
48. Szegedy, C., et al.: Intriguing properties of neural networks. arXiv preprint arXiv:1312.6199 (2013)
49. Tiri, K., Verbauwhede, I.: A logic level design methodology for a secure DPA resistant ASIC or FPGA implementation. In: 2004 Design, Automation and Test in Europe Conference and Exposition (DATE 2004), 16–20 February 2004, Paris, France, pp. 246–251. IEEE Computer Society (2004). https://doi.org/10.1109/DATE.2004.1268856
50. Torres-Huitzil, C., Girau, B.: Fault and error tolerance in neural networks: a review. IEEE Access 5, 17322–17341 (2017)
51. Tramèr, F., Zhang, F., Juels, A., Reiter, M.K., Ristenpart, T.: Stealing machine learning models via prediction APIs. In: 25th USENIX Security Symposium (USENIX Security 16), pp. 601–618 (2016)
52. Velasco-Montero, D., Fernández-Berni, J., Carmona-Galán, R., Rodríguez-Vázquez, Á.: Performance analysis of real-time DNN inference on raspberry pi. In: Real-Time Image and Video Processing 2018, vol. 10670, p. 106700F. International Society for Optics and Photonics (2018)

53. Wei, L., Luo, B., Li, Y., Liu, Y., Xu, Q.: I know what you see: power side-channel attack on convolutional neural network accelerators. In: Proceedings of the 34th Annual Computer Security Applications Conference, ACSAC 2018, San Juan, PR, USA, 03–07 December 2018, pp. 393–406. ACM (2018). https://doi.org/10.1145/3274694.3274696

54. Yan, M., Fletcher, C.W., Torrellas, J.: Cache telepathy: Leveraging shared resource attacks to learn DNN architectures. CoRR abs/1808.04761 (2018). http://arxiv.org/abs/1808.04761

55. Yarom, Y., Falkner, K.: FLUSH+RELOAD: a high resolution, low noise, L3 cache side-channel attack. In: Fu, K., Jung, J. (eds.) Proceedings of the 23rd USENIX Security Symposium, San Diego, CA, USA, 20–22 August 2014, pp. 719–732. USENIX Association (2014). https://www.usenix.org/conference/usenixsecurity14/technical-sessions/presentation/yarom

56. Yu, H., Ma, H., Yang, K., Zhao, Y., Jin, Y.: Deepem: deep neural networks model recovery through em side-channel information leakage. In: HOST (2020)

57. Zhao, P., Wang, S., Gongye, C., Wang, Y., Fei, Y., Lin, X.: Fault sneaking attack: a stealthy framework for misleading deep neural networks. In: 2019 56th ACM/IEEE Design Automation Conference (DAC), pp. 1–6. IEEE (2019)

58. Jovic, A., Jap, D., Papachristodoulou, L., Heuser, A.: Traditional machine learning methods for side-channel analysis. In: Batina, L., Bäck, T., Buhan, I., Picek, S. (eds.) Security and Artificial Intelligence. LNCS, vol. 13049, pp. 25–47. Springer, Cham (2022)

59. Krček, M., et al.: Deep learning on side-channel analysis. In: Batina, L., Bäck, T., Buhan, I., Picek, S. (eds.) Security and Artificial Intelligence. LNCS, vol. 13049, pp. 48–71. Springer, Cham (2022)

Author Index

Printed in the United States
by Baker & Taylor Publisher Services